INTRODUCTION TO THE LITERATURE OF EUROPE IN THE 15th, 16th, AND 17th CENTURIES

INTRODUCTION
TO THE LITERATURE
OF EUROPE
IN THE 15th, 16th, AND
17th CENTURIES

HENRY HALLAM

Volume II

FREDERICK UNGAR PUBLISHING CO.
NEW YORK

Republished 1970
from the edition of 1873
Reprinted from a copy in the collections of
The New York Public Library
Astor, Lenox and Tilden Foundations

Printed in the United States of America

Library of Congress Catalog Card No. 74-118869

ISBN (3-volume set) 0-8044-2331-8
Volume I 0-8044-2332-6
Volume II 0-8044-2333-4
Volume III 0-8044-2334-2

CONTENTS

OF

THE SECOND VOLUME.

———◦◦———

PART II. *continued.*

CHAPTER III.

HISTORY OF SPECULATIVE PHILOSOPHY FROM 1550 TO 1600.

CHAPTER IV.

HISTORY OF MORAL AND POLITICAL PHILOSOPHY AND OF JURISPRUDENCE
FROM 1550 TO 1600.

CHAPTER V.

HISTORY OF POETRY FROM 1550 TO 1600.

CHAPTER VI.

HISTORY OF DRAMATIC LITERATURE FROM 1550 TO 1600.

CHAPTER VII

HISTORY OF POLITE LITERATURE IN PROSE FROM 1550 TO 1600.

CHAPTER VIII.

HISTORY OF PHYSICAL AND MISCELLANEOUS LITERATURE
FROM 1550 TO 1600.

PART III.

ON THE LITERATURE OF THE FIRST HALF OF THE SEVENTEENTH CENTURY.

CHAPTER I.

HISTORY OF ANCIENT LITERATURE IN EUROPE FROM 1600 TO 1650.

CHAPTER II.

HISTORY OF THEOLOGICAL LITERATURE IN EUROPE FROM 1600 TO 1650.

CHAPTER III.

HISTORY OF SPECULATIVE PHILOSOPHY FROM 1600 TO 1650.

CHAPTER IV.

HISTORY OF MORAL AND POLITICAL PHILOSOPHY AND OF JURISPRUDENCE
FROM 1600 TO 1650.

PART II.—*continued.*

ON THE LITERATURE OF THE LATTER HALF OF THE SIXTEENTH CENTURY.

CHAPTER III.

HISTORY OF SPECULATIVE PHILOSOPHY, FROM 1550 TO 1600.

Aristotelian Philosophers — Cesalpin — Opposite Schools of Philosophy — Telesio — Jordano Bruno — Sanchez — Aconcio — Nizolius — Logic of Ramus.

1. THE authority of Aristotle, as the great master of dogmatic philosophy, continued generally predominant Predominance of through the sixteenth century. It has been already Aristotelian observed, that, besides the strenuous support of the philosophy. Catholic clergy, and especially of the Sorbonne, who regarded all innovation with abhorrence, the Aristotelian philosophy had been received, through the influence of Melanchthon, in the Lutheran universities. The reader must be reminded that under the name of speculative philosophy we comprehend not only the logic and what was called ontology of the schools, but those physical theories of ancient or modern date, which, appealing less to experience than to assumed hypotheses, cannot be mingled, in a literary classification, with the researches of true science, such as we shall hereafter have to place under the head of natural philosophy.

2. Brucker has made a distinction between the scholastic and the genuine Aristotelians; the former being Scholastic chiefly conversant with the doctors of the middle and genuine Aristotelians, adopting their terminology, their distinctions, lians. their dogmas, and relying with implicit deference on Scotus or Aquinas, though, in the progress of learning, they might make some use of the original master; while the latter, throwing off the yoke of the schoolmen, prided themselves on an equally complete submission to Aristotle himself. These were chiefly philosophers and physicians, as the former were theologians; and the difference of their objects suffices

to account for the different lines in which they pursued them, and the lights by which they were guided.[a]

3. Of the former class, or successors and adherents of the old schoolmen, it might be far from easy, were it worth while, to furnish any distinct account. Their works are mostly of considerable scarcity; and none of the historians of philosophy, except perhaps Morhof, profess much acquaintance with them. It is sufficient to repeat that, among the Dominicans, Franciscans, and Jesuits, especially in Spain and Italy, the scholastic mode of argumentation was retained in their seminaries, and employed in prolix volumes, both upon theology and upon such parts of metaphysics and natural law as are allied to it. The reader may find some more information in Brucker, whom Buhle, saying the same things in the same order, may be presumed to have silently copied.[b]

The former class little remembered.

4. The second class of Aristotelian philosophers, devoting themselves to physical science, though investigating it with a very unhappy deference to mistaken dogmas, might seem to offer a better hope of materials for history; and in fact we meet here with a very few names of men once celebrated and of some influence over the opinions of their age. But even here their writings prove to be not only forgotten, but incapable, as we may say, on account of their rare occurrence, and the improbability of their republication, of being ever again known.

The others not much better known.

5. The Italian schools, and especially those of Pisa and Padua, had long been celebrated for their adherence to Aristotelian principles, not always such as could justly be deduced from the writings of the Stagirite himself, but opposing a bulwark against novel speculation, as well as against the revival of the Platonic, or any other ancient philosophy. Simon Porta of the former university, and Cæsar Cremonini of the latter, stood at the head of the rigid Aristotelians; the one near the commencement of this period, the other about its close. Both these philosophers have been reproached with the tendency to atheism, so common in the

Schools of Pisa and Padua.

---

[a] Brucker, Hist. Philos., iv. 117 et post.   [b] Brucker, Hist. Philos., i 117 et post. Buhle, ii. 448.

Italians of this period.   A similar imputation has fallen on
another professor of the university of Pisa, Cesalpini, Cesalpini.
who is said to have deviated from the strict system
of Aristotle towards that of Averroes, though he did not
altogether coincide even with the latter.   The real merits of
Cesalpin, in very different pursuits, it was reserved for a
later age to admire.   His ' Quæstiones Peripateticæ,' published in 1575, is a treatise on metaphysics, or the first
philosophy, founded professedly upon Aristotelian principles,
but with considerable deviation.   This work is so scarce
that Brucker had never seen it, but Buhle has taken much
pains to analyse its very obscure contents.   Paradoxical and
unintelligible as they now appear, Cesalpin obtained a high
reputation in his own age, and was denominated, by excellence, the philosopher.   Nicolas Taurellus, a professor at
Altdorf, denounced the ' Quæstiones Peripateticæ' in a book
to which, in allusion to his adversary's name, he gave the
puerile title of Alpes Cæsæ.

6. The system of Cesalpin is one modification of that
ancient hypothesis which, losing sight of all truth Sketch of
and experience in the love of abstraction, substi- his system.
tutes the barren unity of pantheism for religion, and a few
incomprehensible paradoxes for the variety of science.
Nothing, according to him, was substance which was not
animated; but the particular souls which animate bodies
are themselves only substances, because they are parts of
the first substance, a simple, speculative, but not active
intelligence, perfect and immovable, which is God.   The
reasonable soul, however, of mankind is not numerically
one; for matter being the sole principle of plurality, and
human intelligences being combined with matter, they are
plural in number.   He differed also from Averroes in maintaining the separate immortality of human souls; and while
the philosopher of Cordova distinguished the one soul which
he ascribed to mankind from the Deity, Cesalpin considered
the individual soul as a portion, not of this common human
intelligence, which he did not admit, but of the first substance, or Deity.   His system was therefore more incompatible with theism, in any proper sense, than that of Averroes himself, and anticipated in some measure that of Spinoza,

who gave a greater extension to his one substance, by comprehending all matter as well as spirit within it. Cesalpin also denied, and in this he went far from his Aristotelian creed, any other than a logical difference between substances and accidents. I have no knowledge of the writings of Cesalpin except through Buhle; for though I confess that the 'Quæstiones Peripateticæ' may be found in the British Museum,[c] it would scarce repay the labour to examine what is both erroneous and obscure.

7. The name of Cremonini, professor of philosophy for above forty years at Padua, is better know than his writings. These have become of the greatest scarcity. Brucker tells us he had not been able to see any of them, and Buhle had met with but two or three.[d] Those at which I have looked are treatises on the Aristotelian physics; they contain little of any interest; nor did I perceive that they countenance, though they may not repel, the charge of atheism sometimes brought against Cremonini, but which, if at all well-founded, seems rather to rest on external evidence. Cremonini, according to Buhle, refutes the Averroistic notion of an universal human intelligence. Gabriel Naudé, both in his letters, and in the records of his conversation called Naudæana, speaks with great admiration of Cremonini.[e] He had himself passed some years at Padua, and was at that time a disciple of the Aristotelian school in physics, which he abandoned after his intimacy with Gassendi.

Cremonini.

8. Meantime the authority of Aristotle, great in name and respected in the schools, began to lose more and more of its influence over speculative minds. Cesalpin, an Aristotelian by profession, had gone wide in some points from his master. But others waged an open war as philosophical reformers. Francis Patrizzi, in his 'Discussiones Peripateticæ' (1571 and 1581), ap-

Opponents of Aristotle.

Patrizzi.

---

[c] Buhle, ii. 525. Brucker (iv. 222) laments that he had never seen this book. It seems that there were few good libraries in Germany in Brucker's age, or at least that he had no access to them, for it is surprising how often he makes the same complaint. He had, however, seen a copy of the Alpes Cæsæ of Taurellus, and gives rather a long account both of the man and of the book. Ibid. and p. 300.

[d] Buhle, ii. 519.

[e] Some passages in the Naudæana tend to confirm the suspicion of irreligion, both with respect to Cremonini and Naudé himself.

pealed to prejudice with the arms of calumny, raking up the most unwarranted aspersions against the private life of Aristotle, to prepare the way for assailing his philosophy ; a warfare not the less unworthy, that it is often successful.   In the case of Patrizzi it was otherwise : his book was little read ; and his own notions of philosophy, borrowed from the later Platonists, and that rabble of spurious writers who had misled Ficinus and Picus of Mirandola, dressed up by Patrizzi with a fantastic terminology, had little chance of subverting so well-established and acute a system as that of Aristotle.[f]

9. Bernard Telesio, a native of Cosenza, had greater success, and attained a more celebrated name.   System of The first two books of his treatise, ' De Natura Telesio. Rerum juxta Propria Principia,' appeared at Rome in 1565 ; the rest was published in 1586.   These contain an hypothesis more intelligible than that of Patrizzi, and less destitute of a certain apparent correspondence with the phænomena of nature.   Two active incorporeal principles, heat and cold, contend with perpetual opposition for the dominion over a third, which is passive matter.   Of these three all nature consists.   The region of pure heat is in the heavens, in the sun and stars, where it is united with the most subtle matter ; that of cold in the centre of the earth, where matter is most condensed ; all between is their battle-field, in which they continually struggle, and alternately conquer.   These principles are not only active, but intelligent, so far at least as to perceive their own acts and mutual impressions.   Heat is the cause of motion ; cold is by nature immovable, and tends to keep all things in repose.[g]

10. Telesio has been generally supposed to have borrowed this theory from that of Parmenides, in which the antagonist principles of heat and cold had been employed in a similar manner.   Buhle denies the identity of the two systems, and considers that of Telesio as more nearly allied to the Aristotelian, except in substituting heat and cold for the more abstract notions of form and privation.   Heat and cold, it might rather perhaps be said, seem to be merely ill-chosen

---

[f] Buhle, ii. 548.   Brucker, iv. 422.
[g] Brucker iv. 449.   Buhle, ii. 563.   Ginguéné, vii. 501.

names for the hypothetical causes of motion and rest; and the real laws of nature with respect to both of these, were as little discoverable in the Telesian as in the more established theory.   Yet its author perceived that the one possessed an expansive, the other a condensing power; and his principles of heat and cold bear a partial analogy to repulsion and attraction, the antagonist forces which modern philosophy employs.   Lord Bacon was sufficiently struck with the system of Telesio to illustrate it in a separate fragment of the Instauratio Magna, though sensible of its inadequacy to solve the mysteries of nature; and a man of eccentric genius, Campanella, to whom we shall come hereafter, adopted it as the basis of his own wilder speculations.   Telesio seems to have ascribed a sort of intelligence to plants, which his last-mentioned disciple carried to a strange excess of paradox.

11. The name of Telesio is perhaps hardly so well known at present as that of Jordano Bruno. It was far otherwise formerly; and we do not find that the philosophy of this singular and unfortunate man attracted much further notice than to cost him his life.   It may be doubted, indeed, whether the Inquisition at Rome did not rather attend to his former profession of Protestantism and invectives against the church, than to the latent atheism it pretended to detect in his writings, which are at least as innocent as those of Cesalpin.   The self-conceit of Bruno, his contemptuous language about Aristotle and his followers, the paradoxical strain, the obscurity and confusion, in many places, of his writings, we may add, his poverty and frequent change of place, had rendered him of little estimation in the eyes of the world.   But in the last century the fate of Bruno excited some degree of interest about his opinions.   Whether his hypotheses were truly atheistical became the subject of controversy; his works, by which it should have been decided, were so scarce that few could speak with knowledge of their contents; and Brucker, who inclines to think there was no sufficient ground for the imputation, admits that he had only seen one of Bruno's minor treatises.   The later German philosophers, however, have paid more attention to these obscure books,

from a similarity which they sometimes found in Bruno's theories to their own. Buhle has devoted above a hundred pages to this subject.[h] The Italian treatises have within a few years been reprinted in Germany, and it is not uncommon in modern books to find an eulogy on the philosopher of Nola. I have not made myself acquainted with his Latin writings, except through the means of Buhle, who has taken a great deal of pains to explain them. The three principal Italian treatises are entitled, La Cena de li Ceneri, Della Causa, Principio ed Uno, and Dell' Infinito Universo. Each of these is in five dialogues. The Cena de li Ceneri contains a physical theory of the world, in which the author makes some show of geometrical diagrams, but deviates so often into rhapsodies of vanity and nonsense, that it is difficult to pronounce whether he had much knowledge of the science. Copernicus, to whose theory of the terrestrial motion Bruno entirely adheres, he praises as superior to any former astronomer; but intimates that he did not go far beyond vulgar prejudices, being more of a mathematician than a philosopher. The gravity of bodies he treats as a most absurd hypothesis, all natural motion, as he fancies, being circular. Yet he seems to have had some dim glimpse of what is meant by the composition of motions, asserting that the earth has four simple motions, out of which one is compounded.[i]

His Italian works.

Cena de li Ceneri.

12. The second, and much more important treatise, Della Causa, Principio ed Uno, professes to reveal the metaphysical philosophy of Bruno, a system which, at least in pretext, brought him to the stake at Rome, and the purport of which has been the theme of much controversy. The extreme scarcity of his writings has, no doubt, contributed to this variety of judgment; but though his style, strictly speaking, is not obscure, and he seems by no means inclined to conceal his meaning, I am not able to resolve with certainty the problem that Brucker

Della Causa, Principio ed Uno.

---

[h] Vol. ii. p. 604–730.

[i] Dial. v. p. 120 (1830). These dialogues were written, or purport to have been written, in England. He extols Leicester, Walsingham, and especially Sidney.

and those whom he quotes have discussed.[k] Yet the system of Bruno, so far as I understand it from what I have read of his writings, and from Buhle's analysis of them, may be said to contain a sort of double pantheism. The world is animated by an omnipresent intelligent soul, the first cause of every form that matter can assume, but not of matter itself. This soul of the universe is the only physical agent, the interior artist that works in the vast whole, that calls out the plant from the seed and matures the fruit, that lives in all things, though they may not seem to live, and in fact do not, when unorganised, live separately considered, though they all partake of the universal life, and in their component parts may be rendered living. A table as a table, a coat as a coat, are not alive, but inasmuch as they derive their substance from nature, they are composed of living particles.[m] There is nothing so small or so unimportant, but that a portion of spirit dwells in it, and this spiritual substance requires but a proper subject to become a plant or an animal. Forms particular are in constant change; but the first form, being the source of all others, as well as the first matter, are eternal. The soul of the world is the constituent principle of the universe and of all its parts. And thus we have an intrinsic, eternal, self-subsistent principle of form, far better than that which the sophists feigned, whose substances are compounded and corruptible, and, therefore, nothing else than accidents.[n]

---

[k] Brucker, vol. v. 52.

[m] Thus Buhle, or at least his French translator; but the original words are different. Dico dunque che la tavola come tavola non è animata, nè la veste, nè il cuojo come cuojo, nè il vetro come vetro, ma *come cose naturali e composte hanno in se la materia e la forma*. Sia pur cosa quanto piccola e minima si voglia, ha in se parte di sustanza spirituale, la quale, se trova il soggetto disposto, si stende ad esser pianta, ad esser animale, e riceve membri di qual si voglia corpo, che comunemente si dice animato; per chè spirto si trova in tutte le cose, e non è minimo corpusculo, che non contegna cotal porzione in se, che non inanimi, p. 241. Buhle seems not to have understood the words in italics, which certainly

are not remarkably plain, and to have substituted what he thought might pass for meaning.

The recent theories of equivocal generation, held by some philosophers, more on the Continent than in England, according to which all matter, or at least all matter susceptible of organisation by its elements, may become organised and living under peculiar circumstances, seem not very dissimilar to this system of Bruno.

[n] Or, quanto à la causa effettrice, dico l'efficiente fisico universale esser l' intelletto universale, ch' è la prima e principial facultà dell' anima del mondo, la qual è forma universale di quello. . . L' intelletto universale è l' intima più reale e propria facultà, e parte poten-

Forms in particular are the accidents of matter, and we should make a divinity of matter like some Arabian peripatetics, if we did not recur to the living fountain of form —the eternal soul of the world. The first matter is neither corporeal nor sensible, it is eternal and unchangeable, the fruitful mother of forms and their grave. Form and matter, says Bruno, pursuing this fanciful analogy, may be compared to male and female. Form never errs, is never imperfect, but through its conjunction with matter ; it might adopt the words of the father of the human race : Mulier quam mihi dedisti, (la materia, la quale mi hai dato consorte,) me decepit (lei è cagione d' ogni mio peccato). The speculations of Bruno now become more and more subtle, and he admits that our understandings cannot grasp what he pretends to demonstrate—the identity of a simply active and simply passive principle : but the question really is, whether we can see any meaning in his propositions.

13. We have said that the system of Bruno seems to involve a double pantheism. The first is of a simple kind, the hylozoism, which has been exhibited in the preceding paragraph ; it excludes a creative deity, in the strict sense of creation, but leaving an active provident intelligence, cannot be reckoned by any means chargeable with positive atheism. But to this soul of the world Bruno appears not to have ascribed the name of divinity.[o] The first form, and the first matter, and all the forms generated by the two, make, in his theory, but one being, the infinite unchangeable universe, in which is every

Pantheism of Bruno.

---

ziale dell' anima del mondo. Questo è uno medesimo ch' empie il tutto, illumina l' universo, e indrizza la natura à produrre le sue specie, come si conviene, e così ha rispetto à la produzione di cose naturali, come il nostro intelletto è la congrua produzione di specie razionali. . . . . . Questo è nominato da' Platonici fabbro del mondo. P. 235.

Dunque abbiamo un principio intrinseco formale eterno e sussistente, incomparabilmente migliore di quello, che han finto li sophisti, che versano circa gl' accidenti, ignoranti de la sustanza de le cose, e che vengono a ponere le sustanze corrottibili, perchè quello chiamano massimamente, primamente e principal-

mente sustanza, che risulta da la composizione ; il che non è altro ch' uno accidente, che non contiene in se nulla stabilità e verità e si risolve in nulla. P. 242.

[o] Son tre sorti d' intelletto ; il divino, ch' è tutto ; questo mondano, che fà tutto ; gli altri particulari, che si fanno tutte. . . . È vera causa efficiente (l' intelletto mondano) non tanto estrinseca, come anco intrinseca di tutte cose naturali. . . . Mi par, che detrahano à la divina bontà e à l' eccellenza di questo grande animale e simulacro del primo principio quelli, che non vogliano intendere, nè affirmare, il mondo con li suoi membri essere animato. P. 239.

thing, both in power and in act, and which, being all things collectively, is no one thing separately; it is form and not form, matter and not matter, soul and not soul. He expands this mysterious language much farther, resolving the whole nature of the Deity into an abstract, barren, all-embracing unity.[p]

14. These bold theories of Jordano Bruno are chiefly

---

[p] È dunque l' universo uno, infinito, immobile. Una dico è la possibilità assoluta, uno l' atto, una la forma o anima, una la materia o corpo, una la cosa, uno lo ente, uno il massimo e ottimo, il quale non deve posser essere compreso, e però infinibile e interminabile, e per tanto infinito e interminato, e per conseguenza immobile. Questo non si muove localmente; per chè non ha cosa fuor di sè, ove si trasporte, atteso chè sia il tutto. Non si genera; per chè non è altro essere, che lui possa desiderare o aspettare, atteso chè abbia tutto lo essere. Non si corrompe; per chè non è altra cosa, in cui si cangi, atteso chè lui sia ogni cosa. Non può sminuire o crescere, atteso ch' è infinito, a cui come non si può aggiungere, così è da cui non si può sottrarre, per ciò che lo infinito non ha parti proporzionali. Non è alterabile in altra disposizione, per chè non ha esterno, da cui patisca, e per cui venga in qualche affezione. Oltre chè per comprender tutte contrarietadi nell' esser suo, in unità e convenienza, e nessuna inclinazione posser avere ad altro e novo essere, o pur ad altro e altro modo d' essere, non può esser soggetto di mutazione secundo qualità alcuna, nè può aver contrario o diverso, che l' alteri, per chè in lui è ogni cosa concorde. Non è materia, per chè non è figurato, nè figurabile non è terminato, nè terminabile. Non è forma, per chè non informa, nè figura altro, atteso chè è tutto, è massimo, è uno, è universo. Non è misurabile, nè misura. Non si comprende; per chè non è maggior di sè. Non si è compreso; per chè non è minor di se. Non si agguaglia; per chè non è altro e altro, ma uno e medesimo. Essendo medesimo ed uno, non ha essere ed essere; et per chè non ha essere ed essere, non ha parti e parti; e per ciò che non ha parte e parte, non è composto. Questo è termine di sorte, chè non è termine; è talmente forma, chè non è forma; è talmente materia,

chè non è materia; è talmente anima, chè non è anima; per chè è il tutto indifferentemente, e però è uno, l' universo è uno. P. 280.

Ecco, come non è possibile, ma necessario, che l' ottimo, massimo incomprensibile è tutto, è par tutto, è in tutto, per chè come simplice ed indivisibile può esser tutto, esser per tutto, essere in tutto. E così non è stato vanamente detto, che Giove empie tutte le cose, inabita tutte le parti dell' universo, è centro di ciò, che ha l' essere uno in tutto, e per cui uno è tutto. Il quale, essendo tutte le cose, e comprendendo tutto l' essere in se, viene a far, che ogni cosa sia in ogni cosa. Ma mi direste, per chè dunque le cose si cangiano, la materia particolare si forza ad altre forme? vi rispondo, che non è mutazione, che cerca altro essere, ma altro modo di essere. E questa è la differenza tra l' universo e le cose dell' universo; per chè nullo comprende tutto l' essere e tutti modi di essere; di queste ciascuna ha tutto l' essere, ma non tutti i modi di essere. P. 282.

The following sonnet by Bruno is characteristic of his mystical imagination; but we must not confound the personification of an abstract idea with theism:—

Causa, Principio, ed Uno sempiterno,
Onde l' esser, la vita, il moto pende,
E a lungo, a largo, e profondo si stende
Quanto si dice in ciel, terra ed inferno;
    Con senso, con ragion, con mente scerno
Ch' atto, misura e conto non comprende,
Quel vigor, mole e numero, che tende
Oltre ogni inferior, mezzo e superno.
    Cieco error, tempo avaro, ria fortuna,
Sorda invidia, vil rabbia, iniquo zelo,
Crudo cor, empio ingegno, strano ardire,
    Non basteranno a farmi l' aria bruna,
Non mi porann' avanti gl' occhi il velo,
Non faran mai, ch' il mio bel Sol non mire.

If I have quoted too much from Jordano Bruno, it may be excused by the great rarity of his works, which has been the cause that some late writers have not fully seen the character of his speculations.

contained in the treatise Della Causa, Principio ed Uno. In another, entitled Dell' Infinito Universo e Mondi, which, like the former, is written in dia- _{Bruno's other writings.} logue, he asserts the infinity of the universe, and the plurality of worlds. That the stars are suns, shining by their own light, that each has its revolving planets, now become the familiar creed of children, were then among the enormous paradoxes and capital offences of Bruno. His strong assertion of the Copernican theory was, doubtless, not quite so singular, yet this had but few proselytes in the sixteenth century. His other writings, of all which Buhle has furnished us with an account, are numerous; some of them relate to the art of Raymond Lully, which Bruno professed to esteem very highly; and in these mnemonical treatises he introduced much of his own theoretical philosophy. Others are more exclusively metaphysical, and designed to make his leading principles, as to unity, number, and form, more intelligible to the common reader. They are full, according to what we find in Brucker and Buhle, of strange and nonsensical propositions, such as men, unable to master their own crude fancies on subjects above their reach, are wont to put forth. None, however, of his productions has been more often mentioned than the Spaccio della Bestia Trionfante, alleged by some to be full of his atheistical impieties, while others have taken it for a mere satire on the Roman church. This diversity was very natural in those who wrote of a book they had never seen. It now appears that this famous work is a general moral satire in an allegorical form, with little that could excite attention, and less that could give such offence as to provoke the author's death.[q]

15. Upon the whole, we may probably place Bruno in this province of speculative philosophy, though not high, yet above Cesalpin, or any of the school _{General character of his philosophy.} of Averroes. He has fallen into great errors, but they seem to have perceived no truth. His doctrine was not original; it came from the Eleatic philosophers, from Plotinus and the Neo-Platonists,[r] and in some measure from Plato

---

[q] Ginguéné, vol. vii., has given an analysis of the Spaccio della Bestia.

[r] See a valuable analysis of the philosophy of Plotinus in Degerando's His-

himself; and it is ultimately, beyond doubt, of oriental origin. What seems most his own, and I must speak very doubtfully as to this, is the syncretism of the tenet of a pervading spirit, an Anima Mundi, which in itself is an imperfect theism, with the more pernicious hypothesis of an universal Monad, to which every distinct attribute, except unity, was to be denied. Yet it is just to observe that, in one passage already quoted in a note, Bruno expressly says, ' there are three kinds of intelligence: the divine, which is every thing ; the mundane, which does every thing ; and the particular intelligences, which are all made by the second.' The inconceivableness of ascribing intelligence to Bruno's universe, and yet thus distinguishing it as he does from the mundane intelligence, may not perhaps be a sufficient reason for denying him a place among theistic philosophers. But it must be confessed that the general tone of these dialogues conveys no other impression than that of a pantheism, in which every vestige of a supreme intelligence, beyond his soul of the world, is effaced.[s]

16. The system, if so it may be called, of Bruno was

Sceptical theory of Sanchez.

essentially dogmatic, reducing the most subtle and incomprehensible mysteries into positive aphorisms of science. Sanchez, a Portuguese physician, settled as a public instructor at Toulouse, took a different course ; the preface of his treatise, Quod Nihil Scitur, is dated from that city in 1576 ; but no edition is known to have existed before 1581.[t] This work is a mere tissue of sceptical

toire comparée des Systèmes, iii. 357 (edit. 1823). It will be found that his language with respect to the mystic supremacy of unity is that of Bruno himself. Plotin, however, was not only theistic, but intensely religious, and if he had come a century later would, instead of a heathen philosopher, have been one of the first names among the saints of the church. It is probable that his influence, as it is, has not been small in modelling the mystic theology. Scotus Erigena was of the same school, and his language about the first Monad is similar to that of Bruno. Degerando, vol. iv. p. 372.

[s] I can hardly agree with Mr. Whewell in supposing that Jordano Bruno

' probably had a considerable share in introducing the new opinions (of Copernicus) into England.' Hist. of Inductive Sciences, i. 385. Very few in England seem to have embraced these opinions ; and those who did so, like Wright and Gilbert, were men who had somewhat better reasons than the *ipse dixit* of a wandering Italian.

[t] Brucker, iv. 541, with this fact before his eyes, strangely asserts Sanchez to have been born in 1562. Buhle and Cousin copy him without hesitation. Antonio is ignorant of any edition of ' Quod Nihil Scitur' except that of Rotterdam in 1649; and ignorant also that the book contains anything remarkable.

fallacies, propounded, however, with a confident tone not
unusual in that class of sophists. He begins abruptly with
these words : Nec unum hoc scio, me nihil scire, conjector
tamen nec me nec alios.   Hæc mihi vexillum propositio
sit, hæc sequenda venit, Nihil Scitur.   Hanc si probare
scivero, merito concludam nihil sciri ; si nescivero, hoc ipso
melius ; id enim asserebam. A good deal more follows in the
same sophistical style of cavillation. Hoc unum semper
maxime ab aliquo expetivi, quod modo facio, ut vere diceret
an aliquid perfecte sciret; nusquam tamen inveni, præter-
quam in sapiente illo proboque viro Socrate (licet et Pyrrhonii,
Academici et Sceptici vocati, cum Favorino id etiam essere-
rent) quod hoc unum sciebat quod nihil sciret.   Quo solo
dicto mihi doctissimus indicatur ; quanquam nec adhuc
omnino mihi explêrit mentem ; cum et illud unum, sicut
alia, ignoraret.[u]

17. Sanchez puts a few things well; but his scepticism,
as we perceive, is extravagant. After descanting on Montaigne's favourite topic, the various manners and opinions
of mankind, he says, Non finem faceremus si omnes
omnium mores recensere vellemus.   An tu his eandem
rationem, quam nobis, omnino putes ?   Mihi non veri-
simile videtur.   Nihil tamen ambo scimus.   Negabis
forsan tales aliquos esse homines.   Non contendam; sic
ab aliis accepi.[x] Yet, notwithstanding his sweeping denun-
ciation of all science in the boldest tone of Pyrrhonism,
Sanchez comes at length to admit the possibility of a
limited or probable knowledge of truth; and, as might
perhaps be expected, conceives that he had himself attained
it.   'There are two modes,' he observes, ' of discovering
truth, by neither of which do men learn the real nature of
things, but yet obtain some kind of insight into them.
These are experiment and reason, neither being sufficient
alone ; but experiments, however well conducted, do not
show us the nature of things, and reason can only conjecture them.   Hence there can be no such thing as perfect
science ; and books have been employed to eke out the
deficiences of our own experience ; but their confusion,

---

prolixity, multitude, and want of trustworthiness prevent this resource from being of much value, nor is life long enough for so much study. Besides, this perfect knowledge requires a perfect recipient of it, and a right disposition of the subject of knowledge, which two I have never seen. Reader, if you have met with them, write me word.' He concludes the treatise by promising another, ' in which we shall explain the method of knowing truth, as far as human weakness will permit ; ' and, as his self-complacency rises above his affected scepticism, adds, mihi in animo est firman et facilem quantum possim scientiam fundare.

18. This treatise of Sanchez bears witness to a deep sense of the imperfections of the received systems in science and reasoning, and to a restless longing for truth, which strikes us in other writers of this latter period of the sixteenth century. Lord Bacon, I believe, has never alluded to Sanchez, and such paradoxical scepticism was likely to disgust his strong mind; yet we may sometimes discern signs of a Baconian spirit in the attacks of our Spanish philosopher on the syllogistic logic, as being built on abstract and not significant terms, and in his clear perception of the difference between a knowledge of words and one of things.

19. What Sanchez promised, and Bacon gave, a new method of reasoning, by which truth might be better determined than through the common dialectics, had been partially attempted already by Aconcio, mentioned in the last chapter as one of those highly-gifted Italians who fled for religion to a Protestant country. Without openly assailing the authority of Aristotle, he endeavoured to frame a new discipline of the faculties for the discovery of truth. His treatise, De Methodo, sive Recta Investigandarum Tradendarumque Scientiarum Ratione, was published at Basle in 1558, and was several times reprinted, till later works, those especially of Bacon and Des Cartes, caused it to be forgotten. Aconcio defines logic, the right method of thinking and teaching, recta contemplandi docendique ratio. Of the importance of method, or right order in prosecuting our inquiries, he thinks so highly, that if thirty years were to be destined to

Logic of Aconcio.

intellectual labour, he would allot two-thirds of the time to acquiring dexterity in this art, which seems to imply that he did not consider it very easy. To know anything, he tells us, is to know what it is, or what are its causes and effects. All men have the germs of knowledge latent in them, as to matters cognisable by human faculties ; it is the business of logic to excite and develop them : notiones illas seu scintillas sub cinere latentes detegere aptèque ad res obscuras illustrandas applicare.ʸ

20. Aconcio next gives rules at length for constructing definitions, by attending to the genus and differentia. These rules are good, and might very properly find a place in a book of logic ; but whether they contain much that would vainly be sought in other writers, we do not determine. He comes afterwards to the methods of distributing a subject. The analytic method is by all means to be preferred for the investigation of truth, and, contrary to what Galen and others have advised, even for communicating it to others ; since a man can learn that of which he is ignorant, only by means of what is better known, whether he does this himself, or with help of a teacher ; the only process being, a notioribus ad minus nota. In this little treatise of Aconcio there seem to be the elements of a sounder philosophy and a more steady direction of the mind to discover the reality of things than belonged to the logic of the age, whether as taught by the Aristotelians or by Ramus. It has not, however, been quoted by Lord Bacon, nor are we sure that he has profited by it.

21. A more celebrated work than this by Aconcio is one by the distinguished scholar, Marius Nizolius, 'De Veris Principiis et Vera Ratione Philosophandi contra Pseudo-Philosophos.' (Parma, 1553.) It owes, however, what reputation it possesses to Leibnitz, who reprinted it in 1670, with a very able preface, one of his first contributions to philosophy. The treatise itself, he says, was almost strangled in the birth ; and certainly the invectives of Nizolius against the logic and metaphysics of Aristotle could have had little chance of success in a country

Nizolius on the principles of philosophy.

ʸ P. 30.

like Italy, where that authority was more undoubted and durable than in any other. The aim of Nizolius was to set up the best authors of Greece and Rome and the study of philology against the scholastic terminology. But it must be owned that this polite literature was not sufficient for the discovery of truth; nor does the book keep up to the promise of its title, though, by endeavouring to eradicate barbarous sophistry, he may be said to have laboured in the interests of real philosophy. The preface of Leibnitz animadverts on what appeared to him some metaphysical errors of Nizolius, especially an excess of nominalism, which tended to undermine the foundations of certainty, and his presumptuous scorn of Aristotle.[z] His own object was rather to recommend the treatise as a model of philosophical language without barbarism, than to bestow much praise on its philosophy. Brucker has spoken of it rather slightingly, and Buhle with much contempt. I am not prepared by a sufficient study of its contents to pass any judgment; but Buhle's censure has appeared to me somewhat unfair. Dugald Stewart, who was not acquainted with what the latter has said, thinks Nizolius deserving of more commendation than Brucker has assigned

---

[z] Nizolius maintained that universal terms were only particulars—collectivè sumpta. Leibnitz replies, that they are particulars—distributivè sumpta; as, omnis homo est animal means, that every one man is an animal; not that the genus man, taken collectively, is an animal. Nec vero Nizolii error hic levis est; habet enim magnum aliquid in recessu. Nam si universalia nihil aliud sunt quam singularium collectiones, sequitur, scientiam nullam haberi per demonstrationem, quod et infra colligit Nizolius, sed collectionem singularium seu inductionem. Sed ea ratione prorsus evertuntur scientiæ, ac Sceptici vicere. Nam nunquam constitui possunt ea ratione propositiones perfecte universales, quia inductione nunquam certus es, omnia individue a te tentata esse; sed semper intra hanc propositionem subsistes; omnia illa quæ expertus sum sunt talia; cum vero non possit esse ulla ratio universalis, semper manebit possibile innumera quæ tu non sis expertus esse diversa. Hinc jam patet inductionem per se nihil producere, ne cer-

titudinem quidem moralem, sine adminiculo propositionum non ab inductione, sed ratione universali prudentium; nam si essent et adminicula ab inductione, indigerent novis adminiculis, nec haberetur certitudo moralis in infinitum. Sed certitudo moralis ab inductione sperari plane non potest, additis quibuscunque adminiculis, et propositionem hanc, totum magis esse sua parte, sola inductione nunquam perfecte sciemus. Mox enim prodibit, qui negabit ob peculiarem quondam rationem in aliis nondum tentatis veram esse, quemadmodum ex facto scimus Gregorium a Sancto Vincentio negasse totum esse majus sua parte, in angulis saltem contactûs, alios in infinito; et Thomam Hobbes (at quem virum!) cœpisse dubitare de propositione illa geometrica a Pythagora demonstrata, et hecatombæ sacrificio digna habita; quod ego non sine stupore legi. This extract is not very much to the purpose of the text, but it may please some of those who take an interest in such speculations.

to him.[a] He argues against all dialectics, and therefore differs from Ramus ; concluding with two propositions as the result of his whole book :—That as many logicians and metaphysicians as are any where found, so many capital enemies of truth will then and there exist ; and that, so long as Aristotle shall be supreme in the logic and metaphysics of the schools, so long will error and barbarism reign over the mind.   There is nothing very deep or pointed in this summary of his reasoning.

22. The Margarita Antoniana, by Gomez Pereira, published at Medina del Campo in 1554, has been chiefly remembered as the ground of one of the many charges against Des Cartes for appropriating unacknowledged opinions of his predecessors.   The book is exceedingly scarce, which has been strangely ascribed to the efforts of Des Cartes to suppress it.[b]   There is, however, a copy of the original edition in the British Museum, and it has been reprinted in Spain.   It was an unhappy theft, if theft it were ; for what Pereira maintained was precisely the most untenable proposition of the great French philosopher —the absence of sensation in brutes.   Pereira argues against this with an extraordinary disregard of common phænomena, on the assumption of certain maxims which cannot be true, if they contradict inferences from our observation far more convincing than themselves.   We find him give a curious reason for denying that we can infer the sensibility of brutes from their outward actions : namely, that this would prove too much, and lead us to believe them rational beings ; instancing among other stories, true or false, of apparent sagacity, the dog in pursuit of a hare, who, coming where two roads meet, if he traces no scent on the first, takes the other without trial.[c]   Pereira is a rejecter of Aristotelian despotism ; and observes that in matters of speculation and not of faith, no authority is to be respected.[d]   Notwithstand-

Margarita Antoniana of Pereira.

---

[a] Dissertation on Progress of Philosophy, p. 38.

[b] Biogr. univ. Brunet, Manuel du Libraire. Bayle has a long article on Pereira, but though he says the book had been shown to him, he wanted probably the opportunity to read much of it.

According to Brunet, several copies have been sold in France, some of them at no great price. The later editión, of 1749, is of course cheaper.

[c] Fol. 18. This is continually told of dogs ; but does any sensible sportsman confirm it by his own experience? I ask for information only.

[d] Fol. 4.

ing this assertion of freedom, he seems to be wholly enchained
by the metaphysics of the schools : nor should I have thought
the book worthy of notice, but for its scarcity and the circumstance above mentioned about Des Cartes.

23. These are, as far as I know, the only works deserving
of commemoration in the history of speculative philosophy.
A few might easily be inserted from the catalogues of
libraries, or from biographical collections, as well as from
the learned labours of Morhof, Brucker, Tennemann, and
Buhle. It is also not to be doubted, that in treatises of a
different character, theological, moral, or medical, very many
passages, worthy of remembrance for their truth, their
ingenuity, or originality, might be discovered, that bear
upon the best methods of reasoning, the philosophy of the
human mind, the theory of natural religion, or the general
system of the material world.

24. We should not, however, conclude this chapter without
Logic of
Ramus; its
success.
adverting to the dialectical method of Ramus, whom
we left at the middle of the century, struggling
against all the arms of orthodox logic in the university of
Paris. The reign of Henry II. was more propitious to him
than that of Francis. In 1551, through the patronage of
the Cardinal of Lorraine, Ramus became royal professor of
rhetoric and philosophy ; and his new system, which, as has
been mentioned, comprehended much that was important in
the art of rhetoric, began to make numerous proselytes.
Omer Talon, known for a treatise on eloquence, was among
the most ardent of these ; and to him we owe our most
authentic account of the contest of Ramus with the Sorbonne.
The latter were not conciliated, of course, by the success of
their adversary ; and Ramus having adhered to the Huguenot
party in the civil feuds of France, it has been ascribed to the
malignity of one of his philosophical opponents that he
perished in the massacre of St. Bartholomew. He had, however, already, by personally travelling and teaching in Germany, spread the knowledge of his system over that country.
It was received in some of the German universities with
great favour, notwithstanding the influence which Melanchthon's name retained, and which had been entirely thrown
into the scale of Aristotle. The Ramists and anti-Ramists

contended in books of logic through the rest of this century, as well as afterwards; but this was the principal period of Ramus's glory. In Italy he had few disciples; but France, England, and still more Scotland and Germany, were full of them. Andrew Melville introduced the logic of Ramus at Glasgow. It was resisted for some time at St. Andrew's but ultimately became popular in all the Scottish universities.[e] Scarce any eminent public school, says Brucker, can be named, in which the Ramists were not teachers. They encountered an equally zealous militia under the Aristotelian standard; while some, with the spirit of compromise, which always takes possession of a few minds, though it is rarely very successful, endeavoured to unite the two methods, which in fact do not seem essentially exclusive of each other. It cannot be required of me to give an account of books so totally forgotten and so uninteresting in their subjects as these dialectical treatises on either side. The importance of Ramus in philosphical history is not so much founded on his own deserts, as on the effect he produced in loosening the fetters of inveterate prejudice, and thus preparing the way, like many others of his generation, for those who were to be the restorers of genuine philosophy.[f]

---

[e] M'Crie's Life of Melville, ii. 306.   [f] Brucker, v. 576.   Buhle, ii. 601.

CHAPTER IV.

HISTORY OF MORAL AND POLITICAL PHILOSOPHY AND OF
JURISPRUDENCE, FROM 1550 TO 1600.

SECT. I.—ON MORAL PHILOSOPHY.

Soto—Hooker—Essays of Montaigne—Their influence on the Public—
Italian and English Moralists.

1. IT must naturally be supposed that by far the greater
part of what was written on moral obligations in the sixteenth century will be found in the theological quarter of
ancient libraries. The practice of auricular confession
brought with it an entire science of casuistry, which had
gradually been wrought into a complicated system. Many,
once conspicuous writers in this province, belong to the
present period; but we shall defer the subject till we arrive at the next, when it had acquired a more prominent
importance.

2. The first original work of any reputation in ethical
philosophy since the revival of letters, and which,
being apparently designed in great measure for
the chair of the confessional, serves as a sort of link between the class of mere casuistry and the philosophical
systems of morals which were to follow, is by Dominic Soto,
a Spanish Dominican, who played an eminent part in the
deliberations of the Council of Trent, in opposition both to
the papal court and to the theologians of the Scotist, or, as
it was then reckoned by its adversaries, the Semi-Pelagian
school.   This folio volume, entitled De Justitia et Jure, was
first published, according to the Biographie universelle, at
Antwerp, in 1568.   It appears to be founded on the writings

Soto De Justitia.

of Thomas Aquinas, the polar star of every true Dominican. Every question is discussed with that remarkable observation of distinctions, and that unremitting desire both to comprehend and to distribute a subject, which is displayed in many of these forgotten folios, and ought to inspire us with reverence for the zealous energy of their authors, even when we find it impossible, as must generally be the case, to read so much as a few pages consecutively, or when we light upon trifling and insufficient arguments in the course of our casual glances over the volume.

3. Hooker's Ecclesiastical Polity might seem more properly to fall under the head of theology; but the first book of this work being by much the best, Hooker ought rather to be reckoned among those who have weighed the principles, and delineated the boundaries, of moral and political science. I have, on another occasion,[a] done full justice to the wisdom and eloquence of this earliest among the great writers of England, who, having drunk at the streams of ancient philosophy, has acquired from Plato and Tully somewhat of their redundancy and want of precision, with their comprehensiveness of observation and their dignity of soul. The reasonings of Hooker, though he bore in the ensuing century the surname of Judicious, are not always safe or satisfactory, nor, perhaps, can they be reckoned wholly clear or consistent; his learning, though beyond that of most English writers in that age, is necessarily uncritical; and his fundamental principle, the mutability of ecclesiastical government, has as little pleased those for whom he wrote as those whom he repelled by its means.[b]

---

[a] Constitut. Hist. Engl., chap. iv.

[b] [The phrase, 'fundamental principle,' may appear too strong to those who have not paid much attention to the subject, especially when a man of so much ability as the last editor of the Ecclesiastical Polity has laboured to persuade his readers that Hooker maintained the divine right of episcopal government. By a fundamental principle, I mean a leading theorem which determines the character of a book, and gives it its typical form, as distinguished from others which may have the same main object in view. Thus, to take a very different instance, the main object of Homer was to celebrate the prowess of the Greeks in the war of Troy; but the mode in which he presented this, the typical character of the Iliad, was the illustration of one memorable portion of that contest, the quarrel of Achilles with Agamemnon. What the wrath of Achilles was to Homer, that was the mutability of positive laws to Hooker; a leading idea, which gave its peculiar form to his work, and through which his ultimate end, the defence of the ecclesiastical constitution of his country, was to be

But he stood out at a vast height above his predecessors and contemporaries in the English church, and was, perhaps, the first of our writers who had any considerable acquaintance with the philosophers of Greece, not merely displayed in quotation, of which others may have sometimes set an example, but in a spirit of reflection and comprehensiveness which the study of antiquity alone could have infused. The absence of minute ramifications of argument, in which the schoolmen loved to spread out, distinguishes Hooker from the writers who had been trained in those arid dialectics, such as Soto or Suarez: but, as I have hinted, considering the depth and difficulty of several questions that he deals with in the first book of the Polity, we might wish for a little less of the expanded palm of rhetoric, and somewhat of more dialectical precision in the reasoning.[c]

---

effected. It may be inquired of those who think otherwise, why the first book of the Ecclesiastical Polity was written at all? Was it merely to display his reasoning or eloquence upon a subject far more appertaining to philosophy than to theology? Surely this would have been idle ostentation, especially in the very outset of his work. But those who read it can hardly fail to perceive that it is the broad basis of what is to follow in the second and third books; that in laying down the distinction between natural and positive law, and affirming the former alone to be immutable, he prepares the way for denying the main position of his puritan antagonists, that all things contained in Scripture are of perpetual obligation. It is his doctrine, that where God has not declared a positive command to be perpetual, it may be dispensed with by lawful human authority; and in the third book he, in express words, asserts this of ecclesiastical government. Whether he is right or no, we do not here inquire; but those who prefer an honest avowal of truth to that small party-interest which is served by counting all names as on our side, cannot feel any hesitation about his opinion on this point. I repeat, that it may be called his fundamental principle.

I do not, however, deny that, in the seventh book of the Ecclesiastical Polity, written several years after the former, there are signs that Hooker had

in some degree abandoned the broad principle of indifferency, and that he occasionally seems to contend for episcopal government as always best, though not always indispensable. Whether this were owing to the natural effects of controversy, in rendering the mind tenacious of every point it has to maintain, or rather to the bolder course of defence which Saravia and Bancroft had latterly taught the advocates of the church to take, I do not determine. But, even in this book, we shall not find that he ever asserts in terms the perpetual obligation of episcopacy; nor does he, I believe, so much as allude to what is commonly called the apostolical succession, or transmission of spiritual power from one bishop to another; a question wholly distinct from that of mere ecclesiastical government, though perpetually confounded with it.—1842.]

[c] It has been shown with irresistible proof by the last editor of Hooker, that the sixth book of the Ecclesiastical Polity has been lost; that which we read as such being, with the exception of a few paragraphs at the beginning, altogether a different production, though bearing marks of the same author. This is proved, not only by its want of relation to the general object of the work, and to the subject announced in the title of this very book, but by the remarkable fact, that a series of observations by two friends of Hooker on the sixth book are extant, and pub-

4. Hooker, like most great moral writers both of antiquity and of modern ages, rests his positions on His theory of natural law. one solid basis, the eternal obligation of natural law. A small number had been inclined to maintain an arbitrary power of the Deity, even over the fundamental principles of right and wrong ; but the sounder theologians seem to have held that, however the will of God may be the proper source of moral obligation in mankind, concerning which they were not more agreed then than they have been since, it was impossible for him to deviate from his immutable rectitude and holiness. They were unaminous also in asserting the capacity of the human faculties to discern right from wrong, little regarding what they deemed the prejudices or errors that had misled many nations, and more or less influenced the majority of mankind.

5. But there had never been wanting those who, struck by the diversity of moral judgments and behaviour Doubts felt by others. among men, and especially under circumstances of climate, manners, or religion, different from our own, had found it hard to perceive how reason could be an unerring arbiter, when there was so much discrepancy in what she professed to have determined. The relations of travellers, continually pressing upon the notice of Europe in the sixteenth century, and perhaps rather more exaggerated than at present, in describing barbarous tribes, afforded continual aliment to the suspicion. It was at least evident, without

---

lished in the last edition, which were obviously designed for a totally different treatise from that which has always passed for the sixth book of the Ecclesiastical Polity. This can only be explained by the confusion in which Hooker's manuscripts were left at his death, and upon which suspicions of interpolation have been founded. Such suspicions are not reasonable ; and, notwithstanding the exaggerated language which has sometimes been used, I think it very questionable whether any more perfect manuscript was ever in existence. The reasoning in the seventh and eighth books appears as elaborate, the proofs as full, the grammatical structure as perfect, as in the earlier books ; and the absence of those passages of eloquence, which we occasionally find in the former, cannot afford even a presumption that the latter were designed to be written over again. The eighth book is manifestly incomplete, wanting some discussions which the author had announced ; but this seems rather adverse to the hypothesis of a more elaborate copy. The more probable inference is, that Hooker was interrupted by death before he had completed his plan. It is possible also that the conclusion of the eighth book has been lost like the sixth. All the stories on this subject in the Life of Hooker by Walton, who seems to have been a man always too credulous of anecdote, are unsatisfactory to any one who exacts real proof.

any thing that could be called unreasonable scepticism, that these diversities ought to be well explained and sifted before we acquiesced in the pleasant conviction that we alone could be in the right.

6. The Essays of Montaigne, the first edition of which Essays of appeared at Bordeaux in 1580,[d] make in several Montaigne. respects an epoch in literature, less on account of their real importance, or the novel truths they contain, than of their influence upon the taste and the opinions of Europe. They are the first *provocatio ad populum*, the first appeal from the porch and the academy to the haunts of busy and of idle men, the first book that taught the unlearned reader to observe and reflect for himself on questions of moral philosophy. In an age when every topic of this nature was treated systematically, and in a didactic form, he broke out without connection of chapters, with all the digressions that levity and garrulous egotism could suggest, with a very delightful, but, at that time, most unusual rapidity of transition from seriousness to gaiety. It would be to anticipate much of what will demand attention in the ensuing century, were we to mention here the conspicuous writers who, more or less directly, and with more or less of close imitation, may be classed in the school of Montaigne; it embraces, in fact, a large proportion of French and English literature, and especially of that which has borrowed his title of Essays. No prose writer of the sixteenth century has been so generally read, nor probably has given so much delight. Whatever may be our estimate of Montaigne as a philosopher, a name which he was far from arrogating, there will be but one opinion of the felicity and brightness of his genius.

7. It is a striking proof of these qualities, that, in reading Their cha- his Essays, we can hardly help believing him to racteristics. have struck out all his thoughts by a spontaneous effort of his mind, and to have fallen afterwards upon his quotations and examples by happy accident. I have little doubt but that the process was different; and that, either by dint of memory, though he absolutely disclaims the possessing a good one, or by the usual method of common-placing, he

---

[d] This edition contains only the first and second books of the Essays; the third was published in that of Paris, 1588.

had made his reading instrumental to excite his own ingenious and fearless understanding. His extent of learning was by no means great for that age, but the whole of it
was brought to bear on his object; and it is a proof of
Montaigne's independence of mind that, while a vast mass
of erudition was the only regular passport to fame, he read
no authors but such as were most fitted to his own habits of
thinking. Hence he displays an unity, a self-existence,
which we seldom find so complete in other writers. His
quotations, though they perhaps make more than one half of
his Essays, seem parts of himself, and are like limbs of his
own mind, which could not be separated without laceration.
But over all is spread a charm of a fascinating simplicity,
and an apparent abandonment of the whole man to the easy
inspiration of genius, combined with a good-nature, though
rather too epicurean and destitute of moral energy, which,
for that very reason, made him a favourite with men of
similar dispositions, for whom courts, and camps, and country
mansions were the proper soil.

8. Montaigne is superior to any of the ancients in liveliness,
in that careless and rapid style where one thought springs
naturally, but not consecutively, from another, by analogical rather than deductive connection; so that, while the
reader seems to be following a train of arguments, he is im-
perceptibly hurried to a distance by some contingent
association. This may be observed in half his Essays, the
titles of which often give us little insight into their general
scope. Thus the apology for Raymond de Sebonde is soon
forgotten in the long defence of moral Pyrrhonism, which
occupies the twelfth chapter of the second book. He sometimes makes a show of coming back from his excursions; but
he has generally exhausted himself before he does so. This
is what men love to practise (not advantageously for their
severer studies) in their own thoughts; they love to follow the
casual associations that lead them through pleasant labyrinths
—as one riding along the high road is glad to deviate a
little into the woods, though it may sometimes happen
that he will lose his way, and find himself far remote from
his inn. And such is the conversational style of lively and
eloquent old men. We converse with Montaigne, or rather

hear him talk; it is almost impossible to read his Essays
without thinking that he speaks to us; we see his cheerful
brow, his sparkling eye, his negligent but gentlemanly
demeanour; we picture him in his arm-chair, with his few
books round the room, and Plutarch on the table.

9. The independence of his mind produces great part of
the charm of his writing; it redeems his vanity, without
which it could not have been so fully displayed, or, perhaps,
so powerfully felt. In an age of literary servitude, when
every province into which reflection could wander was
occupied by some despot; when, to say nothing of theology,
men found Aristotle, or Ulpian, or Hippocrates, at every
turning to dictate their road, it was gratifying to fall in
company with a simple gentleman who, with much more
reading than generally belonged to his class, had the spirit
to ask a reason for every rule.

10. Montaigne has borrowed much, besides his quotations, from the few ancient authors whom he loved to
study. In one passage he even says that his book is wholly
compiled from Plutarch and Seneca; but this is evidently
intended to throw the critics off their scent. 'I purposely
conceal the authors from whom I borrow,' he says in another
place, 'to check the presumption of those who are apt to
censure what they find in a modern. I am content that they
should lash Seneca and Plutarch through my sides.'e These
were his two favourite authors; and in order to judge of the
originality of Montaigne in any passage, it may often be
necessary to have a considerable acquaintance with their
works. 'When I write,' he says, 'I care not to have books
about me; but I can hardly be without a Plutarch.'f He
knew little Greek, but most editions at that time had a
Latin translation: he needed not for Plutarch to go beyond
his own language. Cicero he did not much admire, except
the epistles to Atticus. He esteemed the moderns very
slightly in comparison with antiquity, though praising
Guicciardini and Philip de Comines. Dugald Stewart observes, that Montaigne cannot be suspected of affectation, and
therefore must himself have believed what he says of the

---

e L. ii. c. 32.   f L. ii. c. 10.

badness of his memory, forgetting, as he tells us, the names
of the commonest things, and even of those he constantly
saw.   But his vanity led him to talk perpetually of himself;
and, as often happens to vain men, he would rather talk of
his own failings than of any foreign subject.   He could not
have had a very defective memory so far as it had been exercised, though he might fall into the common mistake of
confounding his inattention to ordinary objects with weakness of the faculty.

11. Montaigne seldom defines or discriminates ; his mind
had great quickness, but little subtilty ; his carelessness and
impatience of labour rendered his views practically one-
sided ; for though he was sufficiently free from prejudice to
place the objects of consideration in different lights, he
wanted the power, or did not use the diligence, to make that
comparative appreciation of facts which is necessary to distinguish the truth.   He appears to most advantage in
matters requiring good sense and calm observation, as in the
education of children.   The twenty-fourth and twenty-eighth
chapters of the first book, which relate to this subject, are
among that best in the collection.   His excellent temper
made him an enemy to the harshness and tyranny so frequent at that time in the management of children, as his clear
understanding did to the pedantic methods of overloading
and misdirecting their faculties.   It required some courage
to argue against the grammarians who had almost monopo-
lised the admiration of the world.   Of these men Montaigne
observes that, though they have strong memories, their
judgment is usually very shallow ; making only an exception
for Turnebus, who, though in his opinion the greatest
scholar that had existed for a thousand years, had nothing
of the pedant about him but his dress.   In all the remarks
of Montaigne on human character and manners, we find a
liveliness, simplicity, and truth.   They are such as his
ordinary opportunities of observation or his reading suggested ; and though several writers have given proofs of
deeper reflection or more watchful discernment, few are so
well calculated to fall in with the apprehension of the
general reader.

12. The scepticism of Montaigne, concerning which so

much has been said, is not displayed in religion, for he was a steady Catholic, though his faith seems to have been rather that of acquiescence than conviction, nor in such subtilties of metaphysical Pyrrhonism as we find in Sanchez, which had no attraction for his careless nature. But he had read much of Sextus Empiricus, and might perhaps have derived something from his favourite Plutarch. He had also been forcibly struck by the recent narratives of travellers, which he sometimes received with a credulity as to evidence not rarely combined with theoretical scepticism, and which is too much the fault of his age to bring censure on an individual. It was then assumed that all travellers were trustworthy, and, still more, that none of the Greek and Roman authors have recorded falsehoods. Hence he was at a loss to discover a general rule of moral law, as an implanted instinct, or necessary deduction of common reason, in the varying usages and opinions of mankind. But his scepticism was less extravagant and unreasonable at that time than it would be now. Things then really doubtful have been proved, and positions, entrenched by authority which he dared not to scruple, have been overthrown; [g] truth, in retiring from her outposts, has become more unassailable in her citadel.

13. It may be deemed a symptom of wanting a thorough love of truth when a man overrates, as much as when he overlooks, the difficulties he deals with. Montaigne is perhaps not exempt from this failing. Though sincere and candid in his general temper, he is sometimes more ambitious of setting forth his own ingenuity than desirous to come to the bottom of his subject. Hence he is apt to run into the fallacy common to this class of writers, and which La Mothe le Vayer employed much more—that of confounding the variations of the customs of mankind in things morally indifferent with those which affect the principles of duty; and hence the serious writers on philosophy in the next age, Pascal, Arnauld, Malebranche, animadvert with much severity on Montaigne. They considered him, not perhaps

---

[g] Montaigne's scepticism was rightly exercised on witchcraft and other supernatural stories; and he had probably some weight in discrediting those superstitions. See L. iii. c. 11.

unjustly, as an enemy to the candid and honest investigation of truth, both by his sceptical bias and by the great indifference of his temperament; scarcely acknowledging so much as was due the service he had done by chasing away the servile pedantry of the schools, and preparing the road for closer reasoners than himself. But the very tone of their censures is sufficient to prove the vast influence he had exerted over the world.

14. Montaigne is the earliest classical writer in the French language, the first whom a gentleman is ashamed not to have read. So long as an unaffected style and an appearance of the utmost simplicity and good nature shall charm, so long as the lovers of desultory and cheerful conversation shall be more numerous than those who prefer a lecture or a sermon, so long as reading is sought by the many as an amusement in idleness, or a resource in pain, so long will Montaigne be among the favourite authors of mankind. I know not whether the greatest blemish of his Essays has much impeded their popularity; they led the way to the indecency too characteristic of French literature, but in no writer on serious topics, except Bayle, more habitual than in Montaigne. It may be observed, that a larger portion of this quality distinguishes the third book, published after he had attained a reputation, than the two former. It is also more overspread by egotism; and it is not agreeable to perceive that the two leading faults of his disposition became more unrestrained and absorbing as he advanced in life.

15. The Italians have a few moral treatises of this period, but chiefly scarce and little read. The Instituzioni Morali of Alexander Piccolomini, the Instituzioni di Tutta la Vita dell' Uomo Nato Nobile e in Città Libera, by the same author, the Latin treatise of Mazzoni de Triplici Vita, which, though we mention it here as partly ethical, seems to be rather an attempt to give a general survey of all science, are among the least obscure, though they have never been of much reputation in Europe.[h] But a more

Writers on morals in Italy.

---

[h] For these books see Tiraboschi, Corniani, and Ginguéné. Niceron, vol. xxiiii., observes of Piccolomini, that he was the first who employed the Italian language in moral philosophy. This must, however, be taken very strictly, for in a general sense of the word, we have seen earlier instances than his Instituzioni Morali in 1575.

celebrated work, relating indeed to a minor department of
ethics, the rules of polite and decorous behaviour, is the
Galateo of Casa, bishop of Benevento, and an elegant writer
of considerable reputation. This little treatise is not only
accounted superior in style to most Italian prose, but serves
to illustrate the manners of society in the middle of the sixteenth century. Some of the improprieties which he
censures are such as we should hardly have expected to find
in Italy, and almost remind us of a strange but graphic poem
of one Dedekind, on the manners of Germany in the
sixteenth century, called Grobianus. But his own precepts in
other places, though hardly striking us as novel, are more
refined, and relate to the essential principles of social intercourse, rather than to its conventional forms.[1] Casa wrote
also a little book on the duties to be observed between friends
of unequal ranks. The inferior, he advises, should never
permit himself to jest upon his patron ; but if he is himself
stung by any unpleasing wit or sharp word, ought to receive
it with a smiling countenance, and to answer so as to conceal
his resentment. It is probable that this art was understood
in an Italian palace without the help of books.

16. There was never a generation in England which, for
worldly prudence and wise observation of mankind,
In England. stood higher than the subjects of Elizabeth. Rich
in men of strong mind, that age had given them a discipline
unknown to ourselves ; the strictness of the Tudor government, the suspicious temper of the queen, the spirit not only
of intolerance, but of inquisitiveness as to religious dissent,
the uncertainties of the future, produced a caution rather
foreign to the English character, accompanied by a closer
attention to the workings of other men's minds, and their
exterior signs. This, for similar reasons, had long distinguished the Italians ; but it is chiefly displayed, perhaps, in
their political writings. We find it, in a larger and
more philosophical sense, near the end of Elizabeth's
reign, when our literature made its first strong shoot,
prompting the short condensed reflections of Burleigh and

---

[1] Casa inveighs against the punctilious and troublesome ceremonies, introduced, as he supposes, from Spain,
making distinctions in the mode of addressing different ranks of nobility.

Raleigh, or saturating with moral observation the mighty soul of Shakspeare.

17. The first in time, and we may justly say, the first in excellence of English writings on moral prudence, Bacon's are the Essays of Bacon. But these, as we now Essays. read them, though not very bulky, are greatly enlarged since their first publication in 1597. They then were but ten in number:—entitled, 1. Of Studies; 2. Of Discourse; 3. Of Ceremonies and Respects; 4. Of Followers and Friends; 5. Of Suitors; 6. Of Expence; 7. Of Regiment of Health; 8. Of Honour and Reputation; 9. Of Faction; 10. Of Negociating. And even these few have been expanded in later editions to nearly double their extent. The rest were added chiefly in 1612, and the whole were enlarged in 1625. The pith, indeed, of these ten Essays will be found in the edition of 1597; the additions being merely to explain, correct, or illustrate. But, as a much greater number were incorporated with them in the next century, we shall say no more of Bacon's Essays for the present.

Sect. II.—On Political Philosophy.

Freedom of Writing on Government at this Time—Its Causes—Hottoman—Languet—La Boetie—Buchanan—Poynet—Rose—Mariana—The Jesuits—Botero and Paruta—Bodin—Analysis of his Republic.

18. The present period, especially after 1570, is far more fruitful than the preceding in the annals of poli- Number of tical science. It produced several works both of political writers. temporary and permanent importance. Before we come to Bodin, who is its most conspicuous ornament, it may be fit to mention some less considerable books, which, though belonging partly to the temporary class, have in several instances survived the occasion which drew them forth, and indicate a state of public opinion not unworthy of notice.

19. A constant progress towards absolute monarchy, sometimes silent, at other times attended with Oppression of violence, had been observable in the principal governments, kingdoms of Europe for the last hundred years. This had

been brought about by various circumstances which belong
to civil history; but among others, by a more skilful
management, and a more systematic attention to the maxims
of state-craft, which had sometimes assumed a sort of
scientific form, as in The Prince of Machiavel, but were
more frequently inculcated in current rules familiar to the
counsellors of kings. The consequence had been not only
many flagrant instances of violated public right, but in
some countries, especially France, an habitual contempt for
every moral as well as political restraint on the ruler's will.
But oppression is always felt to be such, and the breach of
known laws cannot be borne without resentment, though it
and spirit generated by it. may without resistance; nor were there wanting
several causes that tended to generate a spirit of
indignation against the predominant despotism. Independent of those of a political nature, which varied according
to the circumstances of kingdoms, there were three that
belonged to the sixteenth century as a learned and reflecting age, which, if they did not all exercise a great influence
over the multitude, were sufficient to affect the complexion
of literature, and to indicate a somewhat novel state of
opinion in the public mind.

20. I. From the Greek and Roman poets, orators, or
Derived from classic history. historians, the scholar derived the principles, not
only of equal justice, but of equal privileges; he
learned to reverence free republics, to abhor tyranny, to
sympathise with a Timoleon or a Brutus. A late English
historian, who carried to a morbid excess his jealousy of
democratic prejudices, fancied that these are perceptible in
the versions of Greek authors by the learned of the sixteenth century, and that Xylander or Rhodomann gratified
their spite against the sovereigns of their own time by
mistranslating their text in order, to throw odium on Philip
or Alexander. This is probably unfounded; but it may
still be true that men, who had imbibed notions, perhaps as
indefinite as exaggerated, of the blessings of freedom in
ancient Rome and Greece, would draw no advantageous
contrast with the palpable outrages of arbitrary power
before their eyes. We have seen, fifty years before, a
striking proof of almost mutinous indignation in the

Adages of Erasmus; and I have little doubt that further
evidence of it might be gleaned from the letters and writings
of the learned.

21. II. In proportion as the antiquities of the existing
European monarchies came to be studied, it could From their own and the Jewish.
not but appear that the royal authority had out-
grown many limitations that primitive usage or established
law had imposed upon it; and the farther back these researches extended, the more they seemed, according to some
inquirers, to favour a popular theory of constitutional polity.
III. Neither of these considerations, which affected only the
patient scholar, struck so powerfully on the public mind as
the free spirit engendered by the Reformation, and especially the Judaizing turn of the early Protestants, those at
least of the Calvinistic school, which sought for precedents
and models in the Old Testament, and delighted to recount
how the tribes of Israel had fallen away from Rehoboam,
how the Maccabees had repelled the Syrian, how Eglon
had been smitten by the dagger of Ehud. For many years
the Protestants of France had made choice of the sword,
when their alternative was the stake; and amidst defeat,
treachery, and massacre, sustained an unequal combat with
extraordinary heroism, and a constancy that only a persuasion
of acting according to conscience could impart. That persuasion it was the business of their ministers and scholars
to encourage by argument. Each of these three principles
of liberty was asserted by means of the press in the short
period between 1570 and 1580.

22. First, in order of publication is the Franco-Gallia
of Francis Hottoman, one of the most eminent Franco-Gallia of Hottoman.
lawyers of that age. This is chiefly a collection
of passages from the early French historians, to prove the
share of the people in government, and especially their
right of electing the kings of the first two races. No one,
in such inquiries, would now have recourse to the Franco-
Gallia, which has certainly the defect of great partiality,
and an unwarrantable extension of the author's hypothesis.
But it is also true that Hottoman revealed some facts as to
the ancient monarchy of France, which neither the later
historians, flatterers of the court, nor the lawyers of the

Parliament of Paris, against whom he is prone to inveigh, had suffered to transpire.

23. An anonymous treatise, Vindiciæ contra Tyrannos, Auctore Stephano Junio Bruto Celta, 1579, commonly ascribed to Hubert Languet, the friend of Sir Philip Sidney, breathes the stern spirit of Judaical Huguenotism.[k] Kings, that lay waste the church of God, and support idolatry, kings, that trample upon their subjects' privileges, may be deposed by the states of their kingdom, who indeed are bound in duty to do so, though it is not lawful for private men to take up arms without authority. As kings derive their pre-eminence from the will of the people, they may be considered as feudally vassals of their subjects, so far that they may forfeit their crown by felony against them. Though Languet speaks honourably of ancient tyrannicides, it seems as if he could not mean to justify assassination, since he refuses the right of resistance to private men.

Vindiciæ of Languet.

24. Hottoman and Languet were both Protestants; and, the latter especially, may have been greatly influenced by the perilous fortunes of their religion. A short treatise, however, came out in 1578, written probably near thirty years before, by Stephen de la Boetie, best known to posterity by the ardent praises of his friend Montaigne, and an adherent to the church. This is called Le Contr'Un, ou Discours de la Servitude Volontaire. It well deserves its title. Roused by the flagitious tyranny of many contemporary rulers, and few were worse than Henry II., under whose reign it was probably written, La Boetie pours forth the vehement indignation of a youthful heart, full of the love of virtue and of the brilliant illusions which a superficial knowledge of ancient history creates, against the voluntary abjectness of mankind, who submit as slaves to one no wiser, no braver, no stronger than any of themselves. 'He who so plays the master over you has but two eyes, has but two hands, has but one body, has nothing more than the least among the vast number who dwell in

Contr'Un of Boetie.

---

[k] [Le Clerc has a dissertation printed at the end of the English translation of Bayle's Dictionary, to prove that Du Plessis Mornay wrote the Vindiciæ contra Tyrannos. But the majority have continued to ascribe it to Languet.—1853.]

our cities; nothing has he better than you, save the advantage that you give him, that he may ruin you. Whence has he so many eyes to watch you, but that you give them to him? How has he so many hands to strike you, but that he employs your own? How does he come by the feet which trample on your cities, but by your means? How can he have any power over you, but what you give him? How could he venture to persecute you, if he had not an understanding with yourselves? What harm could he do you, if you were not receivers of the robber that plunders you, accomplices of the murderer who kills you, and traitors to your own selves? You, you sow the fruits of the earth, that he may waste them: you furnish your houses that he may pillage them; you rear your daughters, that they may glut his wantonness, and your sons, that he may lead them at the best to his wars, or that he may send them to execution, or make them the instruments of his concupiscence, the ministers of his revenge. You exhaust your bodies with labour, that he may revel in luxury, or wallow in base and vile pleasures; you weaken yourselves, that he may become more strong, and better able to hold you in check. And yet from so many indignities, that the beasts themselves, could they be conscious of them, would not endure, you may deliver yourselves, if you but make an effort, not to deliver yourselves, but to show the will to do it. Once resolve to be no longer slaves, and you are already free. I do not say that you should assail him, or shake his seat; merely support him no longer, and you will see that, like a great Colossus, whose basis has been removed from beneath him, he will fall by his own weight, and break to pieces.' [m]

25. These bursts of a noble patriotism, which no one who is in the least familiar with the history of that period will think inexcusable, are much unlike what we generally expect from the French writers. La Boetie, in fact, is almost a single instance of a thoroughly republican character till nearly the period of the Revolution. Montaigne, the staun-

---

[m] Le Contr'Un of La Boetie is published at the end of some editions of Montaigne.

chest supporter of church and state, excuses his friend,
'the greatest man, in my opinion, of our age,' assuring us
that he was always a loyal subject, though, if he had been
permitted his own choice, 'he would rather have been born
at Venice than at Sarlat.' La Boetie died young, in 1561;
and his Discourse was written some years before; he might
have lived to perceive how much more easy it is to inveigh
against the abuses of government than to bring about any
thing better by rebellion.

26. The three great sources of a free spirit in politics,
Buchanan,
De Jure
Regni. admiration of antiquity, zeal for religion, and persuasion of positive right, which separately had
animated La Boetie, Languet, and Hottoman, united their
streams to produce, in another country, the treatise of
George Buchanan (De Jure Regni apud Scotos), a scholar,
a Protestant, and the subject of a very limited monarchy.
This is a dialogue elegantly written, and designed, first, to
show the origin of royal government from popular election;
then, the right of putting tyrannical kings to death, according to Scripture, and the conditional allegiance due to the
crown of Scotland, as proved by the coronation oath, which
implies that it is received in trust from the people. The
following is a specimen of Buchanan's reasoning, which
goes very materially farther than Languet had presumed to
do :—' Is there, then,' says one of the interlocutors, ' a mutual
compact between the king and the people ? M. Thus it seems.
—B. Does not he who first violates the compact, and does
anything against his own stipulations, break his agreement?
M. He does.—B. If, then, the bond which attached the king
to the people is broken, all rights he derived from the agreement are forfeited ? M. They are forfeited.—B. And he who
was mutually bound becomes as free as before the agreement?
M. He has the same rights and the same freedom as he had
before.—B. But if a king should do things tending to the
dissolution of human society, for the preservation of which
he has been made, what name should we give him ? M. We
should call him a tyrant.—B. But a tyrant not only possesses
no just authority over his people, but is their enemy ? M.
He is surely their enemy.—B. Is there not a just cause of
war against an enemy who has inflicted heavy and intolerable

injuries upon us? M. There is.—B. What is the nature of a war against the enemy of all mankind, that is, against a tyrant? M. None can be more just.—B. Is it not lawful in a war justly commenced, not only for the whole people, but for any single person, to kill an enemy? M. It must be confessed.—B. What, then, shall we say of a tyrant, a public enemy, with whom all good men are in eternal warfare? may not any one of all mankind inflict on him every penalty of war? M. I observe that all nations have been of that opinion, for Theba is extolled for having killed her husband, and Timoleon for his brother's and Cassius for his son's death.'[n]

27. We may include among political treatises of this class some published by the English and Scottish exiles during the persecution of their religion by the two Maries. They are, indeed, prompted by circumstances, and in some instances have too much of a temporary character to deserve a place in literary history. I will, however, give an account of one, more theoretical than the rest, and characteristic of the bold spirit of these early Protestants, especially as it is almost wholly unknown except by name. This is in the title-page, 'A Short Treatise of Politique Power, and of the true obedience which subjects owe to kings and other civil governors, being an answer to seven questions:—" 1. Whereof politique power groweth, wherefore it was ordained, and the right use and duty of the same? 2. Whether kings, princes, and other governors have an absolute power and authority over their subjects? 3. Whether kings, princes, and other politique governors be subject to God's laws, or the positive laws of their countries? 4. In what things and how far subjects are bound to obey their princes and governors? 5. Whether all the subject's goods be the emperor's or king's own, and that they may lawfully take them for their own? 6. Whether it be lawful to depose an evil governor and kill a tyrant? 7. What confidence is to be given to princes and potentates?"'

Poynet, on Politique Power.

28. The author of this treatise was John Poynet, or Ponnet, as it is spelled in the last edition, bishop of Winchester under Edward VI., and who had a con-

Its liberal theory.

---

[n] P. 96.

siderable share in the Reformation.° It was first published in 1558, and reprinted in 1642, 'to serve,' says Strype, 'the turn of those times.' 'This book,' observes truly the same industrious person, 'was not over favourable to princes.' Poynet died very soon afterwards, so that we cannot determine whether he would have thought it expedient to speak as fiercely under the reign that was to come. The place of publication of the first edition I do not know, but I presume it was at Geneva or Frankfort. It is closely and vigorously written, deserving, in many parts, a high place among the English prose of that age, though not entirely free from the usual fault—vulgar and ribaldrous invective. He determines all the questions stated in the title-page on principles adverse to royal power, contending, in the sixth chapter, that 'the manifold and continual examples that have been, from time to time, of the deposing of kings and killing of tyrants, do most certainly confirm it to be most true, just, and consonant to God's judgment. The history of kings in the Old Testament is full of it; and, as Cardinal Pole truly citeth, England lacketh not the practice and experience of the same; for they deprived King Edward II., because, without law, he killed the subjects, spoiled them of their goods, and wasted the treasures of the realm. And upon what just causes Richard II. was thrust out, and Henry IV. put in his place, I refer it to their own judgment. Denmark also now, in our days, did nobly the like act, when they deprived Christiern the tyrant, and committed him to perpetual prison.

29. 'The reasons, arguments, and laws, that serve for the deposing and displacing of an evil governor, will do Argues for as much for the proof that it is lawful to kill a tyrannicide. tyrant, if they may be indifferently heard. As God hath ordained magistrates to hear and determine private men's matters, and to punish their vices, so also willeth he that the magistrates' doings be called to account and reckoning, and their vices corrected and punished by the body of the whole congregation or commonwealth: as it is manifest by the memory of the ancient office of the High Constable of England, unto whose authority it pertained, not only to summon the king personally before the parliament, or other

---

° Chalmers. Strype's Memorials.

courts of judgment, to answer and receive according to justice, but also upon just occasion to commit him unto ward.[p] Kings, princes, and governors have their authority of the people, as all laws, usages, and policies do declare and testify. For in some places and countries they have more and greater authority ; in some places less ; and in some the people have not given this authority to any other, but retain and exercise it themselves. And is any man so unreasonable to deny that the whole may do as much as they have permitted one member to do, or those that have appointed an office upon trust have not authority upon just occasion (as the abuse of it) to take away what they gave ? All laws do agree that men may revoke their proxies and letters of attorney when it pleaseth them, much more when they see their proctors and attorneys abuse it.

30. ' But now, to prove the latter part of this question affirmatively, that it is lawful to kill a tyrant, there is no man can deny, but that the Ethnics, albeit they had not the right and perfect true knowledge of God, were endued with the knowledge of the law of nature—for it is no private law to a few or certain people, but common to all —not written in books, but grafted in the hearts of men, not made by men, but ordained of God, which we have not learned, received, or read, but have taken, sucked, and drawn it out of nature, whereunto we are not taught, but made, not instructed, but seasoned ;[q] and, as St. Paul saith, " Man's conscience bearing witness of it," ' &c. He proceeds in a strain of some eloquence (and this last passage is not ill-translated from Cicero) to extol the ancient tyrannicides, accounting the first nobility to have been ' those who had revenged and delivered the oppressed people out of the hands of their governors. Of this kind of nobility was Hercules, Theseus, and such like.'[r] It must be owned the worthy bishop is a bold man in assertions of fact. Instances from the Old Testament, of course, follow, wherein Jezebel and Athalia are not forgotten, for the sake of our bloody queen.

31. If too much space has been allowed to so obscure a

---

[p] It is scarcely necessary to observe that this is an impudent falsehood.

[q] Sic. The Latin in Cic. pro Mil. is *imbuti.*

[r] P. 49.

production it must be excused on account of the illustration
The tenets of parties swayed by circumstances. it gives to our civil and ecclesiastical history, though of little importance in literature. It is also well to exhibit an additional proof that the tenets of most men, however general and speculative they may appear, are espoused on account of the position of those who hold them, and the momentary consequences that they may produce. In a few years' time the Church of England, strong in the protection of that royalty which Poynet thus assailed in his own exile, enacted the celebrated homily against rebellion, which denounces every pretext of resistance to governors. It rarely happens that any parties, even the best and purest, will, in the strife to retain or recover their ascendency, weaken themselves by a scrupulous examination of the reasoning or the testimony which is to serve their purpose. Those have lived and read to little advantage who have not discovered this.

32. It might appear that there was some peculiar associa-
Similar tenets among the Leaguers. tion between these popular theories of resistance and the Protestant faith. Perhaps, in truth, they had a degree of natural connexion; but circumstances, more than general principles, affect the opinions of mankind. The rebellion of the League against Henry III., their determination not to acknowledge Henry IV., reversed the state of parties, and displayed, in an opposite quarter, the republican notions of Languet and Buchanan as fierce and as unlimited as any Protestants had maintained them. Henry of Bourbon could only rely upon his legitimate descent, upon the indefeasible rights of inheritance. If France was to choose for herself, France demanded a Catholic king; all the topics of democracy were thrown into that scale; and, in fact, it is well known that Henry had no prospect whatever of success but by means of a conversion, which, though not bearing much semblance of sincerity, the nation thought fit to accept. But during that struggle of a few years we find, among other writings of less moment, one ascribed by some to Rose, Bishop of Senlis, a strenuous partisan of the League, which may perhaps deserve to arrest our attention.[s]

---

[s] The author calls himself Rossæus, and not, as has been asserted, bishop of Senlis. But Pits attributes this book to Rainolds (brother of the more cele-

33. This book, De Justa Reipublicæ Christianæ in Reges
Potestate, published in 1590, must have been partly written
before the death of Henry III. in the preceding year.   He
begins with the origin of human society, which he   Rose on the
treats with some eloquence, and on the principle of   Christian
an election of magistrates by the community, that   Kings.
they might live peaceably, and in enjoyment of their possessions.   The different forms and limitations of government
have sprung from the choice of the people, except where
they have been imposed by conquest.   He exhibits many
instances of this variety: but there are two dangers, one of
limiting too much the power of kings, and letting the
populace change the dynasty at their pleasure; the other,
that of ascribing a sort of divinity to kings, and taking from
the nation all the power of restraining them in whatever
crimes they may commit.   The Scottish Calvinists are an
instance of the first error; the modern advocates of the
house of Valois of the other.   The servile language of those
who preach passive obedience has encouraged not only the
worst Roman emperors, but such tyrants as Henry VIII.,
Edward VI., and Elizabeth of England.

34. The author goes, in the second chapter, more fully into
a refutation of this doctrine, as contrary to the practice of
ancient nations, who always deposed tyrants, to the principles
of Christianity, and to the constitution of European communities, whose kings are admitted under an oath to keep the
laws and to reign justly.   The subject's oath of allegiance
does not bind him, unless the king observe what is stipulated
from him; and this right of withdrawing obedience from
wicked kings is at the bottom of all the public law of Europe.
It is also sanctioned by the church.   Still more has the
nation a right to impose laws and limitations on kings, who

---

brated Dr. John Rainold's), who is said
to have called himself Rossæus. The
Biographie Universelle (art. Rose) says
this opinion has not gained ground; but
it is certainly favoured by M. Barbier
in the Dictionnaire des Anonymes, and
some grounds for it are alleged. From
internal evidence it seems rather the
work of a Frenchman than a foreigner;
but I have not paid much attention to

so unimportant a question. Jugler, in
his Historia Literaria, c. 9, does not
even name Rose. By a passage in
Schelhorn, viii. 465, the book seems to
have been sometimes ascribed to Gene-
brard.—[Herbert names Rainolds as the
author, and says that it is supposed to
have been printed at Edinburgh; but
I cannot think this at all probable.—
1842.]

have certainly no superiority to the law, so that they can transgress it at pleasure.

35. In the third chapter he inquires who is a tyrant ; and, after a long discussion, comes to this result, that a tyrant is one who despoils his subjects of their possessions, or offends public decency by immoral life, but above all, who assails the Christian faith, and uses his authority to render his subjects heretical.   All these characters are found in Henry of Valois. He then urges, in the two following chapters, that all Protestantism is worse than Paganism, inasmuch as it holds out less inducement to a virtuous life, but that Calvinism is much the worst form of the Protestant heresy.   The Huguenots, he proceeds to prove, are neither parts of the French church nor commonwealth.   He infers, in the seventh chapter, that the king of Navarre, being a heretic of this description, is not fit to rule over Christians.   The remainder of the book is designed to show that every king, being schismatic or heretical, may be deposed by the pope, of which he brings many examples ; nor has any one deserved this sentence more than Henry of Navarre.   It has always been held lawful that an heretical king should be warred upon by his own subjects and by all Christian sovereigns ; and he maintains that a real tyrant, who, after being deposed by the wiser part of his subjects, attempts to preserve his power by force, may be put to death by any private person. He adds that Julian was probably killed by a Christian soldier, and quotes several fathers and ecclesiastical historians who justify and commend the act.   He concludes by exhorting the nobility and other orders of France, since Henry is a relapsed heretic, who is not to be believed for any oaths he may make, to rally round their Catholic king, Charles of Bourbon.

36. The principles of Rose, if he were truly the author, both as to rebellion and tyrannicide, belonged natu-

Treatise of Boucher in the same spirit.

rally to those who took up arms against Henry III., and who applauded his assassin.   They were adopted, and perhaps extended, by Boucher, a leaguer still more furious, if possible, than Rose himself, in a book published in 1589, De Justa Henrici III. Abdicatione a Francorum Regno.   This book is written in the spirit of Languet, asserting the general right of the people to depose tyrants, rather than confining it to the case of heresy. The deposing power of the pope, consequently, does not come much into question. He was answered, as well as other writers of the same tenets, by a Scottish Catholic, residing at Paris, William Barclay, father of the more celebrated author of the Argenis, in a treatise ‘ De Regno et Regali Potestate adversus Buchananum, Brutum, Boucherum et Reliquos Monarchomachos,’ 1600. Barclay argues on the principles current in France, that the king has no superior in temporals ; that the people are bound in all cases to obey him ; that the laws owe their validity to his will. The settlement of France by the submission of the League on the one hand, and by the Edict of Nantes on the other, naturally put a stop to the discussion of questions which, theoretical and universal as they might seem, would never have been brought forward but through the stimulating influence of immediate circumstances.

Answered by Barclay.

37. But while the war was yet raging, and the fate of the Catholic religion seemed to hang upon its success, many of the Jesuits had been strenuous advocates of the tyrannicidal doctrine ; and the strong spirit of party attachment in that order renders it hardly uncandid to reckon among its general tenets whatever was taught by its most conspicuous members. The boldest and most celebrated assertion of these maxims was by Mariana, in a book, De Rege et Regis Institutione. The first edition of this remarkable book, and which is of considerable scarcity, was published at Toledo in 1599, dedicated to Philip III., and sanctioned with more than an approbation, with a warm eulogy, by the censor (one of the same order, it may be observed), who by the king's authority had perused the manuscript. It is, however, not such as in an absolute monarchy we should expect to find countenance. Mariana, after inquiring what is the best form of government, and deciding for hereditary monarchy, but only on condition that the prince shall call the best citizens to his councils, and administer all affairs according to the advice of a senate, comes to show the difference between a king and a tyrant. His invectives against the latter prepare us for the sixth

The Jesuits adopt these tenets.

Mariana, De Rege.

chapter, which is entitled, Whether it be lawful to over-throw a tyrant? He begins by a short sketch of the oppression of France under Henry III., which had provoked his assassination. Whether the act of James Clement, 'the eternal glory of France, as most reckon him,'[u] were in itself warrantable, he admits to be a controverted question, stating the arguments on both sides, but placing last those in favour of the murder, to which he evidently leans. All philosophers and theologians, he says, agree that an usurper may be put to death by any one. But in the case of a lawful king, governing to the great injury of the common-wealth or of religion (for we ought to endure his vices so long as they do not reach an intolerable height), he thinks that the states of the realm should admonish him, and on his neglect to reform his life, may take up arms, and put to death a prince whom they have declared to be a public enemy; and any private man may do the same. He con-cludes, therefore, that it is only a question of fact who is a tyrant, but not one of right, whether a tyrant may be killed. Nor does this maxim give a licence to attempts on the lives of good princes; since it can never be applied till wise and experienced men have conspired with the public voice in de-claring the prince's tyranny. 'It is a wholesome thing,' he proceeds, 'that sovereigns should be convinced that, if they oppress the state, and become intolerable by their wicked-ness, their assassination will not only be lawful but glorious to the perpetrator.'[x] This language, whatever indignation it might excite against Mariana and his order, is merely what we have seen in Buchanan.

38. Mariana discusses afterwards the question, whether the power of the king or of the commonwealth be the greater; and after intimating the danger of giving offence, and the difficulty of removing the blemishes which have become inveterate by time (with allusion, doubtless, to the change of the Spanish constitution under Charles and

---

[u] These words, 'æternum Galliæ de-cus,' are omitted in the subsequent edi-tions, but as far as I have compared them there is very little other altera-tion; yet the first alone is in request.

[x] Est salutaris cognitio, ut sit princi-pibus persuasum, si rempublicam op-presserint, si vitiis et fœditate intolerandi erunt, ea conditione vivere, ut non jure tantum sed cum laude et gloria perire possint. p. 77.

Philip), declares in strong terms for limiting the royal power by laws. In Spain, he asserts, the king cannot impose taxes against the will of the people. ' He may use his influence, he may offer rewards, sometimes he may threaten, he may solicit with promises and bribes (we will not say whether he may do this rightly), but if they refuse, he must give way ; and it is the same with new laws, which require the sanction of the people. Nor could they preserve their right of deposing and putting to death a tyrant, if they had not retained the superior power to themselves when they delegated a part to the king. It may be the case in some nations, who have no public assemblies of the states, that of necessity the royal prerogative must compel obedience—a power too great, and approaching to tyranny—but we speak (says Mariana) not of barbarians, but of the monarchy which exists, and ought to exist among us, and of that form of polity which of itself is the best.' Whether any nation has a right to surrender its liberties to a king, he declines to inquire, observing only that it would act rashly in making such a surrender, and the king almost as much so in accepting it.

39. In the second book Mariana treats of the proper education of a prince ; and in the third on the due administration of his government, inveighing vehemently against excessive taxation, and against debasement of the coin, which he thinks ought to be the last remedy in a public crisis. The whole work, even in its reprehensible exaggerations, breathes a spirit of liberty and regard to the common good. Nor does Mariana, though a Jesuit, lay any stress on the papal power to depose princes, which, I believe, he has never once intimated through the whole volume. It is absolutely on political principles that he reasons, unless we except that he considers impiety as one of the vices which constitute a tyrant.[y]

40. Neither of the conflicting parties in Great Britain had neglected the weapons of their contemporaries ; the English Protestants under Mary, the Scots under Popular theories in England.

---

[y] Bayle, art. Mariana, notes G, H, and I, has expatiated upon this notable treatise, which did the Jesuits infinite mischief, though they took pains to disclaim any participation in the doctrine.

her unfortunate namesake, the Jesuits and Catholic priests under Elizabeth, appealed to the natural rights of men, or to those of British citizens. Poynet, Goodman, Knox, are of the first description; Allen and Persons of the second. Yet this was not done, by the latter at least, so boldly, and so much on broad principles, as it was on the Continent; and Persons, in his celebrated Conference, under the name of Doleman, tried the different and rather inconsistent path of hereditary right. The throne of Elizabeth seemed to stand in need of a strongly monarchical sentiment in the nation. Yet we find that the popular origin of government, and the necessity of popular consent to its due exercise, are

Hooker. laid down by Hooker in the first and eighth books of the Ecclesiastical Polity, with a boldness not very usual in her reign, and, it must be owned, with a latitude of expression that leads us forward to the most unalloyed democracy. This theory of Hooker, which he endeavoured in some places to qualify, with little success or consistency, though it excited, perhaps, not much attention at the time, became the basis of Locke's more celebrated Essay on Government, and, through other stages, of the political creed which actuates at present, as a possessing spirit, the great mass of the civilised world.[z]

41. The bold and sometimes passionate writers, who

Political memoirs. possibly will be thought to have detained us too long, may be contrasted with another class more cool and prudent, who sought rather to make the most of what they found established in civil polity than to amend or subvert it. The condition of France was such as to force men into thinking, where nature had given them the capacity of it. In some of the memoirs of the age, such as those of Castelnau or Tavannes, we find an habitual ten-

---

[z] Bilson, afterwards bishop of Winchester, in his ' Difference between Christian Subjection and Unchristian Rebellion,' published in 1585, argues against the Jesuits, that Christian subjects may not bear arms against their princes for any religious quarrel; but admits, ' if a prince should go about to subject his kingdom to a foreign realm, or change the form of the common-wealth from impery to tyranny, or neglect the laws established by common consent of prince and people, to execute his own pleasure, in these and other cases which might be named, if the nobles and commons join together to defend their ancient and accustomed liberty, regiment, and laws, they may not well be counted rebels.' p. 520.

dency to reflect, to observe the chain of causes, and to bring history to bear on the passing time.   De Comines had set a precedent; and the fashion of studying his writings and those of Machiavel conspired with the force of circumstances to make a thoughtful generation.   The political and military discourses of La Noue, being thrown into the form of dissertation, come more closely to our purpose *La Noue.* than merely historical works.   They are full of good sense, in a high moral tone, without pedantry or pretension, and throw much light on the first period of the civil wars.   The earliest edition is referred by the Biographie Universelle to 1587, which I believe should be 1588; but the book seems to have been finished long before.

42. It would carry us beyond the due proportions of this chapter were I to seek out every book belonging to the class of political philosophy, and we are yet *Lipsius.* far from its termination.   The Politica of Justus Lipsius deserve little regard; they are chiefly a digest of Aristotle, Tacitus, and other ancient writers.   Charron has incorporated or abridged the greater part of this work in his own. In one passage Lipsius gave great and just offence to the best of the Protestant party, whom he was about to desert, by recommending the extirpation of heresy by fire and sword.   A political writer of the Jesuit school was Giovanni Botero, whose long treatise, Ragione di *Botero.* Stato, 1589, while deserving of considerable praise for acuteness, has been extolled by Ginguéné, who had never read it, for some merits it is far from possessing.[a]   The tolerant spirit, the maxims of good faith, the enlarged philosophy, which, on the credit of a Piedmontese panegyrist, he ascribes to Botero, will be sought in vain.   This Jesuit justifies the massacre of St. Bartholomew and all other atrocities of that age; observing that the duke of Alba made a mistake in the public execution of Horn and Egmont, instead of getting rid of them privately.[b]   Conservation is with him, as with Machiavel, the great end of government, which is to act so as neither to deserve nor permit opposition.   The imme-

---

[a] Vol. viii. p. 210.
[b] Poteva contentarsi di sbrigarsene con dar morte quanto si può segreta-

mente fosse possibile. This is in another treatise by Botero, Relazioni Universali de' Capitani Illustri.

diate punishment of the leaders of sedition, with as much
silence and secrecy as possible, is the best remedy where the
sovereign is sufficiently powerful.   In cases of danger, it is
necessary to conquer by giving way, and to wait for the cool-
ing of men's tempers, and the disunion that will infallibly
impair their force ; least of all should he absent himself,
like Henry III., from the scene of tumult, and thus give
courage to the seditious, while he diminishes their respect
for himself.

43. Botero had thought and observed much ; he is, in
His remarks
on popula-
tion. extent of reading, second only to Bodin, and his
views are sometimes luminous.   The most remark-
able passage that has occurred to me is on the subject of
population.   No encouragement to matrimony, he observes,
will increase the numbers of the people without providing
also the means of subsistence, and without due care for
breeding children up.   If this be wanting, they either die
prematurely, or grow up of little service to their country.[c]
Why else, he asks, did the human race reach, three thousand years ago, as great a population as exists at present?
Cities begin with a few inhabitants, increase to a certain
point, but do not pass it, as we see at Rome, at Naples, and
in other places.   Even if all the monks and nuns were to
marry, there would not, he thinks, be more people in the
world than there are ; two things being requisite for their
increase—generation and education (or what we should perhaps rather call rearing), and if the multiplication of marriages may promote the one, it certainly hinders the other.[d]
Botero must here have meant, though he does not fully express it, that the poverty attending upon improvident marriages is the great impediment to rearing their progeny.

44. Paolo Paruta, in his Discorsi Politici, Venice, 1599,
Paruta. is perhaps less vigorous and acute than Botero ; yet
he may be reckoned among judicious writers on

---

[c] Concio sia cosa chè se bene senza il
congiungimento dell' uomo e della don-
na non si può il genere umano molti-
plicarsi, non dimeno la moltitudine di
congiungimenti non è sola causa della
moltiplicazione; si ricerca oltre di ciò,
la cura d' allevarli, e la commodità di
sustentarli ; senza la quale o muojono

innanzi tempo, o riescono inutili, e di
poco giovimento alla patria. Lib. viii.
p. 284.
[d] Ibid. Ricercandosi due cose per
la propagazione de popoli, la generazione
e l' educazione, se bene la moltitudine
de matrimonj ajuta forte l' una, impe-
disce però del sicuro l' altro.

general politics.   The first book of these discourses relates
to Roman, the second chiefly to modern history.   His turn
of thinking is independent and unprejudiced by the current
tide of opinion, as when he declares against the conduct
of Hannibal in invading Italy.   Paruta generally states
both sides of a political problem very fairly, as in one of
the most remarkable of his discourses, where he puts the
famous question on the usefulness of fortified towns.   His
final conclusion is favourable to them.   He was a subject of
Venice, and after holding considerable offices, was one of
those historians employed by the Senate, whose writings
form the series entitled Istorici Veneziani.

45. John Bodin, author of several other less valuable
works, acquired so distinguished a reputation by his
Republic, published in French in 1577, and in Latin, Bodin.
with many additions, by himself in 1586,[e] and has in fact so
far outstripped the political writers of his own period, that I
shall endeavour to do justice to his memory by something
like an analysis of this treatise, which is far more known by
name than generally read.   Many have borne testimony to
his extraordinary reach of learning and reflection.   'I know
of no political writer of the same period,' says Stewart, 'whose
extensive, and various, and discriminating reading appears to
me to have contributed more to facilitate and guide the researches of his successors, or whose references to ancient
learning have been more frequently transcribed without acknowledgment.'[f]

---

[e] This treatise, in its first edition,
made so great an impression, that when
Bodin came to England in the service
of the duke of Alençon, he found it explained by lecturers both in London and
Cambridge, but not, as has sometimes
been said, in the public schools of the
university.   This put him upon translating it into Latin himself, to render
its fame more European.   See Bayle,
who has a good article on Bodin.   I am
much inclined to believe that the perusal
of Bodin had a great effect in England.
He is not perhaps very often quoted,
and yet he is named with honour by
the chief writers of the next age ; but
he furnished a store, both of arguments

and of examples, which were not lost on
the thoughtful minds of our countrymen.
Grotius, who is not very favourable to
Bodin, though of necessity he often
quotes the Republic, imputes to him an
incorrectness as to facts, which in some
cases raises a suspicion of ill-faith. Epist.
cccliii.   It would require a more close
study of Bodin than I have made, to
judge of the weight of this charge.
[f] Dissertation on Progress of Philosophy, p. 40.   Stewart, however, thinks
Bodin become so obscure that he makes
an apology for the space he has allotted
to the Republic, though not exceeding
four pages.   He was better known in
the seventeenth century than at present.

46. What is the object of political society? Bodin begins
Analysis of his treatise called The Republic. by inquiring. The greatest good, he answers, of every citizen, which is that of the whole state. And this he places in the exercise of the virtues proper to man, and in the knowledge of things natural, human, and divine. But as all have not agreed as to the chief good of a single man, nor whether the good of individuals be also that of the state, this has caused a variety of laws and customs according to the humours and passions of rulers. This first chapter is in a more metaphysical tone than we usually find in Bodin. He proceeds in the next to the rights of families (jus familiare), and to the distinction between a family and a commonwealth. A family is the right government of many persons under one head, as a commonwealth is that of many Authority of heads of families. families.[g] Patriarchal authority he raises high, both marital and paternal, on each subject pouring out a vast stream of knowledge : nothing that sacred and profane history, the accounts of travellers, or the Roman lawyers could supply, ever escapes the comprehensive researches of Bodin.[h] He intimates his opinion in favour of the right of repudiation, one of the many proofs that he paid more regard to the Jewish than the Christian law,[i] and

---

[g] Familia est plurium sub unius ac ejusdem patris familias imperium subditorum, earumque rerum quæ ipsius propria sunt, recta moderatio. He has an odd theory, that a family must consist of five persons ; in which he seems to have been influenced by some notions of the jurists, that three families may constitute a republic. and that fifteen persons are also the minimum of a community.

[h] Cap. iii. 34. Bodin here protests against the stipulation sometimes made before marriage, that the wife shall not be in the power of the husband ; 'agreements so contrary to divine and human laws, that they cannot be endured, nor are they to be observed even when ratified by oath, since no oath in such circumstances can be binding.'

[i] It has often been surmised that Bodin, though not a Jew by nativity, was such by conviction. This seems to be confirmed by his Republic, wherein he quotes the Old Testament continu-

ally, and with great deference, but seldom or never the New. Several passages might be alleged in proof, but I have not noted them all down. In one place, lib. i. c. 6, he says, Paulus, Christianorum sæculi sui facile princeps, which is at least a singular mode of expression. In another he states the test of true religion so as to exclude all but the Mosaic. An unpublished work of Bodin, called the Heptaplomeres, is said to exist in many manuscripts, both in France and Germany ; in which, after debating different religions in a series of dialogues, he gives the advantage to Deism or Judaism, for those who have seen it seem not to have determined which. No one has thought it worth while to print this production. Jugler, Hist. Literaria, p. 1740. Biogr. Univ. Niceron, xvii. 264.

A posthumous work of Bodin, published in 1596, Universæ Naturæ Theatrum, has been called by some a disguised Pantheism. This did not appear, from what I have read of it, to be the case.

vindicates the full extent of the paternal power in the Roman republic, deducing the decline of the empire from its relaxation.

47. The patriarchal government includes the relation of master to servant, and leads to the question whether slavery should be admitted into a well-constituted commonwealth. Bodin, discussing this with many arguments on both sides, seems to think that the Jewish law, with its limitations as to time of servitude, ought to prevail, since the divine rules were not laid down for the boundaries of Palestine, but being so wise, so salutary, and of such authority, ought to be preferred above the constitutions of men. Slavery, therefore, is not to be permanently established; but where it already exists, it will be expedient that emancipation should be gradual.[k] *Domestic servitude.*

48. These last are the rights of persons in a state of nature, to be regulated, but not created by the law. *Origin of commonwealths.* ' Before there was either city or citizen, or any form of a commonwealth amongst men (I make use in this place of Knolles's very good translation), every master of a family was master in his own house, having power of life and death over his wife and children; but, after that force, violence, ambition, covetousness, and desire of revenge had armed one against another, the issues of wars and combats giving victory unto the one side, made the other to become unto them slaves; and amongst them that overcame, he that was chosen chief and captain, under whose conduct and leading they had obtained the victory, kept them also in his power and command as his faithful and obedient servants, and the other as his slaves. Then that full and entire liberty, by nature given to every man to live as himself best pleased, was altogether taken from the vanquished, and in the vanquishers themselves in some measure also diminished in regard of the conqueror; for that now it concerned every man in private to yield his obedience unto his chief sovereign; and he that would not abate anything of his liberty, to live under the laws and commandments of another, lost all. So the words of lord and servant, of prince and subject, before unknown to the

---

[k] c. 5.

world, were first brought into use.   Yea, reason and the very
light of nature, leadeth us to believe very force and violence
to have given cause and beginning unto commonwealths.'[m]

49. Thus, therefore, the patriarchal simplicity of govern-
Privileges of citizens. ment was overthrown by conquest, of which Nim-
rod seems to have been the earliest instance ; and
now fathers of families, once sovereign, are become citizens.
A citizen is a free man under the supreme government of
another.[n]   Those who enjoy more privileges than others are
not citizens more than they.   ' It is the acknowledgment of
the sovereign by his free subject, and the protection of the
sovereign towards him, that makes the citizen.'   This is one
of the fundamental principles, it may be observed by us in
passing, which distinguish a monarchical from a republican
spirit in constitutional jurisprudence.   Wherever mere subjection, or even mere nativity, is held to give a claim to
citizenship, there is an abandonment of the Republican
principle.   This, always reposing on a real or imaginary
contract, distinguishes the nation, the successors of the first
community, from alien settlers, and, above all, from those
who are evidently of a different race.   Length of time must,
of course, ingraft many of foreign origin upon the native
tree ; but to throw open civil privileges at random to new-
comers is to convert a people into a casual aggregation of
men.   In a monarchy the hereditary principle maintains an
unity of the commonwealth ; which may better permit,
though not entirely without danger, an equality of privileges
among all its subjects.   Thus under Caracalla, but in a
period in which we should not look for good precedents, the
great name, as once it had been, of Roman citizen was extended, east and west, to all the provinces of the empire.

50. Bodin comes next to the relation between patron and
Nature of sovereign power. client, and to those alliances among states which
bear an analogy to it.   But he is careful to distin-
guish patronage or protection from vassalage.   Even in
unequal alliances the inferior is still sovereign ; and, if this
be not reserved, the alliance must become subjection.[o]
Sovereignty, of which he treats in the following chapter, he

---

[m] c. 6.
[n] Est civis nihil aliud quam liber
homo, qui summa alterius potestate
obligatur.
[o] c. 7.

defines a supreme and perpetual power, absolute and subject to no law.[p] A limited prince, except so far as the limitation is confined to the laws of nature, is not sovereign. A sovereign cannot bind his successor, nor can he be bound by his own laws, unless confirmed by oath; for we must not confound the laws and contracts of princes—the former depend upon his will, but the latter oblige his conscience. It is convenient to call parliaments or meetings of states-general for advice and consent, but the king is not bound by them; the contrary notion has done much harm. Even in England, where laws made in parliament cannot be repealed without its consent, the king may reject any new one without regard to the desire of the nation.[q] And though no taxes are imposed in England without consent of parliament, this is the case also in other countries, if necessity does not prevent the meeting of the states. He concludes that the English parliament may have a certain authority, but that the sovereignty and legislative power are solely in the king. Whoever legislates is sovereign, for this power includes all other. Whether a vassal or tributary prince is to be called sovereign, is a question that leads Bodin into a great quantity of feudal law and history; he determines it according to his own theory.[r]

51. The second book of the Republic treats of the different species of civil government. These, according to Bodin, are but three, no mixed form being possible, since sovereignty or the legislative power is indivisible. A democracy he defines to be a government where the majority of the citizens possess the sovereignty. Rome he holds to have been a democratic republic, in which, however, he is not exactly right; and he is certainly mistaken in his general theory, by arguing as if the separate definition of each of the three forms must be applicable after their combination.[s] In his chapter on despotic monarchy, he again denies that governments were founded on

Forms of government.

Despotism and monarchy.

---

[p] Majestas est summa in cives ac subditos legibusque soluta potestas.

[q] Hoc tamen singulare videri possit, quod, quæ leges populi rogatione ac principis jussu feruntur, non aliter quam populi comitiis abrogari possunt. Id enim Dellus Anglorum in Gallia legatus mihi confirmavit; idem tamen confitetur legem probari aut respui consuevisse contra populi voluntatem utcunque principi placuerit.

[r] c. 9 and 10.   [s] lib. ii, c, 1.

original contract. The power of one man, in the origin of
political society, was absolute; and Aristotle was wrong in
supposing a fabulous golden age, in which kings were chosen
by suffrage.[t] Despotism is distinguished from monarchy by
the subjects being truly slaves, without a right over their
properties; but as the despot may use them well, even this
is not necessarily a tyranny.[u] Monarchy, on the other hand,
is the rule of one man according to the law of nature, who
maintains the liberties and properties of others as much as
his own.[x] As this definition does not imply any other
restraint than the will of the prince imposes on himself,
Bodin labours under the same difficulty as Montesquieu.
Every English reader of the Esprit des Lois has been struck
by the want of a precise distinction between despotism and
monarchy. Tyranny differs, Bodin says, from despotism,
merely by the personal character of the prince; but severity
towards a seditious populace is not tyranny; and here he
censures the lax government of Henry II. Tyrannicide he
justifies in respect of an usurper who has no title except
force, but not as to lawful princes, or such as have become
so by prescription.[y]

52. An aristocracy he conceives always to exist where a
smaller body of the citizens governs the greater.[z]
This definition, which has been adopted by some
late writers, appears to lead to consequences hardly compatible with the common use of language. The electors of the
House of Commons in England are not a majority of the
people. Are they, therefore, an aristocratical body ? The
same is still more strongly the case in France, and in most
representative governments of Europe. We might better
say, that the distinguishing characteristic of an aristocracy
is the enjoyment of privileges which are not communicable
to other citizens simply by anything they can themselves do
to obtain them. Thus no government would be properly

Aristocracy.

---

[t] In the beginning of states, quo
societas hominum coalescere cœpit, ac
reipublicæ forma quædam constitui,
unius imperio ac dominatu omnia tene-
bantur. Fallit enim Aristoteles, qui
aureum illud genus hominum fabulis
poeticis quam reipsa illustrius, reges
heroas suffragio creasse prodidit: cum
omnibus persuasum sit ac perspicuum
monarchiam omnium primam in Assyria
fuisse constitutam Nimrodo principe, &c.
[u] c. 2.   [x] c. 3.   [y] c. 4.
[z] Ego statum semper aristocraticum
esse judico, si minor pars civium cæteris
imperat. c. 1.

aristocratical where a pecuniary qualification is alone sufficient to confer political power; nor did the ancients ever
use the word in such a sense.

53. Sovereignty resides in the supreme legislative authority; but this requires the aid of other inferior and Senates and
delegated ministers, to the consideration of which councils of state.
the third book of Bodin is directed. A senate he defines, 'a
lawful assembly of counsellors of state, to give advice to them
who have the sovereignty in every commonwealth: we say,
to give advice, that we may not ascribe any power of
command to such a senate.' A council is necessary in a
monarchy; for much knowledge is generally mischievous in
a king. It is rarely united with a good disposition and with
a moral discipline of mind. None of the emperors were so
illiterate as Trajan, none more learned than Nero. The
counsellors should not be too numerous, and he advises that
they should retain their offices for life. It would be dangerous as well as ridiculous to choose young men for such a
post, even if they could have wisdom and experience, since
neither older persons, nor those of their own age, would
place confidence in them. He then expatiates, in his usual
manner, upon all the councils that have existed in ancient or
modern states.[a]

54. A magistrate is an officer of the sovereign, possessing
public authority.[b] Bodin censures the usual defini- Duties of
tions of magistracy, distinguishing from magistrates magistrates.
both those officers who possess no right of command, and
such commissioners as have only a temporary delegation.
In treating of the duty of magistrates towards the sovereign,
he praises the rule of the law of France, that the judge is not
to regard private letters of the king against the justice of a
civil suit.[c] But after stating the doubt, whether this applies
to matters affecting the public, he concludes that the judge
must obey any direction he receives, unless contrary to the
law of nature, in which case he is bound not to forfeit his
integrity. It is however better, as far as we can, to obey all
the commands of the sovereign, than to set a bad example of
resistance to the people. This has probably a regard to the

---

[a] c. 1.   [b] c. 3.   [c] c. 4.

frequent opposition of the parliament of Paris to what it deemed the unjust or illegal ordinances of the court. Several questions, discussed in these chapters on magistracy, are rather subtle and verbal; and, in general, the argumentative part of Bodin is almost drowned in his erudition.

55. A state cannot subsist without colleges and corpora-
Corporations.   tions, for mutual affection and friendship is the necessary bond of human life. It is true that mischiefs have sprung from these institutions, and they are to be regulated by good laws; but as a family is a community natural, so a college is a community civil, and a commonwealth is but a community governed by a sovereign power; and thus the word community is common unto all three.[d] In this chapter we have a full discussion of the subject; and, adverting to the Spanish Cortes and English House of Commons as a sort of colleges in the state, he praises them as useful institutions, observing, with somewhat more boldness than is ordinary to him, that in several provinces in France there had been assemblies of the states, which had been abolished by those who feared to see their own crimes and peculations brought to light.

56. In the last chapter of the third book, on the degrees
Slaves, part   and orders of citizens, Bodin seems to think that
of the state.   slaves, being subjects, ought to be reckoned parts of the state.[e] This is, as has been intimated, in conformity with his monarchical notions. He then enters upon the different modes of acquiring nobility, and inveighs against making wealth a passport to it; discussing also the derogation to nobility by plebeian occupation. The division into three orders is useful in every form of government.

57. Perhaps the best chapter in the Republic of Bodin is
Rise and fall   the first in the fourth book, on the rise, progress,
of states.   and stationary condition, revolutions, decline, and fall of states. A commonwealth is said to be changed when its form of polity is altered; for its identity is not to be determined by the long standing of the city walls; but when popular government becomes monarchy, or aristocracy is

---

[d] c. 7.

[e] Si mihi tabellæ ac jura suffragiorum in hac disputatione tribuantur, servos æque ac liberos homines civitate donari cupium. By this he may only mean that he would desire to emancipate them.

turned to democracy, the commonwealth is at an end. He thus uses the word *respublica* in the sense of polity or constitution, which is not, perhaps, strictly correct, though sanctioned by some degree of usage, and leaves his proposition a tautological truism. The extinction of states may be natural or violent, but in one way or the other it must happen; since there is a determinate period to all things, and a natural season in which it seems desirable that they should come to an end. The best revolution is that which takes place by a voluntary cession of power.

58. As the forms of government are three, it follows that the possible revolutions from one to another are six. Causes of For anarchy is the extinction of a government, not revolutions. a revolution in it. He proceeds to develop the causes of revolutions with great extent of historical learning and with judgment, if not with so much acuteness or so much vigour of style as Machiavel. Great misfortunes in war, he observes, have a tendency to change popular rule to aristocracy, and success has an opposite effect; the same seems applicable to all public adversity and prosperity. Democracy, however, more commonly ends in monarchy, as monarchy does in democracy, especially when it has become tyrannical; and such changes are usually accompanied by civil war or tumult. Nor can aristocracy, he thinks, be changed into democracy without violence, though the converse revolution sometimes happens quietly, as when the labouring classes and traders give up public affairs to look after their own; in this manner Venice, Lucca, Ragusa, and other cities have become aristocracies. The great danger for an aristocracy is, that some ambitious person, either of their own body or of the people, may arm the latter against them; and this is most likely to occur when honours and magistracy are conferred on unworthy men, which affords the best topic to demagogues, especially where the plebeians are wholly excluded; which, though always grievous to them, is yet tolerable so long as power is intrusted to deserving persons; but when bad men are promoted, it becomes easy to excite the minds of the people against the nobility, above all, if there are already factions among the latter, a condition dangerous to all states, but mostly to an aristocracy. Revolutions are more frequent

in small states, because a small number of citizens is easily
split into parties; hence we shall find in one age more revolutions among the cities of Greece or Italy than have taken
place during many in the kingdoms of France or Spain. He
thinks the ostracism of dangerous citizens itself dangerous,
and recommends rather to put them to death, or to render
them friends. Monarchy, he observes, has this peculiar to it,
that if the king be a prisoner, the constitution is not lost;
whereas, if the seat of government in a republic be taken
it is at an end, the subordinate cities never making resistance.
It is evident that this can only be applicable to the case,
hitherto the more common one, of a republic, in which the
capital city entirely predominates. 'There is no kingdom
which shall not, in continuance of time, be changed, and at
length also be overthrown. But it is best for them who least
feel their changes by little and little made, whether from
evil to good, or from good to evil.'

59. If this is the best, the next is the worst chapter in
Astrological Bodin. It professes to inquire, whether the revolu-
fancies of
Bodin.   tions of states can be foreseen. Here he considers
whether the stars have such an influence on human affairs,
that political changes can be foretold by their means, and
declares entirely against it, with such expressions as would
seem to indicate his disbelief in astrology. If it were true,
he says, that the conditions of commonwealths depended on
the heavenly bodies, there could be yet no certain prediction
of them; since the astrologers lay down their observations
with such inconsistency, that one will place the same star in
direct course at the moment that another makes it retrograde.
It is obvious that any one who could employ this argument
must have perceived that it destroys the whole science of
astrology. But, after giving instances of the blunders and
contradictions of these pretended philosophers, he so far
gives way as to admit that, if all the events from the beginning of the world could be duly compared with the planetary
motions, some inferences might be deduced from them; and
thus, giving up his better reason to the prejudices of his age,
he acknowledges astrology as a theoretical truth. The hypothesis of Copernicus he mentions as too absurd to deserve
refutation; since, being contrary to the tenets of all theolo-

gians and philosophers, and to common sense, it subverts the
foundations of every science.   We now plunge deeper into
nonsense ; Boding proceeding to a long arithmetical disquisition, founded on a passage in Plato, ascribing the fall of
states to want of proportion.[f]

60. The next chapter, on the danger of sudden revolutions
in the entire government, asserts that even the Danger of
most determined astrologers agree in denying that sudden
changes.
a wise man is subjugated by the starry influences, though
they may govern those who are led by passion like wild
beasts.   Therefore a wise ruler may foresee revolutions and
provide remedies.   It is doubtful whether an established law
ought to be changed, though not good in itself, lest it should
bring others into contempt, especially such as affect the
form of polity. These, if possible, should be held immutable ;
yet it is to be remembered, that laws are only made for the
sake of the community, and public safety is the supreme law
of laws.   There is therefore no law so sacred that it may not
be changed through necessity.   But, as a general rule,
whatever change is to be made should be effected gradually.[g]

61. It is a disputed question whether magistrates should
be temporary or perpetual.   Bodin thinks it essen- Judicial
tial that the council of state should be permanent, power of
the sove-
but high civil commands ought to be temporary.[h] reign.
It is in general important that magistrates shall accord in
their opinions ; yet there are circumstances in which their
emulation or jealousy may be beneficial to a state.[i] Whether
the sovereign ought to exercise judicial functions may
seem, he says, no difficult question to those who are agreed
that kings were established for the sake of doing justice.
This, however, is not his theory of the origin of government;
and after giving all the reasons that can be urged in favour
of a monarch-judge, including as usual all historical precedents, he decides that it is inexpedient for the ruler to pronounce the law himself.   His reasons are sufficiently bold,
and grounded on an intimate knowledge of the vices of
courts, which he does not hesitate to pour out.[k]

---

[f] c. 2.   [g] c. 3.   [h] c. 4.
        [i] c. 5.   [k] c. 6.

62. In treating of the part to be taken by the prince, or by
Toleration a good citizen, in civil factions, after a long detail
of religions. from history of conspiracies and seditions, he comes
to disputes about religion, and contends against the permission of reasonings on matters of faith. What can be more
impious, he says, than to suffer the eternal laws of God,
which ought to be implanted in men's minds with the
utmost certainty, to be called in question by probable reasonings? For there is nothing so demonstrable which men
will not undermine by argument. But the principles of
religion do not depend on demonstrations and arguments,
but on faith alone; and whoever attempts to prove them by
a train of reasoning, tends to subvert the foundations of the
whole fabric. Bodin in this sophistry was undoubtedly in-
sincere. He goes on, however, having purposely sacrificed
this cock to Æsculapius, to contend that, if several religions
exist in a state, the prince should avoid violence and persecution; the natural tendency of man being to give his assent
voluntarily, but never by force.[m]

63. The first chapter of the fifth book, on the adaptation
Influence of government to the varieties of race and climate,
of climate has excited more attention than most others, from
on govern-
ment. its being supposed to have given rise to a theory of
Montesquieu. In fact, however, the general principle is
more ancient; but no one had developed it so fully as
Bodin. Of this he seems to be aware. No one, he says, has
hitherto treated on this important subject, which should
always be kept in mind, lest we establish institutions not
suitable to the people, forgetting that the laws of nature
will not bend to the fancy of man. He then investigates the
peculiar characteristics of the northern, middle, and southern
nations, as to physical and moral qualities. Some positions
he has laid down erroneously; but, on the whole, he shows
a penetrating judgment and comprehensive generalisation of
views. He concludes that bodily strength prevails towards
the poles, mental power towards the tropics; and that the
nations lying between partake in a mixed ratio of both.
This is not very just; but he argues from the great armies

---

[m] c. 7.

that have come from the north, while arts and sciences have
been derived from the south.   There is certainly a considerable resemblance to Montesquieu in this chapter; and like
him, with better excuse, Bodin accumulates inaccurate
stories.   Force prevails most with northern nations, reason
with the inhabitants of a temperate or middle climate,
superstition with those of the south; thus astrology, magic,
and all mysterious sciences, have come from the Chaldeans
and Egyptians.   Mechanical arts and inventions, on the
other hand, flourish best in northern countries, and the
natives of the south hardly know how to imitate them, their
genius being wholly speculative, nor have they so much
industry, quickness in perceiving what is to be done, or
worldly prudence.   The stars appear to exert some influence
over national peculiarities; but even in the same latitudes
great variety of character is found, which arises from a
mountainous or level soil, and from other physical circumstances.   We learn by experience, that the inhabitants of
hilly countries and the northern nations generally love freedom, but having less intellect than strength, submit readily
to the wisest among them.   Even winds are not without
some effect on national character.   But the barrenness or
fertility of the soil is more important; the latter producing
indolence and effeminacy, while one effect of a barren soil is
to drive the people into cities, and to the exercise of handi-
crafts for the sake of commerce, as we see at Athens and
Nuremberg, the former of which may be contrasted with
Bœotia.

64. Bodin concludes, after a profusion of evidence drawn
from the whole world, that it is necessary not only to consider the general character of the climate as affecting an
entire region, but even the peculiarities of single districts,
and to inquire what effects may be wrought on the dispositions of the inhabitants by the air, the water, the mountains
and valleys, or prevalent winds, as well as those which depend
on their religion, their customs, their education, their form
of government; for whoever should conclude alike as to all
who live in the same climate would be frequently deceived;
since, in the same parallel of latitude, we may find remarkable differences even of countenance and complexion.   This

chapter abounds with proofs of the comprehension as well as patient research which distinguishes Bodin from every political writer who had preceded him.

65. In the second chapter, which inquires how we may Means of avoid the revolutions which an excessive inequality obviating inequality. of possessions tends to produce, he inveighs against a partition of property, as inconsistent with civil society, and against an abolition of debts, because there can be no justice where contracts are not held inviolable; and observes, that it is absurd to expect a division of all possessions to bring about tranquillity. He objects also to any endeavour to limit the number of the citizens, except by colonisation. In deference to the authority of the Mosaic law, he is friendly to a limited right of primogeniture, but disapproves the power of testamentary dispositions, as tending to inequality, and the admission of women to equal shares in the inheritance, lest the same consequence should come through marriage. Usury he would absolutely abolish, to save the poorer classes from ruin.

66. Whether the property of condemned persons shall be Confisca- confiscated is a problem, as to which, having given tions— rewards. the arguments on both sides, he inclines to a middle course, that the criminal's own acquisitions should be forfeited, but what has descended from his ancestors should pass to his posterity. He speaks with great freedom against unjust prosecutions, and points out the dangers of the law of forfeiture.[n] In the next, being the fourth chapter of this book, he treats of rewards and punishments. All states depend on the due distribution of these; but, while many books are full of the latter, few have discussed the former, to which he here confines himself. Triumphs, statues, public thanks, offices of trust and command, are the most honourable; exemptions from service or tribute, privileges, and the like, the most beneficial. In a popular government, the former are more readily conceded than the latter; in a monarchy, the reverse. The Roman triumph gave a splendour to the republic itself. In modern times the sale of nobility, and of public offices, renders them no longer so honourable as they

---

[n] c. 3.

should be. He is here again very free-spoken as to the conduct of the French, and of other governments.°

67. The advantage of warlike habits to a nation, and the
utility of fortresses, are then investigated. Some
have objected to the latter, as injurious to the   Fortresses.
courage of the people, and of little service against an inva-
der; and also, as furnishing opportunities to tyrants and
usurpers, or occasionally to rebels. Bodin, however, inclines
in their favour, especially as to those on the frontier, which
may be granted as feudal benefices, but not in inheritance.
The question of cultivating a military spirit in the people
depends on the form of polity : in popular states it is necessary; in an aristocracy, unsafe. In monarchies, the position
of the state with respect to its neighbours is to be considered.
The capital city ought to be strong in a republic, because its
occupation is apt to carry with it an entire change in the
commonwealth. But a citadel is dangerous in such a state.
It is better not to suffer castles, or strongholds of private
men, as is the policy of England ; unless when the custom
is so established, that they cannot be dismantled without
danger to the state.ᴾ

68. Treaties of peace and alliance come next under review.
He points out with his usual prolixity the difference   Necessity of
between equal and unequal compacts of this kind.   good faith.
Bodin contends strongly for the rigorous maintenance of
good faith, and reprobates the civilians and canonists who
induced the council of Constance to break their promise towards John Huss. No one yet, he exclaims, has been so
consummately impudent as to assert the right of violating a
fair promise; but one alleges the deceit of the enemy; another, his own mistake ; a third the change of circumstances,
which has rendered it impossible to keep his word ; a fourth,
the ruin of the state which it would entail. But no excuse,
according to Bodin, can be sufficient, save the unlawfulness
of the promise, or the impossibility of fulfilling it. The
most difficult terms to keep are between princes and their
subjects, which generally require the guarantee of other
states. Faith, however, ought to be kept in such cases ; and

° c. 4.   ᴾ c. 5.

he censures, though under an erroneous impression of the fact, as a breach of engagement, the execution of the duke of York in the reign of Henry VI.; adding, that he prefers to select foreign instances, rather than those at home, which he would wish to be buried in everlasting oblivion. In this he probably alludes to the day of St. Bartholomew.[q]

69. The first chapter of the sixth book relates to a perio-
Census of property. dical census of property, which he recommends as too much neglected. The Roman censorship of manners he extols, and thinks it peculiarly required, when all domestic coercion is come to an end. But he would give no coercive jurisdiction to his censors, and plainly intimates his dislike to a similar authority in the church.[r] A more important disquisition follows on public revenues. These may
Public re-venues. be derived from seven sources: namely, national domains; confiscation of enemies' property; gifts of friendly powers; tributes from dependent allies; foreign trade carried on by the state; tolls and customs on exports and imports; or, lastly, taxes directly levied on the people. The first of these is the most secure and honourable; and here we have abundance of ancient and modern learning, while of course the French principle of inalienability is brought forward. The second source of revenue is justified by the rights of war and practice of nations; the third has sometimes occurred; and the fourth is very frequent. It is dishonourable for a prince to be a merchant, and thus gain a revenue in the fifth mode, yet the kings of Portugal do not disdain this; and the mischievous usage of selling offices in some other countries seems to fall under this head. The different taxes on merchandise, or, in our language, of customs and excise, come in the sixth place. Here Bodin advises to lower the import duties on articles with which the people cannot well dispense, but to lay them heavily on manufactured goods, that they may learn to practise these arts themselves.

70. The last species of revenue, obtained from direct taxation, is never to be chosen but from necessity; and as taxes

---

q c. 6. Externa libentius quam do-
mestica recordor, quæ utinam sempi-
terna oblivione sepulta jacerent.
r Lib. vi. c. 1.

are apt to be kept up when the necessity is passed, it is better that the king should borrow money of subjects than impose taxes upon them. He then enters on *Taxation.* the history of taxation in different countries, remarking it as peculiar to France, that the burthen is thrown on the people to the ease of the nobles and clergy, which is the case nowhere except with the French, among whom, as Cæsar truly wrote, nothing is more despised than the common people. Taxes on luxuries, which serve only to corrupt men, are the best of all; those also are good which are imposed on proceedings at law, so as to restrain unnecessary litigation. Borrowing at interest, or by way of annuity, as they do at Venice, is ruinous. It seems, therefore, that Bodin recommends loans without interest, which must be compulsory. In the remainder of this chapter he treats of the best mode of expending the public revenue, and advises that royal grants should be closely examined, and, if excessive, be rescinded, at least after the death of the reigning king.[s]

71. Every adulteration of coin, to which Bodin proceeds, and every change in its value, is dangerous, as it *Adulteration* affects the certainty of contracts, and renders every *of coin.* man's property insecure. The different modes of alloying coin are then explained according to practical metallurgy, and, assuming the constant ratio of gold to silver as twelve to one, he advises that coins of both metals should be of the same weight. The alloy should not be above one in twenty-four; and the same standard should be used for plate. Many curious facts in monetary history will be found collected in this chapter.[t]

72. Bodin next states fully, and with apparent fairness, the advantages and disadvantages both of demo- *Superiority* cracy and aristocracy, and admitting that some *of monarchy.* evils belong to monarchy, contends that they are all much less than in the two other forms. It must be remembered, that he does not acknowledge the possibility of a mixed government; a singular error, which, of course, vitiates his reasonings in this chapter. But it contains many excellent

------

[s] c. 2.   [t] c. 3.

observations on democratical violence and ignorance, which
history had led him duly to appreciate.[u] The best form of
polity he holds to be a monarchy by agnatic succession, such
as, in contradiction to Hottoman, he maintains to have been
always established in France, pointing out also the mischiefs that have ensued in other countries for want of a
Salic law.[x]

73. In the concluding chapter of the work, Bodin, with
too much parade of mathematical language, descants on what he calls arithmetical, geometrical,
and harmonic proportions as applied to political regimen.
As the substance of all this appears only to be, that laws
ought sometimes to be made according to the circumstances
and conditions of different ranks in society, sometimes to be
absolutely equal, it will probably be thought by most rather
incumbered by this philosophy, which, however, he borrowed
from the ancients, and found conformable to the spirit of
learned men in his own time. Several interesting questions
in the theory of jurisprudence are incidentally discussed in
this chapter, such as that of the due limits of judicial discretion.

Conclusion of the work.

74. It must appear, even from this imperfect analysis,
in which much has been curtailed of its fair proportion, and many both curious and judicious observations omitted, that Bodin possessed a highly philosophical mind, united with the most ample stores of history
and jurisprudence. No former writer on political philosophy
had been either so comprehensive in his scheme, or so
copious in his knowledge ; none, perhaps, more original,
more independent and fearless in his inquiries. Two names
alone, indeed, could be compared with his—Aristotle and
Machiavel. Without, however, pretending that Bodin was
equal to the former in acuteness and sagacity, we may say
that the experience of two thousand years, and the maxims
of reason and justice, suggested or corrected by the Gospel
and its ministers, by the philosophers of Greece and Rome,
and by the civil law, gave him advantages, of which his

*Bodin com-
pared with
Aristotle and
Machiavel,*

---

judgment and industry fully enabled him to avail himself. Machiavel, again, has discussed so few, comparatively, of the important questions in political theory, and has seen many things so partially, according to the narrow experience of Italian republics, that, with all his superiority in genius, and still more in effective eloquence, we can hardly say that his Discourses on Livy are a more useful study than the Republic of Bodin.

75. It has been often alleged, as we ·have mentioned above, that Montesquieu owed something, and espe- *and with* cially his theory of the influence of climate, to *Montesquieu.* Bodin. But, though he had unquestionably read the Republic with that advantage which the most fertile minds derive from others, this ought not to detract in our eyes from his real originality. The Republic and the Spirit of Laws bear, however, a more close comparison than any other political systems of celebrity. Bodin and Montesquieu are, in this province of political theory, the most philosophical of those who have read so deeply, the most learned of those who have thought so much. Both acute, ingenious, little respecting authority in matters of opinion, but deferring to it in established power, and hence apt to praise the fountain of waters whose bitterness they exposed ; both in advance of their age, but one so much that his genius neither kindled a fire in the public mind, nor gained in its own due praise, the other more fortunate in being the immediate herald of a generation which he stimulated, and which repaid him by its admiration ; both conversant with ancient and mediæval history, and with the Roman as well as national law; both just, benevolent, and sensible of the great object of civil society, but displaying this with some variation according to their times ; both sometimes seduced by false analogies, but the one rather through respect to an erroneous philosophy, the other through personal thirst of praise and affectation of originality ; both aware that the basis of the philosophy of man is to be laid in the records of his past existence ; but the one prone to accumulate historical examples without sufficient discrimination, and to overwhelm, instead of convincing the reader by their redundancy, the other aiming at an induction from select experience, but hence appearing some

times to reason generally from particular premises, or dazzling the student by a proof that does not satisfy his reason.[y]

Sect. III.—On Jurisprudence.

Golden Age of Jurisprudence — Cujacius—Other Civilians— Anti-Tribonianus of Hottoman—Law of Nations—Franciscus a Victoria—Balthazar Ayala—Albericus Gentilis.

76. THE latter part of the sixteenth century, denominated by Golden age of juris-prudence. Andrès the golden age of jurisprudence, produced the men who completed what Alciat and Augustinus had begun in the preceding generation, by elucidating and reducing to order the dark chaos which the Roman law, enveloped in its own obscurities and those of its earlier commentators, had presented to the student. The most Cujacius. distinguished of these, Cujacius, became professor at Bourges, the chief scene of his renown, and the principal seminary of the Roman law in France, about the year 1555. His works, of which many had been separately published, were collected in 1577, and they make an epoch in the annals of jurisprudence. This greatest of all civil lawyers pursued the track that Alciat had so successfully opened, avoiding all scholastic subtleties of interpretation, for which he substituted a general erudition that rendered the science at once more intelligible and more attractive. Though his works are voluminous, Cujacius has not the reputation of diffuseness; on the contrary, the art of lucid explanation with brevity is said to have been one of his great characteristics. Thus, in the Paratitla on the Digest, a little book which Hottoman,

---

[y] This account of Bodin's Republic will be found too long by many readers; and I ought, perhaps, to apologise for it on the score that M. Lerminier, in his brilliant and agreeable Introduction à l'Histoire Générale du Droit (Paris, 1829), has pre-occupied the same ground. This, however, had escaped my recollection (though I was acquainted with the work of M. L.) when I made my own analysis, which has not been borrowed in a single line from his. The labours of M. Lerminier are not so commonly known in England as to render it unnecessary to do justice to a great French writer of the sixteenth century.

As I have mentioned M. Lerminier, I would ask whether the following is a fair translation of the Latin of Bodin :— Eo nos ipsa ratio deducit, imperia scilicet ac respublicas vi primum coaluisse, *etiam si ab historia deseramur;* quamquam pleni sunt libri, plenæ leges, plena antiquitas. En établissant la théorie de l'origine des sociétés, il déclare qu'il y persiste, *quand même les faits iraient à l'encontre.* Hist. du Droit. pp. 62 and 67.

his rival and enemy, advised his own son to carry constantly about with him, we find a brief exposition, in very good Latin, of every title in order, but with little additional matter. And it is said that he thought nothing requisite for the Institutes but short clear notes, which his thorough admirers afterwards contrasted with the celebrated but rather verbose commentaries of Vinnius.

77. Notwithstanding this conciseness, his works extend to a formidable length. For the civil law itself *Eulogies bestowed upon him.* is, for the most part, very concisely written, and stretches to such an extent, that his indefatigable diligence in illustrating every portion of it could not be satisfied within narrow bounds. 'Had Cujacius been born sooner,' in the words of the most elegant of his successors, 'he would have sufficed instead of every other interpreter. For neither does he permit us to remain ignorant of anything, nor to know any thing which he has not taught. He alone instructs us on every subject, and what he teaches is always his own. Hence, though the learned style of jurisprudence began with Alciat, we shall call it Cujacian.'[z] 'Though the writings of Cujacius are so voluminous,' says Heineccius, 'that scarce any one seems likely to read them all, it is almost peculiar to him, that the longer any of his books is, the more it is esteemed. Nothing in them is trivial, nothing such as might be found in any other; every thing so well chosen that the reader can feel no satiety; and the truth is seen of what he answered to his disciples, when they asked for more diffused commentaries, that his lectures were for the ignorant, his writings for the learned.'[a] A later writer, Gennari, has given a more fully elaborate character of this illustrious lawyer, who might seem to have united every excellence without a failing.[b] But without listening to the

---

[z] Gravina, Origines Juris Civilis, p 219.

[a] Heineccii Opera, xiv. 203. He prefers the Observationes atque Emendationes of Cujacius to all his other works. These contain twenty-eight books, published, at intervals, from the year 1556. They were designed to extend to forty books.

[b] Respublica Jurisconsultorum, p. 237.

Intactum in jurisprudentia reliquit nihil, et quæ scribit, non tam ex aliis excerpta, quam a se inventa, sane fatentur omnes; ita omnia suo loco posita, non nimis protracta, quæ nauseam creant, non arcte ac jejune tractata, quæ explicationis paullo diffusioris pariunt desiderium. Candida perspicuitate brevis, elegans sub amabili simplicitate, caute eruditus, quantum patitur occasio, ubique

enemies whom his own eminence, or the polemical fierceness
of some disputes in which he was engaged, created among
the jurists of that age, it has since been observed, that in his
writings may be detected certain inconsistencies, of which
whole books have been invidiously compiled, and that he was
too prone to abuse his acuteness by conjectural emendations
of the text; a dangerous practice, as Bynkershoek truly remarks, when it may depend upon a single particle whether
the claim of Titius or of Marius shall prevail.[c]

78. Such was the renown of Cujacius that, in the public
schools of Germany, when his name was mentioned,
every one took off his hat.[d] The continual bicker-
ings of his contemporaries, not only of the old Ac-
cursian school, among whom Albericus Gentilis was
prominent in disparaging him, but of those who had been
trained in the steps of Alciat like himself, did not affect this
honest admiration of the general student.[e] But we must not
consider Cujacius exactly in the light of what we now call a
great lawyer. He rejected all modern forensic experience
with scorn, declaring that he had misspent his youth in such
studies. We have, indeed, fifty of his consultations which
appear to be actual cases. But, in general, it is observed by
Gravina, that both he and the greatest of his disciples ' are
but ministers of ancient jurisprudence, hardly deigning to
notice the emergent questions of modern practice. Hence,
while the elder jurists of the school of Bartolus, deficient as
they are in expounding the Roman laws, yet apply them
judiciously to new cases, these excellent interpreters hardly
regard anything modern, and leave to the others the whole
honour of advising and deciding rightly.' Therefore he recommends that the student who has imbibed the elements of
Roman jurisprudence in all their purity from the school of
Cujacius, should not neglect the interpretations of Accursius
in obscure passages; and, above all, should have recourse
to Bartolus and his disciples for the arguments, authorities,

Marginal note: Cujacius an interpreter of law rather than a lawyer.

docens, ne aliqua parte arguatur otiosus,
tam nihil habet inane, nihil inconditum,
nihil curtum, nihil claudicans, nihil re-
dundans, amœnus in Observationibus,
subtilis in Tractatibus, uber ac planus
in Commentariis, generosus in refel-
lendis objectis, accuratus in confingendis
notis, in Paratitlis brevis ac succi plenus,
rectus prudensque in Consultationibus.

  [e] Heinecc. xiv. 209.   Gennari, p. 199.
  [d] Gennari, p. 246.   Biogr. Univ.
  [e] Heineccius, ibid.   Gennari, p. 242.

and illustrations which ordinary forensic questions will require.[f]

79. At some distance below Cujacius, but in places of honour, we find among the great French interpreters of the civil law in this age, Duaren, as devoted to ancient learning as Cujacius, but differing from him by inculcating the necessity of forensic practice to form a perfect lawyer;[g] Govea, who, though a Portuguese, was always resident in France, whom some have set even above Cujacius for ability, and of whom it has been said that he is the only jurist who ought to have written more;[h] Brisson, a man of various learning, who became in the seditions of Paris an unfortunate victim of his own weak ambition; Balduin, a strenuous advocate for uniting the study of ancient history with that of law; Godefroi, whose Corpus Juris Civilis makes an epoch in jurisprudence, being the text-book universally received; and Connan, who is at least much quoted by the principal writers on the law of nature and nations. The boast of Germany was Gifanius.

French lawyers below Cujacius; Govea and others.

80. These 'ministers of ancient jurisprudence' seemed to have no other office than to display the excellences of the old masters in their original purity. Ulpian and Papinian were to them what Aristotle and Aquinas were to another class of worshippers. But the jurists of the age of Severus have come down to us through a compilation in that of Justinian; and Alciat himself had begun to discover the interpolations of Tribonian, and the corruption which, through ignorance or design, had penetrated the vast reservoir of the Pandects. Augustinus, Cujacius, and other French lawyers of the school of Bourges, followed in this track, and endeavoured not only to restore the text from errors introduced by the carelessness of transcribers, a necessary and arduous labour, but from such as had sprung out of the presumptousness of the lawgiver himself, or of those whom he had employed. This excited a vehement opposition, led by some of the chief lawyers of France,

Opponents of the Roman law.

---

[f] Gravina, pp. 222, 230.

[g] Duarenus . . . sine forensis exercitationis præsidio nec satis percipi, nec recte commodeque doceri jus civile existimat. Gennari, p. 479.

[h] Goveanus . . . vir, de quo uno desideretur, plura scripsisse, de cæteris vero, pauciora . . . . quia felix ingenio, naturæ viribus tantum confideret, ut diligentiæ laudem sibi non necessariam, minus etiam honorificam putare videatur. Gennari, p. 281.

jealous of the fame of Cujacius. But, while they pretended to rescue the orthodox vulgate from the innovations of its great interpreter, another sect rose up, far bolder than either, which assailed the law itself. Of these the most determined were Faber and Hottoman.

81. Antony Faber, or Fabre, a lawyer of Savoy, who Faber of became president of the court of Chamberi in 1610, Savoy. acquired his reputation in the sixteenth century. He waged war against the whole body of commentators, and even treated the civil law itself as so mutilated and corrupt, so inapplicable to modern times, that it would be better to lay it altogether aside. Gennari says, that he would have been the greatest of lawyers, if he had not been too desirous to appear such;[i] his temerity and self-confidence diminished the effect of his ability. His mind was ardent and unappalled by difficulties; no one had more enlarged views of jurisprudence, but in his interpretations he was prone to make the laws rather what they ought to have been than what they were. His love of paradox is hardly a greater fault than the perpetual carping at his own master Cujacius, as if he thought the reform of jurisprudence should have been reserved for himself.[k]

82. But the most celebrated production of this party is Anti-Tribonianus of Hottoman. This was nianus of Hottoman. written in 1567, and, though not published in French till 1609, nor in the original till 1647, seems properly to belong to the sixteenth century. He begins by acknowledging the merit of the Romans in jurisprudence, but denies that the compilation of Justinian is to be confounded with the Roman law. He divides his inquiry into two questions: first, whether the study of these laws is useful in France; and, secondly, what are their deficiencies. These laws, he observes by the way, contain very little instruction about Roman history or antiquities, so that in books on those

---

[i] P. 97.

[k] Heineccius, p. 236. Fabre, says Ferrière, as quoted by Terrasson, Hist. de la Jurisprudence, est celui des jurisconsultes modernes qui a porté le plus loin les idées sur le droit. C'étoit un esprit vaste qui ne se rebutoit par de plus grandes difficultés. Mais on l'accuse avec raison d'avoir décidé un peu trop hardiment contre les opinions communes, et de s'être donné souvent trop de liberté de retrancher ou d'ajouter dans les lois. See, too, the article Favre, in Biographie Universelle.

subjects we rarely find them cited. He then adverts to particular branches of the civil law, and shows that numberless
doctrines are now obsolete, such as the state of servitude, the
right of arrogation, the ceremonies of marriage, the peculiar
law of guardianship, while for matters of daily occurrence
they give us no assistance. He points out the useless distinctions between things *mancipi* and *non mancipi*, between
the *dominium quiritarium* and *bonitarium* ; the modes of acquiring property by mancipation, *cessio in jure, usucapio*, and
the like, the unprofitable doctrines about *fidei commissa* and
the *jus accrescendi*. He dwells on the folly of keeping up
the old forms of stipulation in contracts, and those of legal
process, from which no one can depart a syllable without
losing his suit. And on the whole he concludes that not
a twentieth part of the Roman law survives, and of that not
one-tenth can be of any utility. In the second part, Hottoman attacks Tribonian himself for suppressing the genuine
works of great lawyers, for barbarous language, for perpetually mutilating, transposing, and interpolating the passages which he inserts, so that no cohesion or consistency is
to be found in these fragments of materials, nor is it possible
to restore them. The evil has been increased by the herd of
commentators and interpreters since the twelfth century;
those who have lately appeared and applied more erudition
rarely agreeing in their conjectural emendations of the text,
which yet frequently varies in different manuscripts, so as to
give rise to endless disputes. He ends by recommending
that some jurisconsults and advocates should be called
together, in order to compile a good code of laws; taking
whatever is valuable in the Roman system, and adding whatever from other sources may seem worthy of reception,
drawing them up in plain language, without too much
subtilty, and attending chiefly to the principles of equity.
He thinks that a year or two would suffice for the instruction
of students in such a code of laws, which would be completed
afterwards, as was the case at Rome, by forensic practice.

83. These opinions of Hottoman, so reasonable in themselves, as to the inapplicability of much of the   Civil law
Roman law to the actual state of society, were con-   not countenanced in
genial to the prejudices of many lawyers in France.   France.

That law had in fact to struggle against a system already received, the feudal customs which had governed the greater part of the kingdom. And this party so much prevailed, that, by the ordinance of Blois, in 1579, the university of Paris was forbidden to give lectures or degrees in civil law. This was not wholly regarded; but it was not till a century afterwards that public lectures in that science were re-established in the university, on account of the uncertainty which the neglect of the civil law was alleged to have produced.

84. France now stood far pre-eminent in her lawyers. But Italy was not wanting in men once conspicuous, whom we cannot afford time to mention. One of them, Turamini, professor at Ferrara, though his name is not found in Tiraboschi, or even in Gravina, seems to have had a more luminous conception of the relation which should subsist between positive laws and those of nature, as well as of their distinctive provinces, than was common in the great jurists of that generation. His commentary on the title De Legibus, in the first book of the Pandects, gave him an opportunity for philosophical illustration. An account of his writings will be found in Corniani.[m]

Turamini.

85. The canon law, though by no means a province sterile in the quantity of its produce, has not deserved to arrest our attention. It was studied conjointly with that of Rome, from which it borrows many of its principles and rules of proceeding, though not servilely, nor without such variations as the independence of its tribunals and the different nature of its authorities might be expected to produce. Covarruvias and other Spaniards were the most eminent canonists; Spain was distinguished in this line of jurisprudence.

Canon law.

86. But it is of more importance to observe, that in this period we find a foundation laid for the great science of international law, the determining authority in questions of right between independent states. Whatever had been delivered in books on this subject, had rested too much on theological casuistry, or on the analogies of positive and local law, or on the loose practice of nations,

Law of nations. Its early state.

---

and precedents rather of arms than of reason. The fecial law, or rights of ambassadors, was that which had been most respected. The customary code of Europe, in military and maritime questions, as well as in some others, to which no state could apply its particular jurisprudence with any hope of reciprocity, grew up by degrees to be administered, if not upon solid principles, yet with some uniformity. The civil jurists, as being conversant with a system more widely diffused, and of which the equity was more generally recognised than any other, took into their hands the adjudication of all these cases. In the fifteenth and sixteenth centuries, the progress of international relations, and, we may add, the frequency of wars, though it did not at once create a common standard, showed how much it was required. War itself, it was perceived, even for the advantage of the belligerents, had its rules ; an enemy had his rights ; the study of ancient history furnished precedents of magnanimity and justice, which put the more recent examples of Christendom to shame ; the spirit of the Gospel could not be wholly suppressed, at least in theory ; the strictness of casuistry was applied to the duties of sovereigns ; and perhaps the scandal given by the writings of Machiavel was not without its influence in dictating a nobler tone to the morality of international law.

87. Before we come to works strictly belonging to this kind of jurisprudence, one may be mentioned which connects it with theological casuistry. The Relectiones Theologicæ of Francis a Victoria, a professor in Salamanca, and one on whom Nicolas Antonio and many other Spanish writers bestow the highest eulogy, as the restorer of theological studies in their country, is a book of remarkable scarcity, though it has been published at least in four editions. Grotius has been supposed to have made use of it in his own great work ; but some of those who since his time have mentioned Victoria's writings on this subject lament that they are not to be met with. Dupin, however, has given a short account of the Relectiones ; and there are at least two copies in England—one in the Bodleian Library, and another in that of Dr. Williams in Redcross Street. The edition I have used is of Venice, 1626, being probably the latest ; it was published first at Lyons in 1557, at Salamanca

Francis a Victoria.

in 1565, and again at Lyons in 1587, but had become scarce
before its republication at Venice.[n] It consists of thirteen
relections, as Victoria calls them, or dissertations on different
subjects, related in some measure to theology, at least by the
mode in which he treats them.   The fifth, entitled De Indis,
and the sixth, De Jure Belli, are the most important.

88. The third is entitled, De Potestate Civili.   In this he
His opi-   derives government and monarchy from divine in-
nions on
public law.   stitution, and holds that, as the majority of a state
may choose a king whom the minority are bound to obey,
so the majority of Christians may bind the minority by the
choice of an universal monarch.   In the chapter concerning
the Indians, he strongly asserts the natural right of those
nations to dominion over their own property and to sovereignty, denying the argument to the contrary founded on
their infidelity or vices. He treats this question methodically,
in a scholastic manner, giving the reasonings on both sides.
He denies that the emperor, or the pope, is lord of the whole
world, or that the pope has any power over the barbarian
Indians or other infidels.   The right of sovereignty in the
king of Spain over these people he rests on such grounds as
he can find ; namely, the refusal of permission to trade, which
he holds to be a just cause of war, and the cessions made to
him by allies among the native powers.   In the sixth relection on the right of war, he goes over most of the leading
questions, discussed afterwards by Albericus Gentilis and Grotius.   His dissertation is exceedingly condensed, comprising
sixty sections in twenty-eight pages ; wherein he treats of
the general right of war, the difference between public war
and reprisal, the just and unjust causes of war, its proper
ends, the right of subjects to examine its grounds, and many
more of a similar kind. He determines that a war cannot be
just on both sides, except through ignorance ; and also that
subjects ought not to serve their prince in a war which they

---

[n] This is said on the authority of the
Venetian edition. But Nicolas Antonio
mentions an edition at Ingoldstadt in
1580, and another at Antwerp in 1604.
He is silent about those of 1587 and
1626. He also says that the Relectiones
are twelve in number. Perhaps he had
never seen the book, but he does not
advert to its scarcity.   Morhof, who
calls it *Prælectiones*, names the two editions of Lyons, and those of Ingoldstadt
and Antwerp.   Brunet, Watt, and the
Biographie universelle do not mention
Victoria at all.

reckon unjust. Grotius has adopted both these tenets. The whole relection, as well as that on the Indians, displays an intrepid spirit of justice and humanity, which seems to have been rather a general characteristic of the Spanish theologians. Dominic Soto, always inflexibly on the side of right, had already sustained by his authority the noble enthusiasm of Las Casas.

89. But the first book, so far as I am aware, that systematically reduced the practice of nations in the conduct of war to legitimate rules, is a treatise by Balthazar Ayala, judge-advocate (as we use the word) to the Spanish army in the Netherlands, under the prince of Parma, to whom it is dedicated. The dedication bears date 1581, and the first edition is said to have appeared the next year. I have only seen that of 1597, and I apprehend every edition to be very scarce. For this reason, and because it is the opening of a great subject, I shall give the titles of his chapters in a note.[o] It will appear, that the second book of

Ayala on the Rights of War.

---

[o] Balth. Ayalæ, J. C. et exercitus regii apud Belgas supremi juridici, de jure et officiis bellicis disciplina militari, libri tres. Antw. 1597. 12mo. pp. 405.

Lib. i.
c. 1. De Ratione Belli Indicendi, Aliisque Cæremoniis Bellicis.
2. De Bello Justo.
3. De Duello, sive Singulari Certamine.
4. De Pignerationibus, quas vulgo Represalias vocant.
5. De Bello Captis et Jure Postliminii.
6. De Fide Hosti Servanda.
7. De Fœderibus et Induciis.
8. De Insidiis et Fraude Hostili.
9. De Jure Legatorum.
Lib. ii.
c. 1. De Officiis Bellicis.
2. De Imperatore vel Duce Exercitus.
3. Unum non Plures Exercitui Præfici debere.
4. Utrum Lenitate et Benevolentia, an Severitate et Sævitia, plus proficiet Imperator.
5. Temporum Rationem præcipue in Bello Habendam.
6. Contentiosas et Lentas de Rebus Bellicis Deliberationes admodum Noxias esse.

Lib. ii.
7. Dum Res sunt Integræ ne minimum quidem Regi vel Reipublicæ de Majestate sua Concedendum esse ; et errare eos qui Arrogantiam Hostium Modestia et Patientia vinci posse existimant.
8. An præstet Bellum Domi excipere, an vero in Hostilem Agrum inferre.
9. An præstet Initio Prœlii Magno Clamore et Concitato Cursu in Hostes pergere, an vero Loco manere.
c. 10. Non esse Consilii invicem Infensos Civilibus Dissensionibus Hostes Sola Discordia Fretum invadere.
11. Necessitatem Pugnandi Magno Studio Imponendam esse Militibus et Hostibus Remittendam.
12. In Victoria potissimum de Pace Cogitandum.
13. Devictis Hostibus, qua potissimum Ratione Perpetua Pace Quieti obtineri possint [sic].
Lib. iii.
c. 1. De Disciplina Militari.
2. De Officio Legati et Aliorum qui Militibus præsunt.

Ayala relates more to politics and to strategy than to international jurisprudence; and that in the third he treats entirely of what we call martial law. But in the first he aspires to lay down great principles of public ethics; and Grotius, who refers to Ayala with commendation, is surely mistaken in saying that he has not touched the grounds of justice and injustice in war.[p] His second chapter is on this subject, in thirty-four pages; and though he neither sifts the matter so exactly, nor limits the right of hostility so much as Grotius, he deserves the praise of laying down the general principle without subtilty or chicanery. Ayala positively denies, with Victoria, the right of levying war against infidels, even by authority of the pope, on the mere ground of their religion; for their infidelity does not deprive them of their right of dominion; nor was that sovereignty over the earth given originally to the faithful alone, but to every reasonable creature. And this, he says, has been shown by Covarruvias to be the sentiment of the majority of doctors.[q] Ayala deals abundantly in examples from ancient history, and in authorities from the jurists.

90. We find next in order of chronology a treatise by Albericus Gentilis, De Legationibus, published in 1583. Gentilis was an Italian Protestant, who through the Earl of Leicester, obtained the chair of civil law

Albericus Gentilis on Embassies.

Lib. iii.
  3. De Metatoribus sive Mensoribus,
  4. De Militibus, et qui Militare possunt.
  5. De Sacramento Militari.
  6. De Missione.
  7. De Privilegiis Militum.
  8. De Judiciis Militaribus.
  9. De Pœnis Militum.
 10. De Contumacibus et Ducum Dicto non Parentibus.
 11. De Emansoribus.
 12. De Desertoribus.
 13. De Transfugis et Proditoribus.
 14. De Seditiosis.
 15. De Iis qui in Acie Loco cedunt aut Victi Se dedunt.
 16. De Iis qui Arma alienant vel amittunt.
 17. De Iis qui .Excubias deserunt vel minus recte agunt.

Lib. iii.
 18. De Eo qui Arcem vel Oppidum cujus Præsidio impositus est, amittit vel Hostibus dedit.
 19. De Furtis et Aliis Delictis Militaribus.
 20. De Præmiis Militum.

[p] Causas unde bellum justum aut injustum dicitur Ayala non tetigit. De Jure B. et P. Prolegom., § 38.

[q] Bellum adversus infideles ex eo solum quod infideles sunt, ne quidem auctoritate imperatoris vel summi pontificis indici potest; infidelitas enim non privat infideles dominio quod habent jure gentium; nam non fidelibus tantum rerum dominia, sed omni rationabili creaturæ data sunt. . . . Et hæc sententia plerisque probatur, ut ostendit Covarruvias.

at Oxford in 1582. His writings on Roman jurisprudence
are numerous, but not very highly esteemed. This work,
on the Law of Embassy, is dedicated to Sir Philip Sidney,
the patron of so many distinguished strangers. The first
book contains an explanation of the different kinds of embassies, and of the ceremonies anciently connected with
them. His aim, as he professes, is to elevate the importance
and sanctity of ambassadors, by showing the practice of
former times. In the second book he enters more on their
peculiar rights. The envoys of rebels and pirates are not
protected. But difference of religion does not take away
the right of sending ambassadors. He thinks that civil
suits against public ministers may be brought before the
ordinary tribunals. On the delicate problem as to the
criminal jurisdiction of these tribunals over ambassadors
conspiring against the life of the sovereign, Gentilis holds,
that they can only be sent out of the country, as the Spanish
ambassador was by Elizabeth. The civil law, he maintains,
is no conclusive authority in the case of ambassadors, who
depend on that of nations, which in many respects is different from the other. The second book is the most interesting,
for the third chiefly relates to the qualifications required in
a good ambassador. His instances are more frequently taken
from ancient than modern history.

91. A more remarkable work by Albericus Gentilis is his
treatise, De Jure Belli, first published at Lyons, His treatise on the
1589. Grotius acknowledges his obligations to Rights of War.
Gentilis, as well as to Ayala, but in a greater degree to the
former. And that this comparatively obscure writer was of
some use to the eminent founder, as he has been deemed, of
international jurisprudence, were it only for mapping his
subject, will be evident from the titles of his chapters, which
run almost parallel to those of the first and third books of
Grotius.[r] They embrace, as the reader will perceive, the

---

[r] Lib. i.
   c. 1. De Jure Gentium Bellico.
     2. Belli Definitio.
     3. Principes Bellum gerunt.
     4. Latrones Bellum non gerunt.
     5. Bella juste geruntur.
     6. Bellum juste geri utrinque.
     7. De Caussis Bellorum.

Lib. i.
   c. 8. De Caussis Divinis Belli Fa-
      ciendi.
     9. An Bellum Justum sit pro Reli-
      gione.
    10. Si Princeps Religionem Bello
      apud suos juste tuetur.

whole field of public faith, and of the rights both of war and victory. But I doubt whether the obligation has been so extensive as has sometimes been insinuated. Grotius does not, as far as I have compared them, borrow many quotations from Gentilis, though he cannot but sometimes allege the same historical examples. It will also be found in almost every chapter, that he goes deeper into the subject, reasons much more from ethical principles, relies less on the authority of precedent, and is in fact a philosopher where the other is a compiler.

92. Much that bears on the subject of international law

Lib. i.
c. 11. An Subditi bellent contra Principem ex Caussa Religionis.
   12. Utrum sint Caussæ Naturales Belli Faciendi.
   13. De Necessaria Defensione.
   14. De Utili Defensione.
   15. De Honesta Defensione.
   16. De Subditis Alienis contra Dominum Defendendis.
   17. Qui Bellum necessarie inferunt.
   18. Qui utiliter Bellum inferunt.
   19. De Naturalibus Caussis Belli inferendi.
   20. De Humanis Caussis Belli inferendi.
   21. De Malefactis Privatorum.
   22. De Vetustis Caussis non Excitandis.
   23. De Regnorum Eversionibus.
   24. Si in Posteros movetur Bellum.
   25. De Honesta Caussa Belli inferendi.
Lib. ii.
c. 1. De Bello Indicendo.
   2. Si quando Bellum non indicitur.
   3. De Dolo et Stratagematis.
   4. De Dolo Verborum.
   5. De Mendaciis.
   6. De Veneficiis.
   7. De Armis et Mentitis Armis.
   8. De Scævola, Juditha, et Similibus.
   9. De Zopiro et Aliis Transfugis.
   10. De Pactis Ducum.
   11. De Pactis Militum.
   12. De Induciis.
   13. Quando contra Inducias fiat.
   14. De Salvo Conductu.
   15. De Permutationibus et Liberationibus.
   16. De Captivis, et non necandis.

Lib. ii.
c. 17. De His qui se Hosti tradunt.
   18. In Deditos et Captos sæviri.
   19. De Obsidibus.
   20. De Supplicibus.
   21. De Pueris et Fœminis.
   22. De Agricolis, Mercatoribus, Peregrinis, Aliis Similibus.
   23. De Vastitate et Incendiis.
   24. De Cæsis sepeliendis.
Lib. iii.
c. 1. De Belli Fine et Pace.
   2. De Ultione Victoris.
   3. De Sumptibus et Damnis Belli.
   4. Tributis et Agris multari Victos.
   5. Victoris Acquisitio Universalis.
   6. Victos Ornamentis Spoliari.
   7. Urbes diripi, dirui.
   8. De Ducibus Hostium Captis.
   9. De Servis.
   10. De Statu Mutando.
   11. De Religionis Aliarumque Rerum Mutatione.
   12. Si Utile cum Honesto Pugnet.
   13. De Pace Futura Constituenda.
   14. De Jure Conveniendi.
   15. De Quibus cavetur in Fœderibus et in Duello.
   16. De Legibus et Libertate.
   17. De Agris et Postliminio.
   18. De Amicitia et Societate.
   19. Si Fœdus recte contrahitur cum Diversæ Religionis Hominibus.
   20. De Armis et Classibus.
   21. De Arcibus et Præsidiis.
   22. Si Successores Fœderatorum tenentur.
   23. De Ratihabitione, Privatis, Piratis, Exulibus, Adhærentibus.
   24. Quando Fœdus violatur.

may probably be latent in the writings of the jurists Baldus, Covarruvias, Vasquez, especially the two latter, who seem to have combined the science of casuistry with that of the civil law.   Gentilis, and even Grotius, refer much to them ; and the former, who is no great philosopher, appears to have borrowed from that source some of his general principles. It is honourable to these men, as we have already seen in Soto, Victoria, and Ayala, that they strenuously defended the maxims of political justice.

CHAPTER V.

HISTORY OF POETRY FROM 1550 TO 1600.

Sect. I.—On Italian Poetry.

Character of the Italian Poets of this Age—Some of the best enumerated—
Bernardino Rota—Gaspara Stampa—Bernardo Tasso—Gierusalemme
Liberata of Torquato Tasso.

1. The school of Petrarch, restored by Bembo, was preva-
General character of Italian poets in this age. lent in Italy at the beginning of this period. It
would demand the use of a library, formed pecu-
liarly for this purpose, as well as a great expenditure
of time, to read the original volumes which this immensely
numerous class of poets, the Italians of the sixteenth century,
filled with their sonnets. In the lists of Crescimbeni, they
reach the number of 661. We must, therefore, judge of
them chiefly through selections, which, though they may
not always have done justice to every poet, cannot but present to us an adequate picture of the general style of poetry.
Their usual faults. The majority are feeble copyists of Petrarch. Even
in most of those who have been preferred to the
rest, an affected intensity of passion, a monotonous repetition
of customary metaphors, of hyperboles reduced to common-
places by familiarity, of mythological allusions, pedantic
without novelty, cannot be denied incessantly to recur. But,
in observing how much they generally want of that which is
essentially the best, we might be in danger of forgetting that
there is a praise due to selection of words, to harmony of
sound, and to skill in overcoming metrical impediments,
which it is for natives alone to award. The authority of
Italian critics should, therefore, be respected, though not
without keeping in mind both their national prejudice, and

that which the habit of admiring a very artificial style must always generate.

2. It is perhaps hardly fair to read a number of these compositions in succession. Every sonnet has its *Their beauties.* own unity, and is not, it might be pleaded, to be charged with tediousness or monotony, because the same structure of verse, or even the same general sentiment, may recur in an equally independent production. Even collectively taken, the minor Italian poetry of the sixteenth century may be deemed a great repertory of beautiful language, of sentiments and images, that none but minds finely tuned by nature produce, and that will ever be dear to congenial readers, presented to us with exquisite felicity and grace, and sometimes with an original and impressive vigour. The sweetness of the Italian versification goes far towards their charm; but are poets forbidden to avail themselves of this felicity of their native tongue, or do we invidiously detract, as we might on the same ground, from the praise of Theocritus and Bion?

3. 'The poets of this age,' says one of their best critics, 'had, in general, a just taste, wrote with elegance, *Character given by Muratori.* employed deep, noble, and natural sentiments, and filled their compositions with well-chosen ornaments. There may be observed, however, some difference between the authors who lived before the middle of the century and those who followed them. The former were more attentive to imitate Petrarch, and, unequal to reach the fertility and imagination of this great master, seemed rather dry, with the exception, always, of Casa and Costanzo, whom, in their style of composition, I greatly admire. The later writers, in order to gain more applause, deviated in some measure from the spirit of Petrarch, seeking ingenious thoughts, florid conceits, splendid ornaments, of which they became so fond, that they fell sometimes into the vicious extreme of saying too much.'[a]

4. Casa and Costanzo, whom Muratori seems to place in the earlier part of the century, belong, by the date *Poetry of Casa.* of publication at least, to this latter period. The

---

[a] Muratori, della Perfetta Poesia, i. 22.

former was the first to quit the style of Petrarch, which
Bembo had rendered so popular. Its smoothness evidently
wanted vigour, and it was the aim of Casa to inspire a more
masculine tone into the sonnet, at the expense of a harsher
versification. He occasionally ventured to carry on the sense
without pause from the first to the second tercet; an innovation praised by many, but which, at that time, few
attempted to imitate, though in later ages it has become
common, not much perhaps to the advantage of the sonnet.
The poetry of Casa speaks less to the imagination, the heart,
or the ear, than to the understanding.[b]

5. Angelo di Costanzo, a Neapolitan, and author of a well-
known history of his country, is highly extolled by
Of Costanzo. Crescimbeni and Muratori; perhaps no one of these
lyric poets of the sixteenth century is so much in favour with
the critics. Costanzo is so regular in his versification, and
so strict in adhering to the unity of subject, that the Society
of Arcadians, when, towards the close of the seventeenth
century, they endeavoured to rescue Italian poetry from.the
school of Marini, selected him as the best model for imitation.
He is ingenious, but perhaps a little too refined; and by no
means free from that coldly hyperbolical tone in addressing
his mistress, which most of these sonnetteers assume. Costanzo is not to me, in general, a pleasing writer; though
sometimes he is very beautiful, as in the sonnet on Virgil,
' Quella cetra gentil,' justly praised by Muratori, and which
will be found in most collections; remarkable, among higher
merits, for being contained in a single sentence. Another,
on the same subject, ' Cigni felici,' is still better. The
poetry of Camillo Pellegrini much resembles that of Costanzo.[c] The sonnets of Baldi, especially a series on
Baldi.   the ruins and antiquities of Rome, appear to me

---

[b] Casa . . . per poco deviando
dalla dolcezza del Petrarca, a un novello
stile diede principio, col quale le sue
rime compose, intendendo sopra il tutto
alla gravità; per conseguir la quale, si
valse spezialmente del carattere aspro, e
de' raggirati periodi e rotondi, insino a
condurre uno stesso sentimento d'uno in
altro quadernario, e d'uno in altro ter-
zetto; cosa in prima da alcuno non più
tentata; perlochè somma lode ritrasse di

chiunque coltivò in questi tempi la tos-
cana poesia. Ma perchè si fatto stile
era proprio, e adattato all' ingegno del suo
inventore, molto difficile riuscì il segui-
tarlo. Crescimbeni, della Volgar Poesia,
ii. 410. See also Ginguéné, ix. 329.
Tiraboschi, x. 22. Casa is generally,
to my apprehension, very harsh and
prosaic.

[c] Crescimbeni, vol. iv. p. 25.

deserving of a high place among those of the age. They may be read among his poems ; but few have found their way into the collections by Gobbi and Rubbi, which are not made with the best taste. Caro, says Crescimbeni, is less rough than Casa, and more original than Bembo. Salfi extols the felicity of his style, and the harmony ~~Caro.~~ of his versification ; while he owns that his thoughts are often forced and obscure.[d]

6. Among the canzoni of this period, one by Celio Magno on the Deity stands in the eyes of foreigners, ~~Odes of Celio~~ and I believe of many Italians, prominent above ~~Magno.~~ the rest. It is certainly a noble ode.[e] Rubbi, editor of the Parnaso Italiano, says that he would call Celio the greatest lyric poet of his age, if he did not dread the clamour of the Petrarchists. The poetry of Celio Magno, more than one hundred pages extracted from which will be found in the thirty-second volume of that collection, is not in general amatory, and displays much of that sonorous rhythm and copious expression which afterwards made Chiabrera and Guidi famous. Some of his odes, like those of Pindar, seem to have been written for pay, and have somewhat of that frigid exaggeration which such conditions produce. Crescimbeni thinks that Tansillo, in the ode, has no rival but Petrarch.[f] The poetry in general of Tansillo, especially La Balia, which contains good advice to mothers about nursing their infants very prosaically delivered, seems deficient in spirit.[g]

7. The amatory sonnets of this age, forming the greater number, are very frequently cold and affected. ~~Coldness of~~ This might possibly be ascribed in some measure ~~the amatory sonnets.~~

---

[d] Crescimbeni, ii. 429. Ginguéné (continuation par Salfi), ix. 12. Caro's sonnets on Castelvetro, written during their quarrel, are full of furious abuse with no wit. They have the ridiculous particularity that the last line of each is repeated so as to begin the next.

[e] This will be found in the Componimenti Lirici of Mathias ; a collection good on the whole, yet not perhaps the best that might have been made ; nor had the editor at that time so extensive an acquaintance with Italian poetry as he afterwards acquired. Crescimbeni reckons

Celio the last of the good age in poetry; he died in 1612. He praises also Scipio Gaetano (not the painter of that name), whose poems were published, but posthumously, in the same year.

[f] Della Volgar Poesia, ii. 436.

[g] Roscoe republished La Balia, which was very little worth while : the following is an average specimen :—

Questo degenerar, ch' ognor si vede,
Sendo voi caste, donne mie, vi dico,
Che d' altro che dal latte non procede.
L' altrui latte oscurar fa 'l pregio antico
Degli avi illustri e adulterar le razze,
E s' infetta talor sangue pudico.

to the state of manners in Italy, where, with abundant licentiousness, there was still much of jealousy, and public sentiment applauded alike the successful lover and the vindictive husband. A respect for the honour of families, if not for virtue, would impose on the poet who felt or assumed a passion for any distinguished lady, the conditions of Tasso's Olindo, to desire much, to hope for little, and to ask nothing. It is also at least very doubtful whether much of the amorous sorrow of the sonnetteers were not purely ideal.

8. Lines and phrases from Petrarch are as studiously introduced as we find those of classical writers in modern Latin poetry. It cannot be said that this is unpleasing; and to the Italians, who knew every passage of their favourite poet, it must have seemed at once a grateful homage of respect, and an ingenious artifice to bespeak attention. They might well look up to him as their master, but could not hope that even a foreigner would ever mistake the hand through a single sonnet. He is to his disciples, especially those towards the latter part of the century, as Guido is to Franceschini or Elisabetta Serena; an effeminate and mannered touch enfeebles the beauty which still lingers round the pencil of the imitator. If they produce any effect upon us beyond sweetness of sound and delicacy of expression, it is from some natural feeling, some real sorrow, or from some occasional originality of thought in which they cease for a moment to pace the banks of their favourite Sorga. It would be easy to point out not a few sonnets of this higher character, among those especially of Francesco Coppetta, of Claudio Tolomei, of Ludovico Paterno, or of Bernardo Tasso.

Studied imitation of Petrarch.

9. A school of poets, that has little vigour of sentiment, falls readily into description, as painters of history or portrait that want expression of character endeavour to please by their landscape. The Italians, especially in this part of the sixteenth century, are profuse in the song of birds, the murmur of waters, the shade of woods; and, as these images are always delightful, they shed a charm over much of their poetry, which only the critical reader, who knows its secret, is apt to resist, and that to his own

Their fondness for description.

loss of gratification. The pastoral character, which it became customary to assume, gives much opportunity for these secondary, yet very seducing beauties of style. They belong to the decline of the art, and have something of the voluptuous charm of evening. Unfortunately they generally presage a dull twilight, or a thick darkness of creative poetry. The Greeks had much of this in the Ptolemaic age, and again in that of the first Byzantine emperors. It is conspicuous in Tansillo, Paterno, and both the Tassos.

10. The Italian critics, Crescimbeni, Muratori, and Quadrio, have given minute attention to the beauties of particular sonnets culled from the vast stores of the sixteenth century. But as the development of the thought, the management of the four constituent clauses of the sonnet, especially the last, the propriety of every line, for nothing digressive or merely ornamental should be admitted, constitute in their eyes the chief merit of these short compositions, they extol some which in our eyes are not so pleasing, as what a less regular taste might select. Without presuming to rely on my own judgment, defective both as that of a foreigner, and of one not so extensively acquainted with the minor poetry of this age, I will mention two writers, well known, indeed, but less prominent in the critical treatises than some others, as possessing a more natural sensibility and a greater truth of sorrow than most of their contemporaries—Bernardino Rota and Gaspara Stampa.

Judgment of Italian critics.

11. Bernardino Rota, a Neapolitan of ancient lineage and considerable wealth, left poems in Latin as well as Italian : and among the latter his eclogues are highly praised by his editor. But he is chiefly known by a series of sonnets intermixed with canzoni, upon a single subject, Portia Capece, his wife, whom, 'what is unusual among our Tuscan poets (says his editor), he loved with an exclusive affection.' But be it understood, lest the reader should be discouraged, that the poetry addressed to Portia Capece is all written before their marriage, or after her death. The earlier division of the series, 'Rime in Vita,' seems not to rise much above the level of amorous poetry. He wooed, was delayed, complained, and won—the natural

Bernardino Rota.

history of an equal and reasonable love. Sixteen years
intervened of that tranquil bliss which contents the heart
without moving it, and seldom affords much to the poet in
which the reader can find interest.   Her death in 1559 gave
rise to poetical sorrows, as real, and certainly full as rational,
as those of Petrarch, to whom some of his contempories gave
him the second place; rather probably from the similarity
of their subject, than from the graces of his language. Rota
is by no means free from conceits, and uses sometimes
affected and unpleasing expressions, as *mia dolce guerra*,
speaking of his wife, even after her death; but his images
are often striking; [h] and, above all, he resembles Petrarch,
with whatever inferiority, in combining the ideality of a
poetical mind with the naturalness of real grief. It has
never again been given to man, nor will it probably be given,
to dip his pen in those streams of ethereal purity which have
made the name of Laura immortal; but a sonnet of Rota
may be not disadvantageously compared with one of Milton,
which we justly admire for its general feeling, though it
begins in pedantry and ends in conceit.[i]   For my own part,

---

[h] Muratori blames a line of Rota as
too bold, and containing a false thought.

> Feano i begl' occhi a se medesmi giorno.

It seems to me not beyond the limits of
poetry, nor more hyperbolical than many
others which have been much admired.
It is, at least, *Petrarchesque* in a high
degree.

[i] This sonnet is in Mathias, iii. 256.
That of Milton will be remembered by
most readers.

> In lieto e pien di riverenza aspetto,
> Con veste di color bianco e vermiglio,
> Di doppia luce serenato il ciglio,
> Mi viene in sonno il mio dolce diletto.
>   Io me l' inchino, e con cortese affetto
> Seco ragiono e seco mi consiglio.
> Com' abbia a governarmi in quest' esiglio,
> E piango intanto, e la risposta aspetto.
>   Ella m' ascolta fiso, e dice cose
> Veramente celesti, ed io l' apprendo,
> E serbo ancor nella memoria ascose.
>   Mi lascia al fine e parte, e va spargendo
> Per l' aria nel partir viole e rose ;
> Io le porgo la man ; poi mi reprendo.

In one of Rota's sonnets we have the
thought of Pope's epitaph on Gay :—

> Questo cor, questa mente e questo petto
> Sia 'l tuo sepolcro, e non la tomba o 'l sasso ;
> Ch' io ti t' apparecchio qui dogioso e lasso ;
> Non si deve a te, donna, altro ricetto.

He proceeds very beautifully :—

> Ricca sia la memoria e l' intelletto,
> Del ben per cui tutt' altro a dietro io lasso ;
> E mentre questo mar di pianto passo,
> Vadami sempre iunanzi il caro objeto.
>   Alma gentil, dov' abitar solei
> Donna e reina, in terren fascio avvolta,
> Ivi regnar celeste immortal dei.
>   Vantisi pur la morte averti tolta
> Al mondo, a me non già ; ch' a pensier miei
> Una sempre sarai viva e sepolta.

The poems of Rota are separately
published in two volumes. Naples,
1726. They contain a mixture of Latin.
Whether Milton intentionally borrowed
the sonnet on his wife's death,

'Methought I saw my last espoused saint,'

from that above quoted, I cannot pretend
to say ; certainly his resemblances to the
Italian poets often seem more than accidental.   Thus two lines in an indifferent
writer, Girolamo Preti (Mathias, iii.
329), are exactly like one of the sublimest
flights in the Paradise Lost.

> Tu per soffrir della cui luce i rai
> Si fan con l' ale i serafini un velo.

Dark with excessive light thy skirts appear
Yet dazzle Heaven, that brightest seraphim
Approach not, but with both wings veil their
    eyes.

[But it has been suggested to me that

I would much rather read again the collection of Rota's sonnets than those of Costanzo.

12. The sorrows of Gaspara Stampa were of a different kind, but not less genuine than those of Rota. Gaspara Stampa. She was a lady of the Paduan territory, living Her love for near the small river Anaso, from which she Collalto adopted the poetical name of Anasilla. This stream bathes the foot of certain lofty hills, from which a distinguished family, the counts of Collalto, took their appellation. The representative of this house, himself a poet as well as soldier, and, if we believe his fond admirer, endowed with every virtue except constancy, was loved by Gaspara with enthusiastic passion. Unhappily she learned only by sad experience the want of generosity too common to man, and sacrificing, not the honour, but the pride of her sex, by submissive affection, and finally by querulous importunity, she estranged a heart never so susceptible as her own. Her sonnets, which seem arranged nearly in order, begin with the delirium of sanguine love; they are extravagant effusions of admiration, mingled with joy and hope; but soon the sense of Collalto's coldness glides in and overpowers her bliss.[k] After three years' expectation of seeing his promise of marriage fulfilled, and when he had already caused alarm by his indifference, she was compelled to endure the pangs of absence by his entering the service of France. This does not seem to have been of long continuance; but his letters were infrequent, and her complaints, always vented in a sonnet, become more fretful. He returned, and Anasilla exults with tenderness, yet still timid in the midst of her joy.

> Oserò io, con queste fide braccia,
> Cingerli il caro collo, ed accostare
> La mia tremante alla sua viva faccia?

But jealousy, not groundless, soon intruded, and we find her doubly miserable. Collalto became more harsh, is ill reavowed his indifference, forbade her to importune quited.

---

both poets must have alluded to Isaiah, vi. 2. Thus, too, the language of the Jewish liturgies represents the seraphim as veiling their eyes with wings in the presence of God.—1842.]

[k] In an early sonnet she already calls Collalto, 'il Signor, *ch' io amo, e ch' io pavento*;' an expression descriptive enough of the state in which poor Gaspara seems to have lived several years.

him with her complaints, and in a few months espoused another woman. It is said by the historians of Italian literature, that the broken heart of Gaspara sunk very soon under these accumulated sorrows into the grave.[1] And such, no doubt, is what my readers expect, and (at least the gentler of them) wish to find. But inexorable truth to whom I am the sworn vassal, compels me to say that the poems of the lady herself contain unequivocal proofs that she avenged herself better on Collalto—by falling in love again. We find **Her second love.** the acknowledgment of another incipient passion, which speedily comes to maturity; and, while declaring that her present flame is much stronger than the last, she dismisses her faithless lover with the handsome compliment, that it was her destiny always to fix her affections on a noble object. The name of her second choice does not appear in her poems; nor has any one hitherto, it would seem, made the very easy discovery of his existence. It is true that she died young; ' but not of love.'[m]

13. The style of Gaspara Stampa is clear, simple, **Style of Gaspara Stampa.** graceful; the Italian critics find something to censure in the versification. In purity of taste, I should incline to set her above Bernardino Rota, though she has less vigour of imagination. Corniani has applied to her the well-known lines of Horace upon Sappho.[n] But the fires

---

[1] She anticipated her epitaph, on this hypothesis of a broken heart, which did not occur.

> Per amar molto, ed esser poco amata
> Visse e morì infelice; ed or qui giace
> La più fedel amante che sia stata.
>   Pregale, viator, riposo e pace,
> Ed impara da lei si mal trattata
> A non seguire un cor crudo e fugace.

[m] It is impossible to dispute the evidence of Gaspara herself in several sonnets, so that Corniani, and all the rest, must have read her very inattentively. What can we say to these lines?

> Perchè mi par vedere a certi segni
> Ch' ordisci (Amor) nuovi lacci e nuove faci,
> E di ritrarme al giogo tuo t' ingegni.

And afterwards more fully:—

> Qual darai fine, Amor, alle mie pene,
> Se dal cinere estinto d' uno ardore
> Rinasce l' altro, tua mercè, maggiore,
> E si vivace a consumar mi viene?
>   Qual nelle più felici e calde arene

> Nel nido acceso sol di vario odore
> D' una fenice estinta esce poi fuore
> Un verme, che fenice altra diviene.
>   In questo io debbo a' tuoi cortesi strali
> Che sempre è degno, ed onorato oggetto
> Quello, onde mi ferisci, onde m' assali.
>   Ed ora è tale, e tanto, e sì perfetto,
> Ha tante doti alla bellezza eguali,
> Ch' ardor per lui m' è sommo alto diletto.

[n]   . . . spirat adhuc amor
>   Vivuntque commissi calores
>   Æoliæ fidibus puellæ.

Corniani, v. 212, and Salfi in Ginguéné, ix. 406, have done some justice to the poetry of Gaspara Stampa, though by no means more than it deserves. Bouterwek, ii. 150, observes only, viel Poesie zeigt sich nicht in diesen Sonetten; which, I humbly conceive, shows that either he had not read them, or was an indifferent judge; and from his general taste I prefer the former hypothesis.

of guilt and shame, that glow along the strings of the Æolian lyre, ill resemble the pure sorrows of the tender Anasilla. Her passion for Collalto, ardent and undisguised, was ever virtuous ; the sense of gentle birth, though so inferior to his, as perhaps to make a proud man fear disparagement, sustained her against dishonourable submission.

> È ben ver, che 'l desio, con che amo voi,
> È tutto d' onestà pieno, e d' amore ;[o]
> Perchè altrimente non convien tra noi.[p]

But not less in elevation of genius than in dignity of character, she is very far inferior to Vittoria Colonna, or even to Veronica Gambara, a poetess, who, without equalling Vittoria, had much of her nobleness and purity. We pity the Gasparas ; we should worship, if we could find them, the Vittorias.

14. Among the longer poems which Italy produced in this period two may be selected. The Art of Navigation, La Nautica, published by Bernardino Baldi in 1590, is a didactic poem in blank verse, too minute sometimes and prosaic in its details, like most of that class, but neither low, nor turgid, nor obscure, as many others have been. The descriptions, though never very animated, are sometimes poetical and pleasing. Baldi is diffuse ; and this conspires with the triteness of his matter to render the poem somewhat uninteresting. He by no means wants the power to adorn his subject, but does not always trouble himself to exert it, and is tame where he might be spirited. Few poems bear more evident marks that their substance had been previously written down in prose.

La Nautica of Baldi.

15. Bernardo Tasso, whose memory has almost been effaced with the majority of mankind by the splendour of his son, was not only the most conspicuous poet of the age wherein he lived, but was placed by its critics, in some points of view, above Ariosto himself. His minor poetry is of considerable merit. But that to which he owed

Amadigi of Bernardo Tasso.

---

[o] *Sic.* leg. onore ?

[p] I quote these lines on the authority of Corniani, v. 215. But I must own that they do not appear in the two editions of the Rime della Gaspara Stampa which I have searched. I must also add that, willing as I am to believe all things in favour of a lady's honour, there is one very awkward sonnet among those of poor Gaspara, upon which it is by no means easy to put such a construction as we should wish.

[q] 'The character of his lyric poetry is a sweetness and abundance of expressions

most of his reputation is an heroic romance on the story of
Amadis, written about 1540, and first published in 1560.
L'Amadigi is of prodigious length, containing 100 cantos,
and about 57,000 lines. The praise of facility, in the best
sense, is fully due to Bernardo. His narration is fluent,
rapid, and clear; his style not in general feeble or low,
though I am not aware that many brilliant passages will be
found. He followed Ariosto in his tone of relating the story:
his lines perpetually remind us of the Orlando; and I believe
it would appear on close examination that much has been
borrowed with slight change. My own acquaintance, however, with the Amadigi is not sufficient to warrant more than
a general judgment. Ginguéné, who rates this poem very
highly, praises the skill with which the disposition of the
original romance has been altered and its canvas enriched by
new insertions, the beauty of the images and sentiments, the
variety of the descriptions, the sweetness, though not always
free from languor, of the style, and finally recommends its
perusal to all lovers of romantic poetry, and to all who would
appreciate that of Italy.[r] It is evident, however, that the
choice of a subject become frivolous in the eyes of mankind,
not less than the extreme length of Bernardo Tasso's poem,
must render it almost impossible to follow this advice.

16. The satires of Bentivoglio, it is agreed, fall short of
those by Ariosto, though some have placed them
above those of Alamanni.[s] But all these are satires
on the regular model, assuming at least a half-

Satirical and
burlesque
poetry;
Aretin.

---

and images, by which he becomes more
flowing and full (più morbido e più
pastoso, metaphors not translatable by
single English words) than his contemporaries of the school of Petrarch.' Corniani, v. 127.

A sonnet of Bernardo Tasso, so much
admired at the time, that almost every
one, it is said, of a refined taste had it by
heart, will be found in Panizzi's edition
of the Orlando Innamorato, vol. i. p. 376,
with a translation by a lady well known
for the skill with which she has transferred the grace and feeling of Petrarch
into our language. The sonnet, which
begins, Poichè la parte men perfetta e
bella, is not found in Gobbi or Mathias.
It is distinguished from the common

crowd of Italian sonnets in the sixteenth
century by a novelty, truth, and delicacy
of sentiment, which is comparatively rare
in them.

[r] Vol. v. p. 61–108. Bouterwek
(vol. ii. 159) speaks much less favourably of the Amadigi, and, as far as I can
judge, in too disparaging a tone. Corniani, a great admirer of Bernardo, owns
that his *morbidezza* and fertility have
rendered him too frequently diffuse and
flowery. See also Panizzi, p. 393, who
observes that the Amadigi wants interest, but praises its imaginative descriptions as well as its delicacy and softness.

[s] Ginguéné, ix. 198. Biogr. univ.
Tiraboschi, x. 66.

serious tone. A style more congenial to the Italians was
that of burlesque poetry, sometimes poignantly satirical, but
as destitute of any grave aim, as it was light and familiar,
even to popular vulgarity, in its expression, though capable
of grace in the midst of its gaiety, and worthy to employ the
best masters of Tuscan language.[t] But it was disgraced by
some of its cultivators, and by none more than Peter Aretin.
The character of this profligate and impudent person is well
known; it appears extraordinary that, in an age so little
scrupulous as to political or private revenge, some great
princes, who had never spared a worthy adversary, thought
it not unbecoming to purchase the silence of an odious
libeller, who called himself their scourge. In a literary
sense, the writings of Aretin are unequal; the serious are
for the most part reckoned wearisome and prosaic; in his
satires a poignancy and spirit, it is said, frequently breaks
out; and though his popularity, like that of most satirists,
was chiefly founded on the ill-nature of mankind, he gratified
this with a neatness and point of expression, which those
who cared nothing for the satire might admire.[u]

17. Among the writers of satirical, burlesque, or licentious
poetry, after Aretin, the most remarkable are Other bur-
Firenzuola, Casa (one of whose compositions passed lesque
writers.
so much all bounds as to have excluded him from the purple,
and has become the subject of a sort of literary controversy,
to which I can only allude),[x] Franco, and Grazzini, surnamed
Il Lasca. I must refer to the regular historians of Italian
literature for accounts of these, as well as for the styles of
poetry called *macaronica* and *pedantesca*, which appear wholly
contemptible, and the attempts to introduce Latin Attempts
at Latin
metres, a folly with which every nation has been metres.

---

[t] A canzon by Coppetta on his cat, in
the twenty-seventh volume of the Parnaso Italiano, is rather amusing.

[u] Bouterwek, ii. 207. His authority
does not seem sufficient; and Ginguéné,
ix. 212, gives a worse character of the
style of Aretin. But Muratori (Della
Perfetta Poesia, ii. 284) extols one of his
sonnets as deserving a very high place
in Italian poetry.

[x] A more innocent and diverting capi-
tolo of Casa turns on the ill luck of being
named John.

S' io avessi manco quindici o vent' anni,
Messer Gandolfo, io mi sbattezzerei,
Per non aver mai più nome Giovanni.
   Perch' io non posso andar pe' fatti miei,
Nè partirmi di qui per ir sì presso
Ch' io nol senta chiamar da cinque e sei.

He ends by lamenting that no alteration mends the name.

Mutalo, o sminuiscil, se tu sai,
O Nanni, o Gianni, o Giannino, o Giannozzo,
Come più tu lo tocchi, peggio fai,
Che gli è cattivo intero, e peggior mozzo.

inoculated in its turn.[y]   Claudio Tolomei, and Angelo Costanzo himself, by writing sapphics and hexameters, did more honour to so strange a pedantry than it deserved.

18. The translation of the Metamorphoses of Ovid by Anguillara seems to have acquired the highest name with the critics ;[z] but that of the Æneid by Caro is certainly the best known in Europe.   It is not, however, very faithful, though written in blank verse, which leaves a translator no good excuse for deviating from his original; the style is diffuse, and, upon the whole, it is better that those who read it should not remember Virgil.   Many more Italian poets ought, possibly, to be commemorated; but we must hasten forward to the greatest of them all.

Poetical translations.

19. The life of Tasso is excluded from these pages by the rule I have adopted; but I cannot suppose any reader to be ignorant of one of the most interesting and affecting stories that literary biography presents.   It was in the first stages of a morbid melancholy, almost of intellectual derangement, that the Gierusalemme Liberata was finished; it was during a confinement, harsh in all its circumstances, though perhaps necessary, that it was given to the world.   Several portions had been clandestinely published, in consequence of the author's inability to protect his rights ; and even the first complete edition, in 1581, seems to have been without his previous consent.   In the later editions of the same year he is said to have been consulted ; but his disorder was then at a height, from which it afterwards receded, leaving his genius undiminished, and his reason somewhat more sound, though always unsteady. Tasso died at Rome in 1595, already the object of the world's enthusiastic admiration, rather than of its kindness and sympathy.

Torquato Tasso.

20. The Jerusalem is the great epic poem, in the strict sense, of modern times.   It was justly observed by Voltaire,

---

[y] Macaronic verse was invented by one Folengo, in the first part of the century.   This worthy had written an epic poem, which he thought superior to the Æneid.   A friend, to whom he showed the manuscript, paid him the compliment, as he thought, of saying that he had *equalled* Virgil.   Folengo, in a rage, threw his poem into the fire, and sat down for the rest of his life to write Macaronics.   Journal des Savans, Dec. 1831.

[z] Salfi (continuation de Ginguéné), x. 180.   Corniani, vi. 113.

that in the choice of his subject Tasso is superior to Homer. Whatever interest tradition might have attached among the Greeks to the wrath of Achilles and the death of Hector, was slight to those genuine recollections which were associated with the first crusade. It was not the theme of a single people, but of Europe; not a fluctuating tradition, but certain history; yet history so far remote from the poet's time, as to adapt itself to his purpose with almost the flexibility of fable. Nor could the subject have been chosen so well in another age or country; it was still the holy war, and the sympathies of his readers were easily excited for religious chivalry; but, in Italy, this was no longer an absorbing sentiment; and the stern tone of bigotry, which perhaps might still have been required from a Castilian poet, would have been dissonant amidst the soft notes that charmed the court of Ferrara.

The Jerusalem excellent in choice of subject.

21. In the variety of occurrences, the change of scenes and images, and of the trains of sentiment connected with them in the reader's mind, we cannot place the Iliad on a level with the Jerusalem. And again, by the manifest unity of subject, and by the continuance of the crusading army before the walls of Jerusalem, the poem of Tasso has a coherence and singleness, which is comparatively wanting to that of Virgil. Every circumstance is in its place; we expect the victory of the Christians, but acknowledge the probability and adequacy of the events that delay it. The episodes, properly so to be called, are few and short; for the expedition of those who recall Rinaldo from the arms of Armida, though occupying too large a portion of the poem, unlike the fifth and sixth, or even the second and third books of the Æneid, is an indispensable link in the chain of its narrative.

Superior to Homer and Virgil in some points.

22. In the delineation of character, at once natural, distinct, and original, Tasso must give way to Homer, perhaps to some other epic and romantic poets. There are some indications of the age in which he wrote, some want of that truth to nature, by which the poet, like the painter, must give reality to the conceptions of his fancy. Yet here also the sweetness and nobleness of his mind and his fine sense of moral beauty are displayed. The female

Its characters.

warrior had been an old invention; and few, except Homer,
had missed the opportunity of diversifying their battles with
such a character. But it is of difficult management; we
know not how to draw the line between the savage virago,
from whom the imagination revolts, and the gentler fair one,
whose feats in arms are ridiculously incongruous to her
person and disposition. Virgil first threw a romantic charm
over his Camilla; but he did not render her the object of
love. In modern poetry, this seemed the necessary compliment to every lady; but we hardly envy Rogero the possession of Bradamante, or Arthegal that of Britomart.
Tasso alone, with little sacrifice of poetical probability, has
made his readers sympathise with the enthusiastic devotion
of Tancred for Clorinda. She is so bright an ideality, so
heroic, and yet, by the enchantment of verse, so lovely, that
no one follows her through the combat without delight, or
reads her death without sorrow. And how beautiful is the
contrast of this character with the tender and modest
Erminia! The heroes, as has been hinted, are drawn with
less power. Godfrey is a noble example of calm and faultless
virtue, but we find little distinctive character in Rinaldo.
Tancred has seemed to some rather too much enfeebled by
his passion, yet this may be justly considered as part of the
moral of the poem.

23. The Jerusalem is read with pleasure in almost every
canto. No poem, perhaps, if we except the Æneid,
has so few weak or tedious pages; the worst passages are the speeches, which are too diffuse. The native
melancholy of Tasso tinges all his poem; we meet with no
lighter strain, no comic sally, no effort to relieve for an instant the tone of seriousness that pervades every stanza. But
it is probable, that some become wearied by this uniformity
which his metre serves to augment. The ottava rima has its
inconveniences; even its intricacy, when once mastered,
renders it more monotonous, and the recurrence of marked
rhymes, the breaking of the sense into equal divisions, while
they communicate to it a regularity that secures the humblest
verse from sinking to the level of prose, deprive it of that
variety which the hexameter most eminently possesses.
Ariosto lessened this effect by the rapid flow of his language,

Excellence of its style.

and perhaps by its negligence and inequality; in Tasso, who
is more sustained at a high pitch of elaborate expression than
any great poet except Virgil, and in whom a prosaic or feeble
stanza will rarely be found, the uniformity of cadence may
conspire with the lusciousness of style to produce a sense of
satiety in the reader.   This is said rather to account for the
injustice, as it seems to me, with which some speak of Tasso,
than to express my own sentiments; for there are few poems
of great length which I so little wish to lay aside as the
Jerusalem.

24. The diction of Tasso excites perpetual admiration; it
is rarely turgid or harsh; and though more figurative than
that of Ariosto, it is so much less than that of most of our
own or the ancient poets, that it appears simple in our eyes.
Virgil, to whom we most readily compare him, is far superior in energy, but not in grace.   Yet his grace is often too
artificial, and the marks of the file are too evident in the
exquisiteness of his language.   Lines of superior beauty
occur in almost every stanza; pages after pages may be
found, in which, not pretending to weigh the style in the
scales of the Florentine academy, I do not perceive one feeble
verse or improper expression.

25. The conceits so often censured in Tasso, though they
bespeak the false taste that had begun to prevail, do Some faults
not seem quite so numerous as his critics have been in it.
apt to insinuate; but we find sometimes a trivial or affected
phrase, or, according to the usage of the times, an idle
allusion to mythology, when the verse or stanza requires to
be filled up.   A striking instance may be given from the
admirable passage where Tancred discovers Clorinda in the
warrior on whom he has just inflicted a mortal blow—

> La vide, e la conobbe; e restò senza
> E moto e senso——

The effect is here complete, and here he would have desired
to stop.   But the necessity of the verse induced him to finish
it with feebleness and affectation.   *Ahi vista! Ahi conoscenza!*
Such difficult metres as the ottava rima demand these
sacrifices too frequently.   Ariosto has innumerable lines of
necessity.

26. It is easy to censure the faults of this admirable poem.
Defects of the poem. The supernatural machinery is perhaps somewhat in excess; yet this had been characteristic of the romantic school of poetry, which had moulded the taste of Europe, and is seldom displeasing to the reader. A still more unequivocal blemish is the disproportionate influence of love upon the heroic crusaders, giving a tinge of effeminacy to the whole poem, and exciting something like contempt in the austere critics, who have no standard of excellence in epic song but what the ancients have erected for us. But while we must acknowledge that Tasso has indulged too far the inspirations of his own temperament, it may be candid to ask ourselves, whether a subject so grave, and by necessity so full of carnage, did not require many of the softer touches which he has given it. His battles are as spirited and picturesque as those of Ariosto, and perhaps more so than those of Virgil; but to the taste of our times he has a little too much of promiscuous slaughter. The Iliad had here set an unfortunate precedent, which epic poets thought themselves bound to copy. If Erminia and Armida had not been introduced, the classical critic might have censured less in the Jerusalem; but it would have been far less also the delight of mankind.

27. Whatever may be the laws of criticism, every poet will
It indicates the peculiar genius of Tasso. best obey the dictates of his own genius. The skill and imagination of Tasso made him equal to descriptions of war; but his heart was formed for that sort of pensive voluptuousness which most distinguishes his poetry, and which is very unlike the coarser sensuality of Ariosto. He lingers around the gardens of Armida, as though he had been himself her thrall. The Florentine critics vehemently attacked her final reconciliation with Rinaldo in the twentieth canto, and the renewal of their loves; for the reader is left with no other expectation. Nor was their censure unjust; since it is a sacrifice of what should be the predominant sentiment in the conclusion of the poem. But Tasso seems to have become fond of Armida, and could not endure to leave in sorrow and despair the creature of his ethereal fancy, whom he had made so fair and so winning. It is probable that the majority of readers are pleased with

this passage, but it can never escape the condemnation of severe judges.

28. Tasso, doubtless, bears a considerable resemblance to Virgil.　But, independently of the vast advantages Tasso compared to Virgil; which the Latin language possesses in majesty and vigour, and which render exact comparison difficult as well as unfair, it may be said that Virgil displays more justness of taste, a more extensive observation, and, if we may speak thus in the absence of so much poetry which he may have imitated, a more genuine originality.　Tasso did not possess much of the self-springing invention which we find in a few great poets, and which, in this higher sense, I cannot concede to Ariosto ; he not only borrows freely, and perhaps studiously, from the ancients, but introduces frequent lines from earlier Italian poets, and especially from Petrarch.　He has also some favourite turns of phrase, which serve to give a certain mannerism to his stanzas.

29. The Jerusalem was no sooner published than it was weighed against the Orlando Furioso, and neither to Ariosto; Italy nor Europe have yet agreed which scale inclines.　It is indeed one of those critical problems, that admit of no certain solution, whether we look to the suffrage of those who feel acutely and justly, or to the general sense of mankind.　We cannot determine one poet to be superior to the other without assuming premises which no one is bound to grant.　Those who read for a stimulating variety of circumstances, and the enlivening of a leisure hour, must prefer Ariosto ; and he is probably, on this account, a poet of more universal popularity.　It might be said perhaps by some, that he is more a favourite of men, and Tasso of women. And yet, in Italy, the sympathy with tender and graceful poetry is so general, that the Jerusalem has hardly been less in favour with the people than its livelier rival ; and its fine stanzas may still be heard by moonlight from the lips of a gondolier, floating along the calm bosom of the Venetian waters.[a]

---

[a] The following passages may perhaps be naturally compared, both as being celebrated, and as descriptive of sound.　Ariosto has, however, much the advantage ; and I do not think the lines in the Jerusalem, though very famous, are altogether what I should select as a specimen of Tasso.

Aspri concenti, orribile armonia
D' alte querele, d' ululi, e di strida

30. Ariosto must be placed much more below Homer than Tasso falls short of Virgil. The Orlando has not the impetuosity of the Iliad; each is prodigiously rapid, but Homer has more momentum by his weight; the one is a hunter, the other a war-horse. The finest stanzas in Ariosto are fully equal to any in Tasso, but the latter has by no means so many feeble lines. Yet his language, though never affectedly obscure, is not so pellucid, and has a certain refinement which makes us sometimes pause to perceive the meaning. Whoever reads Ariosto slowly, will probably be offended by his negligence; whoever reads Tasso quickly, will lose something of the elaborate finish of his style.

31. It is not easy to find a counterpart among painters to the Bolognese painters. for Ariosto. His brilliancy and fertile invention might remind us of Tintoret; but he is more natural, and less solicitous of effect. If indeed poetical diction be the correlative of colouring in our comparison of the arts, none of the Venetian school can represent the simplicity and averseness to ornament of language which belong to the Orlando Furioso; and it would be impossible, for other reasons, to look for a parallel in a Roman or Tuscan pencil. But with Tasso the case is different; and though it would be an affected expression to call him the founder of the Bolognese school, it is evident that he had a great influence on its chief painters, who came but a little after him. They imbued themselves with the spirit of a poem so congenial to their age, and so much admired in it. No one, I think, can consider their works without perceiving both the analogy of the place each hold in their respective arts, and the traces of a feeling, caught directly from Tasso as their prototype and model. We recognise his spirit in the

---

Della misera gente, che peria
Nel fondo per cagion della sua guida,
Istranamente concordar s' udia
Col fiero suon della fiamma omicida.
Orland. Fur., c. 14.

Chiama gli abitator dell' ombre eterne
Il rauco suon della tartarea tromba;
Treman le spaziose atre caverne,
E l' aer cieco e quel rumor rimbomba.
Nè si stridendo mai dalle superne
Regioni del cielo il folgor piomba;
Nè si scossa giammai trema la terra
Quando i vapori in sen gravida serra.
Gierus. Lib., c. 4.

In the latter of these stanzas there is rather too studied an effort at imitative sound; the lines are grand and nobly expressed, but they do not hurry along the reader like those of Ariosto. In his there is little attempt at vocal imitation, yet we seem to hear the cries of the suffering, and the crackling of the flames.

sylvan shades and voluptuous forms of Albano and Dome-
nichino, in the pure beauty that radiates from the ideal heads
of Guido, in the skilful composition, exact design, and noble
expression of the Caracci. Yet the school of Bologna seems
to furnish no parallel to the enchanting grace and diffused
harmony of Tasso ; and we must, in this respect, look back
to Correggio as his representative.

Sᴇᴄᴛ. II.—Oɴ Sᴘᴀɴɪsʜ Pᴏᴇᴛʀʏ.

Luis de Leon—Herrera—Ercilla—Camoens—Spanish Ballads.

32. Tʜᴇ reigns of Charles and his son have long been
reckoned the golden age of Spanish poetry ; and Poetry culti-
if the art of verse was not cultivated in the latter vated under
period by any quite so successful as Garcilasso Charles and Philip.
and Mendoza, who belonged to the earlier part of the
century, the vast number of names that have been collected
by diligent inquiry show, at least, a national taste which
deserves some attention. The means of exhibiting a full
account of even the most select names in this crowd are not
readily at hand. In Spain itself, the poets of the age of
Philip II., like those who lived under his great enemy in
England, were, with very few exceptions, little regarded till
after the middle of the eighteenth century. The Parnaso
Español of Sedano, the first volumes of which were published
in 1768, made them better known ; but Bouterwek observes,
that it would have been easy to make a superior collection, as
we do not find several poems of the chief writers, with which
the editor seems to have fancied the public to be sufficiently
acquainted. An imperfect knowledge of the language, and
a cursory view of these volumes, must disable me from speaking confidently of Castilian poetry ; so far as I feel myself
competent to judge, the specimens chosen by Bouterwek do
no injustice to the compilation.[b]

---

[b] 'The merit of Spanish poems,' says a critic equally candid and well-informed, 'independently of those in- tended for representation, consists chiefly in smoothness of versification and purity of language, and in facility rather than

33. The best lyric poet of Spain in the opinion of many
Luis de Leon. with whom I venture to concur, was Fra Luis Ponce
de Leon, born in 1527, and whose poems were probably written not very long after the middle of the century.
The greater part are translations, but his original productions
are chiefly religious, and full of that soft mysticism which
allies itself so well to the emotions of a poetical mind. One
of his odes, De La Vida del Cielo, which will be found entire
in Bouterwek, is an exquisite piece of lyric poetry, which, in
its peculiar line of devout aspiration, has perhaps never been
excelled.[c] But the warmth of his piety was tempered by a
classical taste, which he had matured by the habitual imitation of Horace. 'At an early age,' says Bouterwek, 'he became intimately acquainted with the odes of Horace, and
the elegance and purity of style which distinguish those
compositions made a deep impression on his imagination.
Classical simplicity and dignity were the models constantly
present to his creative fancy. He, however, appropriated to
himself the character of Horace's poetry too naturally ever
to incur the danger of servile imitation. He discarded the
prolix style of the canzone, and imitated the brevity of the
strophes of Horace in romantic measures of syllables and
rhymes: more just feeling for the imitation of the ancients
was never evinced by any modern poet. His odes have,
however, a character totally different from those of Horace,
though the sententious air which marks the style of both
authors imparts to them a deceptive resemblance. The
religious austerity of Luis de Leon's life was not to be reconciled with the epicurism of the Latin poet; but notwithstanding this very different disposition of the mind, it is not
surprising that they should have adopted the same form of
poetic expression, for each possessed a fine imagination,
subordinate to the control of a sound understanding. Which
of the two is the superior poet, in the most extended sense
of the word, it would be difficult to determine, as each

strength of imagination.' Lord Holland's Lope de Vega, vol. i. p. 107. He
had previously observed that these poets
were generally voluminous: 'it was
not uncommon even for the nobility of
Philip IV.'s time to converse for some
minutes in extemporaneous poetry; and
in carelessness of metre, as well as in
common-place images, the verses of that
time often remind us of the *improvvisatori* of Italy.'—p. 106.
    [c] P. 248.

formed his style by free imitation, and neither overstepped the boundaries of a certain sphere of practical observation. Horace's odes exhibit a superior style of art; and, from the relationship between the thoughts and images, possess a degree of attraction which is wanting in those of Luis de Leon; but, on the other hand, the latter are the more rich in that natural kind of poetry, which may be regarded as the overflowing of a pure soul, elevated to the loftiest regions of moral and religious idealism.' [d] Among the fruits of these Horatian studies of Luis de Leon, we must place an admirable ode suggested by the prophecy of Nereus, wherein the genius of the Tagus, rising from its waters to Rodrigo, the last of the Gothic kings, as he lay encircled in the arms of Cava, denounces the ruin which their guilty loves were to entail upon Spain.[e]

34. Next to Luis de Leon in merit, and perhaps above him in European renown, we find Herrera, sur- named the Divine. He died in 1578; and his ^Herrera. poems seem to have been first collectively published in 1582. He was an innovator in poetical language, whose boldness was sustained by popularity, though it may have diminished his fame. 'Herrera was a poet,' says Bouterwek, 'of powerful talent, and one who evinced undaunted resolution in pursuing the new path which he had struck out for himself. The novel style, however, which he wished to introduce into Spanish poetry, was not the result of a spontaneous essay, flowing from immediate inspiration, but was theoretically constructed on artificial principles. Thus, amidst traits of real beauty, his poetry everywhere presents marks of affectation. The great fault of his language is too much singularity; and his expression, where it ought to be elevated, is merely far-fetched.'[f] Velasquez observes that, notwithstanding the genius and spirit of Herrera, his extreme care to polish his versification has rendered it sometimes unpleasing to those who require harmony and ease.[g]

---

[d] P. 243.

[e] This ode I first knew many years since by a translation in the poems of Russell, which are too little remembered, except by a few good judges. It has been surmised by some Spanish critics to have suggested the famous vision of the Spirit of the Cape to Camoens; but the resemblance is not sufficient, and the dates rather incompatible.

[f] P. 229.

[g] Geschichte der Spanischen Dichtkunst, p. 207.

35. Of these defects in the style of Herrera I cannot judge; his odes appear to possess a lyric elevation and richness of phrase, derived in some measure from the study of Pindar, or still more, perhaps, of the Old Testament, and worthy of comparison with Chiabrera. Those on the battle of Lepanto are most celebrated; they pour forth a torrent of resounding song, in those rich tones which the Castilian language so abundantly supplies. I cannot so thoroughly admire the ode addressed to Sleep, which Bouterwek as well as Sedano extol. The images are in themselves pleasing and appropriate, the lines steal with a graceful flow on the ear; but we should desire to find something more raised above the common-places of poetry.

36. The poets of this age belong generally, more or less, General tone to the Italian school. Many of them were also of Castilian poetry. translators from Latin. In their odes, epistles, and sonnets, the resemblance of style, as well as that of the languages, make us sometimes almost believe that we are reading the Italian instead of the Spanish Parnaso. There seem, however, to be some shades of difference even in those who trod the same path. The Castilian amatory verse is more hyperbolical, more full of extravagant metaphors, but less subtle, less prone to ingenious trifling, less blemished by verbal conceits than the Italian. Such at least is what has struck me in the slight acquaintance I have with the former. The Spanish poets are also more redundant in descriptions of nature, and more sensible to her beauties. I dare not assert that they have less grace and less power of exciting emotion; it may be my misfortune to have fallen rarely on passages that might repel my suspicion.

37. It is at least evident that the imitation of Italy, propagated by Boscan and his followers, was not the Castillejo. indigenous style of Castile. And of this some of her most distinguished poets were always sensible. In the Diana of Montemayor, a romance which, as such, we shall have to mention hereafter, the poetry, largely interspersed, bears partly the character of the new, partly that of the old or native school. The latter is esteemed superior. Castillejo endeavoured to restore the gay rhythm of the redondilla, and turned into ridicule the imitators of Petrarch.

Bouterwek speaks rather slightingly of his general poetic powers; though some of his canciones have a considerable share of elegance. His genius, playful and witty, rather than elegant, seemed not ill-fitted to revive the popular poetry.[h] But those who claimed the praise of superior talents did not cease to cultivate the polished style of Italy. The most conspicuous, perhaps, before the end of the century, were Gil Polo, Espinel, Lope de Vega, Barahona de Soto, and Figueroa.[i] Several other names, not without extracts, will be found in Bouterwek.

38. Voltaire, in his early and very defective essay on epic poetry, made known to Europe the Araucana of Ercilla, which has ever since enjoyed a certain share of reputation, though condemned by many critics as tedious and prosaic. Bouterwek depreciates it in rather more sweeping a manner than seems consistent with the admissions he afterwards makes.[k] A talent for lively description and for painting situations, a natural and correct diction, which he ascribes to Ercilla, if they do not constitute a claim to a high rank among poets, are at least as much as many have possessed.   An English writer of good taste has placed him in a triumvirate with Homer and Ariosto for power of narration.[m] Raynouard observes that Ercilla has taken Ariosto as his model, especially in the opening of his cantos. But the long digressions and episodes of the Araucana, which the poet has not had the art to connect with his subject, render it fatiguing. The first edition, in 1569, contains but fifteen books; the second part was published in 1578; the whole together in 1590.[n]

Araucana of Ercilla.

39. The Araucana is so far from standing alone in this

---

[h] P. 267.

[i] Lord Holland has given a fuller account of the poetry of Lope de Vega than either Bouterwek or Velasquez and Dieze; and the extracts in his ' Lives of Lope de Vega and Guillen de Castro' will not, I believe, be found in the Parnaso Español, which is contrived on a happy plan of excluding what is best. Las Lagrimas de Angelica, by Barahona de Soto, Lord H. says, ' has always been esteemed one of the best poems in the Spanish language,' vol. i. p. 33.

Bouterwek says he has never met with the book. It is praised by Cervantes in Don Quixote.

The translation of Tasso's Aminta, by Jauregui, has been preferred by Menage as well as Cervantes to the original. But there is no extraordinary merit in turning Italian into Spanish, even with some improvement of the diction.

[k] P. 407.

[m] Pursuits of Literature.

[n] Journal des Savans, Sept. 1824.

class of poetry, that not less than twenty-five epic poems
Many epic poems in Spain. appeared in Spain within little more than half
a century. These will be found enumerated, and,
as far as possible, described and characterised, in Velasquez's
History of Spanish Poetry, which I always quote in the
German translation with the valuable notes of Dieze.[o]
Bouterwek mentions but a part of the number, and a few of
them may be conjectured by the titles not to be properly
epic. It is denied by these writers that Ercilla excelled all
his contemporaries in heroic song. I find, however, a different sentence in a Spanish poet of that age, who names
him as superior to the rest.[p]

40. But in Portugal there had arisen a poet, in comparison of whose glory that of Ercilla is as nothing.
Camoens. The name of Camoens has truly an European
reputation, but the Lusiad is written in a language not
generally familiar. From Portuguese critics it would be
unreasonable to demand want of prejudice in favour of a
poet so illustrious, and of a poem so peculiarly national.
The Æneid reflects the glory of Rome as from a mirror; the
Lusiad is directly and exclusively what its name, ' The
Portuguese' (Os Lusiadas), denotes, the praise of the Lusi-
tanian people. Their past history chimes in, by means of
episodes, with the great event of Gama's voyage to India.
The faults of Camoens, in the management of his fable and
the choice of machinery, are sufficiently obvious; it is, nevertheless, the first successful attempt in modern Europe to
construct an epic poem on the ancient model; for the
Gierusalemme Liberata, though incomparably superior, was
not written or published so soon. In consequence, perhaps,
of this epic form, which, even when imperfectly delineated,

---

[o] P. 376–407. Bouterwek, p. 413.

[p] Oye el estilo grave, el blando acento,
  Y altos concentos del varon famoso
  Que en el heroyco verso fue el primero
  Que honró a su patria, y aun quiza el pos-
    trero.
  Del fuerte Arauco el pecho altivo espanta
  Don Alonso de Ercilla con el mano,
  Con ella lo derriba y lo levanta,
  Vence y honra venciendo al Araucano ;
  Calla sus hechos, los agenos canta,
  Con tal estilo que eclipsó al Toscano :
  Virtud que el cielo para si reserva
  Que en el furor de Marte esté Minerva.

La Casa de la Memoria, por Vicente
Espinel, in Parnaso Español, viii. 352.
  Antonio, near the end of the seventeenth century, extols Ercilla very
highly, but intimates that some did not
relish his simple perspicuity. Ad hunc
usque diem ab iis omnibus avidissime
legitur, qui facile dicendi genus atque
perspicuum admittere vim suam et
nervos, nativaque sublimitate quadam
attolli posse, cothurnatumque ire non
ignorant.

long obtained, from the general veneration for antiquity, a greater respect at the hands of critics than perhaps it deserved, the celebrity of Camoens has always been considerable. In point of fame he ranks among the poets of the south immediately after the first names of Italy; Defects of nor is the distinctive character that belongs to the the Lusiad; poetry of the southern languages anywhere more fully perceived than in the Lusiad. In a general estimate of its merits it must appear rather feeble and prosaic; the geographical and historical details are insipid and tedious; a skilful use of poetical artifice is never exhibited; we are little detained to admire an ornamented diction, or glowing thoughts, or brilliant imagery; a certain negligence disappoints us in the most beautiful passages; and it is not till a second perusal that their sweetness has time to glide into the heart. The celebrated stanzas on Inez de Castro are a proof of this.

41. These deficiencies, as a taste formed in the English school, or in that of classical antiquity, is apt to its excel-account them, are greatly compensated, and doubt- lences. less far more to a native than they can be to us, by a freedom from all that offends, for he is never turgid nor affected, nor obscure, by a perfect ease and transparency of narration, by scenes and descriptions, possessing a certain charm of colouring, and perhaps not less pleasing from the apparent negligence of the pencil, by a style kept up at a level just above common language, by a mellifluous versification, and, above all, by a kind of soft languor which tones, as it were, the whole poem, and brings perpetually home to our minds the poetical character and interesting fortunes of its author. As the mirror of a heart so full of love, courage, generosity, and patriotism, as that of Camoens, the Lusiad can never fail to please us, whatever place we may assign to it in the records of poetical genius.[q]

---

[q] 'In every language,' says Mr. Southey, probably, in the Quarterly Review, xxvii. 38, 'there is a magic of words as untranslatable as the Sesame in the Arabian tale—you may retain the meaning, but if the words be changed the spell is lost. The magic has its effect only upon those to whom the language is as familiar as their mother-tongue, hardly indeed upon any but those to whom it is really such. Camoens possesses it in perfection; it is his peculiar excellence.'

42. The Lusiad is best known in England by the trans-
Mickle's   lation of Mickle, who has been thought to have
translation. done something more than justice to his author,
both by the unmeasured eulogies he bestows upon him,
and by the more substantial service of excelling the original in his unfaithful delineation. The style of Mickle is
certainly more poetical, according to our standard, than that
of Camoens, that is, more figurative and emphatic; but it
seems to me replenished with common-place phrases, and
wanting in the facility and sweetness of the original; in
which it is well known that he has interpolated a great deal
without a pretence.[r]

43. The most celebrated passage in the Lusiad is that
Celebrated   wherein the Spirit of the Cape, rising in the midst
passage in
the Lusiad. of his stormy seas, threatens the daring adventurer
that violates their unploughed waters. In order to judge
fairly of this conception, we should endeavour to forget all
that has been written in imitation of it. Nothing has
become more common-place in poetry than one of its
highest flights, supernatural personification; and, as children draw notable monsters when they cannot come near the
human form, so every poetaster, who knows not how to
describe one object in nature, is quite at home with a
goblin. Considered by itself, the idea is impressive and even
sublime. Nor am I aware of any evidence to impeach its
originality, in the only sense which originality of poetical
invention can bear; it is a combination which strikes us with
the force of novelty, and which we cannot instantly resolve
into any constituent elements. The prophecy of Nereus, to
which we have lately alluded, is much removed in grandeur
and appropriateness of circumstance from this passage of
Camoens, though it may contain the germ of his conception.
It is, however, one that seems much above the genius of its
author. Mild, graceful, melancholy, he has never given in
any other place signs of such vigorous imagination. And
when we read these lines on the spirit of the Cape, it is impossible not to perceive that, like Frankenstein, he is unable

---

[r] Several specimens of Mickle's infi-   liberties ever taken in this way, are
delity in translation, which exceed all   mentioned in the Quarterly Review.

to deal with the monster he has created. The formidable
Adamastor is rendered mean by particularity of description,
descending even to yellow teeth. The speech put into his
mouth is feeble and prolix; and it is a serious objection to
the whole, that the awful vision answers no purpose but that
of ornament, and is impotent against the success and glory
of the navigators. A spirit of whatever dimensions, that can
neither overwhelm a ship, nor even raise a tempest, is incomparably less terrible than a real hurricane.

44. Camoens is still, in his shorter poems, esteemed the
chief of Portuguese poets in this age, and possibly Minor poems
in every other; his countrymen deem him their of Camoens.
model, and judge of later verse by comparison with his. In
every kind of composition then used in Portugal he has left
proofs of excellence. ' Most of his sonnets,' says Bouterwek,
' have love for their theme, and they are of very unequal merit;
some are full of Petrarchic tenderness and grace, and moulded
with classical correctness, others are impetuous and romantic,
or disfigured by false learning, or full of tedious pictures of
the conflicts of passion with reason. Upon the whole,
however, no Portuguese poet has so correctly seized the character of the sonnet as Camoens. Without apparent effort,
merely by the ingenious contrast of the first eight with the
last six lines, he knew how to make these little effusions
convey a poetic unity of ideas and impressions, after the
model of the best Italian sonnets, in so natural a manner,
that the first lines or quartets of the sonnet excite a soft
expectation, which is harmoniously fulfilled by the tercets or
last six lines.' [s] The same writer praises several other of the
miscellaneous compositions of Camoens.

45. But, though no Portuguese of the sixteenth century
has come near to this illustrious poet, Ferreira
endeavoured with much good sense, if not with Ferreira.
great elevation, to emulate the didactic tone of Horace, both
in lyric poems and epistles, of which the latter have been
most esteemed.[t] The classical school formed by Ferreira
produced other poets in the sixteenth century; but it seems
to have been little in unison with the national character.

---

[s] Hist. of Portuguese Literature, p. 187.   [t] Id., p. 111.

The reader will find as full an account of these as, if he is
unacquainted with the Portuguese language, he is likely to
desire, in the author on whom I have chiefly relied.

46. The Spanish ballads or romances are of very different ages. Some of them, as has been observed in
Spanish
ballads. another place, belong to the fifteenth century; and
there seems sufficient ground for referring a small number to
even an earlier date. But by far the greater portion is of
the reign of Philip II., or even that of his successor. The
Moorish romances, in general, and all those on the Cid, are
reckoned by Spanish critics among the most modern. Those
published by Depping and Duran have rarely an air of the
raciness and simplicity which usually distinguish the poetry
of the people, and seem to have been written by poets of
Valladolid or Madrid, the contemporaries of Cervantes, with
a good deal of elegance, though not much vigour. The
Moors of romance, the chivalrous gentlemen of Granada, were
displayed by these Castilian poets in attractive colours;[u] and
much more did the traditions of their own heroes, especially
of the Cid, the bravest and most noble-minded of them all,
furnish materials for their popular songs. Their character, it
is observed by the latest editor, is unlike that of the older
romances of chivalry, which had been preserved orally, as
he conceives, down to the middle of the sixteenth century,
when they were inserted in the Cancionero de Romances
at Antwerp, 1555.[x] I have been informed that an earlier

---

[u] Bouterwek, Sismondi, and others
have quoted a romance, beginning Tanta
Zayda y Adalifa, as the effusion of an
orthodox zeal, which had taken offence
at these encomiums on infidels. Whoever reads this little poem, which may
be found in Depping's collection, will
see that it is written more as a humorous
ridicule on contemporary poets than a
serious reproof. It is much more lively
than the answer, which these modern
critics also quote. Both these poems
are of the end of the sixteenth century.
Neither Bouterwek nor Sismondi have
kept in mind the recent date of the
Moorish ballads.

[x] Duran in the preface to his Ro-
mancero of 1832. These Spanish collections of songs and ballads, called Can-
cioneros and Romanceros, are very

scarce, and there is some uncertainty
among bibliographers as to their editions. According to Duran, this of
Antwerp contains many romances unpublished before, and far older than
those of the fifteenth century, collected
in the Cancionero General of 1516. It
does not appear, perhaps, that the
number which can be referred with probability to a period anterior to 1400 is
considerable, but they are very interesting. Among these are Los Fronterizos,
or songs which the Castilians used in
their incursions on the Moorish frontier.
These were preserved orally like other
popular poetry. We find in these early
pieces, he says, some traces of the
Arabian style, rather in the melancholy
of its tone than in any splendour of
imagery, giving as an instance some

edition, printed in Spain, has lately been discovered. In these there is a certain prolixity and hardness of style, a want of connection, a habit of repeating verses or entire passages from others. They have nothing of the marvellous, nor borrow anything from Arabian sources. In some others of the more ancient poetry, there are traces of the oriental manner, and a peculiar tone of wild melancholy. The little poems scattered through the prose romance, entitled, Las Guerras de Granada, are rarely, as I should conceive, older than the reign of Philip II. These Spanish ballads are known to our public, but generally with inconceivable advantage, by the very fine and animated translations of Mr. Lockhart.[y]

Sect. III.—On French and German Poetry.

French Poetry—Ronsard—His Followers—German Poetry.

47. This was an age of verse in France ; and perhaps in no subsequent period do we find so long a catalogue of her poets. Goujet has recorded not merely the names, but the lives, in some measure, of nearly two hundred whose works were published in this half century. Of this number scarcely more than five or six are much remembered

French poets numerous.

---

lines quoted by Sismondi, beginning, ' Fonte frida, fonte frida, Fonte frida y con amor,' which are evidently very ancient. Sismondi says (Littérature du Midi, iii. 240) that it is difficult to explain the charm of this little poem, but ' by the tone of truth, and the absence of all object;' and Bouterwek calls it very nonsensical. It seems to me that some real story is shadowed in it under images in themselves of very little meaning, which may account for the tone of truth and pathos it breathes.

The older romances are usually in alternate verses of eight and seven syllables, and the rhymes are *consonant*, or real rhymes. The *assonance* is, however, older than Lord Holland supposes, who says (Life of Lope de Vega, vol. ii. p. 12) that it was not introduced till the

end of the sixteenth century. It occurs in several that Duran reckons ancient.

The romance of the Conde Alarcos is probably of the fifteenth century. This is written in octosyllable consonant rhymes, without division of strophes. The Moorish ballads, with a very few exceptions, belong to the reigns of Philip II. and Philip III., and those of the Cid, about which so much interest has been taken, are the latest, and among the least valuable of all. All these are, I believe, written on the principle of assonances.

[y] An admirable romance on a bull-fight, in Mr. Lockhart's volume, is faintly to be traced in one introduced in Las Guerras de Granada; but I have since found it much more at length in another collection. It is still, however, far less poetical than the English imitation.

in their own country. It is possible, indeed, that the
fastidiousness of French critics, or their idolatry of the age of
Louis XIV., and of that of Voltaire, may have led to a little
injustice in their estimate of these early versifiers. Our own
prejudices are apt of late to take an opposite direction.

48. A change in the character of French poetry, about
the commencement of this period, is referable to
the general revolution of literature. The allegorical
personifications which, from the era of the Roman
de la Rose, had been the common field of verse, became far
less usual, and gave place to an inundation of mythology
and classical allusion. The *Désir* and *Reine d'Amour* of the
older school became Cupid with his arrows and Venus with
her doves; the theological and cardinal virtues, which had
gained so many victories over *Sensualité* and *Faux Semblant*,
vanished themselves from a poetry which had generally en-
listed itself under the enemy's banner. This cutting off of
an old resource rendered it necessary to explore other mines.
All antiquity was ransacked for analogies; and where the
images were not wearisomely common-place, they were ab-
surdly far-fetched. This revolution was certainly not in-
stantaneous; but it followed the rapid steps of philological
learning, which had been nothing at the accession of Francis
I., and was every thing at his death.[z] In his court, and in
that of his son, if business or gallantry rendered learning
impracticable, it was at least the mode to affect an esteem
for it. Many names in the list of French poets are conspicuous for high rank, and a greater number are among the
famous scholars of the age. These, accustomed to writing in
Latin, sometimes in verse, and yielding a superstitious homage

Marginal note: Change in the tone of French poetry.

---

[z] [Sainte-Beuve, in his learned Ta-
bleau de la Poésie Française au seizième
siècle, Paris, 1828, speaks of this revolution in taste, which substituted a classical school for that of the middle ages,
kept up as it had been by Marot and his
contemporaries, as almost sudden :—
Tout enfin semble promettre à Marot
une postérité d'admirations encore plus
que de rivaux, et à la poésie un perfec-
tionnement paisible et continu, lorsqu'à
l'improviste la génération nouvelle ré-
clame contre une admiration jusque là
unanime, et, le détachant brusquement
du passé, déclare qu'il est temps de
s'ouvrir par d'autres voies un avenir de
gloire. *L'Illustration de la Langue Française*, par Joachim Dubellay, est comme
le manifeste de cette insurrection sou-
daine, qu'on peut dater de 1549. The
extracts which he proceeds to give from
this work of Dubellay prove that it was
at least intended to recommend the cultivation of style in the native language
through a careful study of classical
models.—1847.]

to the mighty dead of antiquity, thought that they ennobled their native language by destroying her idiomatic purity.

49. The prevalence, however, of this pedantry was chiefly owing to one poet, of great though short-lived renown, Pierre Ronsard. He was the first of seven contemporaries in song under Henry II., then denominated the French Pleiad; the others were Jodelle, Bellay, Baif, Thyard, Dorat, and Belleau. Ronsard, well acquainted with the ancient languages, and full of the most presumptuous vanity, fancied that he was born to mould the speech of his fathers into new forms more adequate to his genius.

Je fis des nouveaux mots,
J'en condamnai les vieux.[a]

His style, therefore, is as barbarous, if the continual adoption of Latin and Greek derivatives renders a modern language barbarous, as his allusions are pedantic. They are more ridiculously such in his amatory sonnets; in his odes these faults are rather less intolerable, and there is a spirit and grandeur which show him to have possessed a poetical mind.[b] The popularity of Ronsard was extensive; and, though he sometimes complained of the neglect of the great, he wanted not the approbation of those whom poets are most ambitious to please. Charles IX. addressed some lines to Ronsard, which are really elegant, and at least do more honour to that prince than anything else recorded of him; and the verses of this poet are said to have lightened the weary hours of Mary Stuart's imprisonment. On his death in 1586 a funeral service was performed in Paris with the best music that the king could command; it was attended by the Cardinal de Bourbon and an immense concourse; eulogies in prose and verse were recited in the university; and in those anxious moments, when the crown of France was almost in its agony, there was leisure to lament that Ronsard had been withdrawn. How differently attended was the grave of Spenser![c]

50. Ronsard was capable of conceiving strongly, and bringing his conceptions in clear and forcible, though seldom in

---

[a] Goujet, Bibliothèque française, xii. 199.   [b] Id. 216.   [c] Id. 207.

pure or well-chosen language, before the mind. The poem
entitled Promesse, which will be found in Auguis's Recueil
des Anciens Poëtes, is a proof of this, and excels what little
besides I have read of this poet.[d] Bouterwek, whose criticism on Ronsard appears fair and just, and who gives him,
and those who belonged to his school, credit for perceiving
the necessity of elevating the tone of French verse above the
creeping manner of the allegorical rhymers, observes that,
even in his errors, we discover a spirit striving upwards, dis-
daining what is trivial, and restless in the pursuit of excellence.[e] But such a spirit may produce very bad and tasteless
poetry. La Harpe, who admits Ronsard's occasional beauties
and his poetic fire, is repelled by his scheme of versification,
full of *enjambemens*, as disgusting to a correct French ear as
they are, in a moderate use, pleasing to our own. After the
appearance of Malherbe, the poetry of Ronsard fell into contempt, and the pure correctness of Louis XIV.'s age was not
likely to endure his barbarous innovations and false taste.[f]
Balzac not long afterwards turns his pedantry into ridicule,
and, admitting the abundance of the stream, adds that it was
turbid.[g] In later times more justice has been done to the
spirit and imagination of this poet, without repealing the
sentence against his style.[h]

---

[d] Vol. iv. p. 135.

[e] Geschichte der Poesie, v. 214.

[f] Goujet, 245. Malherbe scratched
out about half from his copy of Ronsard, giving his reasons in the margin.
Racan one day looking over this, asked
whether he approved what he had not
effaced. Not a bit more, replied Malherbe, than the rest.

[g] Encore aujourd'hui il est admiré par
les trois quarts du parlement de Paris,
et généralement par les autres parlemens
de France. L'université et les Jésuites
tiennent encore son part contre la cour, et
contre l'académie. . . . Ce n'est pas un
poëte bien entier, c'est le commencement
et la matière d'un poëte. On voit, dans
ses œuvres, des parties naissantes, et à
demi animées, d'un corps qui se forme
et qui se fait, mais qui n'a garde d'estre
achevé. C'est une grande source, il faut
l'avouer; mais c'est une source troublée
et boueuse ; une source, où non seule-

ment il y a moins d'eau que de limon
mais où l'ordure empêche de couler l'eau.
Œuvres de Balzac, i. 670, and Goujet,
ubi supra.

[h] La Harpe. Biogr. univ.
[M. Sainte Beuve has devoted a whole
volume to a selection from Ronsard,
Paris, 1828, to whom, without undue
praise, he has restored a more honourable
place than Malherbe and those who took
their tone from him had assigned him.
The extracts are chiefly from his lighter
poetry, in which the pedantry of his
more pompous style does not much appear. Though with little invention, and
indeed a large proportion of these selections is taken from Latin or Greek poets,
Ronsard is often more happy in expression, and more spirited, as well as
gay, in sentement, than we should expect
to find after reading his laboured poems.
—1847.]

51. The remaining stars of the Pleiad, except perhaps Bellay, sometimes called the French Ovid, and whose 'Regrets,' or lamentations for his absence Other French poets. from France during a residence at Rome, are almost as querulous, if not quite so reasonable as those of his proto-type on the Ister,[i] seem scarce worthy of particular notice; for Jodelle, the founder of the stage in France, has deserved much less credit as a poet, and fell into the fashionable ab-surdity of making French out of Greek. Raynouard bestows some eulogy on Baif.[k] Those who came afterwards were sometimes imitators of Ronsard, and, like most imitators of a faulty manner, far more pedantic and far-fetched than himself. An unintelligible refinement, which every nation in Europe seems in succession to have admitted into its poetry, has consigned much then written in France to obli-vion. As large a proportion of the French verse in this period seems to be amatory as of the Italian; and the Italian style is sometimes followed. But a simpler and more livelier turn of language, though without the naïveté of Marot, often distinguishes these compositions. These pass the bounds of decency not seldom; a privilege which seems in Italy to have been reserved for certain Fescennine metres, and is not indulged to the solemnity of the sonnet or canzone. The Italian language is ill-adapted to the epigram, in which the French succeed so well.[m]

52. A few may be selected from the numerous versifiers under the sons of Henry II. Amadis Jamyn, the pupil of Ronsard, was reckoned by his contempora- Du Bartas. ries almost a rival, and is more natural, less inflated and emphatic than his master.[n] This praise is by no means due to a more celebrated poet, Du Bartas. His numerous pro-ductions, unlike those of his contemporaries, turn mostly upon sacred history; but his poem on the Creation, called

---

[i] Goujet, xiii. 128. Auguis.

[k] 'Baif is one of the poets who, in my opinion, have happily contributed by their example to fix the rules of our versification.' Journal des Savans, Feb. 1825.

[m] Goujet devotes three volumes, the twelfth, thirteenth, and fourteenth, of his

Bibliothèque française to the poets of these fifty years. Bouterwek and La Harpe have touched only on a very few names. In the Recueil des Anciens Poëtes, the extracts from them occupy about a volume and a half.

[n] Goujet, xiii. 229. Biog. univ.

La Semaine, is that which obtained most reputation, and by which alone he is now known. The translation by Silvester has rendered it in some measure familiar to the readers of our old poetry; and attempts have been made, not without success, to show that Milton had been diligent in picking jewels from this mass of bad taste and bad writing. Du Bartas, in his style, was a disciple of Ronsard; he affects words derived from the ancient languages, or, if founded on analogy, yet without precedent, and has as little naturalness or dignity in his images as purity in his idiom. But his imagination, though extravagant, is vigorous and original.[o]

53. Pibrac, a magistrate of great integrity, obtained an extraordinary reputation by his quatrains; a series of moral tetrastichs in the style of Theognis. These first appeared in 1574, fifty in number, and were augmented to 126 in later editions. They were continually republished in the seventeenth century, and translated into many European and even oriental languages. It cannot be wonderful that, in the change of taste and manners, they have ceased to be read.[p] An imitation of the sixth satire of Horace, by Nicolas Rapin, printed in the collection of Auguis, is good and in very pure style.[q] Philippe Desportes, somewhat later, chose a better school than that of Ronsard; he rejected its pedantry and affectation, and by the study of Tibullus, as well as by his natural genius, gave a tenderness and grace to the poetry of love which those pompous versifiers had never sought. He has been esteemed the precursor of a better era; and his versification is rather less lawless,[r] according to La Harpe, than that of his predecessors.

Pibrac; Desportes. (marginal note)

---

[o] Goujet, xiii. 304. The Semaine of Du Bartas was printed thirty times within six years, and translated into Latin, Italian, German, and Spanish, as well as English. Id. 312, on the authority of La Croix du Maine.

Du Bartas, according to a French writer of the next century, used methods of exciting his imagination which I recommend to the attention of young poets. L'on dit en France que Du Bartas, auparavant que de faire cette belle description de cheval où il a si bien rencontré,

s'enfermoit quelquefois dans une chambre, et se mettant à quatre pattes, souffloit, hennissoit, gambadoit, tiroit des ruades, alloit l'amble, le trot, le galop, à courbette, et tâchoit par toutes sortes de moyens à bien contrefaire le cheval. Naudé. Considérations sur les Coups d'Estat, p. 47.

[p] Goujet, xii. 266. Biogr. univ.

[q] Recueil des Poëtes, v. 361.

[r] Goujet, xiv. 63. La Harpe Auguis, v. 343—377.

54. The rules of metre became gradually established. Few writers of this period neglect the alternation French metre and versification. of masculine and feminine rhymes;[s] but the open vowel will be found, in several of the earlier. Du Bartas almost affects the *enjambement*, or continuation of the sense beyond the couplet; and even Desportes does not avoid it. Their metres are various; the Alexandrine, if so we may call it, or verse of twelve syllables, was occasionally adopted by Ronsard, and in time displaced the old verse of ten syllables, which became appropriated to the lighter style. The sonnets, as far as I have observed, are regular; and this form, which had been very little known in France, after being introduced by Jodelle and Ronsard, became one of the most popular modes of composition.[t] Several attempts were made to naturalise the Latin metres; but this pedantic innovation could not long have success. Specimens of it may be found in Pasquier.[u]

55. It may be said, perhaps, of French poetry in general, but at least in this period, that it deviates less from General character of French poetry. a certain standard than any other. It is not often low, as may be imputed to the earlier writers, because a peculiar style, removed from common speech, and supposed to be classical, was a condition of satisfying the critics; it is not often obscure, at least in syntax, as the Italian sonnet is apt to be, because the genius of the language and the habits of society demanded perspicuity. But

---

[s] Grevin, about 1558, is an exception. Goujet, xii. 159.

[t] Bouterwek, v. 212.

[u] Recherches de la France, l. vii. c. 11. Baif has passed for the inventor of this foolish art in France, which was more common there than in England. But Prosper Marchand ascribes a translation of the Iliad and Odyssey into regular French hexameters to one Mousset, of whom nothing is known; on no better authority, however, than a vague passage of D'Aubigné, who 'remembered to have seen such a book sixty years ago.' Though Mousset may be imaginary, he furnishes an article to Marchand, who brings together a good deal of learning as to the latinized French metres of the sixteenth century. Dictionnaire Historique.

Passerat, Ronsard, Nicolas Rapin, and Pasquier tried their hands in this style. Rapin improved upon it by rhyming in Sapphics. The following stanzas are from his ode on the death of Ronsard:—

Vous que les ruisseaux d'Hélicon fréquentez,
Vous que les jardins solitaires hantez,
Et le fonds des bois, curieux de choisir
   L'ombre et le loisir.

Qui vivant bien loin de la fange et du bruit,
Et de ces grandeurs que le peuple poursuit,
Estimez les vers que la muse après vous
   Trempe de miel doux.

Notre grand Ronsard, de ce monde sorti,
Les efforts derniers de la Parque a senti;
Ses faveurs n'ont pu le garantir enfin
   Contre le destin, &c. &c.

   PASQUIER, *ubi supra.*

it seldom delights us by a natural sentiment or unaffected grace of diction, because both one and the other were fettered by conventional rules. The monotony of amorous song is more wearisome, if that be possible, than among the Italians.

56. The characteristics of German verse impressed upon German poetry. it by the meister-singers still remained, though the songs of those fraternities seem to have ceased. It was chiefly didactic or religious, often satirical, and employing the veil of apologue. Luther, Hans Sachs, and other more obscure names, are counted among the fabulists; but the most successful was Burcard Waldis, whose fables, partly from Æsop, partly original, were first published in 1548. The Froschmauseler of Rollenhagen, in 1545, is in a similar style of political and moral apologue, with some liveliness of description. Fischart is another of the moral satirists, but extravagant in style and humour, resembling Rabelais, of whose romance he gave a free translation. One of his poems, Die Gluckhafte Schiff, is praised by Bouterwek for beautiful descriptions and happy inventions; but in general he seems to be the Skelton of Germany. Many German ballads belong to this period, partly taken from the old tales of chivalry: in these the style is humble, with no poetry except that of invention, which is not their own; yet they are true-hearted and unaffected, and better than what the next age produced.[x]

Sect. IV.—On English Poetry.

Paradise of Dainty Devices — Sackville—Gascoyne — Spenser's Shepherd's Kalendar — Improvement in Poetry — England's Helicon — Sidney — Shakspeare's Poems—Poets near the close of the Century—Translations— Scotch and English Ballads — Spenser's Faery Queen.

57. The poems of Wyatt and Surrey, with several more, Paradise of Dainty Devices. first appeared in 1557, and were published in a little book entitled Tottel's Miscellanies. But as both of these belonged to the reign of Henry VIII., their

---

[x] Bouterwek, vol. ix. Heinsius, vol. iv.

poetry has come already under our review. It is probable
that Lord Vaux's short pieces, which are next to those of
Surrey and Wyatt in merit, were written before the middle
of the century. Some of these are published in Tottel, and
others in a scarce collection; the first edition of which was
in 1576, quaintly named, The Paradise of Dainty Devices.
The poems in this volume, as in that of Tottel, are not coeval with its publication; it has been supposed to represent
the age of Mary, full as much as that of Elizabeth, and one
of the chief contributors, if not framers of the collection,
Richard Edwards, died in 1566. Thirteen poems are by
Lord Vaux, who certainly did not survive the reign of Mary.

58. We are indebted to Sir Egerton Brydges for the republication, in his British Bibliographer, of the Character
Paradise of Dainty Devices, of which, though there of this
collection.
had been eight editions, it is said that not above six copies
existed.   The poems are almost all short, and by more
nearly thirty than twenty different authors. ' They do not,
it must be admitted,' says their editor, 'belong to the
higher classes; they are of the moral and didactic kind.
In their subject there is too little variety, as they deal very
generally in the common-places of ethics, such as the fickleness and caprices of love, the falsehood and instability of
friendship, and the vanity of all human pleasures. But many
of these are often expressed with a vigour which would do
credit to any era. . . . If my partiality does not mislead me, there is in most of these short pieces some of
that indescribable attraction which springs from the colouring of the heart. The charm of imagery is wanting, but
the precepts inculcated seem to flow from the feelings of
an overloaded bosom.' Edwards he considers, probably
with justice, as the best of the contributors, and Lord
Vaux the next. We should be inclined to give as high a
place to William Hunnis, were his productions all equal to
one little poem;[z] but too often he falls into trivial morality

---

[y] Beloe's Anecdotes of Literature, vol.
v.
[z] This song is printed in Campbell's
Specimens of English Poets, vol. i. p.
117. It begins,
' When first mine eyes did view and mark.'

The little poem of Edwards, called
Amantium Iræ, has often been reprinted
in modern collections, and is reckoned by
Brydges one of the most beautiful in the
language. But hardly any light poem
of this early period is superior to some

and a ridiculous excess of alliteration. The amorous poetry is the best in this Paradise; it is not imaginative or very graceful, or exempt from the false taste of antithetical conceits, but sometimes natural and pleasing; the serious pieces are in general very heavy, yet there is a dignity and strength in some of the devotional strains. They display the religious earnestness of that age with a kind of austere philosophy in their views of life. Whatever indeed be the subject, a tone of sadness reigns through this misnamed Paradise of Daintiness, as it does through all the English poetry of this particular age. It seems as if the confluence of the poetic melancholy of the Petrarchists with the reflective seriousness of the Reformation overpowered the lighter sentiments of the soul; and some have imagined, I know not how justly, that the persecutions of Mary's reign contributed to this effect.

59. But at the close of that dark period, while bigotry might be expected to render the human heart torpid, Sackville's Induction. and the English nation seemed too fully absorbed in religious and political discontent to take much relish in literary amusements, one man shone out for an instant in the higher walks of poetry. This was Thomas Sackville, many years afterwards Lord Buckhurst, and high Treasurer of England, thus withdrawn from the haunts of the Muses to a long and honourable career of active life. The Mirrour for Magistrates, published in 1559, is a collection of stories by different authors, on the plan of Boccaccio's prose work, De Casibus virorum illustrium, recounting the misfortunes and reverses of men eminent in English history. It was designed to form a series of dramatic soliloquies united in one interlude.[a] Sackville, who seems to have planned the scheme, wrote an Induction, or prologue, and also one of the stories, that of the first Duke of Buckingham. The Induction displays best his poetical genius; it is, like much earlier poetry,

---

lines addressed to Isabella Markham by Sir John Harrington, bearing the date of 1564. If these are genuine, and I know not how to dispute it, they are as polished as any written at the close of the queen's reign. These are not in the Paradise of Dainty Devices.

[a] Warton, iv. 40. A copious account of the Mirrour for Magistrates occupies the forty-eighth and three following sections of the History of Poetry, pp. 33—105. In this Warton has introduced rather a long analysis of the Inferno of Dante, which he seems to have thought little known to the English public, as in that age, I believe, was the case.

a representation of allegorical personages, but with a fertility
of imagination, vividness of description, and strength of language, which not only leave his predecessors far behind, but
may fairly be compared with some of the most poetical passages in Spenser. Sackville's Induction forms a link which
unites the school of Chaucer and Lydgate to the Faery
Queen. It would certainly be vain to look in Chaucer,
wherever Chaucer is original, for the grand creations of
Sackville's fancy, yet we should never find any one who
would rate Sackville above Chaucer. The strength of an
eagle is not to be measured only by the height of his place,
but by the time that he continues on the wing. Sackville's
Induction consists of a few hundred lines; and even in these
there is a monotony of gloom and sorrow, which prevents us
from wishing it to be longer. It is truly styled by Campbell
a landscape on which the sun never shines. Chaucer is
various, flexible, and observant of all things in outward
nature, or in the heart of man. But Sackville is far above
the frigid elegance of Surrey; and, in the first days of Elizabeth's reign, is the herald of that splendour in which it was
to close.

60. English poetry was not speedily animated by the example of Sackville. His genius stands absolutely alone   Inferiority of
in the age to which as a poet he belongs. Not   poets in early
years of
that there was any deficiency in the number of ver-   Elizabeth.
sifiers; the Muses were honoured by the frequency, if not by
the dignity, of their worshippers. A different sentence will
be found in some books; and it has become common to elevate the Elizabethan age in one undiscriminating panegyric.
For wise counsellors, indeed, and acute politicians, we could
not perhaps extol one part of that famous reign at the expense of another. Cecil and Bacon, Walsingham, Smith, and
Sadler, belong to the earlier days of the queen. But in a
literary point of view, the contrast is great between the first
and second moiety of her four-and-forty years. We have seen
this already in other subjects than poetry; and in that we
may appeal to such parts of the Mirrour for Magistrates as
are not written by Sackville, to the writings of Churchyard,
or to those of Gouge and Turberville. These writers scarcely
venture to leave the ground, or wander in the fields of fancy.

They even abstain from the ordinary common-places of verse, as if afraid that the reader should distrust or misinterpret their images. The first who deserves to be mentioned as an exception is George Gascoyne, whose Steel Glass, published in 1576, is the earliest instance of English satire, and has strength and sense enough to deserve respect. Chalmers has praised it highly. 'There is a vein of sly sarcasm in this piece which appears to me to be original; and his intimate knowledge of mankind enabled him to give a more curious picture of the dress, manners, amusements, and follies of the times, than we meet with in almost any other author. His Steel Glass is among the first specimens of blank verse in our language.' This blank verse, however, is but indifferently constructed. Gascoyne's long poem, called the Fruits of War, is in the doggerel style of his age; and the general commendations of Chalmers on this poet seem rather hyperbolical. But his minor poems, especially one called The Arraignment of a Lover, have much spirit and gaiety;[b] and we may leave him a respectable place among the Elizabethan versifiers.

Gascoyne.

61. An epoch was made, if we may draw an inference from the language of contemporaries, by the publication of Spenser's Shepherd's Kalendar, in 1579.[c] His primary idea, that of adapting a pastoral to every month of the year, was pleasing and original, though he has frequently neglected to observe the season, even when it was most abundant in appropriate imagery. But his Kalendar is, in another respect, original, at least when compared with the pastoral writings of that age. This species of composition had become so much the favourite of courts, that no language was thought to suit it but that of courtiers, which, with all its false beauties of thought and expression, was transferred to the mouths of shepherds. A striking instance of this had lately been shown in the Aminta; and it was a proof of Spenser's judgment, as well as genius, that he struck out a new line of

Spenser's Shepherd's Kalendar.

---

[b] Ellis's Specimens. Campbell's Specimens, ii. 146.

[c] The Shepherd's Kalendar was printed anonymously. It is ascribed to Sidney by Whetstone in a monody on his death, in 1586. But Webbe, in his Discourse of English Poetry, published the same year, mentions Spenser by name.

pastoral, far more natural, and therefore more pleasing, so far as imitation of nature is the source of poetical pleasure, instead of vying, in our more harsh and uncultivated language, with the consummate elegance of Tasso. It must be admitted, however, that he fell too much into the opposite extreme, and gave a Doric rudeness to his dialogue, which is a little repulsive to our taste. The dialect of Theocritus is musical to our ears, and free from vulgarity; praises which we cannot bestow on the uncouth provincial rusticity of Spenser. He has been less justly censured on another account, for intermingling allusions to the political history and religious differences of his own times; and an ingenious critic has asserted that the description of the grand and beautiful objects of nature, with well-selected scenes of rural life, real but not coarse, constitute the only proper materials of pastoral poetry. These limitations, however, seem little conformable to the practice of poets or the taste of mankind; and if Spenser has erred in the allegorical part of his pastorals, he has done so in company with most of those who have tuned the shepherd's pipe. Several of Virgil's Eclogues, and certainly the best, have a meaning beyond the simple songs of the hamlet; and it was notorious that the Portuguese and Spanish pastoral romances, so popular in Spenser's age, teemed with delineations of real character, and sometimes were the mirrors of real story. In fact, mere pastoral must soon become insipid, unless it borrows something from active life or elevated philosophy. The most interesting parts of the Shepherd's Kalendar are of this description; for Spenser has not displayed the powers of his own imagination, so strongly as we might expect, in pictures of natural scenery. This poem has spirit and beauty in many passages; but is not much read in the present day, nor does it seem to be approved by modern critics. It was otherwise formerly. Webbe, in his Discourse of English Poetry, 1586, calls Spenser 'the rightest English poet he ever read,' and thinks he would have surpassed Theocritus and Virgil, 'if the coarseness of our speech had been no greater impediment to him than their pure native tongues were to them.' And Drayton says, 'Master Edmund Spenser had done enough for the immor-

tality of his name, had he only given us his Shepherd's
Kalendar, a masterpiece, if any.[d]

62. Sir Philip Sidney, in his Defence of Poesie, which may
have been written at any time between 1581 and his
death in 1586, laments that 'poesy thus embraced
in all other places, should only find in our time a bad
welcome in England;' and, after praising Sackville, Surrey,
and Spenser for the Shepherd's Kalendar, does not 'remember to have seen many more that have poetical sinews in
them. For proof whereof, let but most of the verses be put
into prose, and then ask the meaning, and it will be found
that one verse did but beget another, without ordering at the
first what should be at the last; which becomes a confused
mass of words, with a tinkling sound of rhyme, barely accompanied with reason. . . . . . . Truly many of such writings
as come under the banner of irresistible love, if I were a
mistress, would never persuade me they were in love; so
coldly they apply fiery speeches as men that had rather read
lovers' writings, and so caught up certain swelling phrases,
than that in truth they feel those passions.'

Sidney's character of contemporary poets.

63. It cannot be denied that some of these blemishes
are by no means unusual in the writers of the
Elizabethan age, as in truth they are found also in
much other poetry of many countries. But a change
seems to have come over the spirit of English poetry soon
after 1580.   Sidney, Raleigh, Lodge, Breton, Marlowe,
Greene, Watson, are the chief contributors to a collection
called England's Helicon, published in 1600, and comprising
many of the fugitive pieces of the last twenty years.   Davison's Poetical Rhapsody, in 1602,[e] is a miscellany of the
same class.   A few other collections are known to have existed, but are still more scarce than these.   England's
Helicon, by far the most important, has been reprinted in
the same volume of the British Bibliographer as the Paradise of Dainty Devices.   In this juxta-position the difference of their tone is very perceptible.   Love occupies by far
the chief portion of the later miscellany; and love no longer

Improve- ment soon after this time.

---

[d] Preface to Drayton's Pastorals.
[e] [It was much enlarged in 1608 and
1621, and is not now scarce, having
been reprinted by Sir Harris Nicolas in
1826.—1847.]

pining and melancholy, but sportive and boastful. Every one is familiar with the beautiful song of Marlowe, ' Come live with me and be my love ;' and with the hardly less beautiful answer ascribed to Raleigh. Lodge has ten pieces in this collection, and Breton eight. These are generally full of beauty, grace, and simplicity ; and while in reading the productions of Edwards and his coadjutors every sort of allowance is to be made, and we can only praise a little at intervals, these lyrics, twenty or thirty years later, are among the best in our language. The conventional tone is that of pastoral; and thus, if they have less of the depth sometimes shown in serious poetry, they have less also of obscurity and false refinement.[f]

64. We may easily perceive in the literature of the later period of the queen, what our biographical know- Relaxation of moral austerity. ledge confirms, that much of the austerity characteristic of her earlier years had vanished away. The course of time, the progress of vanity, the prevalent dislike, above all, of the Puritans, avowed enemies of gaiety, concurred to this change. The most distinguished courtiers, Raleigh, Essex, Blount, and we must add Sidney, were men of brilliant virtues, but not without licence of morals ; while many of the wits and poets, such as Nash, Greene, Peele, Marlowe, were notoriously of very dissolute lives.

65. The graver strains, however, of religion and philosophy were still heard in verse. The Soul's Errand, Serious poetry. printed anonymously in Davison's Rhapsody, and ascribed by Ellis, probably without reason, to Sylvester, is characterised by strength, condensation, and simplicity.[g]

---

[f] Ellis, in the second volume of his Specimens of English Poets, has taken largely from this collection. It must be owned that his good taste in selection gives a higher notion of the poetry of this age than, on the whole, it would be found to deserve; yet there is so much of excellence in England's Helicon, that he has been compelled to omit many pieces of great merit.

[g] Campbell reckons this, and I think justly, among the best pieces of the Elizabethan age. Brydges gives it to Raleigh without evidence, and we may add, without probability. It is found in manuscripts, according to Mr. Campbell, of the date of 1593. Such poems as this could only be written by a man who had seen and thought much ; while the ordinary Latin and Italian verses of this age might be written by any one who had a knack of imitation and a good ear. [It was published in the second edition of Davison, 1608, with the title, The Lie. In Silvester's works it bears the present title. Its publication therein would of course be presumptive evidence that he was the author, were it

And we might rank in a respectable place among these English poets, though I think he has been lately overrated, one whom the jealous law too prematurely deprived of life, Robert Southwell, executed as a seminary priest in 1591, under one of those persecuting statutes which even the traitorous restlessness of the English Jesuits cannot excuse. Southwell's poetry wears a deep tinge of gloom, which seems to presage a catastrophe too usual to have been unexpected. It is, as may be supposed, almost wholly religious; the shorter pieces are the best.[h]

66. Astrophel and Stella, a series of amatory poems by Sir Philip Sidney, though written nearly ten years before, was published in 1591. These songs and sonnets recount the loves of Sidney and Lady Rich, sister of Lord Essex; and it is rather a singular circumstance that, in her own and her husband's lifetime, this ardent courtship of a married woman should have been deemed fit for publication. Sidney's passion seems indeed to have been unsuccessful, but far enough from being platonic.[i] Astrophel and Stella is too much disfigured by conceits, but is in some places very beautiful; and it is strange that Chalmers, who reprinted Turberville and Warner, should have left Sidney out of his collection of British poets. A poem by the writer just mentioned, Warner, with the quaint title, Albion's England, 1586, has at least the equivocal merit of great length. It is rather legendary than historical; some passages are pleasing, but it is not a work of genius, and the style, though natural, seldom arises above that of prose.

67. Spenser's Epithalamium on his own marriage, written

Poetry of Sidney.

---

not weakened, as Sir Harris Nicolas observes, by the circumstance that it is also published among the poems of the Earl of Pembroke. If it is really found, as Campbell tells us, in a manuscript of 1593, Pembroke's claim must be out of the question.—1847.

[h] I am not aware that Southwell has gained any thing by a republication of his entire poems in 1817. Headley and Ellis had culled the best specimens. St. Peter's Complaint, the longest of his poems, is wordy and tedious; and in reading the volume I found scarce any thing of merit which I had not seen before.

[i] Godwin having several years since made some observations on Sidney's amour with Lady Rich, a circumstance which such biographers as Dr. Zouch take good care to suppress, a gentleman who published an edition of Sidney's Defence of Poetry thought fit to indulge in recriminating attacks on Godwin himself. It is singular that men of sense and education should persist in fancying that such arguments are likely to convince any dispassionate reader.

perhaps in 1594, is of a far higher mood than anything we have named. It is a strain redolent of a bride- Epithala-
mium of
Spenser. groom's joy, and of a poet's fancy. The English language seems to expand itself with a copiousness unknown before, while he pours forth the varied imagery of this splendid little poem. I do not know any other nuptial song, ancient or modern, of equal beauty. It is an intoxication of ecstasy, ardent, noble, and pure. But it pleased not Heaven that these day-dreams of genius and virtue should be undisturbed.

68. Shakspeare's Venus and Adonis appears to have been published in 1593, and his Rape of Lucrece the fol- Poems of
Shakspeare. lowing year. The redundance of blossoms in these juvenile effusions of his unbounded fertility obstructs the reader's attention, and sometimes almost leads us to give him credit for less reflection and sentiment than he will be found to display. The style is flowing, and, in general, more perspicuous than the Elizabethan poets are wont to be. But I am not sure that they would betray themselves for the works of Shakspeare, had they been anonymously published.

69. In the last decad of this century several new poets came forward. Samuel Daniel is one of these. His Daniel and
Drayton. Complaint of Rosamond, and probably many of his minor poems, belong to this period; and it was also that of his greatest popularity. On the death of Spenser, in 1598, he was thought worthy to succeed him as poet-laureate; and some of his contemporaries ranked him in the second place; an eminence due rather to the purity of his language than to its vigour.[k] Michael Drayton, who first tried his shepherd's pipe with some success in the usual style, published his Barons' Wars in 1598. They relate to the last years of Edward II., and conclude with the execution of Mortimer under his son. This poem, therefore, seems to possess a sufficient unity, and, tried by rules of criticism, might be thought not far removed from the class of epic—a dignity, however, to which it has never pretended. But in its conduct Drayton follows history very closely, and we are kept

---

[k] British Bibliographer, vol. ii. Headley remarks that Daniel was spoken of by contemporary critics as the polisher and purifier of the English language.

too much in mind of a common chronicle. Though not very pleasing, however, in its general effect, this poem, The Barons' Wars, contains several passages of considerable beauty, which men of greater renown, especially Milton, who availed himself largely of all the poetry of the preceding age, have been willing to imitate.

70. A more remarkable poem is that of Sir John Davies, afterwards chief-justice of Ireland, entitled, Nosce Teipsum, published in 1599, usually, though rather inaccurately, called, On the Immortality of the Soul. Perhaps no language can produce a poem, extending to so great a length, of more condensation of thought, or in which fewer languid verses will be found. Yet, according to some definitions, the Nosce Teipsum is wholly unpoetical, inasmuch as it shows no passion and little fancy. If it reaches the heart at all, it is through the reason. But since strong argument in terse and correct style fails not to give us pleasure in prose, it seems strange that it should lose its effect when it gains the aid of regular metre to gratify the ear and assist the memory. Lines there are in Davies which far outweigh much of the descriptive and imaginative poetry of the last two centuries, whether we estimate them by the pleasure they impart to us, or by the intellectual vigour they display. Experience has shown that the faculties peculiarly deemed poetical are frequently exhibited in a considerable degree, but very few have been able to preserve a perspicuous brevity without stiffness or pedantry (allowance made for the subject and the times), in metaphysical reasoning, so successfully as Sir John Davies.

Nosce
Teipsum
of Davies.

71. Hall's Satires are tolerably known, partly on account of the subsequent celebrity of the author in a very different province, and partly from a notion, to which he gave birth, by announcing the claim that he was the first English satirist. In a general sense of satire, we have seen that he had been anticipated by Gascoyne; but Hall has more of the direct Juvenalian invective, which he may have reckoned essential to that species of poetry. They are deserving of regard in themselves. Warton has made many extracts from Hall's Satires; he praises in them 'a classical precision, to which English

Satires of
Hall,
Marston,
and Donne

poetry had yet rarely attained;' and calls the versification
'equally energetic and elegant.'[m]   The former epithet may
be admitted; but elegance is hardly compatible with what
Warton owns to be the chief fault of Hall, 'his obscurity,
arising from a remote phraseology, constrained combinations, unfamiliar allusions, elliptical apostrophes, and abrupt-
ness of expression.' Hall is in fact not only so harsh and
rugged that he cannot be read with much pleasure, but so
obscure in very many places that he cannot be understood at
all, his lines frequently bearing no visible connexion in sense
or grammar with their neighbours.   The stream is powerful,
but turbid and often choked.[n]   Marston and Donne may be
added to Hall in this style of poetry, as belonging to the
sixteenth century, though the satires of the latter were not
published till long afterwards.   With as much obscurity as
Hall, he has a still more inharmonious versification, and not
nearly equal vigour.

72. The roughness of these satirical poets was perhaps
studiously affected; for it was not much in unison Modulation
with the general tone of the age.   It requires a verse. of English
good deal of care to avoid entirely the combinations of
consonants that clog our language; nor have Drayton or
Spenser always escaped this embarrassment.   But in the
lighter poetry of the queen's last years, a remarkable sweetness of modulation has always been recognised.   This has
sometimes been attributed to the general fondness for music.
It is at least certain that some of our old madrigals are as
beautiful in language as they are in melody.   Several collections were published in the reign of Elizabeth.[o]   And it
is evident that the regard to the capacity of his verse for
marriage with music, that was before the poet's mind, would
not only polish his metre, but give it grace and sentiment,
while it banished also the pedantry, the antithesis, the prolixity, which had disfigured the earlier lyric poems.   Their

---

[m] Hist. of English Poetry, iv. 383.

[n] Hall's Satires are praised by Campbell, as well as Warton, full as much,
in my opinion, as they deserve. Warton
has compared Marston with Hall, and
concludes that the latter is more 'elegant, exact, and elaborate.'   More so
than his rival he may by possibility be
esteemed; but these three epithets cannot be predicated of his satires in any
but a relative sense.

[o] Morley's Musical Airs, 1594, and
another collection in 1597, contain some
pretty songs.   British Bibliographer, i.
342.   A few of these madrigals will also
be found in Mr. Campbell's Specimens.

measures became more various : though the quatrain, alter-
nating by eight and six syllables, was still very popular, we
find the trochaic verse of seven, sometimes ending with a
double rhyme, usual towards the end of the queen's reign.
Many of these occur in England's Helicon, and in the poems
of Sidney.

73. The translations of ancient poets by Phaier, Golding,
Translation Stanyhurst, and several more, do not challenge our
of Homer by
Chapman; attention; most of them, in fact, being very wretched
performances.[p] Marlowe, a more celebrated name, did not,
as has commonly been said, translate the poem of Hero
and Leander ascribed to Musæus, but expanded it into
what he calls six Sestiads on the same subject; a paraphrase, in every sense of the epithet, of the most licentious
kind. This he left incomplete, and it was finished by Chapman.[q] But the most remarkable productions of this kind
are the Iliad of Chapman and the Jerusalem of Fairfax,
both printed in 1600 : the former, however, containing in
that edition but fifteen books, to which the rest was subsequently added. Pope, after censuring the haste, negligence,
and fustian language of Chapman, observes, ' that which is
to be allowed him, and which very much contributed to
cover his defects, is a free daring spirit that animates his
translation, which is something like what one might imagine
Homer himself would have written before he arrived at years
of discretion.' He might have added that Chapman's translation, with all its defects, is often exceedingly Homeric ; a
praise which Pope himself seldom attained. Chapman deals
abundantly in compound epithets, some of which have retained their place ; his verse is rhymed, of fourteen syllables,
which corresponds to the hexameter better than the deca-
syllable couplet ; he is often uncouth, often unmusical, and
often low ; but the spirited and rapid flow of his metre
makes him respectable to lovers of poetry. Waller, it is
said, could not read him without transport. It must be
added that he is an unfaithful translator, and interpolated
much, besides the general redundancy of his style.[r]

---

[p] Warton, chap liv., has gone very
laboriously into this subject.
[q] Marlowe's poem is republished in
the Restituta of Sir Egerton Brydges.

It is singular that Warton should have
taken it for a translation of Musæus.
[r] Warton, iv. 269. Retrospective
Review, vol. iii. See also a very good

74. Fairfax's Tasso has been more praised, and is better known. Campbell has called it, in rather strong Tasso, Fairfax. terms, ' one of the glories of Elizabeth's reign.' It is not the first version of the Jerusalem, one very literal and prosaic having been made by Carew in 1594.[s] That of Fairfax, if it does not represent the grace of its original, and deviates also too much from its sense, is by no means deficient in spirit and vigour. It has been considered as one of the earliest works, in which the obsolete English, which had not been laid aside in the days of Sackville, and which Spenser affected to preserve, gave way to a style not much differing, at least in point of single words and phrases, from that of the present age. But this praise is equally due to Daniel, to Drayton, and to others of the later Elizabethan poets. The translation of Ariosto by Sir John Harrington, in 1591, is much inferior.

75. An injudicious endeavour to substitute the Latin metres for those congenial to our language met Employment of ancient measures. with no more success than it deserved; unless it may be called success, that Sidney, and even Spenser, were for a moment seduced into approbation of it. Gabriel Harvey, best now remembered as the latter's friend, recommended the adoption of hexameters in some letters which passed between them, and Spenser appears to have concurred. Webbe, a few years afterwards, a writer of little taste or ear for poetry, supported the same scheme, but may be said to have avenged the wrong of English verse upon our great poet, by travestying the Shepherd's Kalendar into Sapphics.[t] Campion, in 1602, still harps upon this foolish pedantry; many instances of which may be found during the Elizabethan period. It is well

---

comparison of the different translations of Homer, in Blackwood's Magazine for 1831 and 1832, where Chapman comes in for his due.

[s] In the third volume of the Retrospective Review, these translations are compared, and it is shown that Carew is far more literal than Fairfax, who has taken great liberties with his original. Extracts from Carew will also be found in the British Bibliographer, i. 30. They are miserably bad. [Carew translated only the first five books of Tasso.— 1847.]

[t] Webbe's success was not inviting to the Latinists. Thus in the second Eclogue of Virgil, for the beautiful lines—

At mecum raucis, tua dum vestigia lustro,
Sole sub ardenti resonant arbusta cicadis,

we have this delectable hexametric version :—

But by the scorched bank-sides i' thy footsteps still I go plodding :
Hedge-rows hot do resound with grasshops mournfully squeaking.

known that in German the practice has been in some measure successful, through the example of a distinguished poet, and through translations from the ancients in measures closely corresponding with their own. In this there is doubtless the advantage of presenting a truer mirror of the original. But as most imitations of Latin measures, in German or English, begin by violating their first principle, which assigns an invariable value in time to the syllables of every word, and produce a chaos of false quantities, it seems as if they could only disgust any one acquainted with classical versification. In the early English hexameters of the period before us, we sometimes perceive an intention to arrange long and short syllables according to the analogies of the Latin tongue. But this would soon be found impracticable in our own, which, abounding in harsh terminations, cannot long observe the law of position.

76. It was said by Ellis, that nearly one hundred names of poets belonging to the reign of Elizabeth might be enumerated, besides many that have left no memorial except their songs. This however was but a moderate computation. Drake has made a list of more than two hundred, some few of whom, perhaps, do not strictly belong to the Elizabethan period.[u] But many of these are only known by short pieces in such miscellaneous collections as have been mentioned. Yet in the entire bulk of poetry, England could not, perhaps, bear comparison with Spain or France, to say nothing of Italy. She had come, in fact, much later to cultivate poetry as a general accomplishment. And, consequently, we find much less of the mechanism of style, than in the contemporaneous verse of other languages. The English sonnetteers deal less in customary epithets and conventional modes of expression. Every thought was to be worked out in new terms, since the scanty precedents of early versifiers did not supply them. This was evidently the cause of many blemishes in the Elizabethan poetry; of much that was false in taste, much that was either too harsh and extravagant or too humble, and of more that was so obscure as to defy all interpretation. But it saved also that mono-

Number of poets in this age.

---

[u] Shakspeare and his Times, i. 674.   plete; it includes, of course, translators.
Even this catalogue is probably incom-

tonous equability that often wearies us in more polished
poetry. There is more pleasure, more sense of sympathy
with another mind, in the perusal even of Gascoyne or
Edwards, than in that of many French and Italian versifiers
whom their contemporaries extolled. This is all that we can
justly say in their favour; for any comparison of the Elizabethan poetry, save Spenser's alone, with that of the nineteenth century would show an extravagant predilection for
the mere name or dress of antiquity.

77. It would be a great omission to neglect in any review
of the Elizabethan poetry, that extensive, though Scots an
anonymous class, the Scots and English ballads. English ballads.
The very earliest of these have been adverted to in our
account of the fifteenth century. They became much more
numerous in the present. The age of many may be determined by historical or other allusions; and from these, availing ourselves of similarity of style, we may fix, with some
probability, the date of such as furnish no distinct evidence.
This however is precarious, because the language has often
been modernised, and passing for some time by oral tradition,
they are frequently not exempt from marks of interpolation.
But, upon the whole, the reigns of Mary and James VI., from
the middle to the close of the sixteenth century, must be
reckoned the golden age of the Scottish ballad; and there
are many of the corresponding period in England.

78. There can be, I conceive, no question as to the superiority of Scotland in her ballads. Those of an historic or
legendary character, especially the former, are ardently
poetical; the nameless minstrel is often inspired with an
Homeric power of rapid narration, bold description, lively
or pathetic touches of sentiment. They are familiar to us
through several publications, but chiefly through the Min-
strelsy of the Scottish Border, by one whose genius these
indigenous lays had first excited, and whose own writings,
when the whole civilised world did homage to his name, never
ceased to bear the indelible impress of the associations that
had thus been generated. The English ballads of the northern
border, or perhaps, of the northern counties, come near in
their general character and cast of manners to the Scottish,
but, as far as I have seen, with a manifest inferiority. Those

again which belong to the south, and bear no trace either
of the rude manners, or of the wild superstitions which the
bards of Ettrick and Cheviot display, fall generally into a
creeping style, which has exposed the common ballad to
contempt. They are sometimes, nevertheless, not devoid of
elegance, and often pathetic. The best are known through
Percy's Reliques of Ancient Poetry ; a collection singularly
heterogeneous, and very unequal in merit, but from the publication of which, in 1765, some of high name have dated
the revival of a genuine feeling for true poetry in the public
mind.

79. We have reserved to the last the chief boast of this
The Faery Queen. period, the Faery Queen. Spenser, as is well known,
composed the greater part of his poem in Ireland,
on the banks of his favourite Mulla. The first three books
were published in 1590; the last three did not appear till
1596. It is a perfectly improbable supposition, that the
remaining part, or six books required for the completion of
his design, have been lost. The short interval before the
death of this great poet was filled up by calamities sufficient
to wither the fertility of any mind.

80. The first book of the Faery Queen is a complete poem,
Superiority of the first book. and, far from requiring any continuation, is rather
injured by the useless re-appearance of its hero in
the second. It is generally admitted to be the finest of the
six. In no other is the allegory so clearly conceived by the
poet, or so steadily preserved, yet with a disguise so delicate,
that no one is offended by that servile setting forth of a moral
meaning we frequently meet with in allegorical poems ; and
the reader has the gratification which good writing in works
of fiction always produces, that of exercising his own ingenuity without perplexing it. That the red-cross knight de-
signates the militant Christian, whom Una, the true church,
loves, whom Duessa, the type of popery, seduces, who is
reduced almost to despair, but rescued by the intervention of
Una, and the assistance of Faith, Hope, and Charity, is what
no one feels any difficulty in acknowledging, but what every
one may easily read the poem without perceiving or remembering. In an allegory conducted with such propriety, and
concealed or revealed with so much art, there can surely be

nothing to repel our taste; and those who read the first book
of the Faery Queen without pleasure, must seek (what others
perhaps will be at no loss to discover for them) a different
cause for their insensibility, than the tediousness or insipid-
ity of allegorical poetry. Every canto of this book teems
with the choicest beauties of imagination; he came to it in
the freshness of his genius, which shines throughout with an
uniformity it does not always afterwards maintain, unsullied
as yet by flattery, unobstructed by pedantry, and unquenched
by languor.

81. In the following books, we have much less allegory;
for the personification of abstract qualities, though
often confounded with it, does not properly belong
to that class of composition; it requires a covert sense beneath an apparent fable, such as the first book contains. But
of this I do not discover many proofs in the second or third,
the legends of Temperance and Chastity; they are contrived
to exhibit these virtues and their opposite vices, but with
little that is not obvious upon the surface. In the fourth
and sixth books there is still less; but a different species of
allegory, the historical, which the commentators have, with
more or less success, endeavoured to trace in other portions
of the poem, breaks out unequivocally in the legend of Justice, which occupies the fifth. The friend and patron of
Spenser, Sir Arthur Grey, Lord Deputy of Ireland, is evidently portrayed in Arthegal; and the latter cantos of this
book represent, not always with great felicity, much of the
foreign and domestic history of the times. It is sufficiently
intimated by the poet himself, that his Gloriana, or Faery
Queen, is the type of Elizabeth; and he has given her another
representative in the fair huntress Belphœbe. Spenser's adulation of her beauty (at some fifty or sixty years of age) may
be extenuated, we can say no more, by the practice of wise
and great men, and by his natural tendency to clothe the
objects of his admiration in the hues of fancy; but its exaggeration leaves the servility of the Italians far behind.

82. It has been justly observed by a living writer of the
most ardent and enthusiastic genius, whose eloquence is as the rush of mighty waters, and has
left it for others almost as invidious to praise in terms of

*The succeed-
ing books.*

*Spenser's
sense of
beauty,*

less rapture, as to censure what he has borne along in the
stream of unhesitating eulogy, that 'no poet has ever had
a more exquisite sense of the beautiful than Spenser.'[x] In
Virgil and Tasso this was not less powerful; but even they,
even the latter himself, do not hang with such a tenderness
of delight, with such a forgetful delay, over the fair creations
of their fancy. Spenser is not averse to images that jar on
the mind by exciting horror or disgust, and sometimes his
touches are rather too strong; but it is on love and beauty,
on holiness and virtue, that he reposes with all the sympathy
of his soul. The slowly sliding motion of his stanza, ' with
many a bout of linked sweetness long drawn out,' beautifully
corresponds to the dreamy enchantment of his description,
when Una, or Belphœbe, or Florimel, or Amoret, is present to
his mind. In this varied delineation of female perfectness,
no earlier poet had equalled him ; nor, excepting Shakspeare,
has he had, perhaps, any later rival.

83. Spenser is naturally compared with Ariosto. 'Fierce
wars and faithful loves did moralise the song ' of
both poets. But in the constitution of their minds,
in the character of their poetry, they were almost the
reverse of each other. The Italian is gay, rapid, ardent;
his pictures shift like the hues of heaven; even while
diffuse, he seems to leave in an instant what he touches,
and is prolix by the number, not the duration, of his images.
Spenser is habitually serious; his slow stanza seems to suit
the temper of his genius; he loves to dwell on the sweetness and beauty which his fancy portrays. The ideal of
chivalry, rather derived from its didactic theory, than
from the precedents of romance, is always before him ; his
morality is pure and even stern, with nothing of the liber-
tine tone of Ariosto. He worked with far worse tools than
the bard of Ferrara, with a language not quite formed,
and into which he rather injudiciously poured an unnecessary archaïsm, while the style of his contemporaries
was undergoing a rapid change in the opposite direction.
His stanza of nine lines is particularly inconvenient and

marginal note: compared to Ariosto.

---

[x] I allude here to a very brilliant
series of papers on the Faery Queen,
published in Blackwood's Magazine,
during the years 1834 and 1835. [They
are universally ascribed to Professor
Wilson.—1842.]

languid in narration, where the Italian octave is sprightly and vigorous; though even this becomes ultimately monotonous by its regularity, a fault from which only the ancient hexameter and our blank verse are exempt.

84. Spenser may be justly said to excel Ariosto in originality of invention, in force and variety of character, in strength and vividness of conception, in depth of reflection, in fertility of imagination, and, above all, in that exclusively poetical cast of feeling, which discerns in every thing what common minds do not perceive. In the construction and arrangement of their fable neither deserves much praise; but the siege of Paris gives the Orlando Furioso, spite of its perpetual shiftings of the scene, rather more unity in the reader's apprehension than belongs to the Faery Queen. Spenser is, no doubt, decidedly inferior in ease and liveliness of narration, as well as clearness and felicity of language. But upon thus comparing the two poets, we have little reason to blush for our countryman. Yet the fame of Ariosto is spread through Europe, while Spenser is almost unknown out of England; and even in this age, when much of our literature is so widely diffused, I have not observed proofs of much acquaintance with him on the Continent.

85. The language of Spenser, like that of Shakspeare, is an instrument manufactured for the sake of the Style of work it was to perform. No other poet had written Spenser. like either, though both have had their imitators. It is rather apparently obsolete by his partiality to certain disused forms, such as the y before the participle, than from any close resemblance to the diction of Chaucer or Lydgate.[y] The enfeebling expletives *do* and *did*, though certainly very common in our early writers, had never been employed with such an unfortunate predilection as by Spenser. Their everlasting recurrence is among the great blemishes of his style. His versification is in many passages beautifully harmonious; but he has frequently permitted himself, whether for the sake

---

[y] 'Spenser,' says Ben Jonson, ' in affecting the ancients writ no language; yet I would have him read for his mat- ter, but as Virgil read Ennius.' This is rather in the sarcastic tone attributed to Jonson.

of variety, or from some other cause, to baulk the ear in the conclusion of a stanza.[z]

86. The inferiority of the last three books to the former is surely very manifest. His muse gives gradual signs of weariness; the imagery becomes less vivid, the vein of poetical description less rich, the digressions more frequent and verbose. It is true that the fourth book is full of beautiful inventions, and contains much admirable poetry; yet even here we perceive a comparative deficiency in the quantity of excelling passages, which becomes far more apparent as we proceed, and the last book falls very short of the interest which the earlier part of the Faery Queen had excited. There is, perhaps, less reason than some have imagined, to regret that Spenser did not complete his original design. The Faery Queen is already in the class of longest poems. A double length, especially if, as we may well suspect, the succeeding parts would have been inferior, might have deterred many readers from the perusal of what we now possess. It is felt already in Spenser, as it is perhaps even in Ariosto, when we read much of either, that tales of knights and ladies, giants and salvage men, end in a satiety which no poetical excellence can overcome. Ariosto, sensible of this intrinsic defect in the epic romance, has enlivened it by great variety of incidents, and by much that carries us away from the peculiar tone of chivalrous manners. The world he lives in is before his eyes, and to please it his aim. He plays with his characters as with puppets that amuse the spectator and himself. In Spenser, nothing is more remarkable than the steadiness of his apparent faith in the deeds of knighthood. He had little turn for sportiveness; and in attempting it, as in the unfortunate instance of Malbecco, and a few shorter passages, we find him dull as well as coarse.

Marginal note: Inferiority of the latter books.

---

[z] Coleridge, who had a very strong perception of the beauty of Spenser's poetry, has observed his alternate alliteration, ‘which when well used is a great secret in melody; as “ *sad* to *see* her *sorrowful* constraint;”—“on the grass her *dainty* limbs *did* lay.”’ But I can hardly agree with him when he proceeds to say, ‘it never strikes any unwarned ear as artificial, or other than the result of the necessary movement of the verse.’ The artifice seems often very obvious. I do not also quite understand, or, if I do, cannot acquiesce in what follows, that ‘Spenser's descriptions are not in the true sense of the word picturesque, but are *composed of a wondrous series of images, as in our dreams.*’ Coleridge's Remains, vol. i. p. 93.

It is in the ideal world of pure and noble virtues that his spirit, wounded by neglect, and weary of trouble, loved to refresh itself without reasoning or mockery ; he forgets the reader, and cares little for his taste, while he can indulge the dream of his own delighted fancy.   It may be here also observed, that the elevated and religious morality of Spenser's poem would secure it, in the eyes of every man of just taste, from the ridicule which the mere romances of knight-errantry must incur, and against which Ariosto evidently guarded himself by the gay tone of his narration.   The Orlando Furioso and the Faery Queen are each in the spirit of its age ; but the one was for Italy in the days of Leo, the other for England under Elizabeth, before, though but just before, the severity of the Reformation had been softened away. The lay of Britomart, in twelve cantos, in praise of chastity, would have been received with a smile at the court of Ferrara, which would have had almost as little sympathy with the justice of Arthegal.

87. The allegories of Spenser have been frequently censured. One of their greatest offences, perhaps, is that they gave birth to some tedious and uninteresting poetry of the same kind.   There is usually something repulsive in the application of an abstract or general name to a person, in which, though with some want of regard, as I have intimated above, to the proper meaning of the word, we are apt to think that allegorical fiction consists. The French and English poets of the middle ages had far too much of this ; and it is to be regretted that Spenser did not give other appellations to his Care and Despair, as he has done to Duessa and Talus.   In fact, Orgoglio is but a giant, Humiltà a porter, Obedience a servant.   The names, when English, suggest something that perplexes us ; but the beings exhibited are mere persons of the drama, men and women, whose office or character is designated by their appellation.

Allegories of the Faery Queen.

88. The general style of the Faery Queen is not exempt from several defects besides those of obsoleteness and redundancy. Spenser seems to have been sometimes deficient in one attribute of a great poet, the continual reference to the truth of nature, so that his fictions should be always such as might exist on the given conditions.   This

Blemishes in the diction.

arises in great measure from copying his predecessors too much in description, not suffering his own good sense to correct their deviations from truth. Thus, in the beautiful description of Una, where she first is introduced to us, riding

> Upon a lowly ass more white than snow;
> *Herself much whiter.*

This absurdity may have been suggested by Ovid's Brachia Sithonia candidiora nive; but the image in this line is not brought so distinctly before the mind as to be hideous as well as untrue; it is merely a hyperbolical parallel.[a] A similar objection lies to the stanza enumerating as many kinds of trees as the poet could call to mind in the description of a forest.

> The sailing pine, the cedar proud and tall,
> The vine-prop elm, the poplar never dry,
> The builder oak, sole king of forests all,
> The aspine good for staves, the cypress funeral,—

with thirteen more in the next stanza. Every one knows that a natural forest never contains such a variety of species; nor indeed could such a medley as Spenser, treading in the steps of Ovid, has brought together from all soils and climates, exist long if planted by the hands of man. Thus, also, in the last canto of the second book, we have a celebrated stanza, and certainly a very beautiful one, if this defect did not attach to it; where winds, waves, birds, voices, and musical instruments are supposed to conspire in one harmony. A good writer has observed upon this, that ' to a person listening to a concert of voices and instruments, the interruption of singing birds, winds, and waterfalls, would be little better than the torment of Hogarth's enraged musician.' [b] But perhaps the enchantment of the Bower of Bliss, where this is feigned to have occurred, may in some degree justify Spenser in this instance, by taking it out of

---

[a] Vincent Bourne, in his translation of William and Margaret, has one of the most elegant lines he ever wrote :—
Candidior nivibus, frigidiorque manus.

But this is said of a ghost.
[b] Twining's Translation of Aristotle's Poetics, p. 14.

the common course of nature. The stanza is translated from
Tasso, whom our own poet has followed with close footsteps
in these cantos of the second book of the Faery Queen—
cantos often in themselves beautiful, but which are rendered
stiff by a literal adherence to the original, and fall very short
of its ethereal grace and sweetness. It would be unjust not
to relieve these strictures, by observing that very numerous
passages might be brought from the Faery Queen of admirable truth in painting, and of indisputable originality. The
cave of Despair, the hovel of Corceca, the incantation of
Amoret, are but a few among those that will occur to the
reader of Spenser.

89. The admiration of this great poem was unanimous
and enthusiastic. No academy had been trained Admiration
of the Faery
to carp at his genius with minute cavilling; no Queen.
recent popularity, no traditional fame (for Chaucer was rather
venerated than much in the hands of the reader) interfered
with the immediate recognition of his supremacy. The
Faery Queen became at once the delight of every accomplished gentleman, the model of every poet, the solace of
every scholar. In the course of the next century, by the
extinction of habits derived from chivalry, and the change
both of taste and language, which came on with the civil
wars and the Restoration, Spenser lost something of his
attraction, and much more of his influence over literature ;
yet, in the most phlegmatic temper of the general reader, he
seems to have been one of our most popular writers. Time,
however, has gradually wrought its work ; and, notwithstanding the more imaginative cast of poetry in the present
century, it may be well doubted whether the Faery Queen is
as much read or as highly esteemed as in the days of Anne.
It is not perhaps very difficult to account for this : those
who seek the delight that mere fiction presents to the mind
(and they are the great majority of readers) have been supplied to the utmost limit of their craving, by stores accommodated to every temper, and far more stimulant than the
legends of Faeryland. But we must not fear to assert, with
the best judges of this and of former ages, that Spenser is
still the third name in the poetical literature of our country,

and that he has not been surpassed, except by Dante, in any other.[c]

90. If we place Tasso and Spenser apart, the English poetry of Elizabeth's reign will certainly not enter into competition with that of the corresponding period in Italy. It would require not only much national prejudice but a want of genuine *æsthetic* discernment to put them on a level. But it may still be said that our own muses had their charms; and even that, at the end of the century, there was a better promise for the future than beyond the Alps. We might compare the poetry of one nation to a beauty of the court, with noble and regular features, a slender form, and grace in all her steps, but wanting a genuine simplicity of countenance, and with somewhat of sickliness in the delicacy of her complexion, that seems to indicate the passing away of the first season of youth; while that of the other would rather suggest a country maiden, newly mingling with polished society, not of perfect lineaments, but attracting beholders by the spirit, variety, and intelligence of her expression, and rapidly wearing off the traces of rusticity, which are still sometimes visible in her demeanour.

General parallel of Italian and English poetry.

---

[c] Mr. Campbell has given a character of Spenser, not so enthusiastic as that to which I have alluded, but so discriminating, and, in general, sound, that I shall take the liberty of extracting it from his Specimens of the British Poets, i. 125. 'His command of imagery is wide, easy, and luxuriant. He threw the soul of harmony into our verse, and made it more warmly, tenderly, and magnificently descriptive than it ever was before, or, with a few exceptions, than it has ever been since. It must certainly be owned that in description he exhibits nothing of the brief strokes and robust power which characterise the very greatest poets; but we shall no where find more airy and expansive images of visionary things, a sweeter tone of sentiment, or a finer flush in the colours of language, than in this Rubens of English poetry. His fancy teems exuberantly in minuteness of circumstance, like a fertile soil sending bloom and verdure through the utmost extremities of the foliage which it nourishes. On a comprehensive view of the whole work, we certainly miss the charm of strength, symmetry, and rapid or interesting progress; for though the plan which the poet designed is not completed, it is easy to see that no additional cantos could have rendered it less perplexed.'

Sect. V.—On Latin Poetry.

In Italy—Germany—France—Great Britain.

91. The cultivation of poetry in modern languages did not as yet thin the ranks of Latin versifiers. They are, *Decline of Latin poetry in Italy.* on the contrary, more numerous in this period than before. Italy, indeed, ceased to produce men equal to those who had flourished in the age of Leo and Clement. Some of considerable merit will be found in the great collection, ' Carmina Illustrium Poetarum' (Florentiæ, 1719); one, too, which, rigorously excluding all voluptuous poetry, makes some sacrifice of genius to scrupulous morality. The brothers Amaltei are perhaps the best of the later period. It is not always easy, at least without more pains than I have taken, to determine the chronology of these poems, which are printed in the alphabetical order of the authors' names. But a considerable number must be later than the middle of the century. It cannot be denied that most of these poets employ trivial images, and do not much vary their forms of expression. They often please, but rarely make an impression on the memory. They are generally, I think, harmonious; and perhaps metrical faults, though not uncommon, are less so than among the Cisalpine Latinists. There appears, on the whole, an evident decline since the preceding age.

92. This was tolerably well compensated in other parts of Europe. One of the most celebrated authors is a *compensated in other countries.* native of Germany, Lotichius, whose poems were *Lotichius.* first published in 1551, and with much amendment in 1561. They are written in a strain of luscious elegance, not rising far above the customary level of Ovidian poetry, and certainly not often falling below it. The versification is remarkably harmonious and flowing, but with a mannerism not sufficiently diversified; the first foot of each verse is generally a dactyle, which adds to the grace, but, so continually repeated, somewhat impairs the strength.[d] Loti-

---

[d] [It is not worth while to turn again to Lotichius; but the first foot in elegiac metre ought to be *generally* a dactyle, though there may be a possible excess.

chius is, however, a very elegant and classical versifier ; and
perhaps equal in elegy to Joannes Secundus, or any Cisalpine
writer of the sixteenth century.[e]   One of his elegies, on the
siege of Magdeburg, gave rise to a strange notion—that he
predicted, by a sort of divine enthusiasm, the calamities of
that city in 1631.   Bayle has spun a long note out of this
fancy of some Germans.[f]   But those who take the trouble,
which these critics seem to have spared themselves, of
attending to the poem itself, will perceive that the author
concludes it with prognostics of peace instead of capture.
It was evidently written on the siege of Magdeburg by
Maurice in 1550.   George Sabinus, son-in-law of Melanchthon, ranks second in reputation to Lotichius among the
Latin poets of Germany during this period.

93. But France and Holland, especially the former, became the more favoured haunts of the Latin muse.
A collection in three volumes by Gruter, under the
fictitious name of Ranusius Gherus, Deliciæ Poetarum Gallorum, published in 1609, contains the principal
writers of the former country, some entire, some in selection.
In these volumes there are about 100,000 lines ; in the Deliciæ Poetarum Belgarum, a similar publication by Gruter,
I find about as many ; his third collection, Deliciæ Poetarum
Italorum, seems not so long, but I have not seen more than
one volume.   These poets are disposed alphabetically ; few,
comparatively speaking, of the Italians seem to belong to
the latter half of the century, but very much the larger
proportion of the French and Dutch.   A fourth collection,
Deliciæ Poetarum Germanorum, I have never seen.   All
these bear the fictitious name of Gherus.   According to
a list in Baillet, the number of Italian poets selected by
Gruter is 203 ; of French, 108 ; of Dutch or Belgic, 129 ;
of German, 211.

Marginal note: Collections of Latin poetry by Gruter.

In Ovid's Epistles, the first foot is a
dactyle in four cases out of five, especially in the pentameter. In the second
book, De Arte Amandi, out of 746 lines,
only 105 begin with a spondee. In the
fourth of the Fasti, out of the first 400
lines, only 65 to 335.—1847.]

[e] Baillet calls him the best poet of
Germany after Eobanus Hessus.

[f] Morhof, l. i. c. 19.   Bayle, art. Lotichius, note G.   This seems to have
been agitated after the publication of
Bayle ; for I find in the catalogue of the
British Museum a disquisition, by one
Krusike, Utrum Petrus Lotichius secun-
dam obsidionem urbis Magdeburgensis
prædixerit ; published as late as 1703.

94. Among the French poets, Beza, who bears in Gruter's collection the name of Adeodatus Seba, deserves Characters high praise, though some of his early pieces are of some Gallo-Latin rather licentious.[g] Bellay is also an amatory poet; poets. in the opinion of Baillet he has not succeeded so well in Latin as in French. The poems of Muretus are perhaps superior. Joseph Scaliger seemed to me to write Latin verse tolerably well, but he is not rated highly by Baillet and the authors whom he quotes.[h] The epigrams of Henry Stephens are remarkably prosaic and heavy. Passerat is very elegant; his lines breathe a classical spirit, and are full of those fragments of antiquity with which Latin poetry ought always to be inlaid, but in sense they are rather feeble.[i] The epistles, on the contrary, of the Chancellor de l'Hospital, in an easy Horatian versification, are more interesting than such insipid effusions, whether of flattery or feigned passion, as the majority of modern Latinists present. They are unequal, and fall too often into a creeping style: but sometimes we find a spirit and nervousness of strength and sentiment worthy of his name; and though keeping in general to the level of Horatian satire, he rises at intervals to a higher pitch, and wants not the skill of descriptive poetry.

95. The best of Latin poets whom France could boast was Sammarthanus (Sainte-Marthe), known also, but less Sammar- favourably, in his own language. His Latin poems thanus. are more classically elegant than any others which met my

---

[g] Baillet, n. 1366, thinks Beza an excellent Latin poet. The Juvenilia first appeared in 1548. The later editions omitted several poems.

[h] Jugemens des Savans, n. 1295. One of Scaliger's poems celebrates that immortal flea, which, on a great festival at Poitiers, having appeared on the bosom of a learned, and doubtless beautiful, young lady, Mademoiselle des Roches, was the theme of all the wits and scholars of the age. Some of their lines, and those of Joe Scaliger among the number, seem designed, by the freedom they take with the fair pucelle, to beat the intruder himself in impudence. See Œuvres de Pasquier, ii. 950.

[i] Among the epigrams of Passerat I have found one which Amaltheus seems to have shortened and improved, retain-

ing the idea, in his famous lines on Acon and Leonilla. I do not know whether this has been observed.

Cætera formosi, dextro est orbatus ocello
   Frater, et est lævo lumine capta seror.
Frontibus adversis ambo si jungitis ora,
   Bina quidem facies, vultus at unus erit.
Sed tu, Carle, tuum lumen transmitte sorori,
   Continuo ut vestrûm fiat uterque Deus.
Plena hæc fulgebit fraterna luce Diana,
   Hujus frater eris tu quoque, cæcus Amor.

This is very good, and Passerat ought to have credit for the invention; but the other is better. Though most know the lines by heart, I will insert them here:—

Lumine Acon dextro, capta est Leonilla sinistro,
   Et potis est forma vincere uterque Deos.
Blande puer, lumen quod habes, concede sorori,
   Sic tu cæcus Amor, sic erit illa Venus.

[I now believe, on the authority of a friend, that this epigram, published in 1576, preceded that of Passerat.—-1842.]

eye in Gruter's collection; and this, I believe, is the general suffrage of critics.[k] Few didactic poems, probably, are superior to his Pædotrophia, on the nurture of children; it is not a little better, which indeed is no high praise, than the Balia of Tansillo on the same subject.[m] We may place Sammarthanus, therefore, at the head of the list; and not far from the bottom of it I should class Bonnefons, or Bonifonius, a French writer of Latin verse in the very worst taste, whom it would not be worth while to mention, but for a certain degree of reputation he has acquired. He might almost be suspected of designing to turn into ridicule the effeminacy which some Italians had introduced into amorous poetry. Bonifonius has closely imitated Secundus, but is much inferior to him in everything but his faults. The Latinity is full of gross and obvious errors.[n]

96. The Deliciæ Poetarum Belgarum appeared to me, on rather a cursory inspection, inferior to the French.
Belgic poets.
Secundus outshines his successors. Those of the younger Dousa, whose premature death was lamented by all the learned, struck me as next in merit. Dominic Baudius is harmonious and elegant, but with little originality or vigour. These poets are loose and negligent in versification, ending too often a pentameter with a polysyllabie, and with feeble effect; they have also little idea of several common rules of Latin composition.

---

[k] Baillet, n. 1401. Some did not scruple to set him above the best Italians, and one went so far as to say that Virgil would have been envious of the Pædotrophia.

[m] The following lines are a specimen of the Pædotrophia, taken much at random :—

Ipsæ etiam Alpinis villosæ in cautibus ursæ,
Ipsæ etiam tigres, et quicquid ubique ferarum
    est,
Debita servandis concedunt ubera natis.
Tu, quam miti animo natura benigna creavit,
Exuperes feritate feras? nec te tua tangant
Pignora, nec querulos puerili e gutture planctus,
Nec lacrymas misereris, opemque injusta re-
    cuses,
Quam præstare tuum est, et quæ te pendet ab
    unâ.
Cujus onus teneris hærebit dulce lacertis
Infelix puer, et molli se pectore sternet?
Dulcia quis primi captabit gaudia risûs
Et primas voces et blæsæ murmura linguæ?
Tunc fruenda alii potes illa relinquere demens,

Tantique esse putas teretis servare papillæ
Integrum decus, et juvenilem in pectore florem ?
          Lib. i. (*Gruter*, iii. 266.)

[n] The following lines are not an unfair specimen of Bonifonius :—

Nympha bellula, nympha mollicella,
Cujus in roseis latent labellis
Meæ deliciæ, meæ salutes, &c.
    *   *   *   *   *
Salvete aureolæ meæ puellæ
Crines aureolique crispulique,
Salvete et mihi vos puellæ ocelli,
Ocelli improbuli protervulique ;
Salvete et Veneris pares papillis
Papillæ teretesque turgidæque ;
Salvete æmula purpuræ labella ;
Tota denique Pancharilla salve.
    *   *   *   *   *
Nunc te possideo, alma Pancharilla,
Turturilla mea et columbililla.

Bonifonius has been thought worthy of several editions, and has met with more favourable judges than myself.

97. The Scots, in consequence of receiving, very frequently, a continental education, cultivated Latin poetry with ardour. It was the favourite amusement of Andrew Melville, who is sometimes a mere scribbler, at others, tolerably classical and spirited. His poem on the Creation, in Deliciæ Poetarum Scotorum, is very respectable. One by Hercules Rollock, on the marriage of Anne of Denmark, is better, and equal, a few names withdrawn, to any of the contemporaneous poetry of France. The Epistolæ Heroidum of Alexander Bodius or Boyd are also good. But the most distinguished among the Latin poets of Europe in this age was George Buchanan, of whom Joseph Scaliger and several other critics have spoken in such unqualified terms, that they seem to place him even above the Italians at the beginning of the sixteenth century.[o] If such were their meaning, I should crave the liberty of hesitating. The best poem of Buchanan, in my judgment, is that on the Sphere, than which few philosophical subjects could afford better opportunities for ornamental digression. He is not, perhaps, in hexameters inferior to Vida, and certainly far superior to Palearius. In this poem Buchanan descants on the absurdity of the Pythagorean system, which supposes the motion of the earth. Many good passages occur in his elegies, though we may not reckon him equal in this metre to several of the Italians. His celebrated translation of the Psalms I must also presume to think overpraised;[p] it is difficult, perhaps, to find one, except the

Scots poets ; Buchanan.

---

[o] Buchananus unus est in tota Europa omnes post se relinquens in Latina poesi. Scaligerana Prima.

Henry Stephens, says Maittaire, was the first who placed Buchanan at the head of all the poets of his age, and all France, Italy, and Germany have since subscribed to the same opinion, and conferred that title upon him. Vitæ Stephanorum, ii. 258. I must confess that Sainte-Marthe appears to me not inferior to Buchanan. The latter is very unequal: if we frequently meet with a few lines of great elegance, they are compensated by others of a different description.

[p] Baillet thinks it impossible that those who wish for what is solid as well as what is agreeable in poetry can prefer any other Latin verse of Buchanan to his Psalms. Jugemens des Savans, n. 1328. But Baillet and several others exclude much poetry of Buchanan on account of its reflecting on popery. Baillet and Blount produce abundant testimonies to the excellence of Buchanan's verses. Le Clerc calls his translation of the Psalms incomparable, Bibl. choisie, viii. 127, and prefers it much to that by Beza, which I am not prepared to question. He extols also all his other poetry, except his tragedies and the poem of the Sphere, which I have praised above the rest. So different are the humours of critics ! But as I have fairly quoted those who do not quite agree with myself, and by both number and reputation ought to weigh more with the reader, he has no right to complain that I mislead his taste.

137th, with which he has taken particular pains, that can be called truly elegant or classical Latin poetry. Buchanan is now and then incorrect in the quantity of syllables, as indeed is common with his contemporaries.

98. England was far from strong, since she is not to claim Buchanan in the Latin poetry of this age. A poem in ten books, De Republica Instauranda, by Sir Thomas Chaloner, published in 1579, has not, perhaps, received so much attention as it deserves, though the author is more judicious than imaginative, and does not preserve a very good rhythm. It may be compared with the Zodiacus Vitæ of Palingenius, rather than any other Latin poem I recollect, to which, however, it is certainly inferior. Some lines relating to the English constitution, which, though the title leads us to expect more, forms only the subject of the last book, the rest relating chiefly to private life, will serve as a specimen of Chaloner's powers,[q] and also explain the principles of our government as an experienced statesman understood them. The Anglorum Prœlia, by Ockland, which was directed by an order of the Privy Council to be read exclusively in schools, is an hexameter poem, versified from the chronicles, in a tame strain, not exceedingly bad, but still farther from good. I recollect no other Latin verse of the queen's reign worthy of notice.

---

[q] Nempe tribus simul ordinibus jus esse sacratas
Condendi leges patrio pro more vetustas
Longo usu sic docta tulit, modus iste rogandi
Haud secus ac basis hanc nostram sic consti-
tuit rem,
Ut si inconsultis reliquis pars ulla superbo
Imperio quicquam statuat, seu tollat, ad omnes
Quod spectat, posthac quo nomine læsa vocetur
Publica res nobis, nihil amplius ipse laboro.
   *   *   *   *   *   *
Plebs primum reges statuit; jus hoc quoque
nostrûm est
Cunctorum, ut regi faveant popularia vota;
(Si quid id est, quod plebs respondet rite
rogata)

Nam neque ab invitis potuit vis unica multis
Extorquere datos concordi munere fasces;
Quin populus reges in publica commoda quon-
dam
Egregios certa sub conditione paravit,
Non reges populum; namque his antiquior ille
est.
   *   *   *   *   *   *
Nec cupiens nova jura ferat, seu condita tollat,
Non prius ordinibus regni de more vocatis,
Ut procerum populique rato stent ordine vota,
Omnibus et positum sciscat conjuncta volun-
tas,

De Rep. Inst. l. 10.

CHAPTER VI.

HISTORY OF DRAMATIC LITERATURE FROM 1550 TO 1600.

Italian Tragedy and Comedy—Pastoral Drama—Spanish Drama—Lope de
Vega—French Dramatists—Early English Drama—Second Era; of
Marlowe and his Contemporaries—Shakspeare—Character of several
of his Plays written within this Period.

1. MANY Italian tragedies are extant belonging to these fifty
years, though not very generally known, nor can I Italian
speak of them except through Ginguéné and Walker, tragedy.
the latter of whom has given a few extracts. The Mari-
anna and Didone of Lodovico Dolce, the Œdipus of Anguillara, the Merope of Torelli, the Semiramis of Manfredi, are
necessarily bounded, in the conduct of their fable, by what
was received as truth. But others, as Cinthio had done,
preferred to invent their story, in deviation from the practice
of antiquity. The Hadriana of Groto, the Acripanda of Decio
da Orto, and the Torrismond of Tasso, are of this kind. In
all these we find considerable beauties of language, a florid
and poetic tone, but declamatory and not well adapted to the
rapidity of action, in which we seem to perceive the germ of
that change from common speech to recitative, which, fixing
the attention of the hearer on the person of the actor rather
than on his relation to the scene, destroyed in great measure
the character of dramatic representation. The Italian tragedies are deeply imbued with horror; murder and cruelty,
with all attending circumstances of disgust, and every pol-
lution of crime, besides a profuse employment of spectral
agency, seem the chief weapons of the poet's armoury to
subdue the spectator. Even the gentleness of Tasso could
not resist the contagion in his Torrismond. These tragedies
still retain the chorus at the termination of every act. Of
the Italian comedies little can be added to what has been said
before; no comic writer of this period is comparable in reputation to Machiavel, Ariosto, or even Aretin.[a] They are rather

---

[a] Ginguéné, vol. vi.

less licentious : and, in fact, the profligacy of Italian manners began, in consequence, probably of a better example in the prelates of the church, to put on some regard for exterior decency in the latter part of the century.

2. These regular plays, though possibly deserving of more
Pastoral
drama. attention than they have obtained, are by no means the most important portion of the dramatic literature of Italy in this age. A very different style of composition has, through two distinguished poets, contributed to spread the fame of Italian poetry, and the language itself, through Europe. The fifteenth and sixteenth centuries were abundantly productive of pastoral verse ; a style pleasing to those who are not severe in admitting its conventional fictions. The pastoral dialogue had not much difficulty in expanding to the pastoral drama. In the Sicilian gossips of Theocritus, and in some other ancient eclogues, new interlocutors supervene, which is the first germ of a regular action. Pastorals of this kind had been written, and possibly represented, in Spain, such as the Mingo Rebulgo, in the middle of the fifteenth century.[b] Ginguéné has traced the progress of similar representations, becoming more and more dramatic in Italy.[c] But it is admitted that the honour of giving the first example of a true pastoral fable to the theatre was due to Agostino Beccari of Ferrara. This piece, named Il Sagrifizio, was acted at that court in 1554. Its priority in a line which was to become famous appears to be its chief merit. In this, as in earlier and more simple attempts at pastoral dialogue, the choruses were set to music.[d]

3. This pleasing, though rather effeminate, species of poetry
Aminta of
Tasso. was carried, more than twenty years afterwards, one or two unimportant imitations of Beccari having intervened, to a point of excellence which perhaps it has never surpassed, in the Aminta of Tasso. Its admirable author was then living at the court of Ferrara, yielding up his heart to those seductive illusions of finding happiness in the favour of the great, and even in ambitious and ill-assorted love, which his sounder judgment already saw through, the

---

[b] Bouterwek's Spanish Literature, i. 129.

[c] vi. 327, et post.
[d] Id. vi. 332.

Aminta bearing witness to both states of mind. In the character of Tirsi he has drawn himself, and seems once (though
with the proud consciousness of genius) to hint at that eccentric melancholy, which soon increased so fatally for his
peace.

> Ne già cose scrivea degne di riso,
> Se ben cose facea degne di riso.

The language of all the interlocutors in the Aminta is alike,
nor is the satyr less elegant or recondite than the learned
shepherds.   It is in general too diffuse and florid, too
uniform and elaborate, for passion; especially if considered
dramatically, in reference to the story and the speakers.
But it is to be read as what it is, a beautiful poem; the
delicacy and gracefulness of many passages rendering them
exponents of the hearer's or reader's feelings, though they
may not convey much sympathy with the proper subject.
The death of Aminta, however, falsely reported to Sylvia,
leads to a truly pathetic scene.   It is to be observed that
Tasso was more formed by classical poetry, and more frequently an imitator of it, than any earlier Italian.   The
beauties of the Aminta are in great measure due to Theocritus,
Virgil, Ovid, Anacreon, and Moschus.

4. The success of Tasso's Aminta produced the Pastor
Fido of Guarini, himself long in the service of the Pastor Fido
duke of Ferrara, where he had become acquainted of Guarini.
with Tasso; though, in consequence of some dissatisfaction
at that court, he sought the patronage of the duke of Savoy.
The Pastor Fido was first represented at Turin in 1585, but
seems not to have been printed for some years afterwards.
It was received with general applause; but the obvious resemblance to Tasso's pastoral drama could not fail to excite
a contention between their respective advocates, which long
survived the mortal life of the two poets.   Tasso, it has
been said, on reading the Pastor Fido, was content to observe that, if his rival had not read the Aminta, he would
not have excelled it.   If his modesty induced him to say no
more than this, very few would be induced to dispute his
claim; the characters, the sentiments are evidently imitated;
and in one celebrated instance a whole chorus is parodied

with the preservation of every rhyme.[e]   But it is far more
questionable whether the palm of superior merit, independent of originality, should be awarded to the later poet.
More elegance and purity of taste belong to the Aminta,
more animation and variety to the Pastor Fido.   The
advantage in point of morality, which some have ascribed to
Tasso, is not very perceptible ; Guarini may transgress
rather more in some passages, but the tone of the Aminta,
in strange opposition to the pure and pious life of its
author, breathes nothing but the avowed laxity of an Italian
court. The Pastor Fido may be considered, in a much greater
degree than the Aminta, a prototype of the Italian opera ;
not that it was spoken in recitative ; but the short and
rapid expressions of passion, the broken dialogue, the frequent
changes of personages and incidents, keep the effect of
representation and of musical accompaniment continually
before the reader's imagination. Any one who glances over
a few scenes of the Pastor Fido will, I think, perceive that it
is the very style which Metastasio, and inferior coadjutors of
musical expression, have rendered familiar to our ears.

5. The great invention, which, though chiefly connected
with the history of music and of society, was by
no means without influence upon literature, the
melodrame, usually called the Italian opera, belongs to the
very last years of this century.   Italy, long conspicuous for
such musical science and skill as the middle ages possessed,
had fallen, in the first part of the sixteenth century, very
short of some other countries, and especially of the Netherlands, from which the courts of Europe, and even of the
Italian princes, borrowed their performers and their instruc-
tors. But a revolution in church music, which had become
particularly dry and pedantic, was brought about by the
genius of Palestrina about 1560 ; and the art, in all its
departments, was cultivated with an increased zeal for all the
rest of the century.[f] In the splendour that environed the

Italian opera.

---

[e] This is that beginning, O bella età
dell' oro.

[f] Ranke, with the musical sentiment
of a German, ascribes a wonderful influence in the revival of religion after
the middle of the century to the compo-

sitions of Palestrina. Church music had
become so pedantic and technical that
the Council of Trent had some doubts
whether it should be retained. Pius IV.
appointed a commission to examine this
question, who could arrive at no decision,

houses of Medici and Este, in the pageants they loved to exhibit, music, carried to a higher perfection by foreign artists, and by the natives who came forward to emulate them, became of indispensable importance; it had already been adapted to dramatic representation in choruses; interludes and pieces written for scenic display were now given with a perpetual accompaniment, partly to the songs, partly to the dance and pantomime which intervened between them.[g] Finally, Ottavio Rinuccini, a poet of considerable genius, but who is said to have known little of musical science, by meditating on what is found in ancient writers on the accompaniment to their dramatic dialogue, struck out the idea of recitative. This he first tried in the pastoral of Dafne, represented privately in 1594; and its success led him to the composition of what he entitled a tragedy for music, on the story of Eurydice. This was represented at the festival on the marriage of Mary of Medicis in 1600. 'The most astonishing effects,' says Ginguéné, 'that the theatrical music of the greatest masters has produced, in the perfection of the science, are not comparable to those of this representation, which exhibited to Italy the creation of a new art.'[h] It is, however, a different question whether this immense enhancement of the powers of music, and consequently of its popularity, has been favourable to the development of poetical genius in this species of composition; and in general it may be said that, if music has, on some occasions, been a serviceable handmaid, and even a judicious monitress, to poetry, she has been apt to prove but a tyrannical mistress. In the melodrame, Corniani well observes, poetry became her vassal, and has been ruled with a despotic sway.

6. The struggle that seemed arduous in the earlier part

The artists said it was impossible to achieve what the church required, a coincidence of expression between the words and the music. Palestrina appeared at this time, and composed the mass of Marcellus, which settled the dispute for ever. Other works by himself and his disciples followed, which elevated sacred music to the highest importance among the accessories of religious worship. Die Päpste, vol. i. p. 498. But a large proportion of the performers, I apprehend, were Germans, especially in theatrical music.

[g] Ginguéné, vol. vi., has traced the history of the melodrame with much pains.

[h] P. 474. Corniani, vii. 31, speaks highly of the poetical abilities of Rinuccini. See also Galluzzi, Storia del Gran Ducato, v. 547.

of this century between the classical and national schools of
dramatic poetry in Spain proved of no long duration. The latter became soon decisively superior;
and before the end of the present period, that
kingdom was in possession of a peculiar and extensive literature, which has attracted the notice of Europe, and has
enriched both the French theatre and our own. The spirit
of the Spanish drama is far different from that which animated the Italian writers; there is not much of Machiavel
in their comedy, and still less of Cinthio in their tragedy.
They abandoned the Greek chorus, which still fettered their
contemporaries, and even the division into five acts, which
later poets, in other countries, have not ventured to renounce.
They gave more complication to the fable, sought more
unexpected changes of circumstance, were not solicitous in
tragedy to avoid colloquial language or familiar incidents,
showed a preference to the tragi-comic intermixture of light
with serious matter, and cultivated grace in poetical diction
more than vigour. The religious mysteries, once common in
other parts of Europe, were devoutly kept up in Spain; and,
under the name of Autos Sacramentales, make no inconsiderable portion of the writings of their chief dramatists.[i]

The national taste revives in the Spanish drama.

7. Andrès, favourable as he is to his country, is far
from enthusiastic in his praises of the Spanish theatre. Its
exuberance has been its ruin; no one, he justly remarks, can
read some thousand plays in the hope of finding a few that
are tolerable, Andrès, however, is not exempt from a strong
prejudice in favour of the French stage. He admits the
ease and harmony of the Spanish versification, the purity of
the style, the abundance of the thoughts, and the ingenious
complexity of the incidents. This is peculiarly the merit of
the Spanish comedy, as its great defect, in his opinion, is the
want of truth and delicacy in the delineation of the passions,
and of power to produce a vivid impression on the reader.
The best work, he concludes rather singularly, of the comic
poets of Spain has been the French theatre.[k]

8. The most renowned of these is Lope de Vega, so
many of whose dramas appeared within the present century,

---

[i] Bouterwek.   [k] Vol. v. p. 138.

that although, like Shakspeare, he is equally to be claimed by the next, we may place his name, once for all, Lope de Vega; in this period. Lope de Vega is called by Cervantes a prodigy of nature; and such he may justly be reckoned; not that we can ascribe to him a sublime genius, or a mind abounding with fine original thought, but his fertility of invention and readiness of versifying his extraordinary fertility; are beyond competition. It was said foolishly, if meant as praise, of Shakspeare, and we may be sure untruly, that he never blotted a line. This may almost be presumed of Vega. 'He required,' says Bouterwek, 'no more than four-and-twenty hours to write a versified drama of three acts in redondillas, interspersed with sonnets, tercets, and octaves, and from beginning to end abounding in intrigues, prodigies, or interesting situations. This astonishing facility enabled him to supply the Spanish theatre with upwards of 2000 original dramas, of which not more than 300 have been preserved by printing. In general the theatrical manager carried away what he wrote before he had even time to revise it; and immediately a fresh applicant would arrive to prevail on him to commence a new piece. He sometimes wrote a play in the short space of three or four hours.' . . . 'Arithmetical calculations have been employed in order to arrive at a just estimate of Lope de Vega's facility in poetic composition. According to his own testimony, he wrote on an average five sheets a day; it has therefore been computed that the number of sheets which he composed during his life must have amounted to 133,225; and that, allowing for the deduction of a small portion of prose, Lope de Vega must have written upwards of 21,300,000 verses. Nature would have overstepped her bounds and have produced the miraculous, had Lope de Vega, along with this rapidity of invention and composition, attained perfection in any department of literature.' [m]

9. This peculiar gift of rapid composition will appear more extraordinary when we attend to the nature of Lope's

---

[m] P. 361, 363. Montalvan, Lope's friend, says, that he wrote 1800 plays and 400 autos. In a poem of his own, written in 1609, he claims 483 plays, and he continued afterwards to write for the stage. Those that remain and have been collected in twenty-five volumes are about 300.

versification, very unlike the irregular lines of our old
_{his versifi-} drama, which it is not perhaps difficult for one well
_{cation;} practised to write or utter extemporaneously. 'The
most singular circumstance attending his verse,' says Lord
Holland, 'is the frequency and difficulty of the tasks which
he imposes on himself. At every step we meet with acros-
tics, echoes, and compositions of that perverted and laborious
kind, from attempting which another author would be deterred by the trouble of the undertaking, if not by the little
real merit attending the achievement. They require no
genius, but they exact much time; which one should think
that such a voluminous poet could little afford to waste.
But Lope made a parade of his power over the vocabulary :
he was not contented with displaying the various order in
which he could dispose the syllables and marshal the rhymes
of his language ; but he also prided himself upon the
celerity with which he brought them to go through the most
whimsical but the most difficult evolutions. He seems to
have been partial to difficulties for the gratification of sur-
mounting them.' This trifling ambition is usual among
second-rate poets, especially in a degraded state of public
taste; but it may be questionable whether Lope de Vega
ever performed feats of skill more surprising in this way
than some of the Italian *improvvisatori*, who have been said
to carry on at the same time three independent sonnets,
uttering, in their unpremeditated strains, a line of each in
separate succession. There is reason to believe that their
extemporaneous poetry is as good as anything in Lope de Vega.

10. The immense popularity of this poet, not limited,
_{his popu-} among the people itself, to his own age, bespeaks
_{larity;} some attention from criticism. 'The Spaniards who
affect fine taste in modern times,' says Schlegel, 'speak with
indifference of their old national poets; but the people retain
a lively attachment to them, and their productions are received on the stage, at Madrid, or at Mexico, with passionate enthusiasm.' It is true that foreign critics have not in
general pronounced a very favourable judgment of Lope de
Vega. But a writer of such prodigious fecundity is ill
appreciated by single plays; the whole character of his
composition manifests that he wrote for the stage, and for

the stage of his own country, rather than for the closet of a foreigner. His writings are divided into spiritual plays, heroic and historical comedies, most of them taken from the annals and traditions of Spain, and, lastly, comedies of real life, or, as they were called, 'of the cloak and sword' (capa y espada), a name answering to the *comœdia togata* of the Roman stage. These have been somewhat better known than the rest, and have, in several instances, found their way to our own theatre, by suggesting plots and incidents to our older writers. The historian of Spanish literature, to whom I am so much indebted, has given a character of these comedies, in which the English reader will perhaps recognise much that might be said also of Beaumont and Fletcher.

11. 'Lope de Vega's comedies de Capa y Espada, or those which may properly be denominated his dramas of intrigue, though wanting in the delineation of character, are romantic pictures of manners, drawn from real life. They present, in their peculiar style, no less interest with respect to situations than his heroic comedies, and the same irregularity in the composition of the scenes. The language, too, is alternately elegant and vulgar, sometimes highly poetic, and sometimes, though versified, reduced to the level of the dullest prose. Lope de Vega seems scarcely to have bestowed a thought on maintaining probability in the succession of the different scenes; ingenious complication is with him the essential point in the interest of his situations. Intrigues are twisted and entwined together, until the poet, in order to bring his piece to a conclusion, without ceremony cuts the knots he cannot untie, and then he usually brings as many couples together as he can by any possible contrivance match. He has scattered through his pieces occasional reflections and maxims of prudence; but any genuine morality, which might be conveyed through the stage, is wanting, for its introduction would have been inconsistent with that poetic freedom on which the dramatic interest of the Spanish comedy is founded. His aim was to paint what he observed, not what he would have approved, in the manners of the fashionable world of his age; but he leaves it to the spectator to draw his own inferences.' [n]

character of his comedies.

---

[n] Bouterwek, p. 375.

12. An analysis of one of these comedies from real life is
Tragedy of Don Sancho Ortiz. given by Bouterwek, and another by Lord Holland.
The very few that I have read appear lively and
diversified, not unpleasing in the perusal, but exciting little
interest, and rapidly forgotten. Among the heroic pieces of
Lope de Vega, a high place appears due to the Estrella de
Sevilla, published with alterations by Triquero, under the
name of Don Sancho Ortiz.° It resembles the Cid in its
subject. The king, Sancho the Brave, having fallen in love
with Estrella, sister of Don Bustos Tabera, and being foiled
by her virtue,ᵖ and by the vigilance of her brother, who had
drawn his sword upon him, as in disguise he was attempting to penetrate into her apartment, resolves to have him
murdered, and persuades Don Sancho Ortiz, a soldier full of
courage and loyalty, by describing the attempt made on his
person, to undertake the death of one whose name is contained in a paper he gives him. Sancho is the accepted
lover of Estrella, and is on that day to espouse her with her
brother's consent. He reads the paper, and after a conflict
which is meant to be pathetic, but in our eyes is merely
ridiculous, determines, as might be supposed, to keep his
word to his sovereign. The shortest course is to contrive a
quarrel with Bustos, which produces a duel, wherein the
latter is killed. The second act commences with a pleasing
scene of Estrella's innocent delight in her prospect of happiness; but the body of her brother is now brought in, and the
murderer, who had made no attempt to conceal himself, soon
appears in custody. His examination before the judges, who
endeavour in vain to extort one word from him in his defence,
occupies part of the third act. The king, anxious to save his
life, but still more so to screen his own honour, requires
only a pretext to pardon the offence. But the noble Castilian
disdains to save himself by falsehood, and merely repeats

° In Lord Holland's Life of Lope de
Vega, a more complete analysis than
what I have offered is taken from the
original play. I have followed the
rifaccimento of Triquero, which is substantially the same.

ᵖ Lope de Vega has borrowed for

Estrella the well-known answer of a
lady to a king of France, told with
several variations of names, and possibly
true of none.

Soy (she says)
Para esposa vuestra poco,
Para dama vuestra mucho.

that he had not slain his friend without cause, and that the action was atrocious, but not criminal.

> Dice que fué atrocidad,
> Pero que no delito.

13. In this embarrassment Estrella appears, demanding not the execution of justice on her brother's murderer, but that he should be delivered up to her. The king, with his usual feebleness, consents to this request, observing that he knows by experience it is no new thing for her to be cruel. She is, however, no sooner departed with the royal order, than the wretched prince repents, and determines to release Sancho, making compensation to Estrella by marrying her to a rico-hombre of Castile. The lady meantime reaches the prison, and in an interview with her unfortunate lover, offers him his liberty, which by the king's concession is in her power. He is not to be outdone in generous sentiments, and steadily declares his resolution to be executed. In the fifth act this heroic emulation is reported by one who had overheard it to the king. All the people of this city, he replies, are heroes, and outstrip nature herself by the greatness of their souls. The judges now enter, and with sorrow report their sentence that Sancho must suffer death. But the king is at length roused, and publicly acknowledges that the death of Bustos had been perpetrated by his command. The president of the tribunal remarks that, as the king had given the order, there must doubtless have been good cause. Nothing seems to remain but the union of the lovers. Here, however, the high Castilian principle once more displays itself. Estrella refuses to be united to one she tenderly loves, but who has brought such a calamity into her family; and Sancho himself, willingly releasing her engagement, admits that their marriage under such circumstances would be a perpetual torment. The lady therefore chooses, what is always at hand in Catholic fiction, the dignified retirement of a nunnery, and the lover departs to dissipate his regrets in the Moorish war.

14. Notwithstanding all in the plan and conduct of this piece, which neither our own state of manners nor the laws of any sound criticism can tolerate, it is very conceivable that

to the factitious taste of a Spanish audience in the age of
Lope de Vega it would have appeared excellent. The character of Estrella is truly noble, and much superior in interest
to that of Chimène. Her resentment is more genuine, and
free from that hypocrisy which, at least in my judgment,
renders the other almost odious and contemptible. Instead
of imploring the condemnation of him she loves, it is as her
own prisoner that she demands Sancho Ortiz, and this for
the generous purpose of setting him at liberty. But the
great superiority of the Spanish play is at the close. Chimène accepts the hand stained with her father's blood, while
Estrella sacrifices her own wishes to a sentiment which the
manners of Spain, and, we may add, the laws of natural
decency required.

15. The spiritual plays of Lope de Vega abound with as
His spiritual plays. many incongruous and absurd circumstances as the
mysteries of our forefathers. The Inquisition was
politic enough to tolerate, though probably the sternness of
Castilian orthodoxy could not approve, these strange representations, which, after all, had the advantage of keeping
the people in mind of the devil, and of the efficacy of holy
water in chasing him away. But the regular theatre, according to Lord Holland, has always been forbidden in Spain
by the church, nor do the kings frequent it.

16. Two tragedies by Bermudez, both on the story of Ines
Numancia of Cervantes. de Castro, are written on the ancient model, with a
chorus, and much simplicity of fable. They are, it
is said, in a few scenes impressive and pathetic, but interrupted by passages of flat and tedious monotony.[q]   Cervantes was the author of many dramatic pieces, some of
which are so indifferent as to have been taken for intentional
satires upon the bad taste of his times, so much of it do they
display. One or two, however, of his comedies have obtained some praise from Schlegel and Bouterwek. But his
tragedy of Numancia stands apart from his other dramas,
and, as I conceive, from anything on the Spanish stage. It
is probably one of his earlier works, but was published for
the first time in 1784. It is a drama of extraordinary power,

----

q Bouterwek, 296.

and may justify the opinion of Bouterwek, that, in different circumstances, the author of Don Quixote might have been the Æschylus of Spain.   If terror and pity are the inspiring powers of tragedy, few have been for the time more under their influence than Cervantes in his Numancia.   The story of that devoted city, its long resistance to Rome, its exploits of victorious heroism, that foiled repeatedly the consular legions, are known to every one.   Cervantes has opened his tragedy at the moment when Scipio Æmilianus, enclosing the city with a broad trench, determines to secure its reduction by famine.   The siege lasted five months, when the Numantines, exhausted by hunger, but resolute never to yield, setting fire to a pile of their household goods, after slaying their women and children, cast themselves into the flame.   Every circumstance that can enhance horror, the complaints of famished children, the desperation of mothers, the sinister omens of rejected sacrifice, the appalling incantations that re-animate a recent corpse to disclose the secrets of its prison-house, are accumulated with progressive force in this tremendous drama.   The love-scenes of Morando and Lira, two young persons whose marriage had been frustrated by the public calamity, though some incline to censure them, contain nothing beyond poetical truth, and add, in my opinion, to its pathos, while they somewhat relieve its severity.

17. Few, probably, would desire to read the Numancia a second time.   But it ought to be remembered that the historical truth of this tragedy, though, as in the Ugolino of Dante, it augments the painfulness of the impression, is the legitimate apology of the author.   Scenes of agony, and images of unspeakable sorrow, when idly accumulated by an inventor at his ease, as in many of our own older tragedies, and in much of modern fiction, give offence to a reader of just taste, from their needlessly trespassing upon his sensibility.   But in that which excites an abhorrence of cruelty and oppression, or which, as the Numancia, commemorates ancestral fortitude, there is a moral power, for the sake of which the sufferings of sympathy must not be flinched from.

18. The Numancia is divided into four jornadas or acts, each containing changes of scene, as on our own stage.   The

metre, by a most extraordinary choice, is the regular octave
stanza, ill-adapted as that is to the drama, intermixed with
the favourite redondilla. The diction, though sometimes
what would seem tame and diffuse to us, who are accustomed
to a bolder and more figurative strain in tragedy than the
southern nations require, rises often with the subject to
nervous and impressive poetry. There are, however, a few
sacrifices to the times. In a finely-imagined prosopopœia,
where Spain, crowned with towers, appears on the scene to
ask the Duero what hope there could be for Numancia, the
river-god, rising with his tributary streams around him,
after bidding her despair of the city, goes into a tedious
consolation, in which the triumphs of Charles and Philip
are specifically, and with as much tameness as adulation,
brought forward as her future recompense. A much worse
passage occurs in the fourth act, where Lira, her brother
lying dead of famine, and her lover of his wounds before her,
implores death from a soldier who passes over the stage.
He replies that some other hand must perform that office ;
he was born only to adore her.[r] This frigid and absurd line,
in such a play by such a poet, is an almost incredible proof of
the mischief which the Provencal writers, with their hyperbolical gallantry, had done to European poetry. But it is
just to observe that this is the only faulty passage, and that
the language of the two lovers is simple, tender, and pathetic.
The material accompaniments of representation on the
Spanish theatre seem to have been full as defective as on
our own. The Numancia is printed with stage directions,
almost sufficient to provoke a smile in the midst of its
withering horrors.

19. The mysteries which had delighted the Parisians for
a century and a half were suddenly forbidden by
the parliament as indecent and profane in 1548.
Four years only elapsed before they were replaced, though
not on the same stage, by a different style of representation.
Whatever obscure attempts at a regular dramatic composition may have been traced in France at an earlier period,

French
theatre ;
Jodelle.

---

[r] Otra mano, otro hierro ha de acabaros,
Que yo solo nació por adoraros.

Jodelle was acknowledged by his contemporaries to be the true father of their theatre. His tragedy of Cléopatre, and his comedy of La Rencontre, were both represented for the first time before Henry II. in 1552. Another comedy, Eugène, and a tragedy on the story of Dido, were published about the same time. Pasquier, who tells us this, was himself a witness of the representation of the two former.[s] The Cléopatre, according to Fontenelle, is very simple, without action or stage effect, full of long speeches, and with a chorus at the end of every act. The style is often low and ludicrous, which did not prevent this tragedy, the first-fruits of a theatre which was to produce Racine, from being received with vast applause. There is, in reality, amidst these raptures that frequently attend an infant literature, something of an undefined presage of the future, which should hinder us from thinking them quite ridiculous. The comedy of Eugène is in verse, and, in the judgment of Fontenelle, much superior to the tragedies of Jodelle. It has more action, a dialogue better conceived, and some traits of humour and nature. This play, however, is very immoral and licentious ; and it may be remarked that some of its satire falls on the vices of the clergy.[t]

20. The Agamemnon of Toutain published in 1557, is taken from Seneca, and several other pieces about the same time, or soon afterwards, seem also to be translations.[u] The Jules César of Grevin was represented in 1560.[x] It contains a few lines that La Harpe has extracted,

Garnier.

---

[s] Cette comédie et la Cléopâtre furent représentées devant le roi Henri à Paris en l'Hostel de Rheims, avec un grand applaudissement de toute la compagnie ; et depuis encore au collège de Boncourt, où toutes les fenestres estoient tapissées d'une infinité de personnages d'honneur, et la cour si pleine d'escoliers que les portes du collège en regorgeoient. Je le dis comme celuy qui y estois présent, avec le grand Tornebus en une mesme chambre. Et les entreparleurs estoient tous hommes de nom. Car même Remy Belleau et Jean de la Peruse jouoient les principaux roullets. Suard tells us that the whole troop of performers, the Confrères de la Passion, whose mysteries had been interdicted, availed themselves of an exclusive privilege granted to them

by Charles VI. in 1400, to prevent the representation of the Cléopatre by public actors. Jodelle was therefore forced to have it performed by his friends. See Recherches de la France, l. vii. c. 6. Fontenelle, Hist. du Théâtre françois (in Œuvres de Font. edit. 1776), vol. iii. p. 52. Beauchamps, Recherches sur les Théâtres de France. Suard, Mélanges de Littérature, vol. iv. p. 59. The last writer, in what he calls Coup-d'œil sur l'Histoire de l'ancien Théâtre français (in the same volume), has given an amusing and instructive sketch of the French drama down to Corneille.

[t] Fontenelle, p. 61.

[u] Beauchamps. Suard.

[x] Suard, p. 73. La Harpe, Cours de Littérature. Grevin also wrote come-

as not without animation.   But the first tragedian that deserves much notice after Jodelle was Robert Garnier, whose
eight tragedies were collectively printed in 1580.   They are
chiefly taken from mythology or ancient history, and are
evidently framed according to a standard of taste which has
ever since prevailed on the French stage.   But they retain
some characteristics of the classical drama which were soon
afterwards laid aside; the chorus is heard between every
act, and a great portion of the events is related by messen-
gers.   Garnier makes little change in the stories he found in
Seneca or Euripides; nor had love yet been thought essential to tragedy.   Though his speeches are immeasurably
long, and overladen with pompous epithets, though they
have often much the air of bad imitations of Seneca's manner, from whom probably, if any one should give himself the
pains to make the comparison, some would be found to have
been freely translated, we must acknowledge that in many
of his couplets the reader perceives a more genuine tone of
tragedy, and the germ of that artificial style which reached
its perfection in far greater men than Garnier.   In almost
every line there is some fault, either against taste or the
present rules of verse; yet there are many which a good poet
would only have had to amend and polish.   The account of
Polyxena's death in La Troade is very well translated from
the Hecuba.   But his best tragedy seems to be Les Juives,
which is wholly his own, and displays no inconsiderable
powers of poetical description.   In this I am confirmed by
Fontenelle, who says that this tragedy has many noble and
touching passages; wherein he has been aided by taking
much from Scripture, the natural sublimity of which cannot
fail to produce an effect.[y]   We find, however, in Les Juives a

---

dies which were very licentious, as those
of the 16th century generally were in
France and Italy, and were not in England, or, I believe, in Spain.

   [y] P. 71.   Suard, who dwells much
longer on Garnier then either Fontenelle
or La Harpe has done, observes, as I
think, with justice: Les ouvrages de
Garnier méritent de faire époque dans
l'histoire du théâtre, non par la beauté
de ses plans; il n'en faut chercher de
bons dans aucune des tragédies du sei-

zième siècle; mais les sentimens qu'il
exprime sont nobles, son style a souvent
de l'élévation sans enflure et beaucoup
de sensibilité; sa versification est facile
et souvent harmonieuse.   C'est lui qui a
fixé d'une manière invariable la succession alternative des rimes masculines et
féminines.   Enfin c'est le premier des
tragiques français dont la lecture pût
être utile à ceux qui voudraient suivre
la même carrière; on a même prétendu
que son Hyppolite avait beaucoup aidé

good deal of that propensity to exhibit cruelty, by which the Italian and English theatres were at that time distinguished. Pasquier says, that every one gave the prize to Garnier above all who had preceded him, and after enumerating his eight plays, expresses his opinion that they would be admired by posterity.[z]

21. We may consider the comedies of Larivey, published in 1579, as making a sort of epoch in the French drama. This writer, of whom little is known, but Larivey. that he was a native of Champagne, prefers a claim to be the first who chose subjects for comedy from real life in France (forgetting in this those of Jodelle), and the first who wrote original dramas in prose. His comedies are six in number, to which three were added in a subsequent edition, which is very rare.[a] These six are Le Laquais, La Veuve, Les Esprits, Le Morfondu, Les Jaloux, and Les Écoliers. Some of them are partly borrowed from Plautus and Terence; and in general they belong to that school, presenting the usual characters of the Roman stage, with no great attempt at originality. But the dialogue is conducted with spirit; and in many scenes, especially in the play called Le Laquais, which, though the most free in all respects, appears to me the most comic and amusing, would remind any reader of the minor pieces of Molière, being conceived, though not entirely executed, with the same humour. All these comedies of Larivey are highly licentious both in their incidents and language. It is supposed in the Biographie universelle that Molière and Regnard borrowed some ideas from Larivey; but both the instances alleged will be found in Plautus.

22. No regular theatre was yet established in France. These plays of Garnier, Larivey, and others of that Theatres class, were represented either in colleges or in pri- in Paris. vate houses. But the Confrères de la Passion, and another

---

Racine dans la composition de Phèdre. Mais s'il l'a aidé, c'est comme l'Hyppo- lite de Sénèque, dont celui de Garnier n'est qu'une imitation, p. 81.

[z] Ibid.

[a] The first edition itself, I conceive, is not very common; for few writers within my knowledge have mentioned Larivey. Fontenelle, I think, could not have read his plays, or he would have given him a place in his brief sketch of the early French stage, as the father of comedy in prose. La Harpe was too superficial to know anything about him. Beauchamps, vol. ii. p. 68, acknowledges his pretensions, and he has a niche in the Biographie universelle. Suard has also done him some justice.

company, the Enfans de Sans Souci, whom they admitted into a participation of their privilege, used to act gross and stupid farces, which few respectable persons witnessed. After some unsuccessful attempts, two companies of regular actors appeared near the close of the century; one, in 1598, having purchased the exclusive right of the Confrères de la Passion, laid the foundations of the Comédie française, so celebrated and so permanent; the other, in 1600, established by its permission a second theatre in the Marais. But the pieces they represented were still of a very low class.[b]

23. England at the commencement of this period could boast of little besides the Scripture mysteries, already losing ground, but which have been traced down to the close of the century, and the more popular moral plays, which furnished abundant opportunities for satire on the times, for ludicrous humour, and for attacks on the old or the new religion. The latter, however, were kept in some restraint by the Tudor government. These moralities gradually drew nearer to regular comedies, and sometimes had nothing but an abstract name given to an individual, by which they could be even apparently distinguished from such. We have already mentioned Ralph Royster Doyster, written by Udal in the reign of Henry VIII., as the earliest English comedy in a proper sense, so far as our negative evidence warrants such a position. Mr. Collier has recovered four acts of another, called Misogonus, which he refers to the beginning of Elizabeth's reign.[c] It is like the former, a picture of London life. A more celebrated piece is Gammar Gurton's Needle, commonly ascribed to John Still, afterwards bishop of Bath and Wells. No edition is known before 1575, but it seems to have been represented in Christ's College at Cambridge, not far from the year 1565.[d] It is impossible for anything to be meaner in subject and characters than this strange farce; but the author had

English stage.

Gammar Gurton's Needle.

---

[b] Suard.

[c] Hist. of Dramatic Poetry, ii. 464.

[d] Mr. Collier agrees with Malone in assigning this date, but it is merely conjectural, as one rather earlier might be chosen with equal probability. Still is said in the biographies to have been born in 1543; but this date seems to be too low. He became Margaret's professor of divinity in 1570. Gammar Gurton's Needle must have been written while the Protestant establishment, if it existed, was very recent, for the parson is evidently a papist.

some vein of humour, and writing neither for fame nor
money, but to make light-hearted boys laugh, and to laugh
with them, and that with as little grossness as the story
would admit, is not to be judged with severe criticism. He
comes, however, below Udal, and perhaps below the writer
of Misogonus. The Supposes of George Gascoyne, acted
at Gray's Inn in 1566, is but a translation in prose from the
Suppositi of Ariosto. It seems to have been published in
the same year.[e]

24. But the progress of literature soon excited in one
person an emulation of the ancient drama. Sack- Gorboduc of
ville has the honour of having led the way. His Sackville.
tragedy of Gorboduc was represented at Whitehall before
Elizabeth in 1562.[f] It is written in what was thought the
classical style, like the Italian tragedies of the same age,
but more inartificial and unimpassioned. The speeches are
long and sententious; the action, though sufficiently full of
incident, passes chiefly in narration; a chorus, but in the
same blank-verse measure as the rest, divides the acts; the
unity of place seems to be preserved, but that of time is
manifestly transgressed. The story of Gorboduc, which is
borrowed from our fabulous British legends, is as full of
slaughter as was then required for dramatic purposes; but
the characters are clearly drawn and consistently sustained;
the political maxims grave and profound; the language not
glowing or passionate, but vigorous; and upon the whole it
is evidently the work of a powerful mind, though in a less
poetical mood than was displayed in the Induction to the
Mirror of Magistrates. Sackville, it has been said, had the
assistance of Norton in this tragedy; but Warton has decided
against this supposition from internal evidence.[g]

---

[e] Warton, iv. 304. Collier, iii. 6.
The original had been first published in
prose, 1525, and from this Gascoyne
took his translation, adopting some of
the changes Ariosto had introduced when
he turned it into verse: but he has inserted little of his own. Ib.

[f] The 18th of January, 1561, to which
date its representation is referred by
Mr. Collier, seems to be 1562, according
to the modern style; and this tallies

best with what is said in the edition of
1571, that it had been played about nine
years before. See Warton, iv. 179.

[g] Hist. of Engl. Poetry, iv. 194. Mr.
Collier supports the claim of Norton to
the first three acts, which would much
reduce Sackville's glory, ii. 481. I incline to Warton's opinion, grounded upon
the identity of style, and the superiority
of the whole tragedy to any thing we
can certainly ascribe to Norton, a coad-

25. The regular form adopted in Gorboduc, though not
Preference given to the irregular form. wholly without imitators, seems to have had little
success with the public.[h] An action passing visibly
on the stage, instead of a frigid narrative, a copious
intermixture of comic buffoonery with the gravest story,
were requisites with which no English audience would dispense. Thus Edwards treated the story of Damon and
Pythias, which, though according to the notions of those
times, it was too bloodless to be called a tragedy at all, belonged to the elevated class of dramatic compositions.[i]
Several other subjects were taken from ancient history ; this
indeed became an usual source of the fable ; but if we may
judge from those few that have survived, they were all constructed on the model which the mysteries had accustomed
our ancestors to admire.

26. The office of Master of the Revels, in whose province
First theatres. it lay to regulate, among other amusements of the
court, the dramatic shows of various kinds, was
established in 1546. The inns of court vied with the royal
palace in these representations, and Elizabeth sometimes
honoured the former with her presence. On her visits to the
universities, a play was a constant part of the entertainment.
Fifty-two names, though nothing more, of dramas acted at
court under the superintendence of the Master of the Revels,
between 1568 and 1580, are preserved.[k] In 1574 a patent
was granted to the Earl of Leicester's servants to act plays
in any part of England, and in 1576 they erected the first
public theatre in Blackfriars. It will be understood, that
the servants of the Earl of Leicester were a company under

jutor of Sternhold in the old version of
the Psalms, and a contributor to the
Mirror of Magistrates.

[h] The Jocasta of Gascoyne, translated
with considerable freedom, in adding,
omitting, and transposing, from the
Phœnissæ of Euripides, was represented
at Gray's Inn in 1566. Warton, iv. 196.
Collier, iii. 7. Gascoyne had the assistance of two obscure poets in this play.

[i] Collier, iii. 2.

[k] Collier, i. 193, et post, iii. 24. Of
these fifty-two plays eighteen were upon

classical subjects, historical or fabulous,
twenty-one taken from modern history
or romance, seven may by their titles,
which is a very fallible criterion, be comedies or farces from real life, and six
may, by the same test, be moralities. It
is possible, as Mr. C. observes, that some
of these plays, though no longer extant
in their integrity, may have formed the
foundation of others ; and the titles of a
few in the list countenance this supposition.

his protection; as we apply the word, Her Majesty's Servants, at this day, to the performers of Drury Lane.[m]

27. As we come down towards 1580, a few more plays are extant. Among these may be mentioned the Promos Plays of Whetstone and others. and Cassandra of Whetstone, on the subject which Shakspeare, not without some retrospect to his predecessor, so much improved in Measure for Measure.[n] But in these early dramas there is hardly anything to praise; or, if they please us at all, it is only by the broad humour of their comic scenes. There seems little reason, therefore, for regretting the loss of so many productions, which no one contemporary has thought worthy of commendation. Sir Philip Sidney, writing about 1583, treats our English stage with great disdain. His censures, indeed, fall chiefly on the neglect of the classical unities, and on the intermixture of kings with clowns.[o] It is amusing to reflect that this contemptuous reprehension of the English theatre (and he had spoken in as disparaging terms of our general poetry) came from the pen of Sidney, when Shakspeare had just arrived at manhood. Had he not been so prematurely cut off, what would have been the transports of that noble spirit which the ballad of Chevy Chase could ' stir as with the sound of a trumpet,' in reading the Faery Queen or Othello!

28. A better era commenced not long after, nearly coincident with the rapid development of genius in other Marlowe and his contemporaries. departments of poetry. Several young men of talent appeared, Marlowe, Peele, Greene, Lily, Lodge, Kyd, Nash, the precursors of Shakspeare, and real founders, as they may in some respects be called, of the English drama.

---

[m] See Mr. Collier's excellent History of Dramatic Poetry to the Time of Shakspeare, vol. i., which having superseded the earlier works of Langbaine, Reid, and Hawkins, so far as this period is concerned, it is superfluous to quote them.

[n] Promos and Cassandra is one of the Six Old Plays reprinted by Steevens. Shakspeare found in it not only the main story of Measure for Measure, which was far from new, and which he felicitously altered, by preserving the chastity of Isabella, but several of the minor circumstances and names, unless even these are to be found in the novels, from which all the dramatists ultimately derived their plot.

[o] ' Our tragedies and comedies, not without cause, are cried out against, observing rules neither of honest civility nor skilful poetry;' and proceeds to ridicule their inconsistencies and disregard to time and place. Defence of Poesy.

Sackville's Gorboduc is in blank verse, though of bad and monotonous construction; but his first followers wrote, as far as we know, either in rhyme or in prose.[p] In the tragedy of Tamburlaine, referred by Mr. Collier to 1586, and the production wholly or principally of Marlowe,[q] a better kind of blank verse is first employed; the lines are interwoven, the occasional hemistich and redundant syllables break the monotony of the measure, and give more of a colloquial spirit to the dialogue. Tamburlaine was ridiculed on account of its inflated style. The bombast, however, which is not so excessive as has been alleged, was thought appropriate to such oriental tyrants. This play has more spirit and poetry than any which, upon clear grounds, can be shown to have preceded it. We find also more action on the stage, a shorter and more dramatic dialogue, a more figurative style, with a far more varied and skilful versification.[r]

Tamburlaine.

If Marlowe did not re-establish blank verse, which is difficult to prove, he gave it at least a variety of cadence, and an easy adaptation of the rhythm to the sense, by which it instantly became in his hands the finest instrument that the tragic poet has ever employed for his purpose, less restricted than that of the Italians, and falling occasionally almost into numerous prose, lines of fourteen syllables being very common in all our old dramatists, but regular and harmonious at other times as the most accurate ear could require.

Blank verse of Marlowe.

29. The savage character of Tamburlaine, and the want of all interest as to every other, render this tragedy a failure in comparison with those which speedily followed from the pen of Christopher Marlowe. The first

Marlowe's Jew of Malta,

---

[p] It may be a slight exception to this, that some portions of the second part of Whetstone's Promos and Cassandra are in blank verse. This play is said never to have been represented. Collier, iii. 64.

[q] Nash has been thought the author of Tamburlaine by Malone, and his inflated style, in pieces known to be his, may give some countenance to this hypothesis. It is mentioned, however, as 'Marlowe's Tamburlaine' in the contemporary diary of Henslow, a manager or proprietor of a theatre, which is preserved at Dulwich College. Marlowe and Nash are allowed to have written 'Dido Queen of Carthage,' in conjunction. Mr. Collier has produced a body of evidence to show that Tamburlaine was written, at least principally, by the former, which leaves no room, as it seems, for further doubt. Vol. iii. p. 113.

[r] Shakspeare having turned into ridicule a passage or two in Tamburlaine, the critics have concluded it to be a

two acts of the Jew of Malta are more vigorously conceived,
both as to character and circumstance, than any other
Elizabethan play, except those of Shakspeare; and perhaps
we may think that Barabas, though not the prototype of
Shylock, a praise of which he is unworthy, may have suggested some few ideas to the inventor. But the latter acts,
as is usual with our old dramatists, are a tissue of uninteresting crimes and slaughter.[s] Faustus is better known:
it contains nothing, perhaps, so dramatic as the first   *and Faustus.*
part of the Jew of Malta; yet the occasional glimpses of
repentance and struggles of alarmed conscience in the chief
character are finely brought in. It is full of poetical
beauties; but an intermixture of buffoonery weakens the
effect, and leaves it on the whole rather a sketch by a great
genius than a finished performance. There is an awful
melancholy about Marlowe's Mephistopheles, perhaps more
impressive than the malignant mirth of that fiend in the
renowned work of Goethe. But the fair form of Margaret is
wanting; and Marlowe has hardly earned the credit of having breathed a few casual inspirations into a greater mind
than his own.[t]

30. Marlowe's Life of Edward II., which was entered on
the books of the Stationers' Company in 1593, has   *His Edward*
been deemed by some the earliest specimen of the   *II.*
historical play founded upon English chronicles. Whether
this be true or not, and probably it is not, it is certainly by
far the best after those of Shakspeare.[u] And it seems probable that the old plays of the Contention of Lancaster and
York, and the True Tragedy of Richard Duke of York,

---

model of bad tragedy. Mr. Collier, iii.
115–126, has elaborately vindicated its
dramatic merits, though sufficiently
aware of its faults.

[s] '*Blood*,' says a late witty writer, 'is
made as light of in some of these old
dramas as *money* in a modern sentimental
comedy; and as *this* is given away till
it reminds us that it is nothing but
counters, so *that* is spilt till it affects us
no more than its representative, the
paint of the property-man in the
theatre.' Lamb's Specimens of Early
Dramatic Poets, i. 19.

[t] The German story of Faust is said

to have been published for the first time
in 1587. It was rapidly translated into
most languages of Europe. We need
hardly name the absurd supposition, that
Fust, the great printer, was intended.

[u] Collier observes, that 'the character
of Richard II. in Shakspeare seems
modelled in no slight degree upon that
of Edward II.' But I am reluctant to
admit that Shakspeare modelled his
characters by those of others; and it is
natural to ask whether there were not
an extraordinary likeness in the dispositions as well as fortunes of the two
kings.

which Shakspeare remodelled in the second and third parts
Plays whence of Henry VI., were in great part by Marlowe, though
Henry VI. was taken. Greene seems to put in for some share in their
composition.[x] These plays claim certainly a very low rank
among those of Shakspeare : his original portion is not inconsiderable ; but it is fair to observe, that some of the
passages most popular, such as the death of Cardinal Beau-
fort, and the last speech of the Duke of York, seem not to
be by his hand.

31. No one could think of disputing the superiority of
Marlowe to all his contemporaries of this early
Peele. school of the English drama. He was killed in a
tavern fray in 1593. There is more room for difference of
tastes as to the second place. Mr. Campbell has bestowed
high praises upon Peele. 'His David and Bethsabe is the
earliest fountain of pathos and harmony that can be traced
in our dramatic poetry. His fancy is rich and his feeling
tender ; and his conceptions of dramatic character have no
inconsiderable mixture of solid veracity and ideal beauty.
There is no such sweetness of versification and imagery to
be found in our blank verse anterior to Shakspeare.'[y]   I

---

[x] These old plays were reprinted by
Steevens in 1766. Malone, on a laborious comparison of them with the second
and third parts of Henry VI., has ascertained that 1771 lines in the latter plays
were taken from the former unaltered,
2373 altered by Shakspeare, while 1899
were altogether his own. It remains to
inquire, who are to claim the credit of
these other plays, so great a portion of
which has passed with the world for the
genuine work of Shakspeare. The solution seems to be given, as well as we
can expect, in a passage often quoted
from Robert Greene's Groat's Worth of
Wit, published not long before his death
in September, 1592. 'Yes,' says he,
addressing himself to some one who has
been conjectured to be Peele, but more
probably Marlowe, 'trust them (the
players) not, for there is an upstart
crow, beautified with our feathers, that
with his tyger's heart wrapped in a
player's hide, supposes he is as well able
to bombast out a blank verse as the best
of you ; and being an absolute Johannes
factotum, is, in his own conceit, the only

Shakescene in a country.' An allusion
is here manifest to the 'tyger's heart,
wrapt in a woman's hide,' which Shakspeare borrowed from the old play, The
Contention of the Houses, and which is
here introduced to hint the particular
subject of plagiarism that prompts the
complaint of Greene. The bitterness he
displays must lead us to suspect that he
had been one himself of those who were
thus preyed upon. But the greater part
of the plays in question is in the
judgment, I conceive, of all competent
critics, far above the powers either of
Greene or Peele, and exhibits a much
greater share of the spirited versification, called by Jonson the 'mighty line,'
of Christopher Marlowe. Malone, upon
second thoughts, gave both these plays
to Marlowe, having, in his dissertation
on the three parts of Henry VI.,
assigned one to Greene, the other to
Peele. None of the three parts have
any resemblance to the manner of
Peele.

[y] Specimens of English Poetry, i. 140.
Hawkins says of three lines in Peele's

must concur with Mr. Collier in thinking these compliments excessive. Peele has some command of imagery, but in every other quality it seems to me that he has scarce any claim to honour; and I doubt if there are three lines together in any of his plays that could be mistaken for Shakspeare's. His Edward I. is a gross tissue of absurdity, with some facility of language, but nothing truly good. It has also the fault of grossly violating historic truth, in a hideous misrepresentation of the virtuous Eleanor of Castile; probably from the base motive of rendering the Spanish nation odious to the vulgar. This play, which is founded on a ballad equally false, is referred to the year 1593. The versification of Peele is much inferior to that of Marlowe; and though sometimes poetical, he seems rarely dramatic.

32. A third writer for the stage in this period is Robert Greene, whose 'Friar Bacon and Friar Bungay' may probably be placed about the year 1590. This Greene. comedy, though savouring a little of the old school, contains easy and spirited versification, superior to Peele, and though not so energetic as that of Marlowe, reminding us perhaps more frequently of Shakspeare.[z] Greene succeeds pretty well in that florid and gay style, a little redundant in images, which Shakspeare frequently gives to his princes and courtiers, and which renders some unimpassioned scenes in his historic plays effective and brilliant. There is great talent shown, though upon a very strange canvas, in Greene's 'Looking Glass for London and England.' His angry allusion to Shakspeare's plagiarism is best explained by sup-

---

David and Bethsabe, that they contain a metaphor worthy of Æschylus:—

At him the thunder shall discharge his bolt;
And his fair spouse with bright and fiery wings
Sit ever burning on his hateful bones.

It may be rather Æschylean, yet I cannot much admire it. Peele seldom attempts such flights. 'His genius was not boldly original; but he had an elegance of fancy, a gracefulness of expression, and a melody of versification which, in the earlier part of his career, was scarcely approached.' Collier, iii. 191.

[z] 'Greene in facility of expression and in the flow of his blank verse is not to be placed below his contemporary Peele. His usual fault, more discoverable in his plays than in his poems, is an absence of simplicity; but his pedantic classical references, frequently without either taste or discretion, he had in common with the other scribbling scholars of the time. It was Shakspeare's good fortune to be in a great degree without the knowledge, and therefore, if on no other account, without the defect.' Collier, iii. 153. Tieck gives him credit for 'a happy talent, a clear spirit, and a lively imagination, which characterise all his writings.' Collier, iii. 148.

posing that he was himself concerned in the two old plays
which had been converted into the second and third parts of
Henry VI.[a] In default of a more probable claimant, I have
sometimes been inclined to assign the first part of Henry VI.
to Greene. But those who are far more conversant with the
style of our dramatists do not suggest this; and we are
evidently ignorant of many names, which might have ranked
not discreditably by the side of these tragedians. The first
part, however, of Henry VI. is, in some passages, not unworthy of Shakspeare's earlier days, nor, in my judgment,
unlike his style; nor in fact do I know any one of his contemporaries who could have written the scene in the Temple
Garden. The light touches of his pencil have ever been
still more inimitable, if possible, than its more elaborate
strokes.[b]

33. We can hardly afford time to dwell on several other
Other writers of this age. writers anterior to Shakspeare. Kyd, whom Mr.
Collier places, as a writer of blank verse, next to
Marlowe,[c] Lodge,[d] Lily, Nash, Hughes, and a few more,

---

[a] Mr. Collier says, iii. 146, Greene
may possibly have had a hand in the
True History of Richard Duke of York.
But why possibly? when he claims it,
if not in express words, yet so as to
leave no doubt of his meaning. See the
note in p. 377.

In a poem written on Greene in 1594,
are these lines:—

Green is the pleasing object of an eye;
Greene pleased the eyes of all that look'd upon
    him;
Green is the ground of every painter's die;
Greene gave the ground to all that wrote upon
    him:
Nay, more, the men that so eclipsed his fame
Purloin'd his plumes; can they deny the same?

This seems an allusion to Greene's
own metaphor, and must be taken for a
covert attack on Shakspeare, who had
by this time pretty well eclipsed the
fame of Greene.

[b] 'These three gifted men' (Peele,
Greene, and Marlowe), says their late
editor, Mr. Dyce (Peele's Works, preface, xxxv.), 'though they often present
to us pictures that in design and colouring outrage the truth of nature, are the
earliest of our tragic writers who exhibit
any just delineation of the workings of
passion; and their language, though now

swelling into bombast, and now sinking
into meanness, is generally rich with
poetry, while their versification, though
somewhat monotonous, is almost always
flowing and harmonious. They as much
excel their immediate predecessors as
they are themselves excelled by Shakspeare.' Not quite as much.

[c] Collier, iii. 207. Kyd is author of
Jeronymo, and of the 'Spanish Tragedy,'
a continuation of the same story.
Shakspeare has selected some of their
aburdities for ridicule, and has left an
abundant harvest for the reader. Parts
of the Spanish Tragedy, Mr. C. thinks,
'are in the highest degree pathetic and
interesting.' This perhaps may be admitted, but Kyd is not, upon the whole,
a pleasing dramatist.

[d] Lodge, one of the best poets of the
age, was concerned, jointly with Greene,
in the Looking Glass for London. In
this strange performance the prophet
Hosea is brought to Nineveh, and the
dramatis personæ, as far as they are
serious, belong to that city; but all the
farcical part relates to London. Of
Lodge, Mr. C. says, that he is 'second
to Kyd in vigour and boldness of conception, but as a drawer of character, so

have all some degree of merit.   Nor do the anonymous
tragedies, some of which were formerly ascribed to Shakspeare, and which even Schlegel, with less acuteness of
criticism than is usual with him, has deemed genuine,
always want a forcible delineation of passion, and a vigorous
strain of verse, though not kept up for many lines.   Among
these are specimens of the domestic species of tragic drama,
drawn probably from real occurrences, such as Arden of
Feversham and the Yorkshire Tragedy, the former of which
especially has very considerable merit.   Its author, I believe, has not been conjectured ; but it may be referred to
the last decad of the century.[e]   Another play of the same
kind, A Woman killed with Kindness, bears the date of
1600, and is the earliest production of a fertile   Heywood's
dramatist, Thomas Heywood.   The language is not   Woman
killed with
much raised above that of comedy, but we can   Kindness.
hardly rank a tale of guilt, sorrow, and death, in that dramatic category.   It may be read with interest and approbation at this day, being quite free from extravagance either
in manner or language, the besetting sin of our earlier dramatists, and equally so from buffoonery.   The subject resembles that of Kotzebue's drama, The Stranger, but is
managed with a nobler tone of morality.   It is true that
Mrs. Frankfort's immediate surrender to her seducer, like
that of Beaumelé in the Fatal Dowry, makes her contemptible ; but this, though it might possibly have originated in

---

essential a part of dramatic poetry, he
unquestionably has the advantage.'—
iii. 214.

[e] The murder of Arden of Feversham
occurred under Edward VI., but the
play was published in 1592.   The impression made by the story must have
been deep, to produce a tragedy so long
afterwards.   It is said by Mr. Collier,
that Professor Tieck has inclined to
think Arden of Feversham a genuine
work of Shakspeare.   I cannot but venture to suspect that, if this distinguished
critic were a native, he would discern
such differences of style as render this
hypothesis improbable.   The speeches
in Arden of Feversham have spirit and
feeling, but there is none of that wit,
that fertility of analogical imagery,

which the worst plays of Shakspeare
display.   The language is also more
plain and perspicuous than we ever find
in him, especially on a subject so full of
passion.   Mr. Collier discerns the hand
of Shakspeare in the Yorkshire Tragedy,
and thinks that 'there are some speeches
which could scarcely have proceeded
from any other pen.'   Collier, iii. 51.
It was printed with his name in 1608 ;
but this, which would be thought good
evidence in most cases, must not be held
sufficient.   It is impossible to explain
the grounds of internal persuasion in
these nice questions of æsthetic criticism ; but I cannot perceive the hand of
Shakspeare in any of the anonymous
tragedies.

the necessity created by the narrow limits of theatrical time, has the good .ffect of preventing that sympathy with her guilt which is reserved for her penitence.

34. Of William Shakspeare,[f] whom, through the mouths of those whom he has inspired to body forth the modifications of his immense mind, we seem to know better than any human writer, it may be truly said that we scarcely know any thing. We see him, so far as we do see him, not in himself, but in a reflex image from the objectivity in which he was manifested : he is Falstaff, and Mercutio, and Malvolio, and Jaques, and Portia, and Imogen, and Lear, and Othello ; but to us he is scarcely a determined person, a substantial reality of past time, the man Shakspeare. The two greatest names in poetry are to us little more than names. If we are not yet come to question his unity, as we do that of ' the blind old man of Scio's rocky isle,' an improvement in critical acuteness doubtless reserved for a distant posterity, we as little feel the power of identifying the young man who came up from Stratford, was afterwards an indifferent player in a London theatre, and retired to his native place in middle life, with the author of Macbeth and Lear, as we can give a distinct historic personality to Homer. All that insatiable curiosity and unwearied diligence have hitherto detected about Shakspeare serves rather to disappoint and perplex us than to furnish the slightest illustration of his character. It is not the register of his baptism, or the draft of his will, or the orthography of his name that we seek. No letter of his writing, no record of his conversation, no character of him drawn with any fulness by a contemporary has been produced.[g]

[f] Though I shall not innovate in a work of this kind, not particularly relating to Shakspeare, I must observe, that Sir Frederick Madden has offered very specious reasons (in the Archæologia, vol. xxvi.) for believing that the poet and his family spelt their name *Shakspere*, and that there are, at least, no exceptions in his own autographs, as has commonly been supposed. A copy of Florio's translation of Montaigne, a book which he had certainly read (see

Malone's note on Tempest, act ii. scene 1), has been lately discovered with the name *W. Shakspere* clearly written in it, and there seems no reason to doubt that it is a genuine signature This book has, very properly, been placed in the British Museum, among the choice κειμηλια of that repository.

[g] [I am not much inclined to qualify this paragraph in consequence of the petty circumstances relating to Shakspeare which have been lately brought

35. It is generally supposed that he settled in London about 1587, being then twenty-three years old. His first writings for the stage. For some time afterwards we cannot trace him distinctly. Venus and Adonis, published in 1593, he describes in his dedication to Lord Southampton, as ‘ the first heir of his invention.’ It is, however, certain that it must have been written some years before, unless we take these words in a peculiar sense, for Greene, in his Groat’s Worth of Wit, 1592, alludes, as we have seen, to Shakspeare as already known among dramatic authors. It appears by this passage, that he had converted the two plays on the wars of York and Lancaster into what we read as the second and third parts of Henry VI. What share he may have had in similar repairs of the many plays then represented cannot be determined. It is generally believed that he had much to do with the tragedy of Pericles, which is now printed among his works, and which external testimony, though we should not rely too much on that as to Shakspeare, has assigned to him ; but the play is full of evident marks of an inferior hand.[h] Its date is unknown ; Drake supposes it to have been his earliest work, rather from its inferiority than on any other ground. Titus Andronicus is now by common consent denied to be, in any sense, a production of Shakspeare ; very few passages, I should think not one, resemble his manner.[i]

36. The Comedy of Errors may be presumed, by an

---

to light, and which rather confirm than otherwise what I have said. But I laud the labours of Mr. Collier, Mr. Hunter, and other collectors of such crumbs; though I am not sure that we should not venerate Shakspeare as much if they had left him undisturbed in his obscurity. To be told that he played a trick to a brother player in a licentious amour, or that he died of a drunken frolic, as a stupid vicar of Stratford recounts (long after the time) in his diary, does not exactly inform us of the man who wrote Lear. If there was a Shakspeare of earth, as I suspect, there was also one of heaven ; and it is of him that we desire to know some'hing.—1842.]

[h] Malone, in a dissertation on the tragedy of Pericles, maintained that it was altogether an early work of Shakspeare. Steevens contended that it was a production of some older poet, improved by him ; and Malone had the candour to own that he had been wrong. The opinion of Steevens is now general. Drake gives the last three acts and part of the former, to Shakspeare ; but I can hardly think his share is by any means so large.

[i] Notwithstanding this internal evidence, Meres, so early as 1598, enumerates Titus Andronicus among the plays of Shakspeare, and mentions no other but what is genuine. Drake, ii. 287. But, in criticism of all kinds, we must acquire a dogged habit of resisting testimony, when *res ipsa per se vociferatur* to the contrary.

allusion it contains, to have been written before the submis-

Comedy of Errors. sion of Paris to Henry IV. in 1594, which nearly put an end to the civil war.[k] It is founded on a very popular subject. This furnishes two extant comedies of Plautus, a translation from one of which, the Menæchmi, was represented in Italy earlier than any other play. It had been already, as Mr. Collier thinks, brought upon the stage in England; and another play, later than the Comedy of Errors, has been reprinted by Steevens. Shakspeare himself was so well pleased with the idea that he has returned to it in Twelfth Night. Notwithstanding the opportunity which these mistakes of identity furnish for ludicrous situations, and for carrying on a complex plot, they are not very well adapted to dramatic effect, not only from the manifest diffi-culty of finding performers quite alike, but because, were this overcome, the audience must be in as great embar-rassment as the represented characters themselves. In the Comedy of Errors there are only a few passages of a poetical vein, yet such perhaps as no other living dramatist could have written ; but the story is well invented and well man-aged ; the confusion of persons does not cease to amuse ; the dialogue is easy and gay beyond what had been hitherto heard on the stage ; there is little buffoonery in the wit, and no absurdity in the circumstances.

37. The Two Gentlemen of Verona ranks above the

Two Gentle-men of Verona. Comedy of Errors, though still in the third class of Shakspeare's plays. It was probably the first English comedy in which characters are drawn from social life, at once ideal and true ; the cavaliers of Verona and their lady-loves are graceful personages, with no transgression of the probabilities of nature ; but they are not exactly the real men and women of the same rank in England. The imagi-nation of Shakspeare must have been guided by some fa-miliarity with romances before it struck out this comedy. It contains some very poetical lines. Though these two plays could not give the slightest suspicion of the depth of thought which Lear and Macbeth were to display, it was already evident that the names of Greene, and even Marlowe,

---

[k] Act iii. scene 2. Some have judged the play from this passage to be written as early as 1591, but on precarious grounds.

would be eclipsed without any necessity for purloining their plumes.

38. Love's Labour Lost is generally placed, I believe, at the bottom of the list. There is indeed little in- Love's Labour Lost. terest in the fable, if we can say that there is any fable at all; but there are beautiful coruscations of fancy, more original conception of character than in the Comedy of Errors, more lively humour than in the Gentlemen of Verona, more symptoms of Shakspeare's future powers as a comic writer than in either. Much that is here but imperfectly developed came forth again in his later plays, especially in As you Like It, and Much Ado about Nothing. The Taming of the Shrew is the only play, except Henry VI., in Taming of the Shrew. which Shakspeare has been very largely a borrower. The best parts are certainly his, but it must be confessed that several passages for which we give him credit, and which are very amusing, belong to his unknown predecessor. The original play, reprinted by Steevens, was published in 1594. I do not find so much genius in the Taming of the Shrew as in Love's Labour Lost; but, as an entire play, it is much more complete.

39. The beautiful play of Midsummer Night's Dream is placed by Malone as early as 1592; its superiority Midsummer Night's Dream. to those we have already mentioned affords some presumption that it was written after them. But it evidently belongs to the earlier period of Shakspeare's genius; poetical, as we account it, more than dramatic; yet rather so because the indescribable profusion of imaginative poetry in this play overpowers our senses till we can hardly observe anything else, than from any deficiency of dramatic excellence. For in reality the structure of the fable, consisting as it does of three if not four actions, very distinct in their subjects and personages, yet wrought into each other without effort or confusion, displays the skill, or rather instinctive felicity, of Shakspeare, as much as in any play he has written. No preceding dramatist had attempted to fabricate a complex

---

[1] Mr. Collier thinks that Shakspeare had nothing to do with any of the scenes where Katherine and Petruchio are not introduced. The underplot resembles, he says, the style of Haughton, author of a comedy called Englishmen for my Money, iii. 78.

plot; for low comic scenes, interspersed with a serious action
upon which they have no influence, do not merit notice.
The Menæchmi of Plautus had been imitated by others as
well as by Shakspeare; but we speak here of original invention.

40. The Midsummer Night's Dream is, I believe, altogether original in one of the most beautiful conceptions that ever visited the mind of a poet, the fairy
machinery. A few before him had dealt in a vulgar and
clumsy manner with popular superstitions; but the sportive,
beneficent, invisible population of the air and earth, long
since established in the creed of childhood, and of those
simple as children, had never for a moment been blended
with 'human mortals' among the personages of the drama.
Lily's Maid's Metamorphosis is probably later than this play
of Shakspeare, and was not published till 1600.[m] It is
unnecessary to observe that the fairies of Spenser, as he has
dealt with them, are wholly of a different race.

*Its ma-
chinery.*

41. The language of Midsummer Night's Dream is equally
novel with the machinery. It sparkles in perpetual
brightness with all the hues of the rainbow, yet
there is nothing overcharged or affectedly ornamented.
Perhaps no play of Shakspeare has fewer blemishes, or is
from beginning to end in so perfect keeping; none in which
so few lines could be erased, or so few expressions blamed.
His own peculiar idiom, the dress of his mind, which began
to be discernible in the Two Gentlemen of Verona, is more
frequently manifested in the present play. The expression
is seldom obscure; but it is never in poetry, and hardly in
prose, the expression of other dramatists, and far less of the
people. And here, without reviving the debated question of
Shakspeare's learning, I must venture to think that he possessed rather more acquaintance with the Latin language
than many believe. The phrases, unintelligible and improper,
except in the sense of their primitive roots, which occur so
copiously in his plays, seem to be unaccountable on the supposition of absolute ignorance. In the Midsummer Night's
Dream these are much less frequent than in his later dramas.

Its language.

---

[m] Collier, iii. 185. Lily had, however, brought fairies, without making
them speak, into some of his earlier
plays. Ibid.

But here we find several instances. Thus, 'things base and vile, holding no *quantity*,' for value; rivers, that 'have over-borne their *continents*,' the *continente ripa* of Horace; '*compact* of imagination;' 'something of great *constancy*,' for consist-ency; 'sweet Pyramus *translated* there;' 'the law of Athens, which by no means we may *extenuate*.' I have considerable doubts whether any of these expressions would be found in the contemporary prose of Elizabeth's reign, which was less overrun by pedantry than that of her successor; but, could authority be produced for Latinisms so forced, it is still not very likely that one who did not understand their proper meaning would have introduced them into poetry. It would be a weak answer that we do not detect in Shakspeare any imitations of the Latin poets. His knowledge of the lan-guage may have been chiefly derived, like that of schoolboys, from the dictionary, and insufficient for the thorough appre-ciation of their beauties. But, if we should believe him well acquainted with Virgil or Ovid, it would be by no means surprising that his learning does not display itself in imita-tation. Shakspeare seems now and then to have a tinge on his imagination from former passages; but he never design-edly imitates, though, as we have seen, he has sometimes adopted. The streams of invention flowed too fast from his own mind to leave him time to accommodate the words of a foreign language to our own. He knew that to create would be easier, and pleasanter, and better.[n]

42. The tragedy of Romeo and Juliet is referred by Malone to the year 1596. Were I to judge by internal evidence, I should be inclined to date this play before the Midsummer Night's Dream; the great frequency of rhymes, the comparative absence of Latinisms, the want of that thoughtful philosophy, which, when it had once germinated in Shakspeare's mind, never ceased to display

Romeo and Juliet.

---

[n] The celebrated essay by Farmer on the learning of Shakspeare put an end to such notions as we find in Warburton and many of the older commentators, that he had imitated Sophocles, and I know not how many Greek authors. Those indeed who agree with what I have said in a former chapter as to the state of learning under Elizabeth will not think it probable that Shakspeare could have acquired any knowledge of Greek. It was not a part of such edu-cation as he received. The case of Latin is different: we know that he was at a grammar school, and could hardly have spent two or three years there without bringing away a certain portion of the language.

itself, and several of the faults that juvenility may best
explain and excuse, would justify this inference.

43. In one of the Italian novels to which Shakspeare had
Its plot. frequently recourse for his fable, he had the good
fortune to meet with this simple and pathetic
subject. What he found he has arranged with great skill.
The incidents in Romeo and Juliet are rapid, various, un-
intermitting in interest, sufficiently probable, and tending
to the catastrophe. The most regular dramatist has hardly
excelled one writing for an infant and barbarian stage. It
is certain that the observation of the unity of time, which
we find in this tragedy, unfashionable as the name of unity
has become in our criticism, gives an intenseness of interest
to the story, which is often diluted and dispersed in a dramatic
history. No play of Shakspeare is more frequently represented, or honoured with more tears.

44. If from this praise of the fable we pass to other
Its beauties considerations, it will be more necessary to modify
and blem-
ishes. our eulogies. It has been said above of the Midsummer Night's Dream, that none of Shakspeare's plays have
fewer blemishes. We can by no means repeat this commendation of Romeo and Juliet. It may be said rather that few,
if any, are more open to reasonable censure ; and we are
almost equally struck by its excellencies and its defects.

45. Madame de Staël has truly remarked, that in Romeo
and Juliet we have, more than any other tragedy, the mere
passion of love; love, in all its vernal promise, full of hope
and innocence, ardent beyond all restraint of reason, but
tender as it is warm. The contrast between this impetuosity
of delirious joy, in which the youthful lovers are first displayed, and the horrors of the last scene, throws a charm of
deep melancholy over the whole. Once alone each of them,
in these earlier moments, is touched by a presaging fear; it
passes quickly away from them, but is not lost on the reader.
To him there is a sound of despair in the wild effusions of
their hope, and the madness of grief is mingled with the
intoxication of their joy. And hence it is that, notwithstanding its many blemishes, we all read and witness this
tragedy with delight. It is a symbolic mirror of the fearful
realities of life, where ' the course of true love ' has so often

' not run smooth,' and moments of as fond illusion as beguiled
the lovers of Verona have been exchanged, perhaps as rapidly,
not indeed for the dagger and the bowl, but for the many-
headed sorrows and sufferings of humanity.

46. The character of Romeo is one of excessive tenderness.   His first passion for Rosaline, which no   The cha-
vulgar poet would have brought forward, serves to   racters.
display a constitutional susceptibility.   There is indeed so
much of this in his deportment and language, that we
might be in some danger of mistaking it for effeminacy, if
the loss of his friend had not aroused his courage.   It seems
to have been necessary to keep down a little the other
characters, that they might not overpower the principal one ;
and though we can by no means agree with Dryden, that if
Shakspeare had not killed Mercutio, Mercutio would have
killed him, there might have been some danger of his killing
Romeo.   His brilliant vivacity shows the softness of the other
a little to a disadvantage.   Juliet is a child, whose intoxication in loving and being loved whirls away the little reason
she may have possessed.   It is however impossible, in my
opinion, to place her among the great female characters of
Shakspeare's creation.

47. Of the language of this tragedy what shall we say ?
It contains passages that every one remembers,   The lan-
that are among the nobler efforts of Shakspeare's   guage.
poetry, and many short and beautiful touches of his pro-
verbial sweetness.   Yet, on the other hand, the faults are in
prodigious number.   The conceits, the phrases that jar on
the mind's ear, if I may use such an expression, and interfere
with the very emotion the poet would excite, occur at least
in the first three acts without intermission.   It seems to
have formed part of his conception of this youthful and
ardent pair, that they should talk irrationally.   The extravagance of their fancy, however, not only forgets reason,
but wastes itself in frigid metaphors and incongruous conceptions ; the tone of Romeo is that of the most bombastic
common-place of gallantry, and the young lady differs only
in being one degree more mad.   The voice of virgin love
has been counterfeited by the authors of many fictions : I
know none who have thought the style of Juliet would

represent it.   Nor is this confined to the happier moments
of their intercourse.   False thoughts and misplaced phrases
deform the whole of the third act.   It may be added that, if
not dramatic propriety, at least the interest of the character,
is affected by some of Juliet's allusions.   She seems indeed
to have profited by the lessons and language of her venerable
guardian; and those who adopt the edifying principle of
deducing a moral from all they read, may suppose that
Shakspeare intended covertly to warn parents against the
contaminating influence of such domestics.   These censures
apply chiefly to the first three acts; as the shadows deepen
over the scene, the language assumes a tone more proportionate to the interest; many speeches are exquisitely beautiful;
yet the tendency to quibbles is never wholly eradicated.

48. The plays we have hitherto mentioned, to which one
Second or two more might be added, belong to the
period of
Shakspeare. earlier class, or as we might say, to his first
manner.   In the second period of his dramatic life, we should
place his historical plays, and such others as were written
before the end of the century or perhaps before the death
of Elizabeth.   The Merchant of Venice, As You Like It,
and Much Ado about Nothing, are among these.   The
versification in these is more studied, the pauses more
artificially disposed, the rhymes, though not quite abandoned,
become less frequent, the language is more vigorous and
elevated, the principal characters are more strongly marked,
more distinctly conceived, and framed on a deeper insight
into mankind.   Nothing in the earlier plays can be compared,
in this respect, with the two Richards, or Shylock, or Falstaff,
or Hotspur.

49. Many attempts had been made to dramatise the
The histo- English chronicles, but, with the single exception
rical plays. of Marlowe's Edward II., so unsuccessfully, that
Shakspeare may be considered as almost an original occupant
of the field.   He followed historical truth with considerable
exactness; and, in some of his plays, as in that of Richard
II., and generally in Richard III. and Henry VIII., admitted
no imaginary personages, nor any scenes of amusement.   The
historical plays have had a great effect on Shakspeare's
popularity.   They have identified him with English feelings

in English hearts, and are very frequently read more in childhood, and consequently better remembered than some of his superior dramas. And these dramatic chronicles borrowed surprising liveliness and probability from the national character and form of government. A prince, and a courtier, and a slave, are the stuff on which the historic dramatist would have to work in some countries; but every class of freemen, in the just subordination without which neither human society, nor the stage, which should be its mirror, can be more than a chaos of huddled units, lay open to the selection of Shakspeare. What he invented is as truly English, as truly historical, in the large sense of moral history, as what he read.

50. The Merchant of Venice is generally esteemed the best of Shakspeare's comedies. This excellent play is referred to the year 1597.° In the management of the plot, which is sufficiently complex without the slightest confusion or incoherence, I do not conceive that it has been surpassed in the annals of any theatre. Yet there are those who still affect to speak of Shakspeare as a barbarian; and others who, giving what they think due credit to his genius, deny him all judgment and dramatic taste. A comparison of his works with those of his contemporaries, and it is surely to them that we should look, will prove that his judgment is by no means the least of his rare qualities. This is not so remarkable in the mere construction of his fable, though the present comedy is absolutely perfect in that point of view, and several others are excellently managed, as in the general keeping of the characters, and the choice of incidents. If Shakspeare is sometimes extravagant, the Marstons and Middletons are seldom otherwise. The variety of characters in the Merchant of Venice, and the powerful delineation of

Merchant of Venice.

° Meres, in his Palladis Tamia, or Wit's Treasury, 1598, has a passage of some value in determining the age of Shakspeare's plays, both by what it contains and by what it omits. 'As Plautus and Seneca are accounted the best for comedy and tragedy among the Latins, so Shakspeare among the English is the most excellent in both kinds for the stage; for comedy witness his Gentlemen of Verona, his Errors, his Love's Labour Lost, his Love's Labour Won [the original appellation of All's Well that Ends Well], his Midsummer Night's Dream, and his Merchant of Venice; for tragedy, his Richard II., his Richard III., Henry IV., King John, *Titus Andronicus*, and his Romeo and Juliet.' Drake, ii. 287.

those upon whom the interest chiefly depends, the effective-
ness of many scenes in representation, the copiousness of the
wit, and the beauty of the language, it would be superfluous
to extol; nor is it our office to repeat a tale so often told
as the praise of Shakspeare. In the language there is the
commencement of a metaphysical obscurity which soon became characteristic; but it is perhaps less observable than
in any later play.

51. The sweet and sportive temper of Shakspeare, though
it never deserted him, gave way to advancing years, and to
the mastering force of serious thought. What he read we
know but very imperfectly; yet in the last years of this
century, when five-and-thirty summers had ripened his
genius, it seems that he must have transfused much of the
wisdom of past ages into his own all-combining mind. In
As You Like several of the historical plays, in the Merchant of
It. Venice, and especially in As You Like It, the philosophic eye, turned inward on the mysteries of human nature,
is more and more characteristic; and we might apply to the
last comedy the bold figure that Coleridge has less appro-
priately employed as to the early poems, that 'the creative
power and the intellectual energy wrestle as in a war-
embrace.' In no other play, at least, do we find the brigLt
imagination and fascinating grace of Shakspeare's youth so
mingled with the thoughtfulness of his maturer age. This
play is referred with reasonable probability to the year 1600.
Few comedies of Shakspeare are more generally pleasing, and
its manifold improbabilities do not much affect us in perusal.
The brave, injured Orlando, the sprightly but modest Rosa-
lind, the faithful Adam, the reflecting Jaques, the serene and
magnanimous Duke, interest us by turns, though the play is
not so well managed as to condense our sympathy, and direct
it to the conclusion.

52. The comic scenes of Shakspeare had generally been
Jonson's drawn from novels, and laid in foreign lands. But
Every Man several of our earliest plays, as has been partly seen,
in his
Humour. delineate the prevailing manners of English life.
None had acquired a reputation which endured beyond their
own time till Ben Johnson in 1596 produced, at the age of
twenty-two, his first comedy, Every Man in his Humour; an

extraordinary monument of early genius, in what is seldom the possession of youth, a clear and unerring description of human character, various and not extravagant beyond the necessities of the stage. He had learned the principles of comedy, no doubt, from Plautus and Terence ; for they were not to be derived from the moderns at home or abroad ; but he could not draw from them the application of living passions and manners ; and it would be no less unfair, as Gifford has justly observed, to make Bobadil a copy of Thraso, than to deny the dramatic originality of Kitely.

53. Every Man in his Humour is perhaps the earliest of European domestic comedies that deserves to be remembered ; for even the Mandragora of Machiavel shrinks to a mere farce in comparison.[p] A much greater master of comic powers than Johnson was indeed his contemporary, and, as he perhaps fancied, his rival ; but, for some reason, Shakspeare had never yet drawn his story from the domestic life of his countrymen.   Johnson avoided the common defect of the Italian and Spanish theatre, the sacrifice of all other dramatic objects to one only, a rapid and amusing succession of incidents : his plot is slight and of no great complexity ; but his excellence is to be found in the variety of his characters, and in their individuality very clearly defined with little extravagance.

---

[p] This would not have been approved by a modern literary historian.   Quelle était, avant que Molière parut et même de son temps, la comédie moderne comparable à la Calandria, à la Mandragore, aux meilleures pièces de l'Arioste, à celles de l'Aretin, du Cecchi, du Lasca, du Bentivoglio, de Francesco d'Ambra, et de tant d'autres ? Ginguéné, vi. 316. This comes of deciding before we know any thing of the facts. Gingnéné might possibly be able to read English, but certainly had no sort of acquaintance with the English theatre.   I should have no hesitation in replying that we could produce at least forty comedies, before the age of Molière, superior to the best of those he has mentioned, and perhaps three times that number as good as the worst.

CHAPTER VII.

HISTORY OF POLITE LITERATURE IN PROSE, FROM 1550 TO 1600.

Sect. I.

Style of best Italian Writers—Those of France—England.

1. I AM not aware that we can make any great distinction
Italian   in the character of the Italian writers of this and
writers.   the preceding period, though they are more numerous in the present. Some of these have been already
mentioned on account of their subjects. In point of style,
            to which we now chiefly confine ourselves, Casa is
Casa.   esteemed among the best.[a] The Galateo is certainly
diffuse, but not so languid as some contemporary works;
nor do we find in it, I think, so many of the inversions which
are common blemishes in the writings of this age.   The prose
            of Tasso is placed by Corniani almost on a level with
Tasso.   his poetry for beauty of diction. 'We find in it,' he
says, 'dignity; rhythm, elegance, and purity without affectation, and perspicuity without vulgarity. He is never trifling
or verbose, like his contemporaries of that century; but
endeavours to fill every part of his discourses with meaning'[b]
These praises may be just, but there is a tediousness in the
moral essays of Tasso, which, like many other productions of
that class, assert what the reader has never seen denied, and
distinguish what he is in no danger of confounding.

---

[a] Corniani, v. 174.   Parini called the Galateo, Capo d' opera di nostra lingua.
[b] Corniani, vi. 240.

2. Few Italian writers, it is said by the editors of the voluminous Milan collection, have united equally Firenzuola. with Firenzuola the most simple naïveté to a Character of Italian delicate sweetness that diffuses itself over the prose. heart of the reader. His dialogue on the Beauty of Women is reckoned one of the best of his works. It is diffuse, but seems to deserve the praise bestowed upon its language. His translation of the Golden Ass of Apuleius is read with more pleasure than the original. The usual style of Italian prose in this, accounted by some its best age, is elaborate, ornate, yet not to excess, with a rhythmical structure apparently much studied, very rhetorical, and for the most part trivial, as we should now think, in its matter. The style of Machiavel, to which, perhaps, the reader's attention was not sufficiently called while we were concerned with his political philosophy, is eminent for simplicity, strength, and clearness. It would not be too much to place him at the head of the prose writers of Italy. But very few had the good taste to emulate so admirable a model. 'They were apt to presume,' says Corniani, 'that the spirit of good writing consisted in the artificial employment of rhetorical figures. They hoped to fertilise a soil barren of argument by such resources. They believed that they should become eloquent by accumulating words upon words, and phrases upon phrases, hunting on every side for metaphors, and exaggerating the most trifling theme by frigid hyperboles.' [c]

3. A treatise on Painting, by Raffaelle Borghino, published in 1584, called Il Riposo, is highly praised Italian for its style by the Milan editors; but it is difficult letter-writers. for a foreigner to judge so correctly of these delicacies of language, as he may of the general merits of composition. They took infinite pains with their letters, great numbers of which have been collected. Those of Annibal Caro are among the best known; [d] but Pietro Aretino,

---

[c] Corniani, vi. 52.

[d] It is of no relevancy to the history of literature, but in one of Caro's letters to Bernardo Tasso, about 1544, he censures the innovation of using the third person in addressing a correspondent.

Tutto questo secolo (dice Monsignor de la Casa) è adulatore; ognuno che scrive dà de le signorie; ognuno, a chi si scrive le vuole; e non pure i grandi, ma i mezzani e i plebei quasi aspirano a questi gran nomi, e si tengono anco per affronto,

Paolo Manuzio, and Bonfadio are also celebrated for their style. The appearance of labour and affectation is still less pleasing in epistolary correspondence than in writings more evidently designed for the public eye; and there will be found abundance of it in these Italian writers, especially in addressing their superiors. Cicero was a model perpetually before their eyes, and whose faults they did not perceive. Yet perhaps the Italian writings of this period, with their flowing grace, are more agreeable than the sententious antitheses of the Spaniards. Both are artificial, but the efforts of the one are bestowed on diction and cadence, those of the other display a constant strain to be emphatic and profound. What Cicero was to Italy, Seneca became to Spain.

4. An exception to the general character of diffuseness is found in the well-known translation of Tacitus by Davanzati. This, it has often been said, he has accomplished in fewer words than the original. No one, for the most part, inquires into the truth of what is confidently said, even where it is obviously impossible. But whoever knows the Latin and Italian languages must know that a translation of Tacitus into Italian cannot be made in fewer words. It will be found, as might be expected, that Davanzati has succeeded by leaving out as much as was required to compensate the difference that articles and auxiliary verbs made against him. His translation is also censured by Corniani,[e] as full of obsolete terms and Florentine vulgarisms.

Davanzati's Tacitus.

5. We can place under no better head than the present that lighter literature which, without taking the form of romance, endeavours to amuse the reader by fanciful invention and gay remark. The Italians have much of this; but it is beyond our province to enumerate

Jordano Bruno.

---

se non gli hanno, e d' errore son notati quelli, che non gli danno. Cosa, che a me pare stranissima e stomachosa, che habbiamo a parlar con uno, come se fosse un altro, e tutta via in astratto, quasi con la idea di colui, con chi si parla, non con la persona sua propria. Pure l' abuso è già fatto, ed è generale, &c., lib. i. p. 122 (edit. 1581). I have found the third person used as early as a letter of Paolo Manuzio to Castelvetro in 1543; but where there was any intimacy with an equal rank, it is not much employed; nor is it always found in that age in letters to men of very high rank from their inferiors.

[e] vi. 58.

productions of no great merit or renown.   Jordano Bruno's
celebrated Spaccio della Bestia Trionfante is one of this
class.   Another of Bruno's light pieces is entitled, La
Cabala del Cavallo Pegaseo, con l' Aggiunta de l' Asino
Cillenico.   This has more profaneness in it than the
Spaccio della Bestia.   The latter, as is well-known, was
dedicated to Sir Philip Sidney ; as was also another little
piece, Gli Eroici Furori.   In this he has a sonnet addressed to the English ladies ; ' Dell' Inghilterra o Vaghe
Ninfe e Belle ;' but ending, of course, with a compliment,
somewhat at the expense of these beauties, to ' l' unica
Diana, Qual' è trà voi quel, che trà gl' astri il sole.'   It
had been well for Bruno if he had kept himself under
the protection of Diana.   The ' chaste beams of that
watery moon ' were less scorching than the fires of the Inquisition.

6. The French generally date the beginning of an easy
and natural style in their own language from the publication
of James Amyot's translation of Plutarch in 1559. French
Some earlier writers, however, have been mentioned Amyot.
in another place, and perhaps some might have been added.
The French style of the sixteenth century is for the most
part diffuse, endless in its periods, and consequently negligent of grammar ; but it was even then lively and unaffected,
especially in narration, the memoirs of that age being still
read with pleasure.   Amyot, according to some, knew Greek
but indifferently, and was perhaps on that account a better
model of his own language ; but if he did not always render
the meaning of Plutarch, he has made Plutarch's reputation,
and that, in some measure, of those who have taken Plutarch
for their guide.   It is well known how popular, more perhaps
than any other ancient, this historian and moralist has been in
France ; but it is through Amyot that he has been read.
The style of his translator, abounding with the native idiom,
and yet enriching the language, not at that time quite
copious enough for its high vocation in literature, with many
words which usage and authority have recognised, has
always been regarded with admiration, and by some, in the
prevalence of a less natural taste, with regret.   It is in French

prose what that of Marot is in poetry, and suggests, not an uncultivated simplicity, but the natural grace of a young person, secure of appearing to advantage, but not at bottom indifferent to doing so. This *naïveté*, a word which, as we have neither naturalised in orthography nor translated it, I must adopt, has ever since been the charm of good writing in France. It is, above all, the characteristic of one who may justly be called the disciple of Amyot, and who extols him above all other writers in the language—Montaigne. The fascination of Montaigne's manner is acknowledged by all who read him; and with a worse style, or one less individually adapted to his character, he would never have been the favourite of the world.[f]

7. In the essays of Montaigne a few passages occur of striking, though simple eloquence. But it must be admitted that the familiar idiomatic tone of Amyot was better fitted to please than to awe, to soothe the mind than to excite it, to charm away the cares of the moment than to impart a durable emotion. It was also so remote from the grand style which the writings of Cicero and the precepts of rhetoric had taught the learned world to admire, that we cannot wonder to find some who sought to model their French by a different standard. The only one of these, so far as I am aware, that falls within the sixteenth century is Du Vair, a man not less distinguished in public life than in literature, having twice held the seals of France under Louis XIII. ' He composed,' says a modern writer, ' many works in which he endeavoured to be eloquent; but he fell into the error, at that time so common, of too much wishing to Latinise our mother-tongue. He has been charged with fabricating words, such as *sponsion, cogitation, contumélie, dilucidité, contemnement,*'[g] &c. Notwithstanding these instances of bad taste which, when collected, seem more monstrous than as they are dispersed in his writings, Du Vair is not devoid of a flowing eloquence, which, whether perfectly congenial to the spirit of the language or not, has

Montaigne; Du Vair.

---

[f] See the articles on Amyot in Baillet, iv. 428. Bayle. La Harpe. Biogr. universelle. Préface aux Œuvres de Pascal, par Neufchâteau.

[g] Neufchâteau, in Préface à Pascal, p. 181. Bouterwek, v. 326, praises Du Vair, but he does not seem a favourite with his compatriot critics.

never wanted its imitators and admirers, and those very successful and brilliant, in French literature.[h] It was of course the manner of the bar and of the pulpit, after the pulpit laid aside its buffoonery, far more than that of Amyot and Montaigne.

8. It is not in my power to communicate much information as to the minor literature of France. One book may be named as being familiarly known, the Satire Menippée. The first edition bears the date of 1593, but is said not to have appeared till 1594, containing some allusions to events of that year. It is a ridicule on the proceedings of the League, who were then masters of Paris, and has commonly been ascribed to Leroy, canon of Rouen, though Passerat, Pithou, Rapin, and others, are said to have had some share in it. This book is historically curious, but I do not perceive that it displays any remarkable degree of humour or invention. The truth appears so much throughout, that it cannot be ranked among works of fiction.[i] _{Satire Menippée.}

9. In the scanty and obscure productions of the English press under Edward and Mary, or in the early years of Elizabeth, we should search, I conceive, in vain for any elegance or eloquence in writing. Yet there _{English writers.}

---

[h] Du Vair's Essay de la Constance et Consolations ès Malheurs publiques, of which the first edition is in 1594, furnishes some eloquent declamation in a style unlike that of Amyot. Repassez en votre mémoire l'histoire de toute l'antiquité; et quand vous trouverez un magistrat qui aura eu grand crédit envers un peuple, ou auprès d'un prince, et qui se sera voulu comporter vertueusement, dites hardiment: Je gage que cestui-ci a été banni, que cestui-ci a été tué, que cestui-ci a été empoisonné. A Athènes, Aristidès, Thémistoclès, et Phocion ; à Rome, infinis desquels je laisse les noms pour n'emplir le papier, me contentant de Camille, Scipion, et Ciceron pour l'antiquité, de Papinien pour les temps des empereurs romains, et de Boëce sous les Gots. Mais pourquoi le prenons-nous si haut ? Qui avons-nous vu de notre siècle tenir les sceaux de France, qui n'ait été mis en cette charge, pour en être déjetté avec contumélie ? Celui qui auroit vu M. le Chancelier Olivier, ou M. le Chancelier de l'Hospital, partir de la cour pour se retirer en leurs maisons, n'auroit jamais envié de tels honneurs, ni de tels charges. Imaginez-vous ces braves et vénérables vieillards, esquels reluisoient toutes sortes de vertus, et esquels entre une infinité de grandes parties vous n'eussiez sçu que choisir, remplis d'érudition, consommez ès affaires, amateurs de leur patrie, vraiment dignes de telles charges, si le siècle eust été digne d'eux. Après avoir longuement et fidèlement servi la patrie, on leur dresse des querelles d'Allemans, et de fausses accusations pour les bannir des affaires, ou plutôt pour en priver les affaires ; comme un navire agité de la conduite dè si sages et experts pilotes, afin de le faire plus aisément briser. p. 76 (edit. 1604).

[i] Biogr. univ. art. Leroy. Vigneul-Marville, i. 197.

is an increasing expertness and fluency; and the language insensibly rejecting obsolete forms, the manner of our writers is less uncouth, and their sense more pointed and perspicuous than before. Wilson's Art of Rhetorique is at least a proof that some knew the merits of a good style, if they did not yet bring their rules to bear on their own language. In Wilson's own manner there is nothing remarkable. The first book which can be worth naming at all is Ascham's Schoolmaster, published in 1570, and probably written some years before. Ascham is plain and strong in his style, but without grace or warmth; his sentences have no harmony of structure. He stands, however, as far as I have seen, above all other writers in the first half of the queen's reign. The best of these, like Reginald Scot, express their meaning well, but with no attempt at a rhythmical structure or figurative language; they are not bad writers, because their solid sense is aptly conveyed to the mind; but they are not good, because they have little selection of words, and give no pleasure by means of style. Puttenham is perhaps the first who wrote a well-measured prose; in his Art of English Poesie, published in 1586, he is elaborate, studious of elevated and chosen expression, and rather diffuse, in the manner of the Italians of the sixteenth century, who affected that fulness of style, and whom he probably meant to imitate. But in these later years of the queen, when almost every one was eager to be distinguished for sharp wit or ready learning, the want of good models of writing in our own language gave rise to some perversion of the public taste. Thoughts and words began to be valued, not as they were just and natural, but as they were removed from common apprehension, and most exclusively the original property of those who employed them. This in poetry showed itself in affected conceits, and in prose led to the pedantry of recondite mythological allusion, and of a Latinized phraseology.

Ascham.

10. The most remarkable specimen of this class is the Euphues of Lilly, a book of little value, but which deserves notice on account of the influence it is recorded to have had upon the court of Elizabeth; an influence also over the public taste, which is manifested in

Euphues of Lilly.

the literature of the age.[k]　It is divided into two parts, having separate titles; the first, 'Ephues, the Anatomy of Wit;' the second, 'Euphues and his England.'　This is a very dull story of a young Athenian, whom the author places at Naples in the first part, and brings to England in the second; it is full of dry commonplaces.　The style which obtained celebrity is antithetical and sententious to affectation; a perpetual effort with no adequate success rendering the book equally disagreeable and ridiculous, though it might not be difficult to find passages rather more happy and ingenious than the rest.　The following specimen is taken at random, and, though sufficiently characteristic, is perhaps rather unfavourable to Lilly, as a little more affected and empty than usual.

11. 'The sharpest north-east wind, my good Euphues, doth never last three days, tempests have but a short time, and the more violent the thunder is, the less permanent it is.　In the like manner it falleth out with jars and carpings of friends, which, begun in a moment, are ended in a moment. Necessary it is that among friends there should be some thwarting, but to continue in anger not convenient: the camel first troubleth the water before he drink; the frank-incense is burned before it smell; friends are tried before they be trusted, lest, shining like the carbuncle as though they had fire, they be found, being touched, to be without fire.　Friendship should be like the wine which Homer, much commending, calleth Maroneum, whereof one pint being mingled with five quarts of water, yet it keepeth his old strength and virtue, not to be qualified by any discurtesie. Where salt doth grow, nothing else can breed; where friendship is built, no offence can harbour.　Then, Euphues, let the falling out of friends be the renewing of affection, that in this we may resemble the bones of the lion, which, lying still and not moved, begin to rot, but, being stricken one against another, break out like fire, and wax green.'

12. 'The lords and gentlemen in that court (of Elizabeth) are also an example,' he says in a subsequent passage, 'for

---

[k] [Ephues, Mr. Collier thinks, was published early in 1579 ; Malone had a copy of that year, which he took to be the second edition.　Watts refers the first edition to 1580.—1842.]

all others to follow, true types of nobility, the only stay and staff of honour, brave courtiers, stout soldiers, apt to revel in peace and ride in war. In fight fierce, not dreading death; in friendship firm, not breaking promise; courteous to all that deserve well, cruel to none that deserve ill. Their adversaries they trust not — that showeth their wisdom; their enemies they fear not — that argueth their courage. They are not apt to proffer injuries, not fit to take any; loth to pick quarrels, but longing to revenge them.' Lilly pays great compliments to the ladies for beauty and modesty, and overloads Elizabeth with panegyric. 'Touching the beauty of this prince, her countenance, her majesty, her personage, I cannot think that it may be sufficiently commended, when it cannot be too much marvailed at; so that I am constrained to say, as Praxiteles did when he began to paint Venus and her son, who doubted whether the world could afford colours good enough for two such fair faces, and I whether my tongue can yield words to blaze that beauty, the perfection whereof none can imagine; which, seeing it is so, I must do like those that want a clear sight, who, being not able to discern the sun in the sky, are enforced to behold it in the water.'

13. It generally happens that a style devoid of simplicity, when first adopted, becomes the object of admiration for its imagined ingenuity and difficulty; and that of Euphues was well-adapted to a pedantic generation who valued nothing higher than far-fetched allusions and sententious precepts. All the ladies of the time, we are told, were Lilly's scholars; 'she who spoke not Euphuism being as little regarded at court as if she could not speak French.' 'His invention,' says one of his editors, who seems well worthy of him, ' was so curiously strung, that Elizabeth's court held his notes in admiration.'[m] Shakspeare has ridiculed this style in Love's Labour's Lost, and Jonson in Every Man out of his Humour; but, as will be seen on comparing the extracts I have given above with the language of Holofernes and Fastidious Brisk, a little in the tone of caricature, which Sir Walter Scott has heightened in one

Its popularity.

---

[m] In Biogr. Britannica, art. Lilly.

of his novels, till it bears no great resemblance to the real
Euphues. I am not sure that Shakspeare has never caught
the Euphuistic style, when he did not intend to make it ridiculous, especially in some speeches of Hamlet.

14. The first good prose writer, in any positive sense of
the word, is Sir Philip Sidney. The Arcadia ap- Sidney's
peared in 1590. It has been said of the author of this Arcadia.
famous romance, to which, as such, we shall have soon to
revert, that 'we may regard the whole literary character of that age as in some sort derived and descended from
him, and his work as the fountain from which all the
vigorous shoots of that period drew something of their
verdure and strength. It was indeed the Arcadia which
first taught to the contemporary writers that inimitable
interweaving and contexture of words, that bold and un-
shackled use and application of them, that art of giving to
language, appropriated to objects the most common and
trivial, a kind of acquired and adventitious loftiness, and to
diction in itself noble and elevated a sort of superadded
dignity, that power of ennobling the sentiments by the
language, and the language by the sentiments, which so
often excites our admiration in perusing the writers of the
age of Elizabeth.'[n] This panegyric appears a good deal too
strongly expressed, and perhaps the Arcadia had not this
great influence over the writers of the latter years of Elizabeth, whose *age* is, in the passage quoted, rather to indefi-
nitely mentioned. We are sometimes apt to mistake an
improvement springing from the general condition of the
public mind for imitation of the one writer who has first
displayed the effects of it. Sidney is, as I have said, our
earliest good writer; but if the Arcadia had never been published, I cannot believe that Hooker or Bacon would have
written worse.

15. Sidney's Defence of Poesie, as has been surmised by
his last editor, was probably written about 1581. I His Defence
should incline to place it later than the Arcadia ;[o] of Poesie.
and he may perhaps allude to himself where he says, 'some

---

[n] Retrospective Review, vol. ii. p. 42.
[o] [Zouch, quoted in Nicolas's edition
of Davison's Rhapsody, says the Arcadia
was written in 1580, and the Defence of
Poesie in 1582.—1847.]

have mingled matters heroical and pastoral.' This treatise is elegantly composed, with perhaps too artificial a construction of sentences; the sense is good, but the expression is very diffuse, which gives it too much the air of a declamation. The great praise of Sidney in this treatise is, that he has shown the capacity of the English language for spirit, variety, gracious idiom, and masculine firmness. It is worth notice that under the word poesy he includes such works as his own Arcadia, or in short any fiction. 'It is not rhyming and versing that maketh poesy; one may be a poet without versing, and a versifier without poetry.'

16. But the finest, as well as the most philosophical, writer of the Elizabethan period is Hooker. The first book of the Ecclesiastical Polity is at this day one of the masterpieces of English eloquence. His periods, indeed, are generally much too long and too intricate, but portions of them are often beautifully rhythmical; his language is rich in English idiom without vulgarity, and in words of a Latin source without pedantry; he is more uniformly solemn than the usage of later times permits, or even than writers of that time, such as Bacon, conversant with mankind as well as books, would have reckoned necessary; but the example of ancient orators and philosophers upon themes so grave as those which he discusses may justify the serious dignity from which he does not depart. Hooker is perhaps the first of such in England who adorned his prose with the images of poetry; but this he has done more judiciously and with more moderation than others of great name; and we must be bigots in Attic severity, before we can object to some of his grand figures of speech. We may praise him also for avoiding the superfluous luxury of quotation, a rock on which the writers of the succeeding age were so frequently wrecked.

Hooker.

17. It must be owned, however, by every one not absolutely blinded by a love of scarce books, that the prose literature of the queen's reign, taken generally, is but very mean. The pedantic Euphuism of Lilly overspread the productions which aspire to the praise of politeness; while the common style of most pieces of circumstance, like those of Martin Mar-prelate and his answerers

Character of Elizabethan writers.

(for there is little to choose in this respect between parties), or of such efforts at wit and satire as came from Greene, Nash, and other worthies of our early stage, is low, and, with few exceptions, very stupid ribaldry. Many of these have a certain utility in the illustration of Shakspeare and of ancient manners, which is neither to be overlooked in our contempt for such trash, nor to be mistaken for intrinsic merit. If it is alleged that I have not read enough of the Elizabethan literature to censure it, I must reply that, admitting my slender acquaintance with the numberless little books that some years since used to be sold at vast prices, I may still draw an inference from the inability of their admirers, or at least pur- chasers, to produce any tolerable specimens. Let the labours of Sir Egerton Brydges, the British Bibliographer, the Cen- sura Literaria, the Restituta, collections so copious, and formed with so much industry, speak for the prose of the queen's reign. I would again repeat, that good sense in plain language was not always wanting upon serious sub- jects; it is to polite writing alone that we now refer.[p] Spenser's dialogue upon the State of Ireland, the Brief Con- ceit of English Policy, and several other tracts, are written as such treatises should be written, but they are not to be counted in the list of eloquent or elegant compositions.

Sect. II.—On Criticism.

State of Criticism in Italy—Scaliger—Castelvetro—Salviati—In other
Countries—England.

18. In the earlier periods with which we have been conver- sant, criticism had been the humble handmaid of   State of the ancient writers, content to explain, or some-   criticism. times aspiring to restore, but seldom presuming to censure

---

[p] It is not probable that Brydges, a man of considerable taste and judgment, whatever some other pioneers in the same track may have been, would fail to select the best portions of the authors he has so carefully perused. And yet I would almost defy any one to produce five passages in prose from his numerous volumes, so far as the sixteenth century is concerned, which have any other merit than that of illustrating some matter of fact, or of amusing by their oddity. I have only noted, in traversing that long desert, two sermons by one Edward Dering, preached before the queen (Bri- tish Bibliographer, i. 260, and 560), which show considerably more vigour than was usual in the style of that age.

their text, or even to justify the superstitious admiration
that modern scholars felt for it.   There is, however, a different and far higher criticism, which excites and guides the
taste for truth and beauty in works of imagination ; a criticism to which even the great masters of language are responsible, and from which they expect their reward.   But of the
many who have sat in this tribunal, a small minority have
been recognised as rightful arbiters of the palms they pretend to confer, and an appeal to the public voice has as often
sent away the judges in dishonour as confirmed their decision.

19. It is a proof at least of the talents and courage which
Scaliger's
Poetics. distinguished Julius Cæsar Scaliger, that he, first
of all the moderns, (or, if there are exceptions, they
must be partial and inconsiderable,) undertook to reduce the
whole art of verse into system, illustrating and confirming
every part by a profusion of poetical literature.   His Poetics
form an octavo of about 900 pages, closely printed.   We can
give but a slight sketch of so extensive a work.   In the first
book he treats of the different species of poems ; in the
second, of different metres ; the third is more miscellaneous,
but relates chiefly to figures and turns of phrase ; the fourth
proceeds with the same subject, but these two are very comprehensive.   In the fifth we come to apply these principles to
criticism ; and here we find a comparison of various poets
one with another, especially of Homer with Virgil.   The
sixth book is a general criticism on all Latin poets, ancient
and modern.   The seventh is a kind of supplement to the
rest, and seems to contain all the miscellaneous matter that
he found himself to have omitted, together with some questions purposely reserved, as he tells us, on account of their
difficulty.   His comparison of Homer with Virgil is very
His prefer-
ence of
Virgil to
Homer. elaborate, extending to every simile or other passage
wherein a resemblance or imitation can be observed,
as well as to the general management of their epic
poems.   In this comparison he gives an invariable preference
to Virgil, and declares that the difference between these
poets is as great as between a lady of rank and the awkward
wife of a citizen.   Musæus he conceives to be far superior to
Homer, according to the testimony of antiquity ; and the

poem of Hero and Leander, which it does not occur to him to
suspect, is the only one in Greek that can be named in competition with Virgil, as he shows by comparison of the said
poem with the very inferior effusions of Homer. If Musæus
had written on the same subject as Homer, Scaliger does not
doubt but that he would have left the Iliad and Odyssey far
behind.[q]

20. These opinions will not raise Scaliger's taste very
greatly in our eyes. But it is not perhaps surprising that
an Italian, accustomed to the polished effeminacy of modern
verse, both in his language and in Latin, should be delighted with the poem of Hero and Leander, which has the
sort of charm that belongs to the statues of Bacchus, and
soothes the ear with voluptuous harmony, while it gratifies
the mind with elegant and pleasing imagery. It is not, however, to be taken for granted that Scaliger is always mistaken
in his judgments on particular passages in these greatest
of poets. The superiority of the Homeric poems is rather
incontestable in their general effect, and in the vigorous
originality of his verse, than in the selection of circumstance,
sentiment, or expression. It would be a sort of prejudice
almost as tasteless as that of Scaliger, to refuse the praise of
real poetic superiority to many passages of Virgil even as
compared with the Iliad, and far more with the Odyssey.
If the similes of the older poet are more picturesque
and animated, those of his imitator are more appropriate
and parallel to the subject. It would be rather whimsical to deny this to be a principal merit in a comparison.

---

[q] Quod si Musæus ea, quæ Homerus
scripsit, scripsisset, longè melius eum
scripturum fuisse judicamus.

The following is a specimen of Scaliger's style of criticism, chosen rather for
its shortness than any other cause:—

Ex vicesimo tertio Iliadis transtulit
versus illos in comparationem;

μάστιγι δ' αἰὲν ἔλαυνε κατωμαδόν· οἱ δέ οἱ ἵπποι
ὑψόσ' ἀειρέσθην ῥίμφα πρήσσοντε κέλευθον.

ἰσχνολογία multa; at in nostro animata
ratio;

Non tam præcipites bijugo certamine campum
Corripuere, ruuntque effusi carcere currus, &c.

Cum virtutibus horum carminum non
est conferenda jejuna illa humilitas; au-
dent præferre tamen grammatici teme-
rarii. Principio, nihil infelicius quam
μάστιγι αἰὲν ἔλαυνεν. Nam continuatio
et equorum diminuit opinionem, et con-
temptum facit verberum. Frequentibus
intervallis stimuli plus proficiunt. Quod
vero admirantur Græculi, pessimum est,
ὑψόσ' ἀειρέσθην. Extento namque, et, ut
milites loquantur, clauso cursu non sub-
siliente opus est. Quare divinus vir,
undantia lora; hoc enim-pro flagro, et
præcipites, et corripuere campum; idque
in præterito, ad celeritatem. Et ruunt,
quasi in diversa, adeo celeres sunt. Illa
vero supra omnem Homerum, proni in
verbera pendent. l. v. c. 3.

Scaliger sacrifices Theocritus as much as Homer at the altar of Virgil, and of course Apollonius has little chance with so partial a judge. Horace and Ovid, at least the latter, are also held by Scaliger superior to the Greeks whenever they come into competition.

21. In the fourth chapter of the sixth book, Scaliger criticises His critique the modern Latin poets, beginning with Marullus; on modern Latin poets. for, what is somewhat remarkable, he says that he had been unable to see the Latin poems of Petrarch. He rates Marullus low, though he dwells at length on his poetry, and thinks no better of Augurellus. The continuation of the Æneid by Maphæus he highly praises; Augerianus not at all; Mantuan has some genius, but no skill; and Scaliger is indignant that some ignorant schoolmasters should teach from him rather than from Virgil. Of Dolet he speaks with great severity; his unhappy fate does not atone for the badness of his verses in the eyes of so stern a critic; 'the fire did not purify him, but rather he polluted the fire.' Palingenius, though too diffuse, he accounts a good poet, and Cotta as an imitator of Catullus. Palearius aims rather to be philosophical than poetical. Castiglione is excellent: Bembus wants vigour, and sometimes elegance; he is too fond, as many others are, of trivial words. Of Politian Scaliger does not speak highly; he rather resembles Statius, has no grace, and is careless of harmony. Vida is reckoned, he says, by most the first poet of our time: he dwells, therefore, long on the Ars Poetica, and extols it highly, though not without copious censure. Of Vida's other poems the Bombyx is the best. Pontanus is admirable for every thing, if he had known where to stop. To Sannazarius and Fracastorius he assigns the highest praise of universal merit, but places the last at the head of the whole band.

22. The Italian language, like those of Greece and Rome, Critical influence of the academies. had been hitherto almost exclusively treated by grammarians, the superior criticism having little place even in the writings of Bembo. But soon after the middle of the century, the academies established in many cities, dedicating much time to their native language, began to point out beauties, and to animadvert on defects beyond the province of grammar. The enthusiastic admiration of

Petrarch poured itself forth in tedious commentaries upon every word of every sonnet; one of which, illustrated with the heavy prolixity of that age, would sometimes be the theme of a volume.   Some philosophical or theological pedants spiritualised his meaning, as had been attempted before : the absurd paradox of denying the real existence of Laura is a known specimen of their refinements.   Many wrote on the subject of his love for her; and a few denied its Platonic purity, which however the academy of Ferrara thought fit to decree.   One of the heretics, by name Cresci, ventured also to maintain that she was married ; but this probable hypothesis had not many followers.[r]

23. Meantime a multitude of new versifiers, chiefly close copyists of the style of Petrarch, lay open to the malice of their competitors, and the strictness of these self-chosen judges of song.   A critical controversy that sprang up about 1558 between two men of letters, very prominent in their age, Annibal Caro and Ludovico Castelvetro, is celebrated in the annals of Italian literature.   The former had published a canzone in praise of the king of France, beginning— *Dispute of Caro and Castelvetro.*

> Venite all' ombra de' gran gigli d' oro.

Castelvetro made some sharp animadversions on this ode, which seems really to deserve a good deal of censure, being in bad taste, turgid, and foolish.   Caro replied with the bitterness natural to a wounded poet.   In this there might be nothing unpardonable, and even his abusive language might be extenuated at least by many precedents in literary story ; but it is imputed to Caro that he excited the Inquisition against his suspected adversary.   Castelvetro had been of the celebrated academy of Modena, whose alleged inclination to Protestantism had proved, several years before, the cause of its dissolution, and of the persecution which some of its members suffered.   Castelvetro, though he had avoided censure at that time, was now denounced about 1560, when the persecution was hottest, to the Inquisition at Rome. He obeyed its summons, but soon found it prudent to make his escape, and reached Chiavenna in the Grison dominions.

---

[r] Crescimbeni, Storia della Volgar Poesia, ii. 295–309.

He lived several years afterwards in safe quarters, but seems
never to have made an open profession of the reformed faith.[s]

24. Castelvetro himself is one of the most considerable
among the Italian critics; but his taste is often
lost in subtilty, and his fastidious temper seems
to have sought nothing so much as occasion for censure.
His greatest work is a commentary upon the Poetics of
Aristotle; and it may justly claim respect, not only as the
earliest exposition of the theory of criticism, but for its
acuteness, erudition, and independence of reasoning, which
disclaims the Stagirite as a master, though the diffuseness
usual in that age, and the microscopic subtilty of the writer's
mind, may render its perusal tedious. Twining, one of the
best critics on the Poetics, has said, in speaking of the
commentaries of Castelvetro, and of a later Italian, Beni,
that 'their prolixity, their scholastic and trifling subtilty,
their useless tediousness of logical analysis, their microscopic
detection of difficulties invisible to the naked eye of common
sense, and their waste of confutation upon objections made
only by themselves, and made on purpose to be confuted—all
this, it must be owned, is disgusting and repulsive. It may
sufficiently release a commentator from the duty of reading
their works throughout, but not from that of examining and
consulting them; for in both these writers, but more especially in Beni, there are many remarks equally acute and
solid; many difficulties will be seen clearly stated, and sometimes successfully removed; many things usefully illustrated
and clearly explained; and if their freedom of censure is now
and then disgraced by a little disposition to cavil, this becomes almost a virtue when compared with the servile and
implicit admiration of Dacier.'[t]

Castelvetro on Aristotle's Poetics.

25. Castelvetro in his censorious humour did not spare
the greatest shades that repose in the laurel groves
of Parnassus, nor even those whom national pride
had elevated to a level with them. Homer is less blamed
than any other; but frequent shafts are levelled at Virgil,
and not always unjustly, if poetry of real genius could ever

Severity of Castelvetro's criticism.

    [s] Muratori, Vita del Castelvetro, 1727.   [t] Twining's Aristotle's Poetics, pre-
Crescimbeni, ii. 431.   Tiraboschi, x. 31.   face, p. 13.
Ginguéné, vii. 365.   Corniani, vi. 61.

bear the extremity of critical rigour, in which a monotonous and frigid mediocrity has generally found refuge.[u]   In
Dante he finds fault with the pedantry that has filled his
poems with terms of science unintelligible and unpleasing
to ignorant men, for whom poems are chiefly designed.[x]
Ariosto he charges with plagiarism, laying unnecessary stress
on his borrowing some stories, as that of Zerbino, from older
books ; and even objects to his introduction of false names of
kings, since we may as well invent new mountains and rivers,
as violate the known truths of history.[y]   This punctilious
cavil is very characteristic of Castelvetro.   Yet he sometimes
reaches a strain of philosophical analysis, and can by no
means be placed in the ranks of criticism below La Harpe, to
whom, by his attention to verbal minuteness, as well as by
the acrimony and self-confidence of his character, he may in
some measure be compared.

26. The Ercolano of Varchi, a series of dialogues, belongs
to the inferior but more numerous class of critical
writings, and after some general observations on
speech and language as common to men, turns to the favourite
theme of his contemporaries, their native idiom.   He is one
who with Bembo contends that the language should not be
called Italian, or even Tuscan, but Florentine, though admitting, what might be expected, that few agree to this except the natives of the city.   Varchi had written on the side
of Caro against Castelvetro, and, though upon the whole he
does not speak of the latter in the Ercolano with incivility,
cannot restrain his wrath at an assertion of the stern critic

marginal note: Ercolano of Varchi.

---

[u] One of his censures falls on the
minute particularity of the prophecy of
Anchises in the sixth Æneid ; peccando
Virgilio nella convenevolezza della pro-
fetia, la quale non suole condescendere a
nomi proprj, ne a cose tanto chiare e
particolari, ma, tacendo i nomi, suole
manifestare le persone, e le loro azioni
con figure di parlare alquanto oscure, si
come si vede nelle profetie della scrittura
sacra e nell' Alessandra di Licophrone,
p. 219 (edit. 1576). This is not unjust
in itself ; but Castelvetro wanted the
candour to own, or comprehensiveness to
perceive, that a prophecy of the Roman
history, couched in allegories, would have
had much less effect on Roman readers.

[x] Rendendola massimamente per questa via difficile ad intendere e meno
piacente a uomini idioti, per gli quali
principalmente si fanno i poemi. P. 597.
But the Comedy of Dante was about as
much written for *gl' idioti*, as the Principia of Newton.

[y] Castelvetro, p. 212. He objects on
the same principle to Giraldi Cinthio,
that he had chosen a subject for tragedy
which never had occurred, nor had been
reported to have occurred, and this of
royal persons unheard of before, il qual
peccato di prendere soggetto tale per
la tragedie non è da perdonare. P. 103.

of Modena, that there were as famous writers in the Spanish and French as in the Italian language. Varchi even denies that there was any writer of reputation in the first of these, except Juan de la Mena, and the author of Amadis de Gaul. Varchi is now chiefly known as the author of a respectable history, which, on account of its sincerity, was not published till the last century. The prejudice that, in common with some of his fellow-citizens, he entertained in favour of the popular idiom of Florence, has affected the style of his history, which is reckoned both tediously diffuse, and deficient in choice of phrase.[z]

27 Varchi, in a passage of the Ercolano having extolled Contro- Dante even in preference to Homer, gave rise to a versy about Dante. controversy wherein some Italian critics did not hesitate to point out the blemishes of their countryman. Bulgarini was one of these. Mazzoni undertook the defence of Dante in a work of considerable length, and seems to have poured out, still more abundantly than his contemporaries, a torrent of philosophical disquisition. Bulgarini replied again to him.[a] Crescimbeni speaks of these discussions as having been advantageous to Italian poetry.[b] The good effects, however, were not very sensibly manifested in the next century.

28. Florence was the chief scene of these critical wars. Academy of Florence. Cosmo I., the most perfect type of the prince of Machiavel, sought by the encouragement of literature in this its most innocuous province, as he did by the arts of embellishment, both to bring over the minds of his subjects a forgetfulness of liberty, and to render them unapt for its recovery. The Academy of Florence resounded with the praises of Petrarch. A few seceders from this body established the more celebrated academy Della Crusca, of the *sieve*, whose appellation bespoke the spirit in which they meant to sift all they undertook to judge. They were soon engaged, and with some loss to their fame, in a controversy upon the Gierusalemme Liberata. Camillo Pellegrino, a Neapolitan, had published in 1584 a dialogue on epic poetry, entitled Il Caraffa, wherein he gave the preference to Tasso above

---

[z] Corniani, vi. 43.   [b] Hist. della Volgar Poesia, ii. 282.
[a] Id. vi. 260. Ginguéné, vii. 491.

Ariosto.　Though Florence had no peculiar interest in this question, the academicians thought themselves guardians of the elder bard's renown; and Tasso had offended the citizens by some reflections in one of his dialogues.　The academy permitted themselves, in a formal reply, to place even Pulci and Boiardo above Tasso.　It was easier to vindicate Ariosto from some of Pellegrino's censures, which are couched in the pedantic tone of insisting with the reader that he ought not to be pleased.　He has followed Castelvetro in several criticisms. The rules of epic poetry so long observed, he maintains, ought to be reckoned fundamental principles, which no one can dispute without presumption.　The academy answer this well on behalf of Ariosto.　Their censures on the Jerusalem apply, in part to the characters and incidents, wherein they are sometimes right, in part to the language, many phrases, according to them, being bad Italian, as *pietose* for *pie* in the first line.[c]

29. Salviati, a verbose critic, who had written two quarto volumes on the style of Boccaccio, assailed the new epic in two treatises, entitled L'Infarinato.　Tasso's Apology followed very soon; but it has been sometimes thought that these criticisms, acting on his morbid intellect, though he repelled them vigorously, might have influenced him to that waste of labour, by which, in the last years of his life, he changed so much of his great poem for the worse. The obscurer insects whom envy stirred up against its glory are not worthy to be remembered.　The chief praise of Salviati himself is that he laid the foundations of the first classical dictionary of any modern language, the Vocabulario della Crusca.[d] *(margin: Salviati's attack on Tasso.)*

---

[c] In the second volume of the edition of Tasso at Venice, 1735, the Caraffa of Pellegrino, the Defence of Ariosto by the Academy, Tasso's Apology, and the Infarinato of Salviati, are cut into sentences, placed to answer each other like a dialogue.　This produces an awkward and unnatural effect as passages are torn from their context to place them in opposition.

The criticism on both sides becomes infinitely wearisome; yet not more so than much that we find in our modern reviews, and with the advantage of being more to the purpose, less ostentatious, and with less pretence to eloquence or philosophy.　An account of the controversy will be found in Crescimbeni, Ginguéné, or Corniani, and more at length in Serassi's Life of Tasso.

[d] Corniani, vi. 204.　The Italian literature would supply several more works on criticism, rhetoric, and grammar. Upon all these subjects it was much richer, at this time, than the French or English.

30. Bouterwek has made us acquainted with a treatise in
Spanish on the art of poetry, which he regards as
the earliest of its kind in modern literature. It
could not be so according to the date of its publication,
which is in 1596; but the author, Alonzo Lopez Pinciano,
was physician to Charles V., and it was therefore written, in
all probability, many years before it appeared from the press.
The title is rather quaint, Philosophia Antigua Poetica, and
it is written in the form of letters. Pinciano is the first who
discovered the Poetics of Aristotle, which he had diligently
studied, to be a fragment of a larger work, as is now generally
admitted. 'Whenever Lopez Pinciano,' says Bouterwek,
'abandons Aristotle, his notions respecting the different
poetic styles are as confused as those of his contemporaries;
and only a few of his notions and distinctions can be deemed
of importance at the present day. But his name is deserving
of honourable remembrance, for he was the first writer of
modern times who endeavoured to establish a philosophic
art of poetry; and, with all his veneration for Aristotle, he
was the first scholar who ventured to think for himself, and
to go somewhat farther than his master.'[e] The Art of
Poetry, by Juan de la Cueva, is a poem of the didactic class,
containing some information as to the history of Spanish
verse.[f] The other critical treatises which appeared in Spain
about this time seem to be of little importance; but we
know by the writings of Cervantes, that the poets of the age
of Philip were, as usual, followed by the animal for whose
natural prey they are designed, the sharp-toothed and keen-
scented critic.

Pinciano's Art of Poetry.

31. France produced very few books of the same class.
The Institutiones Oratoriæ of Omer Talon is an
elementary and short treatise of rhetoric.[g] Baillet
and Goujet give some praise to the Art of Poetry by Pelletier,
published in 1555.[h] The treatise of Henry Stephens, on the
Conformity of the French Language with the Greek, is said
to contain very good observations.[i] But it must be (for I do

French treatises of criticism.

---

[e] Hist. of Span. Lit. p. 323.

[f] It is printed entire in the eighth volume of Parnaso Español.

[g] Gibert, Maîtres de l'Eloquence, printed in Baillet, viii. 181.

[h] Baillet, iii. 351. Goujet, iii. 97. Pelletier had previously rendered Horace's Art of Poetry into French verse, id. 66.

[i] Baillet, iii. 353.

not recollect to have seen it) rather a book of grammar than of superior criticism. The Rhetorique française of Fouquelin (1555) seems to be little else than a summary of rhetorical figures.[k] That of Courcelles, in 1557, is not much better.[m] All these relate rather to prose than poetry. From the number of versifiers in France, and the popularity of Ronsard and his school, we might have expected a larger harvest of critics. Pasquier, in his valuable miscellany, Les Recherches de la France, has devoted a few pages to this subject, but not on an extensive or systematic plan; nor can the two Bibliothèques françaises, by La Croix du Maine and Verdier, both published in 1584, though they contain a great deal of information as to the literature of France, with some critical estimates of books, be reckoned in the class to which we are now adverting.

32. Thomas Wilson, afterwards secretary of state, and much employed under Elizabeth, is the author of an 'Art of Rhetorique,' dated in the preface January, 1553. The rules in this treatise are chiefly from Aristotle, with the help of Cicero and Quintilian, but his examples and illustrations are modern. Warton says that it is the first system of criticism in our language.[n] But in common use of the word it is no criticism at all, any more than the treatise of Cicero de Oratore. It is what it professes to be, a system of rhetoric in the ancient manner; and in this sense, it had been preceded by the work of Leonard Cox, which has been mentioned in another place. Wilson was a man of considerable learning, and his Art of Rhetorique is by no means without merit. He deserves praise for censuring the pedantry of learned phrases, or, as he calls them, 'strange *inkhorn* terms,' advising men 'to speak as is commonly received;' and he censures also what was not less pedantic, the introduction of a French or Italian idiom, which the travelled English affected in order to show their politeness, as the scholars did the former to prove their erudition. Wilson had before published an Art of Logic.

Wilson's Art of Rhetorique.

33. The first English criticism, properly speaking, that I find, is a short tract by Gascoyne, doubtless the poet of

---

[k] Gibert, p. 184.   [m] Ibid. p. 366.   [n] Hist. of Engl. Poetry, iv. 157.

that name, published in 1575; 'Certain Notes of Instruc-
Gascoyne;
Webbe. tion concerning the making of Verse or Rhyme
in English.' It consists only of ten pages, but the
observations are judicious. Gascoyne recommends that the
sentence should, as far as possible, be finished at the close
of two lines in the couplet measure.[o] Webbe, author of a
'Discourse of English Poetry' (1586), is copious in comparison with Gascoyne, though he stretches but to seventy
pages. His taste is better shown in his praise of Spenser
for the Shepherd's Kalendar, than of Gabriel Harvey for his
'reformation of our English verse;' that is, by forcing it
into uncouth Latin measures, which Webbe has himself
most unhappily attempted.

34. A superior writer to Webbe was George Puttenham,
Puttenham's
Art of Poesie. whose 'Art of English Poesie,' published in 1589,
is a small quarto of 258 pages in three books.
It is in many parts very well written, in a measured
prose, rather elaborate and diffuse. He quotes occasionally
a little Greek. Among the contemporary English poets,
Puttenham extols 'for eclogue and pastoral poetry Sir
Philip Sidney and Master Chaloner, and that other gentleman who wrote the late Shepherd's Kalendar. For ditty and
amorous ode I find Sir Walter Rawleigh's vein most lofty,
insolent [uncommon], and passionate; Master Edward Dyer
for elegy most sweet, solemn, and of high conceit; Gascon
[Gascoyne] for a good metre and for a plentiful vein; Phaer
and Golding for a learned and well-connected verse, specially
in translation, clear, and very faithfully answering their
author's intent. Others have also written with much facility,
but more commendably perhaps, if they had not written so
much nor so popularly. But last in recital and first in
degree is the queen our sovereign lady, whose learned, delicate, noble muse easily surmounteth all the rest that have
written before her time or since, for sense, sweetness, and
subtilty, be it in ode, elegy, epigram, or any other kind of
poem, heroic or lyric, wherein it shall please her majesty to
employ her pen, even by so much odds as her own excellent
estate and degree exceedeth all the rest of her most humble

---

[o] Gascoyne, with all the other early
English critics, was republished in a
collection by Mr. Haslewood in two
volumes, 1811 and 1815.

vassals.'[p] On this it may be remarked, that the only specimen of Elizabeth's poetry which, as far as I know, remains is prodigiously bad.[q] In some passages of Puttenham we find an approach to the higher province of philosophical criticism.

Sidney's Defence of Poesy.

35. These treatises of Webbe and Puttenham may have been preceded in order of writing, though not of publication, by the performance of a more illustrious author, Sir Philip Sidney. His Defence of Poesy was not published till 1595. The Defence of Poesy has already been reckoned among the polite writings of the Elizabethan age, to which class it rather belongs than to that of criticism; for Sidney rarely comes to any literary censure, and is still farther removed from any profound philosophy. His sense is good, but not ingenious, and the declamatory tone weakens its effect.

SECT. III.—ON WORKS OF FICTION.

Novels and Romances in Italy and Spain—Sidney's Arcadia.

Novels of Bandello;

36. THE novels of Bandello, three parts of which were published in 1554, and a fourth in 1573, are perhaps the best known and the most admired in that species of composition after those of Boccaccio. They have been censured as licentious, but are far less so than any of preceding times, and the reflections are usually of a moral cast. These, however, as well as the speeches, are very tedious. There is not a little predilection in Bandello for sanguinary stories. Ginguéné praises these novels for just sentiments, adherence to probability, and choice of interesting subjects. In these respects we often find a superiority in the older novels above those of the nineteenth century, the golden age, as it is generally thought, of fictitious story. But, in the management of these subjects, the Italian and Spanish novelists show little skill; they are worse cooks of better

---

[p] Puttenham, p. 51 of Haslewood's edition, or in Censura Litteraria, i. 348.

[q] Ellis's Specimens, ii. 162.

meat; they exert no power over the emotions beyond what
the intrinsic nature of the events related must produce; they
sometimes describe well, but with no great imagination; they
have no strong conception of character, no deep acquaintance
with mankind, not often much humour, no vivacity and
spirit of dialogue.

37. The Hecatomithi, or Hundred Tales, of Giraldi Cinthio
of Cinthio; have become known in England by the recourse
that Shakspeare has had to them in two instances,
Cymbeline and Measure for Measure, for the subjects of his
plays. Cinthio has also borrowed from himself in his own
tragedies. He is still more fond of dark tales of blood than
Bandello. He seems consequently to have possessed an unfortunate influence over the stage, and to him, as well as his
brethren of the Italian novel, we trace those scenes of improbable and disgusting horror from which, though the
native taste and gentleness of Shakspeare for the most part
disdained such helps, we recoil in almost all the other tragedians of the old English school. Of the remaining Italian
novelists that belong to this period it is enough to mention
Erizzo, better known as one of the founders of medallic
science. His Sei Giornate contain thirty-six novels, called
Avvenimenti. They are written with intolerable prolixity,
but in a pure and even elevated tone of morality. This
character does not apply to the novels of Lasca.

38. The French novels, ascribed to Margaret, Queen of
of the Queen Navarre, and first published in 1558, with the title
of Navarre. 'Histoire des Amans fortunés,' are principally taken
from the Italian collections, or from the fabliaux of the trou-
veurs. Though free in language, they are written in a much
less licentious spirit than many of the former, but breathe
throughout that anxiety to exhibit the clergy, especially the
regulars, in an odious or ridiculous light, which the principles of their illustrious authoress might lead us to expect.
Belleforest translated, perhaps with some variation, the
novels of Bandello into French.[r]

39. Few probably will now dispute that the Italian novel,

---

[r] Bouterwek, v. 286, mentions by   the sixteenth century: I do not know
name several other French novelists of   anything of them.

a picture of real life, and sometimes of true circumstances, is perused with less weariness than the Spanish Spanish
romances of
chivalry. romance, the alternative then offered to the lovers of easy reading. But this had very numerous admirers in that generation, nor was the taste confined to Spain. The popularity of Amadis de Gaul and Palmerin of Oliva, with their various continuators, has been already mentioned.[s] One of these, ' Palmerin of England,' appeared in French at Lyons in 1555. It is uncertain who was the original author, or in what language it was first written. Cervantes has honoured it with a place next to Amadis. Mr. Southey, though he condescended to abridge Palmerin of England, thinks it inferior to that Iliad of romantic adventure. Several of the tales of knight-errantry that are recorded to have stood on the unfortunate shelves of Don Quixote belong to this latter part of the century, among which Don Bellianis of Greece is better known by name than any other. These romances were not condemned by Cervantes alone. ' Every poet and prose writer,' says Bouterwek, ' of cultivated talent, laboured to oppose the contagion.'[t]

40. Spain was the parent of a romance in a very different style, but, if less absurd and better written, not per- Diana of
Monte-
mayor. haps much more interesting to us than those of chivalry, the Diana of Montemayor. Sannazaro's beautiful

---

[s] La Noue, a severe Protestant, thinks them as pernicious to the young as the writings of Machiavel had been to the old. This he dwells upon in his sixth discourse. ' De tout temps,' this honest and sensible writer says, ' il y a eu des hommes qui ont esté diligens d'escrire et mettre en lumière des choses vaines. Ce qui plus les y a conviez est, que ils sçavoient que leurs labeurs seroient agréables à ceux de leurs siècles, dont la plus part a toujours heimé [aimé] la vanité, comme le poisson fait l'eau. Les vieux romans dont nous voyons encor les fragmens par-ci et par-là, à savoir de Lancelot du Lac, de Perceforest, Tristan, Giron le courtois, et autres, font foy de ceste vanité antique. On s'en est repeu l'espace de plus de cinq cens ans, jusques à ce que nostre langage estant devenu plus orné et nostres esprits plus frétillans, il a fallu inventer quelque nouveauté pour les égayer. Voilà comment les livres d'Amadis sont venus en évidence parmi nous en ce dernier siècle. Mais pour en parler au vrai, l'Espagne les a engendrez, et la France les a seulement revêtus de plus beaux habillemens. Sous le règne du roy Henry second, ils ont eu leur principale vogue ; et croy que si quelqu'un les eust voulu alors blasmer, on luy eust craché au visage,' &c. p. 153, edit. 1558.

[t] In the opinion of Bouterwek (v. 282) the taste for chivalrous romance declined in the latter part of the century, through the prevalence of a classical spirit in literature, which exposed the mediæval fictions to derision. The number of shorter and more amusing novels might probably have more to do with it ; the serious romance has a terrible enemy in the lively. But it revived, with a little modification, in the next age.

model of pastoral romance, the Arcadia, and some which had
been written in Portugal, take away the merit of originality
from this celebrated fiction.   It formed, however, a school
in this department of literature, hardly less numerous, according to Bouterwek, than the imitators of Amadis.[u]   The
language of Montemayor is neither laboured nor affected,
and, though sometimes of rather too formal a solemnity,
especially in what the author thought philosophy, is remarkably harmonious and elevated ; nor is he deficient in depth
of feeling or fertility of imagination.   Yet the story seems
incapable of attracting any reader of this age.   The Diana,
like Sannazaro's Arcadia, is mingled with much lyric poetry,
which Bouterwek thinks is the soul of the whole composition.
Cervantes indeed condemns all the longer of these poems to
the flames, and gives but limited praise to the Diana.   Yet
this romance, and a continuance of it by Gil Polo, had inspired his own youthful genius in the Galatea.   The chief
merit of the Galatea, published in 1584, consists in the poetry
which the story seems intended to hold together.   In the
Diana of Montemayor, and even in the Galatea, it has been
supposed that real adventures and characters were generally
shadowed—a practice not already without precedent, and
which, by the French especially, was carried to a much
greater length in later times.

41. Spain became celebrated about the end of this century
Novels in
the pica-
resque
style. for her novels in the *picaresque* style, of which
Lazarillo de Tormes is the oldest extant specimen.
The continuation of this little work is reckoned
inferior to the part written by Mendoza himself; but both
together are amusing and inimitably short.[x]   The first edition
Guzman d'
Alfarache. of the most celebrated romance of this class, Guzman
d'Alfarache, falls within the sixteenth century.   It
was written by Matthew Aleman, who is said to have lived
long at court.   He might there have acquired, not a knowledge of the tricks of common rogues, but an experience of
mankind, which is reckoned one of the chief merits of his

---

[u] Hist. Span. Lit. p. 305.

[x] Though the continuation of Lazarillo de Tormes is reckoned inferior to
the original, it contains the only story
in the whole novel which has made its
fortune, that of the man who was exhibited as a sea-monster.

romance. Many of his stories also relate to the manners of a higher class than that of his hero. Guzman d'Alfarache is a sort of prototype of Gil Blas, though, in fact, Le Sage has borrowed very freely from all the Spanish novels of this school. The adventures are numerous and diversified enough to amuse an idle reader, and Aleman has displayed a great deal of good sense in his reflections, which are expressed in the pointed, condensed style affected by most writers of Spain. Cervantes has not hesitated to borrow from him one of Sancho's celebrated adjudications, in the well-known case of the lady, who was less pugnacious in defence of her honour than of the purse awarded by the court as its compensation. This story is, however, if I am not mistaken, older than either of them.[y]

42. It may require some excuse that I insert in this place Las Guerras de Granada, a history of certain Moorish *Las Guerras* factions in the last days of that kingdom, both *de Granada.* because it has been usually referred to the seventeenth century, and because many have conceived it to be a true relation of events. It purports to have been translated by Gines Perez de la Hita, an inhabitant of the city of Murcia, from

---

[y] The following passage, which I extract from the Retrospective Review, vol. v. p. 199, is a fair and favourable specimen of Aleman as a moralist, who is however apt to be tedious, as moralists usually are:—

‘ The poor man is a kind of money that is not current, the subject of every idle housewife's chat, the offscum of the people, the dust of the street, first trampled under foot, and then thrown on the dunghill ; in conclusion, the poor man is the rich man's ass. He dineth with the last, fareth with the worst, and payeth dearest ; his sixpence will not go so far as the rich man's threepence ; his opinion is ignorance, his discretion foolishness, his suffrage scorn, his stock upon the common abused by many, and abhorred by all. If he come into company he is not heard ; if any chance to meet him, they seek to shun him ; if he advise, though never so wisely, they grudge and murmur at him ; if he work miracles, they say he is a witch ; if virtuous, that he goeth about to deceive ; his venial sin is a blasphemy ; his

thought is made treason ; his cause, be it never so just, is not regarded ; and to have his wrongs righted, he must appeal to that other life. All men crush him ; no man favoureth him. There is no man that will relieve his wants ; no man that will bear him company when he is alone and oppressed with grief. None help him, all hinder him ; none give him, all take from him ; he is debtor to none, and yet must make payment to all. O the unfortunate and poor condition of him that is poor, to whom even the very hours are sold which the clock striketh, and payeth custom for the sunshine in. August!'

This is much in the style of our English writers in the first part of the seventeenth century, and confirms what I have suspected, that they formed it in a great measure on the Spanish school. Guzman d'Alfarache was early translated into English, as most other Spanish books were ; and the language itself was more familiar in the reigns of James and Charles than it became afterwards.

an Arabic original of one Aben Hamili. Its late English
translator seems to entertain no doubt of its authenticity;
and it has been sagaciously observed that no Christian could
have known the long genealogies of Moorish nobles which
the book contains. Most of those, however, who read it
without credulity, will feel, I presume, little difficulty in
agreeing with Antonio, who ranks it ' among Milesian fables,
though very pleasing to those who have nothing to do.' The
Zegris and Abencerrages, with all their romantic exploits,
seem to be mere creations of Castilian imagination; nor has
Conde, in his excellent history of the Moors in Spain, once
deigned to notice them even as fabulous; so much did he
reckon this famous production of Perez de la Hita below the
historian's regard. Antonio mentions no edition earlier than
that of Alcala in 1604; the English translator names 1601
for the date of its publication, an edition of which year
is in the Museum; nor do I find that any one has been
aware of an earlier, published at Saragoça in 1595, except
Brunet, who mentions it as rare and little known. It appears
by the same authority that there is another edition of 1598.

43. The heroic and pastoral romance of Spain contributed
Sidney's   something, yet hardly so much as has been supposed,
Arcadia.   to Sir Philip Sidney's Arcadia, the only original
production of this kind worthy of notice which our older
literature can boast. The Arcadia was published in 1590,
having been written, probably, by its highly accomplished
author about ten years before.

44. Walpole, who thought fit to display the dimensions of
Its charac-   his own mind by announcing that he could perceive
ter.   nothing remarkable in Sir Philip Sidney (as if the
suffrage of Europe in what he admits to be an age of heroes
were not a decisive proof that Sidney himself overtopped
those sons of Anak), says of the Arcadia, that it is ' a tedious,
lamentable, pedantic pastoral romance, which the patience
of a young virgin in love cannot now wade through.' We
may doubt whether Walpole could altogether estimate the
patience of a reader so extremely unlike himself; and his
epithets, except perhaps the first, are inapplicable: the
Arcadia is more free from pedantry than most books of that
age; and though we are now so accustomed to a more

stimulant diet in fiction, that few would read it through with
pleasure, the story is as sprightly as most other romances,
sometimes indeed a little too much so, for the Arcadia is not
quite a book for ' young virgins,' of which some of its admirers
by hearsay seem not to have been aware. By the epithet
' pastoral,' we may doubt whether Walpole knew much of
this romance beyond its name ; for it has far less to do with
shepherds than with courtiers, though the idea might probably be suggested by the popularity of the Diana. It does
not appear to me that the Arcadia is more tiresome and
uninteresting than the generality of that class of long
romances, proverbially among the most tiresome of all books ;
and, in a less fastidious age, it was read, no doubt, even as
a story with some delight.[z] It displays a superior mind,
rather complying with a temporary taste than affected by it,
and many pleasing passages occur, especially in the tender
and innocent loves of Pyrocles and Philoclea. I think it,
nevertheless, on the whole, inferior in sense, style, and spirit
to the Defence of Poesy. The following passage has some
appearance of having suggested a well-known poem in the
next age to the lover of Sacharissa ; we may readily believe
that Waller had turned over, in the glades of Penshurst, the
honoured pages of her immortal uncle : [a]—

45. ' The elder is named Pamela, by many men not deemed
inferior to her sister ; for my part, when I marked them both,
methought there was (if at least such perfections may receive
the word of more) more sweetness in Philoclea, but more
majesty in Pamela : methought love played in Philoclea's
eyes, and threatened in Pamela's ; methought Philoclea's
beauty only persuaded, but so persuaded as all hearts must
yield ; Pamela's beauty used violence, and such violence as
no heart could resist, and it seems that such proportion is
between their minds. Philoclea so bashful, as if her excellencies had stolen into her before she was aware ; so humble,

---

[a] ' It appears,' says Drake, ' to have
been suggested to the mind of Sir
Philip by two models of very different ages, and to have been built,
in fact, on their admixture ; these
are the Ethiopic History of Heliodorus, bishop of Tricca in Thessaly,
and the Arcadia of Sannazaro,' p. 549.
A translation of Heliodorus had been
published a short time before.

[a] The poem I mean is that addressed
to Amoret, ' Fair ! that you may truly
know,' drawing a comparison between
her and Sacharissa.

that she will put all pride out of countenance; in sum, such proceeding as will stir hope, but teach hope good manners: Pamela, of high thoughts, who avoids not pride with not knowing her excellencies, but by making that one of her excellencies to be void of pride; her mother's wisdom, greatness, nobility, but, if I can guess aright, knit with a more constant temper.'

46. The Arcadia stands quite alone among English fictions of this century. But many were translated in the reign of Elizabeth from the Italian, French, Spanish, and even Latin, among which Painter's Palace of Pleasure, whence Shakspeare took several of his plots, and the numerous labours of Antony Munday may be mentioned. Palmerin of England in 1580, and Amadis of Gaul in 1592, were among these; others of less value were transferred from the Spanish text by the same industrious hand; and since these, while still new, were sufficient to furnish all the gratification required by the public, our own writers did not much task their invention to augment the stock. They would not have been very successful, if we may judge by such deplorable specimens as Breton and Greene, two men of considerable poetical talent, have left us.[b] The once famous story of the Seven Champions of Christendom, by one Johnson, is of rather a superior class; the adventures are not original, but it is by no means a translation from any single work.[c] Mallory's famous romance, La Morte d'Arthur, is of much earlier date, and was first printed by Caxton. It is, however, a translation from several French romances, though written in very spirited language.

Inferiority of other English fictions.

---

[b] The Mavillia of Breton, the Dorastus and Fawnia of Greene, will be found in the collections of the indefatigable Sir Egerton Brydges. The first is below contempt; the second, if not quite so ridiculous, is written with a quaint, affected, and empty Euphuism. British Bibliographer, i. 508. But as truth is generally more faithful to natural sympathies than fiction, a little tale, called Never too Late, in which Greene has related his own story, is unaffected and pathetic. Drake's Shakspeare and his Times, i. 489.

[c] Drake, i. 529.

CHAPTER VIII.

HISTORY OF PHYSICAL AND MISCELLANEOUS LITERATURE FROM 1500 TO 1600.

Sect. I.—On Mathematical and Physical Science.

Algebraists of this Period—Vieta—Slow Progress of Copernican Theory—
Tycho Brahe—Reform of Calendar—Mechanics—Stevinus—Gilbert.

1. The breach of faith towards Tartaglia, by which Cardan communicated to the world the method of solving Tartaglia cubic equations, having rendered them enemies, the and Cardan. injured party defied the aggressor to a contest, wherein each should propose thirty-one problems to be solved by the other. Cardan accepted the challenge, and gave a list of his problems but devolved the task of meeting his antagonist on his disciple Ferrari. The problems of Tartaglia are so much more difficult than those of Cardan, and the latter's representative so frequently failed in solving them, as to show the former in a high rank among algebraists, though we have not so long a list of his discoveries.[a] This is told by himself in a work of miscellaneous mathematical and physical learning, Quesiti ed invenzioni diverse, published in 1546. In 1555 he put forth the first part of a treatise, entitled Trattato di numeri e misure, the second part appearing in 1560.

2. Pelletier of Mans, a man advantageously known both in literature and science, published a short treatise Algebra of on algebra in 1554. He does not give the method Pelletier. of solving cubic equations, but Hutton is mistaken in supposing that he was ignorant of Cardan's work, which he quotes. In fact he promises a third book, this treatise being divided into two, on the higher parts of algebra; but I do not know whether this be found in any subsequent edition.

---

[a] Montucla, p. 568.

Pelletier does not employ the signs + and −, which had
been invented by Stifelius, using p and m instead, but we
find the sign $\sqrt{}$ of irrationality. What is perhaps the most
original in this treatise is, that its author perceived that, in
a quadratic equation, where the root is rational, it must be
a divisor of the absolute number.[b]

3. In the Whetstone of Wit, by Robert Record, in 1557,
Record's
Whetstone
of Wit. we find the signs + and −, and, for the first time,
that of equality =, which he invented.[c] Record
knew that a quadratic equation has two roots. The scholar,
for it is in dialogue, having been perplexed by this as a difficulty, the master answers, ' That variety of roots doth
declare that one equation in number may serve for two
several questions. But the form of the question may easily
instruct you which of these two roots you shall take for your
purpose. Howbeit, sometimes you may take both.'[d] He
says nothing of cubic equations, having been prevented by
an interruption, the nature of which he does not divulge,
from continuing his algebraic lessons. We owe therefore
nothing to Record but his invention of a sign. As these
artifices not only abbreviate, but clear up the process of
reasoning, each successive improvement in notation deserves,

---

[b] Pelletier seems to have arrived at
this not by observation, but in a scientific method. Comme $x^2 = 2x + 15$ (I
substitute the usual signs for clearness), il est certain que x que nous
cherchons doit estre contenu également
en 15, puisque x^2 est égal à deux x,
et 15 davantage, et que tout nombre
censique (quarré) contient les racines
également et précisément. Maintenant
puisque $2x$ font certain nombre de
racines, il faut donc que 15 fasse
l'achèvement des racines qui sont né-
cessaires pour accomplir x^2. p. 40.
(Lyon, 1554.)

[c] 'And to avoid the tedious repetition of these words, " is equal to," I will
set, as I do often in work use, a pair of
parallels, gemowe lines of one length
thus =, because no two things can be
more equal.' The word gemowe, from
the French gemeau, twin (Cotgrave), is
very uncommon: it was used for a
double ring, a gemel or gemou ring.
Todd's Johnson's Dictionary.

[d] This general mode of expression

might lead us to suppose that Record
was acquainted with negative as well as
positive roots, the fictæ radices of Cardan. That a quadratic equation of a
certain form has two positive roots, had
long been known. In a very modern
book it is said that Mohammed ben
Musa, an Arabian of the reign of Al-
mamon, whose algebra was translated
by the late Dr. Rosen in 1831, observes
that there are two roots in the form
$ax^2 + b = cx$, but that this cannot be in
the other three cases. Libri, Hist. des
Sciences mathématiques en Italie, vol. ii.
(1838). Leonard of Pisa had some notion of this, but did not state it, according to M. Libri, so generally as Ben
Musa. Upon reference to Colebrooke's
Indian Algebra, it will appear that the
existence of two positive roots in some
cases, though the conditions of the problem will often be found to exclude the
application of one of them, is clearly
laid down by the Hindoo algebraists.
But one of them says, ' People do not
approve a negative absolute number.'

even in the most concise sketch of mathematical history, to be remarked. But certainly they do not exhibit any peculiar ingenuity, and might have occurred to the most ordinary student.

4. The great boast of France, and indeed of algebraical science generally, in this period, was Francis Viète, oftener called Vieta, so truly eminent a man that he may well spare laurels which are not his own. It has been observed in another place, that after Montucla had rescued from the hands of Wallis, who claims everything for Harriott, many algebraical methods indisputably contained in the writings of his own countryman, Cossali has come forward, with an equal cogency of proof, asserting the right of Cardan to the greater number of them. But the following steps in the progress of algebra may be justly attributed to Vieta alone. 1. We must give the first place to one less difficult in itself, than important in its results. In the earlier algebra, alphabetical characters were not generally employed at all, except that the Res, or unknown quantity, was sometimes set down R. for the sake of brevity. Stifelius, in 1544, first employed a literal notation, A. B. C., to express unknown quantities, while Cardan, and, according to Cossali, Luca di Borgo, to whom we may now add Leonard of Pisa himself, make some use of letters to express indefinite numbers.[e] But Vieta first applied them as general symbols

Vieta.

His discoveries.

---

[e] Vol. i. p. 54. A modern writer has remarked that Aristotle employs letters of the alphabet to express indeterminate quantities, and says it has never been observed before. He refers to the Physics, in Aristot. Opera, i. 543, 550, 565, &c., but without mentioning any edition. The letters α, β, γ, &c., express force, mass, space, or time. Libri, Hist. des Sciences mathématiques en Italie, i. 104. Upon reference to Aristotle, I find many instances in the sixth book of the Physicæ Auscultationes, and in other places.

Though I am reluctant to mix in my text, which is taken from established writers, any observations of my own on a subject wherein my knowledge is so very limited as in mathematics, I may here remark, that, although Tartaglia and Cardan do not use single letters as

symbols of known quantity, yet, when they refer to a geometrical construction, they employ in their equations double letters, the usual signs of lines. Thus we find, in the Ars Magna, AB*m*AC, where we should put $a - b$. The want of a good algorithm was doubtless a great impediment, but it was not quite so deficient as from reading modern histories of algebraical discovery, without reference to the original writers, we might be led to suppose.

The process by which the rule for solving cubic equations was originally discovered, seems worthy, as I have intimated in another place (vol. i. p. 463), of exciting our curiosity. Maseres has investigated this in the Philosophical Transactions for 1780, reprinted in his Tracts on Cubic and Biquadratic Equations, pp. 55-69, and in

of quantity, and, by thus forming the scattered elements of
specious analysis into a system, has been justly reckoned the
founder of a science which, from its extensive application,
has made the old problems of mere numerical algebra appear
elementary and almost trifling. 'Algebra,' says Kästner,
'from furnishing amusing enigmas to the Cossists,' as he
calls the first teachers of the art, 'became the logic of geometrical invention.'[f] It would appear a natural conjecture,
that the improvement, towards which so many steps had been
taken by others, might occur to the mind of Vieta simply as
a means of saving the trouble of arithmetical operations in
working out a problem. But those who refer to his treatise
entitled De Arte Analytica Isagoge, or even the first page of
it, will, I conceive, give credit to the author for a more
scientific view of his own invention. He calls it logistice
speciosa, as opposed to the logistice numerosa of the older
analysis;[g] his theorems are all general, the given quantities
being considered as indefinite, nor does it appear that he
substituted letters for the known quantities in the investigation of particular problems. Whatever may have suggested
this great invention to the mind of Vieta, it has altogether
changed the character of his science.

5. Secondly, Vieta understood the transformation of equations, so as to clear them from co-efficients or surd roots, or

---

Scriptores Logarithmici, vol. ii. It is
remarkable that he does not seem to
have been aware of what Cardan has
himself told us on the subject in the
sixth chapter of the Ars Magna ; yet he
has nearly guessed the process which
Tartaglia pursued ; that is, by a geometrical construction. It is manifest,
by all that these algebraists have written
on the subject, that they had the clearest
conviction they were dealing with continuous, or geometrical, not merely
with discrete, or arithmetical, quantity.
This gave them an insight into the
fundamental truth, which is unintelligible so long as algebra passes for a
specious *arithmetic*, that *every* value
which the conditions of the problem
admit may be assigned to unknown
quantities, without distinction of ration-
ality and irrationality   To abstract
number itself irrationality is inapplicable.

[f] Geschichte der Mathematik, i. 63.

[g] Forma autem Zetesin ineundi ex
arte propria est, non jam in numeris
suam logicam exercente, quæ fuit osci-
tantia veterum analystarum, sed per lo-
gisticen sub specie noviter inducendam,
feliciorem multo et potiorem numerosa,
ad comparandum inter se magnitudines,
proposita primum homogeniorum lege,
&c. p. i. edit. 1646.

A profound writer on algebra, Mr.
Peacock, has lately defined it, ' the
science of general reasoning by symbolical language.' In this sense there was
very little algebra before Vieta, and it
would be improper to talk of its being
known to the Greeks, Arabs, or Hindoos.
The definition would also include the
formulæ of logic. The original definition of alegebra seems to be the science
of finding an equation between known
and unknown quantities, per oppositio-
nem et restaurationem.

to eliminate the second term.   This, however, is partly
claimed by Cossali for Cardan.   Yet it seems that the process
employed by Cardan was much less neat and short than that
of Vieta, which is still in use.[h] 3. He obtained a solution
of cubic equations in a different method from that of Tartaglia.   4. 'He shows,' says Montucla, 'that when the unknown quantity of any equation may have several positive
values, for it must be admitted that it is only these that he
considers, the second term has for its co-efficient the sum of
these values with the sign — ; the third has the sum of the
products of these values multiplied in pairs ; the fourth the
sum of such products multiplied in threes, and so forth ;
finally, that the absolute term is the product of all the values.
Here is the discovery of Harriott pretty nearly made.' It is
at least no small advance towards it.[i] Cardan is said to have
gone some way towards this theory, but not with much clearness, nor extending it to equations above the third degree.
5. He devised a method of solving equations by approximation, analogous to the process of extracting roots, which has
been superseded by the invention of more compendious rules.[k]
6. He has been regarded by some as the true author of the
application of algebra to geometry, giving copious examples
of the solution of problems by this method, though all belonging to straight lines.   It looks like a sign of the geometrical
relation under which he contemplated his own science, that
he uniformly denominates the first power of the unknown
quantity *latus*.   But this will be found in older writers.[m]

---

[h] It is fully explained in his work De
Recognitione Æquationum, cap. 7.

[i] Some theorems given by Vieta very
shortly, and without demonstration,
show his knowledge of the structure of
equations. I transcribe them from Maseres,
who has expressed them in the usual
algebraic language. Si $a + b \times x - x^2$
æquetur ab, x explicabilis est de qualibet
illarum duarum a vel b. The second
theorem is :—

$$\text{Si } x^3 - b \begin{Bmatrix} a \\ x^2 + ac \\ c \end{Bmatrix} x$$

æquetur abc, x explicabilis est de qualibet illarum trium a, b, vel c. The third
and fourth theorems extend this to
higher equations.

[k] Montucla, i. 600. Hutton's Mathematical Dictionary   Biogr. univers.
art. Viète.

[m] It is certain that Vieta perfectly
knew the relation of algebra to magnitude as well as number, as the first pages
of his In Artem Analyticam Isagoge
fully show. But it is equally certain,
as has been observed before, that Tartaglia and Cardan, and much older
writers, Oriental as well as European,
knew the same; it was by help of
geometry, which Cardan calls *via regia*,
that the former made his great discovery of the solution of cubic equations. Cossali, ii. 147. Cardan, Ars
Magna, ch. xi.

Latus and *radix* are used indifferently

6. 'Algebra,' says a philosopher of the present day, ' was still only an ingenious art, limited to the investigation of numbers; Vieta displayed all its extent, and instituted general expressions for particular results. Having profoundly meditated on the nature of algebra, he perceived that the chief characteristic of the science is to express relations. Newton with the same idea defined algebra an universal arithmetic. The first consequences of this general principle of Vieta were his own application of his specious analysis to geometry, and the theory of curve lines, which is due to Descartes; a fruitful idea, from which the analysis of functions, and the most sublime discoveries, have been deduced. It has led to the notion that Descartes is the first who applied algebra to geometry; but this invention is really due to Vieta; for he resolved geometrical problems by algebraic analysis, and constructed figures by means of these solutions. These investigations led him to the theory of angular sections, and to the general equations which express the values of chords.'[n]

---

for the first power of the unknown quantity in the Ars Magna. Cossali contends that Fra Luca had applied algebra to geometry. Vieta, however, it is said, was the first who taught how to construct geometrical figures by means of algebra. Montucla, p. 604. But compare Cossali, p. 427.

A writer lately quoted, and to whose knowledge and talents I bow with deference, seems, as I would venture to suggest, to have over-rated the importance of that employment of letters to signify quantities, known or unknown, which he has found in Aristotle, and in several of the moderns, and in consequence to have depreciated the real merit of Vieta. Leonard of Pisa, it seems, whose algebra this writer has for the first time published, to his own honour and the advantage of scientific history, makes use of letters as well as lines to represent quantities. Quelquefois il emploie des lettres pour exprimer des quantités indéterminées, connues ou inconnues, sans les représenter par des lignes. On voit ici comment les modernes ont été amenés à se servir des lettres d'alphabet (même pour exprimer des quantités connues) long temps avant Viète, à qui on a attribué à tort une notation qu'il faudrait peut-être faire remonter jusqu'à Aristote, et que tant d'algébristes modernes ont employée avant le géomètre français. Car outre Léonard de Pise, Paciolo, et d'autres géomètres italiens firent usage des lettres pour indiquer les quantités connues, et c'est d'eux plutôt que d'Aristote que les modernes ont appris cette notation. Libri, vol. ii. p. 34. But there is surely a wide interval between the use of a short symbolic expression for particular quantities, as M. Libri has remarked in Aristotle, or even the *partial* employment of letters to designate known quantities, as in the Italian algebraists, and the method of stating general relations by the exclusive use of letters, which Vieta first introduced. That Tartaglia and Cardan, and even, as it now appears, Leonard of Pisa, went a certain way towards the invention of Vieta, cannot much diminish his glory; especially when we find that he entirely apprehended the importance of his own logistice speciosa in science. I have mentioned above, that, as far as my observation has gone, Vieta does not work particular problems by the specious algebra.

[n] M. Fourier, quoted in Biographie universelle.

It has been observed above, that this requires a slight limit-ation as to the solution of problems.

7. The Algebra of Bombelli, published in 1589, is the only other treatise of the kind during this period that seems worthy of much notice. Bombelli saw better than Cardan the nature of what is called the irreducible case in cubic equations. But Vieta, whether after Bombelli or not is not certain, had the same merit.[o] It is remarkable that Vieta seems to have paid little regard to the discoveries of his predecessors. Ignorant, probably, of the writings of Record, and perhaps even of those of Stifelius, he neither uses the sign = of equality, employing instead the clumsy word Æquatio, or rather Æquetur,[p] nor numeral exponents; and Hutton observes that Vieta's algebra has, in consequence, the appearance of being older than it is. He mentions, however, the signs + and − as usual in his own time.

8. Amidst the great progress of algebra through the six-teenth century, the geometers, content with what the ancients had left them, seemed to have had little care but to elucidate their remains. Euclid was the object of their idolatry; no fault could be acknowledged in his elements, and to write a verbose commentary upon a few propositions was enough to make the reputation of a geo-meter. Among the almost innumerable editions of Euclid that appeared, those of Commandin and Clavius, both of them in the first rank of mathematicians for that age, may be distinguished. Commandin, especially, was much in re-quest in England, where he was frequently reprinted, and Montucla calls him the model of commentators for the per-tinence and sufficiency of his notes. The commentary o' Clavius, though a little prolix, acquired a still higher repu-tation. We owe to Commandin editions of the more difficult geometers, Archimedes, Pappus, and Apollonius; but he attempted little, and that without success, beyond the pro-vince of a translator and a commentator. Maurolycus of Messina had no superior among contemporary geometers.

Geometers of this period.

---

[o] Cossali. Hutton.

[p] Vieta uses =, but it is to denote that the proposition is true both of + and − ; where we put ±. It is almost a presumption of copying one from another, that several modern writers say Vieta's word is *æquatio*. I have always found it *æquetur*; a difference not material in itself.

Besides his edition of Archimedes, and other labours on the ancient mathematicians, he struck out the elegant theory, in which others have followed him, of deducing the properties of the conic sections from those of the cone itself. But we must refer the reader to Montucla, and other historical and biographical works, for the less distinguished writers of the sixteenth age.[q]

9. The extraordinary labour of Joachim Rhæticus in his trigonometrical calculations has been mentioned in our first volume. His Opus Palatinum de Triangulis was published from his manuscript by Valentine Otho, in 1594. But the work was left incomplete, and the editor did not accomplish what Joachim had designed. In his tables the sines, tangents, and secants are only calculated to ten, instead of fifteen places of decimals. Pitiscus, in 1613, not only completed Joachim's intention, but carried the minuteness of calculation a good deal farther.[r]

Joachim Rhæticus.

10. It can excite no wonder that the system of Copernicus, simple and beautiful as it is, met with little encouragement for a long time after its promulgation, when we reflect upon the natural obstacles to its reception. Mankind can in general take these theories of the celestial movements only upon trust from philosophers; and in this instance it required a very general concurrence of competent judges to overcome the repugnance of what called itself common sense, and was in fact a prejudice as natural as universal, and as irresistible as could influence human belief. With this was united another, derived from the language of Scripture; and though it might have been sufficient to answer, that phrases implying the rest of the earth and motion of the sun are merely popular, and such as those who are best convinced of the opposite doctrine must employ in ordinary language, this was neither satisfactory to the vulgar, nor recognised by the church. Nor were the astronomers in general much more favourable to the new theory than either the clergy or the multitude. They had taken pains to familiarise their understandings with the Ptolemaic hypothesis; and it may be often observed that those who have

Copernican theory.

<hr>

[q] Montucla. Kästner. Hutton. Biogr. univ.   [r] Montucla, p. 581.

once mastered a complex theory are better pleased with it than with one of more simplicity. The whole weight of Aristotle's name, which, in the sixteenth century, not only biassed the judgment, but engaged the passions, connected as it was with general orthodoxy and the preservation of established systems, was thrown into the scale against Copernicus. It was asked what demonstration could be given of his hypothesis; whether the movements of the heavenly bodies could not be reconciled to the Ptolemaic; whether the greater quantity of motion, and the complicated arrangement which the latter required, could be deemed sufficient objections to a scheme proceeding from the Author of nature, to whose power and wisdom our notions of simplicity and facility are inapplicable; whether the moral dignity of man, and his peculiar relations to the Deity, unfolded in Scripture, did not give the world he inhabits a better claim to the place of honour in the universe, than could be pretended, on the score of mere magnitude, for the sun. It must be confessed, that the strongest presumptions in favour of the system of Copernicus were not discovered by himself.

11. It is easy, says Montucla, to reckon the number of adherents to the Copernican theory during the sixteenth century. After Rhæticus, they may be nearly reduced to Reinhold, author of the Prussian tables; Rothman, whom Tycho drew over afterwards to his own system; Christian Wursticius (Ursticius), who made some proselytes in Italy; finally, Mæstlin, the illustrious master of Kepler. He might have added Wright and Gilbert, for the credit of England. Among the Italian proselytes made by Wursticius, we may perhaps name Jordano Bruno, who strenuously asserts the Copernican hypothesis; and two much greater authorities in physical science, Benedetti and Galileo himself. It is evident that the preponderance of valuable suffrages was already on the side of truth.[s]

12. The predominant disinclination to contravene the apparent testimonies of sense and Scripture had, Tycho perhaps, more effect than the desire of originality Brahe. in suggesting the middle course taken by Tycho Brahe. He

---

[s] Montucla, p. 638.

was a Dane of noble birth, and early drawn, by the impulse
of natural genius, to the study of astronomy.   Frederic III.,
his sovereign, after Tycho had already obtained some reputation, erected for him the observatory of Uraniburg in a
small isle of the Baltic.   In this solitude he passed above
twenty years, accumulating the most extensive and accurate
observations which were known in Europe before the discovery of the telescope and the improvement of astronomical
instruments.   These, however, were not published till 1606,
though Kepler had previously used them in his Tabulæ
Rodolphinæ.   Tycho himself did far more in this essential
department of the astronomer than any of his predecessors ;
his resources were much beyond those of Copernicus, and the
latter years of this century may be said to make an epoch in
physical astronomy.   Frederic, Landgrave of Hesse, was
more than a patron of the science.   The observations of
that prince have been deemed worthy of praise long after
his rank had ceased to avail them.   The emperor Rodolph,
when Tycho had been driven by envy from Denmark, gave
him an asylum and the means of carrying on his observations
at Prague, where he died in 1601.   He was the first in
modern times who made a catalogue of stars, registering
their positions as well as his instruments permitted him.
This catalogue, published in his Progymnasmata in 1602,
contained 777, to which, from Tycho's own manuscripts,
Kepler added 223 stars.[t]

13. In the new mundane system of Tycho Brahe, which,
though first regularly promulgated to the world in
his Progymnasmata, had been communicated in his
His system.
epistles to the Landgrave of Hesse, he supposes the five
planets to move round the sun, but carries the sun itself with
these five satellites, as well as the moon, round the earth.
Though this, at least at the time, might explain the known
phænomena as well as the two other theories, its want of
simplicity always prevented its reception.   Except Longo-
montanus, the countryman and disciple of Tycho, scarce any
conspicuous astronomer adopted an hypothesis which, if it
had been devised some time sooner, would perhaps have met

---

[t] Montucla, p. 653–659.

with better success. But in the seventeenth century, the wise all fell into the Copernican theory, and the many were content without any theory at all.

14. A great discovery in physical astronomy may be assigned to Tycho. Aristotle had pronounced comets to be meteors generated below the orbit of the moon. But a remarkable comet in 1577 having led Tycho to observe its path accurately, he came to the conclusion that these bodies are far beyond the lunar orbit, and that they pass through what had always been taken for a solid firmament, environing the starry orbs, and which plays no small part in the system of Ptolemy. He was even near the discovery of their elliptic revolution, the idea of a curve round the sun having struck him, though he could not follow it by observation.[u]

15. The acknowledged necessity of reforming the Julian calendar gave in this age a great importance to astronomy. It is unnecessary to go into the details Gregorian Calendar. of this change, effected by the authority of Gregory XIII., and the skill of Lilius and Clavius, the mathematicians employed under him. The new calendar was immediately received in all countries acknowledging the pope's supremacy ; not so much on that account, though a discrepancy in the ecclesiastical reckoning would have been very inconvenient, as of its real superiority over the Julian. The Protestant countries came much more slowly into the alteration ; truth being no longer truth when promulgated by the pope. It is now admitted that the Gregorian calendar is very nearly perfect, at least as to the computation of the solar year, though it is not quite accurate for the purpose of finding Easter. In that age it had to encounter the opposition of Mæstlin, an astronomer of deserved reputation, and of Scaliger, whose knowledge of chronology ought to have made him conversant with the subject, but who, by a method of squaring the circle which he announces with great confidence as a demonstration, showed the world that his genius did not guide him to the exact sciences.[x]

16. The science of optics, as well as all other branches of the mixed mathematics, fell very short of astronomy in the

<hr>

[u] Montucla, p. 662.   [x] Id. p. 674–686.

number and success of its promoters.   It was carried not
much farther than the point where Alhazen, Vitello,
Optics. and Roger Bacon left it.   Maurolycus of Messina, in
a treatise published in 1575, though written, according to
Montucla, fifty years before, entitled Theoremata de Lumine
et Umbra, has mingled a few novel truths with error.   He
explains rightly the fact that a ray of light, received through
a small aperture of any shape, produces a circular illumination on a body intercepting it at some distance ; and points
out why different defects of vision are remedied by convex or
concave lenses.   He had, however, mistaken notions as to
the visual power of the eye, which he ascribed not to the
retina but to the crystalline humour ; and, on the whole,
Maurolycus, though a very distinguished philosopher in that
age, seems to have made few considerable discoveries in
physical science.[y]   Baptista Porta, who invented, or at least
made known, the camera obscura, though he dwells on
many optical phenomena in his Magia Naturalis, sometimes
making just observations, had little insight into the principles that explain them.[z]   The science of perspective has
been more frequently treated, especially in this period, by
painters and architects than by mathematicians.   Albert
Durer, Serlio, Vignola, and especially Peruzzi, distinguished
themselves by practical treatises ; but the geometrical principles were never well laid down before the work of Guido
Ubaldi in 1600.[a]

17.   This author, of a noble family in the Apennines,
ranks high also among the improvers of theoretical
Mechanics. mechanics.   This great science, checked, like so
many others, by the erroneous principles of Aristotle, made
scarce any progress till near the end of the century.   Cardan
and Tartaglia wrote upon the subject ; but their acuteness
in abstract mathematics did not compensate for a want of
accurate observation and a strange looseness of reasoning.
Thus Cardan infers that the power required to sustain a
weight on an inclined plane varies in the exact ratio of the
angle, because it vanishes when the plane is horizontal,
and becomes equal to the weight when the plane is perpen-

---

[y] Montucla, p. 695.   [z] Id. p. 698.   [a] Id. p. 708.

dicular. But this must be the case if the power follows any other law of direct variation, as that of the sine of inclination, that is, the height, which it really does.[b] Tartaglia, on his part, conceived that a cannon-ball did not indeed describe two sides of a parallelogram, as was commonly imagined even by scientific writers, but, what is hardly less absurd, that its point-blank direction and line of perpendicular descent are united by a circular arch, to which they are tangents. It was generally agreed till the time of Guido Ubaldi, that the arms of a lever charged with equal weights, if displaced from the horizontal position, would recover it when set at liberty. Benedetti of Turin had juster notions than his Italian contemporaries; he ascribed the centrifugal force of bodies to their tendency to move in a straight line; he determined the law of equilibrium for the oblique lever, and even understood the composition of motions.[c]

18. If, indeed, we should give credit to the sixteenth century for all that was actually discovered, and even reduced to writing, we might now proceed to the great name of Galileo. For it has been said that his treatise Della Scienza Meccanica was written in 1592, though not published for more than forty years afterwards.[d] But as it has been our rule, with not many exceptions, to date books from their publication, we must defer any mention of this remarkable work to the next period. The experiments, however, made by Galileo, when lecturer in mathematics at Pisa, on falling bodies, come strictly within our limits. He was appointed to this office in 1589, and left it in 1592. Among the many unfounded assertions of Aristotle in physics, it was one that the velocity of falling bodies was proportionate to their weights; Galileo took advantage of the leaning tower of Pisa to prove the contrary. But this important, though obvious experiment, which laid open much of the theory of motion, displeased the adherents of Aristotle so highly that they compelled him to leave Pisa. He soon obtained a chair in the university of Padua.

---

[b] Montucla, p. 690.
[c] Id. p. 693.
[d] Playfair has fallen into the mistake of supposing that this treatise was *pub-*
lished in 1592; and those who, on second thoughts, would have known better, have copied him.

19. But on the same principle that we exclude the work

of Galileo on mechanics from the sixteenth century, it seems reasonable to mention that of Simon Stevinus of Bruges; since the first edition of his Statics and Hydrostatics was printed in Dutch as early as 1585, though we can hardly date its reception among the scientific public before the Latin edition in 1608. Stevinus has been chiefly known by his discovery of the law of equilibrium on the inclined plane, which had baffled the ancients, and, as we have seen, was mistaken by Cardan. Stevinus supposed a flexible chain of uniform weight to descend down the sides of two connected planes, and to hang in a sort of festoon below. The chain would be in equilibrio, because if it began to move, there would be no reason why it should not move for ever, the circumstances being unaltered by any motion it could have; and thus there would be a perpetual motion, which is impossible. But the part below, being equally balanced, must, separately taken, be in equilibrio; consequently the part above, lying along the planes, must also be in equilibrio; and hence the weight of the two parts of the chain must be equal, or if that lying along the shorter plane be called the power, it will be to the other as the lengths; or if there be but one plane, and the power hang perpendicularly, as the height to the length.

20. The first discovery made in hydrostatics since the time

of Archimedes is due to Stevinus. He found that the vertical pressure of fluids on a horizontal surface is as the product of the base of the vessel by its height, and showed the law of pressure even on the sides.[e]

21. The year 1600 was the first in which England pro-

duced a remarkable work in physical science: but this was one sufficient to raise a lasting reputation to its author. Gilbert, a physician, in his Latin treatise on the magnet, not only collected all the knowledge which others had possessed on that subject, but became at once the father of experimental philosophy in this island, and by a singular felicity and acuteness of genius, the founder of theories which have been revived after the lapse of ages, and are almost universally received into the creed of the science.

---

[e] Montucla, ii. 180.

The magnetism of the earth itself, his own original hypothesis, nova illa nostra et inaudita de tellure sententia, could not, of course, be confirmed by all the experimental and analogical proof which has rendered that doctrine accepted in recent philosophy ; but it was by no means one of those vague conjectures that are sometimes unduly applauded, when they receive a confirmation by the favour of fortune. He relied on the analogy of terrestrial phænomena to those exhibited by what he calls a *terrella,* or artificial spherical magnet. What may be the validity of his reasonings from experiment it is for those who are conversant with the subject to determine, but it is evidently by the torch of experiment that he was guided. A letter from Edward Wright, whose authority as a mathematician is of some value, admits the terrestrial magnetism to be proved. Gilbert was also one of our earliest Copernicans, at least as to the rotation of the earth ;[f] and with his usual sagacity inferred, before the invention of the telescope, that there are a multitude of fixed stars beyond the reach of our vision.[g]

---

[f] Mr. Whewell thinks that Gilbert was more doubtful about the annual than the diurnal motion of the earth, and informs us that in a posthumous work he seems to hesitate between Tycho and Copernicus. Hist. of Inductive Sciences, i. 389.   Gilbert's argument for the diurnal motion would extend to the annual. Non probabilis modo sed manifesta videtur terræ diurna circumvolutio, cum natura semper agit per pauciora magis quam plura, atque rationi magis consentaneum videtur unum exiguum corpus telluris diurnam volutationem efficere quam mundum totum circumferri.

[g] l. 6. c. 3. The article on Gilbert in the Biographie universelle is discreditable to that publication. If the author was so very ignorant as not to have known any thing of Gilbert, he might at least have avoided the assumption that nothing was to be known.

Sarpi, who will not be thought an incompetent judge, names Gilbert with Vieta, as the only original writers among his contemporaries. Non ho veduto in questo secolo uomo quale abbia scritto cosa sua propria, salvo Vieta in Francia e Gilberti in Inghilterra. Lettere di Fra Paolo, p. 31,

[Griselini, who published some memoirs of Father Paul in 1760, and had seen his manuscripts, thinks fit to claim for him the priority as to all the magnetic observations of Gilbert.   Ora io dico che nel trattato del Gilbert non v'è cosa che non sia stata prima osservata ed experimentata dal Sarpi. Le medesime sono le sue viste ; e riguardo a' fenomeni, tutta la varietà si riduce al modo di esporli, o ne' ragguagli. Frà Paolo è semplice, conciso, e non fa deduzioni sistematiche, e segue la massima inculcata dappoi da Bacone di Verulamio, cioè storia, osservazione e sperienze.   Cited in Vita di F. Paolo Sarpi, per Bianchi Giovini. Bruxelles, 1836. It is for the reader to consider whether Sarpi would have praised Gilbert's originality as he has done, without a hint that he had made the same discoveries.

It may be added, that Griselini was no great master of scientific subjects, as appears in Biographie universelle, art. Sarpi.

This is not said to depreciate the physical science of Sarpi, who was a wonderful man upon almost every subject, and had, I have no doubt, collected much as to magnetism.—1847.]

Sect. II.—On Natural History.

Zoology—Gesner, Aldrovandus.   Botany—Lobel, Cæsalpin, and others.

22. Zoology and botany, in the middle of the sixteenth
<small>Gesner's</small>   century, were as yet almost neglected fields of
<small>Zoology.</small>   knowledge; scarce anything had been added to
the valuable history of animals by Aristotle, and those of
plants by Theophrastus and Dioscorides.   But in the year
1551 was published the first part of an immense work, the
History of Animals, by that prodigy of general erudition,
Conrad Gesner.   This treats of viviparous quadrupeds; the
second, which appeared in 1554, of the oviparous; the third,
in 1555, of birds; the fourth, in the following year, of fishes
and aquatic animals; and one, long afterwards, published
in 1587, relates to serpents.   The first part was reprinted
with additions in 1560, and a smaller work, of woodcuts and
shorter descriptions, called Icones Animalium, appeared in
1553.

23. This work of the first great naturalist of modern times,
<small>Its character</small>   is thus eulogised by one of the latest:—' Gesner's
<small>by Cuvier.</small>   History of Animals,' says Cuvier, 'may be considered
as the basis of all modern zoology; copied almost literally by
Aldrovandus, abridged by Jonston, it has become the foundation of much more recent works; and more than one famous
author has borrowed from it silently most of his learning;
for those passages of the ancients, which have escaped Gesner, have scarce ever been observed by the moderns.   He
deserved their confidence by his accuracy, his perspicuity,
his good faith, and sometimes by the sagacity of his views.
Though he has not laid down any natural classification by
genera, he often points out very well the true relations of
beings.' [h]

24. Gesner treats of every animal under eight heads or
<small>Gesner's ar-</small>   chapters :—1. its name in different languages;
<small>rangement.</small>   2. Its external description and usual place of habit-
ation; 3. Its natural actions, length of life, diseases, &c.;
4. Its disposition, or, as we may say, moral character; 5. Its

---

[h] Biogr. universelle, art. Gesner.

utility, except for food and medicine; 6. Its use as food; 7. Its use in medicine; 8. The philological relations of the name and qualities, their proper and figurative use in language, which is subdivided into several sections. So comprehensive a notion of zoology displays a mind accustomed to encyclopædic systems, and loving the labours of learning for their own sake. Much, of course, would have a very secondary value in the eyes of a good naturalist. His method is alphabetical, but it may be reckoned an alphabet of genera; for he arranges what he deems cognate species together. In the Icones Animalium we find somewhat more of classification. Gesner divides quadrupeds into Animalia Mansueta and Animalia Fera; the former in two, the latter in four orders. Cuvier, in the passage above cited, writing probably from memory, has hardly done justice to Gesner in this respect. The delineations in the History of Animals and in the Icones are very rude; and it is not always easy, with so little assistance from engraving, to determine the species from his description.

25. Linnæus, though professing to give the synonyms of his predecessors, has been frequently careless and unjust towards Gesner; his mention of several quadrupeds (the only part of the latter's work at which I have looked) having been unnoticed in the Systema Naturæ. We do not find, however, that Gesner had made very considerable additions to the number of species known to the ancients; and it cannot be reckoned a proof of his acuteness in zoology, that he placed the hippopotamus among aquatic animals, and the bat among birds. In the latter extraordinary error he was followed by all other naturalists till the time of Ray. Yet he shows some judgment in rejecting plainly fabulous animals. In the edition of 1551 I find but few quadrupeds, except those belonging to the countries round the Mediterranean, or mentioned by Pliny and Ælian.[1] The Rein-deer, which it is doubtful whether the ancients knew, though there seems reason to believe that

His additions to known quadrupeds.

---

[1] In Cardan, De Subtilitate, lib. 10, published in 1550, I find the ant-eater, ursus formicarius, which, if I am not mistaken, Gesner has omitted, though it is in Hernando d'Oviedo; also a cer- copithecus, as large as man, which persists long in standing erect, amat pueros et mulieres, conaturque concumbere, quod nos vidimus. This was probably one of the large baboons of Africa.

it was formerly an inhabitant of Poland and Germany, he
found in Albertus Magnus; and from him, too, Gesner had
got some notion of the Polar Bear. He mentions the Musk-
deer, which was known through the Arabian writers, though
unnoticed by the ancients. The new world furnished him
with a scanty list. Among these is the Opossum, or Simi-
Vulpa (for which Linnæus has not given him credit), an
account of which he may have found in Pinzon or Peter
Martyr;[k] the Manati, of which he found a description in
Hernando's History of the Indies; and the Guinea Pig,
Cuniculus Indus, which he says was, within a few years, first
brought to Europe from the New World, but was become
everywhere common. In the edition of 1560, several more
species are introduced. Olaus Magnus had, in the mean
time, described the Glutton; and Belon had found an Arma-
dillo among itinerant quacks in Turkey, though he knew that
it came from America.[m] Belon had also described the Axis-
deer of India. The Sloth appears for the first time in this
edition of Gesner, and the Sagoin, or Ouistiti, as well as
what he calls Mus Indicus alius, which Linnæus refers to
the Racoon, but seems rather to be the Nasua, or Coati
Mondi. Gesner has given only three cuts of monkeys, but
was aware that there were several kinds, and distinguishes
them in description. I have not presumed to refer his cuts
to particular species, which probably, on account of their

---

[k] In the voyage of Pinzon, the com-
panion of Columbus in his last voyage,
when the continent of Guiana was discovered, which will be found in the
Novus Orbis of Grynæus, a specimen
of the genus Didelphis is mentioned
with the astonishment which the first
appearance of the marsupial type would
naturally excite in an European. Con-
spexere etiamnum ibi animal quadrupes,
prodigiosum quidem; nam pars anterior
vulpem, posterior vero simiam præ-
sentabat, nisi quod pedes effingit humanos; aures autem habet noctuæ, et
infra consuetam alvum aliam habet
instar crumenæ, in qua delitescunt
catuli ejus tantisper, donec tuto prodire
queant, et absque parentis tutela cibatum
quærere, nec unquam exeunt crumenam,
nisi cum sugunt. Portentosum hoc
animal cum catulis tribus Sibiliam dela-

tum est; et ex Sibilia Illiberim, id est
Granatam, in gratiam regum, qui novis
semper rebus oblectantur, p. 116, edit.
1532. In Peter Martyr, De Rebus
Oceanicis, dec. i. lib. 9, we find a longer
account of the monstrosum illud animal
vulpino rostro, cercopithecea cauda,
vespertilioneis auribus, manibus huma-
nius, pedibus simiam æmulans; quod
natos jam filios alio gestat quocunque
proficiscatur utero exteriore in modum
magnæ crumenæ. This animal, he says,
lived some months in Spain, and was
seen by him after its death. Several
species are natives of Guiana.

[m] Tatus, quadrupes peregrina. The
species figured in Gesner is Dasypus
novemcinctus. This animal, however,
is mentioned by Hernando d'Oviedo
under the name Bardati.

rudeness, a good naturalist would not attempt. The Simia
Inuus, or Barbary ape, seems to be one, as we might expect.[n]
Gesner was not very diligent in examining the histories of
the New World. Peter Martyr and Hernando would have
supplied him with several he has overlooked, as the Tapir, the
Pecary, the Ant-eater, and the fetid Polecat.[o]

26. Less acquainted with books but with better opportunities of observing nature than Gesner, his con-   Belon.
temporary Belon made greater accessions to zoology.
Besides his excellent travels in the Levant and Egypt, we
have from him a history of fishes in Latin, printed in 1553,
and translated by the author into French, with alterations
and additions; and one of birds, published in French in
1555, written with great learning, though not without fabulous accounts, as was usual in the earlier period of natural
history. Belon was perhaps the first, at least in modern
times, who had glimpses of a great typical conformity in
nature. In one of his works he places the skeletons of a
man and a bird in apposition, in order to display their essential analogy. He introduced also many exotic plants into
France. Every one knows, says a writer of the last century,
that our gardens owe all their beauty to Belon.[p] The same
writer has satisfactorily cleared this eminent naturalist from
the charge of plagiarism, to which credit had been hastily
given.[q] Belon may, on the whole, be placed by the side of
Gesner.

27. Salviani published in 1558 a history of fishes (Animalium Aquatilium Historia), with figures well ex-   Salviani and
ecuted, but by no means numerous. He borrows   Rondelet's
                                                 Ichthyology.
most of his materials from the ancients, and, having frequently failed in identifying the species they describe, cannot
be read without precaution.[r] But Rondelet (De Piscibus

---

[n] Sunt et cynocephalorum diversa
genera, nec unum genus caudatorum. I
think he knew the leading characteristics founded on the tail, but did not
attend accurately to subordinate distinctions, though he knew them to exist.

[o] The Tapir is mentioned by Peter
Martyr, the rest in Hernando.

[p] Liron, Singularités historiques, i.
456.

[q] Id. p. 438. It had been suspected
that the manuscripts of Gilles, the author
of a compilation from Ælian, who had
himself travelled in the East, fell into
the hands of Belon, who published
them as his own. Gesner has been
thought to insinuate this; but Liron
is of opinion that Belon was not meant
by him.

[r] Biogr. univ. (Cuvier).

Marinis, 1554) was far superior as an ichthyologist, in the judgment of Cuvier, to any of his contemporaries, both by the number of fishes he has known, and the accuracy of his figures, which exceed three hundred for fresh-water and marine species. His knowledge of those which inhabit the Mediterranean Sea was so extensive that little has been added since his time. 'It is the work,' says the same great authority, 'which has supplied almost every thing which we find on that subject in Gesner, Aldrovandus, Willoughby, Artedi, and Linnæus; and even Lacepede has been obliged, in many instances, to depend on Rondelet.' The text, however, is far inferior to the figures, and is too much occupied with an attempt to fix the ancient names of the several species.[s]

28. The very little book of Dr. Caius on British Dogs, published in 1570, the whole of which, I believe, has been translated by Pennant in his British Zoology, is hardly worth mentioning; nor do I know that zoological literature has anything more to produce till almost the close of the century, when the first and second volumes of Aldrovandus's vast natural history was published. These, as well as the third, which appeared in 1603, treat of birds; the fourth is on insects; and these alone were given to the world by the laborious author, a professor of natural history at Bologna. After his death in 1605, nine more folio volumes, embracing with various degrees of detail most other parts of natural history, were successively published by different editors. 'We can only consider the works of Aldrovandus,' says Cuvier, 'as an immense compilation without taste or genius; the very plan and materials being in a great measure borrowed from Gesner; and Buffon has had reason to say that it would be reduced to a tenth part of its bulk by striking out the useless and impertinent matter.'[t] Buffon, however, which Cuvier might have gone on to say, praises the method of Aldrovandus and his fidelity of description, and even ranks his work above every other natural history.[u]

Aldrovandus (side note)

---

[s] Biogr. univ. (Cuvier).   [t] Id.

[u] Hist. naturelle, Premier Discours. The truth is, that all Buffon's censures on Aldrovandus fall equally on Gesner, who is not less accumulative of materials not properly bearing on natural history, and not much less destitute of systematic order. The remarks of Buffon on this waste of learning are very just, and applicable to the works of the sixteenth century on almost every subject as well as zoology.

I am not acquainted with its contents; but according to Linnæus, Aldrovandus, or the editors of his posthumous volumes, added only a very few species of quadrupeds to those mentioned by Gesner, among which are the Zebra, the Jerboa, the Musk Rat of Russia, and the Manis or Scaly Ant-eater.[x]

29. A more steady progress was made in the science of botany, which commemorates, in those living me- *Botany;* morials with which she delights to honour her cul- *Turner.* tivators, several names still respected, and several books that have not lost their utility. Our countryman, Dr. Turner, published the first part of a New Herbal in 1551; the second and third did not appear till 1562 and 1568. 'The arrangement,' says Pulteney, 'is alphabetical according to the Latin names, and after the description he frequently specifies the places and growth. He is ample in his discrimination of the species, as his great object was to ascertain the Materia Medica of the ancients, and of Dioscorides in particular, throughout the vegetable kingdom. He first gives names to many English plants; and allowing for the time when specifical distinctions were not established, when almost all the small plants were disregarded, and the Cryptogamia almost wholly overlooked, the number he was acquainted with is much beyond what could easily have been imagined in an original writer on his subject.'[y]

30. The work of Maranta, published in 1559, on the method of understanding medicinal plants, is, in *Maranta;* the judgment of a late writer of considerable repu- *Botanical Gardens.* tation, nearly at the head of any in that age. The author is independent, though learned, extremely acute in discriminating plants known to the ancients, and has discovered many himself, ridiculing those who dared to add nothing to Dioscorides.[z] Maranta had studied in the private garden, formed by Pinelli at Naples. But public gardens were

---

[x] Collections of natural history seem to have been formed by all who applied themselves to the subject in the sixteenth century; such as Cordus, Mathiolus, Mercati, Gesner, Agricola, Belon, Rondelet, Ortelius, and many others. Hakluyt mentions the cabinets of some English collectors from which he had derived assistance. Beckmann's Hist. of Inventions, ii. 57.

[y] Pulteney's Historical Sketch of the Progress of Botany in England, p. 68.

[z] Sprengel, Historia Rei Herbariæ (1807), i. 345.

common in Italy. Those of Pisa and Padua were the earliest,
and perhaps the more celebrated. One established by the
Duke of Ferrara, was peculiarly rich in exotic plants procured
from Greece and Asia.[a] And perhaps the generous emulation
in all things honourable between the houses of Este and
Medici led Ferdinand of Tuscany, some time afterwards near
the end of the century, to enrich the gardens of Pisa with
the finest plants of Asia and America. The climate of
France was less favourable; the first public garden seems to
have been formed at Montpellier, and there was none at
Paris in 1558.[b] Meantime the vegetable productions of
newly discovered countries became familiar to Europe.
Many are described in the excellent History of the Indies by
Hernando d' Oviedo, such as the Cocos, the Cactus, the
Guiacum. Another Spanish author, Carate, first describes
the Solanum Tuberosum, or potato, under the name of
Papas.[c] It has been said that tobacco is first mentioned, or
at least first well described by Benzoni, in Nova Novi Orbis
Historia (Geneva, 1578).[d] Belon went to the Levant soon
after the middle of the century, on purpose to collect plants;
several other writers of voyages followed before its close.
Among these was Prosper Alpinus, who passed several years
in Egypt, but his principal work, De Plantis Exoticis, is
posthumous, and did not appear till 1627. He is said to be
the first European author who has mentioned coffee.[e]

31. The critical examination of the ancients, the establishment of gardens, the travels of botanists, thus
Gesner.   furnished a great supply of plants; it was now required to compare and arrange them. Gesner first undertook this; he had formed a garden of his own at Zurich, and
has the credit of having discovered the true system of classi-
fying plants according to the organs of fructification; which,
however, he does not seem to have made known, nor were
his botanical writings published till the last century. Gesner

a Sprengel, 360.   b Id. 363.   du café, et en ait décrit la préparation
c Id. 378.   d Id. 373.   avec exactitude. It is possible that this
e Id. 384. Corniani, vi. 25. Biogr.   book of Rauwolf being written in Ger-
univ. Yet, in the article on Rauwolf,   man, and the author being obscure in
a German naturalist, who published an   comparison with Prosper Alpinus, his
account of his travels in the Levant as   prior claim has been till lately over-
early as 1581, he is mentioned as one of   looked.
the first qui ait parlé de l'usage de boire

was the first who mentions the Indian Sugar-cane and the Tobacco, as well as many indigenous plants. It is said that he was used to chew and smoke tobacco, 'by which he rendered himself giddy, and in a manner drunk.'[f] As Gesner died in 1564, this carries back the knowledge of tobacco in Europe several years beyond the above-mentioned treatise of Benzoni.

32. Dodoens, or Dodonæus, a Dutch physician, in 1553, translated into his own language the history of plants by Fuchs, to which he added 133 figures. *Dodoens.* These, instead of using the alphabetical order of his predecessor, he arranged according to a method which he thought more natural. 'He explains,' says Sprengel, 'well and learnedly the ancient botanists, and described many plants for the first time;' among these are the Ulex Europæus and the Hyacinthus non scriptus. The great aim of rendering the modern Materia Medica conformable to the ancient seems to have made the early botanists a little inattentive to objects before their eyes. Dodoens himself is rather a physician than a botanist, and is more diligent about the uses of plants than their characteristics. He collected all his writings, under the title Stirpium Historiæ Pemptades Sex, at Antwerp in 1583, with 1,341 figures, a greater number than had yet been published.

33. The Stirpium Adversaria, by Pena and Lobel, the latter of whom is best known as a botanist, was published at London in 1570. Lobel indeed, though *Lobel.* a native of Lille, having passed most of his life in England, may be fairly counted among our botanists. He had previously travelled much over Europe. 'In the execution of this work,' says Pulteney, 'there is exhibited, I believe, the first sketch, rude as it is, of a natural method of arrangement, which however extends no farther than throwing the plants into large tribes, families, or orders, according to the external appearance or habit of the whole plant or flower, without establishing any definitions or characters. The whole forms forty-four tribes. Some contain the plants of one or two modern genera, others many, and some, it must be owned, very incongruous to each other. On the

---

[f] Sprengel, 373. 390.

whole, they are much superior to Dodoens's divisions.'[g]
Lobel's Adversaria contains descriptions of 1,200 or 1,500
plants, with 272 engravings; the former are not clear or
well expressed, and in this he is inferior to his contemporaries: the latter are on copper, very small, but neat.[h]
In a later work, the Plantarum Historia, Antwerp, 1576, the
number of figures is very considerably greater, but the book
has been less esteemed, being a sort of complement to the
other.   Sprengel speaks more highly of Lobel than the Biographie universelle.

34. Clusius or Lecluse, born at Arras, and a traveller, like
many other botanists, over Europe, till he settled
Clusius.   at Leyden as professor of botany in 1593, is generally reckoned the greatest master of his science whom the
age produced.   His descriptions are remarkable for their
exactness, precision, elegance, and method, though he seems
to have had little regard to natural classification.   He has
added a long list to the plants already known.   Clusius began by a translation of Dodoens into Latin; he published
several other works within the century.[i]

35. Cæsalpin was not only a botanist, but greater in this
than in any other of the sciences he embraced.   He
Cæsalpin.   was the first (the writings of Gesner, if they go so
far, being in his time unpublished,) who endeavoured to
establish a natural order of classification on philosophical
principles.   He founded it on the number, figure, and position of the fructifying parts, observing the situation of the
calix and flower relatively to the germen, the divisions of
the former, and in general what has been regarded in later
systems as the basis of arrangement.   He treats of trees and
of herbs separately, as two grand divisions, but under each
follows his own natural system.   The distinction of sexes he
thought needless in plants, on account of their simplicity;
though he admits it to exist in some, as in the hemp and
the juniper.   His treatise on Plants, in 1583, is divided into
sixteen books; in the first of which he lays down the principles of vegetable anatomy and physiology.   Many ideas,
says Du Petit Thouars, are found there, of which the truth

[g] Historical Sketch, p. 102.   [i] Sprengel, 407. Biogr. univ. Pul-
[h] Sprengel, 399.   teney.

was long afterwards recognised. He analysed the structure
of seeds, which he compares to the eggs of animals ; an
analogy, however, which had occurred to Empedocles among
the ancients. 'One page alone,' the same writer observes,
'in the dedication of Cæsalpin to the duke of Tuscany, con-
centrates the principles of a good botanical system so well,
that, notwithstanding all the labours of later botanists,
nothing material could be added to his sketch, and if this
one page out of all the writings of Cæsalpin remained, it
would be enough to secure him an immortal reputation.'[k]
Cæsalpin unfortunately gave no figures of plants, which
may have been among the causes that his system was so long
overlooked.

36. The Historia Generalis Plantarum by Dalechamps,
in 1587, contains 2,731 figures, many of which, how-   Dalechamps;
ever, appear to be repetitions. These are divided   Bauhin.
into eighteen classes according to their form and size, but
with no natural method. His work is imperfect and faulty;
most of the descriptions are borrowed from his predecessors.[l]
Tabernæmontanus, in a book in the German language, has
described 5,800 species, and given 2,480 figures.[m]   The
Phytopinax of Gerard Bauhin (Basle, 1596) is the first
important work of one who, in conjunction with his brother
John, laboured for forty years in the advancement of botanical knowledge. It is a catalogue of 2,460 plants, including,
among about 250 others that were new, the first accurate
description of the potato, which, as he informs us, was already cultivated in Italy.[n]

37. Gerard's Herbal, published in 1597, was formed on the
basis of Dodoens, taking in much from Lobel and   Gerard's
Clusius; the figures are from the blocks used by   Herbal.
Tabernæmontanus. It is not now esteemed at all by botanists,
at least in this first edition ; 'but,' says Pulteney, 'from its
being well timed, from its comprehending almost the whole
of the subjects then known, by being written in English,

---

[k] Biogr. univ. Sprengel, after giving·
an analysis of the system of Cæsalpin,
concludes: En primi systematis carpo-
logici specimen, quod licet imperfectum
sit, ingenii tamen summi monumentum
et aliorum omnium ad Gærtnerium usque
exemplar est.   P. 430.
[l] Sprengel, 432.
[m] Id. 496.
[n] Id. 451.

and ornamented with a more numerous set of figures than had ever accompanied any work of the kind in this kingdom, it obtained great repute.'[o]

SECT. III.—ON ANATOMY AND MEDICINE.

Fallopius, Eustachius, and other Anatomists—State of Medicine.

Anatomy; Fallopius

38. FEW sciences were so successfully pursued in this period as that of anatomy. If it was impossible to snatch from Vesalius the pre-eminent glory that belongs to him as almost its creator, it might still be said that two men now appeared who, had they lived earlier, would probably have gone as far, and who, by coming later, were enabled to go beyond him. These were Fallopius and Eustachius, both Italians. The former is indeed placed by Sprengel even above Vesalius, and reckoned the first anatomist of the sixteenth century. No one had understood that delicate part of the human structure, the organ of hearing, so well as Fallopius, though even he left much for others. He added several to the list of muscles, and made some discoveries in the intestinal and generative organs.[p]

Eustachius.

39. Eustachius, though on the whole inferior to Fallopius, went beyond him in the anatomy of the ear, in which a canal, as is well known, bears his name. One of his biographers has gone so far as to place him above every anatomist for the number of his discoveries. He has treated very well of the teeth, a subject little understood before, and was the first to trace the vena azygos through all its ramifications. No one as yet had exhibited the structure of the human kidneys, Vesalius having examined them only in dogs.[q] The scarcity of human subjects was in fact an irresistible temptation to take upon trust the identity between quadrupeds and man, which misled the great anatomists of the sixteenth century.[r] Comparative anatomy

---

[o] Hist. Sketch, p. 122.

[p] Portal. Sprengel, Hist. de la Médecine.

[q] Portal.

[r] The church had a repugnance to permit the dissection of dead bodies, but Fallopius tells us that the duke of Tuscany was sometimes obliging enough to

was therefore not yet promoted to its real dignity, both as an indispensable part of natural history, and as opening the most conclusive and magnificent views of teleology.   Coiter, an anatomist born in Holland, but who passed his life in Italy, Germany, and France, was perhaps the first to describe the skeletons of several animals; though Belon, as we have seen, had views far beyond his age in what is strictly comparative anatomy.   Coiter's work bears the date of 1575; in 1566 he had published one on human os-teology, where that of the fœtus is said to be first described, though some attribute this merit to Fallopius.   Coiter is called in the Biographie universelle one of the creators of pathological anatomy. *Coiter.*

40. Columbus (De Re Anatomica, Venice, 1559,) the suc-cessor of Vesalius at Padua, and afterwards profes-sor at Pisa and Rome, has announced the discovery of several muscles, and given the name of vomer to the small bone which sustains the cartilage of the nose, and which Vesalius had taken for a mere process of the sphenoid.   Co-lumbus, though too arrogant in censuring his great prede-cessor, generally follows him.[s]   Arantius, in 1571, is among the first who made known the anatomy of the gravid uterus, and the structure of the fœtus.[t]   He was also conversant, as Vidius, a professor at Paris of Italian birth, as early as 1542, had already been, with the anatomy of the brain.   But this was much improved by Varoli in his Anatomia, published in 1573, who traced the origin of the optic nerves, and gave a better account than any one before him of the eye and of the voice.   Piccolomini (Anatomiæ Prælectiones, 1586) is one of the first who described the cellular tissue, and in other respects has made valuable observations.   Ambrose Paré, a French surgeon, is deemed the founder of chirurgic science, at least in that country.   His works were first collected in 1561, but his treatise on gunshot wounds is as old as 1545.   Several other names are mentioned with respect by the his-torians of medicine and anatomy; such as those of Alberti, Benivieni, Donatus, and Schank.   Never, says Portal, were *Columbus.*

---

send a living criminal to the anatomists, *quem interficimus nostro modo et anato-misamus.* Sprengel suggests that 'nostro modo' meant by opium; but this seems

to be merely a conjecture. Hist. de la Médecine, iv. 11.
[s] Portal, i. 541.
[t] Id. vol. ii. p. 3.

anatomy and surgery better cultivated, with more emulation
or more encouragement, than about the end of the sixteenth
century. A long list of minor discoveries in the human frame
are recorded by this writer and by Sprengel. It will be readily
understood that we give these names, which of itself it is
rather an irksome labour to enumerate, with no other object
than that none of those who by their ability and diligence
carried forward the landmarks of human knowledge should
miss, in a history of general literature, of their meed of
Circulation remembrance. We reserve to the next period those
of the blood. passages in the anatomists of this age which have
seemed to anticipate the great discovery that immortalises
the name of Harvey.

41. These continual discoveries in the anatomical structure
Medicinal of man tended to guide and correct the theory of me-
science. dicine. The observations of this period became more
acute and accurate. Those of Plater and Foresti, especially
the latter, are still reputed classical in medical literature.
Prosper Alpinus may be deemed the father in modern times
of diagnostic science.[u] Plater, in his Praxis Medica, made
the first, though an imperfect attempt, at a classification of
diseases. Yet the observations made in this age, and the
whole practical system, are not exempt from considerable
faults; the remedies were too topical, the symptoms of disease
were more regarded than its cause ; the theory was too simple
and general ; above all, a great deal of credulity and superstition prevailed in the art.[x] Many among the first in science
believed in demoniacal possessions and sorcery, or in astrology. This was most common in Germany, where the school
of Paracelsus, discreditably to the national understanding,
exerted much influence. The best physicians of the century
were either Italian or French.

42. Notwithstanding the bigoted veneration for Hippocrates that most avowed, several physicians, not at all adhering to Paracelsus, endeavoured to set up a rational experience against the Greek school, when they thought them at
variance. Joubert of Montpellier, in his Paradoxes (1566),
was a bold innovator of this class ; but many of his paradoxes

u Sprengel, iii. 173.   x Id. 156.

are now established truths. Botal of Asti, a pupil of Fallopius, introduced the practice of venesection on a scale before unknown, but prudently aimed to show that Hippocrates was on his side. The faculty of medicine, however, at Paris condemned it as erroneous and very dangerous. His method, nevertheless, had great success, especially in Spain.[y]

Sect. IV.—On Oriental Literature.

43. This is a subject over which, on account of my total ignorance of Eastern languages, I am glad to hasten. The first work that appears after the middle of the century is a grammar of the Syriac, Chaldee, and Rabbinical, compared with the Arabic and Ethiopic languages, which Angelo Canini, a man as great in Oriental as in Grecian learning, published at Paris in 1554. In the next year Widmandstadt gave, from the press of Vienna, the first edition of the Syriac version of the New Testament.[z] Several lexicons and grammars of this tongue, which is in fact only a dialect not far removed from the Chaldee, though in a different alphabetical character, will be found in the bibliographical writers. The Syriac may be said to have been now fairly added to the literary domain. The Antwerp Polygot of Arias Montanus, besides a complete Chaldee paraphrase of the Old Testament, the Complutensian having only contained the Pentateuch, gives the New Testament in Syriac, as well as Pagnini's Latin translation of the Old.[a]

Syriac version of New Testament.

44. The Hebrew language was studied, especially among the German Protestants, to a considerable extent, if we may judge from the number of grammatical works published within this period. Among these Morhof selects the Erotemata Linguæ Hebrææ by Neander, printed at Basle in 1567. Tremillius, Chevalier, and Drusius among Protestants, Masius and Clarius in the church of Rome, are

Hebrew critics.

---

[y] Sprengel, iii. p. 215.

[z] Schelhorn, Amœnitates Literariæ, xiii. 234. Biogr. universelle. Andrès, xix. 45. Eichhorn, v. 435. In this edition the Syriac text alone appeared;

Henry Stephens reprinted it with the Greek and with two Latin translations.

[a] Andrès, xix. 49. The whole edition is richer in materials than that of Ximenes.

the most conspicuous names. The first, an Italian refugee, is chiefly known by his translation of the Bible into Latin, in which he was assisted by Francis Junius. The second, a native of France, taught Hebrew at Cambridge, and was there the instructor of Drusius, whose father had emigrated from Flanders on the ground of religion. Drusius himself, afterwards professor of Hebrew at the university of Franeker, has left writings of more permanent reputation than most other Hebraists of the sixteenth century; they relate chiefly to biblical criticism and Jewish antiquity, and several of them have a place in the Critici Sacri and in the collection of Ugolini.[b] Clarius is supposed to have had some influence on the decree of the council of Trent, asserting the authenticity of the Vulgate.[c] Calasio was superior, probably, to them all, but his principal writings do not belong to this period. No large proportion of the treatises published by Ugolini ought, so far as I know their authors, to be referred to the sixteenth century.

45. The Hebrew language had been early studied in England, though there has been some controversy as to the extent of the knowledge which the first translators of the Bible possessed. We find that both Chevalier read lectures on Hebrew at Cambridge not long after the queen's accession, and his disciple Drusius at Oxford, from 1572 to 1576.[d] Hugh Broughton was a deeply learned rabbinical scholar. I do not know that we could produce any other name of marked reputation; and we find that the first Hebrew types, employed in any considerable number, appear in 1592. These are in a book not relating directly to Hebrew, Rheses Institutiones Linguæ Cambro-Britannicæ. But a few Hebrew characters, very rudely cut in wood, are found in Wakefield's Oration, printed as early as 1524.[e]

Its study in England.

---

[b] Drusius is extolled by all critics except Scaliger (Scaligerana Secunda) who seems to have conceived one of his personal prejudices against the Franeker professor, and depreciates his moral character. Simon thinks Drusius the most learned and judicious writer we find in the Critici Sacri. Hist. critique du V. T. p. 498. Biogr. univ. Blount.

[c] Clarius, according to Simon, knew Hebrew but indifferently, and does little more than copy Munster, whose observations are too full of Judaism, as he consulted no interpreters but the rabbinical writers. Masius, the same author says, is very learned, but has the like fault of dealing in rabbinical expositions. p. 499.

[d] Wood's Hist. and Antiquities. In 1574 he was appointed to read publicly in Syriac.

[e] Preface to Herbert's Typographical Antiquities.

46. The Syriac and Chaldee were so closely related to Hebrew, both as languages, and in the theological purposes for which they were studied, that they did not much enlarge the field of Oriental literature. The most copious language, and by far the most fertile of books, was the Arabic. A few slight attempts at introducing a knowledge of this had been made before the middle of the century. An Arabic as well as Syriac press at Vienna was first due to the patronage of Ferdinand I. in 1554, but for a considerable time no fruit issued from it. But the increasing zeal of Rome for the propagation of its faith, both among infidels and schismatics, gave a larger sweep to the cultivation of Oriental languages. Gregory XIII. founded a Maronite College at Rome in 1584, for those Syrian Christians of Libanus who had united themselves to the Catholic church; the cardinal Medici, afterwards grand duke of Florence, established an Oriental press, about 1580, under the superintendence of John Baptista Raimondi; and Sixtus V. in 1588 that of the Vatican, which, though principally designed for early Christian literature, was possessed of types for the chief Eastern languages. Hence the Arabic, hitherto almost neglected, began to attract more attention; the Gospels in that language, were published at Rome in 1590 or 1591; some works of Euclid and Avicenna had preceded; one or two elementary books on grammar appeared in Germany; and several other publications belong to the last years of the century.[f] Scaliger now entered upon the study of Arabic with all his indefatigable activity. Yet, at the end of the century, few had penetrated far into a region so novel and extensive, and in which the subsidiary means of knowledge were so imperfect. . The early grammars are represented by Eichhorn as being very indifferent, and in fact very few Arabic books had been printed. The edition of the Koran by Pagninus in 1529 was unfortunately suppressed, as we have before mentioned, by the zeal of the court of Rome. Casaubon, writing to Scaliger in 1597, declares that no one within his recollection had even touched with the tips of his fingers that language, except Postel in a few rhapsodies;

Marginal note: Arabic begins to be studied.

---

[f] Eichhorn, v. 641, et alibi. Tiraboschi, viii. 195. Ginguéné, vol. vii. p. 258.

and that neither he nor any one else had written anything
on the Persic.[g] Gesner, however, in his Mithridates, 1558,
had given the Lord's prayer in twenty-two languages; to
which Rocca at Rome, in 1591, added three more; and
Megiser increased the number, in a book published next year
at Frankfort, to forty.[h]

SECT. V.—ON GEOGRAPHY.

Voyages in the Indies—Those of the English—Of Ortelius and others.

47. A MORE important accession to the knowledge of Europe
as to the rest of the world, than had hitherto been
made through the press, is due to Ramusio, a Venetian who had filled respectable offices under the republic.
He published, in 1550, the first volume of his well-known
collection of Travels ; the second appeared in 1559, and the
third in 1565. They have been reprinted several times, and
all the editions are not equally complete. No general collection of travels had hitherto been published, except the
Novus Orbis of Grynæus, and though the greater part perhaps of those included in Ramusio's three volumes had
appeared separately, others came forth for the first time.
The Africa of Leo Africanus, a baptized Moor, with which
Ramusio begins, is among these ; and it is upon this work
that such knowledge as we possessed, till very recent times,
as to the interior of that continent, was almost entirely
founded. Ramusio in the remainder of this volume gives
many voyages in Africa, the East Indies, and Indian Archi-
pelago, including two accounts of Magellan's circumnavi-
gation of the world, and one of Japan, which had very lately
been discovered. The second volume is dedicated to travels
through northern Europe and Asia, beginning with that of
Marco Polo, including also the curious, though very ques-

Marginal note: Collection of voyages by Ramusio.

[g] Nostra autem memoria, qui eas lin-
guas vel ακρῳ, quod aiunt, δακτυλῳ atti-
gerit, novi neminem, nisi quod Postellum
nescio quid muginatum esse de lingua
Arabica memini. Sed illa quam tenuia,
quam exilia ! de Persicâ, quod equidem
memini neque ille, neque alius quisquam
vel γρυ το λεγομενον. Epist. ciii.

[h] Biogr. univ. arts. Megiser and
Rocca.

tionable voyage of the Zeni brothers, about 1400, to some
unknown region north of Scotland.   In the third volume we
find the conquests of Cortes and Pizarro, with all that had
already been printed of the excellent work of Hernando
d'Oviedo on the Western world.   Few subsequent collections
of voyages are more esteemed for the new matter they contain than that of Ramusio.[1]

48. The importance of such publications as that of Ramusio
was soon perceived, not only in the stimulus they *Curiosity they awakened.*
gave to curiosity or cupidity towards following up
the paths of discovery, but in calling the attention of reflecting minds, such as Bodin and Montaigne, to so copious a
harvest of new facts, illustrating the physical and social
character of the human species.   But from the want of a
rigid investigation, or more culpable reasons, these early
narratives are mingled with much falsehood, and misled
some of the more credulous philosophers almost as often as
they enlarged their knowledge.

49. The story of the Portuguese conquests in the East,
more varied and almost as wonderful as romance, *Other voyages.*
was recounted in the Asia of Joam de Barros (1552),
and in that of Castanheda in the same and two ensuing
years; these have never been translated.   The great voyage
of Magellan had been written by one of his companions,
Pigafetta.   This was published in Italian in 1556.   The
History of the Indies by Acosta, 1590, may perhaps belong
more strictly to other departments of literature than to
geography.

50. The Romish missionaries, especially the Jesuits, spread
themselves with intrepid zeal during this period over *Accounts of China.*
infidel nations.   Things strange to European preju-
dice, the books, the laws, the rites, the manners, the dresses
of those remote people, were related by them on their return,
for the most part orally, but sometimes through the press.
The vast empire of China, the Cathay of Marco Polo, over
which an air of fabulous mystery had hung, and which ·is
delineated in the old maps with much ignorance of its position and extent, now first was brought within the sphere of

---

[1] Biogr. univ.

European knowledge. The Portuguese had some traffic to Canton; but the relations they gave were uncertain, till, in 1577, two Augustine friars persuaded a Chinese officer to take them into the country. After a residence of four months they returned to Manilla, and, in consequence of their reports, Philip II. sent, in 1580, an embassy to the court of Pekin. The History of China by Mendoza, as it is called, contains all the knowledge that the Spaniards were able to collect by these means; and it may be said, on comparison with later books on the same subject, to be as full and ample an account of China as could have been given in such circumstances. This book was published in 1585, and from that time, but no earlier, do we date our acquaintance with that empire.[k] Maffei, in his History of India, threw all the graces of a pure Latin style over his description of the East. The first part of a scarce and curious collection of voyages to the two Indies, with the names of De Bry and Merian as India and its editors, appeared at Frankfort in 1590. Six other Russia. volumes were published at intervals down to 1634. Possevin, meantime, told us more of a much nearer state, Muscovy, than was before familiar to western Europe, though the first information had been due to England.

51. The spirit of lucre vied with that of religion in penetrating unknown regions. In this the English have English discoveries most to boast; they were the first to pass the Icy in the Cape and anchor their ships in the White Sea. Northern seas. This was in the famous voyage of Chancellor in 1553. Anthony Jenkinson soon afterwards, through the heart of Russia, found his way to Bokhara and Persia. They followed up the discoveries of Cabot in North America; and, before the end of the century, had ascertained much of the coasts about Labrador and Hudson's Bay, as well as those of Virginia, the first colony. These English voyages were recorded in the three parts of the Collection of Voyages, by Hakluyt, published in 1598, 1599, and 1600. Drake, second to Magellan in that bold enterprise, traversed the circumference of the world; and the reign of Elizabeth, quite as much as any

---

[k] Biogr. univ. This was translated into English by R. Parke in 1588; at least I believe it to be the same work, but have never seen the original.

later age, bears witness to the intrepidity and skill, if not strictly to the science, of our sailors. For these undaunted navigators, traversing the unexplored wildernesses of ocean in small ill-built vessels, had neither any effectual assistance from charts, nor the means of making observations themselves, or of profiting by those of others. Hence, when we come to geographical knowledge, in the proper sense of the word, we find it surprisingly scanty, even at the close of the sixteenth century.

52. It had not, however, been neglected, so far as a multiplicity of books could prove a regard to it. Ortelius, Geographical books; in his Theatrum Orbis Terrarum, (the first edition Ortelius. of which was in 1570, augmented afterwards by several maps of later dates,) gives a list of about 150 geographical treatises, most of them subsequent to 1560. His own work is the first general atlas since the revival of letters, and has been justly reckoned to make an epoch in geography, being the basis of all collections of maps since formed, and deserving, it is said, even yet to be consulted, notwithstanding the vast progress of our knowledge of the earth.[m] The maps in the later editions of the sixteenth century bear various dates. That of Africa is of 1590; and though the outline is tolerably given, we do not find the Mauritius Isles, while the Nile is carried almost to the Cape of Good Hope, and made to issue from a great lake. In the map of America, dated 1587, the outline on the N.E. side contains New France, with the *city* of Canada; the St. Lawrence traverses the country, but without lakes; Florida is sufficiently distinguished, but the intervening coast is loosely laid down. Estotiland, the supposed discovery of the Zeni, appears to the North, and Greenland beyond. The outline of South America is worse, the southern parts covering nearly as much longitude as the northern, an error which was in some measure diminished in a map of 1603. An immense solid land, as in all the older maps, connects Terra del Fuego with New Guinea. The delineation of the southern coasts of Asia is not very bad, even in the earlier maps of Ortelius, but some improvement is perceived in his

---

[m] Biogr. univ.

knowledge of China and the adjacent seas in that of the world given in the edition of 1588. The maps of Europe in Ortelius are chiefly defective as to the countries on the Baltic Sea and Russia ; but there is a general incorrectness of delineation which must strike the eye at once of any person slightly experienced in geography.

53. Gerard Mercator, a native of the duchy of Juliers, where he passed the greater part of his life, was perhaps superior to Ortelius. His fame is most diffused by the invention of a well-known mode of delineating hydrographical charts, in which the parallels and meridians intersect each other at right angles. The first of these was published in 1569 ; but the principle of the method was not understood till Edward Wright, in 1599, explained it in his Correction of Errors in Navigation.[n] The Atlas of Mercator, in an edition of 1598, which contains only part of Europe, is superior to that of Ortelius ; and as to England, of which there had been maps published by Lluyd in 1569, and by Saxton in 1580, it may be reckoned very tolerably correct. Lluyd's map, indeed, is published in the Atlas of Ortelius. But in the northern regions of Europe we still find a mass of arbitrary, erroneous conjecture.

54. Botero, the Piedmontese Jesuit mentioned in another place, has given us a cosmography, or general description of as much of the world as was then known, entitled Relazioni Universali ; the edition I have seen is undated, but he mentions the discovery of Nova Zembla in 1594. His knowledge of Asia is very limited, and chiefly derived from Marco Polo. China, he says, extends from 17° to 52° of latitude, and has 22° of longitude. Japan is sixty leagues from China and 150 from America. The coasts, Botero observes, from Bengal to China are so dangerous, that two or three are lost out of every four ships, but the master who succeeds in escaping these perils is sure to make his fortune.

55. But the best map of the sixteenth century is one of uncommon rarity, which is found in a very few copies of the first edition of Hakluyt's Voyages. This contains Davis's Straits (Fretum Davis), Virginia by name, and the lake

---

[n] Montucla, ii. 651. Biogr. univ. art. Mercator.

Ontario. The coast of Chili is placed more correctly than in the prior maps of Ortelius; and it is noticed in the margin that this trending of the coast less westerly than had been supposed was discovered by Drake in 1577, and confirmed by Sarmiento and Cavendish. The huge Terra Australis of the old geography is left out. Corea is represented near its place, and China with some degree of correctness; even the north coast of New Holland is partially traced. The strait of Anian, which had been presumed to divide Asia from America, has disappeared, while a marginal note states that the distance between those two continents in latitude 38° is not less than 1,200 leagues. The Ultra-Indian region is inaccurate; the sea of Aral is still unknown, and little pains have been taken with central and northern Asia. But upon the whole it represents the utmost limit of geographical knowledge at the close of the sixteenth century, and far excels the maps in the edition of Ortelius at Antwerp in 1588.[o]

Sect. VI.—On History.

56. The history of Italy by Guicciardini, though it is more properly a work of the first part of the century, was not published till 1564. It is well known for the solidity of the reflections, the gravity and impartiality with which it is written, and the prolixity of the narration; a fault, however, frequent and not unpardonable in historians contemporary and familiar with the events they relate. If the siege of Pisa in 1508 appeared so uninteresting a hundred years afterwards, as to be the theme of ridicule with Boccalini, it was far otherwise to the citizens of Florence soon after the time. Guicciardini has generally held the first place among Italian historians, though he is by no means equal in literary merit to Machiavel. Adriani, whose continuation of Guicciardini extends to 1574, is little read, nor does he seem to be much recommended by style. No other historian of that country need be mentioned for works published within the sixteenth century.

Guicciardini.

---

[o] [This map is in the British Museum.—1842.]

57. The French have ever been distinguished for those
French
memoirs.
personal memoirs of men more or less conversant
with public life, to which Philip de Comines led the
way.   Several that fell within this period are deserving of
being read, not only for their relation of events, with which
we do not here much concern ourselves, but for a lively
style, and occasionally for good sense and acute thinking.
Those of Montluc may be praised for the former.   Spain had
a considerable historian in Mariana, twenty books of whose
history were published in Latin in 1592, and five more in
1595; the concluding five books do not fall within the
century.   The style is vigorous and classical, the thoughts
judicious.   Buchanan's History of Scotland has already been
praised for the purity of its language.   Few modern histories
are more redolent of an antique air.   We have nothing to
boast in England; our historical works of the Elizabethan
age are mere chronicles, and hardly good even as such.   Nor
do I know any Latin historians of Germany or the Low
Countries who, as writers, deserve our attention.

SECT. VII.—GENERAL STATE OF LITERATURE.

58. THE great Italian universities of Bologna, Padua, Pisa,
Universities
in Italy.
and Pavia, seem to have lost nothing of their
lustre throughout the century.   New colleges, new
buildings in that stately and sumptuous architecture which
distinguishes this period, bore witness to a continual patronage, and a public demand for knowledge.   It is true that the
best days of classical literature had passed away in Italy.
But the revival of theological zeal, and of those particular
studies which it fostered, might perhaps more than compensate in its effect on the industry of the learned for this
decline of philology.   The sciences also of medicine and
mathematics attracted many more students than before.   The
Jesuit colleges, and those founded by Gregory XIII., have
been already mentioned.   They were endowed at a large expense in that palmy state of the Roman see.

59. Universities were founded at Altdorf and Leyden in 1575, at Helmstadt in 1576. Others of less import- In other ance began to exist in the same age. The Uni- countries. versity of Edinburgh derives its origin from the charter of James in 1582. Those of Oxford and Cambridge, reviving as we have seen after a severe shock at the accession of Elizabeth, continued through her reign to be the seats of a progressive and solid erudition. A few colleges were founded in this age. I should have wished to give some sketch of the mode of instruction pursued in these two universities. But sufficient materials have not fallen in my way; what I have been able to glean has already been given to the reader in some pages of the first volume. It was the common practice at Oxford, observed in form down to this century, that every candidate for the degree of bachelor of arts, independently of other exercises, should undergo an examination (become absolutely nominal) in the five sciences of grammar, logic, rhetoric, ethics, and geometry; every one for that of master of arts, in the additional sciences of physics, metaphysics, Hebrew, and some more. These were probably the ancient trivium and quadrivium; enlarged, perhaps after the sixteenth century, according to the increase of learning, and the apparent necessity of higher qualifications.[p] But it would be, I conceive, a great mistake to imagine that the requisitions for academical degrees were ever much insisted upon. The universities sent forth abundance of illiterate graduates in every age. And as they had little influence, at least of a favourable sort, either on philosophy or polite literature, we are not to overrate their importance in the history of the intellectual progress of mankind.[q]

60. Public libraries were considerably enlarged during this period. Those of Rome, Ferrara, and Florence in Italy, of Vienna and Heidelberg in Germany, stood much above any others. Sixtus V. erected the Libraries.

---

[p] ['The quadrivials, I mean arithmetic, music, geometry, and astronomy, are now little regarded in either of the universities.' Harrison's Description of England, p. 252. Hence we may infer that the more modern division in use at Oxford was made after his time.—1842.]

[q] Lord Bacon animadverts (De Cogitatis et Visis) on the fetters which the universities imposed on the investigation of truth; and Morhof ascribes the establishment of the academies in Italy to

splendid repository of the Vatican. Philip II. founded that
of the Escurial, perhaps after 1580, and collected books with
great labour and expense; all who courted the favour of
Spain contributing also by presents of rarities.[r] Ximenes
had established the library of Alcala; and that of Salamanca
is likewise more ancient than this of the Escurial. Every
king of France took a pride in adding to the royal library
of Paris. By an ordinance of 1556, a copy of every book
printed with privilege was to be deposited in this library.
It was kept at Fontainebleau, but transferred to Paris in
1595. During the civil wars its progress was slow.[s] The
first prince of Orange founded the public library of Leyden,
which shortly became one of the best in Europe. The catalogue was published in 1597. That bequeathed by Hum-
phrey, duke of Gloucester, to the University of Oxford, was
dispersed in the general havoc made under Edward VI. At
the close of the century the university had no public library.
But Sir Thomas Bodley had already, in 1597, made the
generous offer of presenting his own, which was carried
into effect in the first years of the ensuing age.[t] In the
colleges there were generally libraries. If we could believe
Scaliger, these were good; but he had never been in England, and there is no reason, I believe, to estimate them
highly.[u] Archbishop Parker had founded, or at least greatly

---

the narrow and pedantic spirit of the
universities. l. i. c. 14.

[r] Mariana, in a long passage wherein
he describes the Escurial palace, gives
this account of the library: Vestibulo
bibliotheca imposita, majori longitudine
omnino pedum centum octoginta quinque, lata pedes triginta duos, libros
servat praesertim Græcos manuscriptos,
præcipuæ plerosque vetustatis; qui ex
omnibus Europæ partibus ad famam
novi operis magno numero confluxerunt:
auro pretiosiores thesauri, *digni quorum
evolvendorum major eruditis hominibus
facultas contingeret.* Quod enim ex captivis et majestate revinctis literis emolu-
mentum? De Rege et Regis Institutione,
l. iii. c. 10. The noble freedom of
Mariana breaks out, we see, in the
midst of his praise of royal magnificence. Few, if any, libraries, except
those of the universities, were accessible

to men of studious habits; a reproach
that has been very slowly effaced. I
have often been astonished, in considering this, that so much learning was
really acquired.

[s] Jugler's Hist. Literaria, c. iii. s. 5.
This very laborious work of the middle
of the last century contains the most
ample account of public libraries
throughout Europe that I have been
able to find. The German libraries,
with the two exceptions of Vienna and
Heidelberg, do not seem to have become
of much importance in the sixteenth
century.

[t] Wood's Hist. and Ant. p. 922.

[u] Scalig. Secunda, p. 236. De mon
temps, he says, in the same place, il y
avoit à Londres douze bibliothèques com-
plètes, et à Paris quatre-vingts. I do not
profess to understand this epithet.

enlarged, the public library of Cambridge. Many private
persons of learning and opulence had formed libraries in
England under Elizabeth ; some of which still subsist in the
mansions of ancient families. I incline to believe that there
was at least as competent a stock of what is generally called
learning among our gentry as in any continental kingdom ;
their education was more literary, their habits more peaceable, their religion more argumentative. Perhaps we should
make an exception for Italy, in which the spirit of collecting
libraries was more prevalent.[x]

61. The last forty years of the sixteenth century were a
period of uninterrupted peace in Italy. Notwith- Collections
standing the pressure of governments always jealous of antiquities in Italy.
and sometimes tyrannical, it is manifest that at least the
states of Venice and Tuscany had grown in wealth, and in
the arts that attend it. Those who had been accustomed to
endure the licence of armies found a security in the rule of
law which compensated for many abuses. Hence that sort
of property, which is most exposed to pillage, became again
a favourite acquisition ; and, among the costly works of art
which adorned the houses of the wealthy, every relic of
antiquity found its place. Gems and medals, which the
books of Vico and Erizzo had taught the owners to arrange
and to appreciate, were sought so eagerly, that, according to
Hubert Goltzius, as quoted by Pinkerton, there were in Italy
380 of such collections. The marbles and bronzes, the
inscriptions of antiquity, were not less in request, and the
well-known word, *virtuosi*, applied to these lovers of what
was rare and beautiful in art or nature, bespoke the honour
in which their pursuits were held. The luxury of literature
displayed itself in scarce books, elegant impressions, and
sumptuous bindings.

62. Among the refined gentlemen, who devoted to these
graceful occupations their leisure and their riches,
none was more celebrated than Gian Vincenzio Pinelli.
Pinelli. He was born of a good family at Naples in 1538.
A strong thirst for knowledge, and the consciousness that
his birth exposed him to difficulties and temptations at home

---

[x] [Morhof, i. 3, mentions several large   that of the younger Aldus Manutius
private libraries in Italy and France :   contained 80,000 volumes.—1842.]

which might obstruct his progress, induced him to seek, at
the age of twenty-four, the university of Padua, at that
time the renowned scene of learning and of philosophy.[y]   In
this city he spent forty-three years, the remainder of his
life.   His father was desirous that he should practise the
law ; but, after a short study of this, Pinelli resumed his
favourite pursuits.   His fortune, indeed, was sufficiently
large to render any sacrifice of them unreasonable ; and it
may have been out of dislike of his compulsory reading, that
in forming this vast library he excluded works of jurisprudence.   This library was collected by the labour of many
years.   The catalogues of the Frankfort fairs, and those of
the principal booksellers in Italy, were diligently perused by
Pinelli ; nor did any work of value appear from the press on
either side of the Alps which he did not instantly add to
his shelves.   This great library was regularly arranged,
and, though he did not willingly display its stores to
the curious and ignorant, they were always accessible to
scholars.   He had also a considerable museum of globes,
maps, mathematical instruments, and fossils ; but he only
collected the scarcer coins.   In his manners, Pinelli was a
finely-polished gentleman, but of weak health, and for this
cause devoted to books, and seldom mingling with gay society, nor even belonging to the literary academies of the
city, but carrying on an extensive correspondence, and continually employed in writing extracts or annotations.   Yet
he has left nothing that has been published.   His own house
was, as it were, a perpetual academy, frequented by the
learned of all nations.   If Pinelli was not a man of great
genius, nor born to be of much service to any science, we
may still respect him for a love of learning, and a nobleness
of spirit, which has preserved his memory.[z]

63.   The literary academies of Italy continued to flourish

---

[y] Animadverterat autem hic noster,
domi, inter amplexus parentum et fami-
liarium obsequia, in urbe deliciarum
plena, militaribus et equestribus, quam
musarum studiis aptiore, non preventu-
rum sese ad eam gloriæ metam quam
sibi destinaverat, ideo gymnasii Patavini
fama permotus, &c.   Gauldi, Vita Pinelli.   This life by a contemporary, or

nearly such, is republished in the Vitæ
Illustrium Virorum by Bates.

[z] Gualdi.   Tiraboschi, vi. 214.   The
library of Pinelli was dispersed and in
great part destroyed by pirates not long
afterwards.   That long since formed by
one of his family is well known to book
collectors.

even more than before; many new societies of the same kind were founded. Several existed at Florence, but all others have been eclipsed by the Della Crusca, established in 1582. Those of another Tuscan city, which had taken the lead in such literary associations, did not long survive its political independence; the jealous spirit of Cosmo extinguished the Rozzi of Sienna in 1568. In governments as suspicious as those of Italy, the sort of secresy belonging to these meetings, and the encouragement they gave to a sentiment of mutual union, might appear sufficient reasons for watchfulness. We have seen how the academy of Modena was broken up on the score of religion. That of Venice, perhaps for the same reason, was dissolved by the senate in 1561, and did not revive till 1593. These, however, were exceptions to the rule; and it was the general policy of governments to cherish in the nobility a love of harmless amusements. All Lombardy and Romagna were full of academies; they were frequent in the kingdom of Naples, and in the ecclesiastical states.[a] They are a remarkable feature in the social condition of Italy, and could not have existed perhaps in any other country. They were the encouragers of a numismatic and lapidary erudition, elegant in itself, and throwing for ever its little sparks of light on the still ocean of the past, but not very favourable to comprehensive observation, and tending to bestow on an unprofitable pedantry the honours of real learning. This, indeed, is the inherent vice of all literary societies, accessible too frequently to those who, for amusement or fashion's sake, love as much knowledge as can be reached with facility, and from the nature of their transactions seldom capable of affording scope for any extensive research.

64. No academy or similar institution can be traced at this time, as far as I know, in France or Germany. But it is deserving of remark, that one sprung up in England, not indeed of the classical and polite character that belonged to the Infiammati of Padua, or

Italian academies.

Society of Antiquaries in England.

---

[a] Tiraboschi, viii. 125–179, is so full on this subject, that I have not recourse to the other writers who have, sometimes with great prolixity, investigated a subject more interesting in its details to the Italians than to us. Ginguéné adds very little to what he found in his predecessor.

the Della Crusca of Florence, yet useful in its objects, and honourable alike to its members and to the country. This was the Society of Antiquaries, founded by Archbishop Parker in 1572. Their object was the preservation of ancient documents, illustrative of history, which the recent dissolution of religious houses, and the shameful devastation attending it, had exposed to great peril. They intended also, by the reading of papers at their meetings, to keep alive the love and knowledge of English antiquity. In the second of these objects this society was more successful than in the first; several short dissertations, chiefly by Arthur Agard, their most active member, have been afterwards published. The Society comprised very reputable names, especially of lawyers, and continued to meet till early in the reign of James, who, from some jealousy, thought fit to dissolve it.[b]

65. The chief cities on this side of the Alps, whence new

New books, and catalogues of them.
editions came forth, were Paris, Basle, Lyons, Leyden, Antwerp, Brussels, Strasburg, Cologne, Heidelberg, Frankfort, Ingoldstadt, and Geneva. In all these, and in many other populous towns, booksellers, who were generally also printers, were a numerous body. In London at least forty or fifty were contemporaneous publishers in the latter part of Elizabeth's reign; but the number elsewhere in England was very small. The new books on the Continent, and within the Alps and Pyrenees, found their principal mart at the annual Frankfort fairs. Catalogues of such books began to be published, according to Beckmann, in 1554.[c] In a collective catalogue of all books offered for sale at Frankfort, from 1564 to 1592, I find the number, in Latin, Greek, and German, to be about 16,000. No Italian or French appear in this catalogue, being probably reserved for another. Of theology in Latin there are 3,200, and in this department the catholic publica-

---

[b] See life of Agard, in Biogr. Brit. and in Chalmers. But the best account is in the Introduction to the first volume of the Archæologia. The present Society of Antiquaries is the representative, but after long intermission, of this Elizabethan progenitor.

[c] Hist. of Inventions, iii. 120. 'George Willer, whom some improperly call Viller, and others Walter, a bookseller at Augsburg, who kept a large shop, and frequented the Frankfort fairs, first fell upon the plan of causing to be printed every fair a catalogue of all the new books, in which the size and printers' names were marked.' There seems to be some doubt whether the first year of these catalogues was 1554 or 1564; the collection mentioned in the text leads us rather to suspect the latter.

tions rather exceed the protestant. But of the theology in
the German language the number is 3,700, not one-fourth of
which is catholic. Scarcely any mere German poetry appears, but a good deal in both languages with musical notes.
Law furnishes about 1,600 works. I reckoned twenty-seven
Greek and thirty-two Latin grammars, not counting different
editions of the same. There are at least seventy editions
of parts of Aristotle. The German books are rather more
than one-third of the whole. Among the Latin I did not
observe one book by a writer of this island. In a compilation by Clessius, in 1602, purporting to be a conspectus of
the publications of the sixteenth century, formed partly from
catalogues of fairs, partly from those of public libraries, we
find, at least in the copy I have examined, but which seems
to want one volume, a much smaller number of productions
than in the former, but probably with more selection. The
books in modern languages are less than 1000, half French,
half Italian. In this catalogue also the catholic theology
rather outnumbers the protestant, which is perhaps not what
we should have expected to find.

66. These catalogues, in the total absence of literary jour-
nals, were necessarily the great means of communicating to all the lovers of learning in Cisalpine
Europe (for Italy had resources of her own) some knowledge
of its progress. Another source of information was the
correspondence of scholars with each other. It was their
constant usage, far more than in modern times, to preserve
an epistolary intercourse. If their enmities were often bitter,
their contentions almost always violent, many beautiful
instances of friendship and sympathy might be adduced on
the other side; they deemed themselves a distinct caste, a
priesthood of the same altar, not ashamed of poverty, nor
disheartened by the world's neglect, but content with the
praise of those whom themselves thought worthy of praise,
and hoping something more from posterity than they obtained
from their own age.

67. We find several attempts at a literary or rather
bibliographical history of a higher character than
these catalogues. The Bibliotheca Universalis of
Gesner was reprinted in 1574, with considerable enlarge-

ments by Simler. Conrad Lycosthenes afterwards made additions to it, and Verdier published a supplement. Verdier was also the author of a Bibliothèque française, of which the first edition appeared in 1584. Another with the same title was published in the same year by La Croix du Maine. Both these follow the strange alphabetical arrangement by Christian instead of family names, so usual in the sixteenth century. La Croix du Maine confines himself to French authors, but Verdier includes all who had been translated. The former is valued for his accuracy and for curious particulars in biography ; the second for the extracts he has given. Doni pretended to give a history of books in his Libreria, but it has not obtained much reputation, and falls, according to the testimony of those who are acquainted with it, below the compilations above mentioned.[d]

68. The despotism of the state, and far more of the church, bore heavily on the press in Italy. Spain, mistress

Restraints on the press.

of Milan and Naples, and Florence under Cosmo I., were jealous governments. Venice, though we are apt to impute a rigid tyranny to its senate, appears to have indulged rather more liberty of writing on political topics to its subjects, on the condition, no doubt, that they should eulogise the wisdom of the republic ; and, comparatively to the neighbouring regions of Italy, the praise both of equitable and prudent government may be ascribed to that aristocracy. It had at least the signal merit of keeping ecclesiastical oppression at a distance ; a Venetian might write with some freedom of the papal court. One of the accusations against Venice, in her dispute with Paul V., was for allowing the publication of books that had been censured at Rome.[e]

69. But Rome struck a fatal blow, and perhaps more deadly than she intended, at literature in the Index

Index Expurgatorius.

Expurgatorius of prohibited books. It had long been the regulation that no book should be printed without a previous licence. This was of course a restraint on the freedom of writing, but it was less injurious to the trade of the printer and bookseller than the subsequent prohibition of what he had published or purchased at his own cost and

---

ᵈ Morhof. Goujet. Biogr. univ.   ᵉ Ranke, ii. 330.

risk. The first list of books prohibited by the church was set forth by Paul IV. in 1559. His Index includes all Bibles in modern languages, enumerating forty-eight editions, chiefly printed in countries still within the obedience of the church. Sixty-one printers are put under a general ban; all works of every description from their presses being forbidden. Stephens and Oporinus have the honour of being among these.[f] This system was pursued and rigorously acted upon by the successors of the imperious Caraffa. The council of Trent had its own list of condemned publications. Philip II. has been said to have preceded the pope himself in a similar proscription. Wherever the sway of Rome and Spain was felt, books were unsparingly burned, and to this cause is imputed the scarcity of many editions.

70. In its principle, which was apparently that of preserving obedience, the prohibitory system might seem to have untouched many great walks of learning *Its effects.* and science. It is of course manifest that it fell with but an oblique blow upon common literature. Yet, as a few words or sentences were sufficient to elicit a sentence of condemnation, often issued with little reflection, it was difficult for any author to be fully secure ; and this inspired so much apprehension into printers, that they became unwilling to incur the hazard of an obnoxious trade. These occupations, says Galluzzi, which had begun to prosper at Florence, never recovered the wound inflicted by the severe regulations of Paul IV. and Pius V.[g] The art retired to Switzerland and Germany. The booksellers were at the mercy of an Inquisition, which every day contrived new methods of harassing them. From an interdiction of the sale of certain prohibited books, the church proceeded to forbid that of all which were not expressly permitted. The Giunti, a firm not so eminent as it had been in the early part of the century, but still the honour of Florence, remonstrated in vain. It seems probable, however, that after the death of Pius V., one of the most rigorous and bigoted pontiffs that ever filled the chair, some degree of relaxation took place.

---

[f] Schelhorn, Amœnit. Liter. vii. 98 ; viii. 342 and 485. The two dissertations on prohibited books here quoted are full of curious information.

[g] Ist. del Gran Ducato, iii. 442.

71. The restraints on the printing and sale of books in
Restric-
tions in
England. England, though not so overpowering as in Italy,
must have stood in the way of useful knowledge
under Elizabeth. The Stationers' Company, founded in
1555, obtained its monopoly at the price of severe restrictions. The Star Chamber looked vigilantly at the dangerous
engine it was compelled to tolerate. By the regulations
it issued in 1585, no press was allowed to be used out of
London, except one at Oxford, and another at Cambridge.
Nothing was to be printed without allowance of the council;
extensive powers both of seizing books and of breaking the
presses were given to the officers of the crown.[h] Thus every
check was imposed on literature, and it seems unreasonable
to dispute that they had some efficacy in restraining its progress, though less, perhaps, than we might in theory expect,
because there was always a certain degree of connivance and
indulgence. Even the current prohibition of importing
popish books, except for the use of such as the council should
permit to use them, must have affected the trade in modern
Latin authors beyond the bounds of theology.

72. These restrictions do not seem to have had any
Latin more
employed
on this
account. material operation in France, in Germany, or the
Low Countries. And they certainly tended very
considerably to keep up the usage of writing in
Latin; or rather, perhaps, it may be said, they were less
rigorously urged in those countries, because Latin continued
to be the customary tongue of scholars. We have seen that
great licence was used in political writings in that language.
The power of reading Latin was certainly so diffused, that
no secrecy could be affected by writing it; yet it seemed to
be a voluntary abstaining from an appeal to the passions of
the multitude, and passed better without censure than the
same sense in a modern dress.

73. The influence of literature on the public mind was
Influence
of litera-
ture. already very considerable. All kinds of reading
had become deeper and more diffused. Pedantry
is the usual, perhaps the inevitable, consequence of a genuine
devotion to learning, not surely in each individual, but in

---

[h] Herbert, iii. 1668.

classes and bodies of men. And this was an age of pedants.
To quote profusely from ancient writers seemed to be a
higher merit than to rival them ; they furnished both authority and ornament, they did honour to the modern, who
shone in these plumes of other birds with little expense
of thought, and sometimes the actual substance of a book is
hardly discernible under this exuberance of rich incrustations. Tacitus, Sallust, Cicero, and Seneca (for the Greeks
were in comparison but little read), and many of the Latin
poets, were the books that, directly, or by the secondary
means of quotation, had most influence over the public
opinion. Nor was it surprising that the reverence for antiquity should be still undiminished; for, though the new
literature was yielding abundant crops, no comparison between the ancients and moderns could as yet fairly arise.
Montaigne, fearless and independent as he was, gave up altogether the pretensions of the latter ; yet no one was more
destined to lead the way to that renunciation of the authority
of the former which the seventeenth century was to witness.
He and Machiavel were the two writers who produced the
greatest effect upon this age. Some others, such as Guevara
and Castiglione, might be full as much read, but they did not
possess enough of original thought to shape the opinions of
mankind. And the former two, to whom we may add Rabelais, seem to be the only writers of the sixteenth century,
setting aside poets and historians, who are now much read
by the world.

PART III.

ON THE LITERATURE OF THE FIRST HALF OF THE
SEVENTEENTH CENTURY.

CHAPTER I.

HISTORY OF ANCIENT LITERATURE IN EUROPE, FROM
1600 TO 1650.

SECT. I.

Decline of merely Philological, especially Greek, Learning—Casaubon—
Viger—Editions of Greek and Latin Classics—Critical Writings—Latin
Style—Scioppius—Vossius—Successive Periods of modern Latinists.

1. IN every period of literary history, if we should listen
to the complaints of contemporary writers, all learn-   Learning of
ing and science have been verging towards extinc-   17th century
less philo-
tion. None remain of the mighty, the race of   logical.
giants is no more ; the lights that have been extinguished
burn in no other hands; we have fallen on evil days, when
letters are no longer in honour with the world, nor are they
cultivated by those who deserve to be honoured.   Such are
the lamentations of many throughout the whole sixteenth
century ; and with such do Scaliger and Casaubon greet that
which opened upon them.   Yet the first part of the seventeenth century may be reckoned eminently the learned age ;
rather, however, in a more critical and exact erudition with
respect to historical fact, than in what is strictly called
philology, as to which we cannot, on the whole, rank this so
high as the preceding period.   Neither Italy nor Germany
maintained its reputation, which, as it has been already
mentioned, had begun to wane towards the close of the
sixteenth century.   The same causes were at work, the same
preference of studies very foreign to polite letters, metaphysical philosophy, dogmatic theology, patristic or mediæval
ecclesiastical history, or, in some countries, the physical

sciences, which were rapidly gaining ground. And to these
we must add a prevalence of bad taste, even among those
who had some pretensions to be reckoned scholars. Lipsius
had set an example of abandoning the purest models; and
its followers had less sense and taste than himself. They
sought obsolete terms from Pacuvius and Plautus, they affected pointed sentences, and a studied conciseness of period,
which made their style altogether dry and jejune.[a] The
universities, and even the gymnasia, or schools of Germany,
grew negligent of all the beauties of language. Latin itself was acquired in a slovenly manner, by help of modern
books, which spared the pains of acquiring any subsidiary
knowledge of antiquity. And this neglect of the ancient
writers in education caused even eminent scholars to write
ill, as we perceive in the supplements of Freinshemius to
Curtius and Livy.[b]

2. A sufficient evidence of this is found in the vast popu-
Popularity   larity which the writings of Comenius acquired in
of Comenius.   Germany. This author, a man of much industry,
some ingenuity, and little judgment, made himself a temporary reputation by his Orbis Sensualium Pictus, and still
more by his Janua Linguarum Reserata, the latter published
in 1631. This contains, in 100 chapters subdivided into
1000 paragraphs, more than 9,300 Latin words, exclusive, of
course, of such as recur. The originality of its method
consists in weaving all useful words into a series of paragraphs, so that they may be learned in a short time, without
the tediousness of a nomenclature. It was also intended to
blend a knowledge of things with one of words.[c] The Orbis
Sensualium Pictus has the same end. This is what has
since been so continually attempted in books of education,
that some may be surprised to hear of its originality. No
one, however, before Comenius seems to have thought of
this method. It must, unquestionably, have appeared to
facilitate the early acquirement of knowledge in a very great
degree; and even with reference to language, if a compendious mode of getting at Latin words were the object, the
works of Comenius would answer the purpose beyond those

---

[a] Biogr. univ. art. Grævius. Eich-   [b] Eichhorn, 326.
horn, iii. l. 320.   [c] Biogr. univ.

of any classical author. In a country where Latin was a
living and spoken tongue, as was in some measure the case
with Germany, no great strictness in excluding barbarous
phrases is either practicable or expedient. But, according
to the received principles of philological literature, they are
such books as every teacher would keep out of the hands of
his pupils. They were, nevertheless, reprinted and translated in many countries; and obtained a general reception,
especially in the German empire, and similarly circumstanced
kingdoms.[d]

3. The Greek language, meantime, was thought unnecessary, and few, comparatively speaking, continued to *Decline of
Greek
learning*
prosecute its study. In Italy it can merely be said
that there were still professors of it in the universities; but
no one Hellenist distinguishes this century. Most of those
who published editions of Greek authors in Germany, and
they were far from numerous, had been formed in the last
age. The decline was progressive; few scholars remained
after 1620, and a long blank ensued, until Fabricius and
Kuster restored the study of Greek near the end of the century. Even in France and Holland, where many were abundantly learned, and some, as we shall see, accomplished
philologers, the Greek language seems to have been either
less regarded, or at least less promoted, by eminent scholars,
than in the preceding century.[e]

---

[d] Baillet, Critiques Grammairiens,
part of the Jugemens des Sçavans (whom
I cite by the number or paragraph, on
account of the different editions), No.
634, quotes Lancelot's remark on the
Janua Linguarum, that it requires a
better memory than most boys possess
to master it, and that commonly the
first part is forgotten before the last is
learned. It excites disgust in the
scholar, because he is always in a new
country, every chapter being filled with
words he has not seen before; and the
successive parts of the book have no
connexion with one another.

Morhof, though he would absolutely
banish the Janua Linguarum from all
schools where good Latinity is required,
seems to think rather better of the Orbis
Sensualium Pictus, as in itself a happy
idea, though the delineations are indifferent, and the whole not so well arranged as it might be. Polyhistor. lib.
ii. c. 4.

[e] Scaliger, even in 1602, says : Quis
hodie aescit Græcè? sed quis est doctus
Græcè? Non dubito esse aliquot, sed
paucos, et quos non novi ne de nomine
quidem. Te unum novi et memoriæ
avorum et nostri sæculi Græcè doctissi-
mum, qui unus in Græcis præstiteris,
quæ post renatas apud nos bonas literas
omnes nunquam præstare potuissent.
He goes on to speak of himself, as standing next to Casaubon, and the only competent judge of the extent of his learning;
qui de præstantia doctrinæ tuæ certo
judicare possit, ego aut unicus sum, aut
qui cæteros hac in re magno intervallo
vinco. Scal. Epist. 72.

4. Casaubon now stood on the pinnacle of critical renown.
His Persius in 1605, and his Polybius in 1609, were
testimonies to his continued industry in this province.[f] But with this latter edition the philological labours
of Casaubon came to an end.   In 1610 he accepted the invitation of James I., who bestowed upon him, though a layman, a
prebend in the church of Canterbury, and, as some, perhaps
erroneously, have said, another in that of Westminster.[g]
He died in England within four years after, having consumed
the intermediate time in the defence of his royal patron
against the Jesuits, and in writing Animadversions on the
Annals of Baronius; works ill-suited to his peculiar talent,
and in the latter of which he is said to have had but little
success.   He laments, in his epistles, the want of leisure for
completing his labours on Polybius ; the king had no taste
but for theology, and he found no library in which he could
pursue his studies.[h] ' I gave up,' he says, ' at last, with
great sorrow, my commentary on Polybius, to which I had
devoted so much time, but the good king must be obeyed.'[i]
Casaubon was the last of the great scholars of the sixteenth
century. Joseph Scaliger, who, especially in his recorded
conversation, was very sparing of praise, says expressly,
' Casaubon is the most learned man now living.' It is not
impossible that he meant to except himself; which would by

Casaubon. (margin note)

---

[f] The translation that Casaubon has
here given of Polybius has generally
passed for excellent, though some have
thought him a better scholar in Greek
than in Latin, and consequently not
always able to render the sense as well
as he conceived it. Baillet, n. 902.
Schweighauser praises the annotations,
but not without the criticism for which
a later editor generally finds room in an
earlier. Reiske, he says, had pointed
out many errors.
[g] The latter is contradicted by Beloe,
Anecdotes of Literature, vol. v. p. 126,
on the authority of Le Neve's Fasti
Ecclesiæ Anglicanæ.
[h] Jacent curæ Polybianæ, et fortasse
æternum jacebunt, neque enim satis
commodus ad illa studia est locus.
Epist. 705. Plura adderem, nisi omni
librorum præsidio meorum deficerer.
Quare etiam de commentariis Polybianis

noli meminisse, quando rationes priorum
meorum studiorum hoc iter mirificè con-
turbavit, ut vix sine suspirio ejus incepti
possim meminisse, quod tot vigiliis mihi
constitit. Sed neque adest mea bibliotheca, neque ea studia multum sunt ad
gustum illius, cujus solius, quamdiu hic
sum futurus, habenda mihi ratio. Ep.
704. (Feb. 1611.) Rex optimus atque
ευσεβεστατος rebus theologicis ita delec-
tatur, ut aliis curis literariis non multum operæ impendat. Ep. 872. Ego
quid hic agam, si cupis scire, hoc unum
respondebo, omnia priora studia mea
funditus interiisse. Nam maximus rex
et liberalissimus unico genere literarum
sic capitur, ut suum et suorum ingenia
in illo detineat. Ep. 753.
[i] Decessi gemens a Polybiano com-
mentario, quem tot laboribus concinna-
veram ; sed regi optimo parendum erat.
Ep. 854. Feb. 1613.

no means be unjust if we take in the whole range of erudition; but in the exactly critical knowledge of the Greek language, Casaubon had not even a rival in Scaliger.

5. A long period ensued, during which no very considerable progress was made in Greek literature. Few books Viger de Idiotismis. occur before the year 1650 which have obtained a durable reputation. The best known, and, as I conceive, by far the best of a grammatical nature, is that of Viger de Idiotismis præcipuis Græcæ Linguæ, which Hoogeveen and Zeunius successively enlarged in the last century. Viger was a Jesuit of Rouen, and the first edition was in 1632. It contains, even as it came from the author, many valuable criticisms, and its usefulness to a Greek scholar is acknowledged. But, in order to determine the place of Viger among grammarians, we should ascertain by comparison with preceding works, especially the Thesaurus of Stephens, for how much he is indebted to their labours. He would probably, after all deductions, appear to merit great praise. His arrangement is more clear, and his knowledge of syntax more comprehensive, than that of Caninius or any other earlier writer; but his notions are not unfrequently imperfect or erroneous, as the succeeding editors have pointed out. In common with many of the older grammarians, he fancied a difference of sense between the two aorists, wherein even Zeunius has followed him.[k]

6. In a much lower rank we may perhaps next place Weller, author of a Greek grammar, published in 1638, of Weller's Greek Grammar. which its late editor, Fischer, says that it has always stood in high repute as a school-book, and been frequently reprinted; meaning, doubtless, in Germany. There is nothing striking in Weller's grammar : it may deserve praise for clearness and brevity, but in Vergara, Caninius, and Sylburgius there is much more instruction for those who are not merely schoolboys. What is most remarkable is, that Weller claims as his own the reduction of the declensions to three, and of the conjugations to one, which, as has

---

[k] An earlier treatise on Greek particles by Devarius, a Greek of the Ionian Islands, might have been mentioned in the last period. It was republished by Reusmann, who calls Devarius, homo olim haud ignobilis, at hodie pæne neglectus. He is thought too subtle in grammar, but seems to have been an excellent scholar. I do not perceive that Viger has borrowed from him.

been seen in another place,[m] is found in the grammar of
Sylburgius, and is probably due to Ramus. This is rather
a piece of effrontery, as he could scarcely have lighted by
coincidence on both these innovations. Weller has given no
syntax; what is added in Fischer's edition is by Lambert
Bos.

7. Philip Labbe, a French Jesuit, was a laborious compiler,
Labbe and among whose numerous works not a few relate to
others. the grammar of the Greek language. He had, says
Niceron, a wonderful talent in multiplying title-pages; we
have fifteen or sixteen grammatical treatises from him, which
might have been comprised in two or three ordinary volumes.
Labbe's Regulæ Accentuum, published in 1635, was once, I
believe, of some repute; but he has little or nothing of his
own.[n] The Greek grammars published in this age by Alexander Scot and others are ill digested, according to Lancelot,
without order or principle, and full of useless and perplexing things;[o] and that of Vossius, in 1642, which is only an
improved edition of Clenardus, appears to contain little
which is not taken from others.[p] Erasmus Schmidt is said
by Eichhorn to be author of a valuable work on Greek
dialects;[q] George Pasor is better known by his writings on
Salmasius the Hellenistic dialect, or that of the Septuagint
de Lingua and New Testament. Salmasius, in his Commen-
Hellenis-
tica. tarius de Hellenistica (Leyden, 1643), has gone very
largely into this subject. This, he says, is a question lately
agitated, whether there be a peculiar dialect of the Greek
Scriptures; for, in the last age, the very name of Hellenistic
was unknown to scholars. It is not above half a century
old. It was supposed to be a Hebrew idiom in Greek
words; which, as he argues elaborately and with great
learning, is not sufficient to constitute a distinct dialect,
none of the ancients having ever mentioned one by this
name. This is evidently much of a verbal dispute, since
no one would apply the word to the scriptural Greek in the
same sense that he does to the Doric and Attic. Salmasius

---

[m] Vol. i. p. 495.
[n] Niceron, vol. xxv.
[o] Baillet, n. 706.

[p] Baillet, n. 711.
[q] Geschichte der Cultur, iii. 325.

lays down two essential characteristics of a dialect: one, that it should be spoken by people of a certain locality; another, that it should be distinguishable by single words, not merely by idiom. A profusion of learning is scattered all round, but not pedantically or impertinently; and this seems a very useful book in Greek or Latin philology. He may perhaps be thought to underrate the peculiarities of language in the Old and New Testament, as if they were merely such as passed current among the contemporary Greeks. The second part of this Commentary relates to the Greek dialects generally, without reference to the Hellenistic. He denies the name to what is usually called the common dialect spoken, or at least written, by the Greeks in general after the time of Alexander. This also is of course a question of words; perhaps Salmasius used a more convenient phraseology than what is often met with in grammarians.

8. Editions of Greek classics are not so numerous as in the former period. The Pindar of Erasmus Schmidt, in 1614, and the Aristotle of Duval, in 1619, may be mentioned; the latter is still in request, as a convenient and complete edition. Meursius was reckoned a good critical scholar, but his works as an editor are not very important. The chief monument of his philological erudition is the Lexicon Græco-Barbarum, a glossary of the Greek of the lower empire. But no edition of a Greek author published in the first part of the seventeenth century is superior, at least in magnificence, to that of Chrysostom by Sir Henry Savile. This came forth, in 1612, from a press established at Eton by himself, provost of that college. He had procured types and pressmen in Holland, and three years had been employed in printing the eight volumes of this great work: one which, both in splendour of execution and in the erudition displayed in it by Savile, who had collected several manuscripts of Chrysostom, leaves immeasurably behind it every earlier production of the English press. The expense, which is said to have been eight thousand pounds, was wholly defrayed by himself, and the tardy sale of so voluminous a work could not have reim-

Greek editions—
Savile's Chrysostom.

bursed the cost.[r]   Another edition, in fact, by a Jesuit,
Fronto Ducæus (Fronton le Duc), was published at Paris
within two years afterwards, having the advantage of a
Latin translation, which Savile had imprudently waived.   It
has even been imputed to Ducæus, that, having procured the
sheets of Savile's edition from the pressmen while it was
under their hands, he printed his own without alteration.
But this seems an apocryphal story.[s]   Savile had the assistance, in revising the text, of the most learned coadjutors he
could find in England.

9. A very few more Greek books were printed at Eton soon
afterwards; and, though that press soon ceased,
some editions of Greek authors, generally for
schools, appeared in England before 1650.   One of these,
the Poetæ Minores of Winterton, is best known, and has
sometimes been reprinted; it appears to differ little, if at
all, from the collection printed by Crispin in 1570, and of
which there had been many subsequent editions, with the
title Vetustissimorum Autorum Georgica, Bucolica et Gno-
monica; but the text, though still very corrupt, has been
amended, and a few notes, generally relating to prosody, have
been subjoined.   The Greek language, however, was now
much studied;[t] the age of James and Charles was truly

---

[r] Beloe's Anecdotes of Literature, vol.
v. p. 103.   The copies sold for 9*l*. each,
a sum equal in command of commodities
to nearly 30*l*. at present, and, from the
relative wealth of the country, to considerably more.   What wonder that the
sale was slow?   Fuller, however, tells
us that, when he wrote, almost half a
century afterwards, the book was become scarce.   Chrysostomus, says Casaubon, a Savilio editur privata impensa,
animo regio.   Ep. 738 (apud Beloe).
The principal assistants of Savile were
Matthew Bust, Thomas Allen, and especially Richard Montagu, afterwards
celebrated in our ecclesiastical history
as bishop of Chichester, who is said to
have corrected the text before it went to
the press.   As this is the first work of
learning, on a great scale, published in
England, it deserves the particular commemoration of those to whom we owe it.

[s] It is told by Fuller, and I do not
know that it has any independent

confirmation.   Savile himself says of
Fronto Ducæus, ' Vir doctissimus, et cui
Chrysostomus noster plurimum debet.'
Fuller, it may be observed, says, that
the Parisian edition followed Savile's
'in a few months,' whereas the time
was two years; and, as Brunet (Manuel
du Libraire) justly observes, there is no
apparent necessity to suppose an unfair
communication of the sheets, even if the
text should be proved to be copied.

[t] It might appear, at first sight, that
Casaubon intended to send his son Meric
to Holland, under the care of Heinsius,
because he could not get a good classical
education in England.   Cupio in Græcis,
Latinis, et Hebraicis literis ipsum serio
exerceri.   Hoc in Anglia posse fieri sperare non possumus; nam hic locupletis-
sima sunt collegia, sed quorum ratio toto
genere diversa est ab institutis omnium
aliorum collegiorum.   Ep. 962 (1614).
But possibly he meant that, on account
of his son's foreign birth, he could not

learned; our writers are prodigal of an abundant erudition, which embraces a far wider range of authors than are now read; the philosophers of every class, the poets, the historians, and orators of Greece, to whom few comparatively had paid regard in the days of Elizabeth, seem as familiar to the miscellaneous writers of her next successors as the fathers of the church are to the theologians. A few, like Jeremy Taylor, are equally copious in their libations from both streams. But though thus deeply read in ancient learning, our old scholars were not very critical in philology.

10. In Latin criticism, the pretensions of the seventeenth century are far more considerable than in Greek. Latin editions — The first remarkable edition, however, that of Torrentius. Horace by Torrentius, a Belgian ecclesiastic, though it appeared in 1602, being posthumous, belongs strictly to the preceding age. It has been said that Dacier borrowed much for his own notes from this editor; but Horace was so profusely illustrated in the sixteenth century that little has been left for later critics except to tamper, as they have largely done, with his text. This period is not generally conspicuous for editions of Latin authors, but some names of high repute in grammatical and critical lore belong to it.

11. Gruter, a native of Antwerp, who became a professor in several German universities, and finally in that Gruter. of Heidelberg, might have been mentioned in our history of the sixteenth century, before the expiration of which some of his critical labours had been accomplished. Many more belong to the first twenty years of the present. No more diligent and indefatigable critic ever toiled in that quarry. His Suspiciones, an early work, in which he has explained and amended miscellaneous passages, his annota-

<hr>

be admitted on the foundation of English colleges, though the words do not clearly express this. At the king's command, however, Meric was sent to Oxford. One of Casaubon's sons went to Eton school; literis dat operam in gymnasio Etoniensi. Ep. 737 (quoted in Beloe's Anecdotes; I had overlooked the passage). Theological learning, in the reign of James, opposed polite letters and philology. Est in Anglia, says Casaubon, theologorum ingens copia; eo enim fere omnes studia sua referunt. Ep. 762. Venio ex Anglia (Grotius writes in 1613), literarum ibi tenuis est merces; theologi regnant, leguleii rem faciunt; unus ferme Casaubonus habet fortunam satis faventem, sed, ut ipse judicat, minus caeteri. Ne huic quidem locus fuisset in Anglia ut literatori, theologum induere debuit. Epist. Grot. p. 751.

tions on the Senecas, on Martial, on Statius, on the Roman historians, as well as another more celebrated compilation which we shall have soon to mention, bear witness to his immense industry. In Greek he did comparatively but little ; yet he is counted among good scholars in that language. All others of his time, it has been said, appear mere drones in comparison with him.[u] Scaliger, indeed, though on intimate terms with Gruter, in one of his usual fits of spleen, charges him with a tasteless indifference to the real merit of the writers whom he explained, one being as good as another for his purpose, which was only to produce a book. In this art Gruter was so perfect that he never failed to publish one every year, and sometimes every month.[y] His eulogists have given him credit for acuteness and judgment, and even for elegance and an agreeable variety, but he seems not to have preserved much repute except for his laborious erudition.

12. Daniel Heinsius, conspicuous as secretary of the synod of Dort, and a Latin poet of distinguished name,
Heinsius.
was also among the first philologers of his age. Many editions of Greek and Latin writers, or annotations upon them, Theocritus, Hesiod, Maximus Tyrius, Aristotle, Horace, Terence, Silius, Ovid, attest his critical skill. He is praised for a judicious reserve in criticism, avoiding the trifles by which many scholars had wearied their readers, and attending only to what really demanded the aid of a critic, as being corrupt or obscure. His learning was very extensive and profound, so that, in the panegyrical tone of the times, he is set above all the living, and almost above all the dead.[z]

13. Grotius contributed much to ancient philology. His editions of Aratus, Stobæus, the fragments of the
Grotius.
lost Greek dramas, Lucan and Tacitus, are but a part of those which he published. In the power of illustrating a writer by parallel or resembling passages from others, his taste and fondness for poetry, as much as his

---

[u] Baillet, n. 483 ; Bayle ; Niceron, vol. ix.

[x] Non curat utrum charta sit cacata, modo libros multos excudat. Scalig. Se-

cunda.

[y] Bayle, art. Gruter, note I.

[z] Baillet, n. 517.

vast erudition, have made him remarkable. In mere critical skill he was not quite so great a master of the Greek as of the Latin language, nor was he equal to restoring the text of the dramatic poets.

14. The Variæ Lectiones of Rutgersius, in 1618, whose premature death cut off a brilliant promise of eru- Rutgersius, dition, are in six books, almost entirely devoted to Reinesius, Barthius. emendation of the text, in such a miscellaneous and desultory series of criticisms as the example of Turnebus and other scholars had rendered usual.[a] Reinesius, a Saxon physician, in 1640, put forth a book with the same title, a thick volume of about 700 pages of multifarious learning, chiefly, but not exclusively, classical. He is more interpretative, and less attentive to restore corrupted texts, than Rutgersius.[b] The Adversaria of Gaspar Barthius are better known. This work is in sixty books, and extends to about 1,500 pages in folio. It is exactly like those of Turnebus and Muretus, an immense repertory of unconnected criticisms and other miscellaneous erudition. The chapters exceed in number the pages, and each chapter contains several articles. There is, however, more connexion, alphabetical or otherwise, than in Turnebus; and they are less exclusively classical, many relating to mediæval and modern writers. The sixtieth book is a commentary on a part of Augustin de Civitate Dei. It is difficult to give a more precise notion of Barthius; he is more *æsthetic* than Turnebus, but less so than Muretus; he explains and corrects fewer intricate texts than the former, but deals more in parallel passages and excursive illustration.[c] Though Greek appears more than in Tur-

---

[a] 'This work,' says Niceron (vol. xxxii.), 'is in esteem: the style is neat and polite, the thoughts are just and refined; it has no more quotations than the subject requires.'

[b] Bayle observes of the writings of Reinesius in general, that 'good judges of literature have no sooner read some pages, but they place him above those philologers who have only a good memory, and rank him with critics who go beyond their reading and know more than books have taught them. The penetration of their understanding makes them draw consequences and form con-

jectures which lead them to discover hidden treasures. Reinesius was one of these, and made it his chief business to find out what others had not said.'

[c] The following are the heads of the fourth chapter of the first book, which may serve as a specimen of the Adversaria:—Ad Victoris Uticensis librum primum notæ et emendationes. Limites. Collimitia, Quantitas. H. Stephanus notatur. Impendere. Totum. Omnimodè. Dextrales. Asta. Francisii Balduini audacia castigatur. Tormenta antiqua. Liguamen Arx Capitis. Memoriæ. Cruciari. Balduinus denuo ali-

nebus, by far the greater part of Barthius's Adversaria relates to Latin, in the proportion of at least fifteen to one.
A few small poems are printed from manuscripts for the first
time. Barthius, according to Morhof, though he sometimes
explains authors very well, is apt to be rash in his alterations, hasty in his judgments, and has too much useless and
frivolous matter. Bayle is not more favourable. Barthius
published an edition of Statius, and another of Claudian.

15. Rigault, or Rigaltius, Petit, Thysius, and several more,
Other critics
—English. do honour to France and the Low Countries during
this period. Spain, though not strong in classical
philology, produced Ramiresius de Prado, whose Πεντη-
κονταρχος, sive quinquaginta militum ductor, 1612, is but a
book of criticism with a quaint title.[d] In Latin literature
we can hardly say that England made herself more conspicuous than in Greek. The notes of John Bond, on Horace,
published in 1606, are properly a work of the age of Elizabeth ; the author was long a schoolmaster in that reign.
These notes are only little marginal scholia for the use of
boys of no great attainments, and in almost every instance,
I believe, taken from Lambinus. This edition of Horace,
though Antony Wood calls the author a most noted critic
and grammarian, has only the merit of giving the observations of another concisely and perspicuously. Thomas
Farnaby is called by Baillet one of the best scholiasts, who
says hardly anything useless, and is very concise.[e] He has
left notes on several of the Latin poets. It is possible that
the notes are compiled, like those of Bond, from the foreign
critics. Farnaby also was a schoolmaster, and schoolmasters
do not write for the learned. He has, however, been acknowledged on the Continent for a diligent and learned
man. Wood says he was 'the chief grammarian, rheto-

---

quoties notatur. It is true that all this
farrago arises out of one passage in
Victor of Utica, and Barthius is far
from being so desultory as Turnebus ;
but 3000 columns of such notes make
but a dictionary without the help of the
alphabet. Barthius tells us himself that
he had finished two other volumes of
Adversaria, besides correcting the first.
See the passage in Bayle, note K. But
he does not stand on very high ground

as a critic, on account of the rapidity
with which he wrote, and for the same
reason has sometimes contradicted himself. Bayle ; Baillet, n. 528 ; Niceron,
vol. vii.; Morhof, lib. v. l. 10.

[d] This has been ascribed by some to
his master Sanctius, author of the Minerva, Ramirez himself having been
thought unequal to such remarks as we
find in it. Baillet, n. 527.

[e] N. 521.

rician, poet, Latinist, and Grecian of his time; and his school
was so much frequented that more churchmen and statesmen
issued thence than from any school taught by one man in
England.'[f]

16. But the greatest in this province of literature was
Claude Saumaise, best known in the Latin form
Salmasius, whom the general suffrage of his com-   Salmasius.
peers placed at their head.   An incredible erudition, so that
it was said, what Salmasius did not know was beyond the
bounds of knowledge, a memory such as none but those great
scholars of former times seem to have possessed, a life
passed, naturally enough, in solitary labour, were sufficient
to establish his fame among the learned.   His intellectual
strength has been more questioned; he wrote, it has been
alleged, on many subjects that he did not well understand,
and some have reduced his merit to that of a grammatical
critic, without altogether rating this so highly as the world
has done.[g]   Salmasius was very proud, self-confident, disdainful, and has consequently fallen into many errors, and
even contradictions, through precipitancy.   In his controversy with Milton, for which he was little fitted, he is rather
feeble, and glad to escape from the severity of his antagonist
by a defence of his own Latinity.[h]   The works of Salmasius
are numerous, and on very miscellaneous subjects; among
the philological, his Annotations on the Historiæ Augustæ
Scriptores seem to deserve mention.   But the most remarkable, besides the commentary on the Hellenistic Dialect, of
which an account has been given, is the Plinianæ Exercitationes, published in 1629.   These remarks, nominally on
Pliny, are, in the first instance, on Solinus.   Salmasius tells
us that he had spent much time on Pliny; but finding it
beyond the powers of one man to write a commentary on
the whole Natural History of that author, he had chosen
Solinus, who is a mere compiler from Pliny, and contains

---

[f] Athenæ Oxonienses, vol. iii.

[g] Baillet, n. 511, is excessively severe
on Salmasius; but the homage due to
his learning by such an age as that in
which he lived cannot be extenuated by
the censure of a man like Baillet, of extensive but rather superficial attainments, and open to much prejudice.

[h] Milton began the attack by objecting
to the use of *persona* for an individual
man; but in this mistaken criticism uttered himself the solecism *vapulandum*.
See Johnson's Lives of the Poets. This
expression had previously been noticed
by Vavasseur.

nothing from any other source. The Plinianæ Exercitationes is a mass of learning on the geography and natural
history of Pliny in more than 900 pages, following the text
of the Polyhistor of Solinus.[1]

17. It had been the desire of those who aspired to repu-

Good writers of Latin.

tation for taste and eloquence to write well in Latin,
the sole language, on this side of the Alps and
Pyrenees, to which the capacity of choice and polished expression was conceded. But when the French tongue was
more cultivated and had a criticism of its own, this became
the natural instrument of polite writers in France, and the
Latin fell to the merely learned, who neglected its beauties.
In England it had never been much studied for the purposes
of style; and though neither in Germany nor the Low
Countries it was very customary to employ the native
language, the current Latin of literature was always careless and often barbarous. Even in Italy the number of
good writers in that language was now very scanty. Two
deserve to be commemorated with praise, both historians of
the same period. The History and Annals of Grotius, in
which he seems to have emulated, with more discretion than
some others, the nervous brevity of Tacitus, though not
always free from a certain hardness and want of flow, nor
equal, consequently, in elegance to some productions of the
sixteenth century, may be deemed a monument of vigorous
and impressive language. The Decads of Famianus Strada,
a Roman Jesuit, contain a history of the Flemish war, not
written certainly in imitation of Tacitus, whom the author
depreciated, but with more classical spirit than we usually
find in that age. Scarcely any Latin, however, of this
period is equal to that of Barclay in the Argenis and
Euphormio. His style, though rather diffuse, and more

---

[1] Nemo adeo ut propriam, suumque
veluti regnum, sibi criticen vindicatum
ivit, ac Claudius Salmasius, qui, quemadmodum nihil unquam scripsit, in quo
non insignia multa artis criticæ vestigia
deprehendas, ita imprimis, ut auctores
cum notis et castigationibus absolutissi-
mis editos taceamus, vasto illo Pliniana-
rum. Exercitationum opere, quantum in
eo eruditionis genere valeret demonstra-

tum dedit. Morhof, liv. v. c. 1, § 12.
The Jesuits, Petavius and Harduin, who
did not cordially praise any Protestant,
charged this book with passing over real
difficulties, while a mass of heterogeneous
matter was foisted in. Le Clerc (or La
Croze) vindicates Salmasius against some
censures of Harduin in Bibl. univ. vol.
iv.

florid than that of the Augustan age, is perhaps better
suited to his subjects, and reminds us of Petronius Arbiter,
who was probably his model.

18. Of the grammatical critics, whose attention was solely
turned to the purity of Latin style, two are conspicuous, Gaspar Scioppius and Gerard Vossius. Scioppius.
The first, one of those restless and angry spirits whose hand
is against all the world, lived a long life of controversy and
satire. His productions, as enumerated by Niceron, mostly
anonymous, are about one hundred, twenty-seven of which,
according to another list, are grammatical.[k] The Protestants whom he had abandoned, and the Jesuits whom he would
not join, are equally the objects of his anger. In literature
he is celebrated for the bitterness of his attacks on Cicero,
whom he spared as little as he did his own contemporaries.
But Scioppius was an admirable master of the Latin language. All that is remembered of his multifarious His Philo-
publications relates to this. We owe to him a much Grammar.
improved edition of the Minerva of Sanctius. His own
Grammatica Philosophica (Milan, 1628), notwithstanding its
title, has no pretensions to be called anything more than
an ordinary Latin grammar. In this I observed nothing remarkable but that he denies the gerund and supine to be
parts of the verb, considering the first as passive participles,
and the second as nouns substantive.

19. The Infamia Famiani of Scioppius was written against
Famianus Strada, whom he hated both as a Jesuit, His In-
and as one celebrated for the beauty of his style. Famiani.
This book serves to show how far those who wrote with some
eloquence, as Strada certainly did, fell short of classical
purity. The faults pointed out are often very obvious to
those who have used good dictionaries. Scioppius is however so fastidious as to reject words employed by Seneca,
Tacitus, and even Phædrus, as of the silver age; and sometimes probably is wrong in his dogmatic assertion of a
negative, that no good authority can be found for them.

20. But his most considerable work is one called Judicium
de Stylo Historico, subjoined to the last, and published

---

[k] Niceron, vol. xxxv.; Biogr. univ.

after his death in 1650. This treatise consists chiefly of
Judicium de Stylo Historico. attacks on the Latin style of Thuanus, Lipsius,
Casaubon, and other recent authors; but in the
course of it we find the remarks of a subtle and severe
observer on the ancients themselves. The *silver* age he
dates from the latter years of Augustus, placing even Ovid
within it. The *brazen* he carries up to Vespasian. In the
silver period he finds many single words as well as phrases
not agreeable to the usage of more ancient authors. As to
the moderns, the Transalpine writers, he says (speaking as
an Italian), are always deficient in purity; they mingle the
phraseology of different ages as preposterously as if they
were to write Greek in a confusion of dialects; they affect
obscurity, a broken structure of periods, a studied use of
equivocal terms. This is particularly perceived in the school
of Lipsius, whose own faults, however, are redeemed by
many beauties even of style.[m] The Italians, on the contrary,

---

[m] Transalpinis hominibus ex quotidiano Latini sermonis inter ipsos usu,
multa sive barbaræ, sive plebeiæ ac de-
terioris notæ, sic adhærescere solent, ut
postea cum stylum arripuere, de Latini-
tate eorum dubitare nequaquam iis in
mentem veniat. Inde fit ut scripta eorum
plerumque minus puritatis habeant,
quamvis gratia et venustas in iis minimè
desideretur. Nam hæc natura duce melius fiebant, quam arte aut studio. Ac-
cedit alia causa cur non æquè pura sit
multorum Transalpinorum oratio, quod
nullo ætatis discrimine ac delectu in
autorum lectione versantur, et ex omnium commixtione varium quoddam ac
multiforme pro suo quisque ingenio dicendi genus effingunt, contempto hoc Fabii
monito: 'Diu non nisi optimus quisque
et qui credentem sibi minime fallat, le-
gendus est, sed diligenter ac pæne ad
scribendi solicitudinem; nec per partes
modo scrutanda omnia, sed perlectus
liber utique ex integro resumendus.'
Itaque genus illud corruptæ orationis,
seu κακοζηλιας, effugere nequeunt, quod
κοινισμον vocant, quæ est quædam mista
ex variarum linguarum ratione oratio,
ut si Atticis Dorica, Ionica, Æolica
etiam dicta confundas; cui simile est si
quis sublimia humilibus, vetera novis,
poetica vulgaribus, Sallustiana Tullianis,
æneæ et ferreæ ætatis vocabula aureis et
argenteis misceat, qui Lipsio deductisque
ab eo viris, solennis et jam olim familiaris est morbus. In quibus hoc amplius, verba maxime impropria, compre-
hensionem obscuram, compositionem
fractam, aut in frustula concisam, vocum
similium aut ambiguarum puerilem cap-
tationem passim animadvertas. Magnis
tamen, non nego, virtutibus vitia sua
Lipsius redimit, imprimis acumine,
venere, salibus (ut excellens viri ingè-
nium ferebat) tum plurimis lectissimis
verbis loquendique modis, ex quibus
non tam facultatem bene scribendi, ejusque, quod melius est, intellectum ei
deesse, quam voluntatem, quo minus
rectiora malit, ambitiuscule, plaususque
popularis studio præpediri intelligas.
Italorum longè dispar ratio. Primum
enim non nisi optimum legere et ad imi-
tandum sibi proponere solent; quod
judicio quo cæteras nationes omnium
consensu superant, imprimis est consentaneum. Deinde nihil non faciunt, ut
evitent omnia unde aliquid injucundæ
et contaminandæ orationis periculi os-
tenditur. Latinè igitur nunquam loquuntur, quod fieri vix posse persuasum
habeant, quin quotidianus ejus linguæ
usus ad instar torrentis lutulentus fluat,
et cujusque modi verborum sordes secum
rapiat, quæ postea quodam familiaritatis
jure sic se scribentibus ingerant, ut

he proceeds to say, read nothing but what is worthy of imitation, and shun every expression that can impair the clearness and purity of a sentence.   Yet even in Manutius and in the Jesuit Maffei he finds instances of barbarism, much more in the French and German scholars of the sixteenth age; expressing contempt upon this account for his old enemy, Joseph Scaliger.   Thuanus, he says, is full of modern idioms; a crime not quite unpardonable, when we remember the immensity of his labour, and the greater importance of other objects that he had in view.

21. Gerard Vossius, a far greater name in general literature than Scioppius, contributed more essentially Gerard Vossius, De Vitiis Sermonis. to these grammatical rules; and to him, perhaps, rather than to any other one man, we may refer the establishment of as much correctness of writing as is attainable in a dead language.   Besides several works on rhetoric and poetry, which, as those topics were usually treated in ages of more erudition than taste or philosophy, resolved themselves into philological disquisitions, looking only to the language of the ancient writers, we have several more strictly within that province.   The long use of Latin in writings on modern subjects, before the classical authors had been studied, had brought in a host of barbarisms, that even yet were not expelled.   His treatise, De Vitiis Sermonis et Glossematis Latino-barbaris, is in nine books; four published in 1645, during the author's life; five in 1685.   The former are by far the most copious.   It is a very large collection of words in use among modern writers, for which there is no adequate authority.   Of these many are plainly barbarous, and taken from the writers of the middle ages, or at best from those of the fifth and sixth centuries.   Few such would be used by any tolerable scholar.   He includes some which, though in themselves good, have a wrong sense

---

etiam diligentissimos fallant, et haud dubie pro Latinis habeantur.   Hoc eorum consilium cum non intelligant Transalpini, id eorum inscitiæ perperam assignant.   Sic rectè Paulo Manutio usu venit, ut quoniam vix tria verba Latina in familiari sermone proferre poterat, eum Germani complures, qui loquentem audituri ad eum venerunt, vehementer præ se contemnerent.   Huic tamen nemo qui sanus sit ad puritatis et elegantiæ Latinæ summam quicquid defuisse dixerit.   P. 65.

given to them. Words however occur, concerning which
one might be ignorant without discredit, especially before
the publication of this treatise, which has been the means of
correcting the ordinary dictionaries.

22. In the five posthumous books, which may be mentioned
in this place, having probably been written before 1650, we
find chiefly what the author had forgotten to notice in the
former, or had since observed. But the most valuable part
relates to the 'falso suspecta,' which fastidious critics have
unreasonably rejected, generally because they do not appear
in the Augustan writers. Those whom he calls ' Nizoliani
verius quam Ciceroniani,' disapproved of all words not found
in Cicero.[n] It is curious to perceive, as Vossius shows us,
how many apparently obvious words do not occur in Cicero ;
yet it would be mere affectation to avoid them. This is
perhaps the best part of Vossius's treatise.

23. We are indebted to Vossius for a still more important
His Aris- work on grammar, the Aristarchus, sive de Arte
tarchus. Grammatica, which first appeared in 1635. This is
in seven books : the first treats of grammar in general, and
especially of the alphabet ; the second of syllables, under
which head he dwells at great length on prosody ;[o] the third
(which, with all the following, is separately entitled De vocum
Analogia) of words generally, and of the genders, numbers,
and cases of nouns. The same subject occupies the fourth
book. In the fifth he investigates verbs ; and in the sixth,
the remaining parts of speech. The last book relates to
syntax. This work is full of miscellaneous observations,
placed for the most part alphabetically under each chapter.
It has been said that Vossius has borrowed almost everything
in this treatise from Sanctius and Scioppius. If this be
true, we must accuse him of unfairness ; for he never mentions the Minerva. But, the edition of this grammar by
Scioppius was not published till after the death of Vossius.

---

[n] Paulus Manutius scrupled to use
words on the authority of Cicero's correspondents, such as Cælius or Pollio ; a
ridiculous affectation, especially when
we observe what Vossius has pointed
out, that many common words do not
occur in Cicero. It is amazing to see
the objections of these Ciceronian critics.

[o] In this we find Vossius aware of the
rule in Terentianus Maurus, but brought
to light by Dawes, and now familiar,
that a final vowel is rarely short before
a word beginning with *s* and a mute consonant.

Salmasius extolled that of the latter above all which had been published.[p]

24. In later times the ambition of writing Latin with accuracy and elegance has so universally declined, that the diligence of Scioppius and Vossius has become hardly valuable except to schoolmasters. It is, however, an art not contemptible, either in respect to the taste and discernment for which it gives scope in composition, or for the enhanced pleasure it reflects on the pages of ancient writers. We may distinguish several successive periods in its cultivation since the first revival of letters. If we begin with Petrarch, since before his time there was no continuous imitation of classical models, the first period will comprise those who desired much, but reached little, the writers of the fourteenth and fifteenth centuries, destitute of sufficient aids, and generally incapable of clearly discriminating the pure from the barbarous in Latin. A better era may be dated from Politian; the ancients were now fully known, and studied with intense labour; the graces of style were frequently caught; yet something was still wanting to its purity and elegance. At the end of a series of improvements, a line marked by Bembus, Sadolet, and Longolius, we arrive at a third period, which we may call that of Paulus Manutius, the golden age of modern Latinity. The diligence in lexicography of Robert Stephens, of Nizolius, of Manutius himself, and the philological treatises of their times, gave a much greater nicety of expression; while the enthusiasm with which some of the best writers emulated the ancients inspired them with a sympathetic eloquence and grace. But towards the end of the century, when Manutius, and Muretus, and Maphæus, and others of that school, had been removed by death, an age of worst taste and perhaps of more negligence in grammar came on, yet one of great scholars, and of

<small>[p] Tuum de grammatica à te accepi exactissimum in hoc genere opus, ac cui nullum priorum aut prisci ævi aut nostri possit comparari. Apud Blount in Vossio. Daunou says of the grammatical and rhetorical writings of Vossius, 'Ces livres se recommandent par l'exactitude, par la méthode, par une littérature très-étendue. Gilbert en convient, mais il trouve de la prolixité. D'autres pourraient n'y voir qu'une instruction sérieuse, souvent austère, et presque toujours profitable.' Biogr. univ.</small>

men powerful even in language — the age of Lipsius, of
Scaliger, of Grotius.   This may be called the fourth period ;
and in this apparently the purity of the language, as well as
its beauty, rather declined.   Finally, the publications of
Scioppius and Vossius mark the beginning of another period,
which we may consider as lasting to the present day.   Grammatical criticism had nearly reached the point at which it
now stands ; the additions, at least, which later philologers,
Perizonius, Burman, Bentley, and many others have made,
though by no means inconsiderable, seem hardly sufficient
to constitute a distinct period, even if we could refer them
properly to any single epoch.   And the praise of eloquent
composition has been so little sought, after the close of the
years passed in education, or attained only in short and
occasional writings which have left no durable reputation
behind, that the Latin language may be said, for this purpose, to have silently expired in the regions of polite literature.

Sect. II.

Antiquities of Rome and Greece—Gruter—Meursius—Chronology.

25. The antiquities of Greece and Rome, though they did
Gruter's
collection
of inscrip-
tions. not occupy so great a relative space in the literature
of this period as of the sixteenth century, were,
from the general increase of erudition, not less frequently the subject of books than before.   This field, indeed, is so vast, that its harvest had in many parts been
scarcely touched, and in others very imperfectly gathered
by those we have already commemorated, the Sigonii, the
Manutii, the Lipsii, and their fellow-labourers in ancient
learning.   The present century opened with a great work,
the Corpus Inscriptionum, by Gruter.   A few endeavours had
long before been made [q] to collect the ancient inscriptions,
of which the countries once Roman, and especially Italy,
were full.   The best work hitherto was by Martin Smetius
of Bruges, after whose death his collection of inscriptions

---

[q] See vol. i. p. 335.

was published at Leyden in 1588, under the superintendence
of Dousa and Lipsius.

26. Scaliger first excited his friend Gruter to undertake
the task of giving an enlarged edition of Smetius.[r] Assisted by
He made the index for this himself, devoting the Scaliger.
labour of the entire morning for ten months (a summo mane
ad tempus cœnæ) to an occupation from which so little glory
could accrue. 'Who,' says Burman, 'would not admire
the liberal erudition and unpretending modesty of the learned
of that age, who, worn as they were by those long and
weary labours, of which they freely complain in their correspondence with each other, though they knew that such occupations as these could gain for them no better name than
that of common clerks or mere drudges, yet hesitated not
to abandon for the advantage of the public those pursuits
which a higher fame might be expected to reward? Who
in these times would imitate the generosity of Scaliger, who,
when he might have ascribed to himself this addition to
the work of Smetius, gave away his own right to Gruter,
and declined to let his name be prefixed either to the index
which he had wholly compiled, or to the many observations
by which he corrects and explains the inscriptions, and desired, in recompense for the industry of Gruter, that he
alone should pass with posterity as the author of the
work?'[s] Gruter, it is observed by Le Clerc, has committed
many faults: he often repeats the same inscriptions, and
still more frequently has printed them from erroneous copies;
his quotations from authors, in whom inscriptions are found,
sometimes want exactness; finally, for which he could not
well be answerable, a vast many have since been brought to
light.[t] In consequence of the publication of Gruter's Inscriptions, the learned began with incredible zeal to examine
old marble inscriptions, and to insert them in any work that

---

[r] Burman in Præfatione ad Gruteri
Corpus Inscript. Several of Scaliger's
epistles prove this, especially the 405th,
addressed to Gruter.

[s] Burman, p. 6.

[t] Bibl. choisie, vol. xiv. p. 51. Burman, ubi supra, gives a strange reason
for reprinting Gruter's Inscriptions with

all their blemishes, even the repetitions;
namely, that it was convenient to preserve the number of pages which had
been so continually referred to in all
learned works, the simple contrivance of
keeping the original numeration in the
margin not having occurred to him,

had reference to antiquity. Reinesius collected as many as make a respectable supplement.[u] But a sort of era in lapidary learning was made, in 1629, by Selden's description of the marbles brought by the Earl of Arundel from Greece, and which now belong to the university of Oxford. These contain a chronology of the early times of Greece, on which great reliance has often been placed, though their antiquity is not accounted very high in comparison with those times.

27. The Jesuit Donati published, in 1633, Roma vetus et nova, which is not only much superior to any-thing previously written on the antiquities of the city, but is preferred by some competent judges to the later and more known work of Nardini. Both these will be found, with others of an earlier date, in the third and fourth volumes of Grævius. The tenth volume of the same collection contains a translation from the history of the Great Roads of the Roman Empire, published in French by Nicolas Bergier in 1622; ill-arranged, it has been said, and diffuse, according to the custom of his age, but inferior, Grævius declares, in variety of learning to no one work that he has inserted in his numerous volumes. Guther, whose treatise on the pontifical law of Rome appears in the fifth volume, was, says the editor, 'a man of various and extended reading, who had made extracts from every class of writers, but had not always digested his learning or weighed what he wrote. Hence much has been found open to criticism in his writings, and there remains a sufficient harvest of the same kind for any one who should care to undertake it.' The best work on Roman dress is by Octavius Ferrarius, published partly in 1642, partly in 1654. This has been called superficial by Spanheim; but Grævius, and several other men of learning, bestow more praise.[x] The Isiac tablet, covered with emblems of Egyptian antiquity, was illustrated by Pignoria, in a work bearing different titles in the successive editions from 1605; and his explanations are still considered probable. Pignoria's other writings were also in high esteem with the antiquaries.[y] It would be

Works on Roman antiquity.

---

[u] Burman, ubi supra.
[x] Niceron, v. 80.   Tiraboschi, xi. 300.
[y] Niceron, vol. xxi.   Biogr. univ.,

tedious to enumerate the less important productions of this kind. A minute and scrupulous criticism, it has been said, distinguished the antiquaries of the seventeenth century. Without, perhaps, the comprehensive views of Sigonius and Panvinius, they were more severely exact. Hence forgery and falsehood stood a much worse chance of success than before. Annius of Viterbo had deceived half the scholars of the preceding age. But when Inghirami, in 1637, published his Etruscarum Antiquitatum Fragmenta, monuments of Etruscan antiquity, which he pretended to have discovered at Volterra, the imposture was speedily detected.[z]

28. The Germania Antiqua of Cluverius was published in 1616, and his Italia Antiqua in 1624. These form a sort of epoch in ancient geography. The latter, especially, has ever since been the great repertory of classical illustration on this subject. Cluverius, however, though a man of acknowledged ability and erudition, has been thought too bold an innovator in his Germany, and to have laid down much on his own conjecture.[a]

Geography of Cluverius.

29. Meursius, a native of Holland, began when very young, soon after the commencement of the century, those indefatigable labours on Grecian antiquity, by which he became to Athens and all Hellas what Sigonius had been to Rome and Italy. Niceron has given a list of his publications, sixty-seven in number, including some editions of ancient writers, but for the most part confined to illustrations of Greek usages; some also treat of Roman. The Græcia feriata, on festivals and games; the Orchestra, on dancing; the Eleusinia, on that deeply interesting, and in his time almost untouched subject, the ancient mysteries, are collected in the works of this very learned person, or scattered through the Thesaurus Antiquitatum Græcarum of Gronovius. 'Meursius,' says his editor, 'was the true and legitimate mystagogue to the sanctuaries of Greece. But his peculiar attention was justly shown to 'the eye of Greece,' Athens. Nothing that bore on her history, her laws and government, her manners and literature, was left

Meursius.

---

[z] Salfi (Continuation de Ginguéné), xi. 358.　　　[a] Blount. Niceron, vol. xxi. Biogr. univ.

by him.   The various titles of his works seem almost to ex-
haust Athenian antiquity: De Populis Atticæ—Athenæ
Atticæ—Cecropia—Regnum Atticum—Archontes Athenien-
ses—Pisistratus—Fortuna Attica—Atticarum Lectionum
Libri IV.—Piræeus—Themis Attica—Solon—Areopagus—
Panathenæa—Eleusinia—Theseus—Æschylus—Sophocles et
Euripides.   It is manifest that all later learning must have
been built upon his foundations.   No one was equal to
Meursius in this province; but the second place is perhaps
Ubbo
Emmius. due to Ubbo Emmius, professor of Greek at Groningen, for his Vetus Græcia Illustrata, 1626.   The
facilities of elucidating the topography of that country were
by no means such as Cluverius had found for Italy; and in
fact little was done in respect to local investigation in order
to establish a good ancient geography till recent times.
Samuel Petit, a man placed by some in the very first list of
the learned, published in 1635 a commentary on the Athenian laws, which is still the chief authority on that subject.

30. In an age so peculiarly learned as this part of the
seventeenth century, it will be readily concluded that many
books must have a relation to the extensive subject of this
section; though the stream of erudition had taken rather a
different course, and watered the provinces of ecclesiastical
and mediæval still more than those of heathen antiquity.
But we can only select one or two which treat of chronology, and that chiefly because we have already given a place
to the work of Scaliger.

31. Lydiat was the first who, in a small treatise on the
Chronology
of Lydiat.
Calvisius. various calendars, 1605, presumed in several respects to differ from that of the dictator of litera-
ture.   He is in consequence reviled in Scaliger's Epistles as
the most stupid and ignorant of the human race, a portentous birth of England, or at best an ass and a beetle, whom
it is below the dignity of the author to answer.[b]   Lydiat

---

[b] Ante aliquot dies tibi scripsi, ut scirem ex te quis sit Thomas Lydiat iste, quo monstro nullum portentosius in vestra Anglia natum puto; tanta est inscitia hominis et confidentia. Ne semel quidem illi verum dicere accidit. And again:—Non est similis morio in orbe terrarum. Paucis asinitatem ejus perstringam ut lector rideat. Nam in tam prodigiosè imperitum scarabæum scribere, neque nostræ dignitatis est, neque otii. Scalig. Epist. 291. Usher nevertheless, if we may trust Wood, thought Scaliger worsted by Lydiat, Ath. Oxon. iii.187.

was, however, esteemed a man of deep learning, and did not flinch from the contest. His Emendatio Temporum, published in 1609, is a more general censure of the Scaligerian chronology, but it is rather a short work for the extent of the subject. A German, Seth Calvisius, on the other hand, is extolled to the skies by Scaliger for a chronology founded on his own principles. These are applied in it to the whole series of events, and thus Calvisius may be said to have made an epoch in historical literature. He made more use of eclipses than any preceding writer; and his dates are reckoned as accurate in modern as in ancient history.[c]

32. Scaliger, nearly twenty years after his death, was assailed by an adversary whom he could not have thought it unworthy of his name to repel. Petau, *Petavius.* or Petavius, a Jesuit of uncommon learning, devoted the whole of the first of two large volumes, entitled Doctrina Temporum, 1627, to a censure of the famous work De Emendatione Temporum. This volume is divided into eight books; the first on the popular year of the Greeks; the second on the lunar; the third on the Egyptian, Persian, and Armenian; the fourth on the solar year; the fifth treats of the correction of the paschal cycle and the calendar; the sixth discusses the principles of the lunar and solar cycles; the seventh is entitled an introduction to computations of various kinds, among which he reckons the Julian period; the eighth is on the true motions of the sun and moon, and on their eclipses. In almost every chapter of the first five books, Scaliger is censured, refuted, reviled. It was a retribution upon his own arrogance; but published thus after his death, with no justice done to his great learning and ability, and scarcely the common terms of respect towards a mighty name, it is impossible not to discern in this work of Petavius both signs of an envious mind, and a partial desire to injure the fame of a distinguished Protestant. His virulence, indeed, against Scaliger becomes almost ridiculous. At the beginning of each of the first five books, he lays it down as a theorem to be demonstrated, that Scaliger is always wrong on the particular subjects to which it relates; and at the close of

---

[c] Blount. Biogr. univ.

each, he repeats the same in geometrical form as having been
proved. He does not even give him credit for the invention
of the Julian period, though he adopts it himself with much
praise, positively asserting that it is borrowed from the Byzantine Greeks.[d] The second volume is in five books, and is
dedicated to the historical part of chronology, and the application of the principles laid down before. A third volume,
in 1630, relating to the same subjects, though bearing a
different title, is generally considered as part of the work.
Petavius, in 1633, published an abridgment of his chronological system, entitled Rationarium Temporum, to which he
subjoined a table of events down to his own time, which in
the larger work had only been carried to the fall of the
empire. This abridgment is better known and more generally
useful than the former.

33. The merits of Petavius as a chronologer have been
Character of
this work. differently appreciated. Many, of whom Huet is
one, from religious prejudices rejoiced in what they
hoped to be a discomfiture of Scaliger, whose arrogance had
also made enemies of a large part of the literary world. Even
Vossius, after praising Petavius, declares that he is unwilling
to decide between men who have done for chronology more
than any others.[e] But he has not always been so favourably
dealt with. Le Clerc observes, that as Scaliger is not very
perspicuous, and Petavius has explained the former's opinions
before he proceeds to refute them, those who compare the
two will have this advantage, that they will understand

---

[d] Lib. vii. c. 7.

[e] Vossius apud Niceron, xxxvii. 111.
Dionysius Petavius permulta post Scali-
gerum optime observavit. Sed nolim
judicium interponere inter eos, quorum
uterque præclare adeo de chronologia
meritus est, ut nullis plus hæc scientia
debeat. . . . Qui sine affectu ac partium
studio conferre volet quæ de temporibus
scripsere, conspiciet esse ubi Scaligero
major laus debeatur, comperiet quoque
ubi longe Petavio malit assentiri; erit
etiam ubi ampliandum videatur; imo
ubi nec facile veritas à quoquam possit
indagari. The chronology of Petavius
was animadverted upon by Salmasius
with much rudeness, and by several

other contemporaries engaged in the
same controversy. If we were to believe Baillet, Petavius was not only the
most learned of the order of Jesuits, but
surpassed Salmasius himself *de plusieurs
coudées*. Jugemens des Sçavans, n. 513.
But to judge between giants we should
be a little taller ourselves than most are.
Baillet, indeed, quotes Henry Valois for
the preference of Petavius to any other
of his age; which, in other words, is
much the same as to call him the most
learned man that ever lived; and Valois
was a very competent judge. The
words, however, are found in a funeral
panegyric.

Scaliger better than before.[f] This is not very complimentary
to his opponent. A modern writer of respectable authority
gives us no reason to consider him victorious. ' Though the
great work of Petavius on chronology,' says M. St. Martin,
' is certainly a very estimable production, it is not less certain
that he has in no degree contributed to enlarge the boundaries
of the science. The author shows too much anxiety to refute
Scaliger, whether right or wrong; his sole aim is to destroy
the edifice perhaps too boldly elevated by his adversary. It
is not unjust to say that Petavius has literally done nothing
for positive chronology; he has not even determined with
accuracy what is most incontestable in this science. Many
of the dates which he considers as well established are still
subject to great doubt, and might be settled in a very different manner. His work is clear and methodical; and,
as it embraces the whole of chronology, it might have become
of great authority; but these very qualities have rendered it
injurious to the science. He came to arrest the flight which,
through the genius of Scaliger, it was ready to take, nor has
it made the least progress ever since; it has produced nothing but conjectures, more or less showy, but with nothing
solid and undeniable for their basis.' [g]

[f] Bibl. choisie, ii. 186. A short abstract of the Petavian scheme of chronology will be found in this volume of

Le Clerc.
[g] Biogr. univ. art. Petavius.

CHAPTER II.

HISTORY OF THEOLOGICAL LITERATURE IN EUROPE, FROM 1600 TO 1650.

Claim of Popes to temporal Power—Father Paul Sarpi—Gradual Decline of papal Power—Unpopularity of Jesuits—Controversy of Catholics and Protestants—Deference of some of the latter to Antiquity—Wavering in Casaubon—Still more in Grotius—Calixtus—An opposite School of Theologians—Daillé—Chillingworth—Hales—Rise of the Arminian Controversy—Episcopius—Socinians—Question as to Rights of Magistrates in Religion—Writings of Grotius on this Subject—Question of Religious Toleration—Taylor's Liberty of Prophesying—Theological Critics and Commentators—Sermons of Donne—and Taylor—Deistical Writers—English Translation of the Bible.

1. THE claim of the Roman see to depose sovereigns was like the retractile claws of some animals, which would be liable to injury were they not usually sheathed. If the state of religion in England and France towards the latter part of the sixteenth century required the assertion of these pretended rights, it was not the policy of a court, guided as often by prudence as by zeal or pride, to keep them for ever before the eyes of the world. Clement VIII. wanted not these latter qualities, but they were restrained by the former; and the circumstances in which the new century opened did not demand any direct collision with the civil power. Henry IV. had been received back into the bosom of the church; he was now rather the ally, the favoured child of Rome, than the object of her proscription. Elizabeth, again, was out of the reach of any enemy but death, and much was hoped from the hereditary disposition of her successor. The temporal supremacy would therefore have been left for obscure and unauthorised writers to vindicate, if an unforeseen circumstance had not called out again its most celebrated champion. After the detection of the gunpowder conspiracy, an oath of allegiance was imposed in England, containing a renunciation, in strong terms, of the tenet that princes excommuni-

Temporal supremacy of Rome.

cated by the pope might be deposed or murdered by their subjects. None of the English Catholics refused allegiance to James; and most of them probably would have felt little scruple at taking the entire oath, which their arch-priest, Blackwell, had approved. But the see of Rome interfered to censure those who took the oath; and a controversy singularly began with James himself in his ' Apology for the Oath of Allegiance.' Bellarmin answered, in 1610, under the name of Matthew Tortus; and the duty of defending the royal author was devolved on one of our most learned divines, Lancelot Andrews, who gave to his reply the quaint title, Tortura Torti.[a] But this favourite tenet of the Vatican was as ill fitted to please the Gallican as the English church. Barclay, a lawyer of Scottish family, had long defended the rights of the crown of France against all opponents. His posthumous treatise on the temporal power of the pope with respect to sovereign princes was published at London in 1609. Bellarmin answered it next year in the ultra-montane spirit which he had always breathed; the parliament of Paris forbad the circulation of his reply.[b]

2. Paul V. was a pope imbued with the arrogant spirit of his predecessors, Paul IV. and Pius V.; no one was more prompt to exercise the despotism which the Jesuits were ready to maintain. After some minor disputes with the Italian states, he came, in 1605, to his famous conflict with the republic of Venice, on the very important question of the immunity of ecclesiastics from the civil tribunals. Though he did not absolve the subjects of Venice

Contest with Venice.

---

[a] Biogr. Britann. art. Andrews. Collier's Ecclesiastical History. Butler's English Catholics, vol. i. Matthew Tortus was the almoner of Bellarmin, whose name he thought fit to assume as a very slight disguise.

[b] Il pretesto, says Father Paul of Bellarmin's book, è di scrivere contra Barclajo ; ma il vero fine si vede esser per ridurre il papa al colmo dell' omnipotente. In questo libro non si tratta altro, che il suddetto argumento, e più di venti cinque volte è replicato, che quando il papa giudica un principe indegno per sua colpa d' aver governo, overo inetto, ò pur conosce, che per il bene della chiesa sia cosa utile, lo può

privare. Dice più volte, che quando il papa comanda, che non sia ubbidito ad un principe privato da lui, non si può dire, che comandi che principe non sia ubbidito, ma che privata persona, perchè il principe privato dal papa non è più principe. E passa tanto inanzi, che viene à dire, il papa può disponere secondo che giudica ispediente di tutti i beni di qual si voglia Christiano, ma tutto sarebbe niente, se solo dicesse che tale è la sua opinione ; dice ch' è un articolo della fede catholica, ch' è eretico, chi non sente così, e questo con tanta petulantia, che non vi si può aggiungere. Lettere di Sarpi, 50.

from their allegiance, he put the state under an interdict,
forbidding the celebration of divine offices throughout its territory. The Venetian clergy, except the Jesuits and some
other regulars, obeyed the senate rather than the pope. The
whole is matter of known history. In the termination of
this dispute, it has been doubted which party obtained the
victory; but in the ultimate result and effect upon mankind,
we cannot, it seems, well doubt that the see of Rome was the
loser.[c] Nothing was more worthy of remark, especially in

Father Paul Sarpi. literary history, than the appearance of one great
man, Fra Paolo Sarpi, the first who, in modern
times and in a Catholic country, shook the fabric not only
of papal despotism, but of ecclesiastical independence and
power. For it is to be observed that in the Venetian business
the pope was contending for what were called the rights of
the church, not for his own supremacy over it. Sarpi was a
man of extraordinary genius, learning, and judgment; his
physical and anatomical knowledge was such as at least to
have caused several great discoveries to be assigned to him;[d]
his reasoning was concise and cogent, his style perspicuous
and animated. A treatise, 'Delle Materie Beneficiarie,' in
other words, on the rights, revenues, and privileges, in secular
matters, of the ecclesiastical order, is a model in its way.
The history is so short and yet so sufficient, the sequence so
natural and clear, the proofs so judiciously introduced, that
it can never be read without delight and admiration of the
author's skill. And this is more striking to those who have
toiled at the verbose books of the sixteenth and seventeenth
centuries, where tedious quotations, accumulated, not selected,
disguise the argument they are meant to confirm. Except
the first book of Machiavel's History of Florence, I do not
remember any earlier summary of facts so lucid and pertinent
to the object. That object was, with Father Paul, neither

---

[e] Ranke is the best authority on this
dispute, as he is on all other matters relating to the papacy in this age. Vol. ii.
p. 324.

[d] He was supposed to have discovered
the valves of the veins, the circulation
of the blood, the expansion and con-
traction of the pupil, the variation of

the compass. A quo, says Baptista
Porta of Sarpi, aliqua didicisse non
solum fateri non erubescimus, sed gloria-
mur, cum eo doctiorem, subtiliorem,
quotquot adhuc videre contigerit, neminem cognovimus ad encyclopædiam.
Magia Naturalis, lib. vii. apud Ranke.

more nor less than to represent the wealth and power of the church as ill-gotten and excessive. The Treatise on Benefices led the way, or rather was the seed thrown into the ground, that ultimately produced the many efforts both of the press and of public authority to break down ecclesiastical privileges.[e]

3. The other works of Sarpi are numerous, but none require our present attention except the most celebrated, his History of the Council of Trent. The manu- History of Council of Trent. script of this having been brought to London by Antonio de Dominis, was there published in 1619, under the name of Pietro Soave Polano, the anagram of Paolo Sarpi Veneto. It was quickly translated into several languages, and became the text-book of Protestantism on the subject. Many incorrectnesses have been pointed out by Pallavicini, who undertook the same task on the side of Rome; but the general credibility of Father Paul's history has rather gained by the ordeal of hostile criticism. Dupin observes that the long list of errors imputed by Pallavicini, which are chiefly in dates and such trifling matters, make little or no difference as to the substance of Sarpi's history; but that its author is more blameable for a malicious disposition to impute political motives to the members of the council, and idle reasonings which they did not employ.[f] Ranke, who has given this a more minute scrutiny than Dupin could have done, comes nearly to the same result. Sarpi is not a fair, but he is, for those times, a tolerably exact historian. His work exhibits the general excellences of his manner; freedom from redundancy, a clear, full, agreeable style; a choice of what is most pertinent and interesting in his materials. Much has been disputed about the religious tenets of Father Paul; it appears to me quite out of doubt, both by the tenor of his history, and still more unequivocally, if possible, by some of his letters, that he was entirely hostile to the church, in the usual sense, as well as to the court of Rome, sympathising in affection, and concurring generally in opinion, with the reformed deno-

---

[e] A long analysis of the Treatise on Benefices will be found in Dupin, who does not blame it very much. The treatise is worth reading through, and has been commended by many good judges of history.

[f] Hist. Eccles. Cent. 17.

mination.[g] But as he continued in the exercise of his functions as a Servite monk, and has always passed at Venice more for a saint than a heretic, some of the Gallican writers have not scrupled to make use of his authority, and to extenuate his heterodoxy. There can be no question but that he inflicted a severe wound on the spiritual power.

4. That power, predominant as it seemed in the beginning

Gallican
liberties.
Richer.

of the seventeenth century, met with adversaries besides Sarpi. The French nation, and especially the parliament of Paris, had always vaunted what were called the liberties of the Gallican church ; liberties, however, for which neither the church itself, nor the king, the two parties interested, were prone to display much regard. A certain canonist, Richer, published in 1611 a book on ecclesiastical

---

[g] The proofs of this it would be endless to adduce from the history ; they strike the eye in every page, though it cannot be expected that he should declare his way of thinking in express terms. Even in his letters he does not this. They were printed, with the date, at least of Verona, in 1673. Sully's fall he laments, ' having become partial to him on account of his firmness in religion.' Lett. 53. Of the republic of the United Provinces he says, La nascenza di quale si come Dio ha favorito con grazie inestimabili, così pare che la malizia del diavolo oppugni con tutte le arti. Lett. 23. After giving an account of one Marsilio, who seems to have been a Protestant, he adds : Credo se non fosse per ragion di stato, si trovarebbono diversi, che saltarebbono da questo fosso di Roma nella cima della riforma ; ma chi teme una cosa, chi un' altra. Dio però par che goda la più minima parte dei pensieri umani. So ch' ella mi intende senza passar più oltre. Lett. 81. Feb. 1612. Sarpi speaks with great contempt of James I., who was occupied like a pedant about Vorstius and such matters. Se il rè d' Inghilterra non fosse dottore, si potrebbe sperare qualche bene, e sarebbe un gran principio, perchè Spagna non si può vincere, se non levato il pretesto della religione, ne questo si leverà se non introducendo i reformati nell' Italia. E se il rè sapesse fare, sarebbe facile e in Torino e qui. Lett. 88. He wrote, however, a remarkable

letter to Casaubon much about this time, hinting at his wish to find an asylum in England, and using rather different language about the king : In eo, rarum, cumulatæ virtutes principis ac viri. Regum idea est, ad quam forte ante actis sæculis nemo formatus fuit. Si ego ejus protectione dignus essem, nihil mihi deesse putarem ad mortalis vitæ felicitatem. Tu, vir præstantissime, nihil te dignius efficere potes, quam tanto principi mea studia commendare. Casaubon, Epist. 811. For *mea* in another edition read *tua* ; but the former seems preferable. Casaubon replied, that the king wished Paul to be a light to his own country ; but if anything should happen, he had written to his ambassador, ut nulla in re tibi desit.

[The above collection of letters, published at Geneva, with the date of Verona, is said by a late biographer of Sarpi, and one very far from Catholic orthodoxy, to have been most incorrectly printed, and even interpolated, for the purpose of giving a more Protestant cast to his opinions ; so that, though in the main his own, they cannot be quoted in evidence. Vita di Sarpi, per Bianchi-Giovini, Bruxelles, 1836, vol. ii. p. 191. But the letter to Casaubon is certainly genuine ; and we have no proof of interpolation in those of Geneva, though we may have of incorrectness. The History, however, is sufficient to demonstrate Sarpi's Protestantism.—1847.]

and political power; in which he asserted the government of the church to be a monarchy tempered with aristocracy; that is, that the authority of the pope was limited in some respects by the rights of the bishops. Though this has since become a fundamental principle among the Cisalpine Catholics, it did not suit the high notions of that age; and the bishops were content to sacrifice their rights by joining in the clamour of the papal party. A synod assembled by Cardinal du Perron, archbishop of Sens, condemned the book of Richer, who was harassed for the rest of his life by the persecution of those he had sought to defend against a servitude which they seemed to covet. His fame has risen in later times. Dupin concludes a careful analysis of Richer's treatise with a noble panegyric on his character and style of writing.[h]

5. The strength of the ultra-montane party in the Gallican church was Perron, a man of great natural capacity, a prodigious memory, a vast knowledge of ecclesiastical and profane antiquity, a sharp wit, a pure and eloquent style, and such readiness in dispute that few cared to engage him.[j] If he did not always reason justly, or upon consistent principles, these are rather failings in the eyes of lovers of truth, than of those, and they are the many, who sympathise with the dexterity and readiness of a partisan. He had been educated as a Protestant, but, like half the learned of that religion, went over from some motive or other to the victorious side. In the conference at Fontainebleau with Du Plessis Mornay, it has been mentioned already that he had a confessed advantage; but victory in debate follows the combatant rather than the cause. The supporters of Gallican liber-

Perron.

---

[h] Hist. Eccles. Cent. 17. l. ii. c. 7. Niceron, vol. xxvii. The Biographie universelle talks of the republican principles of Richer: it must be in an ecclesiastical sense, for nothing in the book, 1 think, relates to civil politics. Father Paul thought Richer's scheme might lead to something better, but did not highly esteem it. Quella mistura del governo ecclesiastico di . monarchia e aristocrazia mi pare una composizione di oglio e acqua, che non possono mai mischiarsi insieme. Lettere di Sarpi, 109. Richer entirely denies the infalli-

bility of the pope in matters of faith, and says there is no authority adduced for it but that of the popes themselves. His work is written on the principles of the Jansenizing Gallicans of the eighteenth century, and probably goes farther than Bossuet, or any who wished to keep on good terms with Rome, would have openly approved. It is prolix, extending to two volumes 4to. Some account of Richer will be found in Histoire de la Mère et du Fils, ascribed to Mezeray, or Richelieu.

[j] Dupin.

ties were discouraged during the life of this cardinal.   He
did not explicitly set himself against them, or deny, perhaps,
the principles of the council of Constance; but by preventing
any assertion of them, he prepared the way, as it was hoped
at Rome, for a gradual recognition of the whole system of
Bellarmin.   Perron, however, was neither a Jesuit nor very
favourable to that order.   Even so late as 1638, a collection
of tracts by the learned brothers Du Puy, on the liberties of
the church, was suppressed at the instance of the nuncio, on
the pretext that it had been published without permission.
It was reprinted some years afterwards, when the power of
Rome had begun to decline.[k]

6. Notwithstandiug the tone still held by the court of
Decline of
papal
power. Rome and its numerous partisans, when provoked
by any demonstration of resistance, they generally
avoided aggressive proceedings, and kept in reserve the
tenets which could not be pleasing to any civil government.
We should doubtless find many assertions of the temporal
authority of the pope by searching into obscure theology
during this period ; but after Bellarmin and Perron were
withdrawn from the stage, no prominent champions of that
cause stood forth ; and it was one of which great talents and
high station alone could overcome the intrinsic unpopularity.
Slowly and silently the power of Rome had much receded
before the middle of the seventeenth century.   Paul V. was
the last of the imperious pontiffs who exacted obedience as
sovereigns of Christendom.   His successors have had recourse
to gentler methods, to a paternal rather than regal authority;
they have appealed to the moral sense, but have rarely or
never alarmed the fears of their church.   The long pontifi-
cate of Urban VIII. was a period of transition from strength
to weakness.   In his first years, this pope was not inactively
occupied in the great cause of subduing the Protestant
heresy.   It has been lately brought to light, that soon after
the accession of Charles I. he had formed a scheme, in conjunction with France and Spain, for conquering and parti-

---

[k] Dupin, l. iii. c. 1.   Grot. Epist.
1105.   Liber de libertatibus ecclesiæ
Gallicanæ ex actis desumptus publicis,
quo regis regnique jura contra molitiones
pontificias defenduntur, ipsius regis jussu
vendi est prohibitus.   See also Epist.
519.

tioning the British islands : Ireland was to be annexed to the
ecclesiastical state, and governed by a viceroy of the Holy
See.[m]   But he afterwards gave up these visionary projects,
and limited his ambition to more practicable views of aggrandisement in Italy.   It is certain that the temporal principality of the popes has often been an useful diversion for
the rest of Europe : the duchy of Urbino was less in our
notions of importance than Germany or Britain ; but it was
quite as capable of engrossing the thoughts and passions of
a pope.

7. The subsidence of Catholic zeal before the middle of this
age deserves especially to be noted at a time when, Unpopula-
in various directions, that church is beginning to Jesuits.
exalt her voice, if not to rear her head, and we are ostenta-
tiously reminded of the sudden revival of her influence in the
sixteenth century.   It did undoubtedly then revive ; but it is
equally manifest that it receded once more.   Among the
leading causes of this decline in the influence, not only of
what are called ultra-montane principles, but of the zeal and
faith that had attended them, a change as visible, and almost
as rapid as the re-action in favour of them which we have
pointed out in the latter part of the sixteenth century, we
must reckon the increasing prejudices against the Jesuit
order.   Their zeal, union, indefatigable devotion to the
cause, had made them the most useful of allies, the most formidable of enemies ; but in these very qualities were involved
the seeds of public hatred and ultimate ruin.   Obnoxious to
Protestant states for their intrigues, to the lawyers, especially in France, for their bold theories of political power
and encroaching spirit, to the Dominicans for the favour they
had won, they had become, long before the close of this
period, rather dangerous supporters of the see of Rome.[n]
Their fate, in countries where the temper of their order had
displayed itself with less restraint, might have led reflecting
men to anticipate the consequences of urging too far the

[m] Ranke, ii. 518. It is not at all
probable that France and Spain would
have seriously coalesced for any object
of this kind : the spoil could not have
been safely divided. But the scheme
serves to show the ambition, at that
time, of the Roman see

[n] Clement VIII. was tired of the
Jesuits, as we are told by Perron, who
did not much love them. Perroniana,
p. 286, 288.

patience of mankind by the ambition of an insulated order
of priests.   In the first part of this century the Jesuits possessed an extensive influence in Japan, and had re-united the
kingdom of Abyssinia to the Roman church.   In the course
of a few years more, they were driven out from both ; their
intriguing ambition had excited an implacable animosity
against the church to which they belonged.

8. Cardinal Richelieu, though himself a theological writer,
Richelieu's   took great care to maintain the liberties of the
care of   French crown and church.   No extravagance of
Gallican
liberties.   Hildebrandic principles would find countenance
under his administration.   Their partisans endeavoured
sometimes to murmur against his ecclesiastical measures ;
it was darkly rumoured that he had a scheme of separating
the Catholic church of France, something in the manner
of Henry VIII., from the supremacy of Rome, though not
from her creed ; and one Hersent published, under the name
of Optatus Gallus, a book so rapidly suppressed as to be of
the greatest rarity, the aim of which was to excite the public
apprehension of this schism.°   It was in defence of the
Gallican liberties, so far as it was yet prudent to assert
them, that De Marca was employed to write a treatise, De
Concordantiâ Sacerdotii et Imperii. This book was censured
at Rome ; yet it does not by any means come up to the
language afterwards used in the Gallican church ; it belongs
to its own age, the transitional period in which Rome had
just ceased to act, but not to speak as a mistress. De Marca
was obliged to make some concessions before he could obtain
the bulls for a bishopric. He rose, however, afterwards to
the see of Paris. The first part of his work appeared in
1641, the second after the death of the author.

9. In this most learned period, according to the sense in
Contro-   which the word was then taken, that Europe has
versy of
Catholics   ever seen, it was of course to be expected that the
and Pro-
testants.   studious ecclesiastics of both the Romish and Protestant denomination would pour forth a prodigal erudition

---

° Biogr. univ. Grot. Epist. 982, 1354.   ligions which were then afloat, and all
By some other letters of Grotius, it ap-   which went on setting the pope nearly
pears that Richelieu tampered with those   aside. Ruarus intimates the same. Epist.
schemes of reconciling the different re-   Ruar. p. 401.

in their great controversy. It had always been the aim of the former to give an historical character to theological inquiry; it was their business to ascertain the faith of the Catholic church as a matter of fact, the single principle of its infallibility being assumed as the basis of all investigation. But their opponents, though less concerned in the issue of such questions, frequently thought themselves competent to dispute the field; and, conversant as they were with ecclesiastical antiquity, found in its interminable records sufficient weapons to protract the war, though not to subdue the foe. Hence, partly in the last years of the sixteenth century, but incomparably more in the present, we find an essential change in the character of theological controversy. It became less reasoning, less scriptural, less general and popular, but far more patristic, that is, appealing to the testimonies of the fathers, and altogether Increased more historical than before. Several consequences respect for the fathers. of material influence on religious opinion sprang naturally from this method of conducting the defence of Protestantism. One was, that it contracted very greatly the circle of those who, upon any reasonable interpretation of the original principle of personal judgment, could exercise it for themselves; it became the privilege of the deeply learned alone. Another that, from the real obscurity and incoherence of ecclesiastical authorities, those who had penetrated farthest into that province of learning were least able to reconcile them; and, however they might disguise it from the world while the pen was in their hands, were themselves necessarily left, upon many points, in an embarrassing state of doubt and confusion. A third effect was, that upon these controversies of Catholic tradition, the church of Rome had very often the best of the argument; and this was occasionally displayed in those wrestling-matches between religious disputants, which were held, publicly or privately, either with the vain hope of coming to an agreement, or to settle the faith of the hearers. And from the two last of these causes it arose, that many Protestants went over to the church of Rome, and that a new theological system was contrived to combine what had been deemed the incompatible tenets of those who had burst from each other with such violence in the preceding century.

10. This retrocession, as it appeared, and as in spirit it *Especially in England. Laud.* was, towards the system abandoned in the first impetuosity of the Reformation, began in England about the conclusion of the sixteenth century. It was evidently connected with the high notions of ecclesiastical power, of an episcopacy by unbroken transmission from the apostles, of a pompous ritual, which the rulers of the Anglican church took up at that time in opposition to the Puritans. It rapidly gained ground in the reign of James, and still more of his son. Andrews, a man far more learned in patristic theology than any of the Elizabethan bishops, or perhaps than any of his English contemporaries except Usher, was, if not the founder, the chief leader of this school. Laud became afterwards, from his political importance, its more conspicuous head; and from him it is sometimes styled. In his conference with the Jesuit Fisher, first published in 1624, and afterwards with many additions in 1639, we find an attempt, not feeble, and we may believe, not feigned, to vindicate the Anglican Protestantism, such as he meant it to be, against the church of Rome, but with much deference to the name of Catholic, and the authority of the ancient fathers.[p] It is unnecessary to observe that this was the prevalent language of the English church in that period of forty years, which was terminated by the civil war; and that it was accompanied by a marked enhancement of religious ceremonies, as well as by a considerable approximation to several doctrines and usages of the Romanists.

11. The progress of the latter church for the first thirty

---

[p] Ce qu'il y a de particulier dans cette conférence, c'est qu'on y cite beaucoup plus les pères de l'église, que n'ont accoutumé de faire les Protestans de deçà la mer. Comme l'église anglicane a une vénération toute particulière pour l'antiquité, c'est par là que les Catholiques romains l'attaquent ordinairement. Bibl. univ. i. 336. Laud, as well as Andrews, maintained 'that the true and real body of Christ is in that blessed sacrament.' Conference with Fisher, p. 299 (edit. 1639). And afterwards, 'for the Church of England, nothing is more plain than that it believes and teaches the true and real presence of Christ in the eucharist. Nothing is more plain than the contrary, as Hall, who belonged to a different school of theology, though the friend of Laud, has in equivalent words observed. Hall's works (Pratt's edition), vol. ix. p. 374.

years of the present century was as striking and uninterrupted as it had been in the final period of the six- Defections
teenth. Victory crowned its banners on every side. to the Ca-
tholic
The signal defeats of the elector-palatine and the church.
king of Denmark, the reduction of Rochelle, displayed an
evident superiority in the ultimate argument to which the
Protestants had been driven, and which silences every other ;
while a rigid system of exclusion from court favour and of
civil discouragement, or even of banishment, and suppression
cf public worship, as in the Austrian dominions, brought
round the wavering and flexible to acquiesce with apparent
willingness in a despotism which they could neither resist
nor escape. The nobility, both in France and Germany, who
at the outset had been the first to embrace a new faith,
became afterwards the first to desert it. Many also of the
learned and able Protestants gave evidence of the jeopardy
of that cause by their conversion. It is not, however, just
to infer that they were merely influenced by this apprehension. Two other causes mainly operated; one, to which
we have above alluded, the authority ascribed to the
traditions of the church as recorded by the writers called
fathers, and with which it was found very difficult to reconcile all the Protestant creed ; another, the intolerance of the
reformed churches, both Lutheran and Calvinistic, which
gave as little latitude as that which they had quitted.

12. The defections, from whatever cause, are numerous in
the seventeenth century. But two, more eminent Wavering of
than any who actually renounced the Protestant Casaubon,
religion, must be owned to have given evident signs of
wavering, Casaubon and Grotius. The proofs of this are
not founded merely on anecdotes which might be disputed,
but on their own language.[q] Casaubon was staggered by

---

[q] In his correspondence with Scaliger, no indications of any vacillation
as to religion appear. Of the unfortunate conference between Du Plessis
Mornay and Du Perron, in the presence
of Henry IV., where Casaubon himself
had been one of the umpires, he speaks
with great regret, though with a full
acknowledgment that his champion had
been worsted. Quod scribis de congressu Diomedis cum Glauco, sic est
omnino, ut tu judicas rectè. Vir optimus, si eum sua prudentia orbi Gallico
satis explorata non defecisset, nunquam
ejus certaminis aleam subiisset. After
much more he concludes : Equidem in
lacrymas prope adducor, quoties subit
animo tristissima illius diei species, cum
de ingenua nobilitate, de excellenti ingenio, de ipsa denique veritate pom-

the study of the fathers, in which he discovered many
things, especially as to the eucharist, which he could not in
any manner reconcile with the tenets of the French Huguenots.[r] Perron used to assail him with arguments he could

paticè adeo vidi triumphatum. Epist.
214. (Oct. 1600.) See also a letter to
Heinsius on the same subject. Casaub.
Epist. 809. In a letter to Perron himself, in 1604, he professed to adhere to
Scripture alóne, against those who
vetustatis auctoritatem pro ratione ob-
tendunt. Epist. 417. A change, however, came gradually over his mind,
and he grew fascinated by this very
authority of antiquity, In 1609 he had,
by the king's command, a conference
on religion with Du Perron, but very
reluctantly, and, as his biographer owns,
quibusdam visus est quodammodo ces-
pitasse. Casaubon was, for several
reasons, no match in such a disputation
for Perron. In the first place, he was
poor and weak, and the other powerful,
which is a reason that might dispense
with our giving any others; but, secondly, he had less learning in the
fathers; and, thirdly, he was entangled
by deference for these same fathers;
finally, he was not a man of as much
acuteness and eloquence as his antagonist. The issue of battle does not follow
the better cause, but the sharper sword;
especially when there is so much *igno-
ratio elenchi* as in this case.

[r] Perron continued to persecute Casaubon with argument, whenever he
met him in the king's library. Je vous
confesse (the latter told Wytenbogart)
qu'il m'a donné beaucoup des scrupules
qui me restent, et auxquels je ne sçais
pas bien répondre . . . il me fâche de
rougir. L'escapade que je prens est que
je n'y puis répondre, mais que j'y pen-
serai. Casauboni Vita (ad edit. Epis-
tolarum, 1709). And in writing to the
same Wytenbogart, Jan. 1610, we find
similar signs of wavering. Me, ne quid
dissimulem, hæc tanta diversitas a fide
veteris ecclesiæ non parum turbat. Ne
de aliis dicam, in re sacramentaria a
majoribus discessit Lutherus, a Luthero
Zuinglius, ab utroque Calvinus, a Cal-
vino qui postea scripserunt. Nam constat mihi ac certissimum est, doctrinam
Calvini de sacra eucharistia longe aliam
esse ab ea quæ in libro observandi viri
Molinæi nostri continetur, et quæ vulgo
in ecclesiis nostris auditur. Itaque Mo-

linæum qui oppugnant, Calvinum illi
non minus objiciunt, quam aliquem è
veteribus ecclesiæ doctoribus. Si sic
pergimus, quis tandem erit exitus? Jam
quod idem Molinæus, omnes veterum
libros suæ doctrinæ contrarios respuit,
ut ὑποβολιμαιους, cui mediocriter docto
fidem faciet? Falsus illi Cyrillus,
Hierosolymorum episcopus; falsus Gre-
gorius Nyssenus, falsus Ambrosius, falsi
omnes. Mihi liquet falli ipsum, et illa
scripta esse verissima, quæ ille pronuntiat ψευδεπιγραφα. Ep. 670. See also
Ep. 1043, written from Paris in the
same year. He came now to England,
and to his great satisfaction found the
church and its prelates exactly what he
would wish. Illud solatio mihi est,
quod in hoc regno speciem agnosco
veteris ecclesiæ, quam ex patrum scriptis
didici. Adde quod episcopis ὁσημεραι
συνδιαγω doctissimis, sapientissimis,
ευσεβεστατοις, et quod novum mihi est,
priscæ ecclesiæ amantissimis. (Lond.
1611.) Ep. 703. His letters are full of
similar language. See 743, 744, 772,
&c. He combined this inordinate respect
for authority with its natural concomitant, a desire to restrain free inquiry.
Though his patristic lore should have
made him not unfavourable to the
Arminians, he writes to Bertius, one of
their number, against the liberty of
conscience they required. Illa quam
passim celebras, prophetandi libertas,
bonis et piis hujus ecclesiæ viris mirum
in modum suspecta res est et odiosa.
Nemo enim dubitat de pietate Christiana
actum esse inter vos, si quod videris
agere, illustrissimis ordinibus fuerit
semel persuasum, ut liberum unicuique
esse velint, via regia relicta semitam ex
animi libidine sibi aliisque aperire.
Atqui veritas, ut scis, in omnibus rebus
scientiis et disciplinis unica est, et το
φωνειν ταυτο inter ecclesiæ veræ notas,
fateantur omnes, non est postrema. Ut
nulli esse dubium possit, quin tot πολυσ-
χιδε.s semitæ totidem sint errorum di-
verticula. Quod olim de politicis rebus
prudentissimi philosophorum dixerunt,
id mihi videtur multo etiam magis in
ecclesiasticis locum habere, την αγαν
ελευθεριαν εις δουλειαν εξ αναγκης τελευτᾶν,

not parry. If we may believe this cardinal, he was on the point of declaring publicly his conversion before he accepted the invitation of James I. to England; and even while in England he promoted the Catholic cause more than the world was aware.[s] This is more than we can readily believe; and we know that he was engaged both in maintaining the temporal rights of the crown against the school of Bellarmin, and in writing animadversions on the ecclesiastical annals of Baronius. But this opposition to the extreme line of the ultra-montanists might be well compatible with a tendency towards much that the reformers had denounced. It seemed, in truth, to disguise the corruptions of the Catholic church by rendering the controversy almost what we might call personal; as if Rome alone, either by usurping the headship of the church, which might or might not have bad consequences, or by its encroachments on the civil power, which were only maintained by a party, were the sole object of that religious opposition, which had divided one-half of Europe from the other. Yet if Casaubon, as he had much inclination to do, being on ill terms with some in England, and disliking the country,[t] had returned to France, it seems pro-

---

et πασαν τυραννιδα αναρχιας esse κρειττην [sic!] et optabiliorem. . . . Ego qui inter pontificios diu sum in patri mea versatus, hoc tibi possum affirmare, nulla re magis stabiliri την τυραννιδα του χξζ, quam dissentionibus nostris et dissidiis.

Meric Casaubon's 'Pietas contra maledicos Patrii Nominis ac Religionis Hostes,' is an elaborate vindication of his father against all charges alleged by his adversaries. The only one that presses is that of wavering in religion. And here Meric candidly owns that his father had been shaken by Perron about 1610. (See this tract subjoined to Almeloveen's edition of the epistles, p. 89.) But afterwards, by dint of theological study, he got rid of the scruples the cardinal had infused into him, and became a Protestant of the new Anglican school, admiring the first six centuries, and especially the period after Constantine: Hoc sæculum cum duobus sequentibus ακμη της εκκλησιας, flos ipse ecclesiæ et ætas illius aurea queat nuncupari. Prolegomena in Exercitationes in Baronium. His friend Scaliger had very different notions of the fathers. 'The

fathers,' says he, in his blunt way, 'are very ignorant, know nothing of Hebrew, and teach us little in theology. Their interpretations of Scripture are strangely perverse. Even Polycarp, who was a disciple of the apostles, is full of errors. It will not do to say that, because they were near the apostolic age, they are never wrong.' Scaligerana Secunda. Le Clerc has some good remarks on the deference shown by Casaubon to the language held by the fathers about the eucharist, which shook his Protestantism. Bibl. choisie, xix. 230.

[s] Perroniana. Grot. Epist. p. 939.

[t] Several of his letters attest his desire of returning. He wrote to Thuanus imploring his recommendation to the queen-regent. But he had given much offence by writing against Baronius, and had very little chance of an indemnity for his prebend of Canterbury, if he had relinquished that on leaving England. This country, however, though he sometimes calls it μακαρων νησος, did not suit his disposition. He was never on good terms with Savile, the most pre-

bable that he would not long have continued in what, according to the principles he had adopted, would appear a schismatical communion.

13. Grotius was from the time of his turning his mind to theology almost as much influenced as Casaubon by primitive authority, and began, even in 1614, to commend the Anglican church for the respect it showed, very unlike the rest of the reformed, to that standard.[u] But the

and of Grotius.

---

sumptuous of the learned, according to him, and most scornful, whom he accused of setting on Montagu to anticipate his animadversions on Baronius, with some suspicion, on Casaubon's part, of stealing from him. Ep. 794, 848, 849. But he seems himself to have become generally unpopular, if we may trust his own account. Ego mores Anglorum non capio. Quoscunque habui notos priusquam huc venirem, jam ego illis sum ignotus, verè peregrinus, barbarus ; nemo illorum me vel verbulo appellat ; *appellatus silet.* Hoc quid sit, non scio. Hic ——— [Henricus Wotton] vir doctissimus ante annos viginti mecum Genevæ vixit, et ex eo tempore literis amicitiam coluimus. Postquam ego e Galliis, ille Venetiis huc convenimus, desii esse illi notus ; meæ quoque epistolæ responsum dedit nullum ; an sit daturus nescio. Ep. 841. It seems difficult to account for so marked a treatment of Casaubon, except on the supposition that he was thought to pursue a course unfavourable to the Protestant interest. He charges the English with despising every one but themselves ; and ascribes this to the vast wealth of their universities; a very discreditable source of pride in our ancestors, if so it were. But Casaubon's philological and critical skill passed for little in this country, where it was not known enough to be envied. In mere ecclesiastical learning he was behind some English scholars.

[u] Casaubon himself hailed Grotius as in the right path. In hodiernis contentionibus in negotio religionis et doctè et piè judicat, et in veneratione antiquitatis cum iis sentit, qui optimè sentiunt. Epist. 883. See also 772, which is addressed to him. This high respect for the fathers and for the authority of the primitive church grew strongly upon him, and the more because he found they were hostile to the Calvinistic

scheme. He was quite delighted at finding Jerome and Chrysostom on his side. Grot. Epist. 29. (1614.) In the next year, writing to Vossius, he goes a great length. Cæterum ego reformatarum ecclesiarum miseriam in hoc maximè deploro, quod cum symbola condere catholicæ sit ecclesiæ, ipsis inter se nunquam eam in rem convenire sit datum, atque interim libelli apologetici ex re nata scripti ad imperatorem, reges, principes, aut ut in concilio œcumenico exhiberentur, trahi cœperint in usum longè alienum. Quid enim magis est alienum ab unitate catholica quam quod diversis in regionibus pastores diversa populo tradere coguntur ? Quam mirata fuisset hoc prodigium pia antiquitas ! Sed hæc aliaque multa mussitanda sunt nobis ob iniquitatem temporum. Epist. 66. He was at this time, as he continued till near the end of his life, when he moved on farther, highly partial to the Anglican church. He was, however, too Erastian for the English bishops of the reign of James, as appears by a letter addressed to him by Overall, who objected to his giving, in his treatise De Imperio circa Sacra, a definitive power in controversies of faith to the civil magistrate, and to his putting episcopacy among non-essentials, which the bishops held to be of divine right. Grotius adhered to his opinion, that episcopacy was not commanded as a perpetual institution, and thought, at that time, that there was no other distinction between bishops and priests than of precedency. Nusquam meminit, he says in one place, Clemens Romanus exsortis illius episcoporum auctoritatis quæ ecclesiæ consuetudine post Marci mortem Alexandriæ, atque eo exemplo alibi, introduci cœpit, sed planè ut Paulus Apostolus, ostendit ecclesias communi presbyterorum, qui iidem omnes et episcopi ipsi Pauloque dicuntur, consilio fuisse gubernatas. Even in his latter

ill usage he sustained at the hands of those who boasted
their independence of papal tyranny, the caresses of the

writings he seems never to have embraced the notions of some Anglican
divines on this subject, but contents
himself, in his remarks on Cassander,
who had said, singularly as it may be
thought, Convenit *inter omnes* olim
Apostolorum ætate inter episcopos et
presbyteros discrimen nullum fuisse,
sed postmodum ordinis servandi et schismatis evitandi causa episcopum presby-
teris fuisse præpositum, with observing,
Episcopi sunt presbyterorum principes ;
et ista προστασια (præsidentia) a Chris o
præmonstrata est in Petro, ab Apostolis
vero, ubicunque fieri poterat, constituta,
et a Spiritu Sancto comprobata in Apo-
calypsi. Op. Theolog. iv. 579, 621.

But to return from this digression to
our more immediate purpose. Grotius
for several years continued in this insulated state, neither approving of the
Reformation nor the church of Rome.
He wrote in 1622 to Episcopius against
those whom he called Cassandrians,
Qui etiam plerosque Romanæ ecclesiæ
errores improbantibus auctores sunt, ne
ab ejus communione discedant. Ep. 181.
He was destined to become Cassandrian
himself, or something more. The infallibility of the church was still no doctrine of his. At illa auctoritas ecclesiæ
αναμαρτητου, quam ecclesiæ, et quidem
suæ, Romanenses ascribunt, cum naturali ratione non sit evidens, nam ipsi
fatentur Judaicam ecclesiam id privile-
gium non habuisse, sequitur ut adversus
negantes probari debeat ex sacris literis.
Epist. secunda series, p. 761. (1620.)
And again : Quæ scribit pater de resti-
tuendis rebus in eum statum, qui ante
concilium Tridentinum fuerat, esset quidem hoc permultum ; sed transubstan-
tiatio et ei respondens adoratio pridem
Lateranensi concilio definita est, et in-
vocatio peculiaris sanctorum pridem in
omnes liturgias recepta. P. 772. (1623.)
Grotius passed most of his latter years
at Paris, in the honourable station of
ambassador from the court of Sweden.
He seems to have thought it a matter
of boast that he did not live as a Protestant. See Ep. 196. The Huguenot
ministers of Charenton requested him
to communicate with them, which he
declined, p. 854, 856. (1635.) He now
was brooding over a scheme of union
among Protestants : the English and

Swedish churches were to unite. and to
be followed by Denmark. Constituto
semel aliquo tali ecclesiarum corpore,
spes est subinde alios atque alios se ag-
gregaturos. Est autem hæc res eo magis
optanda protestantibus, quod quotidie
multi eos deserunt et se cœtibus Ro-
manensium addunt, non alia de causa,
quam quod non unum est eorum corpus,
sed partes distractæ, greges segreges,
propria cuique sua sacrorum communio,
ingens præterea maledicendi certamen.
Epist. 866. (1637.) See also p. 827.
(1630.) He fancied that by such a
weight of authority, grounded on the
ancient church, the exercise of private
judgment, on which he looked with
horror, might be overruled. Nisi interpretandi sacras literas, he writes to Calixtus, libertatem cohibemus intra lineas
eorum, quæ omnes illæ non sanctitate
minus quam primæva vetustate venera-
biles ecclesiæ ex ipsa prædicatione scripturis ubique consentiente hauserint, diu-
que sub crucis maximè magisterio reti-
nuerint, nisi deinde in iis quæ liberam
habuere disputationem fraterna lenitate
ferre alii alios discimus, quis erit letium
sæpe in factiones, deinde in bella erum-
pentium finis ? Ep. 674. (Oct. 1636.)
Qui illam optimam antiquitatem sequuntur ducem, quod te semper fecisse
memini, iis non eveniet, ut multum sibi
ipsis sint discolores. In Angliâ vides
quam bene processerit dogmatum noxio-
rum repurgatio, hac maximè de causa
quod qui id sanctissimum negotium pro-
curandum suscepere nihil admiscuerunt
novi, nihil sui, sed ad meliora sæcula
intentam habuere oculorum aciem. Ep.
966. (1638.)

But he could not be long in perceiving
that this union of Protestant churches
was impossible from the very independence of their original constitution. He
saw that there could be no practicable
re-union except with Rome itself, nor
that, except on an acknowledgment of
her superiority. From the year 1640 his
letters are full of sanguine hopes that
this delusive vision would be realised.
He still expected some concession on the
other side ; but, as usual, would have
lowered his terms according to the pertinacity of his adversaries, if indeed they
were still to be called his adversaries.
He now published his famous annota-

Gallican clergy after he had fixed his residence at Paris, the
growing dissensions and virulence of the Protestants, the

tions on Cassander, and the other tracts
mentioned in the text, to which they
gave rise. In these he defends almost
every thing we deem popery, such as
transubstantiation (Opera Theologica,
iv. 619), stooping to all the nonsensical
evasions of a spiritual mutation of substance and the like; the authority of
the pope (p. 642), the celibacy of the
clergy (p. 645), the communion in one
kind (ibid.), and in fact is less of a Protestant than Cassander. In his epistles
he declares himself decidedly in favour
of purgatory, as at least a probable doctrine. P. 930. In these writings he seems
to have had the countenance of Richelieu. Cardinalis quin ἑνώσεως negotium
in Gallia successurum sit, dubitare se
negat. Epist. sec. series, p. 912. Cardinalis Ricelianus rem successuram pu-
tat. Ita certè loquitur multis. Archie-
piscopus Cantuariensis pœnas dat honesf-
tissimi consilii, quod et aliis bonis sæpe
evenit. P. 911. Grotius is now run away
with by vanity, and fancies all will go
according to his wish, showing much ignorance of the real state of things. He
was left by some from whom he had entertained hopes, and thought the Dutch
Arminians timid. Vossius, ut video,
præ metu, forte et ex Anglia sic jussus,
auxilium suum mihi subtrahit. P. 908.
Salmasius adhuc in consiliis fluctuat. Est
in religionis rebus suæ parti addictior
quam putabatur. P. 912. De Episcopio
doleo; est vir magni ingenii et probus,
sed nimium cupidus alendæ partis. But
it is probable that he had misinterpreted
some language of these great men, who
contemplated with regret the course he
was taking, which could be no longer a
secret. De Grotii ad papam defectione,
a French Protestant of some eminence for
learning writes, tanquam re certa, quod
fama istuc distulit, verum non est. Sed
non sine magno metu eum aliquid istius-
modi meditantem et conantem quotidie
inviti videmus. Inter protestantes cu-
juslibet ordinis nomen ejus ascribi vetat,
quod eos atrocius, sugillavit in Appen-
dice de Antichristo, et Annotatis ad Cassandri consultationem. Sarravii Epistolæ. P. 58. (1642.) And again he expresses his strong disapprobation of one
of the later treatises. Verissimè dixit
ille qui primus dixit Grotium papissare.
P. 196. See also p. 31, 53.

In 1642 Grotius had become wholly
averse to the Reformation. He thought
it had done more harm than good, especially by the habit of interpreting every
thing on the papal side for the worse.
Malos mores qui mansere corrigi æquum
est. Sed an non hoc melius successurum
fuerit, si quisque semet repurgans pro
repurgatione aliorum preces ad Deum
tulisset, et principes et episcopi correc-
tionem desiderantes, non rupta compage,
per concilia universalia in id laborassent.
Dignum est de quo cogitetur. P. 938.
Auratus, as he calls him, that is D'Or,
a sort of chaplain to Grotius, became a
Catholic about this time. The other
only says,—Quod Auratus fecit, idem
fecit antehac vir doctissimus Petrus Pi-
thæus; idem constituerat facere Casaubonus si in Gallia mansisset, affirmavit
enim id inter alios etiam Cordesio. P. 939.
Of Casaubon he says afterwards, Casaubonus multo saniores putabat Catholicos
Galliæ quam Carentonianos. Anglos
autem episcopos putabat a schismatis
culpa posse absolvi. P. 940. Every successive year saw him now draw nearer to
Rome. Reperio autem quicquid com-
muniter ab ecclesia occidentali quæ Romanæ cohæret recipitur, idem reperiri
apud Patres veteres Græcos et Latinos,
quorum communionem retinendam esse
vix quisquam neget. Si quid præter
hoc est, id ad liberas doctorum opina-
tiones pertinet; in quibus suum quis
judicium sequi potest, et communionis
jus non amittere. P. 958. Episcopius
was for limiting articles of faith to the
creed. But Grotius did not agree with
this, and points out that it would not
preserve uniformity. Quam multa jam
sunt de sacramentis, de ecclesiarum regimine, in quibus, vel concordiæ causa,
certi aliquid observari debet. Alioqui
compages ecclesiæ tantopere nobis com-
mendata retineri non potest. P. 941. It
would be endless to quote every passage
tending to the same result. Finally, in
a letter to his brother in Holland, he
expresses his hope that Wytenbogart, the
respectable patriarch of Arminianism,
would turn his attention to the means of
restoring unity to the church. Velim
D. Wytenbogardum, ubi permiserit va-
letudo, nisi id jam fecerit, scriptum aliquid facere de necessitate restituendæ in
ecclesia unitatis, et quibus modis id fieri

choice that seemed alone to be left in their communion, between a fanatical anarchy, disintegrating everything like a

possit. Multi pro remedio monstrant, si necessaria a. non necessariis separentur, in non necessariis sive creditu sive factu relinquatur libertas. At non minor est controversia, quæ sint necessaria quam quæ sint vera. Indicia, aiunt, sunt in scripturis. At certè etiam circa illa loca variat interpretatio. Quare nondum video an quid sit melius, quam ea quæ ad fidem et bona opera nos ducunt retinere, ut sunt in ecclesia catholica; puto enim in iis esse quæ sunt necessaria ad salutem. In cæteris ea quæ conciliorum auctoritate, aut veterum consensu recepta sunt, interpretari eo modo quo interpretati sunt illi qui commodissimè sunt locuti, quales semper aliqui in quaque materia facile reperientur. Si 'quis id a se impetrare non possit, ut taceat, nec propter res de quibus certus non est, sed opinationem tantum quandam habet, turbet unitatem ecclesiæ necessariam, quæ nisi retinetur ubi est, et restituitur ubi non est, omnia ibunt in pejus. P. 960. (Nov. 1643.) Wytenbogart replied very well: Si ita se res habet, ut indicia necessariorum et non necessariorum in scriptura reperiri nequeant, sed quæri debeant in auctoritate conciliorum aut veterum consensu, eo modo quo interpretati sunt illi qui commodissimè locuti sunt, prout Excellentia tua videtur existimare, nescio an viginti quinque anni, etiamsi illi mihi adhuc restarent, omnesque exigui ingenii corporisque mei vires in mea essent potestate, sufficerent ut maturo cum judicio perlegam et expendam omnia quæ eo pertinent. This letter is in the Epistolæ præstantium et eruditorum virorum edited by Limborch in 1683, p. 826. And Grotius's answer is in the same collection. It is that of a man who throws off a mask he had reluctantly worn. There was in fact no other means of repelling Wytenbogart's just observation on the moral impossibility of tracing for ourselves the doctrine of the Catholic church as an historical inquiry. Grotius refers him to a visible standard. Quare considerandum est, an non facilius et æquius sit, quoniam doctrina de gratia, de libero arbitrio, necessitate fidei bonorumque operum obtinuit in ecclesia quæ pro se habet universale regimen et ordinem successionis, privatos se in aliis accommodare, pacis causa, iis quæ universaliter sunt recepta, sive ea aptissimis

explicationibus recipiendo, sive tacendo, quam corpus illud catholicum ecclesiæ se in articulo tolerantiæ accommodare debere uniuscujusque considerationibus et placitis. Exempli gratiâ: Catholica ecclesia nemini præscribit ut precetur pro mortuis, aut opem precum sanctorum vita hac defunctorum imploret; solummodo requirit, ne quis morem adeo antiquum et generalem condemnet. The church does, in fact, rather more than he insinuates.

I have trespassed on the patience of the general reader in this very long note, which may be thought a superfluous digression in a work of mere literature. But the epistles of Grotius are not much read; nor are they in many private libraries. The index is also very indifferent, so that without the trouble I have taken of going over the volume, it might be difficult to find these curious passages. I ought to mention that Burigny has given references to most of them, but with few quotations. Le Clerc, in the first volume of the Bibliothèque universelle, reviewing the epistles of Grotius, slides very gently over his bias towards popery; and I have met with well-informed persons in England, who had no conception of the lengths to which this had led him. It is of far more importance, and the best apology I can offer for so prolix a note, to perceive by what gradual, but, as I think, necessary steps, he was drawn onward by his excessive respect for antiquity, and by his exaggerated notions of Catholic unity, preferring at last to err with the many, than to be right with the few. If Grotius had learned to look the hydra schism in the face, he would have had less fear of its many heads, and at least would have dreaded to cut them off at the neck, lest the source of life should be in one of them.

That Grotius really thought as the fathers of Trent thought upon all points in dispute cannot be supposed. It was not in the power of a man of his learning and thoughtfulness to divest himself of his own judgment, unless he had absolutely subjugated his reason to religious awe, which was far from being the case. His aim was to search for subtle interpretations, by which he might profess to believe the words of the church, though conscious that his sense was not

church on the one hand, and a domination of bigoted and
vulgar ecclesiastics on the other, made him gradually less
and less averse to the comprehensive and majestic unity of
the Catholic hierarchy, and more and more willing to concede some point of uncertain doctrine, or some form of ambiguous expression. This is abundantly perceived, and has
often been pointed out, in his Annotations on the Consulta-
tion of Cassander, written in 1641, in his Animadversions
on Rivet, who had censured the former treatise as inclining
to popery, in the Votum pro Pace Ecclesiasticâ, and in the
Rivetiani Apologetici Discussio ; all which are collected in
the fourth volume of the theological works of Grotius.
These treatises display an uniform and progressive tendency
to defend the church of Rome in everything that can be
reckoned essential to her creed ; and in fact he will be found
to go farther in this direction than Cassander.

14. But if any one could put a different interpretation on
these works, which would require a large measure of prejudice, the epistles of Grotius afford such evidence of his seces-
sion from the Protestant side, as no reasonable understanding
can reject. These are contained in a large folio volume, published in 1687, and amount to 1766 of one series, and 744 of
another. I have quoted the former, for distinction's sake, by
the number, and the latter by the page. Few, we may presume, have taken the pains to go through them, in order to
extract all the passages that bear upon this subject. It will
be found that he began, as I have just said, by extolling the

---

that of the imposers. It is needless to
say that this is not very ingenuous; and
even if it could be justifiable relatively
to the person, would be an abandonment
of the multitude to any superstition and
delusion which might be put upon them.
Via ad pacem expeditissima mihi videtur, si doctrina, communi consensu recepta, commodè explicetur, mores sanæ
doctrinæ adversantes, quantum fieri potest, tollantur, et in rebus mediis accom-
modet se pars ingenio totius. Epist.
1524. Peace was his main object: if
toleration had been as well understood
as it was afterwards, he would perhaps
have compromised less.

Baxter having published a Treatise
of the Grotian Religion, wherein he imputed to Grotius this inclination towards

the church of Rome, Archbishop Bram-
hall replied, after the Restoration, with
a vindication of Grotius, in which he
does not say much to the purpose, and
seems ignorant of the case. The epistles
indeed were not then published.

Besides the passages in these epistles
above quoted, the reader who wishes to
follow this up may consult Epist. 1108,
1460, 1561, 1570, 1706, of the first series ; and in the second series, p. 875,
896, 940, 943, 958, 960, 975. But there
are also many to which I have made no
reference. I do not quote authorities for
the design of Grotius to have declared
himself a convert if he had lived to return to France, though they are easily
found ; because the testimony of his writings is far stronger than any anecdote.

authority of the Catholic or universal church, and its exclusive right to establish creeds of faith.   He some time afterwards ceased to frequent the Protestant worship, but long
kept his middle path, and thought it enough to inveigh
against the Jesuits and the exorbitancies of the see of Rome.
But his reverence for the writers of the fourth and fifth
centuries grew continually stronger; he learned to protest
against the privilege claimed by the reformers, of interpreting Scripture otherwise than the consent of the ancients had
warranted ; visions, first of an union between the Lutheran
and English churches, and then of one with Rome itself,
floated before his eyes; he sought religious peace with the
latter, as men seek it in opposition to civil government, by
the redress of grievances and the subsequent restoration of
obedience.   But in proportion as he perceived how little of
concession was to be obtained, he grew himself more ready
to concede; and though at one time he seems to deny the
infallibility of the church, and at another would not have
been content with placing all things in the state they were
before the council of Trent, he came ultimately to think
such a favourable sense might be put on all the Tridentine
decrees, as to render them compatible with the Confession of
Augsburg.

15. From the year 1640 his course seems to have been
accelerated ; he intimates no disapprobation of those who
went over to Rome; he found, as he tells us, that whatever
was generally received in the Church of Rome had the
authority of those Greek and Latin fathers, whose communion no one would have refused ; and at length, in a remarkable letter to Wytenbogart, bearing date in 1644, he
put it as worthy to be considered, whether it would not be
more reasonable for private men, who find the most essential
doctrines in a church of an universal hierarchy and a legitimate succession, to waive their differences with it for the
sake of peace, by putting the best interpretations they can,
only keeping silence on their own opinions, than that the
Catholic church should accommodate itself to the separate
judgment of such men.   Grotius had already ceased to speak
of the Arminians as if he were one of themselves, though
with much respect for some of their leaders.

16. Upon a dispassionate examination of all these testimonies, we can hardly deem it an uncertain question whether Grotius, if his life had been prolonged, would have taken the easy leap that still remained; and there is some positive evidence of his design to do so. But dying on a journey, and in a Protestant country, this avowed declaration was never made. Fortunately, indeed, for his glory, since his new friends would speedily have put his conversion to the proof, and his latter years might have been spent, like those of Lipsius, in defending legendary miracles, or in waging war against the honoured dead of the reformation. He did not sufficiently remember that a silent neutrality is never indulged to a suspicious proselyte.

17. It appears to me, nevertheless, that Grotius was very far from having truly subjected his understanding to the church of Rome. The whole bent of his mind was to effect an exterior union among Christians; and for this end he did not hesitate to recommend equivocal senses of words, convenient explanations, and respectful silence. He first took up his reverence for antiquity, because he found antiquity unfavourable to the doctrine of Calvin. His antipathy to this reformer and to his followers led him on to an admiration of the episcopal succession, the organized hierarchy, the ceremonial and liturgical institutions, the high notions of sacramental rites, which he found in the ancient church, and which Luther and Zwingle had cast away. He became imbued with the notion of unity as essential to the Catholic church; but he never seems to have gone the length of abandoning his own judgment, or of asserting any positive infallibility to the decrees of man. For it is manifest that, if the councils of Nice or of Trent were truly inspired, it would be our business to inquire what they meant themselves, not to put the most convenient interpretations, nor to search out for some author or another who may have strained their language to our own opinion. The precedent of Grotius, therefore, will not serve those who endeavour to bind the reason of the enlightened part of mankind, which he respected like his own. Two predominant ideas seem to have swayed the mind of this great man in the very gradual transition we have indicated:

one, his extreme reverence for antiquity and for the consent
of the Catholic church ; the other, his Erastian principles
as to the authority of the civil magistrate in matters of religion.   Both conspired to give him an abhorrence of the
' liberty of prophesying,' the right of private men to pro-
mulgate tenets inconsistent with the established faith.   In
friendly conversation or correspondence, even, perhaps, with
due reserve, in Latin writings, much might be indulged to
the learned ; room was to be found for an Erasmus and a
Cassander ; or, if they would themselves consent, for an
Episcopius and a Wytenbogart, at least for a Montagu and
a Laud ; but no pretext was ever to justify a separation.
The scheme of Grotius is, in a modified degree, much the
same as that of Hobbes.

18. In the Lutheran church we find an eminent contemporary of Grotius, who may be reckoned his counterpart in the motives which influenced him to seek for   Calixtus.
an entire union of religious parties, though resembling him
far more in his earlier opinions than in those to which he
ultimately arrived. This was George Calixtus, of the university of Helmstadt, a theologian the most tolerant, mild, and
catholic in his spirit, whom the Confession of Augsburg had
known since Melanchthon. This university, indeed, which
had never subscribed the Form of Concord, was already distinguished by freedom of inquiry, and its natural concomitant, a large and liberal spirit. But in his own church,
generally, Calixtus found as rigid schemes of orthodoxy, and
perhaps a more invidious scrutiny into the recesses of private
opinion, than in that of Rome, with a less extensive basis of
authority. The dream of good men in this age, the re-union
of Christian churches in a common faith, and meanwhile the
tolerance of differences, were ever the aim of Calixtus. But
he fell, like the Anglican divines, into high notions of primitive tradition, placing, according to Eichhorn and Mosheim,
the unanimity of the first six centuries by the side of Scripture itself. He was assailed by the adherents of the Form
of Concord with aggravated virulence and vulgarity ; he was
accused of being a Papist and a Calvinist, reproaches equally
odious in their eyes, and therefore fit to be heaped on his

head; the inconsistency of calumnies being no good reason with bigots against uttering them.[x]

19. In a treatise, published long after his death, in 1697,
His attempts at concord. De tolerantia Reformatorum circa quæstiones inter ipsos et Augustanam confessionem professos controversas consultatio, it is his object to prove that the Calvinists held no such tenets as should exclude them from Christian communion. He does not deny or extenuate the reality of their differences from the Confession of Augsburg. The Lutherans, though many of them, he says, had formerly maintained the absolute decrees of predestination, were now come round to the doctrine of the first four centuries.[y] And he admits that the Calvinists, whatever phrases they may use, do not believe a true and substantial presence in the eucharist.[z] But neither of these errors, if such they are, he takes to be fundamental. In a shorter and more valuable treatise, entitled Desiderium et studium concordiæ ecclesiasticæ, Calixtus proposes some excellent rules for allaying religious heats. But he leans far too much towards the authority of tradition. Every church, he says, which affirms what others deny, is bound to prove its affirmation; first by Scripture, in which whatever is contained must be out of controversy; and, secondly, (as Scripture bears witness to the church that it is the pillar and foundation of truth, and

---

[x] Eichhorn, vol. vi. part ii. p. 20. Mosheim. Biogr. univ.

[y] Nostri e quibus olim multi ibidem absolutum decretum approbarunt, paulatim ad sententiam primorum quatuor sæculorum, nempe decretum juxta præscientiam factum, receperunt. Qua in re multum egregiè laboravit Ægidius Hunnius. Difficile autem est hanc sententiam ita proponere, ne quid Pelagianismo habere affine videatur. P. 14.

[z] Si tamen non tam quid loquantur quam quid sentiant attendimus, certum est eos veri corporis et sanguinis secundum substantiam acceptorum præsentiam non admittere. Rectius autem fuerit utramque partem simpliciter et ingenuè, quod sentit, profiteri, quam alteram alteri ambiguis loquendi formulis imponere. Qualem conciliandi rationem inierunt olim Philippus et Bucerus, nempe ut præscriberentur formulæ, qua-

rum verba utraque pars amplecteretur, sed singulæ suo sensu acciperent ac interpretarentur. Quem conatum, quamvis ex pio eoque ingente concordiæ desiderio et studio profectum, nulla successûs felicitas excepit. P. 70. This observation is very just in the abstract; but in the early period of the reformation there were strong reasons for evading points of difference, in the hope that the truth would silently prevail in the course of time. We, however, who come later, are to follow the advice of Calixtus, and in judging, as well as we can, of the opinions of men, must not altogether regard their words. Upon no theological controversy, probably, has there been so much of studied ambiguity as on that of the eucharist. Calixtus passes a similar censure on the equivocations of some great men of the preceding century in his other treatise mentioned in the text.

especially the primitive church which is called that of the
saints and martyrs,) by the unanimous consent of the ancient
church, above all, where the debate is among learned men.
The agreement of the church is therefore a sufficient evidence
of Christian doctrine, not that of individual writers, who are
to be regarded rather so far as they testify the Catholic doctrine, than as they propound their own.[a] This deference to
an imaginary perfection in the church of the fourth or fifth
century must have given a great advantage to that of Rome,
which is not always weak on such ground, and doubtless
serves to account for those frequent desertions to her banner,
especially in persons of very high rank, which afterwards
occurred in Germany.

20. The tenets of some of those who have been called
High-church Anglicans may in themselves be little High-church
different from those of Grotius and Calixtus. But England.
the spirit in which they have been conceived is altogether opposite. The one is exclusive, intolerant, severe,
dogmatical, insisting on uniformity of faith as well as of
exterior observances : the other Catholic in outward profession, charitable in sentiment, and in fact one mode,
though a mode as imprudent as it was oblique, in which the
latitudinarian principle was manifested. The language both
of Grotius and Calixtus bears this out ; and this ought closely
to be observed, lest we confound the real laxity of one school
with the rigid orthodoxy of the other. One had it in view
to reconcile discordant communions by mutual concession,
and either by such explication of contrarieties as might make
them appear less incompatible with outward unity, or by an
avowed tolerance of their profession within the church ; the

---

[a] Consensu itaque primæ ecclesiæ ex
symbolis et scriptis manifesto doctrina
Christiana rectè confirmatur. Intelligimus autem doctrinam fundamentalem
et necessariam, non quasvis appendices et
quæstiones, aut etiam quorundam scrip-
turæ locorum interpretationes. De tali-
bus enim unanimis et universalis consensus non poterit erui vel proferri. Et
magis apud plerosque spectandum est,
quid tanquam communem ecclesiæ sententiam proponunt, quam quomodo eam
confirmant aut demonstrant. P. 85. I
have not observed in the little I know

of Calixtus any proof of his inclination
towards the church of Rome.

Gerard Vossius, as Episcopius wrote
to Vorstius in 1615, declared in his in-
augural lecture as professor of theology,
his determination to follow the consent
of antiquity, in explicatione Scriptura-
rum et controversiarum diremtionibus
diligenter examinare et expendere catholicum et antiquissimum consensum, cum
sine dubio illud quod a pluribus et anti-
quissimis dictum est, verissimum sit.
Épist. Virorum præstantium, p. 6.

other would permit nothing but submission to its own authority; it loved to multiply rather than to extinguish the risks
of dissent, in order to crush it more effectually; the one was
a pacific negotiator, the other a conquering tyrant.

21. It was justly alarming to sincere Protestants, that so
Daillé on the right use of the Fathers. many brilliant ornaments of their party should either
desert to the hostile side, or do their own so much
injury by taking up untenable ground.[b] Nothing, it appeared to reflecting men, could be trusted to the argument
from antiquity; whatever was gained in the controversy on
a few points was lost upon those of the first importance. It
was become the only secure course to overthrow the tribunal.
Daillé, himself one of the most learned in this patristic
erudition whom the French reformed church possessed, was
the first who boldly attacked the new school of historical theology in their own stronghold, not occupying their
fortress, but razing it to the ground. The design of his
celebrated Treatise concerning the right use of the Fathers,
published in 1628, is, in his own words, to show 'that they
cannot be the judges of the controversies in religion at this
day between the Papist and the Protestant,' nor, by parity
of reasoning, of many others; 1. Because it is, if not an impossible, yet at least a very difficult thing to find out what
their sense hath been touching the same. 2. Because that
their sense and judgment of these things, supposing it to be
certainly and clearly understood, not being infallible, and
without all danger of error, cannot carry with it a sufficient
authority for the satisfying the understanding.'

22. The arguments adduced by Daillé in support of the
former of these two positions, and which occupy the first
book of the treatise, are drawn from the paucity of early

---

[b] It was a poor consolation for so
many losses, that the famous Antonio de
Dominis, archbishop of Spalato, came
over to England, and by his book De
Republica Ecclesiastica, as well as by
his conversation, seemed an undisguised
enemy to the church of Rome. The
object of his work is to prove that the
pope has no superiority over other
bishops. James gave De Dominis the
deanery of Windsor and a living; but
whether he, strictly speaking, belonged
to the church of England, I do not remember to have read. Preferments were
bestowed irregularly in that age. He
returned, however, to the ancient fold ·
but did not avoid suspicion, being thrown
into prison at Rome; and after his death,
the imputations of heresy against him so
much increased that his body was dug
up and burned. Neither party has been
ambitious to claim this vain and insin-
cere, though clever, prelate.

Christian writers, from the nature of the subjects treated by
them having little relation to the present controversies, from
the suspicions of forgery and interpolation affecting many of
their works, the difficulty of understanding their idioms and
figurative expressions, the habit of some of the fathers to
say what they did not believe, their changes of mind, the
peculiar and individual opinions of some among them,
affording little evidence of the doctrine of the church;
finally, the probability that many who differed from those
called the fathers, and whose writings have not descended to
us, may have been of as good authority as themselves.

23. In the second book, which in fact has been very much
anticipated in the first, he shows that neither the testimony
nor the doctrine of the fathers is infallible (by which word he
must be understood to mean that it raises but a slight presumption of truth, proving this by their errors and contradictions. Thus he concludes that, though their negative
authority is considerable, since they cannot be presumed
ignorant of any material doctrine of religion, we are to be
very slow in drawing affirmative propositions from their
writings, and much more so in relying upon them as undoubted verities.

24. It has been said of this treatise on the right use of the
fathers, that its author had pretty well proved they were of
no use at all. This, indeed, is by no means the case : but it
has certainly diminished not only the deference which many
have been wont to pay to the opinion of the primitive writers,
but, what is still more contended for, the value of their testimony, whether as to matters of fact, or as to the prevailing
doctrines of the Christian church. Nothing can be more
certain, though in the warmth of controversy men are apt
to disregard it, than that a witness, who deposes in any one
case what can be disproved, is not entitled to belief in other
assertions which we have no means of confuting, unless it be
shown that the circumstances of his evidence render it more
trustworthy in these points than we have found it before.
Hence such writers as Justin and Irenæus, for example, ought
not, except with great precaution, to be quoted in proof at
all, or at least with confidence ; their falsehood, not probably
wilful, in assertions that have been brought to a test rendering

their testimony very precarious upon any other points. Daillé, it may be added, uses some circumspection, as the times, if not his own disposition, required, in handling this subject, keeping chiefly in view the controversies between the Romish and Protestant churches; nor does he ever indulge in that tone of banter or acrimony which we find in Whitby, Barbeyrac, Jortin, and Middleton; and which must be condemned by every one who reflects that many of these writers exposed their lives, and some actually lost them, in the maintenance and propagation of Christianity.

25. This well-timed and important book met with a good reception from some in England, though it must have been very uncongenial to the ruling party. It was extolled and partly translated by Lord Falkland; and his two distinguished friends, Chillingworth and Hales, found in it the materials of their own bold revolt against church authority. They were both Arminians, and, especially the former, averse in all respects to the Puritan school. But like Episcopius, they scorned to rely, as on these points they might have done, on what they deemed so precarious and inconclusive as the sentiments of the fathers. Chillingworth, as is well known, had been induced to embrace the Romish religion, on the usual ground that a succession of infallible pastors, that is, a collective hierarchy, by adhering to whom alone we could be secure from error, was to be found in that church. He returned again to the Protestant religion on being convinced that no such infallible society could be found. And a Jesuit, by name Knott, having written a book to prove that unrepenting Protestants could not be saved, Chillingworth published, in 1637, his famous answer, The Religion of Protestants a safe way to Salvation. In this he closely tracks the steps of his adversary, replying to every paragraph, and almost every sentence.

Chillingworth's Religion of Protestants.

26. Knott is by no means a despicable writer; he is concise, polished, and places in an adventageous light the great leading arguments of his church. Chillingworth, with a more diffuse and less elegant style, is greatly superior in impetuosity and warmth. In his long parenthetical periods, as in those of other old English writers, in his copiousness, which is never empty or tautological, there is

Character of this work.

an inartificial eloquence springing from strength of intellect and sincerity of feeling, that cannot fail to impress the reader. But his chief excellence is the close reasoning which avoids every dangerous admission, and yields to no ambiguousness of language. He perceived and maintained with great courage, considering the times in which he wrote and the temper of those whom he was not unwilling to keep as friends, his favourite tenet, that all things necessary to be believed are clearly laid down in Scripture. Of tradition, which many of his contemporary Protestants were becoming as prone to magnify as their opponents, he spoke very slightingly; not denying of course a maxim often quoted from Vincentius Lirinensis, that a tradition strictly universal and original must be founded in truth, but being assured that no such could be shown ; and that what came nearest, both in antiquity and in evidence of catholic reception, to the name of apostolical were doctrines and usages rejected alike by all denominations of the church in modern times.[c] It will be readily conceived, that his method of dealing with the controversy is very different from that of Laud in his treatise against Fisher ; wherein we meet chiefly with disputes on passages in the fathers, as to which, especially when they are not quoted at length, it is impossible that any reader can determine for himself. The work of Chillingworth may at least be understood and appreciated without reference to any other ; the condition, perhaps, of real superiority in all productions of the mind.

27. Chillingworth was, however, a man versed in patristical learning, by no means less so, probably, than Laud. But he had found so much uncertainty about this course of theological doctrine, seducing as it generally is to the learned, ' fathers,' as he expresses it, ' being set against fathers, and councils against councils,' that he declares, in a well-known

---

[c] 'If there were anything unwritten which had come down to us with as full and universal a tradition as the unquestioned books of canonical Scripture, that thing should I believe as well as the Scripture ; but I have long sought for some such thing, and yet I am to seek ; nay, I am confident no one point in controversy between Papists and Protestants can go in upon half so fair cards, for to gain the esteem of an apostolic tradition, as those things which are now decried on all hands ; I mean the opinion of the Chiliasts and the communicating infants.' Chap. iii. § 82. He dilates upon this insecurity of tradition in some detached papers, subjoined to the best editions of his work.

passage, the Bible exclusively to be the religion of Protestants; and each man's own reason to be, as from the general
tenor of his volume it appears that he held it, the interpreter
of the Bible.[d] It was a natural consequence that he was a
strenuous advocate not so much for toleration of separate
churches, as for such an 'ordering of the public service of
God, that all who believe the Scripture and live according to
it might, without scruple, or hypocrisy, or protestation
against any part, join in it;'[e] a scheme when practicable,
as it could not perhaps be often rendered, far more eligible
than the separation of sects, and hence the favourite object
of Grotius and Taylor, as well as of Erasmus and Cassander.
And in a remarkable and eloquent passage, Chillingworth
declares that 'Protestants are inexcusable if they did offer
violence to other men's consciences;' which Knott had said
to be notorious, as in fact it was, and as Chillingworth ought
more explicitly to have admitted.[f] 'Certainly,' he observes
in another place, 'if Protestants are faulty in this matter [of
claiming authority], it is for doing it too much and not too
little. This presumptuous imposing of the senses of men
upon the words of God, the special senses of men upon the
general words of God, and laying them upon men's consciences together, under the equal penalty of death and damnation, this vain conceit that we can speak of the things of
God better than in the words of God; this deifying our own
interpretations and tyrannous enforcing them upon others;
this restraining of the word of God from that latitude and
generality, and the understandings of men from that liberty
wherein Christ and the apostles left them, is and hath been
the only fountain of all the schisms of the church, and that
which makes them immortal;[g] the common incendiary of

---

[d] This must always be understood
with the condition, that the reason itself
shall be competently enlightened: if
Chillingworth meant more than this, he
carried his principle too far, as others
have done. The case is parallel in jurisprudence, medicine, mechanics, and
every human science; any one man,
primâ facie, may be a competent judge,
but all men are not so. It is hard to
prove that there is any different rule for
theology; but parties will always contend for extremes; for the rights of
bigots to think for others, and the rights

of the ignorant to think for themselves.
[e] Chap. iii. § 81.
[f] Chap. v. § 96.
[g] 'This persuasion,' he says, in a
note, 'is no singularity of mine, but
the doctrine which I have learned from
divines of great learning and judgment.
Let the reader be pleased to peruse the
7th book of Acontius de Stratagematibus
Satanæ, and Zanchius his last oration
delivered by him after the composing of
the discord between him and Amerba-
chius, and he shall confess as much.'

Christendom, and that which tears in pieces not the coat but the bowels and members of Christ. Take away these walls of separation and all will quickly be one. Take away this persecuting, burning, cursing, damning of men for not subscribing the words of men as the words of God ; require of Christians only to believe Christ, and to call no man master but him only; let those leave claiming infallibility that have no title to it, and let them that in their words disclaim it, disclaim it also in their actions. In a word, take away tyranny,' [h] &c.

28. It is obvious that in this passage, and indeed throughout the volume, Chillingworth contravenes the prevailing theories of the Anglican church, full as distinctly as those of the Roman. He escaped, however, unscathed by the censure of that jealous hierarchy; his private friendship with Laud, the lustre of his name, the absence of factious and sectarian connexions, and still more, perhaps, the rapid gathering of the storms that swept both parties away, may be assigned as his protection. In later times his book obtained a high reputation; he was called the immortal Chillingworth ; he was the favourite of all the moderate and the latitudinarian writers, of Tillotson, Locke, and Warburton. Those of opposite tenets, when they happen to have read his book, can do nothing else but condemn its tendency.

29. A still more intrepid champion in the same cause was John Hales; for his little tract on Schism, not being in any part directed against the Church of Rome, could have nothing to redeem the strong protestations against church authority, ' which,' as he bluntly expresses it, ' is none;' words that he afterwards slightly qualified. The aim of Hales, as well as of Grotius, Calixtus, and Chillingworth, was to bring about a more comprehensive communion; but he went still farther; his language is rough and audacious ; [i]

Hales on Schism.

---

[h] Chap. iv. § 17.

[i] ' I must for my own part confess that councils and synods not only may and have erred, but, considering the means how they are managed, it were a great marvel if they did not err, for what men are they of whom those great meetings do consist? Are they the best, the most learned. the most virtuous, the most likely to walk uprightly? No, the greatest, the most ambitious, and many times men of neither judgment nor learning ; such are they of whom these bodies do consist. Are these men in common equity likely to determine for truth?' Vol. i. p. 60, edit. 1765.

' Universality is such a proof of truth as truth itself is ashamed of ; for universality is but a quainter and a trimmer name to signify the multitude. Now, human authority at the strongest is but weak, but the multitude is the weakest

his theology in some of his other writings has a scent of Racow; and though these crept slowly to light, there was enough in the earliest to make us wonder at the high name, the epithet Ever-memorable, which he obtained in the English church.

30. It is unnecessary to say that few disputes in theology have been so eagerly conducted, or so extensively ramified, as those which relate to the free-will of man, and his capacity of turning himself towards God. In this place nothing more will be expected than a brief statement of the principal question, doing no injustice by a tone of partiality to either side. All shades of opinion, as it seems, may be reduced to two, which have long divided and will long divide the Christian world. According to one of these, the corrupt nature of man is incapable of exerting any power towards a state of acceptance with God, or even of willing it with an earnest desire, until excited by preventing (præveniens) grace; which grace is vouchsafed to some only, and is called free, because God is not limited by any respect of those persons to whom he accords this gift. Whether those who are thus called by the influence of the Spirit are so irresistibly impelled to it, that their perseverance in the faith and good works which are the fruits of their election may surely be relied upon, or, on the other hand, may either at first obdurately resist the divine impulses, or finally swerve from their state of grace, is another question, upon which those who agree in the principal doctrine have been at variance. It is also controverted among those who belong to this class of theologians, whether the election thus freely made out of mankind depends upon

Margin notes: Controversies on grace and free-will. Augustinian scheme.

---

part of human authority; it is the great patron of error; most easily abused and most hardly disabused. The beginning of error may be and mostly is from private persons, but the maintainer and continuer of error is the multitude. Private persons first beget errors in the multitude and make them public; and publicness of them begets them again in private persons. It is a thing which our common experience and practice acquaints us with, that when some private persons have gained authority with the multitude, and infused some error into them

and made it public, the publicness of the error gains authority to it, and interchangeably prevails with private persons to entertain it. The most singular and strongest part of human authority is properly in the wisest and most virtuous, and those I trow are not the most universal,' iii. 164.

The treatise on Schism, from which these last passages are *not* extracted, was printed at Oxford in 1642, with some animadversions by the editor. Wood's Athenæ, iii. 414.

an eternal decree of predestination, or upon a sentence of God following the fall of man.   And a third difference relates to the condition of man after he has been aroused by the Spirit from a state of entire alienation from God; some holding that the completion as well as commencement of the work of conversion is wholly owing to the divine influence, while others maintain a co-operation of the will, so that the salvation of a sinner may in some degree be ascribed to himself.   But the essential principle of all whom we reckon in this category of divines is the necessity of preventing grace, or, in other words, that it is not in the power of man to do any act, in the first instance, towards his own salvation. This, in some or other of its modifications, used to be deemed the orthodox scheme of doctrine; it was established in the Latin church by the influence of Augustin, it was generally held by the schoolmen, by most of the early reformers, and seems to be inculcated by the decrees of the Council of Trent, as much as by the Articles of the church of England.   In a loose and modern acceptation of the word, it often goes by the name of Calvinism, which may perhaps be less improper, if we do not use the term in an exclusive sense; but, if it is meant to imply a particular relation to Calvin, leads to controversial chicane, and a misstatement of the historical part of the question.

31. An opposite class of theological reasoners belong to what is sometimes called the Semi-pelagian school. Semi-pelagian hypo-These concur with the former in the necessity of thesis. assistance from the Spirit to the endeavours of man, towards subduing his evil tendencies, and renewing his heart in the fear and love of God, but conceive that every sinner is capable of seeking this assistance, which will not be refused him, and consequently of beginning the work of conversion by his own will.   They therefore either deny the necessity of preventing grace, except such as is exterior, or, which comes effectively to the same thing, assert that it is accorded in a sufficient measure to every one within the Christian church, whether at the time of baptism, or by some other means.   They think the opposite opinion, whether founded on the hypothesis of an eternal decree or not, irreconcilable with the moral attributes of the Deity, and inconsistent with the general tenor of

Scripture. The Semi-pelagian doctrine is commonly admitted
to have been held by the Greek fathers; but the authority of
Augustin, and the decisions of the Western church, caused it
to assume the character of an heresy. Some of the Scotists
among the schoolmen appear to have made an approach to
it, by their tenet of grace ex congruo. They thought that
the human virtues and moral dispositions of unregenerate
men were the predisposing circumstances which, by a sort of
fitness, made them the objects of the Divine goodness in
according the benefits of his grace. Thus their own free-will,
from which it was admitted that such qualities and actions
might proceed, would be the real, though mediate, cause of
their conversion. But this was rejected by the greater part,
who asserted the absolute irrespective freedom of grace, and
appealed to experience for its frequent efficacy over those who
had no inherent virtues to merit it.

32. The early reformers, and none more than Luther, main-
Tenets of
the reform-
ers.
tained the absolute passiveness of the human will,
so that no good actions even after conversion could
be ascribed in any proper sense to man, but altogether to the
operation of the Spirit. Not only, however, Melanchthon
espoused the synergistic doctrine, but the Lutheran church,
though not in any symbolic book, has been thought to have
gone a good way towards Semi-pelagianism, or what passed
for such with the more rigid party.[k] In the reformed church,
on the contrary, the Supra-lapsarian tenets of Calvin, or the
immutable decrees of election and reprobation from all eternity, were obviously incompatible with any hypothesis that
made the salvation of a sinner depend upon himself. But
towards the close of the sixteenth century, these severer
notions (which it may be observed, by the way, had always
been entirely rejected by the Anabaptists, and by some of
greater name, such as Sebastian Castalio) began to be im-
pugned by a few learned men. This led in England to what
are called the Lambeth articles, drawn up by Whitgift, six
of which assert the Calvinistic doctrine of predestination, and
three deny that of the Semi-pelagians. But these, being not

---

[k] Le Clerc says that the doctrine of
Melanchthon, which Bossuet stigmatises
as Semi-pelagian, is that of the Council
of Trent. Bibl. choisie, v. 341. I
should put a different construction upon
the Tridentine canons; but of course
my practice in these nice questions is
not great.

quite approved by the queen, or by Lord Burleigh, were never
received by authority in our church.   There can nevertheless
be no reasonable or even sincere doubt, that Calvinism, in
the popular sense, was at this time prevalent; even Hooker
adopted the Lambeth articles with verbal modifications that
do not affect their sense.

33. The few who, in England or in the reformed churches
upon the Continent, embraced the novel and hetero- Rise of Ar-
dox opinions, as they were then accounted, within minianism.
the sixteenth century, excited little attention in comparison
with James Arminius, who became professor of theology at
Leyden in 1604.   The controversy ripened in a few years; it
was intimately connected, not, of course, in its own nature,
but by some of those collateral influences which have so often
determined the opinions of mankind, with the political relations between the Dutch clergy and the States of Holland, as
it was afterwards with the still less theological differences of
that government with its Stadtholder; it appealed, on one
side, to reason, on the other, to authority and to force; an
unequal conflict, till posterity restore the balance.   Arminius
died in 1609; he has left works on the main topics of debate;
but in theological literature, the great chief of the Arminian
or Remonstrant church is Simon Episcopius.   The
principles of Episcopius are more widely removed Episcopius.
from those of the Augustinian school than the five articles, so
well known as the leading tenets of Arminius, and condemned
at the synod of Dort.   Of this famous assembly it is difficult
to speak in a few words.   The copious history of Brandt is
perhaps the best authority; though we must own that the
opposite party have a right to be heard.   We are here, however, on merely literary ground, and the proceedings of ecclesiastical synods are not strictly within any province of literary history.

34. The works of Episcopius were collectively published in
1650, seven years after his death.   They form two
volumes in folio, and have been more than once re- His writings.
printed.   The most remarkable are the Confessio Remonstrantium, drawn up about 1624, the Apology for it against
a censure of the opposite party, and what seems to have been
a later work, and more celebrated, his Institutiones Theo-

logicæ. These contain a new scheme of religion, compared
with that of the established churches of Europe, and may
justly be deemed the representative of the liberal or latitudinarian theology. For though the writings of Erasmus,
Cassander, Castalio, and Acontius had tended to the same
purpose, they were either too much weakened by the restraints
of prudence, or too obscure and transitory, to draw much
attention, or to carry any weight against the rigid and exclusive tenets which were sustained by power.

35. The earlier treatises of Episcopius seem to speak on
Their spirit several subjects less unequivocally than the Theo-
and ten-
dency. logical Institutions; a reserve not perhaps to be
censured, and which all parties have thought themselves
warranted to employ, so long as either the hope of agreement
with a powerful adversary, or of mitigating his severity,
should remain. Hence the Confession of the Remonstrants,
explicitly states that they decline the Semi-pelagian controversy, contenting themselves with asserting that sufficient
grace is besowed on all who are called by the Gospel to com-
ply with that divine call and obey its precepts.[m] They used
a form of words, which might seem equivalent to the tenet of
original sin, and they did not avoid or refuse that term. But
Episcopius afterwards denies it, at least in the extended sense
of most theologians, almost as explicitly as Jeremy Taylor.[n]
It was common in the seventeenth century to charge the
Arminians, and especially Episcopius, with Socinianism. Bossuet, who seems to have quarrelled with all parties, and is
neither Molinist nor Jansenist, Calvinist nor Arminian, never
doubting but that there is a firm footing between them, having
attacked Episcopius and Grotius particularly for Semi-pela-

---

[m] Episcop. Opera, vol. i. p. 64. De
eo nemini litem movent Remonstrantes.
I am not sure that my translation is
right; but I think it is what they meant.
By prevenient grace they seemed to have
meant only the exterior grace of the
Gospel's promulgation, which is equivalent to the Semi-pelagian scheme, p. 189.
Grotius latterly came into this opinion,
though he had disclaimed everything of
the kind in his first dealings with theology. I have found the same doctrine
in Calixtus; but I have preserved no
reference as to either.

[n] Instit. Theolog. lib. iv. sect. v. c. 2.
Corruptionis istius universalis nulla sunt
indicia nec signa; imo non pauca sunt
signa ex quibus colligitur naturam totam
humanam sic corruptam non esse. The
whole chapter, Ubi de peccato, quod vocant, originis agitur, et præcipua, S. S.
loca quibus initi creditur, examinantur,
appears to deny the doctrine entirely;
but there may be some shades of distinction which have escaped me. Limborch
(Theolog. Christiana, lib. iii. c. iv.) allows it in a qualified sense.

gianism and Socinianism, Le Clerc entered on their defence. But probably he would have passed himself with Bossuet, and hardly cared if he did pass, for a heretic, at least of the former denomination.[o]

36. But the most distinguishing peculiarity in the writings of Episcopius was his reduction of the fundamental doctrines of Christianity far below the multitudinous articles of the churches; confining them to propositions which no Christian can avoid acknowledging without manifest blame; such, namely, wherein the subject, the predicate, and the connexion of the two are found in Scripture by express or equivalent words.[p] He laid little stress on the authority of the church; notwithstanding the advantage he might have gained by the Anti-Calvinistic tenets of the fathers, admitting, indeed, the validity of the celebrated rule of Vincentius Lirinensis, in respect of tradition, which the upholders of primitive authority have always had in their mouths, but adding that it is utterly impossible to find any instance wherein it can be usefully applied.[q]

Great latitude allowed by them.

37. The Arminian doctrine spread, as is well known, in despite of obloquy and persecution, over much of the Protestant region of Europe. The Lutheran churches were already come into it; and in England there was a predisposing bias in the rulers of the church towards the authority of the primitive fathers, all of whom, before

Progress of Arminianism.

---

[o] Bibl. choisie, vol. v.

[p] Necessaria quæ scripturis continentur talia esse omnia, ut sine manifesta hominis culpa ignorari, negari, aut in dubium vocari nequeant; quia videlicet tum subjectum, tum prædicatum, tum subjecti cum prædicato connexio necessaria in ipsis scripturis est, aut expressè, aut æquipollenter. Inst. Theol. l. iv. c. 9.

[q] Instit. Theolog. l. iv. sect. i. c. 15. Dupin says of Episcopius: Il n'a employé dans ses ouvrages que des passages de l'écriture sainte qu'il possédoit parfaitement. Il avoit aussi lu les rabbins, mais on ne voit pas qu'il eût étudié les pères ni l'antiquité ecclésiastique. Il écrit nettement et méthodiquement, pose des principes, ne dissimule rien des objections qu'on peut faire contre, et y répond du mieux qu'il peut. On voit en

lui une tolérance parfaite pour les Sociniens, quoiqu'il se déclare contre eux; pour le parti d'Arminius, jamais il n'a eu de plus zélé et de plus habile défenseur. Bibliothèque des Auteurs séparés de l'Église romaine, ii. 495.

The life of Episcopius has been written by Limborch. Justice has been done to this eminent person and to the Arminian party which he led, in two recent English works, Nicholls's Calvinism and Arminianism displayed, and Calder's Life of Episcopius (1835). The latter is less verbose and more temperate than the former, and may be recommended, as a fair and useful production, to the general reader. Two theological parties in this country, though opposite in most things, are inveterately prejudiced against the Leyden school.

the age of Augustin, and especially the Greek, are generally
acknowledged to have been on that side which promoted the
growth of this Batavian theology.[r] Even in France, it was
not without considerable influence. Cameron, a divine of
Saumur, one of the chief Protestant seminaries,
Cameron. devised a scheme of conciliation, which, notwithstanding much opposition, gained ground in those churches.
It was supported by some highly distinguished for learning,
Amyraut, Daillé, and Blondel. Of this scheme it is remarkable, that, while in its literal purport it can only seem a
modification of the Augustinian hypothesis, with an awkward
and feeble admixture of the other, yet its tendency was to
efface the former by degrees, and to slide into the Arminian
hypothesis, which ultimately became, I believe, very common
in the reformed church.

38. These perplexities were not confined to Protestant
theology. The church of Rome, strenuous to main-
Rise of
Jansenism. tain the tenets of Augustin, and yet to condemn
those who did the same, has been charged with exerting the
plenitude of her infallibility to enforce the belief of an incoherent syncretism. She had condemned Baius, as giving
too much efficacy to grace; she was on the point of condemning Molina for giving too little. Both Clement VIII.
and Paul V. leaned to the Dominicans against the Jesuits in
this controversy; but the great services and influence of the
latter order prevented a decision which would have humbled
them before so many adversaries. It may, nevertheless, be
said that the Semi-pelagian, or Arminian doctrine, though
consonant to that of the Jesuits, was generally ill received
in the church of Rome, till the opposite hypothesis, that of
Augustin and Calvin, having been asserted by one man in
more unlimited propositions than had been usual, a reaction

---

[r] Gerrard Vossius, in his Historia
Pelagiana, the first edition of which, in
1618, was considerably enlarged afterwards, admitted that the first four centuries did not countenance the predes-
tinarian scheme of Augustin. This
gave offence in Holland; his book was
publicly censured; he was excommu-
nicated, and forbidden to teach in public
or private. Vossius, like others, remembered that he had a large family,
and made, after some years, a sort of
retractation, which of course did not express his real opinion. Le Clerc seems
to doubt whether he acted from this
motive, or from what he calls simplicity,
an expression for weakness. Vossius
was, like his contemporary Usher, a man
of much more learning than strength
of intellect. Bibliothèque universelle,
xvii. 312, 329. Niceron, vol. xiii.

took place, that eventually both gave an apparent triumph to the Molinist party, and endangered the church itself by the schism to which the controversy gave rise. The Augustinus of Jansenius, bishop of Ypres, was published in 1640, and in the very next year was censured at Rome. But as the great controversy that sprang out of the condemnation of this book belongs more strictly to the next period, we shall defer it for the present.

39. The Socinian academy at Racow, which drew to itself several proselytes from other countries, acquired con- Socinus. siderable importance in theological literature after Volkelius. the beginning of the century. It was not likely that a sect regarded with peculiar animosity would escape in the general disposition of the Catholic party in Poland to oppress the dissidents whom they had long feared; the Racovian institution was broken up and dispersed in 1638, though some of its members continued to linger in that country for twenty years longer. The Bibliotheca Fratrum Polonorum, published at Amsterdam (in the title-page, Irenopolis) in 1658, contains chiefly the works of Socinian theologians who belong to this first part of the century. The Prælectiones Theologicæ of Faustus Socinus himself, being published in 1609, after his death, fall within this class. They contain a systematic theology according to his scheme, and are praised by Eichhorn for the acuteness and depth they often display.[s] In these, among his other deviations from the general orthodoxy of Christendom, Socinus astonished mankind by denying the evidences of natural religion, resolving our knowledge even of a deity into revelation. This paradox is more worthy of those who have since adopted it, than of so acute a reasoner as Socinus.[t] It is, in fact, not very congenial to the spirit of his theology, which, rejecting all it thinks incompatible with reason as to the divine attributes, should at least have some established notions of them upon rational principles. The later Socinians, even those nearest to the

---

[s] Eichhorn, vi. part 1, p. 283. Simon, however, observes that Socinus knew little Greek or Hebrew, as he owns himself, though he pretends to decide questions which require a knowledge of these languages. I quote from Bibliothèque universelle, vol. xxiii. p. 498.

[t] Tillotson, in one of his sermons (I cannot give the reference, writing from memory), dissents, as might be expected, from this denial of natural religion, but with such encomiums on Socinus as some archbishops would have avoided.

time did not follow their master in this part of his tenets.[u]
The treatise of Volkelius, son-in-law of Socinus, De vera
Religione, is chiefly taken from the latter's writings.   It was
printed at Racow in 1633, and again in Holland in 1641;
but most of the Dutch impression having been burned by
order of the magistrates, it is a very scarce book, and copies
were formerly sold at great prices.   But the hangman's bon-
fire has lost its charm, and forbidden books, when they happen to occur, are no longer in much request.   The first book
out of five in this volume of Volkelius, on the attributes of
God, is by Crellius.

40. Crellius was, perhaps, the most eminent of the Racovian
Crellius. school in this century.[x]   Many of its members, like
Ruarus.   himself, were Germans, their sect having gained
ground in some of the Lutheran states about this time, as it
did also in the United Provinces.   Grotius broke a lance with
him in his treatise De Satisfactione Christi, to which he
replied in another with the same title.   Each retired from
the field with the courtesies of chivalry towards his antagonist.   The Dutch Arminians in general, though very erroneously supposed to concur in all the leading tenets of the
Racovian theologians, treated them with much respect.[y]
Grotius was often reproached with the intimacies he kept up
among these obnoxious sectaries; and many of his letters, as
well as those of Curcellæus and other leading Arminians,
bear witness to the personal regard they felt for them.[z]

---

[u] Socinum sectæ ejus principes, nuper
Volkelius nunc Ruarus, non probant, in
eo quod circa Dei cognitionem petita e
natura rerum argumenta abdicaverit.
Grot. Epist. 964. See, too, Ruari Epist.
p. 210.

[x] Dupin praises Volkelius highly,
but says of Crellius, Il avoit beaucoup
étudié, mais il n'étoit pas un esprit fort
élevé. Bibl. des Auteurs séparés, ii.
614, v. 628. Simon, on the contrary
(ubi suprà), praises Crellius highly, and
says no other commentator of his party
is comparable to him.

[y] The Remonstrants refused to ana-
thematise the Socinians, Episcopius
says, on account of the apparent arguments in their favour, and the differences
that have always existed on that head.
Apologia Confessionis. Episc. Op. vol. i.

His own tenets were probably what
some would call Arian; thus he says,
Personis his tribus divinitatem tribui,
non collateraliter aut co-ordinatè, sed
subordinatè. Inst. Theol. l. iv. c. 2, 32.
Grotius says, he finds the Catholics
more *tractable* about the Trinity than
the Calvinists.

[z] Grotius never shrunk from defending his intimacy with Ruarus and Crellius, and, after praising the former, concludes, in one of his letters, with this
liberal and honest sentiment: Ego vero
ejus sum animi, ejusque instituti, ut
mihi cum hominibus cunctis præcipue
cum Christianis quantumvis errantibus
necessitudinis aliquid putem interce-
dere, idque me neque dictis neque factis
pigeat demonstrare. Epist. 860. Hæretici nisi aliquid haberent veri ac nobis-

Several proofs of this will be also found in the epistles of Ruarus, a book which throws much light on the theological opinions of the age. Ruarus was a man of acuteness, learning, and piety, not wholly concurring with the Racovians, but not far removed from them.[a] The Commentaries of

---

cum commune, jam hæretici non essent. 2da Series, p. 873. Nihil veri eo factum est deterius, quod in id Socinus incidit. P. 880. This, he thought, was the case in some questions, where Socinus, without designing it, had agreed with antiquity. Neque me pudeat consentire Socino, si quando is in veram veteremque sententiam incidit, ut sanè fecit in controversia de justitia per fidem, et aliis nonnullis. Id. p. 797. Socinus hoc non agens in antiquæ ecclesiæ sensus nonnunquam incidit, et eas partes, ut ingenio valebat, percoluit feliciter. Admiscuit alia quæ etiam vera dicenti auctoritatem detraxere. Epist. 966. Even during his controversy with Crellius he wrote to him in a very handsome manner. Bene autem in epistola tua, quæ mihi longè gratissima advenit, de me judicas, non esse me eorum in numero, qui ob sententias salva pietate dissentientes, alieno a quoquam sim animo, aut boni alicujus amicitiam repudiare. Etiam in libro de vera religione [Volkelii], quem jam percurri, relecturus et posthac, multa invenio summo cum judicio observata; illud vero sæculo gratulor, repertos homines, qui neutiquam in controversiis subtilibus tantum ponunt, quantum in vera vitæ emendatione, et quotidiano ad sanctitatem profectu. Epist. 280. (1631.) He wrote with kindness and regret on the breaking up of the establishment at Racow in 1638. Ep. 1006. Grotius has been as obnoxious on the score of Socinianism as of Popery. His Commentaries on the Scriptures are taxed with it, and in fact he is not in good odour with any but the Arminian divines, nor do they, we see, wholly agree with him.

[a] Ruarus nearly agreed with Grotius, as to the atonement; at least the latter thought so. De satisfactione ita mihi respondit, ut nihil admodum controversiæ relinqueretur. Grot. Epist. 2da Series, p. 881. See also Ruari Epistolæ, p. 148, 282. He paid also more respect to the second century than some of his brethren, p. 100, 439, and even struggles

to agree with the Ante-Nicene fathers, though he cannot come up to them, p. 275, 296. But in answer to some of his correspondents who magnified primitive authority, he well replies : Deinde quæro quis illos fixit veritati terminos? quis duo illa prima sæcula ab omni errore absolvit? Annon ecclesiastica historia satis testatur, nonnullas opiniones portentosas jam tum inter eos qui nomen Christi dederant, invaluisse? Quin ut verum fatear, res ipsa docet nonnullos posterioris ævi acutius in enodandis Scripturis versatos ; et ut de nostra ætate dicam, valde me pœniteret Calvini vestri ac Bezæ si nihilo solidius sacras literas interpretarentur, quam video illos ipsos, quos tu mihi obducis, fecisse. P. 183. He lamented the fatal swerving from protestantism into which reverence for antiquity was leading his friend Grotius : fortassis et antiquitatis veneratio, quæ gravibus quibusdam Pontificiorum erroribus præluxit, ultra lineam eum perduxit, p. 277 (1642); and in answer to Mersenne, who seems to have had some hopes of his conversion, and recommended to him the controversy of Grotius with Rivet, he plainly replies that the former had extenuated some things in the church of Rome which ought to be altered. P. 258. This he frequently laments in the course of his letters, but, in comparison with some of the sterner Socinians, treats him with gentleness. It is remarkable that even he and Crellius seem to have excluded the members of the church of Rome, except the 'vulgus ineruditum et Cassandri gregales,' from salvation ; and this while almost all churches were anathematising themselves in the same way. Ruar. Epist. p. 9, and p. 167.

This book contains two centuries of epistles, the second of which is said to be very scarce, and I doubt whether many have read the first, which must excuse my quotations. The learning, sense, and integrity of Ruarus, as well as the high respect which Calixtus, Curcellæus, and other great men felt for him, render the book of some in-

Grotius on the Scriptures have been also charged with Socinianism: but he pleaded that his interpretations were
those of the fathers.

41. Two questions of great importance, which had been
raised in the preceding century, became still more
interesting in the present, on account of the more
frequent occasion that the force of circumstances gave for
their investigation, and the greater names that were engaged in it. Both of these arose out of the national
establishment of churches, and their consequent relation to
the commonwealth. One regarded the power of the magistrate over the church he recognised; the other involved the
right of his subjects to dissent from it by nonconformity, or
by a different mode of worship.

Erastianism

42. Erastus, by proposing to substitute for the ancient
discipline of ecclesiastical censures, and especially
for excommunication, a perpetual superintendence
of the civil power over the faith and practice of the church,
had given name to a scheme generally denominated Erastianism, though in some respects far broader than anything
he seems to have suggested. It was more elaborately maintained by Hooker in his Ecclesiastical Polity, and had been,
in fact, that on which the English reformation under Henry
was originally founded. But as it was manifestly opposed
to the ultramontane pretensions of the see of Rome, and
even to the more moderate theories of the Catholic church,
being of course destructive of her independence, so did it
stand in equal contradiction to the presbyterian scheme of
Scotland and of the United Provinces. In the
latter country, the States of Holland had been
favourable to the Arminians, so far at least as to repress any
violence against them; the clergy were exasperated and intolerant; and this raised the question of civil supremacy, in
which Grotius by one of his early works, entitled Pietas

*maintained
by Hooker,*

*and Gro-
tius.*

terest. He tells us that while he was
in England, about 1617, a professorship
at Cambridge was offered to him worth
100*l.* per annum, besides as much more
from private pupils. P. 71. But he probably mistook the civil speeches of individuals for an offer: he was not emi-

nent enough for such a proposal on the
part of the university; and at least he
must have been silent about his Socinianism. The morality of the early
Socinians was very strict and even
ascetic, proofs of which appear in these
letters. P. 306, et alibi.

Ordinum Hollandiæ, published in 1613, sustained the right of the magistrate to inhibit dangerous controversies.

43. He returned, after the lapse of some years, to the same theme in a larger and more comprehensive work, De Imperio Summarum Potestatum circa Sacra. It is written upon the Anglican principles of regal supremacy, which had, however, become far less popular with the rulers of our church, than in the days of Cranmer, Whitgift, and Hooker. After stating the question, and proving the ecclesiastical power of the magistrate by natural law, Scripture, established usage, agreement of Heathen and Christian writers, and the reason of the thing, he distinguishes control over sacred offices from their exercise, and proceeds to inquire whether the magistrate may take the latter on himself; which, though practised in the early ages of the world, he finds inconvenient at present, the manners required for the regal and sacerdotal character being wholly different.[b] *His treatise on ecclesiastical power of the state.*

44. Actions may be prescribed or forbidden by natural divine law, positive divine law, or human law; the latter extending to nothing but what is left indefinite by the other two. But though we are bound not to act in obedience to human laws which contradict the divine, we are also bound not forcibly to resist them. We may defend ourselves by force against an equal, not against a superior, as he proves, first, from the Digest, and secondly, from the New Testament.[c] Thus the rule of passive obedience is unequivocally laid down. He meets the recent examples of resistance to sovereigns, by saying that they cannot be approved where the kings have had an absolute power; but where they are bound by compact or the authority of a senate or of estates, since their power is not unlimited, they may be resisted on just grounds by that authority.[d] 'Which I remark,' he proceeds to say, 'lest any one, as I sometimes have known, should disgrace a good cause by a mistaken defence.'

45. The magistrate can alter nothing which is definitely

---

[b] Cap. 4.   [c] Cap. 3.
[d] Sin alicubi reges tales fuere, qui pactis sive positivis legibus et senatus alicujus aut ordinum decretis adstrin- gerentur, in hos, ut summum imperium non obtinent, arma ex optimatum tanquam superiorum sententia sumi justis de causis potuerunt. Ibid.

laid down by the positive law of God; but he may regulate
the circumstantial observance even of such; and as to things
undefined in Scripture he has plenary jurisdiction; such as
the temporalities of the church, the convocation of synods,
the election of pastors. The burden of proof lies on those
who would limit the civil power by affirming anything to be
prescribed by the divine law.[e] The authority attributed in
Scripture to churches does not interfere with the power of
the magistrate, being persuasive and not coercive. The
whole church has no coercive power by divine right.[f] But
since the visible church is a society of divine institution, it
follows that whatever is naturally competent to a lawful
society is competent also to the church, unless it can be
proved to be withdrawn from it.[g] It has, therefore, a legislative government (regimen constitutivum), of which he
gives the institution of the Lord's day as an example. But
this does not impair the sovereign's authority in ecclesiastical matters. In treating of that supremacy, he does not
clearly show what jurisdiction he attributes to the magistrate; most of his instances relating to the temporalities of
the church, as to which no question is likely to arise.[h] But
on the whole he means undoubtedly to carry the supremacy
as far as is done in England.

46. In a chapter on the due exercise of the civil supremacy
over the church, he shows more of a Protestant feeling than
would have been found in him when he approached the latter
years of his life;[i] and declares fully against submission to
any visible authority in matters of faith, so that sovereigns
are not bound to follow the ministers of the church in what
they may affirm as doctrine. Ecclesiastical synods he deems
often useful, but thinks the magistrate is not bound to act
with their consent, and that they are sometimes pernicious.[k]
The magistrate may determine who shall compose such

---

[e] Cap. 3.

[f] Cap. 4.

[g] Quandoquidem ecclesia cœtus est
divina lege non permissus tantum sed et
institutus, de aspectabili cœtu loquor,
sequitur ea omnia quæ cœtibus legitimis
naturaliter competunt, etiam ecclesiæ
competere, quatenus adempta non pro-
bantur. Ibid.

[h] Cap. 5.

[i] Cap. 6. He states the question to
be this: An post apostolorum ætatem
aut persona aut cœtus sit aliquis aspec-
tabilis, de quâ quove certi esse possimus
ac debeamus, quæcunque ab ipsis propo-
nantur, esse indubitatæ veritatis. Ne-
gant hoc Evangelici; aiunt Romanenses.

[k] Cap. 7.

synods;[m] a strong position which he endeavours to prove at great length. Even if the members are elected by the church, the magistrate may reject those whom he reckons unfit; he may preside in the assembly, confirm, reject, annul its decisions. He may also legislate about the whole organisation of the established church.[n] It is for him to determine what form of religion shall be publicly exercised; an essential right of sovereignty as political writers have laid it down. And this is confirmed by experience: 'for if any one shall ask why the Romish religion flourished in England under Mary, the Protestant under Elizabeth, no cause can be assigned but the pleasure of these queens, or, as some might say, of the queens and parliaments.' To the objection from the danger of abuse in conceding so much power to the sovereign, he replies that no other theory will secure us better. On every supposition the power must be lodged in men, who are all liable to error. We must console ourselves by a trust in Divine Providence alone.[o]

47. The sovereign may abolish false religions and punish their professors, which no one else can. Here again we find precedents instead of arguments; but he says that the primitive church disapproved of capital punishments for heresy, which seems to be his main reason for doing the same. The sovereign may also enjoin silence in controversies, and inspect the conduct of the clergy without limiting himself by the canons, though he will do well to regard them. Legislation and jurisdiction, that is, of a coercive nature, do not belong to the church, except as they may be conceded to it by the civil power.[p] He fully explains the various kinds of ecclesiastical law that have been gradually introduced. Even the power of the keys, which is by divine right, cannot be so exercised as to exclude the appellant jurisdiction of the sovereign; as he proves by the Roman law, and by the usage of the parliament of Paris.[q]

---

[m] Designare eos, qui ad synodum sunt venturi.

[n] Cap. 8. Nulla in re magis elucescit vis summi imperii, quam quod in ejus arbitrio est quænam religio publicè exerceatur, idque præcipuum inter majestatis jura ponunt omnes qui politicè scripserunt. Docet idem experientia; si enim quæras cur in Anglia Maria regnante Romana religio, Elizabetha vero imperante, Evangelica viguerit, causa proxima reddi non poterit, nisi ex arbitrio reginarum, aut, ut quibusdam videtur, reginarum ac parlamenti. P. 242.

[o] Cap. 8.   [p] Ibid.

[q] Cap. 9.

48. The sovereign has a control (inspectionem cum imperio) over the ordination of priests, and certainly possesses a right of confirmation, that is, the assignment of an ordained minister to a given cure.[r] And though the election of pastors belongs to the church, this may, for good reasons, be taken into the hands of the sovereign. Instances in point are easily found, and the chapter upon the subject contains an interesting historical summary of this part of ecclesiastical law. In every case the sovereign has a right of annulling an election, and also of removing a pastor from the local exercise of his ministry.[s]

49. This is the full development of an Erastian theory, which Cranmer had early espoused, and which Hooker had maintained in a less extensive manner. Bossuet has animadverted upon it, nor can it appear tolerable to a zealous churchman.[t] It was well received in England by the lawyers, who had always been jealous of the spiritual tribunals, especially of late years, when under the patronage of Laud they had taken a higher tone than seemed compatible with the supremacy of the common law. The scheme, nevertheless, is open to some objections, when propounded in so unlimited a manner, none of which is more striking than that it tends to convert differences of religious opinion into crimes against the state, and furnishes bigotry with new arguments as well as new arms in its conflict with the free exercise of human reason. Grotius, however, feared rather that he had given too little power to the civil magistrate than too much.[u]

Remark upon this theory.

---

[r] Cap. 10. Confirmationem hanc summæ potestati acceptam ferendam nemo sanus negaverit.

[s] Ibid.

[t] See Le Clerc's remarks on what Bossuet has said. Bibliothèque choisie, p. 349.

[u] Ego multo magis vereor, ne minus quam par est magistratibus, aut plusquam par est pastoribus tribuerim, quam ne in alteram partem iterum (?) excesserim, nec sic quidem illis satisfiet qui se ecclesiam vocant. Epist. 42. This was in 1614, after the publication of the Pietas Ordinum Hollandiæ. As he drew nearer to the church of Rome, or that of Canterbury, he must probably have somewhat modified his Erastianism. And yet he seems never to have been friendly to the temporal power of bishops. He writes in August, 1641, Episcopis Angliæ videtur mansurum nomen prope sine re, accisa et opulentia et auctoritate. Mihi non displicet ecclesiæ pastores et ab inani pompa et a curis sæcularium rerum sublevari. P. 1011. He had a regard for Laud, as the restorer of a reverence for primitive antiquity, and frequently laments his fate; but had said, in 1640, Doleo quod episcopi nimium intendendo potentiæ suæ nervos odium sibi potius quam amorem populorum pariunt. Ep. 1390.

50. Persecution for religious heterodoxy, in all its degrees, was in the sixteenth century the principle, as well as the practice, of every church. It was held inconsistent with the sovereignty of the magistrate to permit any religion but his own; inconsistent with his duty to suffer any but the true. The edict of Nantes was a compromise Toleration of religious tenets; between belligerent parties; the toleration of the dissidents in Poland was nearly of the same kind; but no state powerful enough to restrain its sectaries from the exercise of their separate worship had any scruples about the right and obligation to do so. Even the writers of that century, who seemed most strenuous for toleration, Castalio, Celso, and Koornhert had confined themselves to denying the justice of penal, and especially of capital inflictions for heresy; the liberty of public worship had but incidentally, if at all, been discussed. Acontius had developed larger principles, distinguishing the fundamental from the accessory doctrines of the Gospel; which, by weakening the associations of bigotry, prepared the way for a Catholic tolerance. Episcopius speaks in the strongest terms of the treatise of Acontius, De Stratagematibus Satanæ, and says that the remonstrants trod closely in his steps, as would appear by comparing their writings; so that he shall quote no passages in proof, their entire books bearing witness to the conformity.[x]

51. The Arminian dispute led by necessary consequence to the question of public toleration. They sought claimed by the Arminians; at first a free admission to the pulpits, and in an excellent speech of Grotius, addressed to the magistrates of Amsterdam in 1616, he objects to a separate toleration as rending the bosom of the church. But it was soon evident that nothing more could be obtained; and their adversaries refused this. They were driven, therefore, to contend for religious liberty, and the writings of Episcopius are full of this plea. Against capital punishments for heresy he raises his voice with indignant severity, and asserts that the whole Christian world abhorred the fatal precedent of Calvin in the death of Servetus.[y] This indicates a remarkable change

---

[x] Episcop. Opera, i. 301 (edit. 1665).

[y] Calvinus signum primus extulit supra alios omnes, et exemplum dedit in theatro Gebennensi funestissimum, quodque Christianus orbis merito execratur et abominatur; nec hoc contentus tam

already wrought in the sentiments of mankind. No capital
punishments for heresy seem to have been inflicted in Protestant countries after this time ; nor were they as frequently
or as boldly vindicated as before.[z]

52. The Independents claim to themselves the honour of
by the Inde- having been the first to maintain the principles of
pendents;   general toleration, both as to freedom of worship
and immunity from penalties for opinion. But that the Arminians were not as early promulgators of the same noble
tenets seems not to have been proved. Crellius, in his
Vindiciæ pro Religionis Libertate, 1636, contended for the
Polish dissidents, and especially for his own sect.[a] The
principle is implied, if not expressed, in the writings of
Chillingworth, and still more of Hales ; but the first famous
plea in this country for tolerance in religion, on a comprehensive basis and on deep-seated foundations, was the
and by Jere- Liberty of Prophesying by Jeremy Taylor. This
my Taylor.   celebrated work was written, according to Taylor's
dedication, during his retirement in Wales, whither he was
driven, as he expresses it, ' by this great storm which hath
dashed the vessel of the church all in pieces,' and published
in 1647. He speaks of himself as without access to books ;
it is evident, however, from the abundance of his quotations,

---

atroci facinore, cruento simul animo et
calamo parentavit. Apologia pro Confess. Remonstrantium, c. 24, p. 241.
The whole passage is very remarkable,
as an indignant reproof of a party, who,
while living under popish governments,
cry out for liberty of conscience, and
deny the right of punishing opinions ;
yet in all their writings and actions,
when they have the power, display the
very opposite principles. [The council
of Geneva, in 1632, little ashamed of the
death of Servetus, had condemned one
Nicolas Antoine to be strangled and
burned for denying the Trinity. Bibliothèque Raisonnée, ii. 156. I do not
distinctly recollect any later case in Protestant countries of capital punishment
for mere heresy.—1842.]

  [z] De hæreticorum pœnis quæ scripsi,
in iis mecum sentit Gallia et Germania,
ut puto, omnis. Grot. Epist. p. 941.
(1642.) Some years sooner there had
been remains of the leaven in France.
Adversus hæreticidia, he says in 1626,

satis ut arbitror plane locutus sum, certè,
ita ut hic multos ob id offenderim. P. 789.
Our own Fuller, I am sorry to say, in
his Church History, written about 1650,
speaks with some disapprobation of the
sympathy of the people with Legat and
Wightman, burned by James I., in 1614 ;
and this is the more remarkable, as he is
a well-natured and not generally bigoted
writer. I should think he was the latest
Protestant who has tarnished his name
by such sentiments.

  [a] This short tract, which will be found
among the collected works of Crellius,
in the Bibliotheca Fratrum Polonorum,
contains a just and temperate pleading
for religious liberty, but little which can
appear very striking in modern times.
It is said, nevertheless, to have been
translated and republished by D'Hol-
bach about 1760. This I have not seen,
but there must, I presume, have been a
good deal of *condiment* added to make it
stimulating enough for his school.

that he was not much in want of them; and from this, as
well as other strong indications, we may reasonably believe
that a considerable part of his treatise had been committed
to paper long before.

53. The argument of this important book rests on one
leading maxim, derived from the Arminian divines, His Liberty
as it was in them from Erasmus and Acontius, that of Prophesying.
the fundamental truths of Christianity are comprised in
narrow compass, not beyond the Apostles' creed in its literal
meaning; that all the rest is matter of disputation, and too
uncertain, for the most part, to warrant our condemning
those who differ from us, as if their error must be criminal.
This one proposition, much expanded, according to Taylor's
diffuse style, and displayed in a variety of language, pervades the whole treatise, a small part of which, in comparison
with the rest, bears immediately on the point of political
toleration, as a duty of civil governments and of churches
invested with power. In the greater portion, Taylor is
rather arguing against that dogmatism of judgment which
induces men, either singly or collectively, to pronounce with
confidence where only a varying probability can be attained.
This spirit is the religious, though not entirely the political,
motive of intolerance; and by chasing this from the heart,
he inferred, not that he should lay wide the door to universal
freedom, but dispose the magistrate to consider more equit-
ably the claims of every sect. ‘ Whatsoever is against the
foundation of faith, or contrary to good life and the laws of
obedience, or destructive to human society and the public
and just interests of bodies politic, is out of the limits of my
question, and does not pretend to compliance or toleration;
so that I allow no indifferency, nor any countenance to those
religions whose principles destroy government, nor to those
religions, if there be any such, that teach ill life.’

54. No man, as Taylor here teaches, is under any obligation to believe that in revelation, which is not so re- Boldness of
vealed but that wise men and good men have differed his doctrines.
in their opinions about it. And the great variety of opinions
in churches, and even in the same church, ‘ there being none
that is in prosperity,’ as he with rather a startling boldness
puts it, ‘ but changes her doctrines every age, either by

bringing in new doctrines, or by contradicting her old,'
shows that we can have no term of union, but that wherein
all agree, the creed of the apostles.[b]   And hence, though we
may undoubtedly carry on our own private inquiries as much
farther as we see reason, none who hold this fundamental
faith are to be esteemed heretics, nor liable to punishment.
And here he proceeds to reprove all those oblique acts which
are not direct persecutions of men's persons, the destruction
of books, the forbidding the publication of new ones, the
setting out fraudulent editions and similar acts of falsehood,
by which men endeavour to stifle or prevent religious inquiry.   'It is a strange industry and an importune diligence
that was used by our forefathers : of all those heresies which
gave them battle and employment, we have absolutely no
record or monument, but what themselves who are adversaries have transmitted to us; and we know that adversaries,
especially such who observed all opportunities to discredit
both the persons and doctrines of the enemy, are not always
the best records or witnesses of such transactions.   We see it
now in this very age, in the present distemperatures, that
parties are no good registers of the actions of the adverse
side; and if we cannot be confident of the truth of a story
now, now I say that it is possible for any man, and likely
that the interested adversary will discover the imposture,
it is far more unlikely that after ages should know any other
truth, but such as serves the ends of the representers.'[c]

55. None were accounted heretics by the primitive church,
His notions who held by the Apostles' creed, till the council of
of uncer-   Nice defined some things, rightly, indeed, as Taylor
tainty in   professes to believe, but perhaps with too much alter-
theological
tenets.   ation of the simplicity of ancient faith, so that, 'he had need
be a subtle man who understands the very words of the new
determinations.'   And this was carried much farther by
later councils, and in the Athanasian creed, of which, though

---

[b] 'Since no churches believe themselves infallible, that only excepted
which all other churches say is most of
all deceived, it were strange if, in so
many articles, which make up their
several bodies of confessions, they had
not mistaken, every one of them, in

something or other.' This is Taylor's
fearless mode of grappling with his
argument; and any other must give
a church that claims infallibility the
advantage.
   [c] Vol. vii. p. 424. Heber's edition of
Taylor.

protesting his own persuasion in its truth, he intimates not
a little disapprobation. The necessary articles of faith are
laid down clearly in Scripture; but no man can be secure,
as to mysterious points, that he shall certainly understand
and believe them in their true sense. This, he shows,
first, from the great discrepancy of readings in manuscripts
(an argument which he overstates in a very uncritical and
incautious manner), next, from the different senses the words
will bear, which there is no certain mark to distinguish, the
infinity variety of human understandings, swayed, it may be,
by interest, or determined by accidental and extrinsical circumstances, and the fallibility of those means by which men
hope to attain a clear knowledge of scriptural truth. And
after exposing, certainly with no extenuation, the difficulties
of interpretation, he concludes that since these ordinary
means of expounding Scripture are very dubious, 'he that
is the wisest, and by consequence the likeliest to expound
truest, in all probability of reason, will be very far from confidence; and therefore a wise man would not willingly be
prescribed to by others; and if he be also a just man, he will
not impose upon others; for it is best every man should be
left in that liberty, from which no man can justly take him,
unless he could secure him from error; so here there is a
necessity to conserve the liberty of prophesying and interpreting Scripture; a necessity derived from the consideration
of the difficulty of Scripture in questions controverted, and
the uncertainty of any internal medium of interpretation.

56. Taylor would in much of this have found an echo in
the advocates of the church of Rome, and in some His low
opinion of
Protestants of his own communion. But he passes the fathers.
onward to assail their bulwarks. Tradition, or the testimony
of the church, he holds insufficient and uncertain, for the
reasons urged more fully by Daillé; the authority of councils
is almost equally precarious, from their inconsistency, their
liability to factious passions, and the doubtful authenticity of
some of their acts; the pope's claim to infallibility is combated on the usual grounds; the judgment of the fathers is
shown to be inconclusive by their differences among themselves, and their frequent errors; and professing a desire
that ' their great reputation should be preserved as sacred as

it ought,' he refers the reader to Daillé for other things; and,
' shall only consider that the writings of the fathers have been
so corrupted by the intermixture of heretics, so many false
books put forth in their names, so many of their writings
lost which would more clearly have explicated their sense,
and at last an open profession made, and a trade of making
the fathers speak not what themselves thought, but what
other men pleased, that it is a great instance of God's providence and care of his church, that we have so much good
preserved in the writings which we receive from the fathers,
and that all truth is not as clear gone as is the certainty of
their great authority and reputation.' [d]

57. The authority of the church cannot be any longer
Difficulty of finding out truth. alleged when neither that of popes and councils, nor
of ancient fathers, is maintainable; since the diffu-
sive church has no other means of speaking, nor can we distinguish by any extrinsic test the greater or better portion of
it from the worse. And thus, after dismissing respectfully
the pretences of some to expound Scripture by the Spirit, as
impertinent to the question of dictating the faith of others,
he comes to the reason of each man, as the best judge, for
himself, of religious controversies; reason, that may be
exercised either in choosing a guide, if it feel its own incom-
petency, or in examining the grounds of belief. The latter
has great advantages, and no man is bound to know anything
of that concerning which he is not able to judge for himself.
But reason may err, as he goes on to prove, without being
culpable; that which is plain to one understanding being
obscure to another, and among various sources of error which
he enumerates as incidental to mankind, that of education
being ' so great and invincible a prejudice, that he who
masters the inconvenience of it is more to be commended

---

[d] It seems not quite easy to reconcile
this with what Taylor has just before said
of his desire to preserve the reputation of
the fathers sacred. In no writer is it
more necessary to observe the *animus*
with which he writes; for, giving way
to his impetuosity, when he has said any
thing that would give offence, or which
he thought incautious, it was not his
custom, so far as we can judge, to ex-
punge or soften it, but to insert something else of an opposite colour, without
taking any pains to harmonise his context. This makes it easy to quote passages, especially short ones, from Taylor,
which do not exhibit his real way of
thinking; if indeed his way of thinking
itself did not vary with the wind that
blew from different regions of controversy.

than he can justly be blamed that complies with it.' And
thus not only single men, but whole bodies take unhesitat-
ingly and unanimously opposite sides from those who have
imbibed another kind of instruction; and ' it is strange that
all the Dominicans should be of one opinion in the matter of
predestination and immaculate conception, and all the Franciscans of the quite contrary, as if their understandings were
formed in a different mould, and furnished with various principles by their very rule.' These and the like prejudices are
not absolute excuses to everyone, and are often accompanied
with culpable dispositions of mind; but the impossibility of
judging others renders it incumbent on us to be lenient towards all, and neither to be peremptory in denying that those
who differ from us have used the best means in their power
to discover the truth, nor to charge their persons, whatever
we may their opinions, with odious consequences which they
do not avow.

58. This diffuse and not very well arranged vindication of
diversity of judgment in religion, comprised in the Grounds of
first twelve sections of the Liberty of Prophesying, toleration.
is the proper basis of the second part, which maintains the
justice of toleration as a consequence from the former
principle. The general arguments, or prejudices, on which
punishment for religious tenets had been sustained, turned
on their criminality in the eyes of God, and the duty of the
magistrate to sustain God's honour, and to guard his own
subjects from sin. Taylor, not denying that certain and
known idolatry, or any sort of practical impiety, may be
punished corporally, because it is matter of fact, asserts that
no matter of mere opinion, no errors that of themselves are
not sins, are to be persecuted or punished by death or corporal infliction. He returns to his favourite position, ' that
we are not sure not to be deceived;' mingling this, in that
inconsequent allocation of his proofs which frequently occurs
in his writings, with other arguments of a different nature.
The governors of the church, indeed, may condemn and restrain, as far as their power extends, any false doctrine which
encourages evil life, or destroys the foundations of religion;
but if the church meddles farther with any matters of question, which have not this tendency, so as to dictate what

men are to believe, she becomes tyrannical and uncharitable; the Apostles' creed being sufficient to conserve the peace of the church and the unity of her doctrine. And with respect to the civil magistrate, he concludes that he is bound to suffer the profession of different opinions, which are neither directly impious and immoral, nor disturb the public peace.

59. The seventeenth chapter, in which Taylor professes to consider which among the sects of Christendom are to be tolerated, and in what degree, is written in a tone not easily reconciled with that of the rest. Though he begins by saying that diversity of opinions does more concern public peace than religion, it certainly appears, in some passages, that on this pretext of peace, which with the magistrate has generally been of more influence than that of orthodoxy, he withdraws a great deal of that liberty of prophesying which he has been so broadly asserting. Punishment for religious tenets is doubtless not at all the same as restraint of separate worship; yet we are not prepared for the shackles he seems inclined to throw over the latter. Laws of ecclesiastical discipline, which, in Taylor's age, were understood to be binding on the whole community, cannot, he holds, be infringed by those who take occasion to disagree, without rendering authority contemptible; and if there are any as zealous for obedience to the church, as others may be for their opinions against it, the toleration of the latter's disobedience may give offence to the former: an argument strange enough in this treatise! But Taylor is always more prone to accumulate reasons than to sift their efficiency. It is indeed, he thinks, worthy to be considered, in framing a law of church discipline, whether it will be disliked by any who are to obey it; but after it is once enacted, there seems no further indulgence practicable than what the governors of the church may grant to particular persons by dispensation. The laws of discipline are for the public good, and must not so far tolerate a violation of themselves as to destroy the good that the public ought to derive from them.[e]

Inconsistency of one chapter.

---

[e] This single chapter is of itself conclusive against the truth of Taylor's own allegation that he wrote his Liberty of Prophesying in order to procure toleration for the episcopal church of England at the hands of those who had overthrown it. No one ever dreamed of refusing freedom of opinion to that church; it was only about public worship that any difficulty could arise. But, in truth,

60. I have been inclined to suspect that Taylor, for some cause, interpolated this chapter after the rest of the His general defence of toleration. treatise was complete. It has as little bearing upon, and is as inconsistent in spirit with the following sections as with those that precede. To use a familiar illustration, the effect it produces on the reader's mind is like that of coming on deck at sea, and finding that, the ship having been put about, the whole line of coast is reversed to the eye. Taylor, however, makes but a short tack. In the next section he resumes the bold tone of an advocate for freedom; and, after discussing at great length the leading tenet of the Anabaptists, concludes that, resting as it does on such plausible though insufficient grounds, we cannot exclude it by any means from toleration, though they may be restrained from preaching their other notions of the unlawfulness of war, or of oaths, or of capital punishment; it being certain that no good religion teaches doctrines whose consequences would destroy all government. A more remarkable chapter is that in which Taylor concludes in favour of tolerating the Romanists, except when they assert the pope's power of deposing princes, or of dispensing with oaths. The result of all, he says, is this: ' Let the prince and the secular power have a care the commonwealth be safe. For whether such or such a sect of Christians be to be permitted, is a question rather political than religious.'

61. In the concluding sections he maintains the right of particular churches to admit all who profess the Apostles' creed to their communion, and of private men to communicate

---

there is not one word in the whole treatise which could have been written with the view that Taylor pretends.

[It has been suggested, by an anonymous correspondent, that I have put a wrong construction on this seventeenth chapter, and that Taylor's design was to withstand that Puritan party within the church who refused to submit to the established laws of ecclesiastical discipline. It is certain that much which he has said will bear that construction; but, if he meant only this, he has not expressed himself with uniform clearness and consistency, as indeed is too common with him. He is so far from being distinct in the whole treatise as to what he aims at, that his editor, Heber, imagines him to have contended under the name Liberty of Prophesying, not for toleration of sectaries, but of an exemption from fixed articles of faith for the clergy themselves. I conceive this to be a mistake; but Heber was not deficient in acuteness, and could hardly have misunderstood a plain meaning. The hypothesis of my correspondent, it may be observed, strengthens the presumption that the Liberty of Prophesying was chiefly written while the church of England was still in the ascendant.— 1842.]

with different churches, if they require no unlawful condition. But 'few churches, that have framed bodies of confession and articles, will endure any person that is not of the same confession; which is a plain demonstration that such bodies of confession and articles do much hurt.' 'The guilt of schism may lie on him who least thinks it; he being rather the schismatic who makes unnecessary and inconvenient impositions, than he who disobeys them, because he cannot do otherwise without violating his conscience.'[f] The whole treatise on the Liberty of Prophesying ends with the celebrated parable of Abraham, found, as Taylor says, 'in the Jews' books,' but really in an Arabian writer. This story Franklin, as every one now knows, rather unhandsomely appropriated to himself; and it is a strange proof of the ignorance as to our earlier literature which then prevailed, that for many years it continued to be quoted with his name. It was not contained in the first editions of the Liberty of Prophesying; and indeed the book from which Taylor is supposed to have borrowed it was not published till 1651.

62. Such is this great pleading for religious moderation; a production not more remarkable in itself than for the quarter from which it came. In the polemical writings of Jeremy Taylor we generally find a staunch and uncompromising adherence to one party; and from the abundant use he makes of authority we should infer that he felt a great veneration for it. In the Liberty of Prophesying, as has appeared by the general sketch rather than analysis we have just given, there is a prevailing tinge of the contrary turn of mind, more striking than the comparison of insulated passages can be. From what motives, and under what circumstances, this treatise was written, is not easily discerned. In the dedication to Lord Hatton of the collective edition of his controversial writings after the Restoration, he declares that 'when a persecution did arise against the church of England, he intended to make a reservative for his brethren and himself, by pleading for a liberty to our consciences to persevere in that profession, which was warranted by all the laws of God

---

[f] This is said also by Hales, in his tract on Schism, which was published some years before the Liberty of Prophesying. It is, however, what Taylor would have thought without a prompter.

and our superiors.' It is with regret we are compelled to confess some want of ingenuousness in this part of Taylor's proceedings. No one reading the Liberty of Prophesying can perceive that it had the slightest bearing on any toleration that the episcopal church, in the time of the civil war, might ask of her victorious enemies. The differences between them were not on speculative points of faith, nor turning on an appeal to fathers and councils. That Taylor had another class of controversies in his mind is sufficiently obvious to the attentive reader of his work, and I can give no proof in this place to any other.

63. This was the third blow that the new school of Leyden had aimed in England at the positive dogmatists, Effect of this treatise. who, in all the reformed churches, as in that of Rome, laboured to impose extensive confessions of faith, abounding in inferences of scholastic theology, as conditions of exterior communion, and as peremptory articles of faith. Chillingworth and Hales were not less decisive; but the former had but in an incidental manner glanced at the subject, and the short tract on Schism had been rather deficient in proof of its hardy paradoxes. Taylor, therefore, may be said to have been the first who sapped and shook the foundations of dogmatism and pretended orthodoxy; the first who taught men to seek peace in unity of spirit rather than of belief; and, instead of extinguishing dissent, to take away its sting by charity, and by a sense of human fallibility. The mind thus freed from bigotry is best prepared for the public toleration of differences in religion; but certainly the despotic and jealous temper of governments is not so well combated by Taylor as by later advocates of religious freedom.

64. In conducting his argument, he falls not unfrequently into his usual fault. Endowed with a mind of pro- Its defects. digious fertility, which a vast erudition rendered more luxuriant, he accumulates without selection whatever presents itself to his mind; his innumerable quotations, his multiplied reasonings, his prodigality of epithets and appositions are poured along the interminable periods of his writings, with a frequency of repetition, sometimes of the same phrases, which leaves us to suspect that he revised but

little what he had very rapidly composed. Certain it is that, in his different works, he does not quite adhere to himself; and it would be more desirable to lay this on the partial views that haste and impetuosity produce, than on a deliberate employment of what he knew to be insufficient reasoning. But I must acknowledge that Taylor's fairness does not seem his characteristic quality.

65. In some passages of the Liberty of Prophesying, he seems to exaggerate the causes of uncertainty, and to take away from ecclesiastical antiquity even that moderate probability of truth which a dispassionate inquirer may sometimes assign to it. His suspicions of spuriousness and interpolation are too vaguely sceptical, and come ill from one who has no sort of hesitation, in some of his controversies, to allege as authority what he here sets aside with little ceremony. Thus, in the Defence of Episcopacy, published in 1642, he maintains the authenticity of the first fifty of the apostolic canons, all of which, in the Liberty of Prophesying, a very few years afterwards, he indiscriminately rejects. But this line of criticism was not then in so advanced a state as at present; and, from a credulous admission of everything, the learned had come sometimes to more sweeping charges of interpolation and forgery than would be sustained on a more searching investigation. Taylor's language is so unguarded that he seems to leave the authenticity of all the fathers precarious. Doubtless there is a greater want of security as to books written before the invention of printing than we are apt to conceive, especially where independent manuscripts have not been found; but it is the business of a sagacious criticism, by the aid of internal or collateral evidence, to distinguish, not dogmatically as most are wont, but with a rational, though limited assent, the genuine remains of ancient writers from the incrustations of blundering or of imposture.

66. A prodigious reach of learning distinguishes the theologians of these fifty years, far greater than even in the sixteenth century; and also, if I am not mistaken, more critical and pointed, though in these latter qualities it was afterwards surpassed. And in this erudition the Protestant churches, we may perhaps say, were,

Great erudition of this period.

upon the whole, more abundant than that of Rome. But it would be unprofitable to enumerate works which we are incompetent to appreciate. Blondel, Daillé, and Salmasius on the Continent, Usher in England, are the most conspicuous names. Blondel sustained the equality of the apostolic church both against the primacy of Rome, and the episcopacy for which the Anglicans contended; Salmasius and Daillé fought on the same side in that controversy. The writings of our Irish primate, Usher, who main- Usher. tained the antiquity of his order, but not upon such Petavius. high ground as many in England would have desired, are known for their extraordinary learning, in which he has perhaps never been surpassed by an English writer. But for judgment and calm appreciation of evidence, the name of Usher has not been altogether so much respected by posterity as it was by his contemporaries. The church of Rome had its champions of less eminent renown : Gretser, perhaps the first among them, is not very familiar to our ears ; but it is to be remembered, that some of the writings of Bellarmin fall within this period. The Dogmata Theologica of the jesuit Petavius, though but a compilation from the fathers and ancient councils, and not peculiarly directed against the tenets of the reformed, may deserve mention as a monument of useful labour.[g] Labbe, Sirmond, and several others, appear to range more naturally under the class of historical than theological writers. In mere ecclesiastical history—the records of events rather than opinions—this period was far more profound and critical than the preceding. The annals of Baronius were abridged and continued by Spondanus.

67. A numerous list of writers in sacred criticism might easily be produced. Among the Romanists, Corne- Sacred cri- lius à Lapide has been extolled above the rest by ticism his fellow-jesuit Andrès. His Commentaries, published from 1617 to 1642, are reckoned by others too diffuse ; but he seems to have a fair reputation with Protestant critics.[h] The Lutherans extol Gerhard, and especially Glass, author

---

[g] The Dogmata Theologica is not a complete work ; it extends only as far as the head of free-will. It belongs to the class of Loci Communes. Morhof, ii. 539

[h] Andrès, Blount. Simon, however, says he is full of an erudition not to the purpose, which, as his Commentaries on the Scriptures run to twelve volumes, is not wonderful.

of the Philologia Sacra, in hermeneutical theology. Rivet
was the highest name among the Calvinists. Arminius,
Episcopius, the Fratres Poloni, and indeed almost every one
who had to defend a cause, found no course so ready, at
least among Protestants, as to explain the Scriptures consistently with his own tenets. Two natives of Holland, opposite in character, in spirit, and principles of reasoning, and consequently the founders of opposite
schools of disciples, stand out from the rest—Grotius and
Coccejus. Luther, Calvin, and the generality of Protestant
interpreters in the sixteenth century had, in most instances,
rejected with some contempt the allegorical and multifarious
senses of Scripture which had been introduced by the fathers,
and had prevailed through the dark ages of the church.
This adherence to the literal meaning was doubtless promoted by the tenet they all professed, the facility of understanding Scripture. That which was designed for the simple
and illiterate was not to require a key to any esoteric sense.
Grotius, however, in his Annotations on the Old and New
Testament, published in 1633—the most remarkable book of
this kind that had appeared, and which has had a more
durable reputation than any perhaps of its precursors—
carried the system of literal interpretation still farther,
bringing great stores of illustrative learning from profane
antiquity, but merely to elucidate the primary meaning,
according to ordinary rules of criticism. Coccejus followed
a wholly opposite course. Every passage, in his method,
teemed with hidden senses; the narratives, least capable of
any ulterior application, were converted into typical allusion,
so that the Old Testament became throughout an enigmati-
cal representation of the New. He was also remarkable for
having viewed, more than any preceding writer, all the relations between God and man under the form of covenants,
and introduced the technical language of jurisprudence into
theology. This became a very usual mode of treating the
subject in Holland, and afterwards in England. The Cocce-
jans were numerous in the United Provinces, though not
perhaps deemed quite so orthodox as their adversaries, who,
from Gisbert Voet, a theologian of the most inflexible and
polemical spirit, were denominated Voetians. Their disputes

began a little before the middle of the century, and lasted till nearly its close.[i] The Summa Doctrinæ of Coccejus appeared in 1648, and the Dissertationes Theologicæ of Voet in 1649.

68. England gradually took a prominent share in this branch of sacred literature. Among the divines of this period, comprehending the reigns of James and Charles, we may mention Usher, Gataker, Mede, Lightfoot, Jackson, Field, and Leigh.[k] Gataker stood, perhaps, next to Usher in general erudition. The fame of Mede has rested, for the most part, on his interpretations of the Apocalypse. This book had been little commented upon by the reformers; but in the beginning of the seventeenth century, several wild schemes of its application to present or expected events had been broached in Germany. England had also taken an active part, if it be true what Grotius tells us, that eighty books on the prophecies had been published here before 1640.[m] Those of Mede have been received with favour by later interpreters. Lightfoot, with extensive knowledge of the rabbinical writers, poured his copious stores on Jewish antiquities, preceded in this by a more obscure labourer in that region, Ainsworth. Jackson had a considerable name, but I do not think that he has been much quoted in modern times.[n] Field on the Church has been much praised by Coleridge: it is, as it seemed to me, a more temperate work in ecclesiastical theory than some have represented it to be, and written almost wholly against Rome. Leigh's Critica Sacra can hardly be reckoned, nor does it claim to be, more than a compilation from earlier theologians: it is an alphabetical series of words from the Hebrew and Greek Testaments, the author candidly

English commentators.

---

[i] Eichhorn, vi. part i. p. 264. Mosheim.

[k] 'All confess,' says Selden, in the Table-talk, 'there never was a more learned clergy—no man taxes them with ignorance.' In another place, indeed, he is represented to say, 'The jesuits and the lawyers of France, and the Low Country-men, have engrossed all learning; the rest of the world make nothing but homilies.' As far as these sentences are not owing to difference of humour in the time of speaking, he seems to have taken learning in a larger sense the second time than the first. Of learning not theological, the English clergy had no extraordinary portion.

[m] Si qua in re libera esse debet sententia, certè in vaticiniis, præsertim cum jam Protestantium libri prodierint fermè centum (in his octoginta in Anglia sola, ut mihi Anglici legati dixere) super illis rebus, inter se plurimum discordes. Grot. Epist. 895.

[n] [The entire works of Jackson have been reprinted at Oxford within a few years.]—1853.

admitting that he was not very conversant with the Latin language. Leigh, it should be added, was a layman.

69. The style of preaching before the Reformation had been often little else than buffoonery, and seldom respectable. For the most part, indeed, the clergy wrote in Latin what they delivered to the multitude in the native tongue. A better tone began with Luther. His language was sometimes rude and low, but persuasive, artless, powerful. He gave many useful precepts, as well as examples, for pulpit eloquence. Melanchthon and several others, both in the sixteenth and seventeenth centuries, as well in the Lutheran as in the reformed church, endeavoured by systematic treatises to guide the composition of sermons. The former could not, however, withstand the formal, tasteless, and polemical spirit that overspread their theology. In the latter a superior tone is perceived. Of these, according to Eichhorn, the Swiss preachers were most simple and popular, the Dutch most learned and copious, the French had most taste and eloquence, the English most philosophy.[o] It is more than probable that in these characteristics he has meant to comprise the whole of the seventeenth century. Few continental writers, as far as I know, that belong to this its first moiety, have earned any remarkable reputation in this province of theology. In England several might be distinguished out of a large number. Sermons have been much more frequently published here than in any other country; and, from the beginning of the seventeenth century, form a large proportion of our theological literature. But it is of course not requisite to mention more than the very few which may be said to have a general reputation.

Style of preaching.

English sermons.

70. The sermons of Donne have sometimes been praised in late times. They are undoubtedly the productions of a very ingenious and a very learned man; and two folio volumes by such a person may be expected to supply favourable specimens. In their general character, they will not appear, I think, much worthy of being rescued from oblivion. The subtilty of Donne, and his fondness for such inconclusive reasoning as a subtle disputant is apt to

Of Donne.

---

[o] Eichhorn, vi. part ii. p. 219, et post.

fall into, runs through all of these sermons at which I have
looked. His learning he seems to have perverted in order to
cull every impertinence of the fathers and schoolmen, their
remote analogies, their strained allegories, their technical distinctions; and to these he has added much of a similar kind
from his own fanciful understanding. In his theology, Donne
appears often to incline towards the Arminian hypotheses,
which, in the last years of James and the first of his son,
the period in which these sermons were chiefly preached, had
begun to be accounted orthodox at court; but I will not
vouch for his consistency in every discourse. Much, as usual
in that age, is levelled against Rome : Donne was conspi-
cuously learned in that controversy; and, though he talks
with great respect of antiquity, is not induced by it, like
some of his Anglican contemporaries, to make any concession
to the adversary. [p]

71. The sermons of Jeremy Taylor are of much higher
reputation; far, indeed, above any that had preceded Of Jeremy
them in the English church. An imagination essen- Taylor.
tially poetical, and sparing none of the decorations which, by
critical rules, are almost deemed peculiar to verse; a warm tone
of piety, sweetness, and charity ; an accumulation of circumstantial accessories whenever he reasons, or persuades, or describes; an erudition pouring itself forth in quotation till his
sermons become in some places almost a garland of flowers from
all other writers, and especially from those of classical antiquity, never before so redundantly scattered from the pulpit,
distinguish Taylor from his contemporaries by their degree,
as they do from most of his successors by their kind. His
sermons on the Marriage Ring, on the House of Feasting,
on the Apples of Sodom, may be named without disparagement to others, which perhaps ought to stand in equal place.
But they are not without considerable faults, some of which
have just been hinted. The eloquence of Taylor is great, but

---

[p] Donne incurred some scandal by a
book entitled Biathanatos, and considered as a vindication of suicide. It
was published long after his death, in
1651. It is a very dull and pedantic
performance, without the ingenuity and
acuteness of paradox; distinctions, objections, and quotations from the rabble
of bad authors whom he used to read,
fill up the whole of it. It is impossible
to find a less clear statement of argument on either side. No one would be
induced to kill himself by reading such
a book, unless he were threatened with
another volume.

it is not eloquence of the highest class; it is far too Asiatic, too much in the style of the declaimers of the fourth century, by the study of whom he had probably vitiated his taste; his learning is ill-placed, and his arguments often as much so; not to mention that he has the common defect of alleging nugatory proofs; his vehemence loses its effect by the circuity of his pleonastic language; his sentences are of endless length, and hence not only altogether unmusical, but not always reducible to grammar. But he is still the greatest ornament of the English pulpit up to the middle of the seventeenth century; and we have no reason to believe, or rather much reason to disbelieve that he had any competitor in other languages.

72. The devotional writings of Taylor, several of which
Devotional writings of Taylor belong to the first part of the century, are by no means of less celebrity or less value than his sermons. Such are the Life of Christ, the Holy Living and Dying, and the collection of meditations, called the Golden Grove. A writer as distinguished in works of practical piety
and Hall. was Hall. His Art of Divine Meditation, his Contemplations, and indeed many of his writings, remind us frequently of Taylor. Both had equally pious and devotional tempers; both were full of learning, both fertile of illustration; both may be said to have had strong imagination and poetical genius, though Taylor let his predominate a little more. Taylor is also rather more subtle and argumentative; his copiousness has more real variety. Hall keeps more closely to his subject, dilates upon it sometimes more tediously, but more appositely. In his sermons there is some excess of quotation and far-fetched illustration, but less than in those of Taylor. In some of their writings these two great divines resemble each other, on the whole, so much that we might for a short time not discover which we were reading. I do not know that any third writer comes close to either. The Contemplations of Hall are among his most celebrated works. They are prolix, and without much of that vivacity or striking novelty we meet with in the devotional writings of his contemporary, but are perhaps more practical and generally edifying.[q]

---

[q] Some of the moral writings of Hall were translated into French by Chev- reau in the seventeenth century, and had much success. Niceron, xi. 348.

73. The religious treatises of this class, even those which by their former popularity, or their merit, ought to be mentioned in a regular history of theological literature, are too numerous for these pages. A mystical and ascetic spirit diffused itself more over religion, struggling sometimes, as the Lutherans of Germany, against the formal orthodoxy of the church, but more often in subordination to its authority, and co-operating with its functions. The writings of St. Francis de Sales, titular Bishop of Geneva, especially his treatise on the Love of God, published in 1616, make a sort of epoch in the devotional theology of the church of Rome. Those of St. Teresa, in the Spanish language, followed some years afterwards; they are altogether full of a mystical theopathy. But de Sales included charity in his scheme of divine love; and it is to him, as well as others of his age, that not only a striking revival of religion in France, which had been absolutely perverted or disregarded in the sixteenth century, was due, but a reformation in the practices of monastic life, which became more active and beneficent, with less of useless penance and asceticism than before. New institutions sprang up with the spirit of association, and all other animating principles of conventual orders, but free from the formality and torpor of the old.[r]

74. Even in the German churches, rigid as they generally were in their adherence to the symbolical books, some voices from time to time were heard for a more spiritual and effective religion. Arndt's Treatise of True Christianity, in 1605, written on ascetic and devotional principles, and with some deviation from the tenets of the very orthodox Lutherans, has been reckoned one of the first protests against their barren forms of faith;[s] and the mystical theologians, if they had not run into such extravagances as did dishonour to their name, would have been accessions to the same side. The principal mystics or theosophists have generally been counted among philosophers, and will therefore find their place in the next chapter. The German nation is constitutionally disposed to receive those forms of religion which address themselves to the imagination and the heart. Much, therefore, of this character has always been written,

In the Roman

and Lutheran church.

---

[r] Ranke, ii. 430.
[s] Eichhorn, vi. part i. p. 355.   Biogr. univ.   Chalmers.

and become popular, in that language. Few English writings of the practical class, except those already mentioned, can be said to retain much notoriety. Those of George Herbert are best known; his Country Parson, which seems properly to fall within this description, is, on the whole, a pleasing little book; but the precepts are sometimes so overstrained, according to our notions, as to give an air of affectation.

75. The disbelief in revelation, of which several symptoms Infidelity of some writers. Charron. had appeared before the end of the sixteenth century, became more remarkable afterwards both in France and England, involving several names not obscure in literary history. The first of these, in point of date, is Charron. The religious scepticism of this writer has not been generally acknowledged, and indeed it seems repugnant to the fact of his having written an elaborate defence of Christianity; yet we can deduce no other conclusion from one chapter in his most celebrated book, the Treatise on Wisdom. Charron is so often little else than a transcriber, that we might suspect him in this instance also to have drawn from other sources; which, however, would leave the same inference as to his own tenets, and I think this chapter has an air of originality.

76. The name of Charron, however, has not been generally associated with the charge of irreligion. A more Vanini. audacious, and consequently more unfortunate, writer was Lucilio Vanini, a native of Italy, whose book De Admirandis Naturæ Reginæ Deæque Mortalium Arcanis, printed at Paris in 1616, caused him to be burned at the stake by a decree of the parliament of Toulouse in 1619. This treatise, as well as one that preceded it, Amphitheatrum Æternæ Providentiæ, Lyons, 1615, is of considerable rarity, so that there has been a question concerning the atheism of Vanini, which some have undertaken to deny.[t] In the Amphitheatrum I do not perceive anything which leads to such an imputation, though I will not pretend to have read the whole of a book full of the unintelligible metaphysics of the later Aristotelians. It professes, at least, to be a vindi-

---

[t] Brucker, v. 678.

cation of the being and providence of the Deity. But the later work, which is dedicated to Bassompierre, and published with a royal privilege of exclusive sale for six years, is of a very diffent complexion. It is in sixty dialogues, the inter-locutors being styled Alexander and Julius Cæsar, the latter representing Vanini himself. The far greater part of these dialogues relate to physical, but a few to theological subjects. In the fiftieth, on the religion of the heathens, he avows his disbelief of all religion, except such as nature, which is God, being the principle of motion, has planted in the hearts of man; every other being the figment of kings to keep their subjects in obedience, and of priests for their own lucre and honour :[u] observing plainly of his own Amphi-theatrum, which is a vindication of Providence, that he had said many things in it which he did not believe.[x] Vanini

---

[u] In quanam religione verè et piè Deum coli vetusti philosophi existimârunt? In unica Naturæ lege, quam ipsa Natura, quæ Deus est (est enim principium motûs), in ᵕomnium gentium animis inscripsit; cæteras vero leges non nisi figmenta et illusiones esse asserebant, non a cacodæmone aliquo inductas, fabulosum namque illorum genus dicitur a philosophis, sed a principibus ad subditorum pædagogiam excogitatas, et a sacrificulis ob honoris et auri aucupium confirmatas, non miraculis, sed scriptura, cujus nec originale ullibi adinvenitur, quæ miracula facta recitet, et bonarum ac malarum actionum repromissiones polliceatur, in futura tamen vita, ne fraus detegi possit. P. 366.

[x] Multa in eo libro scripta sunt, quibus a me nulla præstatur fides. Cosi va il mondo.—ALEX. Non miror, nam ego crebris vernaculis hoc usurpo sermonibus: Questo mondo è una gabbia de' matti. Reges excipio et Pontifices. Nam de illis scriptum est: Cor Regis in manu Domini, &c. Dial. LVI. p. 428.

The concluding pages are enough to show with what justice Buhle and Tennemann have gravely recorded Vanini among philosophers. Quæso, mi Juli, tuam de animæ immortalitate sententiam explices.—J. C. Excusatum me habeas rogo.—AL. Cur ita?—J. C. Vovi Deo meo quæstionem hanc me non pertractaturum, antequam senex dives et germanus evasero.—AL. Dii tibi Nestoreos pro literariæ reipublicæ emolumento

dies impertiant: vix trigesimum nunc attigisti annum et tot præclaræ eruditionis monumenta admirabili cum laude edidisti.—J. C. Quid hæc mihi prosunt? —AL. Celebrem tibi laudem comparârunt.—J. C. Omnes famæ rumusculos cum uno amasiæ basiolo commutandos plerique philosophi suadent.—AL. At alter ea perfrui potest.—J. C. Quid inde adimit? . . .—AL. Uberrimos voluptatis fructus percepisti in Naturæ arcanis investigandis.—J. C. Corpus mihi est studiis enervatum exhaustumque; neque in hac humana caligine perfectam rerum cognitionem assequi possumus; cum ipsummet Aristotelem philosophorum Deum infinitis propemodum locis hallucinatum fuisse adverto, cumque medicam facultatem præ reliquis certissimam adhuc incertam et fallacem experior, subscribere cuperem Agrippæ libello quem de scientiarum vanitate conscripsit.—AL. Laborum tuorum præmium jam consecutus es; æternitati nomen jam consecrâsti. Quid jucundius in extremo tuæ ætatis curriculo accipere potes, quam hoc canticum? Et superest sine te nomen in orbe tuum.—J. C. Si animus meus una cum corpore, ut Athei fingunt, evanescat, quas ille ex fama post obitum delicias nancisci poterit? Forsitan gloriolæ voculis, et fidiculis ad cadaveris domicilium pertrahatur? Si animus, ut credimus libenter et speramus, interitui non est obnoxius, et ad superos evolabit, tot ibi perfruetur cupediis et voluptatibus, ut illustres ac

was infatuated with presumption, and, if he resembled Jordano Bruno in this respect, fell very short of his acuteness and apparent integrity. His cruel death, and perhaps the scarcity of his works, has given more celebrity to his name in literary history than it would otherwise have obtained.

77. Lord Herbert of Cherbury, in his treatise De Veritate Lord Her- and still more in that De Religione Gentilium, has
bert of
Cherbury. been justly deemed inimical to every positive religion. He admits, indeed, the possibility of immediate revelation from heaven, but denies that any tradition from others can have sufficient certainty. Five fundamental truths of natural religion he holds to be such as all mankind are bound to acknowledge, and damns those heathens who do not receive them as summarily as any theologian.[y]

78. The progress of infidelity in France did not fail to
Grotius de attract notice. It was popular in the court of Louis
Veritate. XIII., and, in a certain degree, in that of Charles I. But this does not belong to the history of literature. Among the writers who may have given some proofs of it we may reckon La Mothe le Vayer, Naudé, and Guy Patin.[z] The

---

splendidas mundi pompas et laudationes nec pili faciat. Si ad purgatorias flammas descendet, gratior erit illi illius orationis, Dies iræ, dies illa, mulierculis gratissima recitatio, quam omnes Tulliani glossuli, dicendique lepores, quam subtilissimæ et pene divinæ Aristotelis ratiocinationes: si Tartareo, quod Deus avertat, perpetuo carceri emancipatur, nullum ibi solatium, nullam redemptionem inveniet.—AL. O utinam in adolescentiæ limine has rationes excepissem!—J. C. Præterita mala ne cogites, futura ne cures, præsentia fugias.—AL. Ah!—J. C. Liberaliter inspiras.—AL. Illius versiculi recordor, Perduto è tutto il tempo, che in amor non si spende.—J. C. Eja quoniam inclinato jam die ad vesperam perducta est disputatio, (cujus singula verba divino Romanæ ecclesiæ oraculo, infallibilis cujus interpres a Spiritu Sancto modo constitutus est Paulus V., serenissimæ Burghesiæ familiæ soboles, subjecta esse volumus, ita ut pro non dictis habeantur, si quæ forsitan sunt, quod vix crediderim, quæ illius placitis ad amussim non consentiant,) laxemus paulisper animos, et a severitate ad hilaritatem risumque traducamus. Heus pueri! lusorias tabulas huc adferte. The wretched man, it seems, had not much reason to think himself a gainer by his speculations; yet he knew not that the worst was still behind.

[y] These five articles are—1. Esse Deum summum.—2. Coli debere.—3. Virtutem pietatemque esse præcipuas partes cultûs divini.—4. Dolendum esse ob peccata, ab iisque resipiscendum.—5. Dari ex bonitate justitiaque divina præmium vel pœnam tum in hac vita, tum post hanc vitam. . . . . Hisce quippe ubi superstitiones figmentaque commiscuerint, vel animas suas criminibus quæ nulla satis eluat pœnitentia, commaculaverint, a seipsis perditio propria, Deo vero summo in æternum sit gloria. De Religione Gentilium, cap. 1.

[z] La Mothe le Vayer has frequently been reckoned among those who carried their general scepticism into religion. And this seems a fair inference, unless the contrary can be shown; for those who doubt of what is most evident, will naturally doubt of what is less so. In La Mothe's fourth dialogue, under the name of Oratius Tubero, he pretends to

writings of Hobbes will be treated at length hereafter. It is probable that this sceptical spirit of the age gave rise to those vindications of revealed religion which were published in the present period. Among these the first place is due to the well-known and extensively circulated treatise of Grotius. This was originally sketched in Dutch verse, and intended for the lower classes of his countrymen. It was published in Latin in 1627.[a] Few, if any, books of the kind have been so frequently reprinted; but some parts being not quite so close and critical as the modern state of letters exacts, and the arguments against the Jews and Mahometans seeming to occupy too much space, it is less read than formerly.

79. This is not a period in which many editions or versions of the Scriptures were published. The English lish translation of the Bible had been several times *English translation of the Bible.* revised, or re-made, since the first edition by Tyndale. It finally assumed its present form under the authority of James I. Forty-seven persons, in six companies, meeting at Westminster, Oxford, and Cambridge, distributed the labour among them, twenty-five being assigned to the Old Testament, fifteen to the New, seven to the Apocrypha. The rules imposed for their guidance by the king were designed, as far as possible, to secure the text against any novel interpretation; the translation, called the Bishop's Bible, being established as the basis, as those still older had been in that; and

---

speak of faith as a gift of God, and not founded on evidence; which was probably but the usual subterfuge. The Naudæana are full of broad intimations that the author was, as he expresses it, *bien déniaisé*; and Guy Patin's letters, except those near the end of his life, lead to a similar conclusion. One of them has certainly the appearance of implicating Gassendi, and has been quoted as such by Sir James Mackintosh, in his Dissertation on Ethical Philosophy. Patin tells us, that Naudé, Gassendi, and he were to sup together the following Sunday. Ce sera une débauche, mais philosophique, et peut-être quelque chose d'avantage, pour être tous trois guéris du loup-garou, et être délivrés du mal des scrupules qui est le

tyran des consciences, nous irons peut-être jusque fort près du sanctuaire. Je fis l'an passé ce voyage de Gentilly avec M. Naudé, moy seul avec luy, tête-à-tête; il n'y avoit point de témoins, aussi n'y en falloit-il point; nous y parlâmes fort librement de tout, sans que personne en ait été scandalisé. P. 32. I should not, nevertheless, lay much stress on this letter, in opposition to the many assertions of belief in religion which the writings of Gassendi contain. One of them, indeed, quoted by Dugald Stewart, in note Q. to his first Dissertation, is rather suspicious, as going too far into a mystical strain for his cold temperament.

[a] Niceron, vol. xix. Biogr. univ.

the work of each person or company being subjected to the review of the rest. The translation, which was commenced in 1607, was published in 1611.[b]

80. The style of this translation is in general so enthu-

siastically praised, that no one is permitted either to qualify or even explain the grounds of his approbation. It is held to be the perfection of our English language. I shall not dispute this proposition; but one remark as to a matter of fact cannot reasonably be censured, that, in consequence of the principle of adherence to the original versions which had been kept up ever since the time of Henry VIII., it is not the language of the reign of James I. It may, in the eyes of many, be a better English, but it is not the English of Daniel, or Raleigh, or Bacon, as any one may easily perceive. It abounds, in fact, especially in the Old Testament, with obsolete phraseology, and with single words long since abandoned, or retained only in provincial use. On the more important question, whether this translation is entirely, or with very trifling exceptions, conformable to the original text, it seems unfit to enter. It is one which is seldom discussed with all the temper and freedom from oblique views which the subject demands, and upon which, for this reason, it is not safe for those who have not had leisure or means to examine it for themselves, to take upon trust the testimony of the learned. A translation of the Old Testament was published at Douay in 1609 for the use of the English Catholics.

---

[b] Fuller's Church History.

CHAPTER III.

HISTORY OF SPECULATIVE PHILOSOPHY FROM 1600 TO 1650.

Sect. I.

Aristotelian Logic—Campanella—Theosophists—Lord Herbert of Cherbury —Gassendi's Remarks upon him.

1. In the two preceding periods, we have had occasion to excuse the heterogeneous character of the chapters that bear this title. The present is fully as much Subjects of this chapter open to verbal criticism; and perhaps it is rather by excluding both moral and mathematical philosophy that we give it some sort of unity, than from a close connexion in all the books that will come under our notice in the ensuing pages. But any tabular arrangement of literature, such as has often been attempted with no very satisfactory result, would be absolutely inappropriate to such a work as the present, which has already to labour with the inconvenience of more subdivisions than can be pleasing to the reader, and would interfere too continually with that general regard to chronology without which the name of history seems incongruous. Hence the metaphysical inquiries that are conversant with the human mind, or with natural theology, the general principles of investigating truth, the comprehensive speculations of theoretical physics, subjects very distinct and not easily confounded by the most thoughtless, must fall, with no more special distribution, within the contents of this chapter. But since, during the period which it embraces, men arose who have laid the foundations of a new philosophy, and thus have rendered it a great epoch in the intellectual history of mankind, we shall not very strictly, though without much devia-

tion, follow a chronological order, and after reviewing some of the less important labourers in speculative philosophy come to the names of three who have most influenced posterity, Bacon, Descartes, and Hobbes.

2. We have seen in a former chapter how little progress

Aristotelians had been made in this kind of philosophy during and Ramists. the sixteenth century. At its close the schools of logic wére divided, though by no means in equal proportion, between the Aristotelians and the Ramists; the one sustained by ancient renown, by civil, or at least academical power, and by the common prejudice against innovation; the other deriving some strength from the love of novelty, and the prejudice against established authority, which the first age of the reformation had generated, and which continued, perhaps, to preserve a certain influence in the second. But neither from one nor the other had philosophy, whether in material or intellectual physics, much to hope; the disputations of the schools might be technically correct; but so little regard was paid to objective truth, or at least so little pains taken to ascertain it, that no advance in real knowledge signalised either of these parties of dialecticians. According, indeed, to a writer of this age, strongly attached to the Aristotelian party, Ramus had turned all physical science into the domain of logic, and argued from words to things still more than his opponents.[a] Lord Bacon, in the bitterest language, casts on him a similar reproach.[b] It seems that he caused this branch of philosophy to retrograde rather than advance.

3. It was obvious, at all events, that from the universi-

---

[a] Keckermann, Præcognita Logica, p. 129. This writer charges Ramus with plagiarism from Ludovicus Vives, placing the passages in apposition, so as to prove his case. Ramus, he says, never alludes to Vives. He praises the former, however, for having attacked the scholastic party, being himself a genuine Aristotelian.

[b] Ne vero, fili, cum hanc contra Aristotelem sententiam fero, me cum rebelli ejus quodam neoterico Petro Ramo conspirasse augurare. Nullum mihi commercium cum hoc ignorantiæ latibulo, perniciosissima literarum tinea, compendiorum patre, qui cum methodi suæ et compendii vinclis res torqueat et premat, res quidem, si qua fuit, elabitur protinus et exsilit; ipse vero aridas et desertissimas nugas stringit. Atque Aquinas quidam cum Scoto et sociis etiam in non rebus rerum varietatem effinxit, hic vero etiam in rebus non rerum solitudinem æquavit. Atque hoc hominis cum sit, humanos tamen usus in ore habet impudens, ut mihi etiam pro [præ?] sophistis prævaricari videatur. Bacon, De Interpretatione Naturæ.

ties, or from the church, in any country, no improvement in philosophy was to be expected : yet those who had strayed from the beaten track, a Paracelsus, a Jordano Bruno, even a Telesio, had but lost them- selves in irregular mysticism, or laid down theories of their own, as arbitrary and destitute of proof as those they en- deavoured to supersede. The ancient philosophers, and especially Aristotle, were, with all their errors and defects, far more genuine high-priests of nature than any moderns of the sixteenth century. But there was a better prospect at its close, in separate though very important branches of physical science. Gilbert, Kepler, Galileo, were laying the basis of a true philosophy ; and they, who do not properly belong to this chapter, laboured very effectually to put an end to all antiquated errors, and to check the reception of novel paradoxes.

No improvement till near the end of the century.

4. We may cast a glance, meantime, on those universities which still were so wise in their own conceit, and maintained a kind of reputation by the multitude of their disciples. Whatever has been said of the scholastic metaphysicians of the sixteenth century, may be understood as being applicable to their successors during the present period. Their method was by no means extinct, though the books which contain it are forgotten. In all that part of Europe which acknowledged the authority of Rome, and in all the universities which were swayed by the orders of Franciscans, Dominicans, and Jesuits, the metaphysics of the thirteenth century, the dialectics of the Peripatetic school, were still taught. If new books were written, as was frequently the case, they were written upon old systems. Brucker, who sometimes transcribes Morhof word for word, but frequently expands with so much more copiousness that he may be presumed to have had a direct acquaintance with many of the books he mentions, has gone most elaborately into this unpropitious subject.[c] The chairs of philosophy in Protestant German universities, except where the Ramists had got possession of them, which was not very common, especially after the first years of this period, were occupied

Methods of the univer- sities.

---

[c] Morhof, vol. ii. 1. 1, c. 13, 14.   Brucker, iv. cap. 2, 3.

by avowed Aristotelians; so that if one should enumerate
the professors of physics, metaphysics, logic, and ethics,
down to the close of the century, he would be almost giving
a list of strenuous adherents of that system.[d] One cause of
this was the ' Philippic method ' or course of instruction in
the philosophical books of Melanchthon, more clear and
elegant, and better arranged than those of Aristotle himself
or his commentators. But this, which long continued to
prevail, was deemed by some too superficial, and tending to
set aside the original authority. Brucker, however, admits,
what seems at least to limit some of his expressions as to
the prevalence of Peripateticism, that many reverted to the
scholastic metaphysics, which raised its head about the
beginning of the seventeenth century, even in the Protestant regions of Germany. The universities of Altdorf and
Helmstadt were the chief nurseries of the genuine Peripateticism.[e]

5. Of the metaphysical writers whom the older philosophy
Scholastic   brought forth we must speak with much ignorance.
writers.   Suarez of Granada is justly celebrated for some of
his other works; but of his Metaphysical Disputations,
published at Mentz, in 1614, in two folio volumes, and several
times afterwards, I find no distinct character in Morhof or
Brucker. They both, especially the former, have praised
Lalemandet, a Franciscan, whose Decisiones Philosophicæ,
on logic, physics, and metaphysics, appeared at Munich, in
1644 and 1645. Lalemandet, says Morhof, has well stated
the questions between the Nominalist and Realist parties;
observing that the difference between them is like that of a
man who casts up a sum of money by figures, and one who
counts the coins themselves.[f] Vasquez, Tellez, and several
more names, without going for the present below the middle
of the century, may be found in the two writers quoted.
Spain was peculiarly the nurse of these obsolete and unprofitable metaphysics.

6. The Aristotelian philosophy, unadulterated by the
figments of the schoolmen, had eminent upholders in the

---

[d] Brucker, iv. 243.
[e] Id. p. 248-253.

[f] Morhof, vol. ii. lib. 1. cap. 14.
sect. 15. Brucker, iv. 129.

Italian universities, especially in that of Padua. Cæsar Cremonini taught in that famous city till his death in 1630. Fortunio Liceto, his successor, was as staunch a disciple of the Peripatetic sect. We have a more full account of these men from Gabriel Naudé, both in his recorded conversation, the Naudæana, and in a volume of letters, than from any other quarter. His twelfth letter, especially, enters into some detail as to the state of the university of Padua, to which, for the purpose of hearing Cremonini, he had repaired in 1625. He does not much extol its condition; only Cremonini and one more were deemed by him safe teachers: the rest were mostly of a common class; the lectures were too few, and the vacations too long. He observes, as one might at this day, the scanty population of the city compared with its size, the grass growing and the birds singing in the streets, and, what we should not find now to be the case, the ' general custom of Italy, which keeps women perpetually locked up in their chambers, like birds in cages.'[g] Naudé in many of these letters speaks in the most panegyrical terms of Cremonini,[h] and particularly for his standing up almost alone in defence of the Aristotelian philosophy, when Telesio, Patrizi, Bruno, and others had been propounding theories of their own. Liceto, the successor of Cremonini, maintained, he afterwards informs us, with little support, the Peripatetic verity. It is probable that, by this time, Galileo, a more powerful adversary than Patrizi or Telesio, had drawn away the students of physical philosophy from Aristotle; nor did Naudé himself long continue in the faith he had imbibed from Cremonini. He became the intimate friend of Gassendi, and embraced a better system without repugnance, though he still kept up his correspondence with Liceto.

7. Logic had never been more studied, according to a writer who has given a sort of history of the science about the beginning of this period, than in the preceding age; and in fact he enumerates above fifty treatises on the subject, between the time of Ramus and his own.[i] The Ramists, though of little importance in Italy, in Spain,

Treatises on logic.

---

[g] Naudæi Epistolæ, p. 52 (edit. 1667).
[h] P. 27, et alibi sæpius.
[i] Keckermann, Præcognita Logica, p. 110 (edit. 1606).

and even in France, had much influence in Germany, England, and Scotland.[k]   None, however, of the logical works of the sixteenth century obtained such reputation as those by Smiglecius, Burgersdicius, and our countryman Crakanthorp, all of whom flourished, if we may use such a word for those who bore no flowers, in the earlier part of the next age.   As these men were famous in their generation, we may presume that they at least wrote better than their predecessors.   But it is time to leave so jejune a subject, though we may not yet be able to produce what is much more valuable.

8. The first name, in an opposite class, that we find in Campa- descending from the sixteenth century, is that of nella; Thomas Campanella, whose earliest writings belong to it.   His philosophy, being wholly dogmatical, must be classed with that of the paradoxical innovators whom he followed and eclipsed.   Campanella, a Dominican friar, and, like his master Telesio, a native of Cosenza, having been accused, it is uncertain how far with truth, of a conspiracy against the Spanish government of his country, underwent an imprisonment of twenty-seven years; during which almost all his philosophical treatises were composed and given to the world.   Ardent and rapid in his mind, and, as has just been seen, not destitute of leisure, he wrote on logic, physics, metaphysics, morals, politics, and grammar.   Upon all these subjects his aim seems to have been to recede as far as possible from Aristotle.   He had early begun to distrust this guide, and had formed a noble resolution to study all schemes of philosophy, comparing them with their archetype, the world itself, that he might distinguish how much exactness was to be found in those several copies, as they ought to be, from one autograph of nature.[m]

9. Campanella borrowed his primary theorems from Telehis theory sio, but enlarged that Parmenidean philosophy by taken from Telesio. the inventions of his own fertile and imaginative genius.   He lays down the fundamental principle, that the perfectly wise and good Being has created certain signs and

---

[k] Keckermann, Præcognita Logica, p. 147 (edit. 1606).
[m] Cypriani Vita Campanellæ, p. 7.

types (statuas atque imagines) of himself, all of which, severally as well as collectively, represent power, wisdom, and love, and the objects of these attributes, namely, existence, truth, and excellence, with more or less evidence. God first created space, the basis of existence, the primal substance, an immovable and incorporeal capacity of receiving body. Next he created matter without form or figure. In this corporeal mass God called to being two workmen, incorporeal themselves, but incapable of subsisting apart from body, the organs of no physical forms, but of their Maker alone. These are heat and cold, the active principles diffused through all things. They were enemies from the beginning, each striving to occupy all material substances itself; each therefore always contending with the other, while God foresaw the great good that their discord would produce.[n] The heavens, he says in another passage, were formed by heat out of attenuated matter, the earth by cold out of condensed matter; the sun, being a body of heat, as he rolls round the earth, attacks the colder substance, and converts part of it into air and vapour.[o] This last part of his theory Campanella must have afterwards changed in words, when he embraced the Copernican system.

10. He united to this physical theory another, not wholly original, but enforced in all his writings with singular confidence and pertinacity, the sensibility of all created beings. All things, he says, feel; else would the world be a chaos. For neither would fire tend upwards, nor stones downwards, nor waters to the sea; but everything would remain where it was, were it not conscious that destruction awaits it by remaining amidst that which is contrary to itself, and that it can only be preserved by seeking that

Notion of universal sensibility.

---

[n] In hac corporea mole tantæ màteria statuæ, dixit Deus, ut nascerentur fabri duo incorporei, sed non potentes nisi a corpore subsistere, nullarum physicarum formarum organa, sed formatoris tantummodo. Idcirco nati calor et frigus, principia activa principalia, ideoque suæ virtutis diffusiva. Statim inimici fuerunt mutuo, dum uterque cupit totam substantiam materialem occupare. Hinc contra se invicem pugnare cœperunt, pro-

vidente Deo ex hujusmodi discordia ingens bonum. Philosophia Realis Epilogistica (Frankfort, 1623), sect. 4.

[o] This is in the Compendium de Rerum Natura pro Philosophia humana, published by Adami in 1617. In his Apology for Galileo, in 1622, Campanella defends the Copernican system, and says that the modern astronomers think they cannot construct good ephemerides without it.

which is of a similar nature. Contrariety is necessary for the decay and reproduction of nature; but all things strive against their contraries, which they could not do, if they did not perceive what is their contrary.[p] God, who is primal power, wisdom, and love, has bestowed on all things the power of existence, and so much wisdom and love as is necessary for their conservation during that time only for which his providence has determined that they shall be. Heat, therefore, has power, and sense, and desire of its own being; so have all other things, seeking to be eternal like God; and in God they are eternal, for nothing dies before him, but is only changed.[q] Even to the world as a sentient being, the death of its parts is no evil, since the death of one is the birth of many. Bread that is swallowed dies to revive as blood, and blood dies, that it may live again in our flesh and bones; and thus as the life of man is compounded out of the deaths and lives of all his parts, so is it with the whole universe.[r] God said, Let all things feel, some more, some less, as they have more or less necessity to imitate my being. And let them desire to live in that which they understand to be good for them, lest my creation should come to nought.[s]

---

[p] Omnia ergo sentiunt; alias mundus esset chaos. Ignis enim non sursum tenderet, nec aquæ in mare, nec lapides deorsum; sed res omnis ubi primo reperiretur, permaneret, cum non sentiret sui destructionem inter contraria nec sui conservationem inter similia. Non esset in mundo generatio et corruptio nisi esset contrarietas, sicut omnes physiologi affirmant. At si alterum contrarium non sentiret alterum sibi esse contrarium, contra ipsum non pugnaret. Sentiunt ergo singula. De Sensu Rerum, l. i. c. 4.

[q] Igitur ipse Deus, qui est prima potentia, prima sapientia, primus amor, largitus est rebus omnibus potentiam vivendi, et sapientiam et amorem quantum sufficit conservationi ipsarum in tanto tempore necessariæ, quantum determinavit ejus mens pro rerum regimine in ipso ente, nec præteriri potest. Calor ergo potest, sentit, amat esse; ita et res omnis, cupitque æternari sicut Deus, et Deo res nulla moritur, sed solummodo mutatur, &c. l. ii. c. 26.

[r] Non est malus ignis in suo esse; terræ autem malus videtur, non autem mundo; nec vipera mala est, licet homini sit mala. Ita de omnibus idem prædico. Mors quoque rei unius si nativitas est multarum rerum, mala non est. Moritur panis manducatus, ut fiat sanguis, et sanguis moritur, ut in carnem nervos et ossa vertatur ac vivat; neque tamen hoc universo displicet animali, quamvis partibus mors ipsa, hoc est, transmutatio dolorifica sit, displiceatque. Ita utilis est mundo transmutatio eorum particularium noxia displicensque illis. Totus homo compositus est ex morte ac vita partialibus, quæ integrant vitam humanam. Sic mundus totus ex mortibus ac vitabus compositus est, quæ totius vitam efficiunt. Philosop. Realis, c. 10.

[s] Sentiant alia magis, alia minus, prout magis minusque opus habent, ut me imitentur in essendo. Ibidem ament omnia vivere in proprio esse præcognito ut bono, ne corruat factura mea. Id.

11. The strength of Campanella's genius lay in his im- His imagina-
agination, which raises him sometimes to flights of tion and
impressive eloquence on this favourite theme. 'The eloquence.
sky and stars are endowed with the keenest sensibility; nor
is it unreasonable to suppose that they signify their mutual
thoughts to each other by the transference of light, and
that their sensibility is full of pleasure. The blessed spirits
that inform such living and bright mansions behold all
things in nature and in the divine ideas; they have also a
more glorious light than their own, through which they are
elevated to a supernatural beatific vision.'[t] We can hardly
read this, without recollecting the most sublime passage,
perhaps, in Shakspeare :—

> Sit, Jessica ; look how the floor of heaven
> Is thick inlaid with patines of bright gold :
> There 's not the smallest orb, which thou behold'st,
> But in his motion like an angel sings,
> Still quiring to the young-eyed cherubim ;
> Such harmony is in immortal souls ;
> But, while this muddy vesture of decay
> Does grossly close us in, we cannot hear it.[u]

12. 'The world is full of living spirits,' he proceeds ;
'and when the soul shall be delivered from this dark cavern,
we shall behold their subtle essences. But now we cannot
discern the forms of the air, and the winds as they rush by
us ; much less the angels and dæmons who people them.
Miserable as we are, we recognise no other sensation than
that which we observe in animals and plants, slow and half
extinguished, and buried under a weight that oppresses it.
We will not understand that all our actions and appetites
and motions and powers flow from heaven. Look at the
manner in which light is diffused over the earth, penetrating
every part of it with endless variety of operation, which we
must believe that it does not perform without exquisite pleasure.'[x] And hence there is no vacuum in nature, except by

---

[t] Animæ beatæ habitantes sic vivas lu-
cidasque mansiones, res naturales vident
omnes divinasque ideas, habent quoque
lumen gloriosius quo elevantur ad visi-
onem supernaturalem beatificam, et veluti apud nos luces plurimæ sese mutuo
tangunt, intersecant, decussant, sentiunt-
que, ita in cœlo luces distinguuntur, uni-
untur, sentiunt. De Sensu Rerum, l. iii.
c. 4.

[u] Merchant of Venice, act v.

[x] Prætervolant in conspectu nostro

violent means; since all bodies delight in mutual contact, and the world no more desires to be rent in its parts than an animal.

13. It is almost a descent in Campanella from these visions of the separate sensibility of nature in each particle, when he seizes hold of some physical fact or analogy to establish a subordinate and less paradoxical part of his theory. He was much pleased with Gilbert's treatise on the magnet, and thought it, of course, a proof of the animation of the earth. The world is an animal, he says, sentient as a whole, and enjoying life in all its parts.[y] It is not surprising that he ascribes intelligence to plants; but he here remarks that we find the male and female sexes in them, and that the latter cannot fructify without the former. This is manifest in siliquose plants and in palms, (which on this account he calls in another place the wiser plants, plantæ sapientiores), in which the two kinds incline towards each other for the purpose of fructification.[z]

14. Campanella, when he uttered from his Neapolitan His works prison these dulcet sounds of fantasy, had the ad- published by Adami. vantage of finding a pious disciple who spread them over other parts of Europe. This was Tobias Adami, initiated, as he tells us, in the same mysteries as himself (nostræ philosophiæ symmysta), who dedicated to the philosophers of Germany his own Prodromus Philosophiæ Instaurandæ, prefixed to his edition of Campanella's Compendium de Rerum Natura, published at Frankfort in 1617. Most of the other writings of the master seem to have pre-

---

venti et aer, at nihil eos videmus, multo minus videmus Angelos Dæmonasque, quorum plenus est mundus.

Infelices qui sensum alium nullum agnoscimus, nisi obtusum animalium plantarumque, tardum, demortuum, aggravatum, sepultum : nec quidem intelligere volumus omnem actionem nostram et appetitum et sensum et motum et vim a cœlo manare. Ecce lux quanto acutissimo expanditur sensu super terram, quo multiplicatur, generatur, amplificatur, idque non sine magna efficere voluptate existimanda est. l. iii. c. 5.

Campanella used to hear, as he tells us, whenever any evil was impending, a voice calling him by his name, sometimes with other words; he doubted whether this were his proper dæmon, or the air itself speaking. It is not wonderful that his imagination was affected by length of confinement.

[y] Mundum esse animal, totum sentiens, omnesque portiones ejus communi gaudere vita. l. i. c. 9.

[z] Inveniemus in plantis sexum masculinum et fœmininum, ut in animalibus, et fœminam non fructificare sine masculi congressu. Hoc patet in siliquis et in palmis, quarum mas fœminaque inclinantur mutuo alter in alterum et sese osculantur, et fœmina impregnatur, nec fructificat sine mare; immo conspicitur dolens, squalida mortuaque, et pulvere illius et odore reviviscit.

ceded this edition ; for Adami enumerates them in his Prodromus.[a] Campanella did not fully obtain his liberty till
1629, and died some years afterwards in France, where he
had experienced the kindness of Peiresc and the patronage
of Richelieu. His philosophy made no very deep impression;
it was too fanciful, too arbitrary, too much tinctured with
marks of an imagination rendered morbid by solitude, to
gain many proselytes in an age that was advancing in severe
science. Gassendi, whose good nature led him to receive
Campanella, oppressed by poverty and ill usage, with every
courteous attention, was of all men the last to be seduced by
his theories. No one, probably, since Campanella, aspiring
to be reckoned among philosophers, has ventured to assert so
much on matters of high speculative importance and to prove
so little. Yet he seems worthy of the notice we have taken of
him, if it were only as the last of the mere dogmatists in philosophy. He is doubtless much superior to Jordano Bruno,
and I should presume, except in mathematics, to Cardan.[b]

15. A less important adversary of the established theory
in physics was Sebastian Basson, in his ' Philosophiæ
Naturalis adversus Aristotelem Libri XII., in quibus
abstrusa veterum physiologia restauratur, et Aristotelis errores solidis rationibus refelluntur. Genevæ, 1621.' This
book shows great animosity against Aristotle, to whom, what
Lord Bacon has himself insinuated, he allows only the credit
of having preserved fragments of the older philosophers, like
pearls in mud. It is difficult to give an account of this long
work. In some places we perceive signs of a just philosophy ;
but in general his explanations of physical phenomena seem
as bad as those of his opponents, and he displays no acquaintance with the writings and the discoveries of his great contemporaries. We find also some geometrical paradoxes ; and
in treating of astronomy he writes as if he had never heard
of the Copernican system.

16. Claude Berigard, born at Moulins, became professor of
natural philosophy at Pisa and Padua. In his Circuli Pisani,

---

[a] [Prodromus Philosophiæ Instaurandæ is only a title-page. Adami contributed a preface to this edition of
Campanella's work ; but the words Prodromus, &c., are meant for the latter,
and not for anything written by the
editor. See Notes and Queries, vol. iv.
p. 27 —1853.]

[b] Brucker (vol. v. p. 106–144) has
given a laborious analysis of the philosophy of Campanella.

published in 1643, he attempted to revive, as it is commonly
said, the Ionic or corpuscular philosophy of Anax-
Berigard.
agoras, in opposition to the Aristotelian.   The book
is rare; but Brucker, who had seen it, seems to have satisfactorily repelled the charge of atheism brought by some
against Berigard.[c] Another Frenchman, domiciled in Italy,
Magnen, trod nearly the same path as Berigard,
Magnen.
professing, however, to follow the modification of
the corpuscular theory introduced by Democritus.[d] It seems
to be óbservable as to these writers, Basson and the others,
that coming with no sufficient knowledge of what had recently been discovered in mathematical and experimental
science, and following the bad methods of the universities,
even when they deviated from their usual doctrines, dogma-
tising and asserting when they should have proved, arguing synthetically from axioms, and never ascending from
particular facts, they could do little good to philosophy, except by contributing, so far as they might be said to have had
any influence, to shake the authority of Aristotle.

17. This authority, which at least required but the deference of modest reason to one of the greatest of man-
Paracelsists.
kind, was ill exchanged, in any part of science, for
the unintelligible dreams of the school of Paracelsus, which
had many disciples in Germany, and a very few in England.
Germany, indeed, has been the native soil of mysticism in
Europe. The tendency to reflex observation of the mind,
characteristic of that people, has exempted them from much
gross error, and given them insight into many depths of
truth, but at the expense of some confusion, some liability to
self-deceit, and to some want of strictness in metaphysical
reasoning. It was accompanied by a profound sense of the
presence of Deity; yet one which, acting on their thoughtful
spirits, became rather an impression than an intellectual
judgment, and settled into a mysterious indefinite theopathy,
when it did not even evaporate in pantheism.

18. The founder, perhaps, of this sect was Tauler of

---

[c] Brucker, iv. 460. Niceron, xxxi., where he is inserted by the name of Beauregard, which is probaMy more correct, but against usage.
[d] Brucker (p. 504) thinks that Mag-

nen misunderstood the atomic theory of Democritus, and substituted one quite different in his Democritus reviviscens, published in 1646.

Strasburg, in the fourteenth century, whose sermons in the native language, which, however, are supposed to and Theo- have been translated from Latin, are full of what sophists. many have called by the vague word mysticism, an intense aspiration for the union of the soul with God. An anonymous work generally entitled The German Theology, written in the fifteenth century, pursues the same track of devotional thought. It was a favourite book with Luther, and was translated into Latin by Castalio.[e] These, indeed, are to be considered chiefly as theological; but the study of them led readily to a state of mental emotion, wherein a dogmatic pseudo-philosophy, like that of Paracelsus, abounding with assertions that imposed on the imagination, and appealing frequently both to Scriptural authority and the evidence of inward light, was sure to be favourably received. The mystics, therefore, and the theosophists belonged to the same class, and it is not uncommon to use the names indifferently.

19. It may appear not here required to dwell on a subject scarcely falling under any province of literary history, but two writers within this period have been suffi- Fludd. ciently distinguished to deserve mention. One of these was Robert Fludd, an English physician, who died in 1637 ; a man of indefatigable diligence in collecting the dreams and follies of past ages, blending them in a portentous combination with new fancies of his own. The Rabbinical and Cabalistic authors, as well as the Paracelsists, the writers on magic, and whatever was most worthy to be rejected and forgotten, formed the basis of his creed. Among his numerous works the most known was his ' Mosaic Philosophy,' in which, like many before his time as well as since, he endeavoured to build a scheme of physical philosophy on the first chapters in Genesis. I do not know whether he found there his two grand principles or forces of nature : a northern force of condensation, and a southern force of dilatation. These seem to be the Parmenidean cold and heat, expressed in a jargon affected in order to make dupes. In peopling the universe with dæmons, and in ascribing all phænomena to their invi-

---

[e] Episcopius places the author of the Theologia Germanica, with Henry Ni- colas and David George, among mere enthusiasts.

sible agency, he pursued the steps of Agrippa and Paracelsus, or rather of the whole school of fanatics and impostors called magical. He took also from older writers, the doctrine of a constant analogy between universal nature, or the macrocosm, and that of man, or the microcosm; so that what was known in one might lead us to what was unknown in the other.[f] Fludd possessed, however, some acquaintance with science, especially in chemistry and mechanics; and his rhapsodies were so far from being universally contemned in his own age, that Gassendi thought it not unworthy of him to enter into a prolix confutation of the Fluddian philosophy.[g]

20. Jacob Behmen, or rather Boehm, a shoemaker of
Jacob Beh-
men.
Gorlitz, is far more generally familiar to our ears than his contemporary Fludd. He was, however, much inferior to him in reading, and in fact seems to have read little but the Bible and the writings of Paracelsus. He recounts the visions and ecstasies during which a supernatural illumination had been conveyed to him. It came indeed without the gift of transferring the light to others; for scarce any have been able to pierce the clouds in which his meaning has been charitably presumed to lie hid. The chief work of Behmen is his Aurora, written about 1612, and containing a record of the visions wherein the mysteries of nature were revealed to him. It was not published till 1641. He is said to have been a man of great goodness of heart, which his writings display; but, in literature, this cannot give a sanction to the incoherencies of madness. His language, as far as I have seen any extracts from his works, is coloured with the phraseology of the alchemists and astrologers; as for his philosophy, so to style it, we find, according to Brucker, who has taken some pains with the subject, manifest traces of the system of emanation, so ancient and so attractive; and from this and several other reasons he is inclined to think the unlearned shoemaker of Gorlitz must have had assistance from men of more education in developing his visions.[h] But the emanative theory is one into which a mind absorbed in

---

[f] This was a favourite doctrine of Paracelsus. Campanella was much too fanciful not to embrace it. Mundus, he says, habet spiritum qui est cœlum, crassum corpus quod est terra, sanguinem qui est mare. Homo igitur compendium epilogusque mundi est. De Sensu Rerum, l. ii. c. 32.

[g] Brucker, iv. 691. Buhle, iii. 157.

[h] Brucker, iv. 698.

contemplation may very naturally fall. Behmen had his disciples, which such enthusiasts rarely want; and his name is sufficiently known to justify the mention of it even in philosophical history.

21. We come now to an English writer of a different class, little known as such at present, but who, without doing much for the advancement of metaphysical philosophy, had at least the merit of devoting to it with a sincere and independent spirit the leisure of high rank, and of a life not obscure in the world—Lord Herbert of Cherbury. The principal work of this remarkable man is his Latin treatise, published in 1624, ' On Truth as it is distinguished from Revelation, from Probability, from Possibility, and from Falsehood.' Its object is to inquire what are the sure means of discerning and discovering truth. This, as, like other authors, he sets out by proclaiming, had been hitherto done by no one, and he treats both ancient and modern philosophers rather haughtily, as being men tied to particular opinions, from which they dare not depart. ' It is not from an hypocritical or mercenary writer that we are to look for perfect truth. Their interest is not to lay aside their mask, or think for themselves. A liberal and independent author alone will do this.'[1] So general an invective, after Lord Bacon, and indeed after others, like Campanella, who could not be charged with following any conceits rather than their own, bespeaks either ignorance of philosophical literature, or a supercilious neglect of it.

Lord Herbert, De Veritate.

22. Lord Herbert lays down seven primary axioms. 1. Truth exists: 2. It is coeval with the things to which it relates: 3. It exists every where: 4. It is self-evident:[k] 5. There are as many truths, as there are differences in things: 6. These differences are made known to us by our natural faculties: 7. There is a truth belonging to these truths: ' Est veritas quædam harum veritatum.'

His axioms.

---

[1] Non est igitur a larvato aliquo vel stipendioso scriptore ut verum consummatum opperiaris: Illorum apprime interest ne personam deponant, vel aliter quidem sentiant. Ingenuus et sui arbitrii ista solummodo præstabit auctor. Epist. ad Lectorem.

[k] Hæc veritas est in se manifesta. He observes that what are called false appearances are true as such, though not true according to the reality of the object: sua veritas apparentiæ falsæ inest, verè enim ita apparebit, vera tamen ex veritate rei non erit.

This axiom he explains as obscurely as it is strangely expressed. All truth he then distinguishes into the truth of the thing or object, the truth of the appearance, the truth of the perception, and the truth of the understanding. The truth of the object is the inherent conformity of the object with itself, or that which makes every thing what it is.[m] The truth of appearance is the conditional conformity of the appearance with the object. The truth of perception is the conditional conformity of our senses (facultates nostras prodromas) with the appearances of things. The truth of understanding is the due conformity between the aforesaid conformities. All truth therefore is conformity, all conformity relation. Three things are to be observed in every inquiry after truth : the thing or object, the sense or faculty, and the laws or conditions by which its conformity or relation is determined. Lord Herbert is so obscure, partly by not thoroughly grasping his subject, partly by writing in Latin, partly perhaps by the 'sphalmata et errata in typographo, quædam fortasse in seipso,' of which he complains at the end, that it has been necessary to omit several sentences as unintelligible, though what I have just given is far enough from being too clear.

23. Truth, he goes on to say, exists as to the object, or Conditions outward thing itself, when our faculties are capable of truth. of dermining every thing concerning it; but though this definition is exact, it is doubtful, he observes, whether any such truth exists in nature. The first condition of discerning truth in things, is that they should have a relation to ourselves (ut intra nostram stet analogiam); since multitudes of things may exist which the senses cannot discover. The three chief constituents of this condition seem to be : 1. That it should be of a proper size, neither immense, nor too small; 2. That it should have its determining difference, or principle of individuation, to distinguish it from other things ; 3. That it should be accommodated to some sense or perceptive faculty. These are the universally necessary conditions of truth (that is, of knowledge) as it regards the

---

[m] Inhærens illa conformitas rei cum seipsa, sive illa ratio, ex qua res unaquæque sibi constat.

object. The truth of appearance depends on others, which
are more particular; as that the object should be perceived
for a sufficient time, through a proper medium, at a due distance, in a proper situation.[n] Truth of perception is conditional also, and its conditions are that the sense should
be sound, and the attention directed towards it. Truth of
understanding depends on the κοιναι εννοιαι, the common
notions possessed by every man of sane mind, and implanted by nature. The understanding teaches us by means
of these, that infinity and eternity exist, though our senses
cannot perceive them. The understanding deals also with
universals, and truth is known as to universals, when the
particulars are rightly apprehended.

24. Our faculties are as numerous as the differences of
things; and thus it is, that the world corresponds
by perfect analogy to the human soul, degrees of
perception being as much distinct from one another as
different modes of it. All our powers may however be reduced to four heads; natural instinct, internal perception,
external sensation, and reason. What is not known by one
of these four means cannot be known at all. Instinctive
truths are proved by universal consent. Here he comes to
his general basis of religion, maintaining the existence of
κοιναι εννοιαι, or common notions of mankind on that subject,
principles against which no one can dispute, without violating the laws of his nature.[o] Natural instinct he defines to
be an act of those faculties existing in every man of sane
mind, by which the common notions as to the relations of
things not perceived by the senses (rerum internarum), and
especially such as tend to the conservation of the individual,
of the species, and of the whole, are formed without any process of reasoning. These common notions, though excited
in us by the objects of sense, are not conveyed to us by them;
they are implanted in us by nature, so that God seems to
have imparted to us not only a part of his image, but of his

> *Instinctive truths.*

---

[n] Lord Herbert defines appearance,
icetypum, seu forma vicaria rei, quæ sub
conditionibus istis cum prototypo suo
conformata, cum conceptu denuo sub
conditionibus etiam suis, conformari et
modo quodam spirituali, tanquam ab
objecto decisa, etiam in objecti absentia
conservari potest.

[o] Principia illa sacrosancta, contra
quæ disputare nefas. p. 44. I have translated this in the best sense I could give
it; but to use *fas* or *nefas*, before we
have defined their meaning, or proved
their existence, is but indifferent logic.

wisdom.[p] And whatever is understood and perceived by all men alike deserves to be accounted one of these notions. Some of them are instinctive, others are deduced from such as are. The former are distinguishable by six marks; priority, independence, universality, certainty, so that no man can doubt them without putting off, as it were, his nature, necessity, that is, usefulness for the preservation of man, lastly, intuitive apprehension, for these common notions do not require to be inferred.[q]

25. Internal perceptions denote the conformity of objects Internal perceptions. with those faculties existing in every man of sane mind, which being developed by his natural instinct, are conversant with the internal relations of things, in a secondary and particular manner, and by means of natural instinct.[r] By this ill-worded definition he probably intends to distinguish the general power, or instinctive knowledge, from its exercise and application in any instance. But I have found it very difficult to follow Lord Herbert. It is by means, he says, of these internal senses that we discern the nature of things in their intrinsic relations, or hidden types of being.[s] And it is necessary well to distinguish the conforming faculty in the mind or internal perception, from the bodily sense. The cloudiness of his expression increases as we proceed, and in many pages I cannot venture to translate or abridge it. The injudicious use of a language in which he did not write with facility, and which is not very well adapted, at the best, to metaphysical disquisition, has doubtless increased the perplexity, into which he has thrown his readers.

26. In the conclusion of this treatise, Herbert lays down Five notions of natural religion. the five common notions of natural religion, implanted, as he conceives, in the breasts of all mankind. 1. That there is a God; 2. That he ought to be worshipped; 3. That virtue and piety are the chief parts of worship; 4. That we are to repent and turn from our sins;

---

[p] P. 48.
[q] P. 60.
[r] Sensus interni sunt actus conformitatum objectorum cum facultatibus illis in omni homine sano et integro existentibus, quæ ab instinctu naturali expo-

sitæ, circa analogiam rerum internam, particulariter, secondario, et ratione instinctûs naturalis versantur. p. 66.

[s] Circa analogiam rerum internam, sive signaturas et characteras rerum penitiores versantur. p. 68.

5. That there are rewards and punishments in another life.[t] Nothing can be admitted in religion which contradicts these primary notions; but if any one has a revelation from heaven in addition to these, which may happen to him sleeping or waking, he should keep it to himself, since nothing can be of importance to the human race which is not established by the evidence of their common faculties. Nor can anything be known to be revealed, which is not revealed to ourselves; or else being tradition and historic testimony, which does not amount to knowledge. The specific difference of man from other animals he makes not reason, but the capacity of religion. It is a curious coincidence that John Wesley has said something of the same kind.[t] It is also remarkable that we find in another work of Lord Herbert, De Religione Gentilium, which dwells again on his five articles of natural religion, essential, as he expressly lays it down, to salvation, the same illustration of the being of a Deity from the analogy of a watch or clock, which Paley has since employed. I believe that it occurs in an intermediate writer.[u]

27. Lord Herbert sent a copy of his treatise De Veritate several years after its publication to Gassendi. We have a letter to the noble author in the third volume of the works of that philosopher, showing, in the candid and sincere spirit natural to him, the objections that struck his

Remarks of Gassendi on Herbert.

---

[t] P. 222.

[t] I have somewhere read a profound remark of Wesley, that, considering the sagacity which many animals display, we cannot fix upon reason as the distinction between them and man; the true difference is, that we are formed to know God, and they are not.

[u] Et quidem si horologium per diem et noctem integram horas signanter indicans, viderit quispiam non mente captus, id consilio arteque summâ factum judicaverit. Ecquis non planè demens, qui hanc mundi machinam non per viginti quatuor horas tantum, sed per tot sæcula circuitus suos obeuntem animadverterit, non id omne sapientissimo utique potentissimoque alicui autori tribuat? De Relig. Gentil. cap. xiii. [The original idea, as has been rightly pointed out to me by M. Alphonse

Borghers, the translator of this work, as well as of my History of the Middle Ages, is in Cicero de Nat. Deorum, ii. 34. Quod si in Scythiam aut in Britanniam, sphæram aliquis tulerit hanc, quam nuper familiaris noster effecit Posidonius, cujus singulæ conversiones idem efficiunt in sole, et in lunâ, et in quinque stellis errantibus, quod efficitur in cœlo singulis diebus et noctibus: quis in illa barbarie dubitet, quin ea sphæra sit perfecta ratione? And with respect to intermediate writers between Lord Herbert and Paley, I have been referred, by two other correspondents, to Hale's Primitive Origination of Mankind, where I had myself suspected it to be, and to Nieuwentyt's Religious Philosopher (English translation, 1730), p. xlvi. of preface.—1842.]

mind in reading the book.[x]   Gassendi observes that the distinctions of four kinds of truth are not new; the veritas rei
of Lord Herbert being what is usually called substance, his
veritas apparentiæ no more than accident, and the other two
being only sense and reason.   Gassendi seems not wholly to
approve, but gives as the best, a definition of truth little differing from Herbert's, the agreement of the cognisant intellect with the thing known: 'Intellectûs cognoscentis cum
re cognita congruentia.'   The obscurity of the treatise De
Veritate could ill suit an understanding like that of Gassendi,
always tending to acquire clear conceptions; and though he
writes with great civility, it is not without smartly opposing
what he does not approve.   The aim of Lord Herbert's work,
he says, is that the intellect may pierce into the nature of
things, knowing them as they are in themselves, without the
fallacies of appearance and sense.   But for himself he confesses that such knowledge he has always found above him,
and that he is in darkness when he attempts to investigate
the real nature of the least thing; making many of the observations on this which we read also in Locke.   And he
well says that we have enough for our use in the accidents
or appearances of things without knowing their substances,
in reply to Herbert, who had declared that we should be
miserably deficient, if, while nature has given us senses to
discern sounds and colours and such fleeting qualities of
things, we had no sure road to internal, eternal, and necessary
truths.[y]   The universality of those innate principles, especially
moral and religious, on which his correspondent had built.
so much, is doubted by Gassendi on the usual grounds, that
many have denied, or been ignorant of them.   The letter is
imperfect, some sheets of the autograph having been lost.

28. Too much space may seem to have been bestowed on
a writer who cannot be ranked high among metaphysicians.
But Lord Herbert was not only a distinguished name, but
may claim the priority among those philosophers in England. If his treatise De Veritate is not as an entire work

---

[x] Gassendi Opera, iii. 411.

[y] Misere nobiscum actum esset, si ad
percipiendos colores, sonos et qualitates
cæteras caducas atque momentaneas sub-
essent media, nulla autem ad veritates
illas internas, æternas, necessarias sine
errore superesset via.

very successful, or founded always upon principles which have stood the test of severe reflection, it is still a monument of an original independent thinker, without rhapsodies of imagination, without pedantic technicalities, and, above all, bearing witness to a sincere love of the truth he sought to apprehend. The ambitious expectation that the real essences of things might be discovered, if it were truly his, as Gassendi seems to suppose, could not be warranted by any thing, at least, within the knowledge of that age. But from some expressions of Herbert I should infer that he did not think our faculties competent to solve the whole problem of *quiddity*, as the logicians called it, or the real nature of any thing, at least, objectively without us.[z] He is, indeed, so obscure, that I will not vouch for his entire consistency. It has been an additional motive to say as much as I have done concerning Lord Herbert, that I know not where any account of his treatise De Veritate will be found. Brucker is strangely silent about this writer, and Buhle has merely adverted to the letter of Gassendi. Descartes has spoken of Lord Herbert's book with much respect, though several of their leading principles were far from the same. It was translated into French in 1639, and this translation he found less difficult than the original.[a]

29. Gassendi himself ought, perhaps, to be counted wholly among the philosophers of this period, since many of his writings were published, and all may have been completed within it. They are contained in six large folio volumes, rather closely printed. The Exercitationes Paradoxicæ, published in 1624, are the earliest. These contain an attack on the logic of Aristotle, the fortress that so many

Gassendi's defence of Epicurus.

---

[z] Cum facultates nostræ ad analogiam propriam terminatæ quidditates rerum intimas non penetrent: ideo quid res naturalis in seipsa sit, tali ex analogia ad nos ut sit constituta, perfecte sciri non potest. p. 165. In another place he says, it is doubtful whether any thing exist in nature, concerning which we have a complete knowledge. The eternal and necessary truths which Herbert contends for our knowing, seem to have been his communes notitiæ, subjectively understood, rather than such as relate to external objects.

[a] Descartes, vol. viii. p. 138 and 168. J'y trouve plusieurs choses fort bonnes, *sed non publici saporis*; car il y a peu de personnes qui soient capables d'entendre la métaphysique. Et, pour le général du livre, il tient un chemin fort différent de celui que j'ai suivi. . . . Enfin, par conclusion, encore que je ne puisse m'accorder en tout aux sentimens de cet auteur, je ne laisse pas de l'estimer beaucoup au-dessus des esprits ordinaires.

bold spirits were eager to assail. But in more advanced life Gassendi withdrew in great measure from this warfare, and his Logic, in the Syntagma Philosophicum, the record of his latest opinions, is chiefly modelled on the Aristotelian, with sufficient commendation of its author. In the study of ancient philosophy, however, Gassendi was impressed with an admiration of Epicurus. His physical theory, founded on corpuscles and a vacuum, his ethics, in their principle and precepts, his rules of logic and guidance of the intellect, seemed to the cool and independent mind of the French philosopher more worthy of regard than the opposite schemes prevailing in the schools, and not to be rejected on account of any discredit attached to the name. Combining with the Epicurean physics and ethics the religious element which had been unnecessarily discarded from the philosophy of the Garden, Gassendi displayed both in a form no longer obnoxious. The Syntagma Philosophiæ Epicuri, published in 1649, is an elaborate vindication of this system, which he had previously expounded in a commentary on the tenth book of Diogenes Laertius. He had already effaced the prejudices against Epicurus himself, whom he seems to have regarded with the affection of a disciple, in a biographical treatise on his life and moral character.

30. Gassendi died in 1656 ; the Syntagma Philosophicum, His chief works after 1650. his greatest as well as last work, in which it is natural to seek the whole scheme of his philosophy, was published by his friend Sorbière in 1658. We may therefore properly defer the consideration of his metaphysical writings to the next period ; but the controversy in which he was involved with Descartes will render it necessary to bring his name forward again before the close of this chapter.

Sect. II.

On the Philosophy of Lord Bacon.

31. It may be judged from what has been said in a former Preparation for the philosophy of chapter, as well as in our last pages, that at the beginning of the seventeenth century, the higher philosophy, which is concerned with general truth, and the

means of knowing it, had been little benefited by the labours of any modern inquirer. It was become, indeed, no strange thing, at least out of the air of a college, to question the authority of Aristotle; but his disciples pointed with scorn at the endeavours which had as yet been made to supplant it, and asked whether the wisdom so long reverenced was to be set aside for the fanatical reveries of Paracelsus, the unintelligible chimæras of Bruno, or the more plausible, but arbitrary, hypotheses of Telesio.

32. Francis Bacon was born in 1561.[b] He came to years of manhood at the time when England was rapidly emerging from ignorance and obsolete methods of study, in an age of powerful minds, full himself of ambition, confidence, and energy. If we think on the public history of Bacon, even during the least public portion of it, philosophy must appear to have been but his amusement; it was by his hours of leisure, by time hardly missed from the laborious study and practice of the law and from the assiduities of a courtier's life, that he became the father of modern science. This union of an active with a reflecting life had been the boast of some ancients, of Cicero and Antonine; but what comparison, in depth and originality, between their philosophy and that of Bacon. Lord Bacon.

33. This wonderful man, in sweeping round the champaign of universal science with his powerful genius, found as little to praise in the recent, as in the ancient methods of investigating truth. He liked as little the empirical presumption of drawing conclusions from a partial experience as the sophistical dogmatism which relied on unwarranted axioms and verbal chicane. All, he thought, was to be constructed anew; the investigation of facts, their arrangement for the purposes of inquiry, the process of eliciting from them the required truth. And for this he saw, that, above all, a thorough purgation of the mind itself would be necessary, by pointing out its familiar errors, their sources, and their remedies. His plan of philosophy.

---

[b] Those who place Lord Bacon's birth in 1560, as Mr. Montagu has done, must be understood to follow the old style, which creates some confusion. He was born the 22nd of January, and died the 9th of April, 1626, in the sixty-sixth year of his age, as we are told in his life by Rawley, the best authority we have.

34. It is not exactly known at what age Bacon first conceived the scheme of a comprehensive philosophy,
but it was, by his own account, very early in life.[c]
Such noble ideas are most congenial to the sanguine spirit of
youth, and to its ignorance of the extent of labour it undertakes. In the dedication of the Novum Organum to James
in 1620, he says that he had been about some such work near
thirty years, 'so as I made no haste.' 'And the reason,' he
adds, 'why I have published it now, specially being imperfect, is, to speak plainly, because I number my days, and

Time of its conception.

---

[c] In a letter to Father Fulgentio, which bears no date in print, but must have been written about 1624, he refers to a juvenile work about forty years before, which he had confidently entitled The Greatest Birth of Time. Bacon says: Equidem memini me quadraginta abhinc annis juvenile opusculum circa has res confecisse, quod magna prorsus fiducia et magnifico titulo, 'Temporis Partum maximum' inscripsi. The apparent vain-glory of this title is somewhat extenuated by the sense he gave to the phrase, Birth of Time. He meant that the lapse of time and long experience were the natural sources of a better philosophy, as he says in his dedication of the Instauratio Magna : Ipse certè, ut ingenue fateor, soleo æstimare hoc opus magis pro partu temporis quam ingenii. Illud enim in eo solummodo mirabile est, initia rei, et tantas de iis quæ invaluerunt suspiciones, alicui in mentem venire potuisse. Cætera non illibenter sequuntur.

No treatise with this precise title appears. But we find prefixed to some of the short pieces a general title, Temporis Partus *Masculus*, sive Instauratio Magna Imperii Universi in Humanum. These treatises, however, though earlier than his great works, cannot be referred to so juvenile a period as his letter to Fulgentio intimates, and I should rather incline to suspect that the *opusculum* to which he there refers has not been preserved. Mr. Montagu is of a different opinion. See his Note I. to the Life of Bacon in vol. xvi. of his edition. The Latin tract De Interpretatione Naturæ Mr. M. supposes to be the germ of the Instauratio, as the Cogitata et Visa are of the Novum Organum. I do not

dissent from this ; but the former bears marks of having been written after Bacon had been immersed in active life. The most probable conjecture appears to be that he very early perceived the meagreness and imperfection of the academical course of philosophy, and of all others which fell in his way, and formed the scheme of affording something better from his own resources ; but that he did not commit *much* to paper, nor had planned his own method till after he was turned of thirty, which his letter to the king intimates.

In a recent and very brilliant sketch of the Baconian philosophy (Edinb. Review, July, 1837), the two leading principles that distinguish it throughout all its parts are justly denominated *utility* and *progress*. To do good to mankind, and do more and more good, are the ethics of its inductive method. We may only regret that the ingenious author of this article has been hurried sometimes into the low and contracted view of the deceitful word *utility*, which regards rather the enjoyments of physical convenience than the general well-being of the individual and the species. If Bacon looked more frequently to the former, it was because so large a portion of his writings relates to physical observation and experiment. But it was far enough from his design to set up physics in any sort of opposition to ethics, much less in a superior light. I dissent also from some of the observations in this article, lively as they are, which tend to depreciate the originality and importance of the Baconian methods. The reader may turn to a note on this subject by Dugald Stewart, at the end of the present section.

would have it saved. There is another reason of my so
doing, which is to try whether I can get help in one intended
part of this work, namely, the compiling of a natural and
experimental history, which must be the main foundation of
a true and active philosophy.' He may be presumed at least
to have made a very considerable progress in his undertaking
before the close of the sixteenth century. But it was first
promulgated to the world by the publication of his Treatise
on the Advancement of Learning in 1605. In this, indeed,
the whole of the Baconian philosophy may be said to be im-
plicitly contained, except perhaps the second book of the
Novum Organum. In 1623, he published his more celebrated Latin translation of this work, if it is not rather to be
deemed a new one, entitled De Augmentis Scientiarum. I
find, upon comparison, that more than two-thirds of this
treatise are a version, with slight interpolation or omission,
from the Advancement of Learning, the remainder being new
matter.

35. The Instauratio Magna had been already published
in 1620, while Lord Bacon was still chancellor. Instauratio
Fifteen years had elapsed since he gave to the Magna.
world his Advancement of Learning, the first fruits of such
astonishing vigour of philosophical genius, that, inconceivable as the completion of the scheme he had even then laid
down in prospect for his new philosophy by any single
effort must appear, we may be disappointed at the great deficiencies which this latter work exhibits, and which he was
not destined to fill up. But he had passed the interval in
active life, and in dangerous paths, deserting, as in truth
he had all along been prone enough to do, the 'shady spaces
of philosophy,' as Milton calls them, for the court of a
sovereign, who, with some real learning, was totally incapable of sounding the depths of Lord Bacon's mind, or even of
estimating his genius.

36. The Instauratio Magna, dedicated to James, is divided,
according to the magnificent ground-plot of its First part:
author, into six parts. The first of these he en- Partitiones
titles Partitiones Scientiarum, comprehending a Scientiarum.
general summary of that knowledge which mankind already
possess ; yet not merely treating this affirmatively, but

taking special notice of whatever should seem deficient or imperfect; sometimes even supplying, by illustration or precept, these vacant spaces of science. This first part he declares to be wanting in the Instauratio. It has been chiefly supplied by the treatise De Augmentis Scientiarum; yet perhaps even that does not fully come up to the amplitude of his design.

37. The second part of the Instauratio was to be, as he

Second part : Novum Organum. expresses it, 'the science of a better and more perfect use of reason in the investigation of things, and of the true aids of the understanding;' the new logic, or inductive method, in which what is eminently styled the Baconian philosophy consists. This, as far as he completed it, is known to all by the name of the Novum Organum. But he seems to have designed a fuller treatise in place of this; the aphorisms into which he has digested it being rather the heads or theses of chapters, at least in many places, that would have been farther expanded.[d] And it is still more important to observe, that he did not achieve the whole of this summary that he had promised; but out of nine divisions of his method we only possess the first, which he denominates 'prærogativæ instantiarum.' Eight others, of exceeding importance to his logic, he has not touched at all, except to describe them by name and to promise more. 'We will speak,' he says, in the first place, of prerogative instances; secondly, of the aids of induction; thirdly, of the rectification of induction; fourthly, of varying the investigation according to the nature of the subject; fifthly, of prerogative natures (or objects), as to investigation, or the choice of what shall be first inquired into; sixthly, of the boundaries of inquiry, or the synoptical view of all natures in the world; seventhly, on the application of inquiry to practice, and what relates to man; eighthly, on the preparations (parascevæ) for inquiry; lastly, on the ascending and descending scale of axioms.'[e]

---

[d] It is entitled by himself, Partis secundæ Summa, digesta in aphorismos.

[e] Dicemus itaque primo loco de prærogativis instantiarum; secundo, de adminiculis inductionis; tertio, de rectificatione inductionis; quarto, de variatione inquisitionis pro natura subjecti; quinto, de prærogativis naturarum quatenus ad inquisitionem, sive de eo quod inquirendum est prius et posterius; sexto, de terminis inquisitionis, sive de synopsi omnium naturarum in universo; septimo, de deductione ad praxin, sive de eo quod est in ordine ad hominem;

All these, after the first, are wanting, with the exception of a few slightly handled in separate parts of Bacon's writings; and the deficiency, which is so important, seems to have been sometimes overlooked by those who have written about the Novum Organum.

38. The third part of the Instauratio Magna was to comprise an entire natural history, diligently and scru- Third part: pulously collected from experience of every kind; Natural History. including under that name of natural history everything wherein the art of man has been employed on natural substances either for practice or experiment; no method of reasoning being sufficient to guide us to truth as to natural things, if they are not themselves clearly and exactly apprehended. It is unnecessary to observe that very little of this immense chart of nature could be traced by the hand of Bacon, or in his time. His Centuries of Natural History, containing about one thousand observed facts and experiments, are a very slender contribution towards such a description of universal nature, as he contemplated: these form no part of the Instauratio Magna, and had been compiled before. But he enumerates one hundred and thirty particular histories which ought to be drawn up for his great work. A few of these he has given in a sort of skeleton, as samples rather of the method of collecting facts, than of the facts themselves; namely, the History of Winds, of Life and Death, of Density and Rarity, of Sound and Hearing.

39. The fourth part, called Scala Intellectûs, is also wanting, with the exception of a very few intro- Fourth ductory pages. ' By these tables,' says Bacon, ' we part: Scala Intellectûs. mean not such examples as we subjoin to the several rules of our method, but types and models, which place before our eyes the entire process of the mind in the discovery of truth, selecting various and remarkable instances.'[f]   These he

---

octavo, de parascevis ad inquisitionem; postremo autem, de scala ascensoria et descensoria axiomatum. lib. ii. 22.

[f] Neque de iis exemplis loquimur, quæ singulis præceptis ac regulis illustrandi gratia adjiciuntur, hoc enim in secunda operis parte abunde præstitimus,

sed plane typos intelligimus ac plasmata, quæ universum mentis processum atque inveniendi continuatam fabricam et ordinem in certis subjectis, iisque variis et insignibus tanquam sub oculos ponant. Etenim nobis venit in mentem in mathematicis, astante machina, sequi demon-

compares to the diagrams of geometry, by attending to
which the steps of the demonstration become perspicuous.
Though the great brevity of his language in this place
renders it rather difficult to see clearly what he understood
by these models, some light appears to be thrown on this
passage by one in the treatise De Augmentis, where he
enumerates among the desiderata of logic what he calls
' traditio lampadis,' or a delivery of any science or particular
truth according to the order wherein it was discovered.[g]
'The methods of geometers,' he there says, 'have some
resemblance to this art;' which is not, however, the case as
to the synthetical geometry with which we are generally
conversant. It is the history of analytical investigation, and
many beautiful illustrations of it have been given since the
days of Bacon in all subjects to which that method of inquiry
has been applied.

40. In a fifth part of the Instauratio Magna Bacon had
Fifth part :
Anticipa-
tiones Phi-
losophiæ. designed to give a specimen of the new philosophy
which he hoped to raise, after a due use of his
natural history and inductive method, by way of
anticipation or sample of the whole. He calls it Prodromi,
sive Anticipationes Philosophiæ Secundæ. And some fragments of this part are published by the names Cogitata et
Visa, Cogitationes de Natura Rerum, Filum Labyrinthi, and
a few more, being as much, in all probability, as he had
reduced to writing. In his own metaphor, it was to be like
the payment of interest till the principal could be raised;
tanquam fœnus reddatur, donec sors haberi possit. For he
Sixth part :
Philosophiæ
Secunda. despaired of ever completing the work by a sixth
and last portion, which was to display a perfect
system of philosophy, deduced and confirmed by a legitimate,

---

strationem facilem et perspicuam; contra
absque hac commoditate omnia videri
involuta et quam revera sunt subtiliora.
    [g] Lib. vi. c. 2. Scientia quæ aliis tan-
quam tela pertexendo traditur, eadem
methodo, si fieri possit, animo alterius
est insinuanda, qua primitus inventa est.
Atque hoc ipsum fieri sane potest in
scientia per inductionem acquisita : sed
in anticipata ista et præmatura scientia,
qua utimur, non facile dicat quis quo
itinere ad eam quam nactus est scientiam

pervenerit. Attamen sane secundum
majus et minus possit quis scientiam
propriam revisere, et vestigia suæ cogni-
tionis simul et consensûs remetiri; atque
hoc facto scientiam sic transplantare in
animum alienum, sicut crevit in suo.
. . . . Cujus quidem generis traditionis,
methodus mathematicorum in eo subjecto similitudinem quandam habet. I
do not well understand the words, in eo
subjecto; he may possibly have referred
to analytical processes.

sober, and exact inquiry according to the method which
he had invented and laid down. ' To perfect this last part
is above our powers and beyond our hopes. We may, as we
trust, make no despicable beginnings, the destinies of the
human race must complete it; in such a manner, perhaps,
as men, looking only at the present, would not readily conceive.   For upon this will depend not only a speculative
good, but all the fortunes of mankind, and all their power.'
And with an eloquent prayer that his exertions may be
rendered effectual to the attainment of truth and happiness,
this introductory chapter of the Instauratio, which announces
the distribution of its portions, concludes.   Such was the
temple, of which Bacon saw in vision before him the stately
front and decorated pediments, in all their breadth of light
and harmony of proportion, while long vistas of receding
columns and glimpses of internal splendour revealed a glory
that it was not permitted him to comprehend.   In the
treatise De Augmentis Scientiarum, and in the Novum Organum, we have less, no doubt, than Lord Bacon, under
different conditions of life, might have achieved; he might
have been more emphatically the high-priest of nature, if
he had not been the chancellor of James I.; but no one man
could have filled up the vast outline which he alone, in that
stage of the world, could have so boldly sketched.

41. The best order of studying the Baconian philosophy
would be to read attentively the Advancement of Course of
Learning; next, to take the treatise De Augmen- Lord Bacon.
tis, comparing it all along with the former, and afterwards to proceed to the Novum Organum.   A less degree
of regard has usually been paid to the Centuries of Natural
History, which are the least important of his writings, or
even to the other philosophical fragments, some of which
contain very excellent passages; yet such, in great measure,
as will be found substantially in other parts of his works.
The most remarkable are the Cogitata et Visa.   It must be
said, that one who thoroughly venerates Lord Bacon will
not disdain his repetitions, which sometimes, by variations
of phrase, throw light upon each other.   It is generally
supposed that the Latin works were translated from the
original English by several assistants, among whom George

Herbert and Hobbes have been named, under the author's
superintendence.[h]   The Latin style of these writings is singularly concise, energetic, and impressive, but frequently
crabbed, uncouth, and obscure; so that we read with more
admiration of the sense than delight in the manner of delivering it.   But Rawley, in his Life of Bacon, informs us
that he had seen about twelve autographs of the Novum
Organum, wrought up and improved year by year, till it
reached the shape in which it was published, and he does
not intimate that these were in English, unless the praise
he immediately afterwards bestows on his English style may
be thought to warrant that supposition.[i]   I do not know that
we have positive evidence as to any of the Latin works
being translations from English, except the treatise De
Augmentis.

42. The leading principles of the Baconian philosophy
are contained in the Advancement of Learning.   These
are amplified, corrected, illustrated, and developed in the
treatise De Augmentis Scientiarum, from the fifth book of
which, with some help from other parts, is taken the first
book of the Novum Organum, and even a part of the second.
I use this language, because, though earlier in publication,
I conceive that the Novum Organum was later in composition.   All that very important part of this fifth book which
relates to Experientia Litterata, or Venatio Panis, as he
calls it, and contains excellent rules for conducting experiments in natural philosophy, is new, and does not appear in
the Advancement of Learning, except by way of promise of
what should be done in it.   Nor is this, at least so fully and
clearly, to be found in the Novum Organum.   The second

---

[h] The translation was made, as Archbishop Tenison informs us, 'by Mr.
Herbert and some others, who were
esteemed masters in the Roman eloquence.'

[i] Ipse reperi in archivis dominationis
suæ, autographa plus minus duodecim
Organi Novi de anno in annum elaborati,
et ad incudem revocati, et singulis annis,
ulteriore lima subinde politi et castigati,
donec in illud tandem corpus adoleverat,
quo in lucem editum fuit; sicut multa ex
animalibus fœtus lambere consuescunt
usque quo ad membrorum firmitudinem

eos perducant.   In libris suis compo-
nendis verborum vigorem et perspicui-
tatem præcipuè sectabatur, non elegan-
tiam aut concinnitatem sermonis, et inter
scribendum aut dictandum sæpe interro-
gavit, num sensus ejus clare admodum
et perspicuè redditus esset?   Quippe qui
sciret æquum esse ut verba famularentur
rebus, non res verbis.   Et si in stylum
forsitan politiorem incidisset, siquidem
apud nostrates eloquii Anglicani artifex
habitus est, id evenit, quia evitare ar-
duum ei erat.

book of this latter treatise he professes not to anticipate. De Novo Organo silemus, he says, neque de eo quicquam prælibamus. This can only apply to the second book, which he considered as the real exposition of his method, after clearing away the fallacies which form the chief subject of the first. Yet what is said of Topica particularis, in this fifth book De Augmentis (illustrated by 'articles of inquiry concerning gravity and levity'), goes entirely on the principles of the second book of the Novum Organum.

43. Let us now see what Lord Bacon's method really was. He has given it the name of induction, but carefully distinguishes it from what bore that name in the old logic, that is, an inference from a perfect enumeration of particulars to a general law of the whole. For such an enumeration, though of course conclusive, is rarely practicable in nature, where the particulars exceed our powers of numbering.[k] Nor, again, is the Baconian method

Nature of the Baconian induction.

---

[k] Inductio quæ procedit per enumerationem simplicem, res puerilis est, et precario concludit, et periculo exponitur ab instantia contradictoria, et plerumque secundum pauciora quam par est, et ex his tantummodo quæ præsto sunt pronuntiat. At inductio quæ ad iuventionem et demonstrationem scientiarum et artium erit utilis, naturam separare debet, per rejectiones et exclusiones debitas; ac deinde post negativas tot quot sufficiunt, super affirmativas concludere; quod adhuc factum non est, nec tentatum certe, nisi tantummodo a Platone, qui ad excutiendas definitiones et ideas, hac certe forma inductionis aliquatenus utitur. Nov. Org. i. 105. In this passage Bacon seems to imply that the enumeration of particulars in any induction is or may be imperfect. This is certainly the case in the plurality of physical inductions; but it does not appear that the logical writers looked upon this as the primary and legitimate sense. Induction was distinguished into the complete and incomplete. 'The word,' says a very modern writer, 'is perhaps unhappy, as indeed it is taken in several vague senses; but to abolish it is impossible. It is the Latin translation of ἐπαγωγή, which word is used by Aristotle as a counterpart to συλλογισμὸς. He seems to consider it in a perfect or dialectic, and in an imperfect or rhetori-

cal sense. Thus if a genus (G.) contained four species (A. B. C. D.), syllogism would argue, that what is true of G. is true of any one of the four; but perfect induction would reason, that what we can prove true of A. B. C. D. separately, we may properly state as true of G., the whole genus. This is evidently a formal argument, as demonstrative as syllogism. But the imperfect or rhetorical induction will perhaps enumerate three only of the species, and then draw the conclusion concerning G., which virtually includes the fourth, or, what is the same thing, will argue, that what is true of the three is to be believed true likewise of the fourth.' Newman's Lectures on Logic, p. 73 (1837.) The same distinction between perfect and imperfect induction is made in the Encyclopédie françoise, art. Induction, and apparently on the authority of the ancients.

It may be observed that this imperfect induction may be put in a regular logical form, and is only vicious in syllogistic reasoning when the conclusion asserts a higher probability than the premises. If, for example, we reason thus: Some serpents are venomous.— This unknown animal is a serpent.— Therefore this is venomous; we are guilty of an obvious paralogism. If we infer only, This may be venomous, our

to be confounded with the less complete form of the inductive process, namely, inferences from partial experience in

reasoning is perfectly valid in itself at
least in the common apprehension of
all mankind, except dialecticians, but
not regular in form. The only means
that I perceive of making it so, is to put
it in some such phrase as the following :
All unknown serpents are affected by a
certain probability of being venomous :
This animal, &c. It is not necessary,
of course, that the probability should be
capable of being estimated, provided we
mentally conceive it to be no other in
the conclusion than in the major term.
In the best treatises on the strict or
syllogistic method, as far as I have seen,
there seems a deficiency in respect to
probable conclusions, which may have
arisen from the practice of taking instances from universal or necessary,
rather than contingent truths, as well as
from the contracted views of reasoning
which the Aristotelian school have always inculcated. No sophisms are so
frequent in practice as the concluding
generally from a partial induction, or
assuming (most commonly tacitly) by
what Archbishop Whately calls 'a kind
of logical fiction,' that a few individuals
are 'adequate samples or representations of the class they belong to.'
These sophisms cannot, in the present
state of things, be practised largely in
physical science or natural history ; but
in reasonings on matter of fact they are
of incessant occurrence. The 'logical
fiction' may indeed frequently be employed, even on subjects unconnected
with the physical laws of nature ; but to
know when this may be, and to what
extent, is just that which, far more
than any other skill, distinguishes what
is called a good reasoner from a bad
one.

[I permit this note to remain as in
former editions ; but it might have been
more fully and more correctly expressed.
The proper nature of induction has been
treated within a few years by Sir William
Hamilton (Edinburgh Review, vol. lvii.),
by Archbishop Whately in his Elements
of Logic, by the author of the article
'Organon' in the Penny Cyclopædia,
by M. de Rémusat, Essais de Philosophie, vol. ii. p. 408, by Dr. Whewell
in the 'History,' and again in the
'Philosophy of the Inductive Sciences,'
and by Mr. Mill, System of Logic, vol. i.

p. 352. The apparently various opinions
of these writers, though in some degree
resolving themselves into differences of
definition, deserve attention from the
philosophical reader ; but it would be
rather too extraneous from the character
of the present work to examine them.
I will only observe, that what has been
called perfect induction, or a complete
enumeration of particulars, is as barren
of new truth as the syllogism itself, to
which indeed, though with some variety
in the formal rules, it properly belongs.
For if we have already enumerated all
species of fish, and asserted them to be
cold-blooded, we advance not a step by
saying this again of a herring or a had-
dock. Mr. Mill, therefore, has well remarked, that 'Induction is a process of
inference ; it proceeds from the known
to the unknown ; and any operation
involving no inference, any process in
which what seems the conclusion is no
wider than the premises from which it is
drawn, does not fall within the meaning
of the term.'—System of Logic, vol. i.
p. 352. But this inference is only rendered logically conclusive, or satisfactory
to the reason, as anything more than a
probable argument, by means of a generalisation, which assumes, on some extra-
logical ground, such as the uniformity of
physical laws, that the partial induction
might have been rendered universal. If
the conclusion contains more than the
premises *imply*, it is manifestly fallacious.
But that the inductive syllogism, ὁ ἐξ
ἐπαγωγῆς συλλογισμὸς (Analyt. Prin. l. ii.
c. 23), can only lead, in *form*, to probable conclusions, even though the enumeration should be complete, appears
from its being in the third figure, though
after a general principle is once established by induction, when we come to
apply it in new cases, the process will
be in the first. Archbishop Whately
and Sir W. Hamilton only differ in appearance as to this, since they look to
different periods of reasoning ; one in
which experience is generalised by the
assumption of something unproved ; another, in which a particular case is
shown to fall within the generalisation.
But the second is not the induction of
Aristotle. What this was I find nowhere more neatly delivered than in an
Arabic treatise on logic, published, with

similar circumstances; though this may be a very sufficient ground for practical, which is probable, knowledge. His own method rests on the same general principle, namely, the uniformity of the laws of nature, so that in certain conditions of phænomena the same effects or the same causes may be assumed; but it endeavours to establish these laws on a more exact and finer process of reasoning than partial experience can effect. For the recurrence of antecedents and consequents does not prove a necessary connexion between them, unless we can exclude the presence of all other conditions which may determine the event. Long and continued experience of such a recurrence, indeed, raises a high probability of a necessary connexion; but the aim of Bacon was to supersede experience in this sense, and to find a shorter road to the result; and for this his methods of exclusion are devised. As complete and accurate a collection of facts, connected with the subject of inquiry, as possible, is to be made out by means of that copious natural history which he contemplated, or from any other good sources. These are to be selected, compared, and scrutinised, according to the rules of natural interpretation delivered in the second book of the Novum Organum, or such others as he designed to add to them; and if experiments are admissible, these are to be conducted according to the same rules. Experience and observation are the guides through the Baconian philosophy, which is the handmaid and interpreter of nature. When Lord Bacon seems to decry experience, which in certain passages he might be thought to do, it is the particular and empirical observation

---

a translation, in the eighth volume of the Asiatic Researches.

'Induction is the process of collecting particulars for the purpose of establishing a general rule respecting the nature of the whole class. Induction is of two kinds, viz. perfect and imperfect. It is perfect induction when the general rule is obtained from an examination of all the parts. For example, all animals are either endowed with speech, or not endowed with speech. But those endowed and those not endowed are both sentient; therefore all animals are sentient. This is an example of perfect induction, which produces certainty.

'It is imperfect induction when a number of individuals of a class being overlooked or excluded, a general rule is thus established respecting the whole. For instance, if it should be assumed that all animals move the under-jaw in eating, because this is the case with man, horses, goats, and sheep, this would be an example of imperfect induction, which does not afford certainty, because it is possible that some animals may not move the under-jaw in eating, as it is reported of the crocodile.' p. 127.—1847.]

of individuals, from which many rash generalisations had
been drawn, as opposed to that founded on an accurate
natural history.   Such hasty inferences he reckoned still
more pernicious to true knowledge than the sophistical
methods of the current philosophy; and in a remarkable
passage, after censuring this precipitancy of empirical conclusions in the chemists, and in Gilbert's Treatise on the
Magnet, utters a prediction that if ever mankind, excited
by his counsels, should seriously betake themselves to seek
the guidance of experience, instead of relying on the dogmatic schools of the sophists, the proneness of the human
mind to snatch at general axioms would expose them to
much risk of error from the theories of this superficial class
of philosophers.[1]

44. The indignation, however, of Lord Bacon is more frequently directed against the predominant philoso-
His dislike of Aristotle. phy of his age, that of Aristotle and the schoolmen.
Though he does justice to the great abilities of the former,
and acknowledges the exact attention to facts displayed in
his History of Animals, he deems him one of the most
eminent adversaries to the only method that can guide us
to the real laws of nature.   The old Greek philosophers,
Empedocles, Leucippus, Anaxagoras, and others of their
age, who had been in the right track of investigation,
stood much higher in the esteem of Bacon than their successors, Plato, Zeno, Aristotle, by whose lustre they had
been so much superseded, that both their works have perished, and their tenets are with difficulty collected.   These
more distinguished leaders of the Grecian schools were in
his eyes little else than disputatious professors (it must be
remembered that he had in general only physical science in
his view) who seemed to have it in common with children,
'ut ad garriendum prompti sint, generare non possint;' so
wordy and barren was their mis-called wisdom.

45. Those who object to the importance of Lord Bacon's
precepts in philosophy that mankind have practised
His method much re- many of them immemorially, are rather confirming
quired. their utility than taking off much from their originality in

---

[1] Nov. Organ. lib. i. 64.   It may be doubted whether Bacon did full justice
to Gilbert.

any fair sense of that term. Every logical method is built
on the common faculties of human nature, which have been
exercised since the creation in discerning, better or worse,
truth from falsehood, and inferring the unknown from the
known. That men might have done this more correctly is
manifest from the quantity of error into which, from want
of reasoning well on what came before them, they have
habitually fallen. In experimental philosophy, to which the
more special rules of Lord Bacon are generally referred,
there was a notorious want of that very process of reasoning
which he has supplied. It is more than probable, indeed,
that the great physical philosophers of the seventeenth century would have been led to employ some of his rules, had
he never promulgated them; but I believe they had been
little regarded in the earlier period of science.[m] It is also a
very defective view of the Baconian method to look only at
the experimental rules given in the Novum Organum. The
preparatory steps of completely exhausting the natural history of the subject of inquiry by a patient and sagacious
consideration of it in every light are at least of equal
importance, and equally prominent in the inductive philosophy.

46. The first object of Lord Bacon's philosophical writings
is to prove their own necessity, by giving an unfavourable impression as to the actual state of most   *Its objects.*
sciences, in consequence of the prejudices of the human
mind, and of the mistaken methods pursued in their cultivation. The second was to point out a better prospect for the
future. One of these occupies the treatise De Augmentis,
and the first book of the Novum Organum. The other, besides many anticipations in these, is partially detailed in the
second book, and would have been more thoroughly developed in those remaining portions which the author did
not complete. We shall now give a very short sketch of
these two famous works, which comprise the greater part of
the Baconian philosophy.

---

[m] It has been remarked, that the
famous experiment of Pascal on the ba-
rometer by carrying it to a considerable
elevation, was 'a *crucial instance,* one of
the first, if not the very first, on record
in physics.' Herschel, p. 229.

47. The Advancement of Learning is divided into two
Sketch of the books only; the treatise De Augmentis into nine.
treatise De
Augmentis. The first of these, in the latter, is introductory, and
designed to remove prejudices against the search after truth,
by indicating the causes which had hitherto obstructed it.
In the second book, he lays down his celebrated partition of
          human learning into history, poetry, and philosophy,
History.
          according to the faculties of the mind respectively
concerned in them, the memory, imagination, and reason.
History is natural or civil, under the latter of which ecclesiastical and literary histories are comprised. These again
fall into regular subdivisions; all of which he treats in a
summary manner, and points out the deficiencies which
ought to be supplied in many departments of history.
          Poetry succeeds in the last chapter of the same
Poetry.
          book, but by confining the name to fictitious narra-
tive, except as to ornaments of style, which he refers to a
different part of his subject, he much limited his views of
that literature; even if it were true, as it certainly is not,
that the imagination alone, in any ordinary use of the word,
is the medium of poetical emotion. The word emotion,
indeed, is sufficient to show that Bacon should either have
excluded poetry altogether from his enumeration of sciences
and learning, or taken into consideration other faculties of
the soul than those which are merely intellectual.

48. Stewart has praised with justice a short but beautiful
Fine passage paragraph concerning poetry (under which title
on poetry. may be comprehended all the various creations of
the faculty of imagination, at least as they are manifested
by words), wherein Bacon 'has exhausted everything that
philosophy and good sense have yet had to offer on the subject of what has since been called the *beau idéal*.' The same
eminent writer and ardent admirer of Bacon observes that
D'Alembert improved on the Baconian arrangement by
classing the fine arts together with poetry. Injustice had
been done to painting and music, especially the former,
when, in the fourth book De Augmentis, they were counted
as mere 'artes voluptariæ,' subordinate to a sort of Epicurean
gratification of the senses, and only somewhat more liberal
than cookery or cosmetics.

49. In the third book, science having been divided into theological and philosophical, and the former, or what regards revealed religion, being postponed for the present, he lays it down that all philosophy relates to God, to nature, or to man. Under natural theology, as a sort of appendix, he reckons the science or theory of angels and superhuman spirits; a more favourite theme, especially as treated independently of revelation, in the ages that preceded Lord Bacon, than it has been since. Natural philosophy is speculative or practical; the former divided into physics, in a particular sense, and metaphysics; 'one of which inquireth and handleth the material and efficient causes; the other handleth the formal and final causes.' Hence physics dealing with particular instances, and regarding only the effects produced, is precarious in its conclusions, and does not reach the stable principles of causation.

Natural theology and metaphysics.

> Limus ut hic durescit, et hæc ut cera liquescit
> Uno eodemque igni.

Metaphysics, to which word he gave a sense as remote from that which it bore in the Aristotelian schools as from that in which it is commonly employed at present, had for its proper object the investigation of forms. It was 'a generally received and inveterate opinion, that the inquisition of man is not competent to find out essential forms or true differences.' 'Formæ inventio,' he says in another place, 'habetur pro desperata.' The word *form* itself, being borrowed from the old philosophy, is not immediately intelligible to every reader. 'In the Baconian sense,' says Playfair, 'form differs only from cause in being permanent, whereas we apply cause to that which exists in order of time.' Form (*natura naturans*, as it was barbarously called) is the general law, or condition of existence, in any substance or quality (*natura naturata*), which is wherever its form is.[n] The conditions of a mathematical figure, prescribed in its

Form of bodies

---

[n] Licet enim in natura nihil vere existat præter corpora individua, edentia actus puros individuos ex lege, in doctrinis tamen illa ipsa lex, ejusque inquisitio, et inventio atque explicatio pro fundamento est tam ad sciendum quam operandum. Eam autem legem ejusque paragraphos Formarum nomine intelligimus; præsertim cum hoc vocabulum invaluerit et familiariter occurrat. Nov. Org. ii. 2.

definition, might in this sense be called its form, if it did not
seem to be Lord Bacon's intention to confine the word to the
laws of particular sensible existences. In modern philosophy,
it might be defined to be that particular combination of
forces which impresses a certain modification upon matter
subjected to their influence.

50. To a knowledge of such forms, or laws of essence and
might some-
times be in-
quired into. existence, at least in a certain degree, it might be
possible, in Bacon's sanguine estimation of his own
logic, for man to attain. Not that we could hope to understand the forms of complex beings, which are almost infinite
in variety, but the simple and primary natures, which are
combined in them. 'To inquire the form of a lion, of an
oak, of gold, nay of water, of air, is a vain pursuit; but to
inquire the forms of sense, of voluntary motion, of vegetation,
of colours, of gravity and levity, of density and tenuity, of
heat, of cold, and all other natures and qualities, which, like
an alphabet, are not many, and of which the essences, upheld
by matter, of all creatures do consist; to inquire, I say, the
true forms of these is that part of metaphysics which we
now define of.'[o] Thus, in the words he soon afterwards
uses, 'of natural philosophy, the basis is natural history;
the stage next the basis is physic; the stage next the vertical
point is metaphysic. As for the vertical point, "Opus quod
operatur Deus a principio usque ad finem," the summary law
of nature, we know not whether man's inquiry can attain
unto it.'[p]

51. The second object of metaphysics, according to Lord
Final causes
too much
slighted. Bacon's notion of the word, was the investigation
of final causes. It is well known that he has spoken
of this, in physics, with unguarded disparagement.[q] 'Like

---

[o] In the Novum Organum he seems
to have gone a little beyond this, and
to have hoped that the form itself of
concrete things might be known. Datæ
autem naturæ formam, sive differentiam
veram, sive naturam naturantem, sive
fontem emanationis (ista enim vocabula
habemus, quæ ad indicationem rei proxi-
me accedunt), invenire opus et intentio
est Humanæ Scientiæ. Lib. ii. 1.

[p] Advancement of Learning, book ii.

This sentence he has scarcely altered in
the Latin.

[q] Causa finalis tantum abest ut prosit,
ut etiam scientias corrumpat, nisi in
hominis actionibus. Nov. Org. ii. 2. It
must be remembered that Bacon had
good reason to deprecate the admixture
of theological dogmas with philosophy,
which had been, and has often since been,
the absolute perversion of all legitimate
reasoning in science. See what Stewart

a virgin consecrated to God, it bears nothing;' one of those witty conceits that sparkle over his writings, but will not bear a severe examination. It has been well remarked that almost at the moment he published this, one of the most important discoveries of his age, the circulation of the blood, had rewarded the acuteness of Harvey in reasoning on the final cause of the valves in the veins.

52. Nature, or physical philosophy, according to Lord Bacon's partition, did not comprehend the human species. Whether this be not more consonant to popular language, adopted by preceding systems of philosophy, than to a strict and perspicuous arrangement, may by some be doubted; though a very respectable authority, that of Dugald Stewart, is opposed to including man in the province of physics. For it is surely strange to separate the physiology of the human body, as quite a science of another class, from that of inferior animals; and if we place this part of our being under the department of physical philosophy, we shall soon be embarrassed by what Bacon has called the 'doctrina de fœdere,' the science of the connexion between the soul of man and his bodily

Man not included by him in physics.

---

has said upon Lord Bacon's objection to reasoning from final causes in *physics*. Philosophy of the Active and Moral Powers, book iii. chap. ii. sect. 4.

[It ought to be more remembered than sometimes it has been, that Bacon solely objects to the confusion of *final* with *efficient* causes, or, as some would say, with antecedent conditions. These alone he considered to fall within the province of physics. But, as a part of metaphysical theology, he gives the former here a place. Stewart has quoted at length the passage, which entirely vindicates Bacon from the charge of depreciating the argument in favour of theism from the structure of the world: a charge not uncommonly insinuated against him in the seventeenth century, but repeated lately with the most dogmatic violence by a powerful writer, Count de Maistre, Examen de la Philos. de Bacon, c. 13, et alibi. Bruxelles, 1838. This work, little known perhaps in England, is from beginning to end a violent attack upon the Baconian philosophy and its author, by a man of extra-ordinary vigour as a polemical writer, quick to discover any weak point, and powerful to throw upon it the light of a remarkably masculine and perspicuous style; second only perhaps in these respects to Bossuet, or rather only falling short of him in elegance of language; but, like him, a mere sworn soldier of one party, utterly destitute of an eclectic spirit in his own philosophy, or even of the power of appreciating with ordinary candour the diversities of opinion in others; repulsive therefore not only to all who have looked with reverence upon those whom he labours to degrade, but to all who abhor party-spirit in the research of truth; yet not unworthy to be read even by them, since he has many just criticisms, and many acute observations; such, however, as ought always to be tried by comparison with the text of Bacon, whom he may not designedly have misrepresented, but, having set out with the conviction that he was a charlatan and an atheist, he naturally is led to exhibit in no other light.—1847.]

frame, a vast and interesting field, even yet very imperfectly explored.

53. It has pleased, however, the author to follow his own Man, in body arrangement. The fourth book relates to the consti-
and mind. tution, bodily and mental, of mankind. In this book he has introduced several subdivisions which, considered merely as such, do not always appear the most philosophical; but the pregnancy and acuteness of his observations under each head silence all criticism of this kind. This book has nearly double the extent of the corresponding pages in the Advancement of Learning. The doctrine as to the substance of the thinking principle having been very slightly touched, or rather passed over, with two curious disquisitions on divination and fascination, he advances in four ensuing books to the intellectual and moral faculties, and those sciences which
Logic; immediately depend upon them. Logic and Ethics are the grand divisions, correlative to the reason and the will of man. Logic, according to Lord Bacon, comprises the sciences of inventing, judging, retaining, and delivering the conceptions of the mind. We invent, that is, discover new arts, or new arguments; we judge by induction or by syllogism; the memory is capable of being aided by artificial methods. All these processes of the mind are the subjects of several sciences, which it was the peculiar aim of Bacon, by his own logic, to place on solid foundations.

54. It is here to be remarked, that the sciences of logic
extent and ethics, according to the partitions of Lord
given it by
Bacon. Bacon, are far more extensive than we are accustomed to consider them. Whatever concerned the human intellect came under the first; whatever related to the will and affections of the mind fell under the head of ethics. Logica de intellectu et ratione, ethica de voluntate appetitu et affectibus disserit; altera decreta, altera actiones progignit. But it has been usual to confine logic to the methods of guiding the understanding in the search for truth; and some, though, as it seems to me, in a manner not warranted by the best usage of philosophers,[r] have endeavoured to exclude

---

[r] In altera philosophiæ parte, quæ est *quærendi* ac disserendi, quæ λογικη dicitur. Cic. de Fin. i. 14.

everything but the syllogistic mode of reasoning from the logical province.   Whether, again, the nature and operations of the human mind, in general, ought to be reckoned a part of physics, has already been mentioned as a disputable question.

55. The science of delivering our own thoughts to others, branching into grammar and rhetoric, and including Grammar · poetry, so far as its proper vehicles, metre and and rhe- toric. diction, are concerned, occupies the sixth book.   In all this he finds more desiderata than, from the great attention paid to these subjects by the ancients, could have been expected. Thus his ingenious collection of antitheta, or common-places in rhetoric, though mentioned by Cicero as to the judicial species of eloquence, is first extended by Bacon himself, as he supposes, to deliberative or political orations.   I do not, however, think it probable that this branch of topics could have been neglected by antiquity, though the writings re- lating to it may not have descended to us; nor can we by any means say there is nothing of the kind in Aristotle's Rhetoric.   Whether the utility of these common-places, when collected in books, be very great, is another question. And a similar doubt might be suggested with respect to the elenchs, or refutations, of rhetorical sophisms, 'colores boni et mali,' which he reports as equally deficient, though a commencement had been made by Aristotle.

56. In the seventh book we come to ethical science.   This he deems to have been insufficiently treated.   He Ethics. would have the different tempers and characters of mankind first considered, then their passions and affections; (neither of which, as he justly observes, find a place in the Ethics of Aristotle, though they are sometimes treated, not so appositely, in his Rhetoric;) lastly, the methods of alter- ing and affecting the will and appetite, such as custom, education, imitation, or society.   'The main and primitive division of moral knowledge seemeth to be into the exemplar or platform of good, and the regiment or culture of the mind; the one describing the nature of good, the other presenting rules how to subdue, apply, and accommodate the will of man thereunto.'   This latter he also calls 'the Georgics of the mind.'   He seems to place 'the platform or essence of

good ' in seeking the good of the whole, rather than that of
the individual, applying this to refute the ancient theories
as to the summum bonum. But perhaps Bacon had not
thoroughly disentangled this question, and confounds, as is
not unusual, the *summum bonum*, or personal felicity, with the
object of moral action, or *commune bonum*. He is right,
however, in preferring, morally speaking, the active to the
contemplative life against Aristotle and other philosophers.
This part is translated in De Augmentis, with little variation,
from the Advancement of Learning ; as is also what follows
on the Georgics, or culture, of the mind. The philosophy of
civil life, as it relates both to the conduct of men in their
mutual intercourse, which is peculiarly termed prudence, and
to that higher prudence which is concerned with the administration of communities, fills up the chart of the
Baconian ethics. In the eighth book, admirable reflections
on the former of these subjects occur at almost every sentence. Many, perhaps most, of these will be found in the
Advancement of Learning. But in this, he had been, for a
reason sufficiently obvious and almost avowed, cautiously
silent upon the art of government, the craft of his king.

Politics. The motives for silence were still so powerful, that
he treats, in the De Augmentis, only of two heads
in political science ; the methods of enlarging the boundaries
of a state, which James I. could hardly resent as an interference with his own monoply, and one of far more importance to the well-being of mankind, the principles of
universal jurisprudence, or rather of universal legislation,
according to which standard all laws ought to be framed.
These he has sketched in ninety-seven aphorisms, or short
rules, which, from the great experience of Bacon in the laws,
as well as his peculiar vocation towards that part of philosophy, deserve to be studied at this day. Upon such topics,
the progressive and innovating spirit of his genius was less
likely to be perceived ; but he is here, as on all occasions,
equally free from what he has happily called in one of his
essays, the ' froward retention of custom,' the prejudice of
mankind, like that of perverse children, against what is
advised to them for their real good, and what they cannot
deny to be conducive to it. This whole eighth book is

pregnant with profound and original thinking. The ninth and last, which is short, glances only at some desiderata in theological science, and is chiefly remark- ^Theology.^ able as it displays a more liberal and catholic spirit than was often to be met with in a period signalised by bigotry and ecclesiastical pride. But as the abjuration of human authority is the first principle of Lord Bacon's philosophy, and the preparation for his logic, it was not expedient to say too much of its usefulness in theological pursuits.

57. At the conclusion of the whole, we may find a summary catalogue of the deficiencies, which, in the course of this ample review, Lord Bacon had found worthy ^Desiderata enumerated by him.^ of being supplied by patient and philosophical inquiry. Of these desiderata, few, I fear, have since been filled up, at least in a collective and systematic manner, according to his suggestions. Great materials, useful intimations, and even partial delineations, are certainly to be found, as to many of the rest, in the writings of those who have done honour to the last two centuries. But with all our pride in modern science, very much even of what, in Bacon's time, was perceived to be wanting, remains for the diligence and sagacity of those who are yet to come.

58. The first book of the Novum Organum, if it is not better known than any other part of Bacon's philosophical ^Novum Organum : first book.^ writings, has at least furnished more of those striking passages which shine in quotation. It is written in detached aphorisms ; the sentences, even where these aphorisms are longest, not flowing much into one another, so as to create a suspicion, that he had formed adversaria, to which he committed his thoughts as they arose. It is full of repetitions ; and indeed this is so usual with Lord Bacon, that whenever we find an acute reflection or brilliant analogy, it is more than an even chance that it will recur in some other place. I have already observed that he has hinted the Novum Organum to be a digested summary of his method, but not the entire system as he designed to develop it, even in that small portion which he has handled at all.

59. Of the splendid passages in the Novum Organum none are perhaps so remarkable as his celebrated division of fallacies, not such as the dialecticians had been accustomed to

refute, depending upon equivocal words, or faulty disposi-

tion of premises, but lying far deeper in the natural or incidental prejudices of the mind itself. These are four in number: *idola tribûs*, to which from certain common weaknesses of human nature we are universally liable; *idola specûs*, which from peculiar dispositions and circumstances of individuals mislead them in different manners; *idola fori*, arising from the current usage of words, which represent things much otherwise than as they really are; and *idola theatri*, which false systems of philosophy and erroneous methods of reasoning have introduced. Hence, as the refracted ray gives us a false notion as to the place of the object whose image it transmits, so our own minds are a refracting medium to the objects of their own contemplation, and require all the aid of a well directed philosophy either to rectify the perception, or to make allowances for its errors.

60. These idola, εἰδωλα, images, illusions, fallacies, or as

Lord Bacon calls them in the Advancement of Learning, false appearances, have been often named in English *idols* of the tribe, of the den, of the market-place. But it seems better, unless we retain the Latin name, to employ one of the synonymous terms given above. For the use of idol in this sense is little warranted by the practice of the language, nor is it found in Bacon himself; but it has misled a host of writers, whoever might be the first that applied it, even among such as are conversant with the Novum Organum. 'Bacon proceeds,' says Playfair, 'to enumerate the causes of error, the *idols*, as he calls them, or false divinities to which the mind had so long been accustomed to bow.' And with a similar misapprehension of the meaning of the word, in speaking of the *idola specûs*, he says, 'Besides the causes of error which are common to all mankind, each individual, according to Bacon, has his own dark cavern or den, into which the light is imperfectly admitted, and in the obscurity of which a tutelary idol lurks, at whose shrine the truth is often sacrificed.'[s] Thus also Dr. Thomas Brown; 'in the inmost sanctuaries of the mind were all the idols which he overthrew;' and a later author on the Novum Organum

---

[s] Preliminary Dissertation to Encyclopædia.

fancies that Bacon 'strikingly, though in his usual quaint
style, calls the prejudices that check the progress of the mind
by the name of idols, because mankind are apt to pay homage
to these, instead of regarding truth.'[t]   Thus, too, in the
translation of the Novum Organum, published in Mr. Basil
Montagu's edition, we find *idola* rendered by idols, without explanation.   We may in fact say that this meaning has
been almost universally given by later writers.   By whom it
was introduced I cannot determine.   Cudworth, in a passage
where he glances at Bacon, has said, ' It is no *idol of the den*,
to use that affected language.'   But, in the pedantic style of
the seventeenth century, it is not impossible that idol may
here have been put as a mere translation of the Greek εἰδωλον,
and in the same general sense of an idea or intellectual
image.[u]   Although the popular sense would not be inapposite
to the general purpose of Bacon in the first part of the Novum
Organum, it cannot be reckoned so exact and philosophical an
illustration of the sources of human error as the unfaithful
image, the shadow of reality, seen through a refracting surface, or reflected from an unequal mirror, as in the Platonic
hypothesis of the cave, wherein we are placed with our backs
to the light, to which he seems to allude in his *idola specûs*.[x]
And as this is also plainly the true meaning, as a comparison
with the parallel passages in the Advancement of Learning
demonstrates, there can be no pretence for continuing to
employ a word which has served to mislead such men as
Brown and Playfair.

---

[t] Introduction to the Novum Organum, published by the Society for the
Diffusion of Useful Knowledge.   Even
Stewart seems to have fallen into the
same error. ' While these idols of the
den maintain their authority, the cultivation of the philosophical spirit is impossible; or rather it is in a renunciation
of this idolatry that the philosophical
spirit essentially consists.' Dissertation,
&c.—The observation is equally true,
whatever sense we may give to *idol*.

[u] In Todd's edition of Johnson's Dictionary this sense is not mentioned. But
in that of the Encyclopædia Metropo-
litana we have these words : ' An *idol*
or image is also opposed to a reality;
thus Lord Bacon (see the quotation from
him) speaks of idols or false appear-

ances.'   The quotation is from the
translation of one of his short Latin
tracts, which was not made by himself.
It is, however, a proof that the word *idol*
was once used in this sense.

[x] Quisque ex phantasiæ suæ cellulis,
tanquam ex specu Platonis, philosopha-
tur.   Historia Naturalis, in præfatione.
Coleridge has some fine lines in allusion
to this hypothesis in that magnificent
effusion of his genius, the introduction
to the second book of Joan of Arc,
but withdrawn, after the first edition,
from that poem; where he describes us
as ' Placed with our backs to bright
reality.'   I am not, however, certain
that Bacon meant this precise analogy
by his *idola specûs*. See De Augmentis,
lib. v. c. 4.

61. In the second book of the Novum Organum we come Second book at length to the new logic, the interpretation of of Novum Organum. nature as he calls it, or the rules for conducting inquiries in natural philosophy according to his inductive method. It is, as we have said, a fragment of his entire system, and is chiefly confined to the ' prerogative in-stances,'[y] or phænomena which are to be selected, for various reasons, as most likely to aid our investigations of nature. Fifteen of these are used to guide the intellect, five to assist the senses, seven to correct the practice. This second book is written with more than usual want of perspicuity, and though it is intrinsically the Baconian philosophy in a pre-eminent sense, I much doubt whether it is very extensively read, though far more so than it was fifty years since. Playfair, however, has given an excellent abstract of it in his Preliminary Dissertation to the Encyclopædia Britannica, with abundant and judicious illustrations from modern science. Sir John Herschel, in his admirable Discourse on Natural Philosophy, has added a greater number from still more recent discoveries, and has also furnished such a luminous development of the difficulties of the Novum Organum, as had been vainly hoped in former times. The commentator of Bacon should be himself of an original genius in philosophy. These novel illustrations are the more useful, because Bacon himself, from defective knowledge of natural phænomena, and from what, though contrary to his precepts, his ardent fancy could not avoid, a premature hastening to explain the essences of things instead of their proximate causes, has frequently given erroneous examples. It is to be observed, on the other hand, that he often antici-pates with marvellous sagacity the discoveries of posterity, and that his patient and acute analysis of the phænomena of heat has been deemed a model of his own inductive reasoning. ' No one,' observes Playfair, ' has done so much in such circumstances.' He was even ignorant of some things that

---

[y] The allusion in ' prærogativæ in-stantiarum ' is not to the English word prerogative, as Sir John Herschel seems to suppose (Discourse on Natural Phi-losophy, p. 182), but to the prærogativa centuria in the Roman comitia, which being first called, though by lot, was generally found, by some prejudice or superstition, to influence the rest, which seldom voted otherwise. It is rather a forced analogy, which is not uncommon with Bacon.

he might have known; he wan'ed every branch of mathematics; and placed in this remote corner of Europe, without many kindred minds to animate his zeal for physical science, seems hardly to have believed the discoveries of Galileo.

62. It has happened to Lord Bacon, as it has to many other writers, that he has been extolled for qualities by no means characteristic of his mind. The first aphorism of the Novum Organum, so frequently quoted, 'Man, the servant and interpreter of nature, performs and understands so much as he has collected concerning the order of nature by observation or reason, nor do his power or his knowledge extend farther,' has seemed to bespeak an extreme sobriety of imagination, a willingness to acquiesce in registering the phænomena of nature without seeking a revelation of her secrets. And nothing is more true than that such was the cautious and patient course of inquiry prescribed by him to all the genuine disciples of his inductive method. But he was far from being one of those humble philosophers who would limit human science to the enumeration of particular facts. He had, on the contrary, vast hopes of the human intellect under the guidance of his new logic. The Latens Schematismus, or intrinsic configuration of bodies, the Latens processus ad formam, or transitional operation through which they pass from one form, or condition of nature, to another, would one day, as he hoped, be brought to light; and this not, of course, by simple observation of the senses, nor even by assistance of instruments, concerning the utility of which he was rather sceptical, but by a rigorous application of exclusive and affirmative propositions to the actual phænomena by the inductive method. ' It appears,' says Playfair, ' that Bacon placed the ultimate object of philosophy too high, and too much out of the reach of man, even when his exertions are most skilfully conducted. He seems to have thought, that by giving a proper direction to our researches, and carrying them on according to the inductive method, we should arrive at the knowledge of the essences of the powers and qualities residing in bodies; that we should, for instance, become acquainted with the essence of heat, of cold, of colour, of transparency. The fact however is, that, in as far as science has yet advanced, no one

Confidence of Bacon.

essence has been discovered, either as to matter in general, or as to any of its more extensive modifications. We are yet in doubt whether heat is a peculiar motion of the minute parts of bodies, as Bacon himself conceived it to be, or something emitted or radiated from their surfaces, or lastly, the vibrations of an elastic medium by which they are penetrated and surrounded.'

63. It requires a very extensive survey of the actual do-

Almost jus-
tified of late; minion of science, and a great sagacity, to judge, even in the loosest manner, what is beyond the possible limits of human knowledge. Certainly, since the time when this passage was written by Playfair, more steps have been made towards realising the sanguine anticipations of Bacon than in the two centuries that had elapsed since the publication of the Novum Organum. We do not yet *know* the real nature of heat, but few would pronounce it impossible or even unlikely that we may know it, in the same degree that we know other physical realities not immediately perceptible, before many years shall have expired. The atomic theory of Dalton, the laws of crystalline substances discovered by Haüy, the development of others still subtler by Mitscherlich, instead of exhibiting, as the older philosophy had done, the idola rerum, the sensible appearances of concrete substance, radiations from the internal glory, admit us, as it were, to stand within the vestibule of nature's temple, and to gaze on the very curtain of the shrine. If, indeed, we could know the internal structure of one primary atom, and could tell, not of course by immediate testimony of sense, but by legitimate inference from it, through what constant laws its component, though indiscerpible, molecules, the atoms of atoms, attract, retain, and repel each other, we should have before our mental vision not only the Latens Schematismus, the real configuration of the substance, but its *form*, or efficient nature, and could give as perfect a definition of any such substance, of gold for example, as we can of a cone or a parallelogram. The recent discoveries of animal and vegetable development, and especially the happy application of the microscope to observing chemical and organic changes in their actual course, are equally remarkable advances towards a knowledge of the Latens processus ad formam, the corpuscular motions by which all change must be accomplished, and are in fact a great deal more than Bacon himself would have deemed possible.[z]

64. These astonishing revelations of natural mysteries, fresh tidings of which crowd in upon us every day, may be likely to overwhelm all sober hesitation as to the capacities of the human mind, and to bring back that confidence which Bacon, in so much less favourable *but should be kept within bounds.* circumstances, has ventured to feel. There seem, however, to be good reasons for keeping within bounds this expectation of future improvement, which, as it has sometimes been announced in unqualified phrases, is hardly more philosophical than the vulgar supposition that the capacities of mankind are almost stationary. The phænomena of nature, indeed, in all their possible combinations, are so infinite, in a popular sense of the word, that during no period, to which the human species can be conceived to reach, would they be entirely collected and registered. The case is still stronger as to the secret agencies and processes by means of which their phænomena are displayed. These have as yet, in no one instance, so far as I know, been fully ascertained. ' Microscopes,' says Herschel, ' have been constructed which magnify more than one thousand times in linear dimension, so that the smallest visible grain of sand may be enlarged to the appearance of one million times more bulky; yet the only impression we receive by viewing it through such a magnifier is that it reminds us of some vast fragment of a rock; while the intimate structure on which depend its colour, its hardness, and its chemical properties, remains still concealed; we do not seem to have made even an approach to a closer analysis of it by any such scrutiny.'[a]

65. The instance here chosen is not the most favourable for the experimental philosopher. He might perhaps hope to gain more knowledge by applying the best microscope to a regular crystal or to an *Limits to our knowledge by sense.* organised substance. But there is evidently a fundamental

---

[z] By the Latens processus, he meant only what is the natural operation by which one form or condition of being is induced upon another. Thus, when the surface of iron becomes rusty, or when water is converted into steam, some change has taken place, a *latent progress* from one form to another. This, in numberless cases, we can now answer, at least to a very great extent, by the science of chemistry.

[a] Discourse on Nat. Philos. p. 191.

limitation of physical science, arising from those of the
bodily senses and of muscular motions. The nicest instruments must be constructed and directed by the human hand ;
the range of the finest glasses must have a limit, not only in
their own natural structure but in that of the human eye.
But no theory in science will be acknowledged to deserve any
regard, except as it is drawn immediately, and by an exclusive process, from the phænomena which our senses report
to us. Thus the regular observation of definite proportions
in chemical combination has suggested the atomic theory ;
and even this has been sceptically accepted by our cautious
school of philosophy. If we are ever to go farther into the
molecular analysis of substances, it must be through the
means and upon the authority of new discoveries exhibited
to our senses in experiment. But the existing powers of
exhibiting or compelling nature by instruments, vast as they
appear to us, and wonderful as has been their efficacy in
many respects, have done little for many years past in
diminishing the number of substances reputed to be simple ;
and with strong reasons to suspect that some of these, at
least, yield to the crucible of nature, our electric batteries
have up to this hour played innocuously round their heads.

66. Bacon has thrown out, once or twice, a hint at a
single principle, a summary law of nature, as if all subordinate causes resolved themselves into one great process,
according to which God works his will in the universe : Opus
quod operatur Deus a principio usque ad finem.   The natural
tendency towards simplification, and what we consider as
harmony, in our philosophical systems, which Lord Bacon
himself reckons among the *idola tribús*, the fallacies incident
to the species, has led some to favour this unity of physical
law. Impact and gravity have each had their supporters.
But we are as yet at a great distance from establishing such
a generalization, nor does it appear by any means probable
that it will ever assume any simple form.

67. The close connexion of the inductive process recom-
Inductive   mended by Bacon with natural philosophy in the
logic ;
whether   common sense of that word, and the general selec-
confined to
physics.   tion of his examples for illustration from that
science, have given rise to a question, whether he compre-

hended metaphysical and moral philosophy within the scope of his inquiry.[b]   That they formed a part of the Instauration of Sciences, and therefore of the Baconian philosophy in the fullest sense of the word, is obvious from the fact that a large proportion of the treatise De Augmentis Scientiarum is dedicated to those subjects; and it is not less so that the *idola* of the Novum Organum are at least as apt to deceive us in moral as in physical argument. The question, therefore, can only be raised as to the peculiar method of conducting investigations, which is considered as his own.   This would, however, appear to have been decided by himself in very positive language. ' It may be doubted, rather than objected, by some, whether we look to the perfection, by means of our method, of natural philosophy alone, or of the other sciences also, of logic, of ethics, of politics. But we certainly mean what has here been said to be understood as to them all ; and as the ordinary logic, which proceeds by syllogism, does not relate to physical only, but to every other science, so ours, which proceeds by induction, comprises them all.   For we as much collect a history and form tables concerning anger, fear, shame, and the like, and also concerning examples from civil life, and as much concerning the intellectual operations of memory, combination, and partition, judgment and the others, as concerning heat and cold, or light, or vegetation, or such things.'   But he proceeds to intimate, as far as I understand the next sentence, that, although his method

---

[b] This question was discussed some years since by the late editor of the Edinburgh Review on one side, and by Dugald Stewart on the other.   See Edinburgh Review, vol. iii. p. 273, and the Preliminary Dissertation to Stewart's Philosophical Essays.

[c] Etiam dubitabit quispiam potius quam objiciet, utrum nos de naturali tantum philosophia, an etiam de scientiis reliquis, logicis, ethicis, politicis, secundum viam nostram perficiendis loquamur. At nos certè de universis hæc, quæ dicta sunt, intelligimus; atque quemadmodum vulgaris logica, quæ regit res per syllogismum, non tantum ad naturales, sed ad omnes scientias pertinet, ita et nostra, quæ procedit per inductionem, omnia complectitur.   Tam enim Historiam et Tabulas Inveniendi conficimus de ira, metu et verecundia et similibus, ac etiam de exemplis rerum civilium ; nec minùs de motibus mentalibus memoriæ, compositionis et divisionis, judicii et reliquorum, quam de calido et frigido, aut luce, aut vegetatione aut similibus.   Sed tamen cum nostra ratio interpretandi, post historiam præparatam et ordinatam, non mentis tantum motus et discursus, ut logica vulgaris, sed et rerum naturam intueatur, ita mentem regimus ut ad rerum naturam se aptis per omnia modis applicare possit. Atque propterea multa et diversa in doctrina interpretationis præcipimus, quæ ad subjecti, de quo inquirimus, qualitatem et conditionem modum inveniendi nonnulla ex parte applicent.   Nov. Org. i. 127.

or logic, strictly speaking, is applicable to other subjects, it
is his immediate object to inquire into the properties of natural things, or what is generally meant by physics.   To this,
indeed, the second book of the Novum Organum and the
portions that he completed of the remaining parts of the
Instauratio Magna bear witness.

68. It by no means follows, because the leading principles
Baconian
philosophy
built on ob-
servation and
experiment. of the inductive philosophy are applicable to other
topics of inquiry than what is usually comprehended
under the name of physics, that we can employ all
the ' prærogativæ instantiarum,' and still less the peculiar
rules for conducting experiments which Bacon has given us
in moral or even psychological disquisitions.   Many of them
are plainly referable to particular manipulations, or at most
to limited subjects of chemical theory.   And the frequent
occurrence of passages which show Lord Bacon's fondness
for experimental processes, seems to have led some to consider his peculiar methods as more exclusively related to such
modes of inquiry than they really are.   But when the Baconian philosophy is said to be experimental, we are to remember
that experiment is only better than what we may call passive observation, because it enlarges our capacity of observing
with exactness and expedition.   The reasoning is grounded
on observation in both cases.   In astronomy, where nature
remarkably presents the objects of our observation without
liability to error or uncertain delay, we may reason on the inductive principle as well as in sciences that require tentative
operations.   The inferences drawn from the difference of time
in the occultation of the satellites of Jupiter at different seasons, in favour of the Corpernican theory and against the in-
stantaneous motion of light, are inductions of the same kind
with any that could be derived from an *experimentum crucis.*
They are exclusions of those hypotheses which might solve many
phænomena, but fail to explain those immediately observed.

69. But astronomy, from the comparative solitariness, if we
Advantages
of the latter. may so say, of all its phænomena, and the simplicity
of their laws, has an advantage that is rarely found
in sciences of mere observation.   Bacon justly gave to experiment, or the interrogation of nature, compelling her to give
up her secrets, a decided preference whenever it can be em-

ployed; and it is unquestionably true that the inductive method is tedious, if not uncertain, when it cannot resort to so compendious a process. One of the subjects selected by Bacon in the third part of the Instauration as specimens of the method by which an inquiry into nature should be conducted, the History of Winds, does not greatly admit of experiments; and the very slow progress of meteorology, which has yet hardly deserved the name of a science, when compared with that of chemistry or optics, will illustrate the difficulties of employing the inductive method without their aid. It is not, therefore, that Lord Bacon's method of philosophising is properly experimental, but that by experiment it is most successfully displayed.

70. It will follow from hence that in proportion as, in any matter of inquiry, we can separate, in what we examine, the determining conditions, or law of form, from every thing extraneous, we shall be more able to use the Baconian method with advantage. In metaphysics, or what Stewart would have called the philosophy of the human mind, there seems much in its own nature capable of being subjected to the inductive reasoning. Such are those facts which, by their intimate connexion with physiology, or the laws of the bodily frame, fall properly within the province of the physician. In these, though exact observation is chiefly required, it is often practicable to shorten its process by experiment. And another important illustration may be given from the education of children, considered as a science of rules deduced from observation; wherein also we are frequently more able to substitute experiment for mere experience, than with mankind in general, whom we may observe at a distance, but cannot control. In politics, as well as in moral prudence, we can seldom do more than this. It seems, however, practicable to apply the close attention enforced by Bacon, and the careful arrangement and comparison of phænomena, which are the basis of his induction, to these subjects. Thus, if the circumstances of all popular seditions recorded in history were to be carefully collected with great regard to the probability of evidence, and to any peculiarity that may have affected the results, it might be easy to perceive such a connexion of antecedent and sub-

sequent events in the great plurality of instances, as would
reasonably lead us to form probable inferences as to similar
tumults when they should occur.   This has sometimes been
done, with less universality, and with much less accuracy than
the Baconian method requires, by such theoretical writers on
politics as Machiavel and Bodin.   But it has been apt to de-
generate into pedantry, and to disappoint the practical statesman, who commonly rejects it with scorn; partly because civil
history is itself defective, seldom giving a just view of events,
and still less frequently of the motives of those concerned in
them; partly because the history of mankind is far less copious
than that of nature, and, in much that relates to politics, has
not yet had time to furnish the groundwork of a sufficient
induction; but partly also from some distinctive circumstances
which affect our reasonings in moral far more than in physical science, and which deserve to be considered, so far at
least as to sketch the arguments that might be employed.

71. The Baconian logic, as has been already said, deduces
universal principles from select observation, that is,
from particular, and, in some cases of experiment,
from singular instances.   It may easily appear to
one conversant with the syllogistic method less legitimate
than the old induction which proceeded by an exhaustive
enumeration of particulars,[d] and at most warranting but a
probable conclusion.   The answer to this objection can only
be found in the acknowledged uniformity of the laws of
nature, so that whatever has once occurred will, under absolutely similar circumstances, always occur again.   This may
be called the suppressed premise of every Baconian enthymem, every inference from observation of phænomena, which
extends beyond the particular case.   When it is once ascertained that water is composed of one proportion of oxygen to
one of hydrogen, we never doubt but that such are its invariable constituents.   We may repeat the experiment to secure
ourselves against the risk of error in the operation, or of some
unperceived condition that may have affected the result; but
when a sufficient number of trials has secured us against this,

Margin note: Induction less conclusive in these subjects.

---

[d] [This is not quite an accurate account of the old induction, which seldom
proceeded to an exhaustive enumeration, but *assumed* a general truth from a
particular one.—1847.]

an invariable law of nature is inferred from the particular instance; nobody conceives that one pint of pure water *can* be of a different composition from another. All men, even the most rude, reason upon this primary maxim; but they reason inconclusively, from misapprehending the true relations of cause and effect in the phænomena to which they direct their attention. It is by the sagacity and ingenuity with which Bacon has excluded the various sources of error, and disengaged the true cause, that his method is distinguished from that which the vulgar practise.

72. It is required, however, for the validity of this method, first, that there should be a strict uniformity in the general laws of nature, from which we can infer that what has been will, in the same conditions, be again; and, secondly, that we shall be able to perceive and estimate all the conditions with an entire and exclusive knowledge. The first is granted in all physical phænomena; but in those which we cannot submit to experiment, or investigate by some such method as Bacon has pointed out, we often find our philosophy at fault for want of the second. Such is at present the case with respect to many parts of chemistry; for example, that of organic substances, which we can analyse, but as yet can in very few instances recompose. We do not know, and, if we did know, could not probably command, the entire conditions of organic bodies, (even structurally, not as living,) the *form*, as Bacon calls it, of blood, or milk, or oak-galls. But in attempting to subject the actions of men to this inductive philosophy, we are arrested by the want of both the necessary requisitions. Matter can only be diverted from its obedience to unvarying laws by the control of mind; but we have to inquire whether mind is equally the passive instrument of any law. We have to open the great problem of human liberty, and must deny even a disturbing force to the will, before we can assume that all actions of mankind must, under given conditions, preserve the same necessary train of sequences as a molecule of matter. But if this be answered affirmatively, we are still almost as far removed from a conclusive result as before. We cannot, without contradicting every-day experience, maintain that all men are determined alike by

Reasons for this difference.

the same *outward* circumstances; we must have recourse to the differences of temperament, of physical constitution, of casual or habitual association. The former alone, however, are, at the best, subject to our observation, either at the time, or, as is most common, through testimony; of the latter, no being, which does not watch the movements of the soul itself, can reach more than a probable conjecture. Sylla resigned the dictatorship—therefore all men, in the circumstances of Sylla, will do the same—is an argument false in one sense of the word circumstances, and useless at least in any other. It is doubted by many, whether meteorology will ever be well understood, on account of the complexity of the forces concerned, and their remoteness from the apprehension of the senses. Do not the same difficulties apply to human affairs? And while we reflect on these difficulties, to which we must add those which spring from the scantiness of our means of observation, the defectiveness and falsehood of testimony, especially what is called historical, and a thousand other errors to which the various 'idola of the world and the cave' expose us, we shall rather be astonished that so many probable rules of civil prudence have been treasured up and confirmed by experience, than disposed to give them a higher place in philosophy than they can claim.

73. It might be alleged in reply to these considerations, Considera- that admitting the absence of a strictly scientific tions on the other side. certainty in moral reasoning, we have yet, as seems acknowledged on the other side, a great body of probable inferences, in the extensive knowledge and sagacious application of which most of human wisdom consists. And all that is required of us in dealing either with moral evidence or with the conclusions we draw from it, is to estimate the probability of neither too high; an error from which the severe and patient discipline of the inductive philosophy is most likely to secure us. It would be added by some, that the theory of probabilities deduces a wonderful degree of certainty from things very uncertain, when a sufficient number of experiments can be made; and thus, that events depending upon the will of mankind, even under circumstances the most anomalous and apparently irreducible to

principles, may be calculated with a precision inexplicable to any one who has paid little attention to the subject. This, perhaps, may appear rather a curious application of mathematical science, than one from which our moral reasonings are likely to derive much benefit, especially as the conditions under which a very high probability can mathematically be obtained involve a greater number of trials than experience will generally furnish. It is nevertheless a field that deserves to be more fully explored : the success of those who have attempted to apply analytical processes to moral probabilities has not hitherto been very encouraging, inasmuch as they have often come to results falsified by experience ; but a more scrupulous regard to all the conditions of each problem may perhaps obviate many sources of error.[e]

74. It seems, upon the whole, that we should neither conceive the inductive method to be useless in regard to any subject but physical science, nor deny the peculiar advantages it possesses in those inquiries rather than others. What must in all studies be important, is the habit of turning round the subject of our investigation in every light, the observation of every thing that is peculiar, the exclusion of all that we find on reflection to be extraneous. In historical and antiquarian researches, in all critical examination which turns upon facts, in the scrutiny of judicial evidence, a great part of Lord Bacon's method, not, of course, all the experimental rules of the Novum Organum, has, as I conceive, a legitimate application.[f] I

Result of the whole.

---

[e] A calculation was published not long since, said to be on the authority of an eminent living philosopher, according to which, granting a moderate probability that each of twelve jurors would decide rightly, the chances in favour of the rectitude of their unanimous verdict were made something extravagantly high, I think about 8000 to 1. It is more easy to perceive the fallacies of this pretended demonstration, than to explain how a man of great acuteness should have overlooked them.   One among many is, that it assumes the giving an unanimous verdict at all to be voluntary; whereas, in practice, the jury must decide one way or the other. We must deduct therefore a fraction expressing the probability that some of the twelve have

wrongly conceded their opinions to the rest. One danger of this rather favourite application of mathematical principles to moral probabilities, as indeed it is of statistical tables (a remark of far wider extent), is that, by considering mankind merely as units, it practically habituates the mind to a moral and social levelling, as inconsistent with a just estimate of men as it is characteristic of the present age.

[f] The *principle* of Bacon's prerogative instances, and perhaps in some cases a very analogous application of them, appear to hold in our inquiries into historical evidence. The fact sought to be ascertained in the one subject corresponds to the physical law in the other. The testimonies as we, though rather laxly, call them, or passages in books from

would refer any one who may doubt this to his History of
Winds, as one sample of what we mean by the Baconian
method, and ask whether a kind of investigation, analogous
to what is therein pursued for the sake of eliciting physical
truths, might not be employed in any analytical process
where general or even particular facts are sought to be
known.   Or if an example is required of such an investigation, let us look at the copious induction from the past and

---

which we infer the fact, correspond to
the observations or experiments from
which we deduce the law.   The necessity of a sufficient induction by searching
for all proof that may bear on the question is as manifest in one case as in the
other.   The exclusion of precarious and
inconclusive evidence is alike indispensable in both.   The selection of prerogative instances, or such as carry with them
satisfactory conviction, requires the same
sort of inventive and reasoning powers.
It is easy to illustrate this by examples.
Thus, in the controversy concerning the
Icon Basilike, the admission of Gauden's
claim by Lord Clarendon is in the nature
of a *prerogative instance*; it renders the
supposition of the falsehood of that claim
highly improbable.   But the many second-
hand and hearsay testimonies which may
be alleged on the other side, to prove
that the book was written by King
Charles, are not prerogative instances,
because their falsehood will be found to
involve very little improbability. So, in a
different controversy, the silence of some
of the fathers as to the text, commonly
called, of the three heavenly witnesses,
even while expounding the context of the
passage, may be reckoned a *prerogative
instance*; a decisive proof that they did
not know it, or did not believe it genuine; because, if they did, no motive
can be conceived for the omission.   But
the silence of Laurentius Valla as to its
absence from the manuscripts on which
he commented is no prerogative instance
to prove that it was contained in them;
because it is easy to perceive that he
might have motives for saying nothing;
and, though the negative argument, as it
is called, or inference that a fact is not
true, because such and such persons have
not mentioned it, is, taken generally,
weaker than positive testimony, it will
frequently supply prerogative instances
where the latter does not.   Launoy, in a

little treatise, De Auctoritate Negantis
Argumenti, which displays more plain
sense than ingenuity or philosophy, lays
it down that a fact of a public nature,
which is not mentioned by any writer
within 200 years of the time, supposing,
of course, that there is extant a competent number of writers who would naturally have mentioned it, is not to be
believed.   The period seems rather arbitrary, and was possibly so considered
by himself; but the general principle is
of the highest importance in historical
criticism.   Thus, in the once celebrated
question of Pope Joan, the silence of all
writers near the time, as to so wonderful
a fact, was justly deemed a kind of *prerogative* argument, when set in opposition to the many repetitions of the story
in later ages.   But the silence of Gildas
and Bede as to the victories of Arthur is
no such argument against their reality,
because they were not under an historical obligation, or any strong motive
which would prevent their silence.   Generally speaking, the more anomalous
and interesting an event is, the stronger
is the argument against its truth from
the silence of contemporaries, on account
of the propensity of mankind to believe
and recount the marvellous; and the
weaker is the argument from the testimony of later times for the same reason.
A similar analogy holds also in jurisprudence.   The principle of our law, rejecting hearsay and secondary evidence, is
founded on the Baconian rule.   Fifty
persons may depose that they have heard
of a fact or of its circumstances; but the
eye-witness is the prerogative instance.
It would carry us too far to develop this
at length, even if I were fully prepared
to do so; but this much may lead us to
think, that whoever shall fill up that
lamentable *desideratum*, the logic of evidence, ought to have familiarised himself with the Novum Organum.

actual history of mankind upon which Malthus established his general theory of the causes which have retarded the natural progress of population. Upon all these subjects before mentioned, there has been an astonishing improvement in the reasoning of the learned, and perhaps of the world at large, since the time of Bacon, though much remains very defective. In what degree it may be owing to the prevalence of a physical philosophy founded upon his inductive logic, it might not be uninteresting to inquire.[g]

75. It is probable that Lord Bacon never much followed up in his own mind that application of his method to psychological, and still less to moral and politi- cal subjects, which he has declared himself to intend. The distribution of the Instauratio Magna, which he has prefixed to it, relates wholly to physical science. He has in no one instance given an example, in the Novum Organum, from moral philosophy, and one only, that of artificial memory, from what he would have called logic.[h] But we must constantly remember that the philosophy of Bacon was left exceedingly incomplete. Many lives would not have sufficed for what he had planned, and he gave only the leisure hours of his own. It is evident that he had turned his thoughts to physical philosophy rather for an exercise of his reasoning faculties, and out of his insatiable thirst for knowledge, than from any peculiar aptitude for their subjects, much less any

Bacon's aptitude for moral subjects.

---

[g] 'The effects which Bacon's writings have hitherto produced, have indeed been far more conspicuous in physics than in the science of mind. Even here, however, they have been great and most important, as well as in some collateral branches of knowledge, such as natural jurisprudence, political economy, criticism, and morals, which spring up from the same root, or rather which are branches of that tree, of which the science of mind is the trunk.' Stewart's Philosophical Essays, Prelim. Dissertation. The principal advantage, perhaps, of those habits of reasoning which the Baconian methods, whether learned directly or through the many disciples of that school, have a tendency to generate, is that they render men cautious and painstaking in the pursuit of truth, and therefore restrain them from deciding too soon. Nemo reperitur qui in rebus ipsis

et experientia moram fecerit legitimam. These words are more frequently true of moral and political reasoners than of any others. Men apply historical or personal experience, but they apply it hastily, and without giving themselves time for either a copious or an exact induction ; the great majority being too much influenced by passion, party-spirit, or vanity, or perhaps by affections morally right, but not the less dangerous in reasoning, to maintain the patient and dispassionate suspense of judgment, which ought to be the condition of our inquiries.

[h] Nov. Organ. ii. 26. It may, however, be observed that we find a few passages in the ethical part of De Augmentis, lib. vii. cap. 3, which show that he had some notions of moral induction germinating in his mind.

advantage of opportunity for their cultivation. He was more
eminently the philosopher of human, than of general nature.
Hence he is exact as well as profound in all his reflections on
civil life and mankind, while his conjectures in natural philosophy, though often very acute, are apt to wander far from
the truth in consequence of his defective acquaintance with
the phænomena of nature. His Centuries of Natural History
give abundant proof of this. He is, in all these inquiries,
like one doubtfully, and by degrees, making out a distant
prospect, but often deceived by the haze. But if we compare
what may be found in the sixth, seventh, and eighth books
De Augmentis, in the Essays, the History of Henry VII.,
and the various short treatises contained in his works, on
moral and political wisdom, and on human nature, from experience of which all such wisdom is drawn, with the Rhetoric,
Ethics, and Politics of Aristotle, or with the historians most
celebrated for their deep insight into civil society and human
character, with Thucydides, Tacitus, Philip de Comines,
Machiavel, Davila, Hume, we shall, I think, find that one
man may almost be compared with all of these together.
When Galileo is named as equal to Bacon, it is to be remembered that Galileo was no moral or political philosopher, and
in this department Leibnitz certainly falls very short of
Bacon. Burke, perhaps, comes, of all modern writers, the
nearest to him; but though Bacon may not be more profound than Burke, he is more copious and comprehensive.

76. The comparison of Bacon and Galileo is naturally
Comparison built upon the influence which, in the same age,
of Bacon and
Galileo. they exerted in overthrowing the philosophy of
the schools, and in founding that new discipline of real science
which has rendered the last centuries glorious. Hume has
given the preference to the latter, who made accessions to
the domain of human knowledge so splendid, so inaccessible
to cavil, so unequivocal in their results, that the majority of
mankind would perhaps be carried along with this decision.
There seems, however, to be no doubt that the mind of Bacon
was more comprehensive and profound. But these compari-
sons are apt to involve *incommensurable* relations. In their
own intellectual characters, they bore no great resemblance
to each other. Bacon had scarce any knowledge of geo-

metry, and so far ranks much below not only Galileo, but
Descartes, Newton, and Leibnitz, all signalised by wonderful
discoveries in the science of quantity, or in that part of
physics which employs it. He has, in one of the profound
aphorisms of the Novum Organum, distinguished the two
species of philosophical genius, one more apt to perceive the
differences of things, the other their analogies. In a mind of
the highest order neither of these powers will be really deficient, and his own inductive method is at once the best
exercise of both, and the best safeguard against the excess of
either. But, upon the whole, it may certainly be said, that
the genius of Lord Bacon was naturally more inclined to collect the resemblances of nature than to note her differences.
This is the case with men like him of sanguine temper, warm
fancy, and brilliant wit; but it is not the frame of mind which
is best suited to strict reasoning.

77. It is no proof of a solid acquaintance with Lord
Bacon's philosophy, to deify his name as the ancient schools
did those of their founders, or even to exaggerate the powers
of his genius. Powers they were surprisingly great, yet
limited in their range, and not in all respects equal; nor
could they overcome every impediment of circumstance.
Even of Bacon it may be said, that he attempted more than
he has achieved, and perhaps more than he clearly apprehended. His objects appear sometimes indistinct, and I am
not sure that they are always consistent. In the Advancement of Learning, he aspired to fill up, or at least to indicate,
the deficiencies in every department of knowledge; he gradually confined himself to philosophy, and at length to
physics. But few of his works can be deemed complete, not
even the treatise De Augmentis, which comes nearer to this
than most of the rest. Hence the study of Lord Bacon is
difficult, and not, as I conceive, very well adapted to those
who have made no progress whatever in the exact sciences,
nor accustomed themselves to independent thinking. They
have never been made a text-book in our universities; though,
after a judicious course of preparatory studies, by which I mean
a good foundation in geometry and the philosophical principles of grammar, the first book of the Novum Organum

might be very advantageously combined with the instruction of an enlightened lecturer.[1]

---

[1] It by no means is to be inferred that because the actual text of Bacon is not always such as can be well understood by very young men, I object to their being led to the real principles of inductive philosophy, which alone will teach them to think, firmly but not presumptuously, for themselves. Few defects, on the contrary, in our system of education are more visible than the want of an adequate course of logic; and this is not likely to be rectified so long as the Aristotelian methods challenge that denomination exclusively of all other aids to the reasoning faculties. The position that nothing else is to be called logic, were it even agreeable to the derivation of the word, which it is not, or to the usage of the ancients, which is by no means uniformly the case, or to that of modern philosophy and correct language, which is certainly not at all the case. is no answer to the question, whether what we call logic does not deserve to be taught at all.

A living writer of high reputation, who has at least fully understood his own subject, and illustrated it better than his predecessors, from a more enlarged reading and thinking, wherein his own acuteness has been improved by the writers of the Baconian school, has been unfortunately instrumental, by the very merits of his treatise on Logic, in keeping up the prejudices on this subject, which have generally been deemed characteristic of the university to which he belonged. All the reflection I have been able to give to the subject has convinced me of the inefficacy of the syllogistic art in enabling us to think rightly for ourselves, or, which is part of thinking rightly, to detect those fallacies of others which might impose on our understanding before we have acquired that art. It has been often alleged, and as far as I can judge, with perfect truth, that no man, who can be worth answering, ever commits, except through mere inadvertence, any paralogisms which the common logic serves to point out. It is easy enough to construct syllogisms which sin against its rules; but the question is, by whom they were employed. For though it is not uncommon, as I am aware, to represent an adversary as reasoning illogically, this is generally effected by putting his

argument into our own words. The great fault of all, over-induction, or the assertion of a general premise upon an insufficient examination of particulars, cannot be discovered or cured by any *logical* skill; and this is the error into which men really fall, not that of omitting to *distribute the middle term*, though it comes in effect, and often in appearance, to the same thing. I do not contend that the rules of syllogism, which are very short and simple, ought not to be learned; or that there may not be some advantage in occasionally stating our own argument, or calling on another to state his, in a regular form (an advantage, however, rather dialectical, which is, in other words, rhetorical, than one which affects the reasoning faculties themselves); nor do I deny that it is philosophically worth while to know that all *general reasoning by words* may be reduced into syllogism, as it is to know that most of plane geometry may be resolved into the superposition of equal triangles; but to represent this portion of logical science as the whole, appears to me almost like teaching the scholar Euclid's axioms, and the axiomatic theorem to which I have alluded, and calling this the science of geometry. The following passage from the Port-Royal logic is very judicious and candid, giving as much to the Aristotelian system as it deserves: Cette partie, que nous avons maintenant à traiter, qui comprend les règles du raisonnement, est estimée la plus importante de la logique, et c'est presque l'unique qu'on y traite avec quelque soin; mais il y a sujet de douter si elle est aussi utile qu'on se l'imagine. La plupart des erreurs des hommes, comme nous avons déjà dit ailleurs, viennent bien plus de ce qu'ils raisonnent sur de faux principes, que non pas de ce qu'ils raisonnent mal suivant leurs principes. Il arrive rarement qu'on se laisse tromper par des raisonnemens qui ne soient faux que parce que la conséquence en est mal tirée; et ceux qui ne seroient pas capables d'en reconnoître la fausseté par la seule lumière de la raison, ne le seroient pas ordinairement d'entendre les règles que l'on en donne, et encore moins de les appliquer. Néanmoins, quand on ne considéreroit ces règles que comme des vérités spéculatives, elles serviroient tou-

78. The ignorance of Bacon in mathematics, and, what was much worse, his inadequate notions of their utility, must be reckoned among the chief defects in his philosophical writings. In a remarkable passage of the Advancement of Learning, he held mathematics to be a part of metaphysics; but the place of this is altered in the Latin, and they are treated as merely auxiliary or instrumental to physical inquiry. He had some

His prejudice against mathematics.

---

jours à exercer l'esprit ; et de plus, on ne peut nier qu'elles n'aient quelque usage en quelques rencontres, et à l'égard de quelques personnes, qui, étant d'un naturel vif et pénétraut, ne se laissent quelquefois tromper par des fausses conséquences, que faute d'attention, à quoi la réflexion qu'ils feroient sur ces règles seroit capable de remédier.' Art de Penser, part iii. How different is this sensible passage from one quoted from some anonymous writer in Whately's Logic, p. 34!—' A fallacy consists of an ingenious mixture of truth and falsehood so entangled, so intimately blended, that the fallacy is, in the chemical phrase, held in solution ; *one drop of sound logic* is that test which immediately disunites them, makes the foreign substance visible, and precipitates it to the bottom.' One fallacy, it might be answered, as common as any, is the *false analogy*, the misleading the mind by a comparison, where there is no real proportion or resemblance. The chemist's test is the *necessary* means of detecting the foreign substance; if the ' drop of sound logic' be such, it is strange that lawyers, mathematicians, and mankind in general, should so sparingly employ it; the fact being notorious, that those most eminent for strong reasoning powers are rarely conversant with the syllogistic method. It is also well known, that these ' intimately blended mixtures of truth and falsehood' perplex no man of plain sense, except when they are what is called *extra-logical*; cases wherein the art of syllogism is of no use.

[The syllogistic logic appears to have been more received into favour of late among philosophers, both here and on the Continent, than it was in the two preceding centuries. The main question, it is to be kept in mind, does not relate to its principles as a science, but to the practical usefulness of its rules as an art.

An able writer has lately observed, that ' he must be fortunate in the clearness of his mind, who, knowing the logical mode, is never obliged to have recourse to it to destroy ambiguity or heighten evidence, and particularly so in his opponents, who, in verbal or written controversy, never finds it necessary to employ it in trying their arguments.' Penny Cyclopædia, art. Syllogism. Every one must judge of this by his own experience ; the profound thinker whose hand seems discernible in this article, has a strong claim to authority in favour of the utility of the syllogistic method ; yet we cannot help remembering that it is very rarely employed even in controversy, where I really believe it to be a valuable weapon against an antagonist, and capable of producing no small effect on the indifferent reader or hearer, especially if he is not of a very sharp apprehension; and moreover that, as I at least believe, the proportion of mathematical, political, or theological reasoners, who have acquired or retained any tolerable expertness in the *technical* part of logic, is far from high, nor am I aware that they fall into fallacies for want of knowledge of it ; but I mean strictly such fallacies as the syllogistic method alone seems to correct. What comes nearest to syllogistic reasoning in practice is that of geometry; as thus, $A = B$; but $C = A$; ergo, $C = B$, is essentially a syllogism, but not according to form. If, however, equality of magnitude may be considered as identity, according to the dictum of Aristotle, ἐν τουτοῖς ἡ ἰσότης ἑνότης, the foregoing is regular in logical form ; and if we take A, B, and C for *ratios*, which are properly identical, not equal, this may justly be called a syllogism. But those who contend most for the formal logic, seldom much regard its use in geometrical science.— 1847.]

prejudice against pure mathematics, and thought they had
been unduly elevated in comparison with the realities of
nature. 'I know not,' he says, 'how it has arisen that
mathematics and logic, which ought to be the serving-maids
of physical philosophy, yet affecting to vaunt the certainty
that belongs to them, presume to exercise a dominion over
her.' It is, in my opinion, erroneous to speak of geometry,
which relates to the realities of space, and to natural objects
so far as extended, as a mere hand-maid of physical philosophy, and not rather a part of it. Playfair has made some
good remarks on the advantages derived to experimental
philosophy itself from the mere application of geometry and
algebra. And one of the reflections which this ought to excite is, that we are not to conceive, as some hastily do, that
there can be no real utility to mankind, even of that kind of
utility which consists in multiplying the conveniences and
luxuries of life, springing from theoretical and speculative
inquiry. The history of algebra, so barren in the days of
Tartaglia and Vieta, so productive of *wealth*, when applied to
dynamical calculations in our own, may be a sufficient
answer.

79. One of the petty blemishes, which, though lost in the
Bacon's
excess of
wit. splendour of Lord Bacon's excellences, it is not
unfair to mention, is connected with the peculiar
characteristics of his mind; he is sometimes too metaphorical
and witty. His remarkable talent for discovering analogies
seems to have inspired him with too much regard to them
as arguments, even when they must appear to any common
reader fanciful and far-fetched. His terminology, chiefly for
the same reason, is often a little affected, and, in Latin,
rather barbarous. The divisions of his prerogative instances
in the Novum Organum are not always founded upon intelligible distinctions. And the general obscurity of the style,
neither himself nor his assistants being good masters of the
Latin language, which at the best is never flexible or copious
enough for our philosophy, renders the perusal of both his
great works too laborious for the impatient reader. Brucker
has well observed that the Novum Organum has been neglected by the generality, and proved of far less service than
it would otherwise have been in philosophy, in consequence

of these very defects, as well as the real depth of the author's mind.[k]

80. What has been the fame of Bacon, 'the wisest, greatest, of mankind,' it is needless to say. What has been his real influence over mankind, how much of our enlarged and exact knowledge may be attributed to his inductive method, what of this again has been due to a thorough study of his writings, and what to an indirect and secondary acquaintance with them, are questions of another kind, and less easily solved. Stewart, the philosopher who has dwelt most on the praises of Bacon, while he conceives him to have exercised a considerable influence over the English men of science in the seventeenth century, supposes, on the authority of Montucla, that he did not 'command the general admiration of Europe,' till the publication of the preliminary discourse to the French Encyclopædia by Diderot and D'Alembert. This, however, is by much too precipitate a conclusion. He became almost immediately known on the Continent. Gassendi was one of his most ardent admirers. Descartes mentions him, I believe, once only, in a letter to Mersenne in 1632;[m] but he was of all men the most unwilling to praise a contemporary. It may be said that these were philosophers, and that their testimony does not imply the admiration of mankind. But writers of a very different character mention him in a familiar manner. Richelieu is said to have highly esteemed Lord Bacon.[n] And it may in some measure be due to this, that in the Sentimens de l'Académie française sur le Cid, he is alluded to, simply

Fame of Bacon on the Continent.

---

[k] Legenda ipsa nobilissima tractatio ab illis est, qui in rerum naturalium inquisitione feliciter progredi cupiunt. Quæ si paulo plus luminis et perspicuitatis haberet, et novorum terminorum et partitionum artificio lectorem non remoraretur, longè plura, quam factum est, contulisset ad philosophiæ emendationem. His enim obstantibus a plerisque hoc organum neglectum est. Hist. Philos. v. 99.

[m] Vol. vi. p. 210, edit. Cousin.

[n] The only authority that I can now quote for this is not very good, that of Aubrey's Manuscripts, which I find in Seward's Anecdotes, iv. 328. But it seems not improbable. The same book quotes Balzac as saying, "Croyons donc, pour l'amour du Chancelier Bacon, que toutes les folies des anciens sont sages; et tous leurs songes mystères, et de celles-là qui sont estimées pures fables, il n'y en a pas une, quelque bizarre et extravagante qu'elle soit, qui n'ait son fondement dans l'histoire, *si l'on en veut croire Bacon*, et qui n'ait été déguisée de la sorte par les sages du vieux temps pour la rendre plus utile aux peuples.'

by the name Bacon, as one well known.[o] Voiture, in a letter
to Costar, about the same time, bestows high eulogy on some
passages of Bacon which his correspondent had sent to him,
and observes that Horace would have been astonished to
hear a barbarian Briton discourse in such a style.[p] The
treatise De Augmentis was republished in France in 1624,
the year after its appearance in England. It was translated
into French as early as 1632; no great proofs of neglect.
Editions came out in Holland, 1645, 1652, and 1662. Even
the Novum Organum, which, as has been said, never became
so popular as his other writings, was thrice printed in Holland, in 1645, 1650, and 1660.[q] Leibnitz and Puffendorf are
loud in their expressions of admiration, the former ascribing
to him the revival of true philosophy as fully as we can at
present.[r] I should be more inclined to doubt whether he
were adequately valued by his countrymen in his own time,
or in the immediately subsequent period. Under the first
Stuarts, there was little taste among studious men but for
theology, and chiefly for a theology which, proceeding with
an extreme deference to authority, could not but generate a
disposition of mind, even upon other subjects, alien to the
progressive and inquisitive spirit of the inductive philosophy.[s]

---

[o] P. 44 (1633).

[p] J'ai trouvé parfaitement beau tout
ce que vous me mandez de Bacon. Mais
ne vous semble-t-il pas qu'Horace, qui
disoit, Visam Britannos hospitibus feros,
seroit bien étonné d'entendre un barbare
discourir comme cela ? Costar is said
by Bayle to have borrowed much from
Bacon. La Mothe le Vayer mentions
him in his Dialogues; in fact, instances
are numerous.

[q] Montagu's Life of Bacon, p. 407.
He has not mentioned an edition at
Strasburg, 1635, which is in the British
Museum.

There is also an edition without time
or place, in the catalogue of the British
Museum.

[r] Brucker, v. 95. Stewart says that
'Bayle does not give above twelve lines
to Bacon;' but he calls him one of the
greatest men of his age, and the length
of an article in Bayle was never designed
to be a measure of the merit of its subject.—[The reception of Bacon's philosophical writings on the Continent has

been elaborately proved against Stewart,
in a dissertation by Mr. Macvey Napier,
published in the eighth volume of the
Transactions of the Royal Society of
Edinburgh.—1842.]

[s] It is not uncommon to meet with
persons, especially who are or have been
engaged in teaching others dogmatically
what they have themselves received in
the like manner, to whom the inductive
philosophy appears a mere school of
scepticism, or at best wholly inapplicable
to any subjects which require entire
conviction. A certain deduction from
certain premises is the only reasoning
they acknowledge. Lord Bacon has a
remarkable passage on this in the 9th
book De Augmentis. Postquam articuli
et principia religionis jam in sedibus suis
fuerint locata, ita ut a rationis examine
penitus eximantur, tum demum conce-
ditur ab illis illationes derivare ac dedu-
cere secundum analogiam ipsorum. In
rebus quidem naturalibus hoc non tenet.
Nam et ipsa principia examini subjici-
untur; per inductionem, inquam, licet

The institution of the Royal Society, or rather the love of
physical science out of which that institution arose, in the
second part of the seventeenth century, made England resound with the name of her illustrious chancellor. Few now
spoke of him without a kind of homage that only the greatest
men receive. Yet still it was by natural philosophers alone
that the writings of Bacon were much studied. The editions
of his works, except the Essays, were few; the Novum Organum never came separately from the English press.[t] They
were not even frequently quoted; for I believe it will be
found that the fashion of referring to the brilliant passages
of the De Augmentis and the Novum Organum, at least in
books designed for the general reader, is not much older
than the close of the last century. Scotland has the merit
of having led the way; Reid, Stewart, Robison, and Playfair
turned that which had been a blind veneration into a rational
worship; and I should suspect that more have read Lord
Bacon within these thirty years than in the two preceding
centuries. It may be an usual consequence of the enthusiastic panegyrics lately poured upon his name, that a more
positive efficacy has sometimes been attributed to his philosophical writings than they really possessed, and it might

---

minime per syllogismum. Atque eadem
illa nullam habent cum ratione repug-
nantiam, ut ab eodem fonte cum primæ
propositiones, tum mediæ, deducantur.
Aliter fit in religione : ubi et primæ propositiones authopystatæ sunt atque per
se subsistentes ; et rursus non reguntur
ab illa ratione quæ propositiones conse-
quentes deducit. Neque tamen hoc fit in
religione sola, sed etiam in aliis scientiis,
tam gravioribus, quam levioribus, ubi
scilicet propositiones humanæ placita
sunt, non posita ; siquidem et in illis
rationis usus absolutus esse non potest.
Videmus enim in ludis, puta schaccorum,
aut similibus, priores ludi normas et
leges merè positivas esse, et ad placitum ;
quas recipi, non in disputationem vocari,
prorsus oporteat; ut vero vincas, et peritè
lusum instituas, ad artificiosum est et rationale. Eodem modo fit et in legibus
humanis ; in quibus haud paucæ sunt
maximæ, ut loquuntur, hoc est, placita

mera juris, quæ auctoritate magis quam
ratione nituntur, neque in disceptationem
veniunt. Quid vero sit justissimum, non
absolutè, sed relativè, hoc est ex analogiâ
illarum maximarum, id demum rationale
est, et latum disputationi campum præbet.
This passage, well weighed, may show us
where, why, and by whom, the synthetic
and syllogistic methods have been preferred to the inductive and analytical.
   [t] The De Augmentis was only once
published after the first edition, in 1638.
An indifferent translation, by Gilbert
Watts, came out in 1640. No edition
of Bacon's works was published in
England before 1730; another appeared
in 1740, and there have been several
since. But they had been printed at
Frankfort in 1665. It is unnecessary to
observe, that many copies of the foreign
editions were brought to this country.
This is mostly taken from Mr. Montagu's account.

be asked whether Italy, where he was probably not much known, were not the true school of experimental philosophy in Europe, whether his methods of investigation were not chiefly such as men of sagacity and lovers of truth might simultaneously have devised. But, whatever may have been the case with respect to actual discoveries in science, we must give to written wisdom its proper meed; no books prior to those of Lord Bacon carried mankind so far on the road to truth; none have obtained so thorough a triumph over arrogant usurpation without seeking to substitute another; and he may be compared to those liberators of nations, who have given them laws by which they might govern themselves, and retained no homage but their gratitude.ᵘ

ᵘ I have met, since this passage was written, with one in Stewart's Life of Reid, which seems to state the *effects* of Bacon's philosophy in a just and temperate spirit, and which I rather quote because this writer has, by his eulogies on that philosophy, led some to an exaggerated notion. 'The influence of Bacon's genius on the subsequent progress of physical discovery has been seldom duly appreciated; by some writers almost entirely overlooked, and by others considered as the sole cause of the reformation in science which has since taken place. Of these two extremes, the latter certainly is the least wide of the truth : for in the whole history of letters no other individual can be mentioned whose exertions have had so indisputable an effect in forwarding the intellectual progress of mankind. On the other hand it must be acknowledged, that before the era when Bacon appeared, various philosophers in different parts of Europe had struck into the right path; and it may perhaps be doubted, whether any one important rule with respect to the true method of investigation be contained in his works,ᵇ of which no hint can be traced in those of his predecessors. His great merit lay in concentrating their feeble and scattered lights; fixing the attention of philosophers on the distinguishing characteristics of true and of false science, by a felicity of illustration peculiar to himself, seconded by the commanding powers of a bold and figurative eloquence. The method of investigation which he recommended had been previously followed in every instance in which any solid discovery had been made with respect to the laws of nature; but it had been followed accidentally and without any regular preconceived design; and it was reserved for him to reduce to rule and method what others had effected, either fortuitously, or from some momentary glimpse of the truth. These remarks are not intended to detract from the just glory of Bacon; for they apply to all those, without exception, who have systematised the principles of any of the arts. Indeed they apply less forcibly to him than to any other philosopher whose studies have been directed to objects analogous to his; inasmuch as we know of no art of which the rules have been reduced successfully into a didactic form, when the art itself was as much in infancy as experimental philosophy was when Bacon wrote.' Account of Life and Writings of Reid, sect. 2.

Sect. III.

On the Metaphysical Philosophy of Descartes.

81. René Descartes was born in 1596, of an ancient family in Touraine.   An inquisitive curiosity into the Early life of nature and causes of all he saw is said to have dis- Descartes. tinguished his childhood, and this was certainly accompanied by an uncommon facility and clearness of apprehension. At a very early age he entered the college of the Jesuits at La Flèche, and passed through their entire course of literature and philosophy. It was now, at the age of sixteen, as he tells us, that he began to reflect, with little satisfaction, on his studies, finding his mind beset with error, and obliged to confess that he had learned nothing but the conviction of his ignorance. Yet he knew that he had been educated in a famous school, and that he was not deemed behind his contemporaries. The ethics, the logic, even the geometry of the ancients, did not fill his mind with that clear stream of truth for which he was ever thirsting. On leaving La Flèche, the young Descartes mingled for some years in the world, and served as a volunteer both under Prince Maurice, and in the Imperial army. Yet during this period there were intervals when he withdrew himself wholly from society, and devoted his leisure to mathematical science. Some germs also of his peculiar philosophy were already ripening in his mind.

82. Descartes was twenty-three years old when, passing a solitary winter in his quarters at Neuburg, on the His begin- Danube, he began to revolve in his mind the futility ning to phi-
losophise. of all existing systems of philosophy, and the discrepancy of opinions among the generality of mankind, which rendered it probable that no one had yet found out the road to real science. He determined, therefore, to set about the investigation of truth for himself, erasing from his mind all preconceived judgments, as having been hastily and precariously taken up. He laid down for his guidance a few fundamental rules of logic, such as to admit nothing as true which he did not clearly perceive, and to proceed from the simpler notion to the more complex, taking the method of geometers, by

which they had gone so much farther than others, for the
true art of reasoning.   Commencing, therefore, with the
mathematical sciences, and observing that, however different
in their subjects, they treat properly of nothing but the relations of quantity, he fell, almost accidentally, as his words
seem to import, on the great discovery that geometrical
curves may be expressed algebraically.[x]   This gave him more
hope of success in applying his method to other parts of
philosophy.

83. Nine years more elapsed, during which Descartes,
He retires to though he quitted military service, continued to
Holland.   observe mankind in various parts of Europe, still
keeping his heart fixed on the great aim he had proposed to
himself, but, as he confesses, without having framed the
scheme of any philosophy beyond those of his contemporaries.
He deemed his time of life immature for so stupendous a
task.   But at the age of thirty-three, with little notice to
his friends, he quitted Paris, convinced that absolute retirement was indispensable for that rigorous investigation
of first principles which he now determined to institute,
and retired into Holland.   In this country he remained
eight years so completely aloof from the distractions of the
world that he concealed his very place of residence, though
preserving an intercourse of letters with many friends in
France.

84. In 1637 he broke upon the world with a volume con-
His publi-   taining the Discourse upon Method, the Dioptrics,
cations.   the Meteors, and the Geometry.   It is only with
the first that we are for the present concerned.[y]   In this discourse, the most interesting, perhaps, of Descartes' writings,
on account of the picture of his life and of the progress of
his studies that it furnishes, we find the Cartesian metaphysics, which do not consist of many articles, almost as
fully detailed as in any of his later works.   In the Medita-
tiones de Prima Philosophia, published in 1641, these fundamental principles are laid down again more at length.   He
invited the criticism of philosophers on these famous Medita-

---

[x] Œuvres de Descartes, par Cousin, Paris, 1824, vol. i. p. 143.
[y] Ibid. p. 121–212.

tions. They did not refuse the challenge, and seven sets of objections, from as many different quarters, with seven replies from Descartes himself, are subjoined to the later editions of the Meditations. The Principles of Philosophy, published in Latin in 1644, contains what may be reckoned the final statement, which occupies most of the first book, written with uncommon conciseness and precision. The beauty of philosophical style which distinguishes Descartes is never more seen than in this first book of the Principia, the translation of which was revised by Clerselier, an eminent friend of the author. It is a contrast at once to the elliptical brevity of Aristotle, who hints, or has been supposed to hint, the most important positions in a short clause, and to the verbose, figurative declamation of many modern metaphysicians. In this admirable perspicuity Descartes was imitated by his disciples Arnauld and Malebranche, especially the former. His unfinished posthumous treatise, the ' Inquiry after Truth by Natural Reason,' is not carried farther than a partial development of the same leading principles of Cartesianism. There is, consequently, a great deal of apparent repetition in the works of Descartes, but such as on attentive consideration will show, not perhaps much real variance, but some new lights that had occurred to the author in the course of his reflections.[z]

85. In pursuing the examination of the first principles of knowledge, Descartes perceived not only that he had cause to doubt of the various opinions which *He begins by doubting all.* he had found current among men, from that very circumstance of their variety, but that the sources of all which he had received for truth themselves, namely, the senses, had afforded him no indisputable certainty. He began to recollect how often he had been misled by appearances, which had at first sight given no intimation of their fallacy, and asked himself in vain by what infallible test he could discern

---

[z] A work has lately been published, Essais philosophiques, suivis de la Métaphysique de Descartes, assemblée et mise en ordre par L. A. Gruyer, 4 vols. Bruxelles, 1832. In the fourth volume we find the metaphysical passages in the writings of Descartes, including his correspondence, arranged methodically in his own words, but with the omission of a large part of the objections to the Meditations and of his replies. I did not, however, see this work in time to make use of it.

the reality of external objects, or at least their conformity to his idea of them. The strong impressions made in sleep led him to inquire whether all he saw and felt might not be in a dream. It was true that there seemed to be some notions more elementary than the rest, such as extension, figure, duration, which could not be reckoned fallacious; nor could he avoid owning that, if there were not an existing triangle in the world, the angles of one conceived by the mind, though it were in sleep, must appear equal to two right angles. But even in this certitude of demonstration he soon found something deficient: to err in geometrical reasoning is not impossible; why might he not err in this? especially in a train of consequences, the particular terms of which are not at the same instant present to the mind. But, above all, there might be a superior being, powerful enough and willing to deceive him. It was no kind of answer to treat this as improbable, or as an arbitrary hypothesis. He had laid down as a maxim that nothing could be received as truth which was not demonstrable; and in one place, rather hyperbolically, and indeed extravagantly in appearance, says that he made little difference between merely probable and false suppositions; meaning this, however, as we may presume, in the sense of geometers, who would say the same thing.

86. But, divesting himself thus of all belief in what the world deemed most unquestionable, plunged in an abyss, as it seemed for a time, he soon found his feet on a rock, from which he sprang upwards to an unclouded sun. Doubting all things, abandoning all things, he came to the question, what is it that doubts and denies? Something it must be; he might be deceived by a superior power, but it was he that was deceived. He felt his own existence; the proof of it was that he did feel it; that he had affirmed, that he now doubted, in a word, that he was a thinking substance. *Cogito; Ergo sum*—this famous enthymem of the Cartesian philosophy veiled in rather formal language that which was to him, and must be to us all, the eternal basis of conviction, which no argument can strengthen, which no sophistry can impair, the consciousness of a self

His first step in knowledge.

within, a percipient indivisible Ego.[a]   The only proof of this
is that it admits of no proof, that no man can pretend to
doubt of his own existence with sincerity, or to express a
doubt without absurd and inconsistent language.

87. The scepticism of Descartes, it appears, which is
merely provisional, is not at all similar to that of
the Pyrrhonists, though some of his arguments   His mind
may have been shafts from their quiver.   Nor did he make
use, which is somewhat remarkable, of the reason-
ings afterwards employed by Berkeley against the   not sceptical.
material world, though no one more frequently distinguished
than Descartes between the objective reality, as it was then
supposed to be, of ideas in the mind, and the external or
sensible reality of things.   Scepticism, in fact, was so far
from being characteristic of his disposition, that his errors
sprang chiefly from the opposite source, little as he was
aware of it, from an undue positiveness in theories which he
could not demonstrate, or even render highly probable.[b]

88. The certainty of an existing Ego easily led him to

---

[a] This word, introduced by the Germans, or originally perhaps by the old
Cartesians, is rather awkward, but far
less so than the English pronoun I, which
is also equivocal in sound.   Stewart has
adopted it as the lesser evil, and it seems
reasonable not to scruple the use of a
word so convenient, if not necessary, to
express the unity of the conscious principle.   If it had been employed earlier,
I am apt to think that some great metaphysical extravagances would have been
avoided, and some fundamental truths
more clearly apprehended.   Fichte is
well known to have made the grand division of *Ich* and *Nicht Ich*, *Ego* and *Non
Ego*, the basis of his philosophy ; in
other words, the difference of subjective
and objective reality.

[b] One of the rules Descartes lays
down in his posthumous art of logic, is
that we ought never to busy ourselves
except about objects concerning which
our understanding appears capable of
acquiring an unquestionable and certain
knowledge, vol. xi. p. 204.   This is at
least too unlimited a proposition, and
would exclude, not indeed all probability,
but all inquiries which must by neces-

sity end in nothing more than probability.   Accordingly we find in the next
pages, that he made little account of any
sciences but arithmetic and geometry, or
such others as equal them in certainty.
' From all this,' he concludes, ' we may
infer, not that arithmetic and geometry
are the only sciences which we must
learn, but that he who seeks the road to
truth should not trouble himself with
any object of which he cannot have as
certain a knowledge as of arithmetical
and geometrical demonstrations.'   It is
unnecessary to observe what havoc this
would make with investigations, even in
physics, of the highest importance to
mankind.

Beattie, in the essay on Truth, part ii.
chap. 2, has made some unfounded criticisms on the scepticism of Descartes,
and endeavours to turn into ridicule his
Cogito ; Ergo sum.   Yet if any one
should deny his own, or our existence, I
do not see how we could refute him,
were he worthy of refutation, but by some
such language ; and in fact, it is what
Beattie himself says, more paraphrasti-
cally, in answering Hume.

that of the operations of the mind, called afterwards by Locke
He arrives at more certainty. ideas of reflection, the believing, doubting, willing,
loving, fearing, which he knew by consciousness,
and indeed by means of which alone he knew that the Ego
existed. He now proceeded a step farther; and, reflecting
on the simplest truths of arithmetic and geometry, saw that
it was as impossible to doubt of them as of the acts of his
mind. But as he had before tried to doubt even of these,
on the hypothesis that he might be deceived by a superior
intelligent power, he resolved to inquire whether such a
power existed, and if it did, whether it could be a deceiver.
The affirmative of the former and the negative of the latter
question Descartes established by that extremely subtle
reasoning so much celebrated in the seventeenth century,
but which has less frequently been deemed conclusive in
later times. It is at least that which no man, not fitted by
long practice for metaphysical researches, will pretend to
embrace.

89. The substance of his argument was this. He found
His proof of a Deity. within himself the idea of a perfect Intelligence,
eternal, infinite, necessary. This could not come
from himself, nor from external things, because both were
imperfect, and there could be no more in the effect than
there is in the cause. And this idea requiring a cause, it
could have none but an actual being, not a possible being,
which is undistinguishable from mere non-entity. If,
however, this should be denied, he inquires whether he, with
this idea of God, could have existed by any other cause, if
there were no God. Not, he argues, by himself; for if he
were the author of his own being, he would have given
himself every perfection, in a word, would have been God.
Not by his parents, for the same might be said of them, and
so forth, if we remount to a series of productive beings.
Besides this, as much power is required to preserve as to
create, and the continuance of existence in the effect implies
the continued operation of the cause.

90. With this argument, in itself sufficiently refined, Des-
Another proof of it. cartes blended another still more distant from
common apprehension. Necessary existence is in-
volved in the idea of God. All other beings are conceivable

in their essence, as things possible; in God alone his essence
and existence are inseparable, Existence is necessary to
perfection; hence a perfect being, or God, cannot be
conceived without necessary existence. Though I do not
know that I have misrepresented Descartes in this result of
his very subtle argument, it is difficult not to treat it as a
sophism. And it was always objected by his adversaries,
that he inferred the necessity of the thing from the necessity
of the idea, which was the very point in question. It seems
impossible to vindicate many of his expressions, from which
he never receded in the controversy to which his Meditations
gave rise. But the long habit of repeating in his mind the
same series of reasonings gave Descartes, as it will always do,
an inward assurance of their certainty, which could not be
weakened by any objection. The former argument for the
being of God, whether satisfactory or not, is to be distinguished from the present.[c]

---

[c] 'From what is said already of the
ignorance we are in of the essence of
mind, it is evident that we are not able
to know whether any mind be necessarily existent by a necessity à priori
founded in its essence, as we have showed
time and space to be. Some philosophers
think that such a necessity may be demonstrated of God from the nature of
perfection. For God being infinitely,
that is, absolutely perfect, they say he
must needs be necessarily existent; because, say they, necessary existence is
one of the greatest of perfections. But I
take this to be one of those false and
imaginary arguments, that are founded
in the abuse of certain terms; and of all
others this word, perfection, seems to
have suffered most this way. I wish I
could clearly understand what these philosophers mean by the word perfection,
when they thus say, that necessity of
existence is perfection. Does perfection
here signify the same thing that it does
when we say that God is infinitely good,
omnipotent, omniscient? Surely perfections are properly asserted of the several powers that attend the essences of
things and not of anything else, but in
a very unnatural and improper sense.
Perfection is a term of relation, and its
sense implies a fitness or agreement to
some certain end, and most properly to

some power in the thing that is denominated perfect. The term, as the etymology of it shows, is taken from the operation of artists. When an artist proposes
to himself to make any thing that shall
be serviceable to a certain effect, his
work is called more or less perfect, according as it agrees more or less with
the design of the artist. From arts, by
a similitude of sense, this word has been
introduced into morality, and signifies
that quality of an agent by which it is
able to act agreeable to the end its actions
tend to. The metaphysicians who reduce
every thing to transcendental considerations have also translated this term into
their science, and use it to signify the
agreement that any thing has with that
idea, which it is required that thing
should answer to. This perfection, therefore, belongs to those attributes that constitute the essence of a thing; and that
being is properly called the most perfect
which has all, the best, and each the
completest in its kind of those attributes,
which can be united in one essence.
Perfection, therefore, belongs to the essence of things, and not properly to their
existence; which is not a perfection of
any thing, no attribute of it, but only the
mere constitution of it *in rerum natura*.
Necessary existence, therefore, which is
a mode of existence, is not a perfection,

91. From the idea of a perfect being Descartes imme-
His deduc-
tions from
this. diately deduced the truth of his belief in an external world, and in the inferences of his reason.
For to deceive his creatures would be an imperfection in
God; but God is perfect. Whatever, therefore, is clearly and
distinctly apprehended by our reason must be true. We have
only to be on our guard against our own precipitancy and
prejudice, or surrender of our reason to the authority of
others. It is not by our understanding, such as God gave it
to us, that we are deceived; but the exercise of our free-will,
a high prerogative of our nature, is often so incautious as to
make us not discern truth from falsehood, and affirm or deny,
by a voluntary act, that which we do not distinctly apprehend. The properties of quantity, founded on our ideas of
extension and number, are distinctly perceived by our minds,
and hence the sciences of arithmetic and geometry are
certainly true. But when he turns his thoughts to the
phænomena of external sensation, Descartes cannot wholly
extricate himself from his original concession, the basis of
his doubt, that the senses do sometimes deceive us. He
endeavours to reconcile this with his own theory, which had
built the certainty of all that we clearly hold certain on the
perfect veracity of God.

92. It is in this inquiry that he reaches that important
Primary and
secondary
qualities. distinction between the primary and secondary
properties of matter, (the latter being modifications
of the former, relative only to our apprehension, but not

---

it being no attribute of the thing no more than existence is, which it is a mode of. But it may be said, that though necessary existence is not a perfection in itself, yet it is so in its cause, upon account of that attribute of the entity from whence it flows; that that attribute must of all others be the most perfect and most excellent, which necessary existence flows from, it being such as cannot be conceived otherwise than as existing. But what excellency, what perfection is there in all this? Space is necessarily existent on account of extension, which cannot be conceived otherwise than as existing. But what perfection is there in space upon this account, which can in no manner act on any thing, which is entirely devoid of all power, wherein I have showed all perfections to consist?

Therefore necessary existence, abstractedly considered, is no perfection; and therefore the idea of infinite perfection does not include, and consequently not prove, God to be necessarily existent. If he be so, it is on account of those attributes of his essence which we have no knowledge of.'

I have made this extract from a very short tract, called Contemplatio Philosophica, by Brook Taylor, which I found in an unpublished memoir of his life printed by the late Sir William Young in 1793. It bespeaks the clear and acute understanding of this celebrated philosopher, and appears to me an entire refutation of the scholastic argument of Descartes; one more fit for the Anselms and such dealers in words, from whom it came, than for himself.

inherent in things,) which, without being wholly new, contradicted the Aristotelian theories of the schools ;[d] and he remarked that we are never, strictly speaking, deceived by our senses, but by the inferences which we draw from them.

93. Such is nearly the substance, exclusive of a great variety of more or less episodical theories, of the three metaphysical works of Descartes, the history of the soul's progress from opinion to doubt, and from doubt to certainty. Few would dispute, at the present day, that he has destroyed too much of his foundations to render his superstructure stable; and to readers averse from metaphysical reflection, he must seem little else than an idle theorist, weaving cob-

---

[d] See Stewart's First Dissertation on the Progress of Philosophy. This writer has justly observed, that many persons conceive *colour* to be inherent in the object, so that the censure of Reid on Descartes and his followers, as having pretended to discover what no one doubted, is at least unreasonable in this respect. A late writer has gone so far as to say, 'Nothing at first can seem a more rational, obvious, and incontrovertible conclusion, than that the colour of a body is an inherent quality, like its weight, hardness, &c.; and that to *see* the object, and to see it of *its own colour*, when nothing intervenes between our eyes and it, are one and the same thing. Yet this is only a prejudice,' &c. Herschel's Discourse on Nat. Philos. p. 82. I almost even suspect that the notion of sounds and smells, being secondary or merely sensible qualities, is not distinct in all men's minds. But after we are become familiar with correct ideas, it is not easy to revive prejudices in our imagination. In the same page of Stewart's Dissertation, he has been led by dislike of the university of Oxford to misconceive, in an extraordinary manner, a passage of Addison in the Guardian, which is evidently a sportive ridicule of the Cartesian theory, and is absolutely inapplicable to the Aristotelian. [The most remarkable circumstance in Reid's animadversion on Descartes, as having announced nothing but what was generally known, is that he had himself, in his Inquiry into the Human Mind, contended very dogmatically in favour of the vulgar notion that secondary qualities exist in bodies, independently of

sensation. 'This scarlet rose which is before me, is still a scarlet rose when I shut my eyes, and was so at midnight when no eye saw it. The colour remains when the appearance ceases; it remains the same when the appearance changes.' Chap. vi. § 4. He even uses similar language as to perfumes, which, indeed, stand on the same ground, though we feel less of the prejudice in favour of their reality than of that of colours. Nothing can be more obvious than the reply: the colour remains only on the tacit hypothesis that some one is looking at the object; at midnight we can hardly say that the rose is red, except by an additional hypothesis, that the day should break. 'We never,' he proceeds, 'as far as I can judge, give the name of colour to the sensation, but to the quality only.' How then do we talk of bright, dull, glaring, gay, dazzling colours? Do not these words refer to a sensation, rather than to a configuration of parts in the coloured body by which it reflects or refracts light? But this first production of Reid, though abounding with acute and original remarks, is too much disfigured by a tendency to halloo on the multitude against speculative philosophy. The appeal to common sense, that is, the crude notions of men who had never reflected, even enough to use language with precision, would have been fatal to psychology. Reid afterwards laid aside the popular tone in writing on philosophy, though, perhaps, he was always too much inclined to cut knots when he could not untie them.'—1847.]

webs for pastime which common sense sweeps away. It is fair, however, to observe, that no one was more careful than Descartes to guard against any practical scepticism in the affairs of life. He even goes so far as to maintain, that a man having adopted any practical opinion on such grounds as seem probable, should pursue it with as much steadiness as if it were founded on demonstration; observing, however, as a general rule, to choose the most moderate opinions among those which he should find current in his own country.[e]

94. The objections adduced against the Meditations are Objections made to his Meditations. in a series of seven. The first are by a theologian named Caterus, the second by Mersenne, the third by Hobbes, the fourth by Arnauld, the fifth by Gassendi, the sixth by some anonymous writers, the seventh by a Jesuit of the name of Bourdin. To all of these Descartes replied with spirit and acuteness. By far the most important controversy was with Gassendi, whose objections were stated more briefly, and, I think, with less skill, by Hobbes. It was the first trumpet in the new philosophy of an ancient war between the sensual and ideal schools of psychology. Descartes had revived, and placed in a clearer light, the doctrine of mind, as not absolutely dependent upon the senses, nor of the same nature as their objects. Stewart does not acknowledge him as the first teacher of the soul's immateriality. 'That many of the schoolmen, and that the wisest of the ancient philosophers, when they described the mind as a spirit, or as a spark of celestial fire, employed these expressions, not with any intention to materialise its essence, but merely from want of more unexceptionable language, might be shown with demonstrative evidence, if this were the proper place for entering into the discussion.'[f] But though it cannot be said that Descartes was absolutely the first who maintained the strict immateriality of the soul, it is manifest to any one who has read his correspondence, that the tenet, instead of being general, as we are apt to presume, was by no means in accordance with the common opinion of his age. The fathers, with the exception, perhaps the single one, of

---

[e] Vol. i. p. 147. Vol. iii. p. 64.   [f] Dissertation, ubi suprà.

Augustin, had taught the corporeity of the thinking substance. Arnauld seems to consider the doctrine of Descartes
as almost a novelty in modern times. 'What you have
written concerning the distinction between the soul and
body appears to me very clear, very evident, and quite
divine; and as nothing is older than truth, I have had
singular pleasure to see that almost the same things have
formerly been very perspicuously and agreeably handled by
St. Augustin in all his tenth book on the Trinity, but chiefly
in the tenth chapter.'[g]   But Arnauld himself, in his objections to the Meditations, had put it as at least questionable,
whether that which thinks is not something extended, which,
besides the usual properties of extended substances, such as
mobility and figure, has also this particular virtue and
power of thinking.[h]   The reply of Descartes removed the
difficulties of the illustrious Jansenist, who became an ardent
and almost complete disciple of the new philosophy.   In a
placard against the Cartesian philosophy, printed in 1647,
which seems to have come from Revius, professor of theology
at Leyden, it is said, 'As far as regards the nature of things,
nothing seems to hinder but that the soul may be either a
substance, or a mode of corporeal substance.'[i]   And More,
who had carried on a metaphysical correspondence with
Descartes, whom he professed to admire, at least at that
time, above all philosophers that had ever existed, without
exception of his favourite Plato, extols him after his death
in a letter to Clerselier, as having best established the foundations of religion. 'For the Peripatetics,' he says, 'pretend
that there are certain substantial forms emanating from
matter, and so united to it that they cannot subsist without
it, to which class these philosophers refer the souls of almost
all living beings, even those to which they allow sensation
and thought; while the Epicureans, on the other hand, who
laugh at substantial forms, ascribe thought to matter itself,
so that it is M. Descartes alone, of all philosophers, who has
at once banished from philosophy all these substantial forms
or souls derived from matter, and absolutely divested matter
itself of the faculty of feeling and thinking.'[k]

---

[g] Descartes, x. 138.
[h] Id. ii. 14.

[i] Id. x. 73.
[k] Id. x. 386.   Even More seems to

95. It must be owned that the firm belief of Descartes in
Theory of
memory
and imagina-
tion. the immateriality of the Ego, or thinking principle, was accompanied with what in later times would have been deemed rather too great concessions to the materialists. He held the imagination and the memory to be portions of the brain, wherein the images of our sensations are bodily preserved ; and even assigned such a motive force to the imagination, as to produce those involuntary actions which we often perform, and all the movements of brutes. 'This explains how all the motions of all animals arise, though we grant them no knowledge of things, but only an imagination entirely corporeal, and how all those operations which do not require the concurrence of reason are produced in us.' But the whole of his notions as to the connexion of the soul and body, and indeed all his physiological theories, of which he was most enamoured, do little credit to the Cartesian philosophy. They are among those portions of his creed which have lain most open to ridicule, and which it would be useless for us to detail. He seems to have expected more advantage to psychology from anatomical researches than in that state of the science, or even probably in any future state of it, anatomy could afford. When asked once where was his library, he replied, showing a calf he was dissecting, 'This is my library.'[m] His treatise on the passions, a subject so important in the philosophy of the human mind, is made up of crude hypotheses, or

---

have been perplexed at one time by the difficulty of accounting for the knowledge and sentiment of disembodied souls, and almost inclined to admit their corporeity. 'J'aimerois mieux dire avec les Platoniciens, les anciens pères, et presque tous les philosophes, que les âmes humaines, tous les génies tant bons que mauvais, sont corporels, et que par conséquent ils ont un sentiment réel, c'est-à-dire, qui leur vient du corps dont ils sont revêtus.' This is in a letter to Descartes in 1649, which I have not read in Latin (vol. x. p. 249). I do not quite understand whether he meant only that the soul, when separated from the gross body, is invested with a substantial clothing, or that there is what we may call an interior body, a

supposed monad, to which the thinking principle is indissolubly united. This is what all materialists mean, who have any clear notions whatever; it is a possible, perhaps a plausible, perhaps even a highly probable, hypothesis, but one which will not prove their theory. The former seems almost an indispensable supposition, if we admit sensibility to phænomena at all in the soul after death ; but it is rather, perhaps, a theological than a metaphysical speculation.

[m] Descartes was very fond of dissection: C'est un exercice où je me suis souvent occupé depuis onze ans, et je crois qu'il n'y a guère de médecins qui y ait regardé de si près que moi. Vol. viii. p. 100, also p. 174 and 180.

at best irrelevant observations, on their physical causes and concomitants.

96. It may be considered as a part of this syncretism, as we may call it, of the material and immaterial hypotheses, that Descartes fixed the seat of the soul in the conarion, or pineal gland, which he selected as the only part of the brain which is not double.   By some means of communication which he did not profess to explain, though later metaphysicians have attempted to do so, the unextended intelligence, thus confined to a certain spot, receives the sensations which are immediately produced through impressions on the substance of the brain.   If he did not solve the problem, be it remembered that the problem has never since been solved.   It was objected by a nameless correspondent, who signs himself Hyperaspistes, that the soul being incorporeal could not leave by its operations a trace on the brain, which his theory seemed to imply.   Descartes answered, in rather a remarkable passage, that as to things purely intellectual, we do not, properly speaking, remember them at all, as they are equally original thoughts every time they present themselves to the mind, except that they are habitually joined, as it were, and associated with certain names, which, being bodily, make us remember them.[n]

Seat of soul in pineal gland.

97. If the orthodox of the age were not yet prepared for a doctrine which seemed so favourable at least to natural religion as the immateriality of the soul, it may be readily supposed, that Gassendi, like Hobbes, had imbibed too much of the Epicurean theory to acquiesce in the spiritualising principles of his adversary. In a sportive style he addresses him, *O anima!* and Descartes replying more angrily, retorts upon him the name *O caro!* which he frequently repeats.   Though we may lament such unhappy efforts at wit in these great men, the

Gassendi's attacks on the Medita-tions.

[n] This passage I must give in French, finding it obscure, and having translated more according to what I guess than literally.   Mais pour ce qui est des choses purement intellectuelles, à proprement parler on n'en a aucun ressouvenir ; et la première fois qu'elles se présentent à l'esprit, on les pense aussi bien que la seconde, si ce n'est peut-être qu'elles ont coutume d'être jointes et comme attachées à certains noms qui, étant corporels, font que nous nous ressouvenons aussi d'elles.   Vol. viii. p. 271.

names to not ill represent the spiritual and carnal philo-
sophies; the school that produced Leibnitz, Kant, and
Stewart, contrasted with that of Hobbes, Condillac, and
Cabanis.

98. It was a matter of course that the vulnerable passages of the six Meditations would not escape the
spear of so skilful an antagonist as Gassendi. But
many of his objections appear to be little more than cavils;
and upon the whole, Descartes leaves me with the impression
of his great superiority in metaphysical acuteness. It was
indeed impossible that men should agree, who persisted in
using a different definition of the important word, *idea*; and
the same source of interminable controversy has flowed ever
since for their disciples. Gassendi adopting the scholastic
maxim, ' Nothing is in the understanding, which has not
been in the sense,' carried it so much farther than those
from whom it came that he denied any thing to be an idea
but what was imagined by the mind. Descartes repeatedly
desired both him and Hobbes, whose philosophy was built
on the same notion, to remark that he meant by idea, whatever can be conceived by the understanding, though not
capable of being represented by the imagination.º Thus we
imagine a triangle, but we can only conceive a figure of a
thousand sides; we know its existence, and can reason about
its properties, but we have no image whatever in the mind,
by which we can distinguish such a polygon from one of a

Superiority of Descartes.

º Par le nom d'idée, il veut seulement qu'on entende ici les images des
choses matérielles dépeintes en la fantaisie corporelle; et cela étant supposé,
il lui est aisé de montrer qu'on ne peut
avoir propre et véritable idée de Dieu
ni d'un ange; mais j'ai souvent averti,
et principalement en celui-là même, que
je prends le nom d'idée pour tout ce qui
est conçu immédiatement par l'esprit;
en sorte que, lorsque je veux et que je
crains, parce que je conçois en même
temps, que je veux et que je crains, ce
vouloir et cette crainte sont mis par moi
en nombre des idées; et je me suis servi
de ce mot, parce qu'il étoit déjà com-
munément reçu par les philosophes pour
signifier les formes des conceptions de
l'entendement divin, encore que nous ne
reconnoissions en Dieu aucune fantaisie
ou imagination corporelle, et je n'en sa-
vois point de plus propre. Et je pense
avoir assez expliqué l'idée de Dieu pour
ceux qui veulent concevoir les sens que
je donne à mes paroles; mais pour ceux
qui s'attachent à les entendre autrement
que je ne fais, je ne le pourrais jamais
assez. Vol. i. p. 404. This is in answer
to Hobbes; the objections of Hobbes,
and Descartes' replies, turn very much
on this primary difference between ideas
as images, which alone our countryman
could understand, and ideas as intellec-
tions, conceptions, νοούμενα, incapable of
being imagined, but not less certainly
known and reasoned upon. The French
is a translation, but made by Clerselier
under the eye of Descartes, so that it
may be quoted as an original.

smaller or greater number of sides. Hobbes in answer to this threw out a paradox which he has not, perhaps, at least in so unlimited a manner, repeated, that by reason, that is, by the process of reasoning, we can infer nothing as to the nature of things, but only as to their names.[p] It is singular that a man conversant at least with the elements of geometry should have fallen into this error. For it does not appear that he meant to speak only of natural substances, as to which his language might seem to be a bad expression of what was afterwards clearly shown by Locke. That the understanding can conceive and reason upon that which the imagination cannot delineate, is evident not only from Descartes' instance of a polygon, but more strikingly by the whole theory of infinites, which are certainly somewhat more than bare words, whatever assistance words may give us in explaining them to others or to ourselves.[q]

99. Dugald Stewart has justly dwelt on the signal service rendered by Descartes to psychological philosophy, by turning the mental vision inward upon itself, and accustoming us to watch the operations of our intellect, which, though employed upon ideas obtained through the senses, are as distinguishable from them as the workman from

Stewart's remarks on Descartes.

---

[p] Que dirons-nous maintenant si peut-être le raisonnement n'est rien autre chose qu'un assemblage et un enchaîne-ment de noms par ce mot *est*? D'où il s'ensuivroit que par la raison nous ne concluons rien de tout touchant la nature des choses, mais seulement touchant leurs appellations, c'est-à-dire que par elle nous voyons simplement si nous assemblons bien ou mal les noms des choses, selon les conventions que nous avons faites à notre fantaisie touchant leurs significations. p. 476. Descartes merely answered :—L'assemblage qui se fait dans le raisonnement n'est pas celui des noms, mais bien celui des choses, signifiées par les noms ; et je m'étonne que le contraire puisse venir en l'esprit. de personne. Descartes treated Hobbes, whom he did not esteem, with less attention than his other corre-spondents. Hobbes could not under-stand what have been called ideas of reflection, such as fear, and thought it was nothing more than the idea of the

object feared. 'For what else is the fear of a lion,' he says, 'than the idea of this lion, and the effect which it pro-duces in the heart, which leads us to run away ?   But this running is not a thought ; so that nothing of our thought ex-ists in fear but the idea of the object.' Descartes only replied, ' It is self-evi-dent that it is not the same thing to see a lion and fear him, that it is to see him only.' p. 483.

[q] I suspect, from what I have since read, that Hobbes had a different, and what seems to me a very erroneous view of infinite, or infinitesimal quan-tities in geometry. For he answers the old sophism of Zeno, Quicquid di-vidi potest in partes infinitas est infini-tum, in a manner which does not meet the real truth of the case : Dividi posse in partes infinitas nihil aliud est quam dividi posse in partes *quotcunque quis velit*. Logica sive Computatio, c. v. p. 38. (edit. 1667).

his work.   He has given, indeed, to Descartes a very proud
title, Father of the experimental philosophy of the human
mind, as if he were to man what Bacon was to nature.[r]   By
patient observation of what passed within him, by holding
his soul, as it were, like an object in a microscope, which is
the only process of a good metaphysician, he became habi-
tuated to throw away those integuments of sense which hide
us from ourselves.   Stewart has censured him for the paradox,
as he calls it, that the *essence* of mind consists in thinking,
and that of matter in extension.   That the act of thinking is
as inseparable from the mind as extension is from matter,
cannot, indeed, be proved ; since, as our thoughts are successive, it is not inconceivable that there may be intervals of
duration between them ; but it can hardly be reckoned a
paradox.   But whoever should be led by the word essence to
suppose that Descartes confounded the percipient thinking
substance, the Ego, upon whose bosom, like that of the ocean,
the waves of perception are raised by every breeze of sense,
with the perception itself, or even, what is scarcely more
tenable, with the reflective action, or thought ; that he anticipated this strange paradox of Hume in his earliest work,
from which he silently withdrew in his Essays, would not only

---

[r] Dissertation on Progress of Philosophy. The word experiment must be
taken in the sense of observation.
Stewart very early took up his admiration for Descartes.   ' He was the first
philosopher who stated in a clear and
satisfactory manner the distinction between mind and matter, and who pointed
out the proper plan for studying the
intellectual philosophy.   It is chiefly in
consequence of his precise ideas with
respect to this distinction, that we may
remark in all his metaphysical writings
a perspicuity which is not observable in
those of any of his predecessors.'   Elem.
of Philos. of Human Mind, vol. i. (published in 1792), note A.   ' When Descartes,' he says in the dissertation
before quoted, ' established it as a
general principle, that *nothing conceivable by the power of imagination could
throw any light on the operations of
thought*, a principle which I consider as
exclusively his own, he laid the foundations of the experimental philosophy
of the human mind.   That the same

truth had been previously perceived
more or less distinctly by Bacon and
others, appears probable from the general complexion of their speculations ;
but which of them has expressed it with
equal precision, or laid it down as a
fundamental maxim in their logic ? '
The words which I have put in italics
seem too vaguely and not very clearly
expressed, nor am I aware that they are
borne out in their literal sense, by any
position of Descartes ; nor do I apprehend the allusion to Bacon.   But it is
certain that Descartes, and still more
his disciples Arnauld and Malebranche,
take better care to distinguish what can
be imagined from what can be conceived
or understood, than any of the school of
Gassendi in this or other countries.
One of the great merits of Descartes as
a metaphysical writer, not unconnected
with this, is that he is generally careful
to avoid figurative language in speaking
of mental operations, wherein he has
much the advantage over Locke.

do great injustice to one of the acutest understandings that
ever came to the subject, but overlook several clear assertions
of the distinction, especially in his answer to Hobbes. 'The
thought,' he says, 'differs from that which thinks, as the
mode from the substance.'[s]   And Stewart has in his earliest
work justly corrected Reid in this point as to the Cartesian
doctrine.[t]

100. Several singular positions which have led to an undue
depreciation of Descartes in general as a philosopher   Paradoxes
occur in his metaphysical writings. Such was his   of Descartes.
denial of thought, and, as is commonly said, sensation to
brutes, which he seems to have founded on the mechanism of
the bodily organs, a cause sufficient, in his opinion, to explain
all the phænomena of the motions of animals, and to obviate
the difficulty of assigning to them immaterial souls;[u] his

---

[s] Vol. i. p. 470. Arnauld objected,
in a letter to Descartes, Comment se
peut il faire que la pensée constitue
l'essence de l'esprit, puisque l'esprit est
une substance, et que la pensée semble
n'en être qu'un mode ? Descartes replied that thought in general, la pensée,
ou la nature qui pense, in which he placed
the essence of the soul, was very different from such or such particular acts of
thinking. Vol. vi. p. 153, 160.

[t] Philosophy of Human Mind, vol. i.
note A. See the Principia, § 63.

[u] It is a common opinion that Descartes denied all life and sensibility to
brutes. But this seems not so clear.
Il faut remarquer, he says in a letter to
More, where he has been arguing against
the existence in brutes of any thinking
principle, que je parle de la pensée, non
de la vie, ou du sentiment ; car je n'ôte
la vie à aucun animal, ne la faisant con-
sister que dans la seule chaleur du cœur.
Je ne leur refuse pas même le sentiment
autant qu'il dépend des organes du corps.
Vol. x. p. 208. In a longer passage, if
he does not express himself very clearly,
he admits passions in brutes, and it seems
impossible that he could have ascribed
passions to what has no sensation.
Much of what he here says is very good.
Bien que Montaigne et Charron aient
dit, qu'il y a plus de différence d'homme
à homme que d'homme à bête, il n'est
toutefois jamais trouvé aucune bête si
parfaite, qu'elle ait usé de quelque signe
pour faire entendre à d'autres animaux

quelque chose qui n'eût point de rapport
à ses passions ; et il n'y a point d'homme
si imparfait qu'il n'en use ; en sorte que
ceux qui sont sourds et muets inventent
des signes particuliers par lesquels ils
expriment leurs pensées ; ce qui me
semble un très-fort argument pour prouver que ce qui fait que les bêtes ne parlent point comme nous, est qu'elles n'ont
aucune pensée, et non point que les organes leur manquent. Et on ne peut
dire qu'elles parlent entre elles, mais que
nous ne les entendons pas ; car *comme
les chiens et quelques autres animaux nous
expriment leurs passions*, ils nous expri-
meroient aussi bien leurs pensées s'ils en
avoient.   Je sais bien que les bêtes font
beaucoup de choses mieux que nous,
mais je ne m'en étonne pas ; car cela
même sert à prouver qu'elles agissent
naturellement, et par ressorts, ainsi qu'un
horloge ; laquelle montre bien mieux
l'heure qu'il est que notre jugement
nous l'enseigne. . . . .   On peut
seulement dire que, bien que les bêtes ne
fassent aucune action qui nous assure
qu'elles pensent, toutefois, à cause que
les organes de leurs corps ne sont pas
fort différens des nôtres, on peut conjec-
turer qu'il y a quelque pensée jointe à
ces organes, ainsi que nous expérimen-
tons en nous, bien que la leur soit beaucoup moins parfaite ; à quoi je n'ai rien
à répondre, si non que si elles pensoient
aussi que nous, elles auroient une âme
immortelle aussi bien que nous ; ce qui
n'est pas vraisemblable, à cause qu'il n'y

rejection of final causes in the explanation of nature, as far
above our comprehension, and unnecessary to those who had
the internal proof of God's existence; his still more paradoxical tenet, that the truth of geometrical theorems, and
every other axiom of intuitive certainty, depended upon the
will of God; a notion that seems to be a relic of his original
scepticism, but which he pertinaciously defends throughout
his letters.[x] From remarkable errors men of original and
independent genius are rarely exempt; Descartes had pulled
down an edifice constructed by the labours of near two thousand years, with great reason in many respects, yet perhaps
with too unlimited a disregard of his predecessors; it was
his destiny, as it had been theirs, to be sometimes refuted
and depreciated in his turn.   But the single fact of his having
first established, both in philosophical and popular belief, the
proper immateriality of the soul, were we even to forget the
other great accessions which he made to psychology, would
declare the influence he has had on human opinion.   From
this immateriality, however, he did not derive the tenet of its
immortality.   He was justly contented to say, that from the
intrinsic difference between mind and body, the dissolution
of the one could not necessarily take away the existence of
the other, but that it was for God to determine whether it
should continue to exist; and this determination, as he
thought, could only be learned from his revealed will.   The
more powerful arguments, according to general apprehension,
which reason affords for the sentient being of the soul after
death, did not belong to the metaphysical philosophy of Descartes, and would never have been very satisfactory to his

---

a point de raison pour le croire de quelques animaux, sans le croire de tous, et
qu'il y en a plusieurs trop imparfaits
pour pouvoir croire cela d'eux, comme
sont les huîtres, les éponges, etc.   Vol.
ix. p. 425.   I do not see the meaning of
une âme immortelle in the last sentence ;
if the words had been une âme imma-
térielle, it would be to the purpose.
More, in a letter to which this is a reply,
had argued as if Descartes took brutes
for insensible machines, and combats
the paradox with the arguments which
common sense furnishes. He would even
have preferred ascribing immortality to
them, as many ancient philosophers did.

But surely Descartes, who did not acknowledge any proofs of the immortality
of the human soul to be valid, except
those founded on revelation, needed not to
trouble himself much about this difficulty.

[x] C'est en effet parler de Dieu comme
d'un Jupiter ou d'un Saturne, et l'assu-
jettir au Styx et aux destinées, que de
dire que ces vérités sont indépendantes
de lui.   Ne craignez point, je vous prie,
d'assurer et de publier partout que c'est
Dieu qui a établi ces lois en la nature,
ainsi qu'un roi établit les lois en son roy-
aume.   Vol. vi. p. 109.   He argues as
strenuously the same point in p. 132
and p. 307.

mind. He says, in one of his letters, that 'laying aside what faith assures us of, he owns that it is more easy to make conjectures for our own advantage, and entertain promising hopes, than to feel any confidence in their accomplishment.'[y]

101. Descartes was perhaps the first who saw that definitions of words, already as clear as they can be made, His just are nugatory or impracticable. This alone would notion of definitions. distinguish his philosophy from that of the Aristotelians, who had wearied and confused themselves for twenty centuries with unintelligible endeavours to grasp by definition what refuses to be defined. 'Mr. Locke,' says Stewart, 'claims this improvement as entirely his own, but the merit of it unquestionably belongs to Descartes, although it must be owned that he has not always sufficiently attended to it in his researches.'[z] A still more decisive passage to this effect than that referred to by Stewart in the Principia will be found in the posthumous dialogue on the Search after Truth. It is objected by one of the interlocutors, as it had actually been by Gassendi, that, to prove his existence by the act of thinking, he should first know what existence and what thought is. 'I agree with you,' the representative of Descartes replies, 'that it is necessary to know what doubt is, and what thought is, before we can be fully persuaded of this reasoning—I doubt, therefore I am—or what is the same—I think, therefore I am. But do not imagine that for this purpose you must torture your mind to find out

---

[y] Vol. ix. p. 369.

[z] Dissertation, ubi suprà. Stewart, in his Philosophical Essays, note A, had censured Reid for assigning this remark to Descartes and Locke, but without giving any better reason than that it is found in a work written by Lord Stair ; earlier, certainly, than Locke, but not before Descartes. It may be doubtful, as we shall see hereafter, whether Locke has not gone beyond Descartes, or at least distinguished undefinable words more strictly.

[Sir William Hamilton remarks on this passage, where Reid assigns the observation to Descartes and Locke: 'This is incorrect. Descartes has little, and Locke no praise for this observation. It had been made by Aristotle, and after him by many others ; while, subsequently to

Descartes, and previous to Locke, Pascal, and the Port-Royal logicians, to say nothing of a paper of Leibnitz in 1684, had reduced it to a matter of commonplace. In this instance, Locke can indeed be proved a borrower.' Hamilton's edition of Reid, p. 220. But this very learned writer quotes no passage from Aristotle to this effect, and certainly the practice of that philosopher and his followers was to attempt definitions of every thing. Nor could Aristotle, or even Descartes, have distinguished undefinable words by their expressing simple ideas of sense or reflection, as Locke has done, when they have not made that classification of ideas into simple and complex, which forms so remarkable a part of his philosophy.—1847.]

the next genus, or the essential differences, as the logicians, talk and so compose a regular definition. Leave this to such as teach or dispute in the schools. But whoever will examine things by himself, and judge of them according to his understanding, cannot be so senseless as not to see clearly, when he pays attention, what doubting, thinking, being, are, or to have any need to learn their distinctions. Besides, there are things which we render more obscure in attempting to define them, because, as they are very si n] and very clear, we cannot know and comprehend them better than by themselves. And it should be reckoned among the chief errors that can be committed in science for men to fancy that they can define that which they can only conceive, and distinguish what is clear in it from what is obscure, while they do not see the difference between that which must be defined before it is understood, and that which can be fully known by itself. Now, among things which can thus be clearly known by themselves, we must put doubting, thinking, being. For I do not believe any one ever existed so stupid as to need to know what being is before he could affirm that he is; and it is the same of thought and doubt. Nor can he learn these things except by himself, nor be convinced of them but by his own experience, and by that consciousness and inward witness which every man finds in himself when he examines the subject. And as we should define whiteness in vain to a man who can see nothing, while one who can open his eyes and see a white object requires no more, so to know what doubting is, and what thinking is, it is only necessary to doubt and to think.'[a] Nothing could more tend to cut short the verbal cavils of the schoolmen, than this limitation of their favourite exercise, definition. It is due, therefore, to Descartes, so often accused of appropriating the discoveries of others, that we should establish his right to one of the most important that the new logic has to boast.

102. He seems, at one moment, to have been on the point of taking another step very far in advance of his age. 'Let us take,' he says, ' a piece of wax from

His notion of substances.

---

the honey-comb: it retains some taste and smell, it is hard, it is cold, it has a very marked colour, form, and size. Approach it to the fire; it becomes liquid, warm, inodorous, tasteless; its form and colour are changed, its size is increased. Does the same wax remain after these changes? It must be allowed that it does; no one doubts it, no one thinks otherwise. What was it then that we so distinctly knew to exist in this piece of wax? Nothing certainly that we observed by the senses, since all that the taste, the smell, the sight, the touch reported to us has disappeared, and still the same wax remains.' This something which endures under every change of sensible qualities cannot be imagined; for the imagination must represent some of these qualities, and none of them are essential to the thing; it can only be conceived by the understanding.[b]

103. It may seem almost surprising to us, after the writings of Locke and his followers on the one ~not quite~ hand, and the chemist with his crucible on the ~correct.~ other, have chased these abstract substances of material objects from their sanctuaries, that a man of such prodigious acuteness and intense reflection as Descartes should not have remarked that the identity of wax after its liquefaction is merely nominal, and depending on arbitrary language, which in many cases gives new appellations to the same aggregation of particles after a change of their sensible qualities; and that all we call substances are but aggregates of resisting movable corpuscles, which by the laws of nature are capable of affecting our senses differently, according to the combinations they may enter into, and the changes they may successively undergo. But if he had distinctly seen this, which I do not apprehend that he did, it is not likely that he would have divulged the discovery. He had already given alarm to the jealous spirit of orthodoxy by what now appears to many so self-evident, that they have treated the supposed paradox as a trifling with words, the doctrine that colour, heat, smell, and other secondary qualities, or accidents of bodies, do not exist in them, but in our own minds, and are the effects of their

---

[b] Méditation seconde, i. 256.

intrinsic or primary qualities. It was the tenet of the schools that these were sensible realities, inherent in bodies; and the church held as an article of faith that the substance of bread being withdrawn from the consecrated wafer, the accidents of that substance remained as before, but independent, and not inherent in any other. Arnauld raised this objection, which Descartes endeavoured to repel by a new theory of transubstantiation ; but it always left a shade of suspicion, in the Catholic church of Rome, on the orthodoxy of Cartesianism.

104. 'The paramount and indisputable authority which, in His notions of intuitive truth. all our reasonings concerning the human mind, he ascribes to the evidence of consciousness,' is reckoned by Stewart among the great merits of Descartes. It is certain that there are truths which we know, as it is called, intuitively, that is, by the mind's immediate inward glance. And reasoning would be interminable, if it did not find its ultimate limit in truths which it cannot prove. Gassendi imputed to Descartes, that, in his fundamental enthymem, Cogito, ergo sum, he supposed a knowledge of the major premise, Quod cogitat, est. But Descartes replied that it was a great error to believe that our knowledge of particular propositions must always be deduced from universals, according to the rules of logic ; whereas, on the contrary, it is by means of our knowledge of particulars that we ascend to generals, though it is true that we descend again from them to infer other particular propositions.[c] It is probable that Gassendi did not make this objection very seriously.

105. Thus the logic of Descartes, using that word for principles that guide our reasoning, was an instrument of defence both against the captiousness of ordinary scepticism, that of the Pyrrhonic school, and against the disputatious dogmatism of those who professed to serve under the banner of Aristotle. He who reposes on his own consciousness, or

----

[c] Vol. ii. p. 305. See, too, the passage quoted above, in his posthumous dialogue.

[Perhaps the best answer might have been, that Cogito, ergo sum, though thrown into the form of an enthymem, was not meant so much for a logical in-ference, as an assertion of consciousness. It has been observed, that Cogito is equivalent to Sum cogitans, and involves the conclusion. It is impossible to employ rules of logic upon operations of the mind which are anterior to all reasoning. —1847.]

who recurs to first principles of intuitive knowledge, though
he cannot be said to silence his adversary, should have the
good sense to be silent himself, which puts equally an end to
debate.   But so far as we are concerned with the investigation of truth, the Cartesian appeal to our own consciousness,
of which Stewart was very fond, just as it is in principle,
may end in an assumption of our own prejudices as the
standard of belief.   Nothing can be truly self-evident but
that which a clear, an honest, and an experienced understanding in another man acknowledges to be so.

106. Descartes has left a treatise highly valuable, but not
very much known, on the art of logic, or rules for Treatise on
the conduct of the understanding.[d]   Once only, in a art of logic.
letter, he has alluded to the name of Bacon.[e]   There are,
perhaps, a few passages in this short tract that remind us of
the Novum Organum.   But I do not know that the coincidence is such as to warrant a suspicion that he was indebted
to it; we may reckon it rather a parallel, than a derivative
logic; written in the same spirit of cautious, inductive pro-
cedure, less brilliant and original in its inventions, but of
more general application than the Novum Organum, which
is with some difficulty extended beyond the province of natural philosophy.   Descartes is as averse as Bacon to syllogis-

---

[d] M. Cousin has translated and republished two works of Descartes, which
had only appeared in Opera Posthuma
Cartesii, Amsterdam, 1701. Their authenticity, from external and intrinsic
proofs, is out of question. One of these
is that mentioned in the text, entitled,
' Rules for the Direction of the Understanding;' which, though logical in its
subject, takes most of its illustrations
from mathematics. The other is a dialogue, left imperfect, in which he sustains the metaphysical principles of his
philosophy. Of these two little tracts
their editor has said, ' that they equal in
vigour and perhaps surpass in arrangement the Meditations and Discourse on
Method. We see in these more unequivocally the main object of Descartes,
and the spirit of the revolution which
has created modern philosophy, and
placed in the understanding itself the
principle of all certainty, the point of de-
parture for all legitimate inquiry. They

might seem written but yesterday, and
for the present age.' Vol. xi. preface,
p. i. I may add to this, that I consider
the Rules for the Direction of the Understanding as one of the best works on
logic (in the enlarged sense) which I
have ever read; more practically useful, perhaps, to young students, than the
Novum Organum; and though, as I
have said, his illustrations are chiefly
mathematical, most of his rules are applicable to the general discipline of the
reasoning powers. It occupies little more
than one hundred pages, and I think
that I am doing a service in recommending it Many of the rules will, of course,
be found in later books; some possibly
in earlier. This tract, as well as the
dialogue which follows it, is incomplete,
a portion being probably lost.

[e] Si quelqu'un de cette humeur vou-
loit entreprendre d'écrire l'histoire des
apparences célestes selon la méthode de
Vérulamius. Vol. vi. p. 210,

tic forms. 'Truth,' he says, 'often escapes from these fetters, in which those who employ them remain entangled. This is less frequently the case with those who make no use of logic, experience showing that the most subtle of sophisms cheat none but sophists themselves, not those who trust to their natural reason. And to convince ourselves how little this syllogistic art serves towards the discovery of truth, we may remark that the logicians can form no syllogism with a true conclusion, unless they are already acquainted with the truth that the syllogism develops. Hence it follows that the vulgar logic is wholly useless to him who would discover truth for himself, though it may assist in explaining to others the truth he already knows, and that it would be better to transfer it as a science from philosophy to rhetoric.[f]

107. It would occupy too much space to point out the many profound and striking thoughts which this treatise on the conduct of the understanding, and indeed most of the writings of Descartes, contain. 'The greater part of the questions on which the learned dispute are but questions of words. These occur so frequently that, if philosophers would agree on the signification of their words, scarce any of their controversies would remain.' This has been continually said since ; but it is a proof of some progress in wisdom, when the original thought of one age becomes the truism of the next. No one had been so much on his guard against the equivocation of words, or knew so well their relation to the operations of the mind. And it may be said generally, though not without exception, of the metaphysical writings of Descartes, that we find in them a perspicuity which springs from his unremitting attention to the logical process of inquiry, admitting no doubtful or ambiguous position, and never requiring from his reader a deference to any authority but that of demonstration. It is a great advantage in reading such writers that we are able to discern when they are manifestly in the wrong. The sophisms of Plato, of Aristotle, of the schoolmen, and of a great many recent metaphysicians, are disguised by their obscurity ; and while they creep insidiously into the mind of

Merits of his writings.

---

[f] Vol. xi. p. 255.

the reader, are always denied and explained away by partial disciples.

108. Stewart has praised Descartes for having recourse to the evidence of consciousness in order to prove the His notions of free-will. liberty of the will. But he omits to tell us that the notions entertained by this philosopher were not such as have been generally thought compatible with free agency in the only sense that admits of controversy. It was an essential part of the theory of Descartes that God is the cause of all human actions. 'Before God sent us into the world,' he says in a letter, 'he knew exactly what all the inclinations of our will would be; it is he that has implanted them in us; it is he also that has disposed all other things, so that such or such objects should present themselves to us at such or such times, by means of which he has known that our free-will would determine us to such or such actions, and he has willed that it should be so; but he has not willed to compel us thereto.' [g] 'We could not demonstrate,' he says at another time, 'that God exists, except by considering him as a being absolutely perfect; and he could not be absolutely perfect, if there could happen any thing in the world which did not spring entirely from him. . . . . Mere philosophy is enough to make us know that there cannot enter the least thought into the mind of man, but God must will and have willed from all eternity that it should enter there.' [h] This is in a letter to his highly intelligent friend, the Princess Palatine Elizabeth, grand-daughter of James I.; and he proceeds to declare himself strongly in favour of predestination, denying wholly any particular providence, to which she had alluded, as changing the decrees of God, and all efficacy of prayer, except as one link in the chain of his determinations. Descartes, therefore, whatever some of his disciples may have become, was far enough from an Arminian theology. 'As to free-will,' he says elsewhere, 'I own that thinking only of ourselves we cannot but reckon it independent, but when we think of the infinite power of God we cannot but believe that all things depend on him, and that consequently our free-will must do so too. . . . But since our knowledge of the existence of God should not hinder

---

[g] Vol. ix. p. 374.   [h] Id. p. 246.

us from being assured of our free-will, because we feel and are conscious of it in ourselves, so that of our free-will should not make us doubt of the existence of God. For the independence which we experience and feel in ourselves, and which is sufficient to make our actions praiseworthy or blamable, is not incompatible with a dependence of another nature, according to which all things are subject to God.'[1]

109. A system so novel, so attractive to the imagination by its bold and brilliant paradoxes as that of Descartes, could not but excite the attention of an age already roused to the desire of a new philosophy, and to the scorn of ancient authority. His first treatises appeared in French; and, though he afterwards employed Latin, his works were very soon translated by his disciples, and under his own care. He wrote in Latin with great perspicuity; in French with liveliness and elegance. His mathematical and optical writings gave him a reputation which envy could not take away, and secured his philosophy from that general ridicule which sometimes overwhelms an obscure author. His very enemies, numerous and vehement as they were, served to enhance the celebrity of the Cartesian system, which he seems to have anticipated by publishing their objections to his Meditations with his own replies. In the universities, bigoted for the most part to Aristotelian authority, he had no chance of public reception; but the influence of the universities was much diminished in France, and a new theory had perhaps better chances in its favour on account of their opposition. But the Jesuits, a more powerful body, were in general adverse to the Cartesian system, and especially some time afterwards, when it was supposed to have the countenance of several leading Jansenists. The Epicurean school, led by Gassendi and Hobbes, presented a formidable phalanx; since it in fact comprehended the wits of the world, the men of indolence and sensuality, quick to discern the many weaknesses of Cartesianism, with no capacity for its excellences. It is unnecessary to say how predominant this class was in the seventeenth and eighteenth centuries, both in France and England.

Fame of his system, and attacks upon it.

---

[1] Vol. ix. p. 368. This had originally been stated in the Principia with less confidence, the free-will of man and pre- determination of God being both asserted as true, but their co-existence incomprehensible. Vol. iii. p. 86.

110. Descartes was evidently in considerable alarm lest the church should bear with its weight upon his philosophy.[k]　He had the censure on Galileo before Controversy with Voet. his eyes, and certainly used some chicane of words as to the earth's movement upon this account. It was, however, in the Protestant country which he had chosen as his harbour of refuge that he was doomed to encounter the roughest storm.　Gisbert Voet, an eminent theologian in the university of Utrecht, and the head of the party in the church of Holland, which had been victorious in the synod of Dort, attacked Descartes with all the virulence and bigotry characteristic of his school of divinity.　The famous demonstration of the being of God he asserted to be a cover for atheism, and thus excited a flame of controversy, Descartes being not without supporters in the university, especially Regius, professor of medicine.　The philosopher was induced by these assaults to change his residence from a town in the province of Utrecht to Leyden.　Voet did not cease to pursue him with outrageous calumny, and succeeded in obtaining decrees of the senate and university of Utrecht, which interdicted Regius from teaching that ' new and unproved (præsumpta) philosophy' to his pupils. The war of libels on the Voetian side did not cease for some years, and Descartes replied with no small acrimony against Voet himself.　The latter had recourse to the civil power, and instituted a prosecution against Descartes, which was quashed by the interference of the Prince of Orange.　But many in the university of Leyden, under the influence of a notable theologian of that age, named Trigandius, one of the stoutest champions of Dutch orthodoxy, raised a cry against the Cartesian philosophy as being favourable to Pelagianism and popery, the worst names that could be given in Holland ; and it was again through the protection of the Prince of Orange that he escaped a public censure. Regius, the most zealous of his original advocates, began to swerve from the fidelity of a sworn disciple, and published a

---

[k] On a tellement assujetti la théologie à Aristote, qu'il est impossible d'expliquer une autre philosophie qu'il ne semble d'abord qu'elle soit contre la foi. Et à propos de ceci, je vous prie de me mander s'il n'y a rien de déterminé en la foi touchant l'étendue du monde : savoir s'il est fini ou plutôt infini, et si tout ce qu'on appelle espaces imaginaires soient des corps créés et véritables.　Vol. vi. p. 73.

book containing some theories of his own, which Descartes
thought himself obliged to disavow. Ultimately he found,
like many benefactors of mankind, that he had purchased
reputation at the cost of peace; and, after some visits to
France, where, probably, from the same cause, he never designed to settle, found an honourable asylum and a premature death at the court of Christina. He died in 1651,
having worked a more important change in speculative
philosophy than any who had preceded him since the revival
of learning; for there could be no comparison in that age,
between the celebrity and effect of his writings and those of
Lord Bacon.[m]

111. The prejudice against Descartes, especially in his own
country, was aggravated by his indiscreet and not
very warrantable assumption of perfect originality.[n]

Charges of plagiarism.

No one, I think, can fairly refuse to own, that the Cartesian
metaphysics, taken in their consecutive arrangement, form
truly an original system; and it would be equally unjust to
deny the splendid discoveries he developed in algebra and
optics. But upon every one subject which Descartes treated,
he has not escaped the charge of plagiarism; professing
always to be ignorant of what had been done by others, he
falls perpetually into their track; more, as his adversaries
maintained, than the chances of coincidence could fairly explain. Leibnitz has summed up the claims of earlier writers
to the pretended discoveries of Descartes; and certainly it is

---

[m] The life of Descartes was written,
very fully and with the warmth of a disciple, by Baillet, in two volumes quarto,
1691, of which he afterwards published
an abridgment. In this we find at length
the attacks made on him by the Voetian
theologians. Brucker has given a long
and valuable account of the Cartesian
philosophy, but not favourable, and perhaps not quite fair. Vol. v. p. 200–334.
Buhle is, as usual, much inferior to
Brucker. But those who omit the mathematical portion will not find the original works of Descartes very long, and
they are well worthy of being read.

[n] I confess, he says in his logic, that
I was born with such a temper, that the
chief pleasure I find in study is not from
learning the arguments of others, but

by inventing my own. This disposition
alone impelled me in youth to the study
of science; hence, whenever a new book
promised by its title some new discovery,
before sitting down to read it, I used to
try whether my own natural sagacity
could lead me to any thing of the kind,
and I took care not to lose this innocent
pleasure by too hasty a perusal. This
answered so often that I at length perceived that I arrived at truth, not as
other men do, after blind and precarious
guesses, by good luck rather than skill,
but that long experience had taught me
certain fixed rules, which were of surprising utility, and of which I afterwards made use to discover more truths.
Vol. xi. p. 252.

a pretty long bill to be presented to any author. I shall insert this passage in a note, though much of it has no reference to this portion of the Cartesian philosophy.[o] It may perhaps be thought by candid minds, that we cannot apply the doctrine of chances to coincidence of reasoning in men of acute and inquisitive spirits, as fairly as we may to that of style or imagery; but, if we hold strictly that the old writer may claim the exclusive praise of a philosophical discovery,

---

[o] Dogmata ejus metaphysica, velut circa ideas a sensibus remotas, et animæ distinctionem a corpore, et fluxam per se rerum materialium fidem, prorsus Platonica sunt. Argumentum pro existentia Dei, ex eo, quod ens perfectissimum, vel quo majus intelligi non potest, existentiam includit, fuit Anselmi, et in libro ' Contra insipientem ' inscripto extat inter ejus opera, passimque a scholasticis examinatur. In doctrina de continuo, pleno et loco Aristotelem noster secutus est, Stoicosque in re morali penitus expressit, floriferis ut apes in saltibus omnia libant. In explicatione rerum mechanica Leucippum et Democritum præeuntes habuit qui et vortices ipsos jam docuerant. Jordanus Brunus easdem fere de magnitudine universi ideas habuisse dicitur, quemadmodum et notavit V. CC. Stephanus Spleissius, ut de Gilberto nil dicam, cujus magneticæ considerationes tum per se, tum ad systema universi applicatæ, Cartesio plurimum profuerunt. Explicationem gravitatis per materiæ solidioris rejectionem in tangente, quod in physica Cartesiana prope pulcherrimum est, didicit ex Keplero, qui similitudine palearum motu aquæ in vase gyrantis ad centrum contrusarum rem explicuit primus. Actionem lucis in distans, similitudine baculi pressi jam veteres adumbravere. Circa iridem a M. Antonio de Dominis non parum lucis accepit. Keplerum fuisse primum suum in dioptricis magistrum, et in eo argumento omnes ante se mortales longo intervallo antegressum, fatetur Cartesius in epistolis familiaribus; nam in scriptis, quæ ipse edidit, longè abest a tali confessione aut laude ; tametsi illa ratio, quæ rationum directionem explicat, ex compositione nimirum duplicis conatûs perpendicularis ad superficiem et ad eandem paralleli, disertè apud Keplerum extet, qui eodem, ut Cartesius, modo æqualitatem angulorum incidentiæ et reflexionis hinc

deducit. Idque gratam mentionem ideo merebatur, quod omnis prope Cartesii ratiocinatio huic innititur principio. Legem refractionis primum invenisse Willebroodum Snellium, Isaacus Vossius patefecit, quanquam non ideo negare ausim, Cartesium in eadem incidere potuisse de suo. Negavit in epistolis Vietam sibi lectum, sed Thomæ Harrioti Angli libros analyticos posthumos anno 1631 editos vidisse multi vix dubitant ; usque adeo magnus est eorum consensus cum calculo geometriæ Cartesianæ. Sane jam Harriotus æquationem nihilo æqualem posuit, et hinc derivavit, quomodo oriatur æquatio ex multiplicatione radicum in se invicem, et quomodo radicum auctione, diminutione, multiplicatione aut divisione variari æquatio possit, et quomodo proinde natura, et constitutio æquationum et radicum cognosci possit ex terminorum habitudine. Itaque narrat celeberrimus Wallisius, Robervalium, qui miratus erat, unde Cartesio in mentem venisset palmarium illud, æquationem ponere æqualem nihilo ad instar unius quantitatis, ostenso sibi a Domino de Cavendish libro Harrioti exclamasse, il l'a vu ! il l'a vu ! vidit, vidit. Reductionem quadrato-quadratæ æquationis ad cubicam superiori jam sæculo invenit Ludovicus Ferrarius, cujus vitam reliquit Cardanus ejus familiaris. Denique fuit Cartesius, ut a viris doctis dudum notatum est, et ex epistolis nimium apparet, immodicus contemptor aliorum, et famæ cupiditate ab artificiis non abstinens, quæ parum generosa videri possunt. Atque hæc profecto non dico animo, obtrectandi viro, quem mirificè æstimo, sed eo consilio, ut cuique suum tribuatur, nec unus omnium laudes absorbeat ; justissimum enim est, ut inventoribus suus honos constet, nec sublatis virtutum præmiis præclara faciendi studium refrigescat. Leibnitz, apud Brucker, v. 255.

we must regret to see such a multitude of feathers plucked from the wing of an eagle.

112. The name of Descartes as a great metaphysical writer has revived in some measure of late years; and this has been chiefly owing, among ourselves, to Dugald Stewart; in France, to the growing disposition of their philosophers to cast away their idols of the eighteenth century. 'I am disposed,' says our Scottish philosopher, 'to date the origin of the true philosophy of mind from the Principia (why not the earlier works?) of Descartes, rather than from the Organum of Bacon, or the Essays of Locke; without, however, meaning to compare the French author with our two countrymen, either as a contributor to our stock of *facts* relating to the intellectual phænomena, or as the author of any important conclusion concerning the general laws to which they may be referred.' The excellent edition by M. Cousin, in which alone the entire works of Descartes can be found, is a homage that France has recently offered to his memory, and an important contribution to the studious both of metaphysical and mathematical philosophy. I have made use of no other, though it might be desirable for the inquirer to have the Latin original at his side, especially in those works which had not been seen in French by their author.

Recent increase of his fame.

Sect. IV.

On the Metaphysical Philosophy of Hobbes.

113. The metaphysical philosophy of Hobbes was promulgated in his treatise on Human Nature, which appeared in 1650. This, with his other works, De Cive and De Corpore Politico, were fused into that great and general system, which he published in 1651 with the title of Leviathan. The first part of the Leviathan, 'Of Man,' follows the several chapters of the treatise on Human Nature with much regularity; but so numerous are the enlargements or omissions, so many are the variations with which the author has expressed the same positions, that they should much

Metaphysical treatises of Hobbes.

rather be considered as two works, than as two editions of the same. They differ more than Lord Bacon's treatise, De Augmentis Scientiarum, does from his Advancement of Learning. I shall, however, blend the two in a single analysis, and this I shall generally give, as far as is possible, consistently with my own limits, in the very words of Hobbes. His language is so lucid and concise, that it would be almost as improper to put an algebraical process in different terms as some of his metaphysical paragraphs. But as a certain degree of abridgment cannot be dispensed with, the reader must not take it for granted, even where inverted commas denote a closer attention to the text, that nothing is omitted, although, in such cases, I never hold it permissible to make any change.

114. All single thoughts, it is the primary tenet of Hobbes, are representations or appearances of some quality His theory of a body without us, which is commonly called an of sensation object. 'There is no conception in a man's mind, which hath not at first totally, or by parts, been begotten upon the organs of sense. The rest are derived from that original.' [p] In the treatise on Human Nature he dwells long on the immediate causes of sensation; and if no alteration had been made in his manuscript since he wrote his dedication to the Earl of Newcastle in 1640, he must be owned to have anticipated Descartes in one of his most celebrated doc- coincident trines. 'Because the image in vision, consisting in with Descartes. colour and shape, is the knowledge we have of the qualities of the object of that sense, it is no hard matter for a man to fall into this opinion, that the same colour and shape are the very qualities themselves; and for the same cause, that sound and noise are the qualities of the bell, or of the air. And this opinion hath been so long received, that the contrary must needs appear a great paradox; and yet the introduction of species visible and intelligible (which is necessary for the maintenance of that opinion), passing to and fro from the object, is worse than any paradox, as being a plain impossibility. I shall, therefore, endeavour to make plain these points: 1. That the subject wherein colour and image are

---

[p] Leviathan, c. 1.

inherent is not the object or thing seen. 2. That there is nothing without us (really) which we call an image or colour. 3. That the said image or colour is but an apposition unto us of the motion, agitation or alteration, which the object worketh in the brain, or spirits, or some external substance of the head. 4. That, as in vision, so also in conceptions that arise from the other senses, the subject of their inherence is not the object, but the sentient.' [q] And this he goes on to prove. Nothing of this will be found in the Discours sur la Méthode, the only work of Descartes then published; and, even if we believe Hobbes to have interpolated this chapter after he had read the Meditations, he has stated the principle so clearly, and illustrated it so copiously, that, so far especially as Locke and the English metaphysicians took it up, we may almost reckon him another original source.

115. The second chapter of the Leviathan, 'On Imagi-

Imagination and memory. nation,' begins with one of those acute and original observations we often find in Hobbes: 'That when a thing lies still, unless somewhat else stir it, it will lie still for ever, is a truth that no man doubts of. But that when a thing is in motion, it will eternally be in motion, unless somewhat stay it, though the reason be the same, namely, that nothing can change itself, is not so easily assented to. For men measure, not only other men, but all other things, by themselves; and because they find themselves subject after motion to pain and lassitude, think everything else grows weary of motion and seeks repose of its own accord.' The physical principle had lately been established, but the reason here given for the contrary prejudice, though not the sole one, is ingenious and even true. Imagination he defines to be ' conception remaining, and by little and little decaying after the act of sense.'[r] This he afterwards expressed less happily, 'the gradual decline of the motion in which sense consists;' his phraseology becoming more and more tinctured with the materialism which he affected in all his philosophy. Neither definition seems at all applicable to the imagination which calls up long past perceptions. ' This decaying sense when we would express the thing itself (I mean fancy itself),

---

[q] Hum. Nat. c. 2.   [r] Id. c. 3.

we call imagination, but when we would express the decay, and signify that the sense is fading, old and past, it is called memory. So that imagination and memory are but one thing, which for divers considerations hath divers names.' It is however evident that imagination and memory are distinguished by something more than their names.' The second fundamental error of Hobbes in his metaphysics, his extravagant nominalism, if so it should be called, appears in this sentence, as the first, his materialism, does in that previously quoted.

116. The phænomena of dreaming and the phantasms of waking men are considered in this chapter with the keen observation and cool reason of Hobbes.[t] I am not sure that he has gone more profoundly into psychological speculations in the Leviathan than in the earlier treatise; but it bears witness more frequently to what had probably been the growth of the intervening period, a proneness to political and religious allusion, to magnify civil and to depreciate ecclesiastical power. 'If this superstitious fear of spirits were taken away, and with it prognostics from dreams, false prophecies, and many other things depending thereon, by which crafty and ambitious persons abuse the simple people, men would be much more fitted than they are for civil obedience. And this ought to be the work of the schools; but they rather nourish such doctrine.'[u]

117. The fourth chapter on Human Nature, and the corresponding third chapter of the Leviathan, entitled On Discourse, or the Consequence and Train of Imagination, are among the most remarkable in Hobbes, as they contain the elements of that theory of association, which was slightly touched afterwards by Locke, but developed and pushed to a far greater extent by Hartley. ' The cause,' he says, ' of the coherence or consequence of one conception to another is their first coherence or consequence at that time when they are produced by sense; as for instance, from St. Andrew the mind runneth to St. Peter, because their names are read together; from St. Peter to a stone, from the same cause ; from stone to foundation, because we see them

Discourse or train of imagination.

---

* Lev. c. 2.   [t] Hum. Nat. c. 3.   [u] Id. ibid.

together; and for the same cause from foundation to church, and from church to people, and from people to tumult; and according to this example the mind may run almost from any thing to any thing.'[x] This he illustrates in the Leviathan by the well-known anecdote of a question suddenly put by one, in conversation about the death of Charles I., 'What was the value of a Roman penny?' Of this *discourse*, as he calls it, in a larger sense of the word than is usual with the logicians, he mentions several kinds; and after observing that the remembrance of succession of one thing to another, that is, of what was antecedent and what consequent and what concomitant, is called an experiment, adds, that 'to have had many experiments, is what we call experience, which is nothing else but remembrance of what antecedents have been followed by what consequents.'[y]

118. 'No man can have a conception of the future, for the future is not yet, but of our conceptions of the past we make a future, or rather call past future relatively.'[z] And again: 'The present only has a being in nature; things past have a being in the memory only, but things to come have no being at all; the future being but a fiction of the mind, applying the sequels of actions past to the actions that are present, which with most certainty is done by him that has most experience, but not with certainty enough. And though it be called prudence, when the event answereth our expectation, yet in its own nature it is but presumption.'[a] When we have observed antecedents and consequents frequently associated, we take one for a sign of the other, as clouds foretell rain, and rain is a sign there have been clouds. But signs are but conjectural, and their assurance is never full or evident. For though a man have always seen the day and night to follow one another hitherto, yet can he not thence conclude they shall do so, or that they have done so, eternally. Experience concludeth nothing universally. But those who have most experience conjecture best, because they have most signs to conjecture by; hence old men, cæteris paribus, and men of quick parts, conjecture

Experience.

---

[x] Hum. Nat. c. 4, § 2.
[y] Id.

[z] Hum. Nat. c. 4, § 7.
[a] Lev. c. 3.

better than the young or dull.'[b]   'But experience is not to be
equalled by any advantage of natural and extemporary wit,
though perhaps many young men think the contrary.' There
is a presumption of the past as well as the future founded on
experience, as when from having often seen ashes after fire,
we infer from seeing them again that there has been fire.
But this is as conjectural as our expectations of the future.[c]

119. In the last paragraph of the chapter in the Leviathan
he adds, what is a very leading principle in the phi-   Unconceiv-
losophy of Hobbes, but seems to have no particular   ableness of
infinity.
relation to what has preceded.   ' Whatsoever we imagine is
finite ; therefore there is no idea or conception of anything
we call infinite.   No man can have in his mind an image of
infinite magnitude, nor conceive infinite swiftness, infinite
time, or infinite force, or infinite power.   When we say anything is infinite, we signify only that we are not able to conceive the ends and bounds of the things named, having no
conception of the thing, but of our own inability.   And therefore the name of God is used, not to make us conceive him,
for he is incomprehensible and his greatness and power are
inconceivable, but that we may honour him.   Also because
whatsoever, as I said before, we conceive, has been perceived
first by sense, either all at once, or by parts ; a man can
have no thought, representing anything, not subject to sense.
No man, therefore, can conceive anything, but he must conceive it in some place, and indeed with some determinate
magnitude, and which may be divided into parts, nor that
anything is all in this place and all in another place at the
same time, nor that two or more things can be in one and
the same place at once.   For none of these things ever have,
or can be incident to sense, but are absurd speeches, taken
upon credit without any signification at all, from deceived
philosophers, and deceived or deceiving schoolmen.'   This,
we have seen in the last section, had been already discussed
with Descartes.   The paralogism of Hobbes consists in his
imposing a limited sense on the word idea or conception, and
assuming that what cannot be conceived according to that
sense has no signification at all.

---

[b] Hum. Nat. c. 4.   [c] Lev. c. 3.

120. The next chapter being the fifth in one treatise, and
Origin of   the fourth in the other, may be reckoned, perhaps,
language.   the most valuable as well as original in the writings
of Hobbes. It relates to speech and language. 'The invention of printing,' he begins by observing, 'though ingenious,
compared with the invention of letters, is no great matter.
. . . . But the most noble and profitable invention of all
others was that of speech, consisting of names or appellations, and their connexion, whereby men register their
thoughts, recall them when they are past, and also declare
them one to another for mutual utility and conversation;
without which there had been amongst men neither commonwealth, nor society, nor content nor peace, no more than
among lions, bears, and wolves. The first author of speech
was God himself, that instructed Adam how to name such
creatures as he presented to his sight; for the Scripture
goeth no further in this matter. But this was sufficient to
direct him to add more names, as the experience and use
of the creatures should give him occasion, and to join them
in such manner by degrees, as to make himself understood;
and so by succession of time so much language might be
gotten as he had found use for, though not so copious as an
orator or philosopher has need of.'[d]

121. This account of the original of language appears in
His political general as probable as it is succinct and clear. But
theory
interferes.   the assumption that there could have been no society
or mutual peace among mankind without language, the ordinary instrument of contract, is too much founded upon his
own political speculations. Nor is it proved by the comparison to lions, bears, and wolves, even if the analogy could
be admitted; since the state of warfare which he here intimates to be natural to man, does not commonly subsist in
these wild animals of the same species. *Sœvis inter se convenit
ursis*, is an old remark. But taking mankind with as much
propensity to violence towards each other as Hobbes could
suggest, is it speech, or reason and the sense of self-interest,
which has restrained this within the boundaries imposed on
it by civil society? The position appears to be that man,

---

[d] Leviathan, c. 4.

with every other faculty and attribute of his nature, except language, could never have lived in community with his fellows. It is manifest, that the mechanism of such a community would have been very imperfect. But possessing his rational powers, it is hard to see why he might not have devised signs to make known his special wants, or why he might not have attained the peculiar prerogative of his species and foundation of society, the exchange of what he liked less for what he liked better.

122. This will appear more evident, and the exaggerated notions of the school of Hobbes as to the absolute necessity of language to the mutual relations of mankind will be checked, by considering what was not so well understood in his age as at present, the intellectual capacities of those who are born deaf, and the resources which they are able to employ. It can hardly be questioned, but that a number of families thrown together in this unfortunate situation, without other intercourse, could by the exercise of their natural reason, as well as the domestic and social affections, constitute themselves into a sort of commonwealth, at least as regular as that of ants and bees. But those whom we have known to want the use of speech have also wanted the sense of hearing, and have thus been shut out from many assistances to the reasoning faculties, which our hypothesis need not exclude. The fair supposition is that of a number of persons merely dumb; and although they would not have laws or learning, it does not seem impossible that they might maintain at least a patriarchal, if not a political, society for many generations. Upon the lowest supposition, they could not be inferior to the Chimpanzees, who are said to live in communities in the forests of Angola.

Necessity of speech exaggerated.

123. The succession of conceptions in the mind depending wholly on that which they had one to another when produced by the senses, they cannot be recalled at our choice and the need we have of them, 'but as it chanceth us to hear and see such things as shall bring them to our mind. Hence brutes are unable to call what they want to mind, and often, though they hide food, do not know where to find it. But man has the power to set up marks or

Use of names.

sensible objects, and remember thereby somewhat past. The
most eminent of these are names or articulate sounds, by
which we recall some conception of things to which we give
those names; as the appellation white bringeth to remembrance the quality of such objects as produce that colour or
conception in us. It is by names that we are capable of
science, as for instance that of number ; for beasts cannot
number for want of words, and do not miss one or two out
of their young, nor could a man without repeating orally
or mentally the words of number know how many pieces
of money may be before him.' ᵉ We have here another
assumption, that the numbering faculty is not stronger
in man than in brutes, and also that the former could not
have found out how to divide a heap of coins into parcels
without the use of words of number. The experiment might
be tried with a deaf and dumb child.

124. Of names some are proper, and some common to
many or universal, there being nothing in the world
universal but names, for the things named are every
one of them individual and singular. ' One universal name
is imposed on many things for their similitude in some
quality or other accidents ; and whereas a proper name
bringeth to mind one thing only, universals recall any one
of those many.' ᶠ ' The universality of one name to many
things hath been the cause that men think the things are
themselves universal, and so seriously contend that besides
Peter and John, and all the rest of the men that are, have
been, or shall be in the world, there is yet something else
that we call man, viz. man in general, deceiving themselves
by taking the universal or general appellation for the thing it
signifieth.ᵍ For if one should desire the painter to make

Marginal note: Names universal not
realities.

ᵉ Hum. Nat. c. 5.
ᶠ Lev. c. 4.
ᵍ 'An universal,' he says in his
Logic, 'is not a name of many things
collectively, but of each taken separately
(sigillatim sumptorum). Man is not the
name of the human species in general,
but of each single man, Peter, John, and
the rest, separately. Therefore this universal name is not the name of any thing
existing in nature, nor of any idea or
phantasm formed in the mind, but always

of some word or name. Thus when an
animal, or a stone, or a ghost (spectrum),
or any thing else is called universal, we
are not to understand that any man or
stone or any thing else was, or is, or can
be, an universal, but only that these
words animal, stone, and the like, are universal names, that is, names common to
many things, and the conceptions corresponding to them in the mind are the
images and phantasms of single animals
or other things. And therefore we do not

him the picture of a man, which is as much as to say, of a man in general, he meaneth no more but that the painter should choose what man he pleaseth to draw, which must needs be some of them that are, or have been, or may be, none of which are universal. But when he would have him to draw the picture of the king, or any particular person, he limiteth the painter to that one person he chooseth. It is plain, therefore, that there is nothing universal but names, which are therefore called indefinite.'[h]

125. 'By this imposition of names, some of larger, some of stricter signification, we turn the reckoning of How imthe consequences of things imagined in the mind posed. into a reckoning of the consequences of appellations.'[i] Hence he thinks that though a man born deaf and dumb might by meditation know that the angles of one triangle are equal to two right ones, he could not, on seeing another triangle of different shape, infer the same without a similar process. But by the help of words, after having observed the equality is not consequent on any thing peculiar to one triangle, but on the number of sides and angles which is common to all, he registers his discovery in a proposition. This is surely to confound the antecedent process of reasoning with what he calls the registry, which follows it. The instance, however, is not happily chosen, and Hobbes has conceded the whole point in question, by admitting that the truth of the proposition could be *observed*, which cannot require the use of words.[k] He expresses the next sentence

---

need, in order to understand what is meant by an universal, any other faculty than that of imagination, by which we remember that such words have excited the conception in our minds sometimes of one particular thing, sometimes of another.' Cap. 2, § 9. Imagination and memory are used by Hobbes almost as synonyms.

[h] Hum. Nat. c. 5.

[i] It may deserve to be remarked that Hobbes himself, nominalist as he was, did not limit reasoning to comparison of propositions, as some later writers have been inclined to do, and as in his objections to Descartes he might seem to do himself. This may be inferred from the sentence quoted in the text, and more

expressly, though not quite perspicuously, from a passage in the Computatio, sive Logica, his Latin treatise published after the Leviathan.   Quomodo autem animo *sine verbis tacita cogitatione ratiocinando addere et subtrahere solemus* uno aut altero exemplo ostendendum est. Si quis ergo e longinquo aliquid obscurè videat, etsi nulla sint imposita vocabula, habet tamen ejus rei ideam eandem propter quam impositis nunc vocabulis dicit eam rem esse corpus. Postquam autem propius accesserit, videritque eandem rem certo quodam modo nunc uno, nunc alio in loco esse, habebit ejusdem ideam novam, propter quam nunc talem rem *animatam* vocat, &c. p. 2.

[k] The demonstration of the thirty-

with more felicity. 'And thus the consequence found in one particular comes to be registered and remembered as an universal rule, and discharges our mental reckoning of time and place; and delivers us from all labour of the mind saving the first, and makes that which was found true here and now to be true in all times and places.'[m]

126. The equivocal use of names makes it often difficult

The subject continued.

to recover those conceptions for which they were designed 'not only in the language of others, wherein we are to consider the drift and occasion and contexture of the speech, as well as the words themselves, but in our own discourse, which being derived from the custom and common use of speech, representeth unto us not our own conceptions. It is, therefore, a great ability in a man, out of the words, contexture, and other circumstances of language, to deliver himself from equivocation, and to find out the true meaning of what is said; and this is it we call understanding.'[n] 'If speech be peculiar to man, as for aught I know it is, then is understanding peculiar to him also; understanding being nothing else but conception caused by speech.'[o] This definition is arbitrary, and not conformable to the usual sense. 'True and false,' he observes afterwards, 'are attributes of speech, not of things; where speech is not, there is neither truth nor falsehood, though there may be error. Hence as truth consists in the right ordering of names in our affirmations, a man that seeks precise truth hath need to remember what every word he uses stands for, and place it accordingly. In geometry, the only science hitherto known, men begin by definitions. And every man

---

second proposition of Euclid could leave no one in doubt whether this property were common to all triangles, after it had been proved in a single instance. It is said, however, to be recorded by an ancient writer, that this discovery was first made as to equilateral, afterwards as to isosceles, and lastly as to other triangles. Stewart's Philosophy of Human Mind, vol. ii. chap. iv. sect. 2. The mode of proof must have been different from that of Euclid. And this might possibly lead us to suspect the truth of the tradition. For if the equality of the angles of a triangle to two right angles admitted

of any *elementary* demonstration, such as might occur in the infancy of geometry, without making use of the property of parallel lines, assumed in the twelfth axiom of Euclid, the difficulties consequent on that assumption would readily be evaded. See the Note on Euclid, i. 29, by Playfair, who has given a demonstration of his own, but one which involves the idea of motion rather more than was usual with the Greeks in their elementary propositions.

[m] Lev.

[n] Hum. Nat.

[o] Lev.

who aspires to true knowledge should examine the definitions of former authors, and either correct them or make them anew. For the errors of definitions multiply themselves, according as the reckoning proceeds, and lead men into absurdities, which at last they see, but cannot avoid without reckoning anew from the beginning in which lies the foundation of their errors. . . . . In the right definition of names, lies the first use of speech, which is the acquisition of science. And in wrong or no definitions lies the first abuse from which proceed all false and senseless tenets, which make those men that take their instruction from the authority of books, and not from their own meditation, to be as much below the condition of ignorant men, as men endued with true science are above it. For between true science and erroneous doctrine, ignorance is in the middle. Words are wise men's counters—they do but reckon by them; but they are the money of fools.'[p]

127. ' The names of such things as affect us, that is, which please and displease us, because all men be not alike affected with the same thing, nor the same man at all times, are in the common discourse of men of inconstant signification. For seeing all names are imposed to signify our conceptions, and all our affections are but conceptions, when we conceive the same thoughts differently, we can hardly avoid different naming of them. For though the nature of that we conceive be the same, yet the diversity of our reception of it, in respect of different constitutions of body and prejudices of opinion, gives every thing a tincture of our different passions. And therefore, in reasoning, a man must take heed of words, which, besides the signification of what we imagine of their nature, have a signification also of the nature, disposition, and interest of the speaker; such as are the names of virtues and vices; for one man calleth wisdom what another calleth fear, and one cruelty what another justice; one prodigality what another magnanimity, and one gravity what another stupidity, &c. And therefore such names can never be true grounds of any ratiocination. No more can metaphors and tropes of ·speech, but these are

Names differently imposed.

---

[p] Lev.

less dangerous, because they profess their inconstancy, which the other do not.'[q] Thus ends this chapter of the Leviathan, which, with the corresponding one in the treatise on Human Nature, are, notwithstanding what appear to me some erroneous principles, as full, perhaps, of deep and original thoughts as any other pages of equal length on the art of reasoning and philosophy of language. Many have borrowed from Hobbes without naming him; and in fact he is the founder of the Nominalist school in England. He may probably have conversed with Bacon on these subjects; we see much of that master's style of illustration. But as Bacon was sometimes too excursive to sift particulars, so Hobbes has sometimes wanted a comprehensive view.

128. 'There are,' to proceed with Hobbes, 'two kinds of knowledge; the one, sense, or knowledge original, and remembrance of the same; the other, science, or knowledge of the truth of propositions, derived from understanding. Both are but experience, one of things from without, the other from the proper use of words in language, and experience being but remembrance, all knowledge is remembrance. Knowledge implies two things, truth and evidence; the latter is the concomitance of a man's conception with the words that signify such conception in the act of ratiocination.' If a man does not annex a meaning to his words, his conclusions are not evident to him. 'Evidence is to truth as the sap to the tree, which, so far as it creepeth along with the body and branches, keepeth them alive; when it forsaketh them they die; for this evidence, which is meaning with our words, is the life of truth.' 'Science is evidence of truth, from some beginning or principle of sense. The first principle of knowledge is that we have such and such conceptions; the second, that we have thus and thus named the things whereof they are conceptions; the third is, that we have joined those names in such manner as to make true propositions; the fourth and last is, that we have joined these propositions in such manner as they be concluding, and the truth of the conclusion said to be known.'[r]

Knowledge.

---

[q] Lev.

[r] Hum. Nat. c. 6.

129. Reasoning is the addition or subtraction of parcels.
'In whatever matter there is room for addition and
subtraction, there is room for reason ; and where _{Reasoning.} these have no place, then reason has nothing at all to do.'[s]
This is neither as perspicuously expressed, nor as satisfac-
torily illustrated, as is usual with Hobbes ; but it is true
that all syllogistic reasoning is dependent upon quantity
alone, and consequently upon that which is capable of addition and subtraction. This seems not to have been clearly
perceived by some writers of the old Aristotelian school, or
perhaps by some others, who, as far as I can judge, have a
notion that the relation of a genus to a species, or a predicate to its subject, considered merely as to syllogism or
deductive reasoning, is something different from that of a
whole to its parts ; which would deprive that logic of its
chief boast, its axiomatic evidence. But, as this would
appear too dry to some readers, I shall pursue it farther in
a note.[t]

---

[s] Lev. c. 5.

[t] Dugald Stewart (Elements of Philosophy, &c. vol. ii. ch. ii. sec. 2) has
treated this theory of Hobbes on reasoning, as well as that of Condillac,
which seems much the same, with great
scorn, as 'too puerile to admit of (*i. e.*
require) refutation.' I do not myself
think the language of Hobbes, either
here, or as quoted by Stewart from his
Latin treatise on Logic, so perspicuous
as usual. But I cannot help being of
opinion that he is substantially right.
For surely, when we assert that A is B,
we assert that all things which fall under
the class B, taken collectively, comprehend A ; or, that B = A + X : B being
here put, it is to be observed, not for the
res prædicata itself, but for the concrete,
de quibus prædicandum est. I mention
this, because this elliptical use of the
word predicate seems to have occasioned
some confusion in writers on logic.
The predicate, strictly taken, being an
attribute or quality, cannot be said to
include or contain the subject. But
to return, when we say B = A + X, or
B − X = A, since we do not compare, in
such a proposition as is here supposed,
A with X, we only mean that A = A,
or, that a certain part of B is the same
as itself. Again, in a particular affirmative, Some A is B, we assert that part of

A, or A − Y, is contained in B, or that
B may be expressed by $\overline{A - Y} + X$.
So also when we say, Some A is not
B, we equally divide the class or genus
B into A − Y and X, or assert that
$B = \overline{A - Y} + X$; but in this case, the
subject is no longer A − Y, but the remainder, or other part of A, namely Y ;
and this is not found in either term of
the predicate. Finally, in the universal
negative, No. A (neither $\overline{A - Y}$ nor Y)
is B, the $\overline{A - Y}$ of the predicate vanishes or has no value, and B becomes
equal to X, which is incapable of mea-
surement with A, and consequently with
either A − Y or Y, which make up A.
Now if we combine this with another
proposition, in order to form a syllogism,
and say that C is A, we find, as before,
that $\overline{A} = C + Z$; and substituting this
value of A in the former proposition, it
appears that B = C + Z + X. Then, in
the conclusion, we have, C is B ; that
is, C is a part of C + Z + X. And the
same in the three other cases or moods
of the figure. This seems to be, in
plainer terms, what Hobbes means by
addition or subtraction of parcels, and
what Condillac means by rather a lax
expression, that equations and propositions are at bottom the same, or, as
he phrases it better, 'l'évidence de rai-

130. A man may reckon without the use of words in particular things, as in conjecturing from the sight
of anything what is likely to follow; and if he
reckons wrong, it is error. But in reasoning on general

---

son consiste uniquement dans l'identité.'
If we add to this, as he probably intended, non-identity, as the condition of
all negative conclusions, it seems to be
no more than is necessarily involved in
the fundamental principle of syllogism,
the *dictum de omni et nullo*; which may
be thus reduced to its shortest terms :
' Whatever can be divided into parts, includes all those parts, and nothing else.'
This is not limited to mathematical
quantity but includes every thing which
admits of more and less. Hobbes has a
good passage in his Logic on this : Non
putandum est computationi, id est, ratio-
cinationi in numeris tantum locum esse,
tanquam homo a cæteris animantibus,
quod censuisse narratur Pythagoras, sola
numerandi facultate distinctus esset ; nam
et ·magnitudo magnitudini, corpus cor-
pori, motus motui, tempus tempori, gra-
dus qualitatis gradui, actio actioni, con-
ceptus conceptui, proportio proportioni,
oratio 'orationi, nomen nomini, in quibus
omne philosophiæ genus continetur, ad-
jici adimique potest.

But it does not follow by any means
that we should assent to the strange passages quoted by Stewart from Condillac
and Diderot, which reduce all *knowledge*
to identical propositions. Even in geometry, where the objects are strictly
magnitudes, the countless variety in
which their relations may be exhibited
constitutes the riches of that inexhaus-
tible science ; and in moral or physical
propositions, the relation of quantity
between the subject and predicate, as
concretes, which enables them to be
compared, though it is the sole foundation of all *general deductive reasoning*, or
syllogism, has nothing to do with the
other properties or relations, of which
we obtain a knowledge by means of that
comparison. In mathematical reasoning,
we infer as to quantity through the medium of quantity ; in other reasoning,
we use the same medium, but our inference is as to truths which do not lie
within that category. Thus in the hack-
neyed instance, All men are mortal; that
is, mortal creatures include men and
something more, it is absurd to assert,

that we only know that men are men.
It is true that our knowledge of the
truth of the proposition comes by the
help of this comparison of men in the
subject with men as implied in the predicate ; but the very nature of the proposition discovers a constant relation
between the individuals of the human
species and that mortality which is predicated of them along with others ; and
it is in this, not in an identical equation,
as Diderot seems to have thought, that
our *knowledge* consists.

The remarks of Stewart's friend, M.
Prevost of Geneva, on the principle of
identity as the basis of mathematical
science, and which the former has candidly subjoined to his own volume, appear to me very satisfactory. Stewart
comes to admit that the dispute is nearly
verbal ; but we cannot say that he originally treated it as such ; and the principle itself, both as applied to geometry
and to logic, is, in my opinion, of some
importance to the clearness of our conceptions as to those sciences. It may be
added that Stewart's objection to the
principle of identity as the basis of geometrical reasoning is less forcible in its
application to syllogism. He is willing
to admit that magnitudes capable of coincidence by immediate superposition
may be reckoned identical, but scruples
to apply such a word to those which are
dissimilar in figure, as the rectangles of
the means and extremes of four propor-
tional lines. Neither one nor the other
are, in fact, identical as real quantities,
the former being necessarily conceived
to differ from each other by position in
space, as much as the latter ; so that the
expression he quotes from Aristotle, ἐν
τούτοις ἡ ἰσότης ἑνότης, or any similar
one of modern mathematicians, can only
refer to the abstract magnitude of their
areas, which being divisible into the
same number of equal parts, they are
called the same. And there seems no
real difference in this respect between
two circles of equal radii and two such
rectangles as are supposed above, the
identity of their magnitudes being a distinct truth, independent of any consi-

words, to fall on a false inference is not error, though often

deration either of their figure or their position. But, however this may be, the identity of the subject with part of the predicate in an affirmative proposition is never fictitious, but real. It means that the persons or things in the one are strictly the same beings with the persons or things to which they are compared in the other, though, through some difference of relations, or other circumstance, they are expressed in different language. It is needless to give examples, as all those who can read this note at all will know how to find them.

I will here take the liberty to remark, though not closely connected with the present subject, that Archbishop Whately is not quite right in saying (Elements of Logic, p. 46), that in affirmative propositions the predicate is *never* distributed. Besides the numerous instances where this is, in point of fact, the case, all which he justly excludes, there are many in which it is involved in the very form of the proposition. Such are those which assert identity or equality, and such are all definitions. Of the first sort are all the theorems in geometry, asserting an equality of magnitudes or ratios, in which the subject and predicate may always change places. It is true that in the instance given in the work quoted, that equilateral triangles are equiangular, the converse requires a separate proof, and so in many similar cases. But in these the predicate is not distributed by the form of the proposition; they assert no equality of magnitude.

The position, that where such equality is affirmed, the predicate is not *logically* distributed, would lead to the consequence that it can only be *converted* into a particular affirmation. Thus after proving that the square of the hypotenuse, in all right-angled triangles, is equal to those of the sides, we could only infer that the squares of the sides are *sometimes* equal to that of the hypotenuse, which could not be maintained without rendering the rules of logic ridiculous. The most general mode of considering the question is to say, as we have done above, that, in an universal affirmative, the predicate B (that is, the class of which B is predicated) is composed of A the subject, and X, an unknown remainder. But if, by the very

nature of the proposition, we perceive that X is nothing, or has no value, it is plain that the subject measures the entire predicate, and vice versâ, the predicate measures the subject; in other words, each is taken universally, or distributed.

[A critic upon the first edition has observed, 'that nothing is clearer than that in these propositions the predicate is not necessarily distributed;' and even hints a doubt whether I understood the terms rightly. Edinburgh Review, vol. lxxxii. p. 219. This suspicion of my ignorance as to the meaning of the two commonest words in logic I need not probably repel; as to the peremptory assertion of this critic, without any proof beyond his own authority, that in propositions denoting equality of magnitude, the predicate is not *necessarily* distributed, if his own reflections do not convince him, I can only refer him to Aristotle's words: ἐν τούτοις ἡ ἰσότης ἑνότης; and I presume he does not doubt that in identical propositions of the form, A est A, the distribution of the predicate, or the convertibility of the proposition, which is the same thing, is manifest.—1842.]

[Reid observes, in his Brief Account of Aristotle's Logic, that 'the doctrine of the conversion of propositions is not so complete as it appears. How, for instance, shall we convert this proposition, God is omniscient?' Sir W. Hamilton, who, as editor of Reid, undertakes the defence against him of every thing in the established logic, rather curiously answers, in his notes on this passage: 'By saying, An, or The, omniscient is God.' (Hamilton's edition of Reid, p. 697.) The rule requires, 'An Omniscient,' a conversion into the particular; but, as this would be shocking, he substitutes, as an alternative, *the*, which is to take generally or distribute the predicate in the first proposition; and to this the nature of the proposition leads us, as it does in innumerable cases. However, as logical writers, especially the recent, commonly exclude all consideration of the subject-matter of propositions, it may be correct to say, with Archbishop Whately, that, as a rule of syllogism, the predicate is not distributed. Aristotle himself, though he lays this down as a formal rule, does not hesitate to say, that where the predicate is the *proprium* (ἴδιον) or characteristic of the subject, and of nothing

so called, but absurdity.[u] 'If a man should talk to me of
a round quadrangle, or accidents of bread in cheese, or
immaterial substances, or of a free subject, a free will, or
any free, but free from being hindered by opposition, I should
not say he were in error, but that his words were without
meaning, that is to say, absurd.' Some of these propositions, it will occur, are intelligible in a reasonable sense, and
not contradictory, except by means of an arbitrary definition
which he who employs them does not admit. It may be
observed here, as we have done before, that Hobbes does not
confine reckoning, or reasoning, to universals, or even to
words.

131. Man has the exclusive privilege of forming general
theorems. But this privilege is allayed by another,
that is, by the privilege of absurdity, to which no
living creature is subject, but man only. And of men those
are of all most subject to it, that profess philosophy. . . For
there is not one that begins his ratiocination from the
definitions or explications of the names they are to use,
which is a method used only in geometry, whose conclusions
have thereby been made indisputable. He then enumerates
seven causes of absurd conclusions; the first of which is the
want of definitions, the others are erroneous imposition of
names. If we can avoid these errors, it is not easy to fall
into absurdity (by which he of course only means any wrong
conclusion) except perhaps by the length of a reasoning.
'For all men,' he says, 'by nature reason alike, and well,

*Its fre-
quency.*

---

else, it may be reciprocated (ἀντικατηγο-
ρεῖται) with the subject; as if it is the
proprium of a man to be capable of learning grammar, all men are capable of
being grammarians, and all who are such
are men. Topica, i. 4. And in the well-
known passage upon inductive syllogism,
Analyt. Prior. l. ii. c. 23, he shows the
minor premise to be convertible into an
universal affirmative, by which alone
such a syllogism differs from the logical
form called Darapti. But as Aristotle
notoriously considers syllogisms in their
matter as well as form, the modern
writers, who confine themselves to the
latter, are not concluded by his authority.
Their theory, which not only reduces
all logic to syllogism, but all syllogism

to a very few rules of form, so that we
may learn everything that can be learned
in this art through the letters A, B, and
C, without any examples at all, appears
to render it more jejune and unprofitable
than ever. The comparison which some
have made of this literal logic with algebra is surely not to the purpose, for
we cannot move a step in algebra without
known as well as unknown quantities.
As soon as we substitute real examples,
we must perceive that the predicate *is*
sometimes distributed in affirmative propositions by the sense of the propositions
themselves, and without any extrinsic
proof, which is all that I meant.—
1847.]

[u] Lev. c. 5.

when they have good principles. Hence it appears that reason is not as sense and memory born with us, nor gotten by experience only, as prudence is, but attained by industry, in apt imposing of names, and in getting a good and orderly method of proceeding from the elements to assertions, and so to syllogisms. Children are not endued with reason at all till they have attained the use of speech, but are called reasonable creatures, for the possibilty of having the use of reason hereafter. And reasoning serves the generality of mankind very little, though with their natural prudence without science they are in better condition than those who reason ill themselves, or trust those who have done so.'[x] It has been observed by Buhle, that Hobbes had more respect for the Aristotelian forms of logic than his master Bacon. He has in fact written a short treatise, in his Elementa Philosophiæ, on the subject; observing, however, therein, that a true logic will be sooner learned by attending to geometrical demonstrations than by drudging over the rules of syllogism, as children learn to walk not by precept but by habit.[y]

132. 'No discourse whatever,' he says truly in the seventh chapter of the Leviathan, 'can end in absolute knowledge of fact, past or to come. For as to the knowledge of fact, it is originally sense; and ever after memory. And for the knowledge of consequence, which I have said before is called science, it is not absolute but conditional. No man can know by discourse that this or that is, has been, or will be, which is to know absolutely; but only that if this is, that is; if this has been, that has been; if this shall be, that shall be; which is to know conditionally, and that not the consequence of one thing to another, but of one name of a thing to another *(margin: Knowledge of fact not derived from reasoning.)*

---

[x] Lev. c. 5.

[y] Citius multo veram logicam discunt qui mathematicorum demonstrationibus, quam qui logicorum syllogizandi præceptis legendis tempus conterunt, haud aliter quam parvuli pueri gressum formare discunt non præceptis sed sæpe gradiendo. C. iv. p. 30. Atque hæc sufficiunt (he says afterwards) de syllogismo, qui est tanquam gressus philosophiæ;

nam et quantum necesse est ad cognoscendum unde vim suam habeat omnis argumentatio legitima, tantum diximus; et omnia accumulare quæ dici possunt, æque superfluum esset ac si quis ut dixi puerulo ad gradiendum præcepta dare velit; acquiritur enim ratiocinandi ars non præceptis sed usu et lectione eorum librorum in quibus omnia severis demonstrationibus transiguntur. C. v. p. 35.

name of the same thing.   And therefore when the discourse is put into speech and begins with the definitions of words, and proceeds by connexion of the same into general affirmations, and of those again into syllogisms, the end or last sum is called the conclusion, and the thought of the mind by it signified is that conditional knowledge of the consequence of words which is commonly called science.   But if the first ground of such discourse be not definitions ; or if definitions be not rightly joined together in syllogisms, then the end or conclusion is again opinion, namely, of the truth of somewhat said, though sometimes in absurd and senseless words, without possibility of being understood.'[z]

133. ' Belief, which is the admitting of propositions upon trust, in many cases is no less free from doubt than perfect and manifest knowledge; for as there is nothing whereof there is not some cause, so when there is doubt, there must be some cause thereof conceived.   Now there be many things which we receive from the report of others, of which it is impossible to imagine any cause of doubt; for what can be opposed againt the consent of all men, in things they can know and have no cause to report otherwise than they are, such as is great part of our histories, unless a man would say that all the world had conspired to deceive him ?'[a]   Whatever we believe on the authority of the speaker, he is the object of our faith. Consequently when we believe that the Scriptures are the Word of God, having no immediate revelation from God himself, our belief, faith, and trust is in the church, whose word we take and acquiesce therein.   Hence all we believe on the authority of men, whether they be sent from God or not, is faith in men only.[b]   We have no certain knowledge of the truth of Scripture, but trust the holy men of God's church succeeding one another from the time of those who saw the wondrous works of God Almighty in the flesh.   And as we believe the Scriptures to be the word of God on the authority of the church, the interpretation of the Scripture in case of controversy ought to be trusted to the church rather than private opinion.[c]

Belief.

---

[z] Lev. c. 7.   [b] Lev. c. 7.
[a] Hum. Nat. c. 6.   [c] Hum. Nat. c. 11.

134. The ninth chapter of the Leviathan contains a synoptical chart of human science or 'knowledge Chart of of consequences,' also called philosophy. He di- science. vides it into natural and civil, the former into consequences from accidents common to all bodies, quantity and motion, and those from qualities otherwise called physics. The first includes astronomy, mechanics, architecture, as well as mathematics. The second he distinguishes into consequences from qualities of bodies transient, or meteorology, and from those of bodies permanent, such as the stars, the atmosphere, or terrestrial bodies. The last are divided again into those without sense, and those with sense; and these into animals and men. In the consequences from the qualities of animals generally he reckons optics and music; in those from men we find ethics, poetry, rhetoric, and logic. These altogether constitute the first great head of natural philosophy. In the second, or civil philosophy, he includes nothing but the rights and duties of sovereigns and their subjects. This chart of human knowledge is one of the worst that has been propounded, and falls much below that of Bacon.[d]

135. This is the substance of the philosophy of Hobbes, so far as it relates to the intellectual faculties, and Analysis of especially to that of reasoning. In the seventh passions. and two following chapters of the treatise on Human Nature, in the ninth and tenth of the Leviathan, he proceeds to the analysis of the passions. The motion in some internal substance of the head, if it does not stop there, producing mere conceptions, proceeds to the heart, helping or hindering the vital motions, which he distinguishes from the voluntary, exciting in us pleasant or painful affections, called passions. We are solicited by these to draw near to that which pleases us, and the contrary. Hence pleasure, love, appetite, desire, are divers names for divers considerations of the same thing. As all conceptions we have immediately by the sense are delight or pain or appetite or fear, so are all the imaginations after sense. But as they are weaker imaginations, so are they also weaker pleasures or weaker pains.[e] All delight is appetite, and presupposes a further end. There is no utmost

---

[d] Lev. c. 9.   [e] Hum. Nat. c. 7.

end in this world, for while we live we have desires, and
desire presupposes a further end.   We are not therefore to
wonder that men desire more, the more they possess : for
felicity, by which we mean continual delight, consists not in
having prospered, but in prospering.[f]   Each passion, being,
as he fancies, a continuation of the motion which gives rise
to a peculiar conception, is associated with it.   They all,
except such as are immediately connected with sense, consist
in the conception of a power to produce some effect.   To
honour a man, is to conceive that he has an excess of power
over some one with whom he is compared; hence qualities
indicative of power, and actions significant of it, are honourable ; riches are honoured as signs of power, and nobility is
honourable as a sign of power in ancestors.[g]

136. 'The constitution of man's body is in perpetual
Good and   mutation, and hence it is impossible that all the
evil relative
terms.   same things should always cause in him the same
appetites and aversions ; much less can all men consent in
the desire of any one object.   But whatsoever is the object
of any man's appetite or desire, that is it which he for his
part calls good, and the object of his hate and aversion, evil,
or of his contempt, vile and inconsiderable.   For these words
of good, evil, and contemptible are ever used with relation
to the person using them ; there being nothing simply and
absolutely so ; nor any common rule of good and evil, to be
taken from the nature of the objects themselves, but from
the person of the man, where there is no commonwealth, or
in a commonwealth from the person that represents us, or
from an arbitrator or judge, whom men disagreeing shall
by consent set up, and make his sentence the rule thereof.'[h]

137. In prosecuting this analysis all the passions are re-
His para-   solved into self-love, the pleasure that we take in
doxes.   our own power, the pain that we suffer in wanting
it.   Some of his explications are very forced.   Thus weeping
is said to be from a sense of our want of power.   And here
comes one of his strange paradoxes.   'Men are apt to weep
that prosecute revenge, when the revenge is suddenly stopped
or frustrated by the repentance of their adversary ; *and such*

---

[f] Hum. Nat. c. 7.   Lev. c. 11.   [g] Hum. Nat. c. 8.   [h] Lev. c. 6.

are the tears of reconciliation.'[k]   So resolute was he to resort
to anything the most preposterous, rather than admit a
moral feeling in human nature.   His account of laughter is
better known, and perhaps more probable, though not explaining the whole of the case.   After justly observing that
whatsoever it be that moves laughter, it must be new and
unexpected, he defines it to be ' a sudden glory arising from
a sudden conception of some eminency in ourselves, by comparison with the infirmity of others, or with our own formerly, for men laugh at the follies of themselves past.'   It
might be objected, that those are most prone to laughter
who have least of this glorying in themselves, or under-
valuing of their neighbours.

138. ' There is a great difference between the desire of a
man when indefinite, and the same desire limited   His notion
to one person, and this is that love which is the   of love.
great theme of poets.   But notwithstanding their praises, it
must be defined by the word need; for it is a conception a
man hath of his need of that one person desired.'[m]   ' There is
yet another passion sometimes called love, but more properly
good-will or charity.   There can be no greater argument to
a man of his own power than to find himself able not only to
accomplish his own desires, but also to assist other men in
theirs; and this is that conception wherein consists charity.
In which first is contained that natural affection of parents
towards their children, which the Greeks call στοργὴ, as also
that affection wherewith men seek to assist those that adhere
unto them.   But the affection wherewith men many times
bestow their benefits on strangers is not to be called charity,
but either contract, whereby they seek to purchase friendship, or fear, which makes them to purchase peace.'[n]   This
is equally contrary to notorious truth, there being neither
fear nor contract in generosity towards strangers.   It is,
however, not so extravagant as a subsequent position, that
in beholding the danger of a ship in a tempest, though there
is pity, which is grief, yet ' the delight in our own security
is so far predominant, that men usually are content in such
a case to be spectators of the misery of their friends.'[o]

---

[k] Hum Nat. c. 9.   Lev. c. 6 and 10.   [n] Id. ibid.
[m] Hum Nat. c. 9.   [o] Id. ibid. This is an exaggeration

139. As knowledge begins from experience, new experience
is the beginning of new knowledge. Whatever,
Curiosity.
therefore, happens new to a man gives him the
hope of knowing somewhat he knew not before. This
appetite of knowledge is curiosity. It is peculiar to man;
for beasts never regard new things, except to discern how
far they may be useful, while man looks for the cause and
beginning of all he sees.[p] This attribute of curiosity seems
rather hastily denied to beasts. And as men, he says, are
always seeking new knowledge, so are they always deriving
some new gratification. There is no such thing as perpetual
tranquillity of mind while we live here, because life itself is
but motion, and can never be without desire, nor without
fear, no more than without sense. ' What kind of felicity
God hath ordained to them that devoutly honour him, a
man shall no sooner know than enjoy, being joys that now
are as incomprehensible, as the word of schoolmen, beatifical
vision, is unintelligible.'[q]

140. From the consideration of the passions Hobbes advances to inquire what are the causes of the dif-
Difference
of intellec-   ference in the intellectual capacities and dispositions
tual capa-
cities.   of men.[r]   Their bodily senses are nearly alike,
whence he precipitately infers there can be no great difference in the brain. Yet men differ much in their bodily
constitution, whence he derives the principal differences in
their minds; some being addicted to sensual pleasures are
less curious as to knowledge, or ambitious as to power.
This is called dulness, and proceeds from the appetite of
bodily delight. The contrary to this is a quick ranging of
mind accompanied with curiosity in comparing things that
come into it, either as to unexpected similitude, in which
fancy consists, or dissimilitude in things appearing the
same, which is properly called judgment; ' for to judge is
nothing else but to distinguish and discern. And both
fancy and judgment are commonly comprehended under the
name of wit, which seems to be a tenuity and agility of

---

of some well-known lines of Lucretius,   [q] Lev. c. 6 and c. 11.
which are themselves exaggerated.   [r] Hum. Nat. c. 10.
[p] Hum. Nat. c. 9.

spirits, contrary to that restiness of the spirits supposed in those who are dull.'*

141. We call it levity, when the mind is easily diverted, and the discourse is parenthetical; and this proceeds from curiosity with too much equality and indifference; for when all things make equal impression and delight, they equally throng to be expressed. A different fault is indocibility, or difficulty of being taught; which must arise from a false opinion that men know already the truth of what is called in question; for certainly they are not otherwise so unequal in capacity as not to discern the difference of what is proved and what is not, and therefore if the minds of men were all of white paper, they would all most equally be disposed to acknowledge whatever should be in right method, and by right ratiocination delivered to them. But when men have once acquiesced in untrue opinions, and registered them as authentical records in their minds, it is no less impossible to speak intelligibly to such men than to write legibly on a paper already scribbled over. The immediate cause, therefore, of indocibility is prejudice, and of prejudice false opinion of our own knowledge.[t]

142. Intellectual virtues are such abilities as go by the name of a good wit, which may be natural or acquired. 'By natural wit,' says Hobbes, 'I mean   Wit and fancy. not that which a man hath from his birth, for that is nothing else but sense; wherein men differ so little from one another, and from brute beasts, as it is not to be reckoned among virtues. But I mean that wit which is gotten by use only and experience, without method, culture, or instruction, and consists chiefly in celerity of imagining and steady direction. And the difference in this quickness is caused by that of men's passions that love and dislike some one thing, some another, and therefore some men's thoughts run one way, some another; and are held to, and observe differently the things that pass through their imagination.' Fancy is not praised without judgment and discretion, which is properly a discerning of times, places, and persons; but judgment

---

          * Hum. Nat.   t Ibid.

and discretion is commended for itself without fancy: without steadiness and direction to some end, a great fancy is one kind of madness, such as they have who lose themselves in long digressions and parentheses. If the defect of discretion be apparent, how extravagant soever the fancy be, the whole discourse will be taken for a want of wit.[u]

143. The causes of the difference of wits are in the passions; and the difference of passions proceeds partly from the different constitution of the body and partly from different education. Those passions are chiefly the desire of power, riches, knowledge, or honour; all which may be reduced to the first, for riches, knowledge, and honour are but several sorts of power. He who has no great passion for any of these, though he may be so far a good man as to be free from giving offence, yet cannot possibly have either a great fancy or much judgment. To have weak passions is dulness, to have passions indifferently for every thing giddiness and distraction, to have stronger passions for any thing than others have is madness. Madness may be the excess of many passions; and the passions themselves, when they lead to evil, are degrees of it. He seems to have had some notion of what Butler is reported to have thrown out as to the madness of a whole people. 'What argument for madness can there be greater, than to clamour, strike, and throw stones at our best friends? Yet this is somewhat less than such a multitude will do. For they will clamour, fight against, and destroy those by whom all their lifetime before they have been protected, and secured from injury. And if this be madness in the multitude, it is the same in every particular man.'[x]

Differences in the passions.

Madness.

144. There is a fault in some men's habit of discoursing which may be reckoned a sort of madness, which is when they speak words with no signification at all. 'And this is incident to none but those that converse in questions of matters incomprehensible as the schoolmen, or in questions of abstruse philosophy. The common sort of men seldom speak insignificantly, and are therefore by those other egregious persons counted idiots. But to be

Unmeaning language.

---

[u] Lev. c. 8.   [x] Id. c. 8.

assured their words are without any thing correspondent to them in the mind, there would need some examples; which if any man require, let him take a schoolman into his hands, and see if he can translate any one chapter concerning any difficult point, as the Trinity, the Deity, the nature of Christ, transubstantiation, free-will, &c., into any of the modern tongues, so as to make the same intelligible, or into any tolerable Latin, such as they were acquainted with that lived when the Latin tongue was vulgar.' And after quoting some words from Suarez, he adds, ' When men write whole volumes of such stuff, are they not mad, or intend to make others so ? ' [y]

145. The eleventh chapter of the Leviathan, on manners, by which he means those qualities of mankind which concern their living together in peace and ^{Manners.} unity, is full of Hobbes's caustic remarks on human nature. Often acute, but always severe, he ascribes overmuch to a deliberate and calculating selfishness. Thus the reverence of antiquity is referred to ' the contention men have with the living, not with the dead, to these ascribing more than due that they may obscure the glory of the other.' Thus, also, ' to have received from one to whom we think ourselves equal, greater benefits than we can hope to requite, disposes to counterfeit love, but really to secret hatred, and puts a man into the estate of a desperate debtor, that in declining the sight of his creditor, tacitly wishes him where he might never see him more. For benefits oblige, and obligation is thraldom; and unrequitable obligation perpetual thraldom, which is to one's equal hateful.' He owns, however, that to have received benefits from a superior, disposes us to love him ; and so it does where we can hope to requite even an equal. If these maxims have a certain basis of truth, they have at least the fault of those of Rochefoucault; they are made too generally characteristic of mankind.

146. Ignorance of the signification of words disposes men to take on trust not only the truth they know not, ^{Ignorances and prejudice.} but also errors and nonsense. For neither can be detected without a perfect understanding of words. ' But

---

[y] Lev.

ignorance of the causes and original constitution of right, equity, law, and justice, disposes a man to make custom and example the rule of his actions, in such manner as to think that unjust which it has been the custom to punish, and that just, of the impunity and approbation of which they can produce an example, or, as the lawyers which only use this false measure of justice barbarously call it, a precedent.' 'Men appeal from custom to reason, and from reason to custom, as it serves their turn, receding from custom when their interest requires it, and setting themselves against reason as oft as reason is against them; which is the cause that the doctrine of right and wrong is perpetually disputed both by the pen and the sword; whereas the doctrine of lines and figures is not so, because men care not in that subject what is truth, as it is a thing that crosses no man's ambition, profit, or lust. For I doubt not, but if it had been a thing contrary to any man's right of dominion, or to the interest of men that have dominion, that the three angles of a triangle should be equal to two angles of a square, that doctrine should have been, if not disputed, yet by the burning of all books of geometry, suppressed, as far as he whom it concerned was able.'[z] This excellent piece of satire has been often quoted, and sometimes copied, and does not exaggerate the pertinacity of mankind in resisting the evidence of truth, when it thwarts the interests and passions of any particular sect or community. In the earlier part of the paragraph it seems not so easy to reconcile what Hobbes has said with his general notions of right and justice; since if these resolve themselves, as is his theory, into mere force, there can be little appeal to reason, or to any thing else than custom and precedent, which are commonly the exponents of power.

147. In the conclusion of this chapter of the Leviathan as well as in the next, he dwells more on the nature of religion than he had done in the former treatise, and so as to subject himself to the imputation of absolute atheism, or at least of a denial of most attributes which we assign to the Deity. 'Curiosity about causes,' he says, 'led men to search out, one after the other, till they came to

His theory of religion.

---

[z] Lev. c. 11.

this necessary conclusion, that there is some eternal cause
which men call God. But they have no more idea of his
nature, than a blind man has of fire, though he knows that
there is something that warms him. So by the visible things
of this world and their admirable order, a man may conceive
there is a cause of them, which men call God, and yet not
have an idea or image of him in his mind. And they that
make little inquiry into the natural causes of things are
inclined to feign several kinds of powers invisible, and to
stand in awe of their own imaginations. And this fear of
things invisible is the natural seed of that which every one
in himself calleth religion, and in them that worship or fear
that power otherwise than they do, superstition.'

148. 'As God is incomprehensible, it follows that we can
have no conception or image of the Deity; and consequently
all his attributes signify our inability or defect of power to
conceive any thing concerning his nature, and not any conception of the same, excepting only this, that there is a God.
Men that by their own meditation arrive at the acknowledgment of one infinite, omnipotent, and eternal God, choose
rather to confess this is incomprehensible and above their
understanding, than to define his nature by spirit incorporeal,
and then confess their definition to be unintelligible.'[a] For
concerning such spirits he holds that it is not possible by
natural means only to come to the knowledge of so much as
that there are such things.[b]

149. Religion he derives from three sources—the desire
of men to search for causes, the reference of every Its supposed
thing that has a beginning to some cause, and the sources.
observation of the order and consequence of things. But
the two former lead to anxiety, for the knowledge that there
have been causes of the effects we see, leads us to anticipate
that they will in time be the causes of effects to come; so
that every man, especially such as are over-provident, is
'like Prometheus, the prudent man, as his name implies,
who was bound to the hill Caucasus, a place of large prospect, where an eagle feeding on his liver devoured as much
by day as was repaired by night; and so he who looks too

---

[a] Lev. c. 12.   [b] Hum. Nat. c. 11.

far before him, has his heart all day long gnawed by the
fear of death, poverty, or other calamity, and has no repose nor
pause but in sleep.' This is an allusion made in the style of
Lord Bacon. The ignorance of causes makes men fear some
invisible agent, like the gods of the Gentiles; but the investigation of them leads us to a God eternal, infinite, and omnipotent. This ignorance, however, of second causes, conspiring
with three other prejudices of mankind, the belief in ghosts, or
spirits of subtile bodies, the devotion and reverence generally
shown towards what we fear as having power to hurt us,
and the taking of things casual for prognostics, are altogether the natural seed of religion, which by reason of the
different fancies, judgments, and passions of several men
hath grown up into ceremonies so different that those which
are used by one man are for the most part ridiculous to
another. He illustrates this by a variety of instances from
ancient superstitions. But the forms of religion are changed
when men suspect the wisdom, sincerity, or love of those
who teach it, or its priests.[c] The remaining portion of the
Leviathan, relating to moral and political philosophy, must
be deferred to our next chapter.

150. The Elementa Philosophiæ were published by Hobbes
in 1655, and dedicated to his constant patron the Earl of
Devonshire. These are divided into three parts: entitled
De Corpore, De Homine, and De Cive. And the first part
has itself three divisions; Logic, the First Philosophy, and
Physics. The second part, De Homine, is neither the treatise of Human Nature, nor the corresponding part of the
Leviathan, though it contains many things substantially
found there. A long disquisition on optics and the nature
of vision, chiefly geometrical, is entirely new. The third
part, De Cive, is the treatise by that name, reprinted, as far
as I am aware, without alteration.

151. The first part of the first treatise, entitled Computatio sive Logica, is by no means the least valuable among
the philosophical writings of Hobbes. In forty pages the
subject is very well and clearly explained, nor do I know that
the principles are better laid down, or the rules more suffi-

---

[c] Lev. c. 12.

ciently given, in more prolix treatises. Many of his observations, especially as to words, are such as we find in his English
works, and perhaps his nominalism is more clearly expressed
than it is in them. Of the syllogistic method, at least for
the purpose of demonstration, or teaching others, he seems
to have entertained a favourable opinion, or even to have held
it necessary for real demonstration, as his definition shows.
Hobbes appears to be aware of what I do not remember to
have seen put by others, that in the natural process of reasoning, the minor premise commonly precedes the major.[d]
It is for want of attending to this, that syllogisms, as usually
stated, are apt to have so formal and unnatural a construction.
The process of the mind in this kind of reasoning is explained, in general, with correctness, and, I believe, with
originality, in the following passage, which I shall transcribe from the Latin, rather than give a version of my own;
few probably being likely to read the present section, who are
unacquainted with that language. The style of Hobbes,
though perspicuous, is concise, and the original words will
be more satisfactory than any translation.

152. Syllogismo directo cogitatio in animo respondens est
hujusmodi. Primo concipitur phantasma rei nominatæ cum
accidente sive affectu ejus propter quem appellatur eo nomine
quod est in minore propositione subjectum; deinde animo
occurrit phantasma ejusdem rei cum accidente sive affectu

---

[d] In Whately's Logic, p. 90, it is
observed, that 'the *proper order* is to
place the major premise first, and the
minor second; but this does not constitute the major and minor premises,' &c.
It may be the proper order in one sense,
as exhibiting better the foundation of
syllogistic reasoning; but it is not that
which we commonly follow, either in
thinking, or in proving to others. In
the rhetorical use of syllogism it can
admit of no doubt, that the opposite
order is the most striking and persuasive; such as in Cato, 'If there be a
God, he must delight in virtue; And that
which he delights in must be happy.'
In Euclid's demonstrations this will be
found the form usually employed. And,
though the rules of grammar are generally illustrated by examples, which is
beginning with the major premise, yet
the process of reasoning which a boy
employs in construing a Latin sentence
is the reverse. He observes a nominative
case, a verb in the third person, and then
applies his general rule, or major, to the
particular instance, or minor, so as to
infer their agreement. In criminal jurisprudence, the Scots begin with the
major premise, or relevancy of the in-
dictment, when there is room for doubt;
the English with the minor, or evidence
of the fact, reserving the other for what
we call motion in arrest of judgment.
Instances of both orders are common,
but by far the most frequent are of that
which the Archbishop of Dublin reckons
the less proper of the two. Those logicians who fail to direct the student's
attention to this, really do not justice to
their own favourite science.

propter quem appellatur, quod est in eadem propositione praedicatum. Tertio redit cogitatio rursus ad rem nominatam cum affectu propter quem eo nomine appellatur, quod est in praedicato propositionis majoris. Postremo cum meminerit eos affectus esse omnes unius et ejusdem rei, concludit tria illa nomina ejusdem quoque rei esse nomina; hoc est, conclusionem esse veram. Exempli causa, quando fit syllogismus hic, Homo est Animal, Animal est Corpus, ergo Homo est Corpus, occurrit animo imago hominis loquentis vel differentis [sic, sed lege disserentis], meminitque id quod sic apparet vocari hominem. Deinde occurrit eadem imago ejusdem hominis sese moventis, meminitque id quod sic apparet vocari animal. Tertio recurrit eadem imago hominis locum aliquem sive spatium occupantis, meminitque id quod sic apparet vocari corpus.[e] Postremo cum meminerit rem illam quae et extendebatur secundum locum, et loco movebatur, et oratione utebatur, unam et eandem fuisse, concludit etiam nomina illa tria, Homo, Animal, Corpus, ejusdem rei esse nomina, et proinde, Homo est Corpus, esse propositionem veram. Manifestum hinc est conceptum sive cogitationem quae respondens syllogismo ex propositionibus universalibus in animo existit, nullam esse in iis animalibus quibus deest usus nominum, cum inter syllogizandum oporteat non modo de re sed etiam alternis vicibus de diversis rei nominibus, quae propter diversas de re cogitationes adhibitae sunt, cogitare.

153. The metaphysical philosophy of Hobbes, always bold and original, often acute and profound, without producing an immediate school of disciples like that of Descartes, struck,

---

[e] This is the questionable part of Hobbes's theory of syllogism. According to the common and obvious understanding, the mind, in the major premise, Animal est Corpus, does not reflect on the subject of the minor, Homo, as occupying space, but on the subject of the major, Animal, which includes, indeed, the former, but is mentally substituted for it. It may sometimes happen, that where this predicate of the minor term is *manifestly* a collective word that comprehends the subject, the latter is not as it were absorbed in it, and may be contemplated by the mind distinctly in the major; as if we say, John is a man; a man feels; we may perhaps have no image in the mind of any man but John. But this is not the case where the predicated quality appertains to many things visibly different from the subject; as in Hobbes's instance, Animal est Corpus, we may surely consider other animals as being extended and occupying space besides men. It does not seem that otherwise there could be any ascending scale from particulars to generals, as far as the reasoning faculties, independent of words, are concerned. And if we begin with the major premise of the syllogism, this will be still more apparent.

perhaps, a deeper root in the minds of reflecting men, and
has influenced more extensively the general tone of speculation.   Locke, who had not read much, had certainly read
Hobbes, though he does not borrow from him so much as has
sometimes been imagined.   The French metaphysicians of
the next century found him nearer to their own theories than
his more celebrated rival in English philosophy.   But the
writer who has built most upon Hobbes, and may be reckoned,
in a certain sense, his commentator, if he who fully explains
and develops a system may deserve that name, was Hartley.
The theory of association is implied and intimated in many
passages of the elder philosopher, though it was first expanded and applied with a diligent, ingenious, and comprehensive research, if sometimes in too forced a manner by his
disciple.   I use this word without particular inquiry into the
direct acquaintance of Hartley with the writings of Hobbes;
the subject had been frequently touched in intermediate
publications, and, in matters of reasoning, as I have intimated above, little or no presumption of borrowing can be
founded on coincidence.   Hartley also resembles Hobbes in
the extreme to which he has pushed the nominalist theory,
in the proneness to materialise all intellectual processes, and
either to force all things mysterious to our faculties into
something imaginable, or to reject them as unmeaning, in
the want, much connected with this, of a steady perception of the difference between the Ego and its objects, in
an excessive love of simplifying and generalising, and in a
readiness to adopt explanations neither conformable to reason
nor experience, when they fall in with some single principle,
the key that was to unlock every ward of the human soul.

154. In nothing does Hobbes deserve more credit than in
having set an example of close observation in the philosophy
of the human mind.   If he errs, he errs like a man who goes
a little out of the right track, not like one who has set out
in a wrong one.   The eulogy of Stewart on Descartes, that
he was the father of this experimental psychology, cannot be
strictly wrested from him by Hobbes, inasmuch as the publications of the former are of an earlier date; but we may
fairly say that the latter began as soon, and prosecuted his
inquiries farther.   It seems natural to presume that Hobbes,

who is said to have been employed by Bacon in translating some of his works into Latin, had at least been led by him to the inductive process which he has more than any other employed. But he has seldom mentioned his predecessor's name; and indeed his mind was of a different stamp; less excursive, less quick in discovering analogies, and less fond of reasoning from them, but more close, perhaps more patient, and more apt to follow up a predominant idea which sometimes becomes one of the 'idola specûs' that deceive him.

CHAPTER IV.

HISTORY OF MORAL AND POLITICAL PHILOSOPHY AND OF JURISPRUDENCE, FROM 1600 TO 1650.

Sect. I.—On Moral Philosophy.

Casuists of the Roman Church—Suarez on Moral Law—Selden—Charron —La Mothe le Vayer—Bacon's Essays—Feltham—Browne's Religio Medici—Other Writers.

1. In traversing so wide a field as moral and political philosophy, we must still endeavour to distribute the subject according to some order of subdivision, so far at least as the contents of the books themselves which come before us will permit. And we give the first place to those which, relating to the moral law both of nature and revelation, connect the proper subject of the present chapter with that of the second and third.

2. We meet here a concourse of volumes occupying no small space in old libraries, the writings of the casuists, chiefly within the Romish church. None perhaps in the whole compass of literature are more neglected by those who do not read with what we may call a professional view; but to the ecclesiastics of that communion they have still a certain value, though far less than when they were first written. The most vital discipline of that church, the secret of the power of its priesthood, the source of most of the good and evil it can work, is found in the confessional. It is there that the keys are kept; it is there that the lamp burns, whose rays diverge to every portion of human life. No church that has relinquished this prerogative can ever establish a permanent dominion over mankind; none that retains it in effective use can lose the hope or the prospect of being their ruler.

3. It is manifest that in the common course of this rite
Necessity of rules for the confessor. no particular difficulty will arise, nor is the confessor likely to weigh in golden scales the scruples or excuses of ordinary penitents. But peculiar circumstances might be brought before him, wherein there would be a necessity for possessing some rule, lest by sanctioning the guilt of the self-revealing party he should incur as much of his own. Treatises therefore of casuistry were written as guides to the confessor, and became the text-books in every course of ecclesiastical education. These were commonly digested in a systematic order, and, what is the unfailing consequence of system, or rather almost part of its definition, spread into minute ramifications, and aimed at comprehending every possible emergency. Casuistry is itself allied to jurisprudence, especially to that of the canon law; and it was natural to transfer the subtilty of distinction and copiousness of partition usual with the jurists, to a science which its professors were apt to treat upon very similar principles.

4. The older theologians seem, like the Greek and Roman
Increase of casuistical literature. moralists, when writing systematically, to have made general morality their subject, and casuistry but their illustration. Among the monuments of their ethical philosophy, the Secunda Secundæ of Aquinas is the most celebrated. Treatises, however, of casuistry, which is the expansion and application of ethics, may be found both before and during the sixteenth century; and while the confessional was actively converted to so powerful an engine, they could not conveniently be wanting. Casuistry, indeed, is not much required by the church in an ignorant age; but the sixteenth century was not an age of ignorance. Yet it is not till about the end of that period that we find casuistical literature burst out, so to speak, with a profusion of fruit. 'Uninterruptedly afterwards,' says Eichhorn, 'through the whole seventeenth century, the moral and casuistical literature of the church of Rome was immensely rich; and it caused a lively and extensive movement in a province which had long been at peace. The first impulse came from the Jesuits, to whom the Jansenists opposed themselves. We must

distinguish from both the theological moralists, who remained faithful to their ancient teaching.' [a]

5. We may be blamed, perhaps, for obtruding a pedantic terminology, if we make the most essential distinction in morality, and one for want of which, more than any other, its debatable controversies have arisen, that between the subjective and objective rectitude of actions; in clearer language, between the provinces of conscience and of reason, between what is well meant and what is well done. The chief business of the priest is naturally with the former. The walls of the confessional are privy to the whispers of self-accusing guilt. No doubt can ever arise as to the subjective character of actions which the conscience has condemned, and for which the penitent seeks absolution. Were they even objectively lawful, they are sins in him according to the unanimous determination of casuists. But though what the conscience reclaims against is necessarily wrong, relatively to the agent, it does not follow that what it may fail to disapprove is innocent. Choose whatever theory we may please as to the moral standard of actions, they must have an objective rectitude of their own. independently of their agent, without which there could be no distinction of right and wrong, nor any scope for the dictates of conscience. The science of ethics, as a science, can only be conversant with objective morality. Casuistry is the instrument of applying this science, which, like every other, is built on reasoning, to the moral nature and volition of man. It rests for its validity on the great principle, that it is our duty to know, as far as lies in us, what is right, as well as to do what we know to be such. But its application was beset with obstacles; the extenuations of ignorance and error were so various, the difficulty of representing the moral position of the penitent to the judgment of the confessor by any process of language so insuperable, that the most acute understanding might be foiled in the task of bringing home a conviction of guilt to the self-deceiving sinner. Again, he might aggravate needless scruples, or disturb the tranquil repose of innocence.

Marginal note: Distinction of subjective and objective morality.

---

[a] Geschichte der Cultur, vol. vi. part i. p. 390.

6. But though past actions are the primary subject of
Directory office of the confessor. auricular confession, it was a necessary consequence that the priest would be frequently called upon to advise as to the future, to bind or loose the will in incomplete or meditated lines of conduct. And as all without exception must come before his tribunal, the rich, the noble, the counsellors of princes, and princes themselves, were to reveal their designs, to expound their uncertainties, to call, in effect, for his sanction in all they might have to do, to secure themselves against transgression by shifting the responsibility on his head. That this tremendous authority of direction, distinct from the rite of penance, though immediately springing from it, should have produced a no more overwhelming influence of the priesthood than it has actually done, great as that has been, can only be ascribed to the reaction of human inclinations which will not be controlled, and of human reason which exerts a silent force against the authority it acknowledges.

7. In the directory business of the confessional, far more
Difficulties, of casuistry. than in the penitential, the priest must strive to bring about that union between subjective and objective rectitude in which the perfection of a moral act consists, without which in every instance, according to their tenets, some degree of sinfulness, some liability to punishment remains, and which must at least be demanded from those who have been made acquainted with their duty. But when he came from the broad lines of the moral law, from the decalogue and the Gospel, or even from the ethical systems of theology, to the indescribable variety of circumstance which his penitents had to recount, there arose a multitude of problems, and such as perhaps would most command his attention, when they involved the practice of the great, to which he might hesitate to apply an unbending rule. The questions of casuistry, like those of jurisprudence, were often found to turn on the great and ancient doubt of both sciences, whether we should abide by the letter of a general law, or let in an equitable interpretation of its spirit. The consulting party would be apt to plead for the one ; the guide of conscience would more securely adhere to the other. But he might also perceive the severity of those rules of obligation which con-

duce, in the particular instance, to no apparent end, or even defeat their own principle. Hence there arose two schools of casuistry, first in the practice of confession, and afterwards in the books intended to assist it ; one strict and uncomplying, the other more indulgent and flexible to circumstances.

8. The characteristics of these systems were displayed in almost the whole range of morals. They were, how- Strict and ever, chiefly seen in the rules of veracity, and espe- of it. cially in promissory obligations. According to the fathers of the church, and to the rigid casuists in general, a lie was never to be uttered, a promise was never to be broken. The precepts especially of Revelation, notwithstanding their brevity and figurativeness, were held complete and literal. Hence promises obtained by mistake, fraud, or force, and above all, gratuitous vows, where God was considered as the promisee, however lightly made, or become intolerably onerous by supervenient circumstances, were strictly to be fulfilled, unless the dispensing power of the church might sometimes be sufficient to release them. Besides the respect due to moral rules, and especially those of Scripture, there had been from early times in the Christian church a strong disposition to the ascetic scheme of religious morality ; a prevalent notion of the intrinsic meritoriousness of voluntary self-denial, which discountenanced all regard in man to his own happiness, at least in this life, as a sort of flinching from the discipline of suffering. And this had doubtless its influence upon the severe casuists.

9. But there had not been wanting those who, whatever course they might pursue in the confessional, found Convenience the convenience of an accommodating morality in of the latter. the secular affairs of the church. Oaths were broken, engagements entered into without faith, for the ends of the clergy, or of those whom they favoured in the struggles of the world. And some of the ingenious sophistry, by which these breaches of plain rules are usually defended, was not unknown before the Reformation. But casuistical writings at that time were comparatively few. The Jesuits have the credit of first rendering public a scheme of false morals, which has been denominated from them, and enhanced the obloquy that overwhelmed their order. Their volumes of

casuistry were exceedingly numerous ; some of them belong
to the last twenty years of the sixteenth, but a far greater
part to the following century.

10. The Jesuits were prone for several reasons to embrace
Favoured by
the Jesuits. the laxer theories of obligation. They were less
tainted than the old monastic orders with that
superstition which had flowed into the church from the East,
the meritoriousness of self-inflicted suffering for its own
sake. They embraced a life of toil and danger, but not of
habitual privation and pain. Dauntless in death and torture, they shunned the mechanical asceticism of the con-
vent. And, secondly, their eyes were bent on a great end,
the good of the Catholic church, which they identified with
that of their own order. It almost invariably happens that
men who have the good of mankind at heart, and actively
prosecute it, become embarrassed, at some time or other, by
the conflict of particular duties with the best method of promoting their object. An unaccommodating veracity, an un-
swerving good faith, will often appear to stand, or stand
really, in the way of their ends ; and hence the little confidence we repose in enthusiasts, even when, in a popular
mode of speaking, they are most sincere; that is, most convinced of the rectitude of their aim.

11. The course prescribed by Loyola led his disciples not
The causes
of this. to solitude, but to the world. They became the
associates and councillors, as well as the confes-
sors of the great. They had to wield the powers of the
earth for the service of heaven. Hence, in confession itself,
they were often tempted to look beyond the penitent, and
to guide his conscience rather with a view to his usefulness than his integrity. In questions of morality, to abstain from action is generally the means of innocence, but to
act is indispensable for positive good. Thus their casuistry
had a natural tendency to become more objective, and to
entangle the responsibility of personal conscience in an in-
extricable maze of reasoning. They had also to retain
their influence over men not wholly submissive to religious
control, nor ready to abjure the pleasant paths in which
they trod ; men of the court and the city, who might serve
the church though they did not adorn it, and for whom

it was necessary to make some compromise in furtherance of the main design.

12. It must also be fairly admitted, that the rigid casuists went to extravagant lengths. Their decisions were often not only harsh, but unsatisfactory; the reason demanded in vain a principle of their iron law; and the common sense of mankind imposed the limitations, which they were incapable of excluding by anything better than a dogmatic assertion. Thus, in the cases of promissory obligation, they were compelled to make some exceptions, and these left it open to rational inquiry whether more might not be found. They diverged unnecessarily, as many thought, from the principles of jurisprudence; for the jurists built their determinations, or professed to do so, on what was just and equitable among men; and though a distinction, frequently very right, was taken between the *forum exterius* and *interius*, the provinces of jurisprudence and casuistry, yet the latter could not, in these questions of mutual obligation, rest upon wholly different ground from the former.

Extravagance of the strict casuists.

13. The Jesuits, however, fell rapidly into the opposite extreme. Their subtilty in logic, and great ingenuity in devising arguments, were employed in sophisms that undermined the foundations of moral integrity in the heart. They warred with these arms against the conscience which they were bound to protect. The offences of their casuistry, as charged by their adversaries, are very multifarious. One of the most celebrated is the doctrine of equivocation; the innocence of saying that which is true in a sense meant by the speaker, though he is aware that it will be otherwise understood. Another is that of what was called probability; according to which it is lawful, in doubtful problems of morality, to take the course which appears to ourselves least likely to be right, provided any one casuistical writer of good repute has approved it. The multiplicity of books, and want of uniformity in their decisions, made this a broad path for the conscience. In the latter instance, as in many others, the *subjective* nature of moral obligation was lost sight of; and to this the scientific treatment of casuistry inevitably contributed.

Opposite faults of Jesuits.

14. Productions so little regarded as those of the jesuitical casuists cannot be dwelt upon. Thomas Sanchez of Cordova is author of a large treatise on matrimony, published in 1592 ; the best, as far as the canon law is concerned, which has yet been published. But in the casuistical portion of this work the most extraordinary indecencies occur, such as have consigned it to general censure.[b] Some of these, it must be owned, belong to the rite of auricular confession itself, as managed in the church of Rome, though they give scandal by their publication and apparent excess beyond the necessity of the case. The Summa Casuum Conscientiæ of Toletus, a Spanish Jesuit and Cardinal, which, though published in 1602, belongs to the sixteenth century, and the casuistical writings of Less, Busenbaum, and Escobar, may just be here mentioned. The Medulla Casuum Conscientiæ of the second (Munster, 1645) went through fifty-two editions, the Theologia Moralis of the last (Lyon, 1646) through forty.[c] Of the opposition excited by the laxity in moral rules ascribed to the Jesuits, though it began in some manner during this period, we shall have more to say in the next.

15. Suarez of Granada, by far the greatest man in the department of moral philosophy whom the order of Loyola produced in this age, or perhaps in any other, may not improbably have treated of casuistry in some part of his numerous volumes. We shall, however, gladly leave this subject to bring before the reader a large treatise of Suarez, on the principles of natural law, as well as of all positive jurisprudence. This is entitled, Tractatus de legibus ac Deo legislatore in decem libros distributes utriusque fori hominibus non minus utilis, quam necessarius. It might with no great impropriety, perhaps, be placed in any of the three sections of this chapter, relating not only to moral philosophy, but to politics in some degree, and to jurisprudence.

Suarez De Legibus.

16. Suarez begins by laying down the position, that all legislative, as well as all paternal, power is derived from God,

---

[b] Bayle, art. Sanchez, expatiates on this, and condemns the Jesuit, Catilina Cethegum. The later editions of San-

chez De Matrimonio are *castigate.*
[c] Ranke, Die Päpste, vol. iii.

and that the authority of every law resolves itself into his. For either the law proceeds immediately from God, Titles of his ten books. or, if it be human, it proceeds from man as his vicar and minister.   The titles of the ten books of this large treatise are as follows: 1. On the nature of law in general, and on its causes and consequences; 2. On eternal, natural law, and that of nations; 3. On positive human law in itself, considered relatively to human nature, which is also called civil law; 4. On positive ecclesiastical law; 5. On the differences of human laws, and especially of those that are penal, or in the nature of penal; 6. On the interpretation, the alteration, and the abolition of human laws; 7. On unwritten law, which is called custom; 8. On those human laws which are called favourable, or privileges; 9. On the positive divine law of the old dispensations; 10. On the positive divine law of the new dispensation.

17. This is a very comprehensive chart of general law, and entitles Suarez to be accounted such a precursor of Heads of the second book. Grotius and Puffendorf as occupied most of their ground, especially that of the latter, though he cultivated it in a different manner.   His volume is a closely printed folio of 700 pages in double columns.   The following heads of chapters in the second book will show the questions in which Suarez dealt, and in some degree his method of stating and conducting them: 1. Whether there be any eternal law, and what is its necessity; 2. On the subject of eternal law, and on the acts it commands; 3. In what act the eternal law exists (existit), and whether it be one or many; 4. Whether the eternal law be the cause of other laws, and obligatory through their means; 5. In what natural law consists; 6. Whether natural law be a preceptive divine law; 7. On the subject of natural law, and on its precepts; 8. Whether natural law be one; 9. Whether natural law bind the conscience; 10. Whether natural law obliges not only to the act (actus) but to the mode (modum) of virtue.   This obscure question seems to refer to the subjective nature, or motive, of virtuous actions, as appears by the next; 11. Whether natural law obliges us to act from love or charity (ad modum operandi ex caritate); 12. Whether natural law not only prohibits certain actions, but invalidates them when done;

13. Whether the precepts of the law of nature are intrinsically immutable; 14. Whether any human authority can alter or dispense with the natural law; 15. Whether God by his absolute power can dispense with the law of nature; 16. Whether an equitable interpretation can ever be admitted in the law of nature; 17. Whether the law of nature is distinguishable from that of nations; 18. Whether the law of nations enjoins or forbids any thing; 19. By what means we are to distinguish the law of nature from that of nations; 20. Certain corollaries; and that the law of nations is both just, and also mutable.

18. These heads may give some slight notion to the reader of the character of the book, as the book itself may serve as a typical instance of that form of theology, of metaphysics, of ethics, of jurisprudence, which occupies the unread and unreadable folios of the sixteenth and seventeenth centuries, especially those issuing from the church of Rome, and may be styled generally the scholastic method. Two remarkable characteristics strike us in these books, which are sufficiently to be judged by reading their table of contents, and by taking occasional samples of different parts. The extremely systematic form they assume and the multiplicity of divisions render this practice more satisfactory than it can be in works of less regular arrangement. One of these characteristics is that spirit of system itself, and another is their sincere desire to exhaust the subject by presenting it to the mind in every light, and by tracing all its relations and consequences. The fertility of those men who, like Suarez, superior to most of the rest, were trained in the scholastic discipline, to which I refer the methods of the canonists and casuists, is sometimes surprising; their views are not one-sided; they may not solve objections to our satisfaction, but they seldom suppress them; they embrace a vast compass of thought and learning; they write less for the moment, and are less under the influence of local and temporary prejudices than many who have lived in better ages of philosophy. But, again, they have great defects; their distinctions confuse instead of giving light; their systems being not founded on clear principles become embarrassed and incoherent; their method is not always sufficiently con-

Character of such scholastic treatises.

secutive; the difficulties which they encounter are too arduous
for them; they labour under the multitude, and are entangled
by the discordance, of their authorities.

19. Suarez, who discusses all these important problems of
his second book with acuteness, and, for his circum- _{Quotations}
stances, with an independent mind, is weighed down _{of Suarez.}
by the extent and nature of his learning. If Grotius quotes
philosophers and poets too frequently, what can we say of
the perpetual reference to Aquinas, Cajetan, Soto, Turrecre-
mata, Vasquius, Isidore, Vincent of Beauvais or Alensis, not
to mention the canonists and fathers, which Suarez employs
to prove or disprove every proposition? The syllogistic forms
are unsparingly introduced. Such writers as Soto or Suarez
held all kinds of ornament not less unfit for philosophical
argument than they would be for geometry. Nor do they
ever appeal to experience or history for the rules of determination. Their materials are nevertheless abundant, consisting of texts of Scripture, sayings of the fathers and schoolmen,
established theorems in natural theology and metaphysics,
from which they did not find it hard to select premises which,
duly arranged, gave them conclusions.

20. Suarez, after a prolix discussion, comes to the conclusion, that ' eternal law is the free determination of _{His defi-}
_{nition of}
the will of God, ordaining a rule to be observed, _{etern aw.}
either, first, generally by all parts of the universe as a means
of a common good, whether immediately belonging to it in
respect of the entire universe, or at least in respect of the
singular parts thereof; or, secondly, to be specially observed
by intellectual creatures in respect of their free operations.' [d]
This is not instantly perspicuous; but definitions of a complex
nature cannot be rendered such. It is true, however, what
the reader may think curious, that this crabbed piece of
scholasticism is nothing else in substance, than the celebrated
sentence on law, which concludes the first book of Hooker's
Ecclesiastical Polity. Whoever takes the pains to understand

---

[d] Legem æternam esse decretum liberum voluntatis Dei statuentis ordinem
servandum, aut generaliter ab omnibus
partibus universi in ordine ad commune
bonum, vel immediatè illi conveniens
ratione totius universi, vel saltem ratione singularum specierum ejus, aut spe-
cialiter servandum a creaturis intel-
lectualibus quoad liberas operationes
earum. c. 3, § 6. Compare with Hooker:
Of Law no less can be said than that
her throne is the bosom of God, &c.

Suarez, will perceive that he asserts exactly that which is unrolled in the majestic eloquence of our countryman.

21. By this eternal law God is not necessarily bound. But this seems to be said rather for the sake of avoiding phrases which were conventionally rejected by the scholastic theologians, since, in effect, his theory requires the affirmative, as we shall soon perceive ; and he here says that the law is God himself (Deus ipse), and is immutable. This eternal law is not immediately known to man in this life, but either, ' in other laws, or through them,' which he thus explains. ' Men, while pilgrims here (viatores homines), cannot learn the divine will in itself, but only as much as by certain signs or effects is proposed to them ; and hence it is peculiar to the blessed in heaven that, contemplating the divine will, they are ruled by it as by a direct law. The former know the eternal law, because they partake of it by other laws, temporal and positive; for, as second causes display the first, and creatures the Creator, so temporal laws (by which he means laws respective of man on earth), being streams from that eternal law, manifest the fountain whence they spring. Yet all do not arrive even at this degree of knowledge, for all are not able to infer the cause from the effect. And thus, though all men necessarily perceive some participation of the eternal laws in themselves, since there is no one endowed with reason who does not in some manner acknowledge that what is morally good ought to be chosen, and what is evil rejected, so that in this sense men have all some notion of the eternal law, as St. Thomas, and Hales, and Augustin say ; yet nevertheless they do not all know it formally, nor are aware of their participation of it, so that it may be said the eternal law is not universally known in a direct manner. But some attain that knowledge, either by natural reasoning, or, more properly, by revelation of faith ; and hence we have said that it is known by some only in the inferior laws, but by others through the means of those laws.' [e]

22. In every chapter Suarez propounds the arguments of Whether God is a legislator? doctors on either side of the problem, ending with his own determination, which is frequently a middle course. On the question, ' Whether natural law is of itself

---

[e] Lib. ii. c. 4, § 9.

perceptive, or merely indicative of what is intrinsically right or wrong? or, in other words, whether God, as to this law, is a legislator? he holds this middle line with Aquinas and most theologians (as he says); contending that natural law does not merely indicate right and wrong, but commands the one and prohibits the other on divine authority; though this will of God is not the whole ground of the moral good and evil which belongs to the observance or transgression of natural law, inasmuch as it presupposes a certain intrinsic right and wrong in the actions themselves, to which it superadds the special obligation of a divine law. God therefore may be truly called a legislator in respect of natural law.'[f]

23. He next comes to a profound but important inquiry, closely connected with the last, Whether God could have permitted by his own law actions against natural reason? Ockham and Gerson had resolved this in the affirmative, Aquinas the contrary way. Suarez assents to the latter, and thus determines that the law is strictly immutable. It must follow of course that the pope cannot alter or dispense with the law of nature, and he might have spared the fourteenth chapter, wherein he controverts the doctrine of Sanchez and some casuists who had maintained so extraordinary a prerogative.[g] This, however, is rather episodical. In the fifteenth chapter he treats more at length the question, Whether God can dispense with the law of nature? which is not, perhaps, decided in denying his power to repeal it. He begins by distinguishing three classes of moral laws. The first are the most general, such as that good is to be done rather than evil; and with these it is agreed that God cannot dispense. The second is of such as the precepts of the decalogue, where the chief difficulty had arisen. Ockham, Peter d'Ailly, Gerson, and others, incline to say that he can dispense with all these, inasmuch as they are only prohibitions which he has himself imposed. This

Whether God could permit or commend wrong actions?

---

[f] Hæc Dei voluntas, prohibitio aut præceptio non est tota ratio bonitatis et malitiæ quæ est in observatione vel transgressione legis naturalis, sed supponit in ipsis actubus necessariam quandam honestatem vel turpitudinem, et illis adjungit specialem legis divinæ obligationem. c. 6, § 11.

[g] Nulla potestas humana, etiamsi pontificia sit, potest proprium aliquod præceptum legis naturalis abrogare, nec illud proprie et in se minuere, neque in ipso dispensare. § 8.

tenet, Suarez observes, is rejected by all other theologians as
false and absurd.   He decidedly holds that there is an intrinsic goodness or malignity in actions independent of the
command of God.   Scotus had been of opinion that God
might dispense with the commandments of the second table,
but not those of the first.   Durand seems to have thought
the fifth commandment (our sixth) more dispensable than
the rest, probably on account of the case of Abraham.   But
Aquinas, Cajetan, Soto, with many more, deny absolutely the
dispensability of the decalogue in any part.   The Gordian
knot about the sacrifice of Isaac is cut by a distinction, that
God did not act here as a legislator, but in another capacity, as
lord of life and death, so that he only used Abraham as an
instrument for that which he might have done himself.   The
third class of moral precepts is of those not contained in the
decalogue, as to which he decides also, that God cannot dispense with them, though he may change the circumstances
upon which their obligation rests, as when he releases a vow.

24. The Protestant churches were not generally attentive
to casuistical divinity, which smelt too much of the
opposite system.   Eichhorn observes that the first
book of that class, published among the Lutherans,
was by a certain Baldwin of Wittenberg, in 1628.[h]   A few
books of casuistry were published in England during this
period, though nothing, as well as I remember, that can be
reckoned a system, or even a treatise, of moral philosophy.
Perkins, an eminent Calvinistic divine of the reign of Elizabeth, is the first of these in point of time.   His Cases of
Conscience appeared in 1606. Of this book I can say nothing
from personal knowledge.   In the works of Bishop Hall
several particular questions of this kind are treated, but not
with much ability.   His distinctions are more than usually
feeble.   Thus usury is a deadly sin, but it is very difficult to
commit it unless we love the sin for its own sake ; for almost
every possible case of lending money will be found by his
limitations of the rule to justify the taking a profit for the
loan.[i]   His casuistry about selling goods is of the same description ; a man must take no advantage of the scarcity of

English casuists— Perkins, Hall.

the commodity, unless there should be just reason to raise the price, which he admits to be often the case in a scarcity. He concludes by observing that, in this, as in other well-ordered nations, it would be a happy thing to have a regulation of prices. He decides, as all the old casuists did, that a promise extorted by a robber is binding. Sanderson was the most celebrated of the English casuists. His treatise, De Juramenti Obligatione, appeared in 1647.

25. Though no proper treatise of moral philosophy came from any English writer in this period, we have one *Selden,* which must be placed in this class, strangely as the *De Jure Naturali* subject has been handled by its distinguished author. *juxta Hebraeos.* Selden published in 1640 his learned work, De Jure Naturali et Gentium juxta Disciplinam Ebræorum.[k] The object of the author was to trace the opinions of the Jews on the law of nature and nations, or of moral obligation, as distinct from the Mosaic law ; the former being a law to which they held all mankind to be bound. This theme had been of course untouched by the Greek and Roman philosophers, nor was much to be found upon it in modern writers. His purpose is therefore rather historical than argumentative ; but he seems so generally to adopt the Jewish theory of natural law that we may consider him the disciple of the rabbis as much as their historian.

·26. The origin of natural law was not drawn by the Jews, as some of the jurists imagined it ought to be, *Jewish* from the habits and instincts of all animated beings, *theory of natural law.* quod natura omnia animalia docuit, according to the definition of the Pandects. Nor did they deem, as many have done, the consent of mankind and common customs of nations to be a sufficient basis for so permanent and invariable a standard. Upon the discrepancy of moral sentiments and practices among mankind Selden enlarges in the tone which Sextus Empiricus had taught scholars, and which the world had learned from Montaigne. Nor did unassisted reason seem equal to determine moral questions, both from its natural feebleness, and because reason alone does not create an

---

[k] *Juxta* for *secundum*, we need hardly say, is bad Latin : it was, however, very common, and is even used by Joseph Scaliger, as Vossius mentions in his treatise, De Vitiis Sermonis.

obligation, which depends wholly on the command of a superior.[m] But God, as the ruler of the universe, has partly implanted in our minds, partly made known to us by exterior
revelation, his own will, which is our law. These positions
he illustrates with a superb display of erudition, especially
Oriental, and certainly with more prolixity, and less regard
to opposite reasonings, than we should desire.

27. The Jewish writers concur in maintaining that certain
Seven pre-
cepts of the
sons of
Noah.
short precepts of moral duty were orally enjoined by
God on the parent of mankind, and afterwards on
the sons of Noah. Whether these were simply preserved by tradition, or whether, by an innate moral faculty,
mankind had the power of constantly discerning them, seems
to have been an unsettled point. The principal of these
divine rules are called, for distinction, The Seven Precepts
of the Sons of Noah. There is, however, some variance in
the lists, as Selden has given them from the ancient writers.
That most received consists of seven prohibitions ; namely,
of idolatry, blasphemy, murder, adultery, theft, rebellion, and
cutting a limb from a living animal. The last of these, the
sense of which, however, is controverted, as well as the third,
but no other, are indicated in the ninth chapter of Genesis.

28. Selden pours forth his unparalleled stores of erudition
Character
of Selden's
work.
on all these subjects, and upon those which are suggested in the course of his explanations. These digressions are by no means the least useful part of his long
treatise. They elucidate some obscure passages of Scripture.
But the whole work belongs far more to theological than to
philosophical investigation ; and I have placed it here chiefly
out of conformity to usage ; for undoubtedly Selden, though a
man of very strong reasoning faculties, had not greatly turned
them to the principles of natural law. His reliance on the
testimony of Jewish writers, many of them by no means ancient, for those primæval traditions as to the sons of Noah,
was in the character of his times, but it will scarcely suit the
more rigid criticism of our own. His book, however, is excellent for its proper purpose, that of representing Jewish

---

[m] Selden says, in his Table Talk,
that he can understand no law of nature
but a law of God. He might mean this
in the sense of Suarez, without denying an intrinsic distinction of right and
wrong.

opinion, and is among the greatest achievements in erudition that any English writer has performed.

29. The moral theories of Grotius and Hobbes are so much interwoven with other parts of their philosophy, in the treasise De Jure Belli and in the Leviathan, that it would be dissecting those works too much, were we to separate what is merely ethical from what falls within the provinces of politics and jurisprudence. The whole must therefore be reserved for the ensuing sections of this chapter. Nor is there much in the writings of Bacon or of Descartes which falls, in the sense we have hitherto been considering it, under the class of moral philosophy. We may, therefore, proceed to another description of books, relative to the passions and manners of mankind, rather than, in a strict sense, to their duties, though of course there will frequently be some intermixture of subjects so intimately allied.

Grotius and Hobbes.

30. In the year 1601, Peter Charron, a French ecclesiastic, published his treatise on Wisdom. The reputation of this work has been considerable; his countrymen are apt to name him with Montaigne; and Pope has given him the epithet of 'more wise' than his predecessor, on account, as Warburton expresses it, of his 'moderating everywhere the extravagant Pyrrhonism of his friend.' It is admitted that he has copied freely from the Essays of Montaigne; in fact, a very large portion of the treatise on Wisdom, not less, I should conjecture, than one-fourth, is extracted from them with scarce any verbal alteration. It is not the case that he moderates the sceptical tone which he found there; on the contrary, the most remarkable passages of that kind have been transcribed; but we must do Charron the justice to say, that he has retrenched the indecencies, the egotism, and the superfluities. Charron does not dissemble his debts. 'This,' he says in his preface, ' is the collection of a part of my studies; the form and method are my own. What I have taken from others, I have put in their words, not being able to say it better than they have done.' In the political part he has borrowed copiously from Lipsius and Bodin, and he is said to have obligations to Duvair.[n] The ancients also must

Charron on Wisdom.

---

[n] Biogr. universelle.

have contributed their share.   It becomes, therefore, difficult
to estimate the place of Charron as a philosopher, because we
feel a good deal of uncertainty whether any passage may be his
own.   He appears to have been a man formed in the school of
Montaigne, not much less bold in pursuing the novel opinions
of others, but less fertile in original thoughts, so that he often
falls into the common-places of ethics ; with more reading than
his model, with more disciplined habits as well of arranging
and distributing his subject as of observing the sequence of an
argument ; but, on the other hand, with far less of ingenuity
in thinking, and of sprightliness of language.

31. A writer of rather less extensive celebrity than Charron belongs full as much to the school of Montaigne,
La Mothe
le Vayer.
His Dia-
logues.
though he does not so much pillage his Essays. This
was La Mothe le Vayer, a man distinguished by his
literary character in the court of Louis XIII., and ultimately
preceptor both to the Duke of Orleans and the young king
(Louis XIV.) himself.   La Mothe was habitually and universally a sceptic.   Among several smaller works we may chiefly
instance his Dialogues, published many years after his death
under the name of Horatius Tubero.   They must have been
written in the reign of Louis XIII., and belong, therefore, to
the present period.   In attacking every established doctrine,
especially in religion, he goes much farther than Montaigne,
and seems to have taken some of his metaphysical system
immediately from Sextus Empiricus. He is profuse of quotation, especially in a dialogue entitled Le Banquet sceptique,
the aim of which is to show that there is no uniform taste of
mankind as to their choice of food.   His mode of arguing
against the moral sense is entirely that of Montaigne, or, if
there be any difference, is more full of the two fallacies by
which that lively writer deceives himself : namely, the accumulating examples of things arbitrary and fanciful, such as
modes of dress and conventional usages, with respect to which
no one pretends that any natural law can be found ; and,
when he comes to subjects more truly moral, the turning our
attention solely to the external action, and not to the motive
or principle, which under different circumstances may prompt
men to opposite courses.

32. These dialogues are not unpleasing to read, and ex-

hibit a polite though rather pedantic style, not uncommon
in the seventeenth century. They are, however, very diffuse,
and the sceptical paradoxes become merely common-place by
repetition. One of them is more grossly indecent than any
part of Montaigne. La Mothe le Vayer is not, on the whole,
much to be admired as a philosopher; little appears to be
his own, and still less is really good. He contributed, no
question, as much as any one, to the irreligion and contempt
for morality prevailing in that court where he was in high
reputation. Some other works of this author may be classed
under the same description.

33. We can hardly refer Lord Bacon's Essays to the
school of Montaigne, though their title may lead   Bacon's
us to suspect that they were in some measure sug-   Essays.
gested by that most popular writer. The first edition, containing ten essays only, and those much shorter than as
we now possess them, appeared, as has been already mentioned, in 1597. They were reprinted with very little variation in 1606. But the enlarged work was published in
1612, and dedicated to Prince Henry. He calls them, in
this dedication, ' certain brief notes, set down rather signifi-
cantly than curiously, which I have called Essays. The
word is late, but the thing is ancient; for Seneca's Epistles
to Lucilius, if you mark them well, are but Essays, that
is, dispersed meditations, though conveyed in the form of
epistles.' The resemblance, at all events, to Montaigne, is
not greater than might be expected in two men equally
original in genius, and entirely opposite in their characters
and circumstances. One, by an instinctive felicity, catches
some of the characteristics of human nature; the other, by
profound reflection, scrutinises and dissects it. One is too
negligent for the inquiring reader, the other too formal
and sententious for one who seeks to be amused. We
delight in one, we admire the other; but this admiration has
also its own delight. In one we find more of the sweet
temper and tranquil contemplation of Plutarch, in the other
more of the practical wisdom and somewhat ambitious pro-
spects of Seneca. It is characteristic of Bacon's philosophical
writings, that they have in them a spirit of movement, a
perpetual reference to what man is to do in order to an end,

rather than to his mere speculation upon what is. In his
Essays this is naturally still more prominent. They are, as
quaintly described in the title-page of the first edition,
'places (loci) of persuasion and dissuasion ;' counsels for those
who would be great as well as wise. They are such as sprang
from a mind ardent in two kinds of ambition, and hesitating
whether to found a new philosophy, or to direct the vessel
of the state. We perceive, however, that the immediate
reward attending greatness, as is almost always the case,
gave it a preponderance in his mind ; and hence his Essays
are more often political than moral ; they deal with mankind, not in their general faculties or habits, but in their
mutual strife, their endeavours to rule others, or to avoid
their rule. He is more cautious and more comprehensive,
though not more acute, than Machiavel, who often becomes
too dogmatic through the habit of referring every thing to
a particular aspect of political societies. Nothing in the
Prince or the Discourses on Livy is superior to the Essays
on Seditions, on Empire, on Innovations, or generally those
which bear on the dexterous management of a people by
their rulers. Both these writers have what to our more
liberal age appears a counselling of governors for their own
rather than their subjects' advantage : but as this is generally
represented to be the best means, though not, as it truly is,
the real end, their advice tends, on the whole, to promote
the substantial benefits of government.

34. The transcendent strength of Bacon's mind is visible
in the whole tenor of these Essays, unequal as they
must be from the very nature of such compositions.

Their excel-
lence.

They are deeper and more discriminating than any earlier,
or almost any later, work in the English language, full of
recondite observation, long matured and carefully sifted. It
is true that we might wish for more vivacity and ease :
Bacon, who had much wit, had little gaiety ; his Essays are
consequently stiff and grave, where the subject might have
been touched with a lively hand ; thus it is in those on
Gardens and on Building. The sentences have sometimes
too apophthegmatic a form, and want coherence ; the historical instances, though far less frequent than with Montaigne, have a little the look of pedantry to our eyes. But

it is from this condensation, from this gravity, that the work derives its peculiar impressiveness. Few books are more quoted, and what is not always the case with such books, we may add that few are more generally read. In this respect they lead the van of our prose literature; for no gentleman is ashamed of owning that he has not read the Elizabethan writers; but it would be somewhat derogatory to a man of the slightest claim to polite letters, were he unacquainted with the Essays of Bacon. It is indeed little worth while to read this or any other book for reputation's sake; but very few in our language so well repay the pains, or afford more nourishment to the thoughts. They might be judiciously introduced, with a small number more, into a sound method of education, one that should make wisdom, rather than mere knowledge, its object, and might become a text-book of examination in our schools.

35. It is rather difficult to fix upon the fittest place for bringing forward some books, which, though moral Feltham's in their subject, belong to the general literature of Resolves. the age, and we might strip the province of polite letters of what have been reckoned its chief ornaments. I shall therefore select here such only as are more worthy of consideration for their matter than for the style in which it is delivered. Several that might range, more or less, under the denomination of moral essays, were published both in English and in other languages. But few of them are now read, or even much known by name. One, which has made a better fortune than the rest, demands mention, the Resolves of Owen Feltham. Of this book, the first part of which was published in 1627, the second not till after the middle of the century, it is not uncommon to meet with high praises in those modern writers who profess a faithful allegiance to our older literature. For myself, I can only say that Feltham appears not only a laboured and artificial, but a shallow writer. Among his many faults none strikes me more than a want of depth, which his pointed and sententious manner renders more ridiculous. There are certainly exceptions to this vacuity of original meaning in Feltham; it would be possible to fill a few pages with extracts not undeserving of being read, with thoughts just and judicious, though never deriving

much lustre from his diction.   He is one of our worst writers
in point of style: with little vigour, he has less elegance;
his English is impure to an excessive degree, and full of
words unauthorized by any usage.   Pedantry, and the novel
phrases which Greek and Latin etymology was supposed to
warrant, appear in most productions of this period; but
Feltham attempted to bend the English idiom to his own
affectations.   The moral reflections of a serious and thoughtful mind are generally pleasing, and to this perhaps is partly
owing the kind of popularity which the Resolves of Feltham
have obtained; but they may be had more agreeably and
profitably in other books.[o]

36. A superior genius to that of Feltham is exhibited in
Browne's   the Religio Medici of Sir Thomas Browne.   This
Religio Me-   little book made a remarkable impression; it was
dici.
soon translated into several languages, and is highly extolled
by Conringius and others, who could only judge through
these versions.   Patin, though he rather slights it himself,
tells us in one of his letters that it was very popular at Paris.
The character which Johnson has given of the Religio Medici
is well known; and, though perhaps rather too favourable,
appears in general just.[p]   The mind of Browne was fertile,
and, according to the current use of the word, ingenious;
his analogies are original, and sometimes brilliant; and as

---

[o] This is a random sample of Feltham's style:—'Of all objects of sorrow a distressed king is the most pitiful,
because it presents us most the frailty of
humanity, and cannot but most *midnight*
the soul of him that is fallen.   The sorrows of a deposed king are like the *distor-
quements* of a *darted* conscience, which
none can know but he that hath lost a
crown.' Cent. i. 61. We find not long after
the following precious phrase:—'The
nature that is *arted* with the subtleties of
time and practice.' i. 63.   In one page
we have *obnubilate, nested, parallel* (as a
verb), *fails* (failings), *uncurtain, deprav-
ing* (calumniating). i. 50.   And we are
to be disgusted with such vile English,
or properly no English, for the sake of
the sleepy saws of a trivial morality.
Such defects are not compensated by the
better and more striking thoughts we
may occasionally light upon. In reading

Feltham, nevertheless, I seemed to perceive some resemblance to the tone and
way of thinking of the Turkish Spy,
which is a great compliment to the
former; for the Turkish Spy is neither
disagreeable nor superficial. The resemblance must lie in a certain contemplative
melancholy, rather serious than severe,
in respect to the world and its ways;
and as Feltham's Resolves seem to have
a charm, by the editions they have gone
through, and the good name they have
gained, I can only look for it in this.

[p] 'The Religio Medici was no sooner
published than it excited the attention
of the public by the novelty of paradoxes,
the dignity of sentiment, the quick succession of images, the multitude of
abstruse allusions, the subtlety of disquisition, and the strength of language.'
Life of Browne (in Johnson's Works,
xii. 275).

his learning is also in things out of the beaten path, this
gives a peculiar and uncommon air to all his writings, and
especially to the Religio Medici. He was, however, far removed from real philosophy, both by his turn of mind and
by the nature of his erudition; he seldom reasons, his
thoughts are desultory, sometimes he appears sceptical or
paradoxical, but credulity and deference to authority prevail.
He belonged to the class, numerous at that time in our
church, who halted between Popery and Protestantism; and
this gives him, on all such topics, an appearance of vacillation and irresoluteness which probably represents the real
state of his mind. His paradoxes do not seem very original,
nor does he arrive at them by any process of argument;
they are more like traces of his reading casually suggesting
themselves, and supported by his own ingenuity. His style
is not flowing, but vigorous; his choice of words not elegant,
and even approaching to barbarism as English phrase; yet
there is an impressiveness, an air of reflection and sincerity
in Browne's writings, which redeem many of their faults.
His egotism is equal to that of Montaigne, but with this
difference, that it is the egotism of a melancholy mind,
which generally becomes unpleasing. This melancholy temperament is characteristic of Browne. ' Let's talk of graves
and worms and epitaphs' seems his motto. His best written
work, the Hydriotaphia, is expressly an essay on sepulchral
urns; but the same taste for the circumstances of mortality
leavens also the Religio Medici.

37. The thoughts of Sir Walter Raleigh on moral prudence are few, but precious. And some of the   Selden's
bright sallies of Selden recorded in his Table Talk   Table Talk.
are of the same description, though the book is too miscellaneous to fall under any single head of classification. The
editor of this very short and small volume, which gives,
perhaps, a more exalted notion of Selden's natural talents
than any of his learned writings, requests the reader to distinguish times, and ' in his fancy to carry along with him
the when and the why many of these things were spoken.'
This intimation accounts for the different spirit in which he
may seem to combat the follies of the prelates at one time,
and of the presbyterians or fanatics at another. These

sayings are not always, apparently, well reported; some
seem to have been misunderstood, and in others the limiting
clauses to have been forgotten. But on the whole they are
full of vigour, raciness, and a kind of scorn of the half-
learned, far less rude, but more cutting than that of Scaliger.
It has been said that the Table Talk of Selden is worth
all the Ana of the Continent. In this I should be disposed
to concur; but they are not exactly works of the same class.

38. We must now descend much lower, and could find
Osborn's little worth remembering. Osborn's Advice to his
Advice to
his Son. Son may be reckoned among the moral and political
writings of this period. It is not very far above mediocrity,
and contains a good deal that is common-place, yet with a
considerable sprinkling of sound sense and observation. The
style is rather apophthegmatic, though by no means more
so than was then usual.

39. A few books, English as well as foreign, are purposely
John Valen- deferred for the present; I am rather apprehensive
tine Andreæ. that I shall be found to have overlooked some not
unworthy of notice. One written in Latin by a German
writer has struck me as displaying a spirit which may claim
for it a place among the livelier and lighter class, though
with serious intent, of moral essays. John Valentine Andreæ
was a man above his age, and a singular contrast to the
narrow and pedantic herd of German scholars and theologians. He regarded all things around him with a sarcastic
but benevolent philosophy, keen in exposing the errors of
mankind, yet only for the sake of amending them. It has
been supposed by many that he invented the existence of
the famous Rosicrucian society, not so much, probably, for
the sake of mystification, as to suggest an institution so
praiseworthy and philanthropic as he delineated for the
imitation of mankind. This, however, is still a debated
problem in Germany.[q] But among his numerous writings,
that alone of which I know anything is entitled, in the original
Latin, Mythologiæ Christianæ, sive Virtutum et Vitiorum
Vitæ Humanæ Imaginum Libri Tres. (Strasburg, 1618.)
Herder has translated a part of this book in the fifth volume

---

q Brucker, iv. 735.   Biogr. univ. art. Andreæ, et alibi.

of his Zerstreute Blätter; and it is here that I have met with it. Andreæ wrote, I believe, solely in Latin, and his works appear to be scarce, at least in England. These short apologues, which Herder has called Parables, are written with uncommon terseness of language, a happy and original vein of invention, and a philosophy looking down on common life without ostentation and without passion. He came, too, before Bacon, but he had learned to scorn the disputes of the schools, and had sought for truth with an entire love, even at the hands of Cardan and Campanella. I will give a specimen, in a note, of the peculiar manner of Andreæ, but my translation does not, perhaps, justice to that of Herder. The idea, it may be observed, is now become more trite.[r]

Sect. II.—On Political Philosophy.

Change in the Character of Political Writings—Bellenden and others—Patriarchal Theory refuted by Suarez—Althusius—Political Economy of Serra—Hobbes—and Analysis of his Political Treatises.

40. THE recluse philosopher, who, like Descartes in his country-house near Utrecht, investigates the properties of

---

[r] 'The Pen and the Sword strove with each other for superiority, and the voices of the judges were divided. The men of learning talked much and persuaded many; the men of arms were fierce, and compelled many to join their side. Thus nothing could be determined; it followed that both were left to fight it out, and settle their dispute in single combat.

'On one side books rustled in the libraries, on the other arms rattled in the arsenals; men looked on in hope and fear, and waited the end.

'The Pen, consecrated to truth, was notorious for much falsehood; the Sword, a servant of God, was stained with innocent blood; both hoped for the aid of heaven, both found its wrath.

'The State, which had need of both, and disliked the manners of both, would put on the appearance of caring for the weal and woe of neither. The Pen was weak, but quick, glib, well exercised, and very bold, when one provoked it. The Sword was stern, implacable, but less compact and subtle, so that on both sides the victory remained uncertain. At length, for the security of both, the common weal pronounced that both in turn should stand by her side and bear with each other. For that only is a happy country where the Pen and the Sword are faithful servants, not where either governs by its arbitrary will and passion.'

If the touches in this little piece are not always clearly laid on, it may be ascribed as much, perhaps, to their having passed through two translations, as to the fault of the excellent writer. But in this early age we seldom find the entire neatness and felicity which later times attained.

quantity, or the operations of the human mind, while nations are striving for conquest and factions for ascendancy, hears that tumultuous uproar but as the dash of the ocean waves at a distance, and it may even serve, like music that falls upon the poet's ear, to wake in him some new train of high thought, or at the least to confirm his love of the absolute and the eternal, by comparison with the imperfection and error that beset the world. Such is the serene temple of philosophy, which the Roman poet has contrasted with the storm and the battle, with the passions of the great and the many, the perpetual struggle of man against his fellows. But if he who might dwell on this vantage-ground descends into the plain, and takes so near a view of the world's strife that he sees it as a whole very imperfectly, while the parts to which he approaches are magnified beyond their proportion; if especially he mingles with the combat, and shares its hopes and its perils, though in many respects he may know more than those who keep aloof, he will lose something of that faculty of equal and comprehensive vision, in which the philosophical temper consists. Such has very frequently, or more or less, perhaps, in almost every instance, been the fate of the writer on general politics; if his pen has not been solely employed with a view to the questions that engage attention in his own age, it has generally been guided in a certain degree by regard to them.

41. In the sixteenth century, we have seen that notions of popular rights, and of the admissibility of sovereign power for misconduct, were alternately broached by the two great religious parties of Europe, according to the necessity in which they stood for such weapons against their adversaries. Passive obedience was preached as a duty by the victorious, rebellion was claimed as a right by the vanquished. The history of France and England, and partly of other countries, was the clue to these politics. But in the following period, a more tranquil state of public opinion, and a firmer hand upon the reins of power, put an end to such books as those of Languet, Buchanan, Rose, and Mariana. The last of these, by the vindication of tyrannicide, in his treatise De Rege, contributed to bring about a re-action in political

Abandonment of anti-monarchical theories.

literature. The Jesuits in France, whom Henry IV. was inclined to favour, publicly condemned the doctrine of Mariana in 1606. A book by Becanus, and another by Suarez, justifying regicide, were condemned by the parliament of Paris, in 1612.[s] The assassination, indeed, of Henry IV., committed by one, not perhaps, metaphysically speaking, sane, but whose aberration of intellect had evidently been either brought on or nourished by the pernicious theories of that school, created such an abhorrence of the doctrine, that neither the Jesuits nor others ventured afterwards to teach it. Those also who magnified, as far as circumstances would permit, the alleged supremacy of the See of Rome over temporal princes, were little inclined to set up, like Mariana, a popular sovereignty, a right of the multitude not emanating from the Church, and to which the Church itself might one day be under the necessity of submitting. This became, therefore, a period favourable to the theories of absolute power; not so much shown by means of their positive assertion through the press as by the silence of the press, comparatively speaking, on all political theories whatever.

42. The political writings of this part of the seventeenth century assumed in consequence more of an historical, or, as we might say, a statistical character. Learning was employed in systematical analyses of ancient or modern forms of government, in dissertations explanatory of institutions, in copious and exact statements of the true, rather than arguments upon the right or the expedient. Some of the very numerous works of Herman Conringius, a professor at Helmstadt, seem to fall within this description. But none are better known than a collection, made by the Elzevirs, at different times near the middle of this century, containing accounts, chiefly published before, of the political constitutions of European commonwealths. This collection, which is in volumes of the smallest size, may be called for distinction the Elzevir Republics. It is very useful in respect of the knowledge of facts it imparts, but rarely contains anything of a philosophical

Political literature becomes historical.

---

[s] Mezeray, Hist. de la Mère et du Fils.

nature. Statistical descriptions of countries are much allied to these last; some indeed are included in the Elzevir series. They were as yet not frequent; but I might have mentioned, while upon the sixteenth century, one of the earliest, the Description of the Low Countries by Ludovico Guicciardini brother of the historian.

43. Those, however, were not entirely wanting who took
Bellenden de Statu. a more philosophical view of the social relations of mankind. Among these a very respectable place should be assigned to a Scotsman, by name Bellenden, whose treatise De Statu, in three Books, is dedicated to Prince Charles in 1615. The first of these books is entitled De Statu prisci orbis in religione, re politica et literis; the second, Ciceronis Princeps, sive de statu principis et imperii; the third, Ciceronis Consul, Senator, Senatusque Romanus, sive de statu reipublicæ et urbis imperantis orbi. The first two books are, in a general sense, political; the last relates entirely to the Roman polity, but builds much political precept on this. Bellenden seems to have taken a more comprehensive view of history in his first book, and to have reflected more philosophically on it, than perhaps any one had done before; at least, I do not remember any work of so early an age which reminds me so much of Vico and the Grandeur et Décadence of Montesquieu. We can hardly make an exception for Bodin, because the Scot is so much more regularly historical, and so much more concise. The first book contains little more than forty pages. Bellenden's learning is considerable, and without that pedantry of quotation which makes most books of the age intolerable. The latter parts have less originality and reach of thought. This book was reprinted, as is well known, in 1787; but the celebrated preface of the editor has had the effect of eclipsing the original author: Parr was constantly read and talked of, Bellenden never.

44. The Politics of Campanella are warped by a desire to
Campanella's Politics. please the court of Rome, which he recommends as fit to enjoy an universal monarchy, at least by supreme control: and observes, with some acuteness, that no prince had been able to obtain an universal ascendant over Christendom, because the presiding vigilance of the Holy

See has regulated their mutual contentions, exalting one
and depressing another, as seemed expedient for the good of
religion.[t] This book is pregnant with deep reflection on
history; it is enriched, perhaps, by the study of
Bodin, but is much more concise. In one of the
Dialogues of La Mothe le Vayer, we find the fallacy of some
general maxims in politics drawn from a partial induction
well exposed, by showing the instances where they have
wholly failed.   Though he pays high compliments to Louis
XIII. and to Richelieu, he speaks freely enough, in his
sceptical way, of the general advantages of monarchy.

La Mothe le Vayer.

45. Gabriel Naudé, a man of extensive learning, acute
understanding, and many good qualities, but rather
lax in religious and moral principle, excited some
attention by a very small volume, entitled Considérations sur
les Coups d'État, which he wrote while young, at Rome, in
the service of the Cardinal de Bagne.   In this he maintains
the bold contempt of justice and humanity in political
emergencies which had brought disgrace on the Prince of
Machiavel, blaming those who, in his own country, had
abandoned the defence of the St. Bartholomew massacre.
The book is in general heavy and not well written, but
coming from a man of cool head, clear judgment, and considerable historical knowledge, it contains some remarks
not unworthy of notice.

Naudé's Coups d'État.

46. The ancient philosophers, the civil lawyers, and by far
the majority of later writers, had derived the origin
of government from some agreement of the com-
munity.   Bodin, explicitly rejecting this hypothesis, referred
it to violent usurpation.   But, in England, about the beginning of the reign of James, a different theory gained ground
with the church; it was assumed, for it did not admit of
proof, that a patriarchal authority had been transferred by
primogeniture to the heir-general of the human race; so
that kingdoms were but enlarged families, and an indefeasible
right of monarchy was attached to their natural chief,
which, in consequence of the impossibility of discovering him,

Patriarchal theory of government.

---

[t] Nullus hactenus Christianus princeps monarchiam super cunctos Chris-
tianos populos sibi conservare potuit.
Quoniam papa præest illis, et dissipat
erigitque illorum conatus prout religioni
expedit. C. 8.

devolved upon the representative of the first sovereign who
could be historically proved to have reigned over any nation.
This had not perhaps hitherto been maintained at length in
any published book, but will be found to have been taken
for granted in more than one. It was of course, in favour
with James I., who had a very strong hereditary title; and
it might seem to be countenanced by the fact of Highland
and Irish clanship, which does really affect to rest on a
patriarchal basis.

47. This theory as to the origin of political society, or
one akin to it, appears to have been espoused by
some on the Continent. Suarez, in the second book
of his great work on law, observes, in a remarkable passage,
that certain canonists hold civil magistracy to have been
conferred by God on some prince, and to remain always in
his heirs by succession; but 'that such an opinion has
neither authority nor foundation. For this power, by its
very nature, belongs to no one man, but to a multitude of
men. This is a certain conclusion, being common to all our
authorities, as we find by St. Thomas, by the civil laws, and
by the great canonists and casuists; all of whom agree that
the prince has that power of law-giving which the people
have given him. And the reason is evident, since all men
are born equal, and consequently no one has a political
jurisdiction over another, nor any dominion; nor can we
give any reason from the nature of the thing, why one man
should govern another rather than the contrary. It is true
that one might allege the primacy which Adam at his creation necessarily possessed, and hence deduce his government
over all men, and suppose that to be derived by some one,
either through primogenitary descent, or through the special
appointment of Adam himself. Thus Chrysostom has said
that the descent of all men from Adam signifies their subordination to one sovereign. But in fact we could only infer
from the creation and natural origin of mankind that Adam
possessed a domestic or patriarchal (œconomicam), not a
political, authority; for he had power over his wife, and
afterwards a paternal power over his sons till they were
emancipated; and he might even in course of time have
servants and a complete family, and that power in respect

Refuted by Suarez.

of them which is called patriarchal. But after families began
to be multiplied, and single men who were heads of families
to be separated, they had each the same power with respect
to their own families. Nor did political power begin to
exist till many families began to be collected into one entire
community. Hence, as that community did not begin by
Adam's creation, nor by any will of his, but by that of all
who formed it, we cannot properly say, that Adam had
naturally a political headship in such a society; for there
are no principles of reason from which this could be inferred,
since by the law of nature it is no right of the progenitor
to be even king of his own posterity. And if this cannot
be proved by the principles of natural law, we have no
ground for asserting that God has given such a power by a
special gift or providence, inasmuch as we have no revelation
or Scripture testimony to the purpose.'[u] So clear, brief,
and dispassionate a refutation might have caused our English divines, who became very fond of this patriarchal theory,
to blush before the Jesuit of Granada.

48. Suarez maintains it to be of the essence of a law that it
be enacted for the public good. An unjust law is no
law, and does not bind the conscience.[x] In this he
breathes the spirit of Mariana. But he shuns some of his
bolder assertions. He denies the right of rising in arms
against a tyrant, unless he is an usurper; and though he is
strongly for preserving the concession made by the kings of
Spain to their people, that no taxes shall be levied without
the consent of the Cortes, does not agree with those who lay
it down as a general rule, that no prince can impose taxes
on his people by his own will.[y] Suarez asserts the direct
power of the church over heretical princes, but denies it as
to infidels.[z] In this last point, as has been seen, he follows
the most respectable authorities of his nation.

His opinion of law.

49. Bayle has taken notice of a systematic treatise on
Politics by John Althusius, a native of Germany. Of this I
have only seen an edition published at Groningen in 1615,
and dedicated to the states of West Friesland. It seems,
however, from the article in Bayle, that there was one

---

[u] Lib. ii. c. 2, § 3.   [y] Lib. v. c. 17.
[x] Lib. i. c. 7; and lib. iii. c. 22.   [z] Lib. iii. c. 10.

printed at Herborn in 1603. Several German writers inveigh against this work as full of seditious principles, inimical to every government. It is a political system, taken chiefly from preceding authors, and very freely from Bodin; with great learning, but not very profitable to read. The ephori, as he calls them, by which he means the estates of a kingdom, have the right to resist a tyrant. But this right he denies to the private citizen. His chapter on this subject is written more in the tone of the sixteenth than of the seventeenth century, which indeed had scarcely commenced.[a] He answers in it Albericus Gentilis, Barclay, and others who had contended for passive obedience, not failing to draw support from the canonists and civilians whom he quotes. But the strongest passage is in his dedication to the States of Friesland. Here he declares his principle, that the supreme power or sovereignty (jus majestatis) does not reside in the chief magistrate, but in the people themselves, and that no other is proprietor or usufructuary of it, the magistrate being the administrator of this supreme power, but not its owner, nor entitled to use it for his benefit. And these rights of sovereignty are so much confined to the whole community, that they can no more alienate them to another, whether they will or not, than a man can transfer his own life.[b]

50. Few, even among the Calvinists, whose form of government was in some cases republican, would in the seventeenth century have approved this strong language of Althusius. But one of their noted theologians, Paræus, incurred the censure of the university of Oxford in 1623, for some passages in his commentary on the Epistle to the Romans, which seemed to impugn their orthodox tenet of unlimited submission. He merely holds that subjects, when not private men, but inferior magistrates, may defend themselves, and the state, and the true religion, even by arms against the sovereign under certain conditions; because

---

[a] Cap. 38. De tyrannide et ejus remediis.

[b] Administratorem, procuratorem, gubernatorem jurium majestatis, principem agnosco. Proprietarium vero et usufructuarium majestatis nullum alium quam populum universum in corpus unum symbioticum ex pluribus minoribus consociationibus consociatum, &c.

these superior magistrates are themselves responsible to the
laws of God and of the state.[c] It was, in truth, impossible
to deny the right of resistance in such cases without 'brand-
ing the unsmirched brow' of Protestantism itself; for by
what other means had the reformed religion been made to
flourish in Holland and Geneva, or in Scotland? But in
England, where it had been planted under a more auspicious
star, there was little occasion to seek this vindication of the
Protestant church, which had not, in the legal phrase, come
in by disseisin of the state, but had united with the state to
turn out of doors its predecessor. That some of the Anglican
refugees under Mary were ripe enough for resistance, or even
regicide, has been seen in another place by an extract from
one of their most distinguished prelates.

51. Bacon ought to appear as a prominent name in
political philosophy, if we had never met with it
in any other. But we have anticipated much of ^{Bacon.}
his praise on this score; and it is sufficient to repeat generally
that on such subjects he is among the most sagacious of mankind. It would be almost ridiculous to descend from Bacon,
even when his giant shadow does but pass over our scene,
to the feebler class of political moralists, such as Saavedra,
author of Idea di un Principe politico, a wretched effort of
Spain in her degeneracy; but an Italian writer must not be
neglected, from the remarkable circumstance that he is
esteemed one of the first who have treated the science of
political œconomy. It must, however, be under- Political
stood that, besides what may be found on the sub- œconomy.
ject in the ancients, many valuable observations which must
be referred to political œconomy occur in Bodin, that the
Italians had, in the sixteenth century, a few tracts on coin-
age, that Botero touches some points of the science, and
that in England there were, during the same age, pamphlets

---

[c] Subditi non privati, sed in magis-
tratu inferiori constituti, adversus supe-
riorem magistratum se et rempublicam
et ecclesiam seu veram religionem etiam
armis defendere jure possunt, his positis
conditionibus : 1. Cum superior magis-
tratus degenerat in tyrannum ; 2. Aut
ad manifestam idololatriam atque blas-
phemias ipsos vel subditos alios vult
cogere ; 3. Cum ipsis atrox infertur injuria ; 4. Si aliter incolumes fortunis
vita et conscientia esse non possint;
5. Ne prætextu religionis aut justitiæ
sua quærant ; 6. Servata semper ἐπιεικειᾳ
et moderamine inculpatæ tutelæ juxta
leges. Paræus in Epist. ad Roman.
col. 1350.

on public wealth, especially one entitled, A Brief Conceit of
English Policy.[d]

52. The author to whom we allude is Antonio Serra, a
Serra on the
means of ob-
taining mo-
ney without
mines. native of Cosenza, whose short treatise on the
causes which may render gold and silver abundant
in countries that have no mines is dedicated to the
Count de Lemos ' from the prison of Vicaria this tenth day
of July, 1613.' It has hence been inferred, but without a
shadow of proof, that Serra had been engaged in the conspiracy of his fellow-citizen Campanella fourteen years before.
The dedication is in a tone of great flattery, but has no
allusion to the cause of his imprisonment, which might have
been any other. He proposes, in his preface, not to discuss
political government in general, of which he thinks that the
ancients have treated sufficiently, if we well understood their
works, and still less to speak of justice and injustice, the
civil law being enough for this, but merely of what are the
causes that render a country destitute of mines abundant in
gold and silver, which no one has ever considered, though
some have taken narrow views, and fancied that a low rate
of exchange is the sole means of enriching a country.

53. In the first part of this treatise, Serra divides the
His causes of
wealth. causes of wealth, that is, of abundance of money,
into general and particular accidents (accidenti
communi e proprj), meaning by the former circumstances
which may exist in any country, by the latter such as are
peculiar to some. The common accidents are four; abundance of manufactures, character of the inhabitants, extent
of commerce, and wisdom of government. The peculiar are,
chiefly, the fertility of the soil, and convenience of geographical position. Serra prefers manufactures to agriculture; one of his reasons is their indefinite capacity of
multiplication; for no man whose land is fully cultivated by
sowing a hundred bushels of wheat, can sow with profit a
hundred and fifty; but in manufactures he may not only
double the produce, but do this a hundred times over, and

---

[d] This bears the initials of W. S.,
which some have idiotically taken for
William Shakspeare. I have some reason
to believe that there was an edition considerably earlier than that of 1584, but,
from circumstances unnecessary to mention, cannot produce the manuscript authority on which this opinion is founded.
It has been reprinted more than once, if
I mistake not, in modern times.

that with less proportion of expense. Though this is now
evident, it is perhaps what had not been much remarked
before.

54. Venice, according to Serra, held the first place as a
commercial city, not only in Italy, but in Europe; His praise of
' for experience demonstrates that all the merchan- Venice.
dises which come from Asia to Europe pass through Venice,
and thence are distributed to other parts.' But as this
must evidently exclude all the traffic by the Cape of Good
Hope, we can only understand Serra to mean the trade with
the Levant. It is, however, worthy of observation, that we
are apt to fall into a vulgar error in supposing that Venice
was crushed, or even materially affected, as a commercial
city, by the discoveries of the Portuguese.[e] She was in fact
more opulent, as her buildings of themselves may prove, in
the sixteenth century, than in any preceding age. The
French trade from Marseilles to the Levant, which began
later to flourish, was what impoverished Venice, rather than
that of Portugal with the East Indies. This republic was the
perpetual theme of admiration with the Italians. Serra
compares Naples with Venice; one, he says, exports grain
to a vast amount, the other imports its whole subsistence;
money is valued higher at Naples, so that there is a profit in
bringing it in, its export is forbidden; at Venice it is free;
at Naples the public revenues are expended in the kingdom;
at Venice they are principally hoarded. Yet Naples is poor
and Venice rich. Such is the effect of her commerce and of
the wisdom of her government, which is always uniform,
while in kingdoms, and far more in viceroyalties, the system
changes with the persons. In Venice the method of choosing

---

[e] [Perhaps it is too much to say
that Venice was not materially affected
by the Portuguese commerce with India;
when, though she became positively
richer in the sixteenth century than before, her progress would have been more
rapid, had the monopoly of the spice
trade remained in her hands. A remarkable proof of the apprehensions which
the discovery of the passage by the Cape
excited at Venice, appears by a letter of
Luigi da Porto, author of the novel on
Romeo and Juliet, written so early as
1509, just ten years after the voyage of
Vasco di Gama. One ·of the senators
recommended his colleagues to employ
their money in inducing the Sultan of
Egypt to obstruct the voyages of the
Portuguese to Calicut, so that the state
might possess again the whole commerce
in spices: il che è stato sin quà gran
parte della ricchezza nostra, e 'l non
poter più farlo, fra breve dovrà esser
cagione della nostra povertà e della nostra rovina. Lettere di L. da Porto,
1832, vol. ii. p. 476.—1847.]

magistrates is in such perfection, that no one can come in by corruption or favour, nor can any one rise to high offices who has not been tried in the lower.

55. All causes of wealth, except those he has enumerated, Serra holds to be subaltern or temporary; thus the low rate of exchange is subject to the common accidents of commerce. It seems, however, to have been a theory of superficial reasoners on public wealth, that it depended on the exchanges far more than is really the case; and in the second part of this treatise Serra opposes a particular writer, named De Santis, who had accounted in this way alone for abundance of money in a state. Serra thinks that to reduce the weight of coin may sometimes be an allowable expedient, and better than to raise its denomination. The difference seems not very important. The coin of Naples was exhausted by the revenues of absentee proprietors, which some had proposed to withhold; a measure to which Serra justly objects. This book has been reprinted at Milan in the collection of Italian œconomists, and, as it anticipates the principles of what has been called the mercantile theory, deserves some attention in following the progress of opinion. The once celebrated treatise of Mun, England's Treasure by foreign Trade, was written before 1640; but not being published till after the Restoration, we may postpone it to the next period.

Low rate of exchange not essential to wealth.

56. Last in time among political philosophers before the middle of the century we find the greatest and most famous, Thomas Hobbes. His treatise De Cive was printed in 1642 for his private friends. It obtained, however, a considerable circulation, and excited some animadversion. In 1647 he published it at Amsterdam, with notes to vindicate and explain what had been censured. In 1650 an English treatise, with the Latin title, De Corpore Politico, appeared; and in 1651 the complete system of his philosophy was given to the world in the Leviathan. These three works bear somewhat the same relation to one another that the Advancement of Learning does to the treatise De Augmentis Scientiarum; they are in effect the same; the same order of subjects, the same arguments, and in most places either the same words, or such variations as occurred

Hobbes. His political works.

to the second thoughts of the writer; but much is more copiously illustrated and more clearly put in the latter than
in the former; while much also, from whatever cause, is
withdrawn or considerably modified. Whether the Leviathan
is to be reckoned so exclusively his last thoughts that we
should presume him to have retracted the passages that do
not appear in it, is what every one must determine for himself. I shall endeavour to present a comparative analysis of
the three treatises, with some preference to the last.

57. Those, he begins by observing, who have hitherto
written upon civil policy have assumed that man is Analysis of
an animal framed for society; as if nothing else his three treatises.
were required for the institution of commonwealths, than
that men should agree upon some terms of compact which
they call laws. But this is entirely false. That men do
naturally seek each other's society, he admits by a note in
the published edition of De Cive ; but political societies
are not mere meetings of men, but unions founded on the
faith of covenants. Nor does the desire of men for society
imply that they are fit for it. Many may desire it who will
not readily submit to its necessary conditions.[f] This he
left out in the two other treatises, thinking it, perhaps, too
great a concession to admit any desire of society in man.

58. Nature has made little odds among men of mature age
as to strength or knowledge. No reason, therefore, can be
given why one should by any intrinsic superiority command
others, or possess more than they. But there is a great
difference in their passions; some through vainglory seeking pre-eminence over their fellows, some willing to allow
equality, but not to lose what they know to be good for
themselves. And this contest can only be decided by battle,
showing which is the stronger.

59. All men desire to obtain good and to avoid evil,
especially death. Hence they have a natural right to preserve their own lives and limbs, and to use all means necessary for this end. Every man is judge for himself of the

---

[f] Societates autem civiles non sunt
meri congressus, sed fœdera, quibus fa-
ciendis fides et pacta necessaria sunt.
. . . Alia res est appetere, alia esse ca-
pacem. Appetunt enim illi qui tamen
conditiones æquas, sine quibus societas
esse non potest, accipere per superbiam
non dignantur.

necessity of the means, and the greatness of the danger.
And hence he has a right by nature to all things, to do what
he wills to others, to possess and enjoy all he can. For he
is the only judge whether they tend or not to his preservation. But every other man has the same right. Hence there
can be no injury towards another in a state of nature. Not
that in such a state a man may not sin against God, or
transgress the laws of nature.[g] But injury, which is doing
any thing without right, implies human laws that limit
right.

60. Thus the state of man in natural liberty is a state of
war, a war of every man against every man, wherein the notions of right and wrong, justice and injustice, have no place.
Irresistible might gives of itself right, which is nothing but
the physical liberty of using our power as we will for our
own preservation and what we deem conducive to it. But
as, through the equality of natural powers, no man possesses
this irresistible superiority, this state of universal war is contrary to his own good, which he necessarily must desire.
Hence his reason dictates that he should seek peace as far
as he can, and strengthen himself by all the helps of war
against those with whom he cannot have peace. This then
is the first fundamental law of nature. For a law of nature
is nothing else than a rule or precept found out by reason
for the avoiding what may be destructive to our life.

61. From this primary rule another follows, that a man
should be willing, when others are so too, as far forth as for
peace and defence of himself he shall think it necessary, to
lay down his right to all things, and to be contented with so
much liberty against other men, as he would allow to other
men against himself. This may be done by renouncing his
right to any thing, which leaves it open to all, or by transferring it especially to another. Some rights, indeed, as
those to his life and limbs, are inalienable, and no man lays
down the right of resisting those who attack them. But, in
general, he is bound not to hinder those to whom he has

---

[g] Non quod in tali statu peccare in
Deum, aut leges naturales violare im-
possibile sit. Nam injustitia erga homines supponit leges humanas, quales in
statu naturali nullæ sunt. De Cive, c. 1.
This he left out in the later treatises.
He says afterward (sect. 28), omne damnum homini illatum legis naturalis vio-
latio atque in Deum injuria est.

granted or abandoned his own right, from availing themselves of it; and such hinderance is injustice or injury; that is, it is *sine jure*, his *jus* being already gone. Such injury may be compared to absurdity in argument, being in contradiction to what he has already done, as an absurd proposition is in contradiction to what the speaker has already allowed.

62. The next law of nature, according to Hobbes, is that men should fulfil their covenants. What contracts and covenants are, he explains in the usual manner. None can covenant with God, unless by special revelation; therefore vows are not binding, nor do oaths add anything to the swearer's obligation. But covenants entered into by fear he holds to be binding in a state of nature, though they may be annulled by the law. That the observance of justice, that is, of our covenants, is never against reason, Hobbes labours to prove; for if ever its violation may have turned out successful, this being contrary to probable expectation ought not to influence us. 'That which gives to human actions the relish of justice, is a certain nobleness or gallantness of courage rarely found; by which a man scorns to be beholden for the contentment of his life to fraud or breach of promise.' [h] A short gleam of something above the creeping selfishness of his ordinary morality!

63. He then enumerates many other laws of nature, such as gratitude, complaisance, equity, all subordinate to the main one of preserving peace by the limitation of the natural right, as he supposes, to usurp all. These laws are immutable and eternal; the science of them is the only true science of moral philosophy. For that is nothing but the science of what is good and evil in the conversation and society of mankind. In a state of nature private appetite is the measure of good and evil. But all men agree that peace is good, and therefore the means of peace, which are the moral virtues or laws of nature, are good also, and their contraries evil. These laws of nature are not properly called such, but conclusions of reason as to what should be done or abstained from; they are but theorems concerning what conduces to conservation and defence; whereas law is strictly the word

---

[h] Leviathan, c. 15.

of him that by right has command over others. But so
far as these are enacted by God in Scripture, they are truly
laws.

64. These laws of nature, being contrary to our natural
passions, are but words of no strength to secure any one without a controlling power. For till such a power is erected,
every man will rely on his own force and skill. Nor will the
conjunction of a few men or families be sufficient for security,
nor that of a great multitude guided by their own particular
judgments and appetites. ' For if we could suppose a great
multitude of men to consent in the observation of justice and
other laws of nature without a common power to keep them
all in awe, we might as well suppose all mankind to do the
same, and then there neither would be, nor need to be, any
civil government or commonwealth at all, because there would
be peace without subjection.[1] Hence it becomes necessary to
confer all their power on one man, or assembly of men, to
bear their person or represent them ; so that every one shall
own himself author of what shall be done by such representative. It is a covenant of each with each, that he will
be governed in such a manner, if the other will agree to the
same. This is the generation of the great Leviathan, or
mortal God, to whom, under the immortal God, we owe our
peace and defence. In him consists the essence of the
commonwealth, which is one person, of whose acts a great
multitude by mutual covenant have made themselves the
authors.

65. This person (including, of course, an assembly as well
as an individual) is the sovereign, and possesses sovereign
power. And such power may spring from agreement or
from force. A commonwealth by agreement or institution is
when a multitude do agree and covenant one with another
that whatever the major part shall agree to represent them,
shall be the representative of them all. After this has been
done, the subjects cannot change their government without
its consent, being bound by mutual covenant to own its
actions. If any one man should dissent, the rest would
break their covenant with him. But there is no covenant

---

[1] Leviathan, c. 17.

with the sovereign. He cannot have covenanted with the whole multitude as one party, because it has no collective existence till the commonwealth is formed ; nor with each man separately, because the acts of the sovereign are no longer his sole acts, but those of the society, including him who would complain of the breach. Nor can the sovereign act unjustly towards a subject ; for he who acts by another's authority cannot be guilty of injustice towards him ; he may, it is true, commit iniquity, that is violate the laws of God and nature, but not injury.

66. The sovereign is necessarily judge of all proper means of defence, of what doctrines shall be taught, of all disputes and complaints, of rewards and punishments, of war and peace with neighbouring commonwealths, and even of what shall be held by each subject in property. Property, he admits in one place, existed in families before the institution of civil society ; but between different families there was no *meum* and *tuum*. These are by the law and command of the sovereign ; and hence, though every subject may have a right of property against his fellow, he can have none against the sovereign. These rights are incommunicable, and inseparable from the sovereign power ; there are others of minor importance, which he may alienate ; but if any one of the former is taken away from him, he ceases to be truly sovereign.

67. The sovereign power cannot be limited nor divided. Hence there can be but three simple forms of commonwealth ; monarchy, aristocracy, and democracy. The first he greatly prefers. The king has no private interest apart from the people, whose wealth, honour, security from enemies, internal tranquillity, are evidently for his own good. But in the other forms each man may have a private advantage to seek. In popular assemblies, there is always an aristocracy of orators, interrupted sometimes by the temporary monarchy of one orator. And though a king may deprive a man of all he possesses to enrich a flatterer or favourite, so may also a democratic assembly, where there may be as many Neros as orators, each with the whole power of the people he governs. And these orators are usually more powerful to hurt others than to save them. A king may receive counsel of whom

he will, an assembly from those only who have a right to belong to it, nor can their counsel be secret. They are also more inconstant both from passion and from their numbers; the absence of a few often undoing all that had been done before. A king cannot disagree with himself, but an assembly may do so, even to producing civil war.

68. An elective or limited king is not the sovereign, but the sovereign's minister; nor can there be a perfect form of government, where the present ruler has not power to dispose of the succession. His power, therefore, is wholly without bounds, and correlative must be the people's obligation to obey. Unquestionably there are risks of mischiefs and inconveniences attending a monarchy; but these are less than in the other forms; and the worst of them is not comparable to those of civil war, or the anarchy of a state of nature, to which the dissolution of the commonwealth would reduce us.

69. In the exercise of government the sovereign is to be guided by one maxim, which contains all his duty: Salus populi suprema lex. And in this is to be reckoned not only the conservation of life, but all that renders it happy. For this is the end for which men entered into civil society, that they might enjoy as much happiness as human nature can attain. It would be therefore a violation of the law of nature, and of the trust reposed in them, if sovereigns did not study, as far as by their power it may be, that their subjects should be furnished with every thing necessary, not for life alone, but for the delights of life. And even those who have acquired empire by conquest must desire to have men fit to serve them, and should, in consistency with their own aims, endeavour to provide what will increase their strength and courage. Taxes, in the opinion of Hobbes, should be laid equally, and rather on expenditure than on revenue; the prince should promote agriculture, fisheries, and commerce, and in general whatever makes men happy and prosperous. Many just reflections on the art of government are uttered by Hobbes, especially as to the inexpediency of interfering too much with personal liberty. No man, he observes in another place, is so far free as to be exempted from the sovereign power; but if liberty consists in the paucity of

restraining laws, he sees not why this may not be had in monarchy as well as in a popular government. The dream of so many political writers, a wise and just despotism, is pictured by Hobbes as the perfection of political society.

70. But, most of all, is the sovereign to be free from any limitation by the power of the priesthood. This is chiefly to be dreaded, that he should command anything under the penalty of death, and the clergy forbid it under the penalty of damnation. The pretensions of the see of Rome, of some bishops at home, and those of even the lowest citizens to judge for themselves and determine upon public religion, are dangerous to the state and the frequent cause of wars. The sovereign therefore is alone to judge whether religions are safely to be admitted or not. And it may be urged, that princes are bound to cause such doctrine as they think conducive to their subjects' salvation to be taught, forbidding every other, and that they cannot do otherwise in conscience. This, however, he does not absolutely determine. But he is clearly of opinion that, though it is not the case where the prince is infidel,[k] the head of the state, in a Christian commonwealth, is head also of the church; that he rather than any ecclesiastics is the judge of doctrines; that a church is the same as a commonwealth under the same sovereign, the component members of each being precisely the same. This is not very far removed from the doctrine of Hooker, and still less from the practice of Henry VIII.

71. The second class of commonwealths, those by forcible acquisition, differ more in origin than in their subsequent character from such as he has been discussing. The rights of sovereignty are the same in both. Dominion is acquired by generation or by conquest; the one parental, the other despotical. Parental power, however, he derives not so much from having given birth to, as from having preserved, the child; and, with originality and acuteness, thinks it belongs by nature to the mother rather than to the father, except where there is some contract between the parties to the con-

---

[k] Imperantibus autem non Christianis in temporalibus quidem omnibus eandem deberi obedientiam etiam a cive Christiano extra controversiam est: in spiritualibus vero, hoc est, in iis quæ pertinent ad modum colendi Dei sequenda est ecclesia aliqua Christianorum. De Cive, c. 18, § 3.

trary. The act of maintenance and nourishment conveys, as he supposes, an unlimited power over the child, extending to life and death, and there can be no state of nature between parent and child. In his notion of patriarchal authority he seems to go as far as Filmer; but, more acute than Filmer, perceives that it affords no firm basis for political society. By conquest and sparing the lives of the vanquished they become slaves; and so long as they are held in bodily confinement, there is no covenant between them and their master; but in obtaining corporal liberty they expressly or tacitly covenant to obey him as their lord and sovereign.

72. The political philosophy of Hobbes had much to fix the attention of the world and to create a sect of admiring partisans. The circumstances of the time, and the character of the passing generation, no doubt powerfully conspired with its intrinsic qualities; but a system so original, so intrepid, so disdainful of any appeal but to the common reason and common interests of mankind, so unaffectedly and perspicuously proposed, could at no time have failed of success. From the two rival theories, on the one hand, that of original compact between the prince and people, derived from antiquity, and sanctioned by the authority of fathers and schoolmen; on the other, that of an absolute patriarchal transmuted into an absolute regal power, which had become prevalent among part of the English clergy, Hobbes took as much as might conciliate a hearing from both, an original covenant of the multitude, and an unlimited authority of the sovereign. But he had a substantial advantage over both these parties, and especially the latter, in establishing the happiness of the community as the sole final cause of government, both in its institution and its continuance; the great fundamental theorem upon which all political science depends, but sometimes obscured or lost in the pedantry of theoretical writers.[m]

---

[m] [It was imputed to Hobbes by some of the royalists, that he had endeavoured to conciliate Cromwell, and make his own residence in England secure, by the unlimited doctrine of submission to power that he lays down. This is said by Clarendon: but I had been accustomed to look on it as an unfounded conjecture. In the curious poem, however, which Hobbes wrote at the age of eighty-four, on his own life, we have some confirmation of it :

Militat ille liber nunc regibus omnibus, et qui
    Nomine sub quovis regia jura tenent.

He owns that he was accused to the king of favouring Cromwell.

Nam regi accusor falso, quasi facta probarem
    Impia Cromwelli, jus scelerique darem.

73. In the positive system of Hobbes we find less cause for praise. We fall in at the very outset with a strange and indefensible paradox ; the natural equality of human capacities, which he seems to have adopted rather in opposition to Aristotle's notion of a natural right in some men to govern, founded on their superior qualities, than because it was at all requisite for his own theory. By extending this alleged equality, or slightness of difference, among men to physical strength, he has more evidently shown its incompatibility with experience. If superiority in mere strength has not often been the source of political power, it is for two reasons : first, because, though there is a vast interval between the strongest man and the weakest, there is generally not much between the former and him who comes next in vigour ; and, secondly, because physical strength is multiplied by the aggregation of individuals, so that the stronger few may be overpowered by the weaker many ; while in mental capacity, comprehending acquired skill and habit as well as natural genius and disposition, both the degrees of excellence are removed by a wider distance, and what is still more important, the aggregation of the powers of individuals does not regularly and certainly augment the value of the whole. That the real or acknowledged superiority of one man to his fellows has been the ordinary source of power is sufficiently evident from what we daily see among children, and must, it should seem, be admitted by all who derive civil authority from choice or even from conquest, and therefore is to be inferred from the very system of Hobbes.

74. That a state of nature is a state of war, that men, or at least a very large proportion of men, employ force of every kind in seizing to themselves what is in the possession of others, is a proposition for which Hobbes incurred as much obloquy as for any one in his writings ; yet it is one not easy to con-

---

Creditur ; adversis in partibus esse videbar ;
   Perpetuo jubeor regis abesse domo.
    *   *   *   *
In patriam rideo tutelæ non bene certus,
   Sed nullo potui tutior esse loco.
    *   *   *   *
Londinum veniens, ne clam venisse viderer,
   Concilio statûs [sic] conciliandus eram.
    *   *   *   *
Omnia miles erat, committier omnia et uni
   Poscebat ; tacitè Cromwell is unus erat

Regia conanti calamo defendere jura,
   Quis vitio vertat regia jura petens ?

The last two lines were an admission of the charge. This poem is worth reading, and is of course an extraordinary performance at eighty-four. Hobbes (Sir W. Molesworth's edition), vol. i. p. xciii.—1853.]

trovert. But soon after the publication of the Leviathan, a dislike of the Calvinistic scheme of universal depravity, as well as of his own, led many considerable men into the opposite extreme of elevating too much the dignity of human nature; if by that term they meant, and in no other sense could it be applicable to this question, the real practical character of the majority of the species. Certainly the sociableness of man is as much a part of his nature as his selfishness; but whether this propensity to society would necessarily or naturally have led to the institution of political communities, may not be very clear; while we have proof enough in historical traditions, and in what we observe of savage nations, that mutual defence by mutual concession, the common agreement not to attack the possessions of each other, or to permit strangers to do so, has been the true basis, the final aim, of those institutions, be they more or less complex, to which we give the appellation of commonwealths.

75. In developing, therefore, the origin of civil society, Hobbes, though not essentially differing from his predecessors, has placed the truth in a fuller light. It does not seem equally clear, that his own theory of a mutual covenant between the members of an unanimous multitude to become one people and to be represented, in all time to come, by such a sovereign government as the majority should determine, affords a satisfactory groundwork for the rights of political society. It is, in the first place, too hypothetical as a fact. That such an agreement may have been sometimes made by independent families, in the first coming together of communities, it would be presumptuous to deny—it carries upon the face of it no improbability, except as to the design of binding posterity, which seems too refined for such a state of mankind as we must suppose; but it is surely possible to account for the general fact of civil government in a simpler way; and what is most simple, though not always true, is on the first appearance most probable. If we merely suppose an agreement, unanimous of course in those who concur in it, to be governed by one man, or by one council, promising that they shall wield the force of the whole against any one who shall contravene their commands issued for the public good, the foundation is as well laid, and the commonwealth

as firmly established, as by the double process of a mutual
covenant to constitute a people, and a popular determination
to constitute a government. It is true that Hobbes distinguishes a commonwealth by institution, which he supposes to
be founded on this unanimous consent, from one by acquisition, for which force alone is required. But as the force of
one man goes but a little way towards compelling the obedience of others, so as to gain the name of sovereign power,
unless it is aided by the force of many who voluntarily conspire to its ends, this sort of commonwealth by conquest will
be found to involve the previous institution of the more peaceable kind.

76. This theory of a mutual covenant is defective also in a
most essential point. It furnishes no adequate basis for any
commonwealth beyond the lives of those who established it.
The right, indeed, of men to bind their children, and through
them a late posterity, is sometimes asserted by Hobbes, but
in a very transient manner, and as if he was aware of the
weakness of his ground. It might be inquired whether the
force on which alone he rests the obligation of children to
obey, can give any right beyond its own continuance; whether
the absurdity he imputes to those who do not stand by their
own engagements is imputable to such as disregard the
covenants of their forefathers; whether, in short, any law of
nature requires our obedience to a government we deem
hurtful, because, in a distant age, a multitude whom we
cannot trace bestowed unlimited power on some unknown
persons from whom that government pretends to derive its
succession.

77. A better ground for the subsisting rights of his Leviathan is sometimes suggested, though faintly, by Hobbes
himself. ' If one refuse to stand to what the major part
shall ordain, or make protestation against any of their decrees,
he does contrary to his covenant, and therefore unjustly :
and whether he be of the congregation or not, whether his
consent be asked or not, he must either submit to their decrees, or be left in the condition of war he was in before,
wherein he might without injustice be destroyed by any man
whatsoever.'[n] This renewal of the state of war which is the

---

[n] Lev. c. 18.

state of nature, this denial of the possibility of doing an injury to any one who does not obey the laws of the commonwealth, is enough to silence the question why we are obliged still to obey. The established government and those who maintain it, being strong enough to wage war against gainsayers, give them the option of incurring the consequences of such warfare or of complying with the laws. But it seems to be a corollary from this, that the stronger part of a commonwealth, which may not always be the majority, have not only a right to despise the wishes but the interests of dissentients. Thus the more we scrutinise the theories of Hobbes, the more there appears a deficiency of that which only a higher tone of moral sentiment can give, a security for ourselves against the appetites of others, and for them against our own. But it may be remarked that his supposition of a state of war, not as a permanent state of nature, but as just self-defence, is perhaps the best footing on which we can place the right to inflict severe, and especially capital, punishment upon offenders against the law.

78. The positions so dogmatically laid down as to the impossibility of mixing different sorts of government were, even in the days of Hobbes, contradicted by experience. Several republics had lasted for ages under a mixed aristocracy and democracy; and there had surely been sufficient evidence that a limited monarchy might exist, though, in the revolution of ages, it might, one way or other, pass into some new type of polity. And these prejudices in favour of absolute power are rendered more dangerous by paradoxes unusual for an Englishman, even in those days of high prerogative when Hobbes began to write, that the subject has no property relatively to the sovereign, and, what is the fundamental error of his whole system, that nothing done by the prince can be injurious to any one else. This is accompanied by the other portents of Hobbism, scattered through these treatises, especially the Leviathan, that the distinctions of right and wrong, moral good and evil, are made by the laws, that no man can do amiss who obeys the sovereign authority, that though private belief is of necessity beyond the prince's control, it is according to his will, and in no other way, that we must worship God.

79. The political system of Hobbes, like his moral system, of which, in fact, it is only a portion, sears up the heart. It takes away the sense of wrong, that has consoled the wise and good in their dangers, the proud appeal of innocence under oppression, like that of Prometheus to the elements, uttered to the witnessing world, to coming ages, to the just ear of Heaven. It confounds the principles of moral approbation, the notions of good and ill desert, in a servile idolatry of the monstrous Leviathan it creates, and after sacrificing all right at the altar of power, denies to the Omnipotent the prerogative of dictating the laws of his own worship.

SECT. III.

Roman Jurisprudence—Grotius on the Laws of War and Peace—Analysis of this Work—Defence of it against some Strictures.

80. In the Roman jurisprudence we do not find such a cluster of eminent men during this period as in the Civil jurists sixteenth century; and it would of course be out of of this period. our province to search for names little now remembered, perhaps, even in forensic practice. Many of the writings of Fabre of Savoy, who has been mentioned in the present volume, belong to the first years of this century. Farinacci, or Farinaceus, a lawyer of Rome, obtained a celebrity, which, after a long duration, has given way in the progress of legal studies, less directed than formerly towards a superfluous erudition.[o] But the work of Menochius de præsumptionibus, or, as we should express it, on the rules of evidence, is said to have lost none of its usefulness, even since the decline of the civil law in France.[p] No book, perhaps, belonging to this period is so generally known as the commentaries of Vinnius on the Institutes, which, as far as I know, has not been superseded by any of later date. Conringius of Helmstadt may be reckoned in some measure among the writers on jurisprudence, though chiefly in the line of historical illustration. The Elementa Juris Civilis, by Zouch, is a mere

---

[o] Biogr. univ.   [p] Id.

epitome, but neatly executed, of the principal heads of the Roman law, and nearly in its own words. Arthur Duck, another Englishman, has been praised even by foreigners, for a succinct and learned, though elementary and popular, treatise on the use and authority of the civil law in different countries of Europe. This little book is not disagreeably written; but it is not, of course, from England that much could be contributed towards Roman jurisprudence.

81. The larger principles of jurisprudence, which link that science with general morals, and especially such as relate to the intercourse of nations, were not left untouched in the great work of Suarez on laws. I have not however made myself particularly acquainted with this portion of his large volume. Spain appears to have been the country in which these questions were originally discussed upon principles broader than precedent, as well as upon precedents themselves; and Suarez, from the general comprehensiveness of his views in legislation and ethics, is likely to have said well whatever he may have said on the subject of international law. But it does not appear that he is much quoted by later writers.

Suarez on laws.

82. The name of Suarez is obscure in comparison of one who soon came forward in the great field of natural jurisprudence. This was Hugo Grotius, whose famous work, De Jure Belli et Pacis, was published at Paris, in 1625. It may be reckoned a proof of the extraordinary diligence as well as quickness of parts which distinguished this writer, that it had occupied a very short part of his life. He first mentions, in a letter to the younger Thuanus in August, 1623, that he was employed in examining the principal questions which belong to the law of nations.[q] In the same year he recommends the study of that law to another of his correspondents in such terms as bespeak his own attention to it.[r] According to one of his letters to Gassendi,

Grotius De Jure Belli et Pacis.

---

[q] Versor in examinandis controversiis præcipuis quæ ad jus gentium pertinent. Epist. 75. This is not from the folio collection of his epistles, so often quoted in a preceding chapter of this volume (Part III., Chap. II.), but from one antecedently published in 1648, and entitled Grotii Epistolæ ad Gallos.

[r] Hoc spatio exacto, nihil restat quod tibi æque commendem atque studium juris, non illius privati, ex quo leguleii et rabulæ victitant, sed gentium ac publici; quam præstabilem scientiam Cicero vocans consistere ait in fœderibus, pactionibus, conditionibus populorum, regum, nationum, in omni denique jure belli et

quoted by Stewart, the scheme was suggested to him by Peiresc.

83. It is acknowledged by every one that the publication of this treatise made an epoch in the philosophical, Success of and almost we might say in the political history of this work. Europe. Those who sought a guide to their own conscience or that of others, those who dispensed justice, those who appealed to the public sense of right in the intercourse of nations, had recourse to its copious pages for what might direct or justify their actions. Within thirty or forty years from its publication, we find the work of Grotius generally received as authority by professors of the continental universities, and deemed necessary for the student of civil law, at least in the Protestant countries of Europe. In England, from the difference of laws and from some other causes which might be assigned, the influence of Grotius was far slower, and even ultimately much less general. He was, however, treated with great respect as the founder of the modern law of nations, which is distinguished from what formerly bore that name by its more continual reference to that of nature. But when a book is little read it is easily misrepresented; and as a new school of philosophers rose up, averse to much of the principles of their predecessors, but, above all things, to their tediousness, it became the fashion not so much to dispute the tenets of Grotius as to set aside his whole work, among the barbarous and obsolete schemes of ignorant ages. For this purpose various charges have been alleged against it by men of deserved eminence, not, in my opinion, very candidly, or with much real knowledge of its contents. They have had, however, the natural effect of creating a prejudice, which, from the sort of oblivion fallen upon the book, is not likely to die away. I shall, therefore, not think myself performing an use-

---

pacis. Hujus juris principia quomodo ex morali philosophia petenda sunt, monstrare poterunt Platonis ac Ciceronis de legibus liber. Sed Platonis summas aliquas legisse suffecerit. Neque pœniteat ex scholasticis Thomam Aquinatem, si non perlegere, saltem inspicere secunda parte secundæ partis libri, quem Summam Theologiæ inscripsit; præsertim ubi de justitia agit ac de legibus. Usum propius monstrabunt Pandectæ, libro primo atque ultimo; et codex Justinianeus, libro primo et tribus postremis. Nostri temporis juris consulti pauci juris gentium ac publici controversias attigere, eoque magis eminent, qui id fecere, Vasquius, Hottomannus, Gentilis. Epist. xvi. This passage is useful in showing the views Grotius himself entertained as to the subject and groundwork of his treatise,

less task in giving an analysis of the treatise De Jure Belli et
Pacis; so that the reader, having seen for himself what it is,
may not stand in need of any arguments or testimony to refute
those who have represented it as it is not.

84. The book may be considered as nearly original, in its
Its origin-   general platform, as any work of man in an advanced
ality.   stage of civilisation and learning can be. It is more
so, perhaps, than those of Montesquieu and Smith. No one
had before gone to the foundations of international law so as
to raise a complete and consistent superstructure; few had
handled even separate parts, or laid down any satisfactory
rules concerning it. Grotius enumerates a few preceding
writers, especially Ayala and Albericus Gentilis, but does not
mention Soto in this place. Gentilis, he says, is wont, in
determining controverted questions, to follow either a few
precedents not always of the best description, or even the
authority of modern lawyers, in their answers to cases, many
of which are written with more regard to what the consulting
parties desire, than to what real justice and equity demand.

85. The motive assigned for this undertaking is the noblest.
Its motive   'I saw,' he says, 'in the whole Christian world a
and object. licence of fighting, at which even barbarians might
blush, wars begun on trifling pretexts or none at all, and
carried on without reverence for any divine or human law, as
if that one declaration of war let loose every crime.' The
sight of such a monstrous state of things had induced some,
like Erasmus, to deny the lawfulness of any war to a Christian.
But this extreme, as he justly observes, is rather pernicious
than otherwise; for when a tenet so paradoxical and impracticable is maintained, it begets a prejudice against the
more temperate course which he prepares to indicate. 'Let,
therefore,' he says afterwards, 'the laws be silent in the
midst of arms; but those laws only which belong to peace,
the laws of civil life and public tribunals, not such as are
eternal, and fitted for all seasons, unwritten laws of nature,
which subsist in what the ancient form of the Romans denominated " a pure and holy war." 's

86. 'I have employed in confirmation of this natural and

---

* Eas res puro pioque duello repe-   giously frequent in the opinion of the
tundas censeo. It was a case prodi-   Romans.

national law the testimonies of philosophers, of historians, of poets, lastly, even of orators; not that we should indiscriminately rely upon them; for they are apt His autho-
rities. to say what may serve their party, their subject, or their cause; but because when many at different times and places affirm the same thing for certain, we may refer this unanimity to some general cause, which in such questions as these can be no other than either a right deduction from some natural principle or some common agreement. The former of these denotes the law of nature, the latter that of nations; the difference whereof must be understood, not by the language of these testimonies, for writers are very prone to confound the two words, but from the nature of the subject. For whatever cannot be clearly deduced from true premises, and yet appears to have been generally admitted, must have had its origin in free consent. . . . . The sentences of poets and orators have less weight than those of history; and we often make use of them not so much to corroborate what we say, as to throw a kind of ornament over it.' 'I have abstained,' he adds afterwards, 'from all that belongs to a different subject, as what is expedient to be done; since this has its own science, that of politics, which Aristotle has rightly treated by not intermingling any thing extraneous to it, while Bodin has confounded that science with this which we are about to treat. If we sometimes allude to utility, it is but in passing, and distinguishing it from the question of justice.'[t]

87. Grotius derives the origin of natural law from the sociable character of mankind. 'Among things Foundation
of natural
law. common to mankind is the desire of society, that is, not of every kind of society, but of one that is peaceable and ordered according to the capacities of his nature with others of his species. Even in children, before all instruction, a propensity to do good to others displays itself, just as pity in that age is a spontaneous affection.' We perceive by this remark that Grotius looked beyond the merely rational basis of natural law to the moral constitution of human nature. The conservation of such a sociable life is the source of that

---

[t] Prolegomena in librum de Jure Belli.

law which is strictly called natural; which comprehends, in the first place, the abstaining from all that belongs to others, and the restitution of it if by any means in our possession, the fulfilment of promises, the reparation of injury, and the right of human punishment. In a secondary sense, natural law extends to prudence, temperance, and fortitude, as being suitable to man's nature. And in a similar lax sense we have that kind of justice itself called distributive (διανεμητικὴ), which prefers a better man to a worse, a relation to a stranger, a poorer man to a richer, according to the circumstances of the party and the case.[u] And this natural law is properly defined, 'the dictate of right reason, pointing out a moral guilt or rectitude to be inherent in any action, on account of its agreement or disagreement with our rational and social nature; and consequently that such an action is either for bidden or enjoined by God the author of nature.'[x]   It is so immutable, that God himself cannot alter it; a position which he afterwards limits by a restriction we have seen in Suarez, that if God command any one to be killed, or his goods to be taken, this would not render murder or theft lawful, but, being commanded by the lord of life and all things, it would cease to be murder or theft. This seems little better than a sophism unworthy of Grotius; but he meant to distinguish between an abrogation of the law of nature, and a dispensation with it in a particular instance. The original position, in fact, is not stated with sufficient precision or on a right principle.

88. Voluntary or positive law is either human or revealed.

Positive law.   The former is either that of civil communities, which are assemblages of freemen, living in society for the sake of laws and common utility, or that of nations, which derives its obligation from the consent of all or many nations; a law which is to be proved, like all unwritten law, by continual usage and the testimony of the learned. The revealed law he divides in the usual manner, but holds that no part of the Mosaic, so far as it is strictly a law, is at

---

[u] Prolegomena in librum de Jure Bellum.

[x] Jus naturale est dictatum rectæ rationis, indicans actui alicui, ex ejus convenientia aut disconvenientia cum ipsa natura rationali ac sociali, inesse moralem turpitudinem aut necessitatem moralem, ac consequenter ab auctore naturæ Deo talem actum aut vetari aut præcipi. L. i. c. i. § 10.

present binding upon us. But much of it is confirmed by the
Christian Scriptures, and much is also obligatory by the law
of nature. This last law is to be applied, *à priori*, by the conformity of the act in question to the natural and social nature
of man ; *à posteriori*, by the consent of mankind ; the latter
argument, however, not being conclusive, but highly probable,
when the agreement is found in all, or in all the more civilised
nations.[y]

89. Perfect rights, after the manner of the jurists, he distinguishes from imperfect. The former are called Perfect and
sua, our own, properly speaking, the objects of what imperfect
rights.
they styled commutative justice—the latter are denominated
fitnesses (aptitudines), such as equity, gratitude, and domestic
affection prescribe, but which are only the objects of distributive or equitable justice. This distinction is of the highest
importance in the immediate subject of the work of Grotius ;
since it is agreed on all hands that no law gives a remedy for
the denial of these, nor can we justly, in a state of nature,
have recourse to arms in order to enforce them.[z]

90. War, however, as he now proceeds to show, is not
absolutely unlawful either by the law of nature or Lawful cases
that of nations, or of revelation. The proof is, as of war.
usual with Grotius, very diffuse ; his work being in fact a
magazine of arguments and examples with rather a super-
erogatory profusion.[a] But the Anabaptist and Quaker superstition has prevailed enough to render some of his refutation
not unnecessary. After dividing war into public and private,
and showing that the establishment of civil justice does not
universally put an end to the right of private war, since cases
may arise when the magistrate cannot be waited for, and
others where his interference cannot be obtained, he shows
that the public war may be either solemn and regular according to the law of nations, or less regular on a sudden emergency of self-defence ; classing also under the latter any war
which magistrates not sovereign may in peculiar circumstances levy.[b] And this leads him to inquire what constitutes
sovereignty ; defining, after setting aside other descriptions,
that power to be sovereign whose acts cannot be invalidated

y Lib. i. c. 1.   a C. 2.
z Id. ibid.   b C. 3.

at the pleasure of any other human authority, except one, which, as in the case of a successor, has exactly the same sovereignty as itself.[c]

91. Grotius rejects the opinion of those who hold the *Resistance by subjects unlawful.* people to be everywhere sovereign, so that they may restrain and punish kings for misgovernment; quoting many authorities for the irresponsibility of kings. Here he lays down the principles of non-resistance, which he more fully inculcates in the next chapter. But this is done with many distinctions as to the nature of the principality, which may be held by very different conditions. He speaks of patrimonial kingdoms, which, as he supposes, may be alienated like an inheritance. But where the government can be traced to popular consent, he owns that this power of alienation should not be presumed to be comprised in the grant. Those, he says, are much deceived who think that in kingdoms where the consent of a senate or other body is required for new laws, the sovereignty itself is divided; for these restrictions must be understood to have been imposed by the prince on his own will, lest he should be entrapped into something contrary to his deliberate intention.[d] Among other things in this chapter, he determines that neither an unequal alliance, that is, where one party retains great advantages, nor a feudal homage takes away the character of sovereignty from the inferior, so far at least as authority over his own subjects is concerned.

92. In the next chapter, Grotius dwells more at length on the alleged right of subjects to resist their governors, and altogether repels it, with the exception of strict self-defence, or the improbable case of a hostile spirit, on the prince's part, extending to the destruction of his people. Barclay, the opponent of Buchanan and the Jesuits, had admitted the right of resistance against enormous cruelty. If the king has abdicated the government, or manifestly relinquished it, he may, after a time, be considered merely a private person. But mere negligence in government is by no means to be reckoned a relinquishment.[e] And he also observes that, if

---

[c] Summa potestas illa dicitur, cujus actus alterius juri non subjacet, ita ut alterius voluntatis humanæ arbitrio irriti possint reddi. § 7.
[d] § 18.
[e] Si rex aut alius quis imperium ab-

the sovereignty be divided between a king and part of his
subjects, or the whole, he may be resisted by force in usurping their share, because he is no longer sovereign as to that;
which he holds to be the case, even if the right of war be in
him, since that must be understood of a foreign war, and it
could not be maintained that those who partake the sovereignty have not the right to defend it; in which predicament
a king may lose even his own share by the right of war. He
proceeds to the case of usurpation ; not such as is warranted
by long prescription, but while the circumstances that led to
the unjust possession subsist. Against such an usurper he
thinks it lawful to rebel, so long as there is no treaty or voluntary act of allegiance, at least if the government de jure
sanctions the insurrection. But where there may be a doubt
whether the lawful ruler has not acquiesced in the usurpation,
a private person ought rather to stand by possession, than to
take the decision upon himself.[f]

93. The right of war, which we must here understand in
the largest sense, the employment of force to resist All men na-
force, though by private men, resides in all man- turally have
                                                   right of war.
kind. Solon, he says, taught us that those commonwealths
would be happy wherein each man thought the injuries of
others were like his own.[g] The mere sociability of human
nature ought to suggest this to us. And, though Grotius
does not proceed with this subject, he would not have doubted
that we are even bound by the law of nature, not merely that
we have a right, to protect the lives and goods of others
against lawless violence, without the least reference to positive law or the command of a magistrate.[h] If this has been
preposterously doubted, or affected to be doubted, in England
of late years, it has been less owing to the pedantry which
demands an express written law upon the most pressing
emergency, than to lukewarmness, at the best, in the public
cause of order and justice. The expediency of vindicating
these by the slaughter of the aggressors must depend on the

dicavit, aut manifeste habet pro derelicto, in eum post id tempus omnia li-
cent, quæ in privatum. Sed minimè
pro derelicto habere rem censendus est,
qui eam tractat negligentius. C. 4, § 9.
  [f] § 20.

[g] Εν ἡ̑ των αδικουμενων ουχ ἡττον οἱ μη
αδικουμενοι προβαλλονται και κολαζουσι
τους αδικουντας. Ut cætera desint vincula,
sufficit humanæ naturæ communio.
  [h] He lays this down expressly afterwards. L. ii. c. 20.

peculiar circumstances; but the right is paramount to any
positive laws, even if, which with us is not the case, it were
difficult to be proved from them.

94. We now arrive at the first and fundamental inquiry,
Right of self-
defence. what is the right of self-defence, including the defence of what is our own. There can, says Grotius,
be no just cause of war (that is, of using force, for he is now
on the most general ground) but injury. For this reason he
will not admit of wars to preserve the balance of power. An
imminent injury to ourselves or our property renders repulsion of the aggressor by force legitimate. But here he
argues rather weakly and inconsistently through excess of
charity, and acknowledging the strict right of killing one
who would otherwise kill us, thinks it more praiseworthy to
accept the alternative.[i] The right of killing one who inflicts
a smaller personal injury he wholly denies; and with respect
to a robber, while he admits he may be slain by natural law,
is of opinion that the Gospel has greatly limited the privilege
of defending our property by such means. Almost all jurists
and theologians of his day, he says, carry it farther than he
does.[k] To public warfare he gives a greater latitude than to
private self-defence, but without assigning any satisfactory
reason; the true reason being that so rigid a scheme of ethics
would have rendered his book an Utopian theory, instead of
a practicable code of law.

95. Injury to our rights, therefore, is a just cause of war.
But what are our rights? What is property? whence
does it come? what may be its subjects? in whom does it
reside? Till these questions are determined, we can have
but crude and indefinite notions of injury, and consequently
of the rights we have to redress it. The disquisition is
necessary, but it must be long; unless, indeed, we acquiesce
in what we find already written, and seek for no stable principles upon which this grand and primary question in civil
society, the rights of property and dominion, may rest. Here
then begins what has seemed to many the abandonment by
Grotius of his general subject, and what certainly suspends

---

[i] Lib. ii. c. 1, § 8. Gronovius observes pithily and truly on this: melius
occidi quam occidere injuria; non melius
occidi injuria quam occidere jure.

[k] Hodie omnes ferme tam juriscon-
sulti quam theologi doceant recte homines a nobis interfici rerum defendenda-
rum causa. § 13.

for a considerable time the inquiry into international law, but still not, as it seems to me, an episodical digression, at least for the greater part, but a natural and legitimate investigation, springing immediately from the principal theme of the work, connected with it more closely at several intervals, and ultimately reverting into it. But of this the reader will judge as we proceed with the analysis.

96. Grotius begins with rather too romantic a picture of the early state of the world, when men lived on the spontaneous fruits of the earth, with no property except in what each had taken from the common mother's lap. But this happy condition did not, of course, last very long, and mankind came to separate and exclusive possession, each for himself and against the world. Original occupancy by persons, and division of lands by the community he rightly holds to be the two sources of territorial propriety. Occupation is of two sorts, one by the community (per universitatem), the other (per fundos) by several possession. What is not thus occupied is still the domain of the state. Grotius conceives that mankind have reserved a right of taking what belongs to others in extreme necessity. It is a still more remarkable limitation of the right of property, that it carries very far his notions of that of transit, maintaining that not only rivers, but the territory itself of a state may be peaceably entered, and that permission cannot be refused, consistently with natural law, even in the case of armies; nor is the apprehension of incurring the hostility of the power who is thus attacked by the army passing through our territory a sufficient excuse.[m] This of course must now be exploded. Nor can, he thinks, the transit of merchandise be forbidden or impeded by levying any further tolls than are required for the incident expenses. Strangers ought to be allowed to settle, on condition of obeying the laws, and even to occupy any waste tracts in the territory;[n] a position equally untenable. It is less unreasonably that he maintains the general right of mankind to buy what they want, if the other party can spare it; but he extends too far his principle that no nation can be excluded by another from privileges

Its origin and limitations.

---

[m] Sic etiam metus ab eo in quem bellum justum movet is qui transit, ad   negandum transitum non valet. Lib. ii. c. 2, § 13.   [n] § 16, 17.

which it concedes to the rest of the world. In all these positions, however, we perceive the enlarged and philanthropic
spirit of the system of Grotius, and his disregard of the
usages of mankind, when they clashed with his Christian principles of justice. But as the very contrary supposition has
been established in the belief of the present generation, it
may be doubtful whether his own testimony will be thought
sufficient.

97. The original acquisition of property was, in the infancy of human societies, by division or by occupancy; it is now by occupancy alone. Paullus
has reckoned as a mode of original acquisition, if we have
caused anything to exist, si quid ipsi, ut in rerum natura
esset, fecimus. This, though not well expressed, must mean
the produce of labour. Grotius observes, that this resolves
itself into a continuance of a prior right, or a new one by
occupancy, and therefore no peculiar mode of acquisition.
In those things which naturally belong to no one, there
may be two sorts of occupation, dominion or sovereignty,
and property. And in the former sense at least, rivers and
bays of the sea are capable of occupation. In what manner
this may be done he explains at length.[o] But those who
occupy a portion of the sea have no right to obstruct others
in fishing. This had been the subject of a controversy of
Grotius with Selden; the one in his Mare Liberum denying,
the other in his Mare Clausum sustaining, the right of
England, to exclude the fishermen of Holland from the
seas which she asserted to be her own.

98. The right of occupancy exists as to things derelict or
abandoned by their owners. But it is of more importance to consider the presumptions of such relinquishment by sovereign states, as distinguished from mere
prescription. The non-claim of the owner during a long
period seems the only means of giving a right where none
originally existed. It must be the silent acquiescence of one
who knows his rights and has his free will. But when this
abandonment has once taken place, it bars unborn claim-
ants; for he who is not born, Grotius says, has no rights ;
ejus qui nondum est natus nullum est jus.[p]

Right of occupancy.

*Relinquish-
ment of it.*

---

[o] C. 3.   [p] Id 4.

99. A right over persons may be acquired in three ways, by generation, by their consent, by their crime. In children we are to consider three periods; that of imperfect judgment, or infancy, that of adult age in the father's family, and that of emancipation or forisfamiliation, when they have ceased to form a part of it. In the first of these, a child is capable of property in possession, but not in enjoyment. In the second, he is subject to the parent only in actions which affect the family. In the third, he is wholly his own master. All beyond this is positive law. The paternal power was almost peculiar to the Romans, though the Persians are said to have had something of the same. Grotius, we perceive, was no ally of those who elevated the patriarchal power, in order to found upon it a despotic polity; nor does he raise it by any means so high as Bodin. The customs of Eastern nations would, perhaps, have warranted somewhat more than he concedes.[q]

Right over persons. By generation.

100. Consent is the second mode of acquiring dominion. The consociation of male and female is the first species of it, which is principally in marriage, for which the promise of the woman to be faithful is required. But he thinks that there is no mutual obligation by the law of nature; which seems designed to save the polygamy of the patriarchs. He then discusses the chief questions as to divorce, polygamy, clandestine marriages, and incest; holding, that no unions are forbidden by natural law except in the direct line. Concubines, in the sense of the Roman jurisprudence, are true Christian wives.[r]

By consent. In marriage.

101. In all other consociations except marriage, it is a rule that the majority can bind the minority. Of these the principal is a commonwealth. And here he maintains the right of every citizen to leave his country, and that the state retains no right over those whom it has banished. Subjection, which may arise from one kind of consent, is either private or public; the former is of several species, among which adoption, in the Roman sense, is the noblest, and servitude the meanest. In the latter case, the master has not the right of life and death over his servants,

In commonwealths.

---

q C. 5.   r Id.

though some laws give him impunity. He is perplexed about the right over persons born in slavery, since his theory of its origin will not support it. But, in the case of public subjection, where one state becomes voluntarily subject to another, he finds no difficulty about the unborn, because the people is the same, notwithstanding the succession of individuals; which seems paying too much deference to a legal fiction.[s]

102. The right of alienating altogether the territory he grants to patrimonial sovereigns. But he denies that a part can be separated from the rest without its consent, either by the community, or by the sovereign, however large his authority may be. This he extends to subjection of the kingdom to vassalage. The right of alienating private property by testament is founded, he thinks, in natural law;[t] a position wherein I can by no means concur. In conformity with this, he derives the right of succession by intestacy from the presumed intention of the deceased, and proceeds to dilate on the different rules of succession established by civil laws. Yet the rule that paternal and maternal heirs shall take respectively what descended from the ancestors on each side, he conceives to be founded in the law of nature, though subject to the right of bequest.[u]

Right of alienating subjects.

Alienation by testament.

103. In treating of the acquisition of property by the law of nations, he means only the arbitrary constitutions of the Roman and other codes. Some of these he deems founded in no solid reason, though the lawgivers of every country have a right to determine such matters as they think fit. Thus the Roman law recognises no property in animals *feræ naturæ*, which that of modern nations gives, he says, to the owner of the soil where they are found, not unreasonably any more than the opposite maxim is unreasonable. So of a treasure found in the earth, and many other cases, wherein it is hard to say that

Rights of property by positive law.

---

[s] C. 5.
[t] Id. 6, § 14.
[u] Id. 7. In this chapter Grotius decides that parents are not bound by strict justice to maintain their children. The

case is stronger the other way, in return for early protection. Barbeyrac thinks that aliment is due to children by strict right during infancy.

the law of nature and reason prescribes one rule more than another.[x]

104. The rights of sovereignty and property may termi-
nate by extinction of the ruling or possessing Extinction
family without provision of successors. Slaves of rights.
then become free, and subjects their own masters. For
there can be no new right by occupancy in such. But a
people or community may cease to exist, though the
identity of persons or even of race is not necessary for its
continuance. It may expire by voluntary dispersion, or by
subjugation to another state. But mere change of place by
simultaneous emigration will not destroy a political society,
much less a change of internal government. Hence a republic becoming a monarchy, it stands in the same relation to other communities as before, and, in particular, is
subject to all its former debts.[y]

105. In a chapter on the obligations which the right of
property imposes on others than the proprietor, we Some casu-
find some of the more delicate questions in the tions.
casuistry of natural law, such as relate to the bonâ fide
possessor of another's property. Grotius always siding with
the stricter moralists, asserts that he is bound not only to
restore the substance but the intermediate profits, without any
claim for the valuable consideration which he may have paid.
His commentator, Barbeyrac, of a later and laxer school
of casuistry, denies much of this doctrine.[z]

106. That great branch of ethics which relates to the
obligation of promises has been so diffusively handled by the

[x] § 8.
[y] § 2. At the end of this chapter, Grotius unfortunately raises a question, his
solution of which laid him open to censure. He inquires to whom the countries formerly subject to the Roman
empire belong? And here he comes to
the inconceivable paradox that that empire and the rights of the citizens of
Rome still subsist. Gronovius bitterly
remarks, in a note on this passage : Mirum est hoc loco summum virum, cum
in præcipua questione non male sentiret,
in tot salebras se conjecisse, totque mon-
stra et chimæras confinxisse, ut aliquid
novum diceret, et Germanis potius ludi-
brium deberet, quam Gallis et Papæ

parum placeret. This, however, is very
uncandid, as Barbeyrac truly points out;
since neither of these could take much
interest in a theory which reserved a
supremacy over the world to the Roman
people. It is probably the weakest
passage in all the writings of Grotius,
though there are too many which do not
enhance his fame.
[z] C. 10. Our own jurisprudence goes
upon the principles of Grotius, and even
denies the possessor by a bad title,
though bonâ fide, any indemnification
for what he may have laid out to the
benefit of the property, which seems
hardly consonant to the strictest rules
of natural law.

casuists, as well as philosophers, that Grotius deserves much
Promises. credit for the brevity with which he has laid down
the simple principles, and discussed some of the more
difficult problems. That mere promises, or *nuda pacta*, where
there is neither mutual benefit, nor what the jurists call
synallagmatic contract, are binding on the conscience,
whatever they may be, or ought to be, in law, is maintained
against a distinguished civilian, Francis Connan; nor does
Barbeyrac seem to dispute this general tenet of moral philosophers. Puffendorf however says, that there is a tacit
condition in promises of this kind, that they can be performed
without great loss to the promiser, and Cicero holds them to
be released, if their performance would be more detrimental
to one party, than serviceable to the other. This gives a
good deal of latitude; but perhaps they are in such cases
open to compensation without actual fulfilment. A promise
given without deliberation, according to Grotius himself, is not
binding. Those founded on deceit or error admit of many
distinctions; but he determines, in the celebrated question of
extorted promises, that they are valid by the natural, though
their obligation may be annulled by the civil law. But
the promisee is bound to release a promise thus unduly
obtained.[a] These instances are sufficient to show the spirit
in which Grotius always approaches the decision of moral
questions; serious and learned, rather than profound in
seeking a principle, or acute in establishing a distinction.
In the latter quality he falls much below his annotator Barbeyrac, who had, indeed, the advantage of coming nearly a
century after him.

107. In no part of his work has Grotius dwelt so much on
Contracts. the rules and distinctions of the Roman law, as in
his chapter on contracts, nor was it very easy or

---

[a] C. 11, § 7. It is not very probable
that the promisee will fulfil this obligation in such a case; and the decision of
Grotius, though conformable to that of
the theological casuists in general, is
justly rejected by Puffendorf and Barbeyrac, as well as by many writers of the
last century. The principle seems to be
that right and obligation in matters of
agreement are correlative, and where
the first does not arise, the second cannot

exist. Adam Smith and Paley incline
to think the promise ought, under certain
circumstances, to be kept; but the reasons they give are not founded on the
justitia expletrix, which the proper obligation of promises, as such, requires. It
is also a proof how little the moral sense
of mankind goes along with the rigid
casuists in this respect, that no one is
blamed for defending himself against
a bond given through duress or illegal

desirable to avoid it.[b]   The wisdom of those great men, from
the fragments of whose determinations the existing jurisprudence of Europe, in subjects of this kind, has been chiefly
derived, could not be set aside without presumption, nor
appropriated without ingratitude.   Less fettered, at least
in the best age of Roman jurisprudence, by legislative interference than our modern lawyers have commonly been,
they resorted to no other principles than those of natural
justice.   That the Roman law, in all its parts, coincides
with the best possible platform of natural jurisprudence it
would be foolish to assert; but that in this great province,
or rather demesne land, of justice, the regulation of contracts between man and man, it does not considerably
deviate from the right line of reason, has never been disputed by anyone in the least conversant with the Pandects.

108. It will be manifest, however, to the attentive reader
of Grotius in this chapter, that he treats the subject of contract as a part of ethics rather than Considered ethically.
of jurisprudence; and it is only by the frequent parallelism
of the two sciences that the contrary could be suspected.
Thus he maintains that, equality being the principle of the
contract by sale, either party is forced to restore the difference arising from a misapprehension of the other, even
without his own fault; and this whatever may be the amount,
though the civil law gives a remedy only where the difference
exceeds one-half of the price.[c]   And in several other places
he diverges equally from that law.   Not that he ever contemplated what Smith seems to have meant by 'natural
jurisprudence,' a theory of the principles which ought to run
through and to be the foundation of the laws of all nations.
But he knew that the judge in the tribunal, and the inward
judge in the breast, even where their subjects of determination
appear essentially the same, must have different boundaries
to their jurisdiction; and that, as the general maxims, and
inflexible forms of external law, in attempts to accommodate
themselves to the subtilties of casuistry, would become un-

---

violence, if the plea be a true one.
 In a subsequent passage, l. iii. c. 19,
§ 4, Grotius seems to carry this theory
of the duty of releasing an unjust promise so far, as to deny the obligation of

the latter, and thus circuitously to agree
with the opposite class of casuists.
 [b] C. 12.
 [c] § 12.

certain and arbitrary, so the finer emotions of the conscience would lose all their moral efficacy, by restraining the duties of justice to that which can be enforced by the law. In the course of this twelfth chapter we come to a question much debated in the time of Grotius, the lawfulness of usury. After admitting, against the common opinion, that it is not repugnant to the law of nature, he yet maintains the prohibition in the Mosaic code to be binding on all mankind.[d] An extraordinary position, it would seem, in one who had denied any part of that system to be truly an universal law. This was, however, the usual determination of casuists; but he follows it up, as was also usual, with so many exceptions as materially relax and invalidate the application of his rule.

109. The next chapter, on promissory oaths, is a corollary to the last two. It was the opinion of Grotius, Promissory oaths. as it had been of all theologians, and, in truth, of all mankind, that a promise or contract not only becomes more solemn, and entails on its breach a severer penalty, by means of this adjuration of the Supreme Being, but may even acquire a substantial validity by it in cases where no prior obligation would subsist.[e] This chapter is distinguished by a more than usually profuse erudition. But notwithstanding the rigid observance of oaths which he deems incumbent by natural and revealed law, he admits of a considerable authority in the civil magistrate, or other superior, as a husband or father, to annul the oaths of inferiors beforehand, or to dispense with them afterwards; not that they can release a moral obligation, but that the obligation itself is incurred under a tacit condition of their consent. And he seems, in rather a singular manner, to hint a kind of approval of such dispensations by the church.[f]

110. Whatever has been laid down by Grotius in the Engagements of kings towards subjects. last three chapters as to the natural obligations of mankind, has an especial reference to the main purport of this great work, the duties of the

---

[d] § 20. [e] C. 13.

[f] § 20. Ex hoc fundamento defendi possunt absolutiones juramentorum, quæ olim a principibus, nunc ipsorum principum voluntate, quo magis cautum sit pietati, ab ecclesiæ præsidibus exercentur.

supreme power. But the engagements of sovereigns give rise to many questions which cannot occur in those of private men. In the chapter which ensues, on the promises, oaths, and contracts of sovereigns, he confines himself to those engagements which immediately affect their subjects. These it is of great importance, in the author's assumed province of the general confessor or casuist of kings, to place on a right footing; because they have never wanted subservient counsellors, who would wrest the law of conscience, as well as that of the land, to the interests of power. Grotius, in denying that the sovereign may revoke his own contracts, extends this case to those made by him during his minority, without limitation to such as have been authorised by his guardians.[g] His contracts with his subjects create a true obligation, of which they may claim, though not enforce, the performance. He hesitates whether to call this obligation a civil or only a natural one; and in fact it can only be determined by positive law.[h] Whether the successors of a sovereign are bound by his engagements must depend, he observes, on the political constitution, and on the nature of the engagement. Those of an usurper he determines not to be binding, which should probably be limited to domestic contracts, though his language seems large enough to comprise engagements towards foreign states.[i]

111. We now return from what, in strict language, may pass for a long digression, though not a needless one, to the main stream of international law. The title of the fifteenth chapter is on public treaties. After several divisions, which it would at present be thought unnecessary to specify so much at length, Grotius enters on a question not then settled by theologians, whether alliances with infidel powers were in any circumstances lawful. Francis I. had given great scandal in Europe by his league with the Turk. And though Grotius admits the general lawfulness of such alliances, it is under limitations which would hardly have borne out the court of France in promoting the aggrandisement of the common enemy of

Public treaties.

---

[g] C. 14, § 1.   [h] § 6.

[i] Contractibus vero eorum qui sine jure imperium invaserunt, non tene-

buntur populi aut veri reges, nam hi jus obligandi populum non habuerunt. § 14.

Christendom.   Another and more extensive head in the
casuistry of nations relates to treaties that have been concluded without the authority of the sovereign.   That he is
not bound by these engagements is evident as a leading
rule ; but the course which, according to natural law,
ought to be taken in such circumstances is often doubtful.
The famous capitulation of the Roman army at the Cau-
dine Forks is in point.   Grotius, a rigid casuist, determines that the senate were not bound to replace their
army in the condition from which the treaty had delivered
them.   And this seems to be a rational decision, though
the Romans have sometimes incurred the censure of ill
faith for their conduct.   But if the sovereign has not only
by silence acquiesced in the engagement of his ambassador or general, which of itself, according to Grotius, will
not amount to an implied ratification, but recognised it by
some overt act of his own, he cannot afterwards plead the
defect of sanction.[k]

112. Promises consist externally in words, really in the
Their inter- intention of the parties.   But as the evidence of
pretation. this intention must usually depend on words, we
should adapt our general rules to their natural meaning.
Common usage is to determine the interpretation of agreements, except where terms of a technical sense have been
employed.   But if the expressions will bear different
senses, or if there is some apparent inconsistency in different clauses, it becomes necessary to collect the meaning
conjecturally, from the nature of the subject, from the
consequences of the proposed interpretation, and from its
bearing on other parts of the agreement.   This serves to
exclude unreasonable and unfair constructions from the
equivocal language of treaties, such as was usual in former
times to a degree which the greater prudence of contracting parties, if not their better faith, has rendered impossible in modern Europe.   Among other rules of interpretation, whether, in private or public engagements, he lays
down one, familiar to the jurists, but concerning the
validity of which some have doubted, that things favourable, as they style them, or conferring a benefit, are to be

---

[k] C. 15.

construed largely; things odious, or onerous to one party
are not to be stretched beyond the letter. Our own law,
as is well known, adopts this distinction between remedial
and penal statutes; and it seems (wherever that which is
favourable in one sense is not odious in another) the most
equitable principle in public conventions. The celebrated
question, the cause, or, as Polybius more truly calls it, the
pretext of the second Punic war, whether the terms of a
treaty binding each party not to attack the allies of the
other shall comprehend those who have entered subsequently into alliance, seems, but rather on doubtful grounds,
to be decided in the negative. Several other cases from
history are agreeably introduced in this chapter.[1]

113. It is often, he observes, important to ascertain
whether a treaty be personal or real, that is, whether it
affect only the contracting sovereign or the state. The
treaties of republics are always real or permanent, even if
the form of government should become monarchical; but
the converse is not true as to those of kings, which are to
be interpreted according to the probable meaning where
there are no words of restraint or extension. A treaty
subsists with a king though he may be expelled by his
subjects : nor is it any breach of faith to take up arms
against an usurper with the lawful sovereign's consent.
This is not a doctrine which would now be endured.[m]

114. Besides those rules of interpretation which depend
on explaining the words of an engagement, there are others
which must sometimes be employed to extend or limit the
meaning beyond any natural construction. Thus in the
old law case, a bequest, in the event of the testator's
posthumous son dying, was held valid, where none was born,
and instances of this kind are continual in the books of
jurisprudence. It is equally reasonable sometimes to restrain the terms of a promise, where they clearly appear to
go beyond the design of the promiser, or where supervenient
circumstances indicate an exception which he would infallibly have made. A few sections in this place seem,
perhaps, more fit to have been inserted in the eleventh
chapter.

---

[1] C. 16.   [m] § 17.

115. There is a natural obligation to make amends for
Obligation to repair injury. injury to the natural rights of another, which is extended by means of the establishment of property and of civil society to all which the laws have accorded him.[n] Hence a correlative right arises, but a right which is to be distinguished from fitness or merit. The jurists were accustomed to treat expletive justice, which consists in giving to every one what is strictly his own, separately from attributive justice, the equitable and right dispensation of all things according to desert. With the latter Grotius has nothing to do; nor is he to be charged with introducing the distinction of perfect and imperfect rights, if indeed those phrases are as objectionable as some have accounted them. In the far greater part of this chapter he considers the principles of this important province of natural law, the obligation to compensate damage, rather as it affects private persons than sovereign states. As, in most instances, this falls within the jurisdiction of civil tribunals, the rules laid down by Grotius may to a hasty reader seem rather intended as directory to the judge, than to the conscience of the offending party. This, however, is not by any means the case; he is here, as almost every where else, a master in morality and not in law. That he is not obsequiously following the Roman law will appear by his determining against the natural responsibility of the owner for injuries committed, without his fault, by a slave or a beast.[o] But sovereigns, he holds, are answerable for the piracies and robberies of their subjects when they are able to prevent them. This is the only case of national law which he discusses. But it is one of high importance, being in fact one of the ordinary causes of public hostility. This liability, however, does not exist, where subjects having obtained a lawful commission by letters of marque become common pirates, and do not return home.

116. Thus far, the author begins in the eighteenth chapter, we have treated of rights founded on natural law,

---

[n] C. 17.

[o] This is against what we read in the 8th title of the 4th book of the Institutes. Si quadrupes pauperiem fecerit.

Pauperies, in the legal sense, which has also some classical authority, means damnum sine injuria.

with some little mixture of the arbitrary law of nations. We come now to those which depend wholly on _{Rights by law of} the latter. Such are the rights of ambassadors. _{nations.} We have now, therefore, to have recourse more to the usage of civilised people than to theroretical principles. The practice of mankind has, in fact, been so much more uniform as to the privileges of ambassadors than other _{Those of ambassa-} matters of national intercourse, that they early _{dors.} acquired the authority and denomination of public law. The obligation to receive ambassadors from other sovereign states, the respect due to them, their impunity in offences committed by their principles or by themselves, are not indeed wholly founded on custom, to the exclusion of the reason of the case; nor have the customs of mankind, even here, been so unlike themselves as to furnish no contradictory precedents; but they afford perhaps the best instance of a tacit agreement, distinguishable both from moral right and from positive convention, which is specifically denominated the law of nations. It may be mentioned, that Grotius determines in favour of the absolute impunity of ambassadors, that is, their irresponsibility to the tribunals of the country where they reside, in the case of personal crimes, and even of conspiracy against the government. This, however, he founds altogether upon what he conceives to have been the prevailing usage of civilised states.[p]

117. The next chapter, on the right of sepulture, appears more excursive than any other in the whole treatise. _{Right of} The right of sepulture can hardly become a _{sepulture.} public question, except in time of war, and as such it might have been shortly noticed in the third book. It supplies Grotius, however, with a brilliant prodigality of classical learning.[q] But the next is far more important. It _{Punish-} is entitled, On Punishments. The injuries done to _{ments.} us by others give rise to our right of compensation and to our right of punishment. We have to examine the latter with the more care, that many have fallen into mistakes from not duly apprehending the foundation and nature of punishment. Punishment is, as Grotius rather quaintly de-

fines it, Malum passionis, quod infligitur ob malum actionis,
evil inflicted on another for the evil which he has committed.
It is not a part of attributive and hardly of expletive justice;
nor is it, in its primary design, proportioned to the guilt of
the criminal, but to the magnitude of the crime. All men
have naturally a right to punish crimes, except those who
are themselves equally guilty; but though the criminal would
have no ground to complain, the mere pleasure of revenge is
not a sufficient motive to warrant us; there must be an useful
end to render punishment legitimate. This end may be the
advantage of the criminal himself, or of the injured party, or
of mankind in general. The interest of the injured party
here considered is not that of reparation, which, though it
may be provided for in punishment, is no proper part of it,
but security against similar offences of the guilty party or of
others. All men may naturally seek this security by punishing the offender, and though it is expedient in civil society
that this right should be transferred to the judge, it is not
taken away, where recourse cannot be had to the law. Every
man may even, by the law of nature, punish crimes by which
he has sustained no injury; the public good of society requiring security against offenders, and rendering them common enemies.[r]

118. Grotius next proceeds to consider whether these
rights of punishment are restrained by revelation, and concludes that a private Christian is not at liberty to punish
any criminal, especially with death, for his own security or
that of the public, but that the magistrate is expressly em-
powered by Scripture to employ the sword against male-
factors. It is rather an excess of scrupulousness, that he
holds it unbecoming to seek offices which give a jurisdiction
in capital cases.[s]

119. Many things essentially evil are not properly pun-
ishable by human laws. Such are thoughts and intentions,
errors of frailty, or actions from which, though morally
wrong, human society suffers no mischief; or the absence
of such voluntary virtues as compassion and gratitude.
Nor is it always necessary to inflict lawful punishment,

---

many circumstances warranting its remission. The ground
of punishment is the guilt of the offender, its motive is
the advantage expected from it. No punishment should
exceed what is deserved, but it may be diminished according to the prospect of utility, or according to palliating circumstances. But though punishments should bear proportion to offences, it does not follow that the criminal should
suffer no more evil than he has occasioned, which would
give him too easy a measure of retribution. The general
tendency of all that Grotius has said in this chapter is
remarkably indulgent and humane, beyond the practice or
even the philosophy of his age.[t]

120. War is commonly grounded upon the right of
punishing injuries, so that the general principles upon
which this right depends upon mankind ought well to be
understood before we can judge of so great a matter of
national law. States, Grotius thinks, have a right, analogous to that of individuals out of society, to punish heinous
offences against the law of nature or of nations, though not
affecting themselves, or even any other independent community. But this is to be done very cautiously, and does not
extend to violations of the positive divine law, or to any
merely barbarous and irrational customs. Wars undertaken
only on this score are commonly suspicious. But he goes on
to determine that war may be justly waged against those who
deny the being and providence of God, though not against
idolators, much less for the sake of compelling any nation
to embrace Christianity, unless they prosecute its professors,
in which case they are justly liable to punishment. He
pronounces strongly in this place against the prosecution of
heretics.[u]

121. This is the longest chapter in the work of Grotius.
Several of his positions, as the reader may probably have
observed, would not bear a close scrutiny; the rights of
individuals in a state of nature, of magistrates in civil society,
and of independent communities, are not kept sufficiently
distinct; the equivocal meaning of right, as it exists cor-
relatively between two parties, and as it comprehends the

---

[t] C. 20.   [u] Id.

general obligations of moral law, is not always guarded against. It is, notwithstanding these defects, a valuable commentary, regard being had to the time when it appeared, on the principles both of penal jurisprudence and of the rights of war.

122. It has been a great problem, whether the liability to punishment can be transmitted from one person to another. This may be asked as to those who have been concerned in the crime, and those who have not. In the first case, they are liable as for their own offence, in having commanded, connived at, permitted, assisted, the actors in the crime before or after its perpetration. States are answerable for the delinquencies of their subjects when unpunished. They are also bound either to punish, or to deliver up, those who take refuge within their dominions from the justice of their own country. He seems, however, to admit afterwards, that they need only command such persons to quit the country. But they have a right to inquire into and inform themselves of the guilt alleged, the ancient privileges of suppliants being established for the sake of those who have been unjustly persecuted at home. The practice of modern Europe, he owns, has limited this right of demanding the delivery or punishment of refugees within narrow bounds. As to the punishment of those who have been wholly innocent of the offence, Grotius holds it universally unjust, but distinguishes it from indirect evil, which may often fall on the innocent. Thus, when the estate of a father is confiscated, his children suffer, but are not punished; since their succession was only a right contingent on his possession at his death.[x] It is a consequence from this principle, that a people so far subject to its sovereign as to have had no control upon his actions, cannot justly incur punishment on account of them.

Their responsibility.

---

[x] C. 21, § 10. Hence it would follow, by the principle of Grotius, that our law of forfeiture in high treason is just, being part of the direct punishment of the guilty; but that of attainder, or corruption of blood, is unjust, being an infliction on the innocent alone. I incline to concur in this distinction, and think it at least plausible, though it was seldom or never taken in the discussions concerning those two laws. Confiscation is no more unjust towards the posterity of an offender than fine, from which of course it only differs in degree; and, on the other hand, the law has as much right to exclude that posterity from enjoying property at all, as from enjoying that which descends from a third party through the blood, as we call it, of a criminal ancestor.

123. After distinguishing the causes of war into pretexts and motives, and setting aside wars without any assignable justification as mere robberies, he men- tions several pretexts which he deems insufficient, such as the aggrandisement of a neighbour, his construction of for- tresses, the right of discovery, where there is already a pos- sessor, however barbarous, the necessity of occupying more land. And here he denies, both to single men and to a people, the right of taking up arms in order to recover their liberty. He laughs at the pretended right of the emperor or of the pope to govern the world; and concludes with a sin- gular warning against wars undertaken upon any pretended explanation of Scriptural prophecies.[y] It will be anticipated from the scrupulousness of Grotius in all his casuistry, that he enjoins sovereigns to abstain from war in a doubtful cause, and to use all convenient methods of avoiding it by conference, arbitration, or even by lot. Single combat itself, as a mode of lot, he does not wholly reject in this place. In answer to a question often put, Whether a war can be just on both sides? he replies that, in relation to the cause or subject, it cannot be so, since there cannot be two opposite rights; but since men may easily be deceived as to the real right, a war may be just on both sides with respect to the agents.[z] In another part of his work, he ob- serves that resistance, even where the cause is not originally just, may become such by the excess of the other party.

(marginal note: Insufficient causes of war.)

(marginal note: Duty of avoiding it.)

124. The duty of avoiding war, even in a just cause, as long as possible, is rather part of moral virtue in a large sense, than of mere justice. But, besides the obligations imposed on us by humanity and by Christian love, it is often expedient for our own interests to avoid war. Of this, however, he says little, it being plainly a matter of civil prudence with which he has no concern.[a] Dismissing, therefore, the subject of this chapter, he comes to the justice of wars undertaken for the sake of others. Sovereigns, he conceives, are not bound to take up arms in defence of any one of their subjects who may be unjustly treated. Hence, a state may abandon those whom

(marginal note: And expe- diency.)

(marginal note: War for the sake of other subjects.)

---

[y] C. 22.   [z] Id. 23.   [a] Id. 24.

it cannot protect without great loss to the rest; but whether
an innocent subject may be delivered up to an enemy is a
more debated question. Soto and Vasquez, casuists of great
name, had denied this; Grotius, however, determines it
affirmatively. This seems a remarkable exception from the
general inflexibility of his adherence to the rule of right.
For on what principle of strict justice can a people, any more
than private persons, sacrifice, or put in jeopardy, the life
of an innocent man? Grotius is influenced by the supposition, that the subject ought voluntarily to surrender himself
into the hands of the enemy for the public good; but no man
forfeits his natural rights by refusing to perform an action
not of strict social obligation.[b]

125. Next to subjects are allies, whom the state has bound
itself to succour; and friendly powers, though with-
Allies.   out alliance, may also be protected from unjust attack. This extends even to all mankind; though war in
behalf of strangers is not obligatory. It is also
Strangers.   lawful to deliver the subjects of others from extreme manifest oppression of their rulers; and though this
has often been a mere pretext, we are not on that account to
deny the justice of an honest interference. He even thinks
the right of foreign powers, in such a case, more unequivocal
than that of the oppressed people themselves. At the close
of this chapter he protests strongly against those who serve
in any cause for the mere sake of pay, and holds them worse
than the common executioner, who puts none but criminals
to death.[c]

126. In the twenty-sixth and concluding chapter of this
None to   second book, Grotius investigates the lawfulness
serve in an
unjust war.   of bearing arms at the command of superiors,
and determines that subjects are indispensably bound not
to serve in a war which they conceive to be clearly unjust. He even inclines, though admitting the prevailing
opinion to be otherwise, to think that, in a doubtful cause,
they should adhere to the general moral rule in case of
doubt, and refuse their personal service. This would evidently be impracticable, and ultimately subversive of poli-

---

        [b] C. 25.   [c] Id.

tical society. It, however, denotes the extreme scrupulosity
of his mind. One might smile at another proof of this,
where he determines that the hangman, before the performance of his duty, should satisfy himself as to the justice of
the sentence.[d]

127. The rights of war, that is, of commencing hostility,
have thus far been investigated with a comprehen-   Rights in
siveness that has sometimes almost hidden the sub-   war.
ject. We come now, in the third book, to rights in war.
Whatever may be done in war is permitted either by the
law of nature or that of nations. Grotius begins with the
first. The means morally, though not physically, necessary
to attain a lawful end are themselves lawful; a proposition
which he seems to understand relatively to the rights of
others, not to the absolute moral quality of actions; distinctions which are apt to embarrass him. We have, therefore,
a right to employ force against an enemy, though it may be
the cause of suffering to innocent persons. The principles
of natural law authorise us to prevent neutrals from furnishing an enemy with the supplies of war, or with any thing
else essential for his resistance to our just demands of redress,
such as provisions in a state of siege. And it is remarkable
that he refers this latter question to natural law, because he
had not found any clear decision of it by the positive law of
nations.[e]

128. In acting against an enemy force is the nature of
war. But it may be inquired, whether deceit is not   Use of
also a lawful means of success? The practice of   deceit.
nations and the authority of most writers seem to warrant it.
Grotius dilates on different sorts of artifice, and after admitting the lawfulness of such as deceive by indications, comes
to the question of words equivocal or wholly false. This he
first discusses on the general moral principle of veracity,
more prolixly, and with more deference to authority, than
would suit a modern reader; yet this basis is surely indispensable for the support of any decision in public casuistry.
The right, however, of employing falsehood towards an
enemy, which he generally admits, does not extend to pro-

---

[d] C. 26.   [e] L. iii. c. 1.

mises, which are always to be kept, whether express or implied, especially when confirmed by oath. And more greatness of mind, as well as more Christian simplicity, would be
shown by abstaining wholly from falsehood in war. The
law of nature does not permit us to tempt any one to do that
which in him would be criminal, as to assassinate his sovereign,
or to betray his trust. But we have a right to make use of
his voluntary offers.[f]

129. Grotius now proceeds from the consideration of na-
Rules and
customs of
nations.
Reprisals. tural law or justice to that of the general customs
of mankind, in which, according to him, the arbi-
trary law of nations consists. By this, in the first
place, though naturally no one is answerable for another, it
has been established that the property of every citizen is, as
it were, mortgaged for the liabilities of the state to which
he belongs. Hence, if justice is refused to us by the sovereign, we have a right to indemnification out of the property
of his subjects. This is commonly called reprisals; and it is
a right which every private person would enjoy, were it not
for the civil laws of most countries, which compel him to
obtain the authorisation of his own sovereign, or of some
tribunal. By an analogous right the subjects of a foreign
state have sometimes been seized in return for one of our
own subjects unjustly detained by their government.[g]

130. A regular war, by the law of nations, can only be
Declarations
of war. waged between political communities. Wherever
there is a semblance of civil justice and fixed law,
such a community exists, however violent may be its actions.
But a body of pirates or robbers are not one. Absolute independence, however, is not required for the right of war.
A formal declaration of war, though not necessary by the
law of nature, has been rendered such by the usage of civilised nations. But it is required, even by the former, that
we should demand reparation for an injury, before we seek
redress by force. A declaration of war may be conditional
or absolute; and it has been established as a ratification of
regular hostilities, that they may not be confounded with the
unwarranted acts of private men. No interval of time is
required for their commencement after declaration.[h]

---

[f] L. iii. c. 1   [g] C. 2.   [h] Id. 3.

131. All is lawful during war, in one sense of the word, which by the law and usage of nations is dispunish- *Rights by* able. And this, in formal hostilities, is as much the *law of na-* *tions over* right of one side as of the other. The subjects of *enemies.* our enemy, whether active on his side or not, become liable to these extreme rights of slaughter and pillage ; but it seems that, according to the law of nations, strangers should be exempted from them, unless by remaining in the country they serve his cause. Women, children, and prisoners may be put to death ; quarter or capitulation for life refused. On the other hand, if the law of nations is less strict in this respect than that of nature, it forbids some things which naturally might be allowable means of defence, as the poisoning an enemy, or the wells from which he is to drink. The assassination of an enemy is not contrary to the law of nations, unless by means of traitors, and even this is held allowable against a rebel or robber, who are not protected by the rules of formal war. But the violation of women is contrary to the law of nations.[i] The rights of war with respect to enemies' property are unlimited, without exception even of churches or sepulchral monuments, sparing always the bodies of the dead.

132. By the law of nature, Grotius thinks that we acquire a property in as much of the spoil as is sufficient to indemnify us, and to punish the aggressor. But the law of nations carries this much farther, and gives an unlimited property in all that has been acquired by conquest, which mankind are bound to respect. This right commences as soon as the enemy has lost all chance of recovering his losses ; which is, in movables, as soon as they are in a place within our sole power. The transfer of property in territories is not so speedy. The goods of neutrals are not thus transferred, when found in the cities or on board the vessels of an enemy. Whether the spoil belongs to the captors, or to their sovereign, is so disputed a question, that it can hardly be reckoned a part of that law of nations, or universal usage, with which Grotius is here concerned. He thinks, however, that what is taken in public enterprises appertains to the state ; and

---

[i] C. 4.   [k] Id. 5.

that this has been the general practice of mankind. The
civil laws of each people may modify this, and have frequently done so.[m]

133. Prisoners, by the law of nations, become slaves of
Prisoners become slaves. the captor, and their posterity also. He may treat
them as he pleases with impunity. This has been
established by the custom of mankind, in order that the
conqueror might be induced to spare the lives of the vanquished. Some theologians deny the slave, even when taken
in an unjust war, the right of making his escape, from whom
Grotius dissents. But he has not a right, in conscience, to
resist the exercise of his master's authority. This law of
nations as to the slavery of prisoners, as he admits, has not
been universally received, and is now abolished in Christian
countries out of respect to religion.[n] But, strictly, as an individual may be reduced into slavery, so may a whole conquered people. It is of course at the discretion of the conqueror to remit a portion of his right, and to leave as much
of their liberties and possessions untouched as he pleases.[o]

134. The next chapter relates to the right of postliminium,
Right of postlimi-nium. one depending so much on the peculiar fictions of
the Roman jurists, that it seems strange to discuss
as part of an universal law of nations at all. Nor does
it properly belong to the rights of war, which are between
belligerent parties. It is certainly consonant to natural
justice that a citizen returning from captivity should be fully
restored to every privilege and all property that he had
enjoyed at home. In modern Europe there is little to which
the jus postliminii can even by analogy be applied. It has
been determined, in courts of admiralty, that vessels re-
captured after a short time do not revert to their owner.
This chapter must be reckoned rather episodical.[p]

135. We have thus far looked only at the exterior right,
Moral limit-ation of rights in war. accorded by the law of nations to all who wage
regular hostilities in a just or unjust quarrel. This
right is one of impunity alone, but before our own
conscience, or the tribunal of moral approbation in mankind,
many things hitherto spoken of as lawful must be condemned.

   ᵐ C. 6.   ⁿ Id. 7.   ᵒ Id. 8.   ᵖ Id. 9.

In the first place, an unjust war renders all acts of force committed in its prosecution unjust, and binds the aggressor before God to reparation. Every one, general or soldier, is responsible in such cases for the wrong he has commanded or perpetrated. Nor can any one knowingly retain the property of another obtained by such a war, though he should come to the possession of it with good faith.[q] And as nothing can be done, consistently with moral justice, in an unjust war, so, however legitimate our ground for hostilities may be, we are not at liberty to transgress the boundaries of equity and humanity. In this chapter, Grotius, after dilating with a charitable abundance of examples and authorities in favour of clemency in war, even towards those who have been most guilty in provoking it, specially indicates women, old men, and children, as always to be spared, extending this also to all whose occupations are not military. Prisoners are not to be put to death, nor are towns to be refused terms of capitulation. He denies that the law of retaliation, or the necessity of striking terror, or the obstinate resistance of an enemy, dispenses with the obligation of saving his life. Nothing but some personal crime can warrant the refusal of quarter or the death of a prisoner. Nor is it allowable to put hostages to death.[r]

136. All unnecessary devastation ought to be avoided, such as the destruction of trees, of houses, especially ornamental and public buildings, and of every-thing not serviceable in war, nor tending to prolong it, as pictures and statues. Temples and sepulchres are to be spared for the same or even stronger reasons. Though it is not the object of Grotius to lay down any political maxims, he cannot refrain in this place from pointing out several considerations of expediency, which should induce us to restrain the licence of arms within the limits of natural law.[s] There is no right by nature to more booty, strictly speaking, than is sufficient for our indemnity, wherein are included the expenses of the war. And the property of innocent persons, being subjects of our enemies, is only liable in failure of those who are primarily aggressors.[t]

Moderation required as to spoil.

---

q C. 10.   r Id. 11.   s Id. 12.   t Id. 13.

137. The persons of prisoners are only liable, in strict
And as to   moral justice, so far as is required for satisfaction
prisoners.   of our injury. The slavery into which they may
be reduced ought not to extend farther than an obligation of
perpetual servitude in return for maintenance. The power
over slaves by the law of nature is far short of what the
arbitrary law of nations permits, and does not give a right
of exacting too severe labour, or of inflicting punishment
beyond desert. The peculium, or private acquisitions of a
slave by economy or donation, ought to be reckoned his
property. Slaves, however, captured in a just war, though
one in which they have had no concern, are not warranted in
conscience to escape and recover their liberty. But the
children of such slaves are not in servitude by the law of
nature, except so far as they have been obliged to their
master for subsistence in infancy. With respect to prisoners,
the better course is to let them redeem themselves by a
ransom, which ought to be moderate.[u]

138. The acquisition of that sovereignty which was en-
Also in con-   joyed by a conquered people, or by their rulers, is
quest.   not only legitimate, so far as is warranted by the
punishment they have deserved, or by the value of our
own loss, but also so far as the necessity of securing ourselves
extends. This last is what is often unsafe to remit out of clemency. It is a part of moderation in victory to incorporate
the conquered with our own citizens on equal terms, or
to leave their independence on reasonable precautions for our
own security. If this cannot be wholly conceded, their civil
laws and municipal magistracies may be preserved, and, above
all, the free exercise of their religion. The interests of con-
querors are as much consulted, generally, as their reputation,
by such lenient use of their advantages.[x]

139. It is consonant to natural justice that we should
And in re-   restore to the original owners all of which they have
stitution to   been despoiled in an unjust war, when it falls into our
right
owners.   hands by a lawful conquest, without regard to the
usual limits of postliminium. Thus, if an ambitious state
comes to be stripped of its usurpations, this should be not for

----

          [u] C. 14.   [x] Id. 15.

the benefit of the conqueror, but of the ancient possessors.
Length of time, however, will raise the presumption of
abandonment.[y]   Nothing should be taken in war from
neutral states, except through necessity and with compensation.   The most ordinary case is that of the passage of
troops.   The neutral is bound to strict impartiality in a war
of doubtful justice.[z]   But it seems to be the opinion of
Grotius, that, by the law of nature, every one, even a private
man, may act in favour of the innocent party as far as the
rights of war extend, except that he cannot appropriate to
himself the possessions of the enemy; that right being one
founded on indemnification.   But civil and military laws have
generally restrained this to such as obey the express order of
their government.[a]

140. The licence of war is restrained either by the laws of
nature and nations, which have been already dis- Promises to
cussed, or by particular engagement. The obligation enemies and pirates.
of promises extends to enemies, who are still parts of the
great society of mankind.   Faith is to be kept even with
tyrants, robbers, and pirates. He here again adverts to the
case of a promise made under an unjust compulsion; and
possibly his reasoning on the general principle is not quite
put in the most satisfactory manner.   It would now be
argued that the violation of engagements towards the worst
of mankind, who must be supposed to have some means of
self-defence, on account of which we propose to treat with
them, would produce a desperation among men in similar
circumstances injurious to society.   Or it might be urged,
that men do not lose by their crimes a right to the perform-
mance of all engagements, especially when they have fulfilled
their own share in them, but only of such as involve a positive
injustice towards the other party.   In this place he repeats
his former doctrine, that the most invalid promise may be
rendered binding by the addition of an oath.   It follows,
from the general rule, that a prince is bound by his engagements to rebel subjects; above all, if they have had the
precaution to exact his oath.   And thus a change in the
constitution of a monarchy may legitimately take place, and

---

[y] C. 16.   [z] Id. 17.   [a] Id. 19.

it may become mixed instead of absolute by the irrevocable
concession of the sovereign. The rule, that promises made
under an unjust compulsion are not obligatory, has no application in a public and regular war.[b] Barbeyrac remarks on
this, that if a conqueror, like Alexander, subdues an un-
offending people with no specious pretext at all, he does not
perceive why they should be more bound in conscience to
keep the promises of obedience they may have been compelled
to enter into, than if he had been an ordinary bandit. And
this remark shows us, that the celebrated problem in casuistry,
as to the obligation of compulsory promises, has far more
important consequences than the payment of a petty sum to
a robber. In two cases, however, Grotius holds that we are
dispensed from keeping an engagement towards an enemy.
One of these is, when it has been conditional, and the other
party has not fulfilled his part of the convention. This is of
course obvious, and can only be open to questions as to the
precedence of the condition. The other case is where we
retain what is due to us by way of compensation, notwithstanding our promise. This is permissible in certain instances.[c]

141. The obligation of treaties of peace depends on their
being concluded by the authority which, according
to the constitution of the state, is sovereign for this
purpose. Kings who do not possess a patrimonial
sovereignty cannot alienate any part of their dominions
without the consent of the nation or its representatives;
they must even have the consent of the city or province
which is thus to be transferred. In patrimonial kingdoms,
the sovereign may alienate the whole, but not always a part,
at pleasure. He seems, however, to admit an ultimate right
of sovereignty, or *dominium eminens,* by which all states may
dispose of the property of their subjects, and consequently
alienate it for the sake of a great advantage, but subject to
the obligation of granting them an indemnity. He even
holds that the community is naturally bound to indemnify

Treaties con-
cluded by
competent
authority.

---

[b] C. 19, § 11. There seems, as has
been intimated above, to be some inconsistency in the doctrine of Grotius with
respect to the general obligation of such

promises, which he maintains in the second book; and now, as far as I collect
his meaning, denies by implication.
  [c] C. 19.

private subjects for the losses they sustain in war, though
this right of reparation may be taken away by civil laws.
The right of alienation by a treaty of peace is only questionable between the sovereign and his subjects; foreign states
may presume its validity in their own favour.[d]

142. Treaties of peace are generally founded on one of two
principles; that the parties shall return to the con- Matters re-
dition wherein they were before the commencement lating to them.
of hostilities, or that they shall retain what they possess at
their conclusion. The last is to be presumed in a case of
doubtful interpretation. A treaty of peace extinguishes all
public grounds of quarrel, whether known to exist or not,
but does not put an end to the claims of private men subsisting before the war, the extinguishment of which is never to
be presumed. The other rules of interpretation which he
lays down are, as usual with him, derived rather from natural
equity than the practice of mankind, though with no neglect
or scorn of the latter. He maintains the right of giving an
asylum to the banished, but not of receiving large bodies of
men who abandon their country.[e]

143. The decision of lot may be adopted in some cases,
in order to avoid a war, wherein we have little chance of resisting an enemy. But that of single combat, according to
Grotius's opinion, though not repugnant to the law of nature, is incompatible with Christianity; unless in the case
where a party, unjustly assailed, has no other means of defence. Arbitration by a neutral power is another method of
settling differences, and in this we are bound to acquiesce.
Wars may also be terminated by implicit submission or by
capitulation. The rights which this gives to a conqueror
have been already discussed. He concludes this chapter
with a few observations upon hostages and pledges. With
respect to the latter he holds that they may be reclaimed
after any lapse of time, unless there is a presumption of tacit
abandonment.[f]

144. A truce is an interval of war, and does not require a
fresh declaration at its close. No act of hostility Truces and
is lawful during its continuance; the infringement conventions.

---

[d] C. 20.   [e] Id.   [f] Id.

of this rule by either party gives the other a right to take
up arms without delay. Safe-conducts are to be construed
liberally, rejecting every meaning of the words which does
not reach their spirit. Thus a safe-conduct to go to a place
implies the right of returning unmolested. The ransom of
prisoners ought to be favoured.[g] A state is bound by the
conventions in war made by its officers, provided they are
such as may reasonably be presumed to lie within their delegated authority, or such as they have a special commission
to warrant, known to the other contracting party. A state
is also bound by its tacit ratification in permitting the
execution of any part of such a treaty, though in itself not
obligatory, and also by availing itself of any advantage
thereby. Grotius dwells afterwards on many distinctions
relating to this subject, which however, as far as they do not
resolve themselves into the general principle, are to be considered on the ground of positive regulation.[h]

145. Private persons, whether bearing arms or not, are
Those of private persons. as much bound as their superiors by the engagements they contract with an enemy. This applies
particularly to the parole of a prisoner. The engagement
not to serve again, though it has been held null by some
jurists, as contrary to our obligation towards our country, is
valid. It has been a question, whether the state ought to
compel its citizens to keep their word towards the enemy?
The better opinion is that it should do so; and this has been
the practice of the most civilised nations.[i] Those who put
themselves under the protection of a state engage to do nothing hostile towards it. Hence such actions as that of
Zopyrus, who betrayed Babylon under the guise of a refugee,
are not excusable. Several sorts of tacit engagements are
established by the usage of nations, as that of raising a white
flag in token of a desire to suspend arms. These are exceptions from the general rule which authorises deceit in war.[k]
In the concluding chapter of the whole treatise Grotius
briefly exhorts all states to preserve good faith and to seek
peace at all times, upon the mild principles of Christianity.[m]

146. If the reader has had the patience to make his way

---

[g] C. 21.   [h] Id. 22.   [i] Id. 23.
[k] C. 24.   [m] Id. 25.

through the abstract of Grotius, De Jure Belli, that we have
placed before him, he will be fully prepared to judge Objections to Grotius made by Paley un- reasonable.
of the criticisms made upon this treatise by Paley
and Dugald Stewart. ' The writings of Grotius
and Puffendorf,' says the former, ' are of too forensic a
cast, too much mixed up with civil law and with the jurisprudence of Germany, to answer precisely the design of a
system of ethics, the direction of private consciences in the
general conduct of human life.' But it was not the intention
of Grotius (we are not at present concerned with Puffendorf)
to furnish a system of ethics; nor did any one ever hold
forth his treatise in this light. Upon some most important
branches of morality he has certainly dwelt so fully as to
answer the purpose of ' directing the private conscience in
the conduct of life.' The great aim, however, of his inquiries
was to ascertain the principles of natural right applicable to
independent communities.

147. Paley, it must be owned, has a more specious ground
of accusation in his next charge against Grotius for the profusion of classical quotations. ' To any thing more than
ornament they can make no claim. To propose them as
serious arguments, gravely to attempt to establish or fortify
a moral duty by the testimony of a Greek or Roman poet, is
to trifle with the reader, or rather take off his attention from
all just principles in morals.'

148. A late eminent writer has answered this from the
text of Grotius, but in more eloquent language than Reply of Mackintosh.
Grotius could have employed. ' Another answer,
says Mackintosh, 'is due to some of those who have criticised
Grotius, and that answer might be given in the words of
Grotius himself. He was not of such a stupid and servile
cast of mind, as to quote the opinions of poets or orators, of
historians and philosophers, as those of judges from whose
decision there was no appeal. He quotes them, as he
tells us himself, as witnesses, whose conspiring testimony,
mightily strengthened and confirmed by their discordance on
almost every other subject, is a conclusive proof of the unanimity of the whole human race on the great rules of duty
and the fundamental principles of morals. On such matters,
poets and orators are the most unexceptionable of all wit-

nesses; for they address themselves to the general feelings and sympathies of mankind; they are neither warped by system, nor perverted by sophistry; they can attain none of their objects; they can neither please nor persuade, if they dwell on moral sentiments not in unison with those of their readers. No system of moral philosophy can surely disregard the general feelings of human nature, and the according judgment of all ages and nations. But where are these feelings and that judgment recorded and preserved? In those very writings which Grotius is gravely blamed for having quoted. The usages and laws of nations, the events of history, the opinions of philosophers, the sentiments of orators and poets, as well as the observation of common life, are, in truth, the materials out of which the science of morality is formed; and those who neglect them are justly chargeable with a vain attempt to philosophise without regard to fact and experience, the sole foundation of all true philosophy.' [n]

149. The passage in Grotius which has suggested this noble defence will be found above. It will be seen on reference to it, that he proposes to quote the poets and orators cautiously, and rather as ornamental than authoritative supports of his argument. In no one instance, I believe, will he be found to ' enforce a moral duty,' as Paley imagines, by their sanction. It is nevertheless to be fairly acknowledged, that he has sometimes gone a good deal farther than the rules of a pure taste allow in accumulating quotations from the poets; and that, in an age so impatient of prolixity as the last, this has stood much in the way of the general reader.

150. But these criticisms of Paley contain very trifling censure in comparison with the unbounded scorn poured on Grotius by Dugald Stewart, in his first Dissertation on the Progress of Philosophy. I have never read these pages of an author whom I had unfortunately not the opportunity of personally knowing, but whose researches have contributed so much to the delight and advantage of mankind, without pain and surprise. It would be too much to say that, in several parts of this Dissertation, by no means in the first class of Stewart's writings, other proofs of

Censures of Stewart.

---

[n] Mackintosh, Discourse on the Study of the Law of Nature and Nations, p. 23 (edit. 1828).

precipitate judgment do not occur; but that he should have
spoken of a work so distinguished by fame, and so effective,
as he himself admits, over the public mind of Europe, in terms
of unmingled depreciation, without having done more than
glanced at some of its pages, is an extraordinary symptom of
that tendency towards prejudices, hasty but inveterate, of
which this eminent man seems to have been not a little susceptible.   The attack made by Stewart on those who have
taken the law of nature and nations as their theme, and
especially on Grotius, who stands forward in that list, is pro-
tracted for several pages, and it would be tedious to examine
every sentence in succession.   Were I to do so, it is not, in
my opinion, an exaggeration to say that almost every successive sentence would lie open to criticism.   But let us take
the chief heads of accusation.

151. 'Grotius,' we are told, 'under the title, De Jure
Belli ac Pacis, has aimed at a complete system of Answer to
natural law.   Condillac says, that he chose the title them.
in order to excite a more general curiosity.'   The total
erroneousness of this passage must appear to every one who
has seen what Grotius declares to have been his primary
object.   He chose the title because it came nearest to express
that object—the ascertainment of laws binding on independent communities in their mutual relations, whether of war
or peace.   But as it was not possible to lay down any solid
principles of international right till the notions of right, of
sovereignty, of dominion over things and persons, of war
itself, were clearly established, it became indispensable to
build upon a more extensive basis than later writers on the
law of nations, who found the labour performed to their
hands, have thought necessary.   All ethical philosophy, even
in those parts which bear a near relation to jurisprudence
and to international law, was in the age of Grotius a chaos
of incoherent and arbitrary notions, brought in from various
sources; from the ancient schools, from the Scriptures, the
fathers, the canons, the casuistical theologians, the rabbins,
the jurists, as well as from the practice and sentiments of
every civilised nation, past and present, the Jews, the Greeks
and Romans, the trading republics, the chivalrous kingdoms
of modern Europe.   If Grotius has not wholly disentangled

himself from this bewildering maze, through which he pain-
fully traces his way by the lights of reason and revelation, he
has at least cleared up much, and put others still oftener in
the right path, where he has not been able to follow it. Condillac, as here quoted by Stewart, has anticipated Paley's
charge against Grotius, of labouring to support his conclusions by the authority of others, and of producing a long
string of quotations to prove the most indubitable propositions. In what degree this very exaggerated remark is true
we have already seen. But it should be kept in mind, that
neither the disposition of the age in which Grotius lived, nor
the real necessity of illustrating every part of his inquiries by
the precedent usages of mankind, would permit him to treat
of moral philosophy as of the abstract theorems of geometry.
If his erudition has sometimes obstructed or misled him,
which perhaps has not so frequently happened as these critics
assume, it is still true that a contemptuous ignorance of what
has been done or has been taught, such as belonged to the
school of Condillac and to that of Paley, does not very well
qualify the moral philosopher for inquiry into the principles
which are to regulate human nature.

152. ' Among the different ideas,' Stewart observes, ' which
have been formed of natural jurisprudence, one of the most
common, especially in the earlier systems, supposes its object to be—to lay down those rules of justice which would be
binding on men living in a social state without any positive
institutions ; or, as it is frequently called by writers on this
subject, living together in a state of nature. This idea of the
province of jurisprudence seems to have been uppermost in
the mind of Grotius in various parts of his treatise.' After
some conjectures on the motives which led the early writers
to take this view of national law, and admitting that the
rules of justice are in every case precise and indispensable,
and that their authority is altogether independent of that of
the civil magistrate, he deems it ' obviously absurd to spend
much time in speculating about the principles of this natural
law, as applicable to men before the institution of governments.' It may possibly be as absurd as he thinks it. But
where has Grotius shown that this condition of natural
society was uppermost in his thoughts ? Of the state of

nature, as it existed among individuals before the foundation of any civil institutions, he says no more than was requisite in order to exhibit the origin of those rights which spring from property and government. But that he has, in some part especially of his second book, dwelt upon the rules of justice binding on men subsequent to the institution of property, but independently of positive laws, is most certain; nor is it possible for any one to do otherwise, who does not follow Hobbes in confounding moral with legal obligation; a theory to which Mr. Stewart was of all men the most averse.

153. Natural jurisprudence is a term that is not always taken in the same sense. It seems to be of English origin; nor am I certain, though my memory may deceive me, that I have ever met with it in Latin or in French. Strictly speaking, as jurisprudence means the science of law, and is especially employed with respect to the Roman, natural jurisprudence must be the science of morals, or the law of nature. It is, therefore, in this sense, co-extensive with ethics, and comprehends the rules of temperance, liberality, and benevolence, as much as those of justice. Stewart, however, seems to consider this idea of jurisprudence as an arbitrary extension of the science derived from the technical phraseology of the Roman law. ' Some vague notion of this kind,' he says, ' has manifestly given birth to many of the digressions of Grotius.' It may have been seen by the analysis of the entire treatise of Grotius above given, that none of his digressions, if such they are to be called, have originated in any vague notion of an identity, or proper analogy, between the strict rules of justice and those of the other virtues. The Aristotelian division of justice into commutative and distributive, which Grotius has adopted, might seem in some respect to bear out this supposition; but it is evident, from the context of Stewart's observations, that he was referring only to the former species, or justice in its more usual sense, the observance of perfect rights, whose limits may be accurately determined, and whose violation may be redressed.

154. Natural jurisprudence has another sense imposed upon it by Adam Smith. According to this sense, its object,

in the words of Stewart, is 'to ascertain the general principles of justice which ought to be recognised in every municipal code, and to which it ought to be the aim of every legislator to accommodate his institutions.' Grotius, in Smith's opinion, was 'the first who attempted to give the world any thing like a system of those principles which ought to run through, and to be the foundation of, the laws of all nations; and his treatise on the laws of peace and war, with all its imperfections, is perhaps at this day the most complete book that has yet been given on the subject.'

155. The first probably, in modern times, who conceived this idea of an universal jurisprudence was Lord Bacon. He places among the desiderata of political science, the province of universal justice, or the sources of law. 'Id nunc agatur, ut fontes justitiæ et utilitatis publicæ petantur, et in singulis juris partibus character quidam et idea justi exhibeatur, ad quem particularium regnorum et rerumpublicarum leges probare, atque inde emendationem moliri, quisque, cui hæc cordi erit et curæ, possit.'° The maxims which follow are an admirable illustration of the principles which should regulate the enactment and expression of laws, as well as of much that should guide, in a general manner, the decision of courts of justice. They touch very slightly, if at all, any subject which Grotius has handled ; but certainly come far closer to natural jurisprudence, in the sense of Smith, inasmuch as they contain principles which have no limitation to the circumstances of particular societies. These maxims of Bacon, and all others that seem properly to come within the province of jurisprudence in this sense, which is now become not uncommon, the science of universal *law*, are resolvable partly into those of natural justice, partly into those of public expediency. Little, however, could be objected against the admission of universal jurisprudence, in this sense, among the sciences. But if it is meant that any systematic science, whether by the name of jurisprudence or legislation, can be laid down as to the principles which ought to determine the institutions of all nations, or that, in other words, the laws of each separate community ought to be regulated by any uni-

---

° De Augmentis, lib. viii.

versal standard, in matters not depending upon eternal justice, we must demur to receiving so very disputable a proposition.   It is probable that Adam Smith had no thoughts of asserting it; yet his language is not very clear, and he seems to have assigned some object to Grotius, distinct from the establishment of natural and international law.   'Whether this was,' says Stewart, 'or was not, the leading object of Grotius, it is not material to decide; but if this was his object, it will not be disputed that he has executed his design in a very desultory manner, and that he often seems to have lost sight of it altogether, in the midst of those miscellaneous speculations on political, ethical, and historical subjects, which form so large a portion of his treatise, and which so frequently succeed each other without any apparent connexion or common aim.'

156. The unfairness of this passage it is now hardly incumbent upon me to point out.   The reader has been enabled to answer that no political speculation will be found in the volume, De Jure Belli ac Pacis, unless the disquisition on the origin of human society is thus to be denominated; that the instances continually adduced from history are always in illustration of the main argument; and that what are here called ethical speculations are in fact the real subject of the book, since it avowedly treats of obligations on the conscience of mankind, and especially of their rulers.   Whether the various topics in this treatise ' succeed each other without apparent connexion or common aim,' may best be seen by the titles of the chapters, or by the analysis of their contents. There are certainly a very few of these that have little in common, even by deduction or analogy, with international law, though scarce any, I think, which do not rise naturally out of the previous discussion.   Exuberances of this kind are so common in writers of great reputation, that where they do not transgress more than Grotius has done, the censure of irrelevancy has been always reckoned hypercritical.

157. 'The Roman system of jurisprudence,' Mr. Stewart proceeds, 'seems to have warped in no inconsiderable degree the notions of Grotius on all questions connected with the theory of legislation, and to have diverted his attention from that philosophical idea of law so well expressed by Cicero:

' Non a prætoris edicto, neque a duodecim tabulis, sed penitus ex intima philosophia hauriendam juris disciplinam.' In this idolatry, indeed, of the Roman law, he has not gone so far as some of his commentators, who have affirmed that it is only a different name for the law of nature: but that his partiality for his professional pursuits has often led him to overlook the immense difference between the state of society in ancient and modern Europe will not, I believe, now be disputed.' It is probable that it will be disputed by all who are acquainted with Grotius. The questions connected with the theory of legislation which he has discussed are chiefly those relating to the acquisition and alienation of property in some of the earlier chapters of the second book. That he has not, in these disquisitions, adopted all the determinations of the Roman jurists is certain; whether he may in any particular instance have adhered to them more than the best theory of legislation would admit, is a matter of variable opinion. But Stewart, wholly unacquainted with the civil laws, appears to have much underrated their value. In most questions of private right, they form the great basis of every modern legislation; and, as all civilised nations, including our own, have derived a large portion of their jurisprudence from this source, so even the theorists, who would disdain to be ranked as disciples of Paullus and Papinian, are not ashamed to be their plagiaries.

158. It has been thrown out against Grotius by Rousseau,[p] and the same insinuation may be found in other writers, that he confounds the fact with the right, and the duties of nations with their practice. How little foundation there is for this calumny is sufficiently apparent to our readers. Scrupulous, as a casuist, to an excess hardly reconcilable with the security and welfare of good men, he was the first, beyond the precincts of the confessional or the church, to pour the dictates of a saint-like innocence into the ears of princes. It is true that in recognising the legitimacy of slavery, and in carrying too far the principles of obedience to government, he may be thought to have deprived mankind of some of their security against injustice; but this is exceedingly different from a sanction to it. An

Grotius vindicated against Rousseau.

---

[p] Contrat social.

implicit deference to what he took for divine truth was the
first axiom in the philosophy of Grotius. If he was occasionally deceived in his application of this principle, it was but
according to the notions of his age; but those who wholly
reject the authority must of course want a common standard
by which his speculations in moral philosophy can be reconciled with their own.

159. I must now quit a subject upon which, perhaps, I
have dwelt too long. The high fame of Dugald Stewart has
rendered it a sort of duty to vindicate from his hasty censures the memory of one still more illustrious in reputation,
till the lapse of time, and the fickleness of literary fashion,
conspired with the popularity of his assailants to magnify his
defects, and meet the very name of his famous treatise with
a kind of scornful ridicule. That Stewart had never read
much of Grotius, or even gone over the titles of his chapters,
is very manifest; and he displays a similar ignorance as to
the other writers on natural law, who for more than a century
afterwards, as he admits himself, exercised a great influence
over the studies of Europe. I have commented upon very
few, comparatively, of the slips which occur in his pages on
this subject.

160. The arrangement of Grotius has been blamed as
unscientific by a more friendly judge, Sir James *His arrange-*
Mackintosh. Though I do not feel very strongly *ment.*
the force of his objections, it is evident that the law of nature
might have been established on its basis, before the author
passed forward to any disquisition upon its reference to independent communities. This would have changed a good
deal the principal object that Grotius had in view, and
brought his treatise, in point of method, very near to that of
Puffendorf. But assuming, as he did, the authority recognised by those for whom he wrote, that of the Scriptures, he
was less inclined to dwell on the proof which reason affords
for a natural law, though fully satisfied of its validity even
without reference to the Supreme Being.

161. The real faults of Grotius, leading to erroneous determinations, seem to be rather an unnecessary scrupulousness, and somewhat of old theological preju- *His defects.*
dice, from which scarce any man in his age, who was not

wholly indifferent to religion, had liberated himself. The notes of Barbeyrac seldom fail to correct this leaning. Several later writers on international law have treated his doctrine of an universal law of nations founded on the agreement of mankind as an empty chimera of his invention. But if he only meant by this the tacit consent, or, in other words, the general custom of civilised nations, it does not appear that there is much difference between his theory and that of Wolf or Vattel.

END OF THE SECOND VOLUME.